Evidence and Faith

Philosophy and Religion since the Seventeenth Century

Charles Taliaferro has written a dynamic narrative history of philosophical reflection on religion from the seventeenth century to the present, with an emphasis on shifting views of faith and the nature of evidence. The book begins with the movement called Cambridge Platonism, which formed a bridge between the ancient and medieval worlds and early modern philosophy. While the book provides a general overview of different movements in philosophy, it also offers a detailed exposition and reflection on key arguments, and the scope is broad, from Descartes to contemporary feminist philosophy of religion.

Written with clarity and verve, this book will appeal to professionals and students in the philosophy of religion, religious studies, and the history of ideas, as well as informed lay readers.

Charles Taliaferro is Professor of Philosophy at St. Olaf College, Minnesota.

THE EVOLUTION OF MODERN PHILOSOPHY

General Editors:
Paul Guyer and Gary Hatfield (*University of Pennsylvania*)

Roberto Torretti: *The Philosophy of Physics*
David Depew and Marjorie Grene: *The Philosophy of Biology*

Forthcoming:
Paul Guyer: *Aesthetics*
Gary Hatfield: *The Philosophy of Psychology*
Stephen Darwall: *Ethics*
T. R. Harrison: *Political Philosophy*
William Ewald and Michael J. Hallett: *The Philosophy of Mathematics*
Michael Losonsky: *The Philosophy of Language*

Why has philosophy evolved in the way that it has? How have its subdisciplines developed, and what impact has this development exerted on the way that the subject is now practiced? Each volume of "The Evolution of Modern Philosophy" will focus on a particular subdiscipline of philosophy and examine how it has evolved into the subject as we now understand it. The volumes will be written from the perspective of a current practitioner in contemporary philosophy, whose point of departure will be the question: How did we get from there to here? Cumulatively the series will constitute a library of modern conceptions of philosophy and will reveal how philosophy does not in fact comprise a set of timeless questions but has rather been shaped by broader intellectual and scientific developments to produce particular fields of inquiry addressing particular issues.

Evidence and Faith

Philosophy and Religion since the Seventeenth Century

CHARLES TALIAFERRO

St. Olaf College

CAMBRIDGE
UNIVERSITY PRESS

CAMBRIDGE UNIVERSITY PRESS
Cambridge, New York, Melbourne, Madrid, Cape Town, Singapore, São Paulo

Cambridge University Press
40 West 20th Street, New York, NY 10011-4211, USA

www.cambridge.org
Information on this title: www.cambridge.org/9780521790277

First published 2005

Printed in the United States of America

A catalog record for this publication is available from the British Library.

Library of Congress Cataloging in Publication data

Taliaferro, Charles.
    Evidence and faith : philosophy and religion since the seventeenth century /
Charles Taliaferro.
        p.   cm. – (The evolution of modern philosophy)
    Includes bibliographical references and index.
    ISBN 0-521-79027-1 (alk. paper) – ISBN 0-521-79375-0 (pbk. : alk. paper)
    1. Philosophy and religion – History.   2. Philosophy, Modern.   I. Title.   II. Series.
BD573.T35   2005
210–dc22

                                                                                    2004054538

            ISBN-13   978-0-521-79027-7 hardback
            ISBN-10   0-521-79027-1 hardback

            ISBN-13   978-0-521-79375-9 paperback
            ISBN-10   0-521-79375-0 paperback

Contents

Acknowledgments

I thank Paul Guyer and Gary Hatfield for inviting me to undertake this project and Terence Moore for his support and guidance. I thank St. Olaf College and especially the Department of Philosophy for ongoing support. My colleague and dean, Rick Fairbanks, has been especially generous. For hospitality, conversation, and library use in 1998–1999, I thank the Department of Philosophy at New York University, especially Thomas Nagel, Roy Sorenson, and Peter Unger; the Department of Religion at Columbia University, especially Wayne Proudfoot and Matthew Bagger; the Department of Religion at Princeton University, especially Jeffrey Stout; the American Academy in Rome; and the General Theological Seminary in New York City. I thank Paula Schanilec for her generous work in helping me prepare this manuscript for publication. I also thank Rachel Traughber, Kate Monson, Adam Goldhammer, Jerrae Swanson, Andrea Gatzke, April Carlson, Michael Littell, Sarah Campbell, Ashley Miller, Erik Chrisopherson, Dan Sinykin, and Amber Griffioen. For critical comments on earlier versions of this manuscript, I thank Pamela Sue Anderson, Kelly Clark, Brian Davies, Gary DeKrey, Stewart Goetz, Geoffrey Gorham, Paul Griffiths, Paul Guyer, James Harris, William Hasker, Michael Murray, Phillip Quinn, Paul Reasoner, Anthony Rudd, and Corliss Swain. I am also very grateful for the expert assistance of Brian MacDonald and Stephanie Achard of Cambridge University Press.

This book is dedicated to Nicholas Shears, Alex Marcell, and Francesca Lowe with love. And to Jil, with love always.

Introduction

Philosophy of religion is, I believe, one of the most fascinating and profound areas of philosophy, in part because it asks basic questions about our place in the cosmos and about the possibility of a reality that may *transcend* the cosmos. Is the cosmos created or uncreated? Alternatively, should the natural world itself be thought of as sacred or divine? What is the relationship between (apparently) competing concepts of God found in different religions and even in the same religion? Is a Buddhist concept of the self or a Christian view of the soul credible in light of modern science? A philosophical exploration of these and other questions requires an investigation into the nature and limits of human thought.

Philosophy of religion is also a robust, important undertaking due to its breadth. Religious traditions are so comprehensive and all-encompassing that almost every domain of philosophy may be drawn upon in the philosophical exploration of their coherence, justification, and value. I can think of few areas of philosophy that lack religious implications. Any philosophical account of knowledge, values, reason, human nature, language, science, and the like will have a bearing on how one views God or the sacred; religious values and practices; the religious treatment of birth, history, and death; the varieties of religious experience; the relationship between science and religion; and other substantial terrain. At least two other factors contribute to the importance of philosophy of religion.

Because it explores embedded social and personal practices, philosophy of religion is relevant to practical concerns; its subject matter is not all abstract theory. Given the vast percentage of the world population that is either aligned with religion or affected by it, philosophy of religion has a secure role in addressing people's values and commitments.[1] A chief point of reference in much philosophy of religion revolves not around hypothetical, highly abstract thought experiments but around the shape and content of living traditions. Because of this practical embeddedness, philosophy of religion involves issues of great political and cultural significance. Questions are raised about the relationship between religious and secular values; religious toleration and liberty; and the religious implications and duties concerning medicine, the economy, public art, education, sexual ethics, and environmental responsibility.

Finally, for those interested in the history of ideas in the modern era, there is an inescapable reason for studying philosophy of religion: most modern philosophers explicitly address religious topics. One cannot undertake a credible history of modern philosophy without taking philosophy of religion seriously.

This book follows the custom of taking the "modern era" to begin with the birth of modern science.[2] I start to build a history of modern philosophy of religion in the middle of seventeenth-century Europe when Isaac Newton enters the scene. Beginning the book in the mid-seventeenth century provides a view of philosophical work on religion in the midst of debate over the religious importance of an emerging, powerful empirical science. It also shows philosophy of religion being carried out in the context of tumultuous political and social changes that help define the centuries that follow.

In the first volume of the series "The Evolution of Modern Philosophy," Roberto Torretti offers an account of modern physics, noting that his topic differs from philosophy of religion and other areas in terms of its continuity with the past. "While the modern philosophies of art, language, politics, religion, and so on seek to elucidate manifestations of human life that are much older and probably will last much longer than the philosophical will for lucidity, the modern philosophy of physics has

---

[1] Reliable statistics on religion are difficult to obtain, but I note the following figures on some world religions from the *Britannica Book of the Year, 2003*: Christianity – more than 2 billion (32.9%); Islam – more than 1.2 billion (19.8%); Hinduism – more than 800 million (13.3%); Buddhism – more than 360 million (5.9%); Judaism – more than 14 million (.2%). The *Britannica* has a useful overview of adherents to sixteen religions.

[2] There are other customs; some pinpoint the beginning of the "modern era" or "modernity" in the late 1700s at the time of the French Revolution. Alternatively, "modern" and "modernism" have been used to describe a system of logic (*via moderna*) in the fourteenth to sixteenth century in contrast to older systems (*via antiqua*).

to do with modern physics, an intellectual enterprise that began in the seventeenth century as a central piece of history itself."[3] Unlike Torretti's modern physics, there are significant connections between philosophy of religion today and earlier philosophy, including philosophy in ancient Greece. In planning a starting point for this book, I wanted to appeal to one or more philosophers who had deep roots in earlier philosophical traditions but who were also party to modern science. I kept thinking of the ancient Roman pictures of the keeper of doorways, Janus, the god of beginnings. He has two faces, one looking to the past, the other to the future. I settled on a cluster of philosophers known as the Cambridge Platonists, who flourished at Cambridge University in the seventeenth century, to begin this narrative.

The Cambridge Platonists occupy an important middle ground in the history of ideas. They understood the power of modern science (there is reason to believe one of the members of this movement, Henry More, influenced Newton's science), and yet they worked in allegiance with an important Platonic philosophical and religious heritage spanning ancient, medieval, and Renaissance philosophy. They forged an extraordinary synthesis designed to incorporate modern science while retaining what they believed to be the best of Greek and Hebrew wisdom. Like Janus, the Cambridge Platonists invite us to adopt that double vision of looking both to the past and to the future. I believe that they are also deserving of more than a passing glance because of their work to promote nonviolent political life and toleration in a time of war and bitter political and sectarian struggle. Their goal of synthesizing ancient and modern wisdom may or may not be tenable and, looking back, we may readily conclude that their case for toleration did not go far enough, but I believe their critique of religious persecution and their respect for liberty of conscience (both philosophical and political) is a good place to begin.

The Cambridge Platonists are also a promising starting point because in their literature one may see almost all the themes that define early modern philosophical work on religion, as well as themes that occupy the philosophy of religion up to the present day. Among the many subjects addressed by the Cambridge Platonists is a topic that bears not just on philosophy of religion but on philosophy of science, philosophy of art, and other subfields of philosophy. A philosophy of X,

---

[3] Roberto Torretti, *The Philosophy of Physics* (Cambridge: Cambridge University Press, 1999), xiii.

be it religion, science, art, history, or whatever, may be in radical opposition to X as it is practiced. So, a philosopher of religion may think of religion as intellectually and morally bankrupt, just as some philosophers
of art find some contemporary "art" either not art at all or aesthetically
abominable. Unfortunately, the obvious point needs to be made that a
philosophy of X must be accurately apprised of X.[4] Some artists, scientists, and religious practitioners complain that philosophy of art, science,
and religion utilize misleading pictures of the way art, science, and religion are actually practiced. For better or for worse, the Cambridge
Platonists were *philosophers* of religion and, at the same time, committed to the practice of religion. They *practiced* the very thing they
were *studying* and *philosophically reflecting on,* and in that respect the
Cambridge Platonists were like artists or scientists working out a philosophy of art or science. They also thereby raise questions about the roles
of detachment and religious commitment in the course of philosophical
inquiry.[5]

---

[4] Regrettably, it is not unusual to see an observation like the following in philosophy of
science and other areas of philosophy: "Philosophers of science nowadays tend to be
much better informed than their predecessors about the details of the sciences they are
philosophizing about, and this, I have no doubt, has led to important improvements in
the field," from John Worrall, "Philosophy and the Natural Sciences," in *Philosophy 2,*
ed. A. C. Grayling (Oxford: Oxford University Press, 1998), 243. To those new to
philosophy as a field, it must seem bizarre that philosophers of science, art, religion,
and the like would be unacquainted with the history and current practice that define
their subject matter.

[5] On the importance of philosophers of religion looking to the way religion is practiced,
see M. Jamie Ferreira, "Normativity and Reference in a Wittgensteinian Philosophy
of Religion," *Faith and Philosophy* 18:4 (2001): 443–464. In *The Religious* (Oxford:
Blackwell, 2002), John Caputo charges that some philosophy of religion "prove to
be almost completely irrelevant to anyone with the least experience of religious matters, which beg to be treated differently and on their own terms" (3). The Cambridge
Platonists had a great deal of experience in religious matters as well as matters philosophical. On the advantage of combining the philosophy of X – be it religion or
art – with practice, consider Arthur Danto's comment on how aesthetics has bene-
fited from contributors who truly wrestle with art rather than just write about it.
"The dreariness has been driven out of aesthetics, it seems to me, by virtue of the
fact that it is more and more written by philosophers engaged in the raw world of
artistic conflict" (*The Body/Body Problem* [Berkeley: University of California Press,
1999], 245). Like Danto's nondreary philosophers of art, the Cambridge Platonists offer us an *engaged* philosophy of religion. On the advantage of such engaged work, see
also Basil Mitchell's *The Justification of Religious Belief* (London: Macmillan, 1973),
especially 103.

A further reason for my starting point is that there is now a revival of the kind of philosophy of religion advanced by the Cambridge Platonists. Beginning and ending this book with Cambridge Platonism offers one way to take stock of the history of the field. (With all these reasons for giving prominence to this philosophical movement, I want to assure readers that the narrative that follows does not construe the history of philosophy of religion as a series of footnotes on Cambridge Platonism!)

Several other features of this narrative history need to be highlighted. In order to prevent this book from becoming too encyclopedic or dispersed, I use the concept of evidence and its associates (justification, entitlement, warrant, reason to believe, and so on) as recurring reference points. This is the reason behind the title of the book, *Evidence and Faith* (recommended to me by my editor Paul Guyer) rather than the more generic *The Evolution of Modern Philosophy of Religion*. I am concerned with questions such as these:

> What do different philosophies of religion count as evidence for their viability?
>
> How does concern for evidence or intellectual legitimacy relate to moral and religious values?
>
> What standards of evidence or legitimization may be employed in religious views of the subjects cited at the outset of this Introduction – alternative pictures of the divine, for example?
>
> Can you or I have a justified "true experience" or apprehension of God?
>
> Is evidence something normative or objective, or is it relative to specific religious traditions, communities, and gender?
>
> How important is it to have evidence for or against religious beliefs?

I keep one eye on these and other, similar questions throughout the text. Philosophy of religion involves far more than the theory of knowledge and the justification and critique of religious beliefs and practices. Still, the concept of "evidence" (understood in very broad terms) serves as a useful reference point because questions of justification and entitlement are customarily addressed in the modern philosophical exploration of virtually all religious topics. Moreover, to discuss when or if evidence is vital for the legitimization of religious belief and practice inevitably involves taking on such important topics as the trustworthiness of our cognitive faculties, concepts of truth, responsibility, the reliability of testimony, the difference (if any) between fact and interpretation, the limits of inquiry, burdens of proof, and fundamental questions of values.[6]

"Evidence" is only a touchstone in this narrative history, not the dominating, exclusive subject. So, in the exploration of the seventeenth-century Cambridge Platonists in Chapter 1, I seek to bring to the fore their views of faith and reason while at the same time not bypassing their philosophy of human nature and their conception of God's relation to the world. In a sense, the Cambridge Platonist chapter explicitly underscores the difficulty of writing a history of the concept of evidence or a history of what is categorized as "religion" or "religious," in complete isolation from other concerns. The Cambridge Platonists did not simply work with a barren concept of evidence but with a whole scheme of ideas, culminating in a conception of ourselves in the world in which we are so created in order to enable the fruitful exercise of reason.[7] Their view of reason had an important moral and religious role in the (eventual) British opposition to slavery.

In order to keep this book to a manageable length, I center the narrative more on themes and arguments rather than give pride of place to the biographical details of individuals. Biographies, autobiographies, and other texts are suggested for further study. Most of the figures

---

[6] For better or worse, the list is not exhaustive. In the course of my research, I have been struck by how the history of theories of evidence is intertwined with philosophy of religion. Just as a history of philosophy of religion may use the topic of evidence as a reference point, a history of theories of evidence may give prominence to philosophy of religion. William Twining, one of the leading figures in the field of evidence scholarship, notes that the history of evidence theory in law is linked to debate in philosophy of religion; see *Theories of Evidence: Bentham and Wigmore* (London: Weidenfield and Nicolson, 1985), 1. Also see "Some Skepticism about Some Skepticism," in *Rethinking Evidence* (Oxford: Basil Blackwell, 1990), chap. 4, in which Twining explores the legal ramifications of different forms of skepticism, some of which are central topics in philosophy of religion.

[7] The difficulty of addressing evidence in a solitary, narrow fashion may be driven home by taking account of all the presuppositions behind interesting questions about evidence. The question "Are your beliefs supported by evidence?" presumes (at a minimum) that there is a subject, you, and such things as beliefs. Moreover, if someone calls out to you, "Make sure you act in accord with the evidence," I suspect you will respond to different cues and at different speeds depending on what you take to be your circumstances – whether, for example, you have jumped out of a plane and are trying to open your parachute, or you are thinking through Euclidian geometry in tranquillity. Given the right conditions, you also might even like to ask the person hailing you: "Who are you?" "Why this request *now*?" So, questions of evidence very quickly generate other questions about the nature and role of circumstance.

covered in this book have been and still are the subject of enormous study, and often heated, contentious debate. I flag some of the salient points in dispute and suggest some routes into the secondary literature. I am also selective about locating places to address specific arguments in detail; for example, rather than examine the argument from design in many different chapters, I take note of the argument in Chapter 1 and elsewhere, but I make it central to Chapter 4 (on Humean philosophy of religion) and discuss it only briefly in other places. The first chapter references many arguments and claims that are singled out for in-depth discussion later.

I assume some acquaintance with the common terms employed in philosophy of religion but no more than what may be gleaned from standard introductions to the field.[8] *Evidence and Faith* is not chiefly addressed to those already in the field but to those with a background in philosophy who are interested in this vital area of inquiry. To facilitate your engagement with (and contribution to) philosophy of religion, there is an appendix of relevant journals, book series, centers, and societies. I believe that philosophy of religion is best done in collaboration, and my hope is that this book may be of use in drawing more people to the field.

It needs to be stressed that I make no claim to be telling *the* definitive story of modern philosophy of religion. I offer *a* reading of the field in terms that I hope will invite further (including *contrary*) philosophical investigation and the development of different interpretations of modern philosophy of religion. The goal I do *not* have in this historical study is the sequential construction of monuments to movements that serve only historical interests. I believe that many of the struggles from the seventeenth century onward are relevant today. The book is largely a narrative of figures and ideas in their setting, but the text also includes observations on subsequent philosophy and suggested lines of reasoning to further debate. In brief, *Evidence and Faith* is my best effort at locating material for philosophical reflection on the nature and value

---

[8] For an introduction, see my *Contemporary Philosophy of Religion* (Oxford: Blackwell, 1998). Most of the main academic presses have introductions to the field that provide a guide to the common terms used in the philosophical study of religion. The following authors have introductions, any one of which would provide a reasonable background for this history: W. Abraham, S. Brown, K. J. Clark, R. Creel, Brian Davies, C. S. Evans, J. C. A. Gaskin, J. Hick, A. O'Hear, M. Peterson et al., B. R. Tilgman, T. V. Morris, K. Yandell.

of religion in the past and present. Most of the chapters include the reconstruction of at least one relevant argument (along with objections and replies), which I hope will have a bearing on projects some readers will engage and perhaps rework (critically or constructively) in the field today.

Although I am writing primarily for those with only some background in the field, a word needs to be said to and about seasoned scholars. The history of philosophy as a field has increased in caliber dramatically over the past thirty years. There is now considerable scorn for making huge generalizations about eras in philosophy, as well as in employing some of the standard categories like rationalism and empiricism. In a recent exchange among four prominent historians in the *Journal of History of Philosophy*, Richard Watson notes how many histories of philosophy are more a matter of shadows than accurate accounts of what "really" happened.

> The shadow history of philosophy is a kind of received view consisting of stories of philosophy that most philosophers accept even though they know that these stories are not really quite precisely right. For example, everyone knows that the division between Continental Rationalists and British Empiricists is bogus. There are strong rationalist elements in Berkeley and strong empiricist elements in Descartes. And so on. Loeb says, "No serious scholar subscribes to [this] standard theory." But most historians continue to teach courses in Rationalism and Empiricism, even if they change the course titles to, say, Early Modern Philosophy or The British Tradition.[9]

I take heed of the need for a more careful use of terms and seek to employ the big "-isms," as in empiricism, idealism, and the like, only for the purpose of a very general organization of some of the material.[10]

---

[9] "Shadow History in Philosophy," *Journal of the History of Philosophy* 3:1 (January 1993): 97.

[10] As an aside, it is interesting to note that many of the standard textbook categories such as empiricism, rationalism, and idealism do not fade away; they remain useful, notwithstanding the frustrations of some scholars over precise definitions. In an important study in the 1930s, *Idealism: A Critical Survey* (London: Methuen, 1933), A. C. Ewing lamented the use of "idealism" and made this prediction: "My view is that the term will soon die out except as a name for a past movement, since most philosophers of the present day seem to feel that it is better not to label themselves expressly as idealists or realists, while they still draw on the resources of either or, better, both schools" (5). For better or for worse, the term "idealism" is alive and very much in currency today. Here are two representative titles of recent, important works:

I also underscore a point that I am certain Watson would not deny: a narrative history needs to include not only work on what we now think philosophers were *actually* getting at, but also material on how they were treated by their contemporaries and in the following centuries. In this book I address the philosophers themselves, as well as the shadows they cast.[11]

It is perhaps obvious that someone setting out to write a focused history of philosophy is at least somewhat optimistic about the possibility of describing (or, given the task of covering 350 years in just over 400 pages, *sketching*) some of what took place from the seventeenth century onward. As it happens, I am not skeptical about the viability of historical inquiry. I do not share the dictum that all history is really about the present and our contemporary projections. Still, I am writing this book for you, my contemporaries, and not as a timeless record of events. In what follows, then, I cross-reference works of the past with the present – mentioning, for example, how seventeenth-century Cambridge Platonist views of human nature differ from current, twenty-first-century views. Sometimes, in order to bring past philosophical debates into view, current projects need to be mentioned in order to set them explicitly to one side, lest they implicitly color our judgment.

Philosophy of religion as it is practiced today includes cross-cultural studies and sustained work on widely divergent, nontheistic traditions. This is an exciting development, and yet it is a *development*. Much of the initial modern era was centered mainly on theism and its alternatives (usually what today we would call deism, naturalism, agnosticism, and skepticism). The Cambridge Platonists had a keen interest in non-Christian traditions; for example, Leibniz was fascinated by Confucianism, and Spinoza's God is not theistic, but it is not until later that nontheistic notions of God, and work in and on Hindu, Buddhist, Taoist, and African philosophy definitively enlarge the practice of philosophy of religion in the West. *Evidence and Faith*

T. L. S. Sprigge, *The Vindication of Absolute Idealism* (Edinburgh: University Press, 1983), and John Foster, *The Case for Idealism* (London: Routledge and Kegan Paul, 1982).

[11] For example, some current historians have offered very different pictures of some philosophers (e.g., Descartes, Hume, Kant) from the ways in which they have been interpreted in the past. I reference some of the more promising projects that recast the "received view" while also offering some of the "standard" interpretations.

narrates the expansion of philosophy of religion, beginning with a theistic philosophy in mid-seventeenth-century England and ending with today's pluralistic, some would say tumultuous, environment. In a narrative history beginning with ancient Asian philosophy of religion, there would be a parallel story of the expansion of Asian philosophy to include the encounter with Abrahamic faiths (Judaism, Christianity, and Islam). At present, the expansive, amplified practice of philosophy of religion worldwide has initiated a vibrant era for both the history and practice of philosophy, as scholars engage important theistic *and* nontheistic philosophical religious traditions.

Most chapters begin with a brief sketch, a kind of snapshot, of a historic event. The first one is an address to the House of Commons during the tragic English Civil War in 1647.

✦

ONE

The Sovereignty of the Good in Seventeenth-Century Philosophy of Religion

Divine truth allwaies carried it's own light and evidence; so as that the mind receiving itt is illuminated, edified, satisfied. . . . It speaks for itt sfelfe, it recommendes itt selfe to its owne enterteinment, by it's owne excellencie. It adde allsoe, that the persuasion of the holie spirit contributes to the minde's assurance and satisfaction.

Benjamin Whichcote[1]

Plato and the English Civil War

On March 31, 1647, Ralph Cudworth of Cambridge University addressed the House of Commons in Westminster, England. Civil war had broken out five years earlier. Parliamentary troops had recently occupied Cambridge, and negotiations between king and Parliament were breaking down. In all, the civil war resulted in 190,000 deaths, just under 4 percent of the population, and the decimation of at least 150 towns and villages.[2] In the midst of this political and social turmoil, Cudworth commended a lesson from one of Plato's dialogues: "Virtue and holiness in creatures, as Plato well discourses in his *Euthyphro*, are not therefore Good, because God loves them, and will have them be

---

[1] Excerpt from a letter in J. D. Roberts, *From Puritanism to Platonism in Seventeenth Century England* (The Hague: Martinus Nijhoff, 1968), 67. Although I have kept the seventeenth-century English here, I employ modern spelling subsequently. The title of this chapter is in the spirit of Iris Murdoch's *The Sovereignty of Good* (New York: Schocken Books, 1971). See P. Conrad, "Platonism in Iris Murdoch," in *Platonism and the English Imagination*, ed. A. Baldwin and S. Hutton (Cambridge: Cambridge University Press, 1994).

[2] Graham E. Seel, *Regicide and Republic – England, 1603–1660* (Cambridge: Cambridge University Press, 2001), 104, 176.

accounted such; but rather, God therefore loves them because they are in themselves simply good."[3] Cudworth told the House of Commons that goodness, not self-love or appetites and desires, is sovereign. To think of God in terms of sheer power is a harmful projection, a base reflection of human vice. Worshiping a God of sheer power, uninformed by goodness, celebrates vanity; it is symptomatic of a community incapable of conceiving of a good that transcends self-will. "And it is another mistake which sometimes we have of God by shaping him out according to the model of ourselves, when we make him nothing but a blind, dark, impetuous Self-will, running through the world; such as we ourselves are furiously acted with, that have not the ballast of absolute goodness to poise and settle us."[4] Evil is an ugly deformity of life, an aberration, whereas beauty and goodness are natural and woven together. "God is beauty."[5] Cudworth drew on Plato's dialogue *Euthydemus* in his portrait of moral and religious education. To bolster his case, Cudworth employed the Christian Bible as well as Plato, Plotinus, and Epictetus.

Cudworth's address to the House of Commons was not an academic paper in philosophy of religion. He was delivering a sermon; it was more exhortation or plea than argument.[6] Considering the execution of

---

[3] Cudworth, "A Sermon Preached before the House of Commons," in *The Cambridge Platonists*, ed. C. A. Patrides (Cambridge: Cambridge Univeristy Press, 1970), 102. Alison Teply and I have coedited a collection of Cambridge Platonist works, *Cambridge Platonist Spirituality* (Mahwah, N.J.: Paulist Press, 2005), which includes the full text of Cudworth's address.

[4] Cudworth, "A Sermon Preached," 102.

[5] Ibid., 113.

[6] For readers who may worry that this book begins with a preacher rather than a philosopher, Cudworth's philosophical credentials are impeccable, as testified to by Locke, Leibniz, Shaftesbury, Price, Reid, et al. See, for example, J. Locke, *Some Thoughts Concerning Education*, ed. John Yolton and Jean Yolton (Oxford: Oxford University Press, 1989), 248, and John Passmore, *Ralph Cudworth: An Interpretation* (Cambridge: Cambridge University Press, 1992), 91–95. Hume places Cudworth alongside Clarke and Locke (*Enquiry*, parts I and VII, and parts II and III). He is credited by J. H. Muirhead as the first to use the term "philosophy of religion" in English; see *The Platonic Tradition in Anglo-Saxon Philosophy* (New York: Macmillan, 1931), 28. The *Oxford English Dictionary* credits Cudworth for the first use of "theism" in English. In the *Times Literary Supplement*, June 14, 2002, Kenneth Winkler (current editor of *Hume Studies*) writes: "Ralph Cudworth's *True Intellectual System of the Universe* (1678) is one of the first great works of philosophy written in the English language" (8). For evidence of Cudworth's relevance today, see B. Hooker, "Cudworth and Quinn," *Analysis* 61 (2001): 333–335. There is an accessible entry by Cudworth in J. B. Schneewind's collection *Moral Philosophy from Montaigne to Kant*

King Charles I two years later and Cromwell's military excursion into Ireland (three thousand Irish were killed at Drogheda, two thousand at Wexford), the effectiveness of Cudworth's invocation to restrain political power with justice and humility is not obvious. Still, the address displays some of the salient themes that come to be refined and articulated in Cudworth's mature philosophical work in which goodness and beauty, education and faith are in profound concord. Cudworth's address to the House of Commons also reflects four important features of early modern philosophy of religion.

First, philosophy of religion was often carried out with an eye on politics and morality. In the mid-seventeenth century, "religion" was commonly seen as the source or guardian of moral and political wisdom. A philosopher of religion could remain completely free of the political theater no more than a politician could act without regard for religious concerns – the pursuit of justified true beliefs about God and the good were bound together. In *A Treatise Concerning Eternal and Immutable Morality*, Cudworth's opposition to praising God solely for God's pure power carried clear political implications. He countered the thesis "that there is no act evil but as it is prohibited by God, and which cannot be made good if it be commanded by God."[7] By implication Cudworth also stood against the exultation of any monarch or parliament that would arrogate to itself the power to settle by command what is good or evil. "When things exist, they are what they are, this or that, absolutely or relatively, not by will or arbitrary command, but by the necessity of their own nature. . . . Wherefore the natures of justice and injustice cannot be arbitrary things, that may be applicable by will indifferently to any actions or dispositions whatsoever."[8] During Cudworth's lifetime, beliefs

---

(Cambridge: Cambridge University Press, 2003), 275–292. For an interesting study of the theory of human nature behind Cudworth's address to the House of Commons, see Alan Gabbey, "Cudworth, More and the Mechanical Analogy," in *Philosophy, Science, and Religion in England*, ed. R. Kroll et al. (Cambridge: Cambridge University Press, 1992).

[7] *A Treatise Concerning Eternal and Immutable Morality, with a Treatise on Free Will*, ed. Sarah Hutton (Cambridge: Cambridge University Press, 1996), 14. Cudworth attributes the view he is attacking to William of Ockham (1290–1349). Interpretations of Ockham vary. For a good study on this point, see Marilyn Adams's two-volume work, *William Ockham* (Notre Dame: University of Notre Dame Press, 1987). For a good survey of the politics surrounding Cambridge Platonism, see G. A. J. Rogers, "The Other-Worldly Philosophers and the Real World: The Cambridge Platonists, Theology, and Politics," in *The Cambridge Platonists in Philosophical Context*, ed. G. A. J. Rogers et al. (Dordrecht: Kluwer, 1997).

[8] Ibid., 17.

about divine power ran parallel to beliefs about political institutions of power, whether it be the church, Parliament, or crown.[9]

A second point to observe at the beginning of this book is that in seventeenth-century literature (as in the works of most medieval authors) the lines demarcating philosophy and theology are not clear, and established parameters identifying philosophy of religion as a subfield of philosophy are lacking. In exploring the seventeenth-century literature, we do well to see the intellectual climate as heterogeneous and as rife with philosophy of religion as it was with politics, theology, apologetics, science, and philosophy of science. There were proposals to sequester religious concerns from philosophy, science, and other fields, but Cudworth opposed such a split, completely rejecting the dictum that religion is not philosophy (*Religio non est philosophia*). The seventeenth and eighteenth centuries seem to vindicate Cudworth, at least on the point that philosophical and religious themes were frequently intertwined and rarely treated in complete isolation.

Third, the formats for engaging different philosophies of religion were much more varied than our twenty-first-century conventions. Early modern philosophy of religion may be found in essays, treatises, lectures, and letters, as well as in poetry, biography and autobiography, dialogues, aphorisms, pamphlets, travel literature, and even sermons before the House of Commons.

Fourth, philosophical reflection on religion was increasingly practiced outside the single religious tradition or church that had sovereign European authority. Earlier, in medieval philosophical inquiry into God, God's relation to the world, and the practice of religion, philosophy was sometimes carried out at the crossroads of Christianity, Judaism, and Islam. But until the Reformation, Western European philosophy was undertaken in a Roman Catholic climate.[10] By the seventeenth century, however, Protestant as well as Catholic philosophers were

---

[9] See "The Absolute and Ordained Power of God and King in Sixteenth and Seventeenth Centuries: Philosophy, Science, Politics, and Law," *Journal of the History of Ideas* 59 (1998): 669–690, and "The Absolute and Ordained Power of God in Sixteenth and Seventeenth Century Theology," *Journal of the History of Ideas* 59 (1998): 436–461, both by Francis Oakley.

[10] In a book of this size, it is impossible to include an extensive treatment of the medieval background. I offer some observations at different points on links between early modern philosophy and medieval work; for a brilliant overview of the medievals (Christians, Jews, and Muslims), see A. S. McGrade, ed., *The Cambridge Companion to Medieval Philosophy* (Cambridge: Cambridge University Press, 2003).

publishing important works. Cudworth, for example, and many of the subsequent English-speaking contributors to philosophy of religion were Protestants.

Ralph Cudworth (1617–1688) was one of several philosophers who became known collectively as the Cambridge Platonists. Others in this school of philosophy include Benjamin Whichcote (1609–1683), Henry More (1614–1687), John Smith (1616–1672), and Nathaniel Culverwell (1618–1713).[11] Whichcote was the major inspiration of this movement, but Cudworth and More are its better-known philosophers. Ralph Cudworth's daughter Damaris Cudworth Masham (1659–1708) and Anne Viscountess Conway (1631–1679) also advocated and advanced a broadly Cambridge Platonist philosophy.[12]

Platonism, Christianity, and Some Divine Arguments

A central motif for the Cambridge Platonists was "the candle of the Lord," a descriptive term they took from the Old Testament Proverbs 20:27: "The spirit of man is the candle of the Lord." They believed that human nature – in fact, nature as a whole – was created and conserved in existence by an all-good, omnipotent, omniscient, necessarily existing God. In More's terms: "God is a spirit Eternal, Infinite in Essence and Goodness, Omniscient, Omnipotent, and of himself necessarily Existent."[13] Our reasoning functions as a candle of the Lord in that through reasoning we can reflect on a God of essential goodness

---

[11] Still others associated with this circle include Jeremy Taylor (1613–1667), Peter Sterry (1613–1672), George Rust (d. 1670), Joseph Glanvill (1636–1680), and John Norris (1657–1711).

[12] For two fine bibliographies of work by and about Cambridge Platonists, see Rogers et al., *The Cambridge Platonists in Philosophical Context*, and R. Crocker's "A Bibliography of Henry More," in Sarah Hutton's splendid *Henry More (1610–1687): Tercentenary Studies* (Dordrecht: Kluwer, 1990). Crocker also has a useful biographical essay in the Hutton volume. For an overview of the relevant seventeenth-century manuscripts, see the appendix to Passmore's *Ralph Cudworth: An Interpretation*. There is also a good "Essay on Bibliography" by Aaron Lichtenstein in his *Henry More: The Rational Theology of a Cambridge Platonist* (Cambridge, Mass.: Harvard University Press, 1962). For a general look at the religious and cultural ideas behind Cambridge Platonism, see Rosalie Colie's *Light and Enlightenment* (Cambridge: Cambridge University Press, 1957).

[13] Chapter 4 in *The Immortality of the Soul*, p. 23 in the Garland facsimile *Henry More: A Collection of Several Philosophical Writings*, ed. Rene Welleck, vol. 1 (New York: Garland, 1978). See also *An Antidote against Atheism*, in ibid., 20.

and beauty.[14] Our very rational, sensory, and bodily lives are divinely bestowed gifts that provide evidence of our Creator.

Cudworth, More, Whichcote, Culverwell, and Smith are called *Cambridge* Platonists because of their academic appointments at Cambridge University. They are *Platonists* because of their philosophical bent but only in the general sense that covers many philosophers in the Christian tradition from Clement of Alexandria (150–215), Origen (185–254), and Augustine (354–430) to Marsilio Ficino (1433–1499), each of whom left marks on the Cambridge school. The Platonism of Cudworth and his companions amounted to a vision of goodness (or the Good) as the preeminent attribute of God – a goodness toward which we are constitutionally oriented.[15] We are so constituted that we naturally seek goodness, and this search finds its consummation in a relationship with God. The Good, and ultimately God, are the objects of our natural desire. Although some of their other convictions may be understood as "Platonic" as opposed to Aristotelian, on many issues this Cambridge school did not follow the historical Plato. Plato, for example, treated God as a finite demiurge who worked on preexisting matter. Clement, Ficino, and the Cambridge Platonists embraced a more exalted view of God's creative power.[16]

Cambridge Platonism links British philosophy with Christian humanism and Platonism. Humanism flowered during the Renaissance of northern Europe in the work of Erasmus of Rotterdam (1463–1494), while Platonism won followers in southern Europe, where Pico Della Mirandola (1463–1494) and Ficino brought together classical

---

[14] For the Platonic background on beauty, see Marsilio Ficino's commentary on Plato's *Symposium*.

[15] Marsilio Ficino (and other Christian Platonists) describes God as the Supreme or Highest Good, the Good of all goods. See Ficino's *Meditations on the Soul*, trans. Language Department, School of Economic Science, London (Rochester: Inner Traditions International, 1997). For a related but different view in the Thomistic tradition, see R. Garrigou-Lagrange, *God: His Existence and His Nature*, vol. 2 (London: B. Herder Book, 1949), chap. 1.

[16] For Plato's view of the demiurge, see A. E. Taylor, *A Commentary on Plato's Timaeus* (Oxford: Clarendon, 1928). Two general treatments of Platonism within Christianity are Muirhead's *The Platonic Tradition in Anglo-Saxon Philosophy* and W. R. Inge's *The Platonic Tradition in English Religious Thought* (London: Longmans, Green, 1926). Nicholas Sagovsky offers a constructive portrait of Plato's contribution to Christianity in *Ecumenism, Christian Origins and the Practice of Communion* (Cambridge: Cambridge University Press, 2000), chap. 2, "Plato's Vision." For a classic study, see C. Bigg, *The Christian Platonists of Alexandria* (Oxford: Clarendon, 1968).

philosophy and Christian convictions. In this ethos, Erasmus warmly promoted pre-Christian philosophy while also commending what he called the philosophy of Christ (*Philosophia Christi*). To take stock of the Renaissance background to the Cambridge Platonists, they should be read in relation to Thomas More (1478–1535), rather than, say, the Renaissance political philosopher Niccolo Machiavelli (1469–1527), for whom classical notions of power take precedence over Christian virtues. Cudworth's address to the House of Commons in 1647 is the mirror opposite of Machiavelli's *The Prince* (1513), which makes a brazen recommendation of fearsome power rather than charity. While Cudworth, like Erasmus, counseled the exercise of power only with scrupulous attention to justice, humility, and charity, Machiavelli commended stealthy self-advancement and subterfuge. In Machiavelli's *The Prince*, reason has a largely instrumental role. Given that one wants political power, the role of reason is to pinpoint the best means to reach that goal. Cudworth, in the tradition of Plato and Augustine, held instead that philosophical reflection can disclose to us a host of goods beyond self-will, which warrant our pursuit and allegiance.

To what grounds did the Cambridge Platonists appeal in articulating and securing their harmonious, God-filled picture of humanity and the cosmos? By and large, the Cambridge Platonists did not assume that their philosophy of God and their treatment of values could be established with irresistible force. More and Cudworth held that theism deserves "full assent from any unprejudiced mind," but they did not maintain that the truth of theism could be confirmed infallibly.[17] More offered this analogy:

> For I conceive that we may give *full* assent to that which notwithstanding may possibly be otherwise: which I shall illustrate by several examples. Suppose two men got to the top of Mount Athos, and there viewing a stone in the form of an altar with ashes on it, and the footsteps of men on these ashes, or some words, if you will, as Optimo Maximo.[18] . . . or the like, written or scrawled out on the ashes; and one of them should cry out, Assuredly there have been some men here that have done this: but the other more nice than wise should reply, Nay, it may possibly be otherwise; for this stone may have naturally grown into this very shape, and the seeming ashes may be no ashes, that is, no remainders of any

---

[17] Chap. 2 in Henry More's *An Antidote against Atheism*, 10.

[18] *Optimo Maximo*: the Greatest and Best, as used of the Divine. The initials DOM, for Deo Optimo Maximo, are sometimes imprinted on the doors of churches.

fuel burnt there, but some inexplicable and imperceptive motions of the air, or some other particles of the matter into the form and nature of ashes, and have fridg'd and played about so, that they have also figured those intelligible characters in the same. But would not any body deem it a piece of weakness no less than dotage for the other man one wit to recede from his former apprehension, but as fully as ever to agree with what he pronounced first, notwithstanding this bare possibility of being otherwise.[19]

This analogy is instructive as it reveals the Cambridge Platonist motive to employ "plain reason" – that is, a form of reasoning that accords with the ordinary ways in which we measure evidence and draw conclusions about the world.[20] Their understanding of reasoning in philosophical theology is consistent with their view of reason in general, which includes – but is not limited to – reflections on mathematics and geometry. As such, our philosophical conclusions about religion are not to be assessed exclusively by comparison with grasping, abstract logical entailments. The atheist's description and explanation of *Optimo Maximo* are not *logically* absurd, although they are unreasonable. The analogy that More employs also testifies to the Cambridge Platonists' intent to secure their philosophy in terms of overall coherence. In the end, their views of God and human nature were recommended on the grounds that they were intelligible in light of a host of factors, just as one might infer that a message was intentionally spelled out in ashes in light of one's acquaintance with language, one's expectations about people, one's beliefs about ashes, and so on.

Henry More builds a case for theism in his *An Antidote against Atheism* (1652). His first argument in *An Antidote* is a version of what today would be called an "ontological argument," which he complements with other arguments to build a cumulative case for theism. More's work is one of the earliest formulations of an ontological and design argument by an English-speaking philosopher. The ontological argument that follows resembles (and is indebted to) one advanced by Descartes that we consider in the next chapter.[21] The argument may be

---

[19] *An Antidote against Atheism*, 10–11.

[20] Ibid., 2.

[21] Descartes' version influenced More's, but I cite More's first because of its place in the overall system of Cambridge Platonism. (See the Introduction for my rationale for beginning with the Cambridge Platonists.) One other reason for beginning with More's version is that there is less confusion and controversy about identifying More's line

described as proceeding *a priori* (from what is earlier), as it proceeds from investigating the concept of God rather than from experience. Arguments *a posteriori* (from what comes after) proceed on the basis of experience; yet here the distinction is not a sharp one, for More's reflection on the concept of God sometimes blends with his claim of experiencing the divine.

More, like Cudworth, begins with the concept of God, not as brute power, but as supremely valuable and perfect. "I define God therefore thus, An essence or being fully and absolutely perfect. I say, fully and absolutely perfect, in counter distinction to such perfection as is not full and absolute, but the perfection of this or that species or kind of finite being, suppose of a lion, horse, or tree."[22] God, then, is neither a finite entity nor merely one member of the category "Divinity." God, if God exists, is not like a perfect lion whose perfection may be relative to kind – for example, possessing a muscular body or large head. Rather, to conceive of God is to conceive of a unique reality of maximal excellence or overriding perfection. In this philosophical theology, God's excellence and perfection is unsurpassable.[23] The divine attributes of goodness, power, knowledge, necessary existence, and eternity are then derived from the concept of perfection or unsurpassable greatness. Power, knowledge, and the other attributes are advanced as attributes of a perfect being.[24] A being that has one but not another of these great-making qualities would be imperfect. A being with omniscience and goodness but which is finite and subject to corruption is less great than an omniscient, good, omnipotent, eternal, necessarily existing being: "Knowledge without goodness is but dry subtlety or mischievous craft; goodness with knowledge devoid of power is but lame and ineffectual."[25] Perfect lions, horses, trees, islands, and the like, however glorious, are not equal to the concept of a being of overriding perfection, capable of creating any such lions, horses, and so on.

---

of reasoning. A great deal more scholarly dispute has arisen from Descartes' *Meditations*. The lineage of the ontological argument goes back to Anselm of Canterbury (1033–1109). For an overview of its history, see A. C. McGill and J. Hick, eds., *The Many Faced Argument* (New York: Macmillan, 1967). Cudworth sought to bolster the ontological argument by appeal to an argument from design.

[22] *An Antidote against Atheism*, 13.

[23] For a contemporary articulation of such philosophical theology, see T. V. Morris, "Perfect Being Theology," *Nous* 21 (1987).

[24] *An Antidote against Atheism*, 16.

[25] Ibid., 16.

Henry More claims that the idea of God as perfect being, with the entailment of great-making attributes, is a natural idea and inference. Just as we are driven to accept necessary truths about shapes and mathematics (e.g., every number is either even or odd), we likewise naturally conceive of perfection in terms of these divine attributes. This inference is described by More as our natural, noncapricious, native understanding of God. "There is in man an Idea of a Being absolutely and fully perfect, which we frame out by attributing all conceivable perfection to it whatsoever that implies no contradiction. And this Notion is naturall and essential to the Soul of man and cannot be washt out, nor conveigh'd away by any force or trick of wit whatsoever, so long as the Mind of man is not craz'd but hath the ordinary use of her own Faculties."[26] More then reasons that God qua perfect being either does truly necessarily exist or is impossible or contingent. Yet a perfect being could not be contingent, as contingency would mar its seeming perfection. In More's view, the fact that we naturally conceive of perfection as a necessary reality is evidence that God's reality is indeed possible and therefore not impossible.[27] The conclusion is that God does truly exist necessarily.

Henry More's initial move concerns the idea of God, but he is proposing that the idea of God is the idea of a being whose necessary existence is not a function of our ideas nor is in any way derived from some other reality. So, More does not understand divine necessity in the way in which one might secure necessary entailments through definitions. Given the definition of *grandmother* as "a female whose child has a child," it follows necessarily that if Jane Doe is a grandmother, then Jane is a female whose child has a child. This definitional necessity falls short of attributing to Jane the essential property of *being a grandmother*; Jane might not have had a child. The necessity of God, for More, is not something accidental to God or the result of how we define God, such that the being who is God could become contingent or cease to exist necessarily. God's necessary or essential existence is not derived from or constituted by any human conceptual or linguistic framework. Even if More fails to

---

[26] Ibid., chap. 3.

[27] This move from conceivability to possibility is one that we need to revisit at different places in the history of modern philosophy (especially in Chapters 4 and 8). For a superb collection of some of the latest work on this, see T. S. Gendler and J. Hawthorne, eds., *Conceivability and Possibility* (Oxford: Clarendon, 2002). I defend the use of thought experiments to justify claims about possibility in "Sensibility and Possibilia," *Philosophia Christi* 3:2 (January 2002).

secure his conclusion of God's actual existence, he has sought to paint a portrait of what he sees as a divine reality independent of any human intervention; God is seen in terms of noncontingent excellence in goodness, power, and knowledge.

The argument requires extensive further articulation to be successful; one must clarify the concept of necessity and face up to challenges about whether God's existence is a bona fide possibility. I do not comment on the validity or soundness of the argument here, as we meet ontological arguments in several chapters; I offer some constructive suggestions later about the argument in connection with Hume and Kant. What I underscore now is *the way* More argues: he begins with the apprehension of God as supreme value; he construes this as evident to our very souls and then works from this interior notion to recognizing God as an exterior, transcendent reality.

> If we were traveling in a desolate wilderness, where we could discover neither man nor house, and should meet with herds of cattle or flocks of sheep upon whose bodies there were branded certain marks or letters, we should without hesitancy conclude that these have been under the hand of some man or other that has set his name upon them. And verily when we see in our souls in such legible characters the name, or rather the nature and idea of God, why should we be so slow and backward from making the like reasonable inference?[28]

Essentially More sees us bearing within us a sign that should lead us to recognize the One who made us and to whom we belong.[29] The coordination between the inner sign of God's presence and the external sign of God in the world is confirmed in the world's apparent design.

> Wherefore we being so well furnished for the voyage, I would have my atheist to take shipping with me, and looking from this particular speculation of our own inward nature, to launch out into that vast ocean ... of the external phenomena of universal nature, or walk with me a while on the wide theatre of the outward world, and diligently to attend to those many and most manifest marks and signs that I shall point him to in this outward frame of things, that naturally signify unto us *That there is a God*.[30]

---

[28] *An Antidote against Atheism*, 27.

[29] See also Descartes' *Meditations on First Philosophy*, third meditation. For an exposition of Descartes' argument, see Chapter 2.

[30] *An Antidote against Atheism*, 37–38.

More's extensive development of an argument from design can be found in the *Divine Dialogues*, a work that is a prime example of popular philosophy of religion in the seventeenth century. In his biography of More, Richard Ward writes, "For ten years together, after the return of King Charles the Second, the Mystery of Godliness and Dr. More's other works, ruled all the booksellers in London."[31]

The dialogue features an exchange between Philotheus (the one who loves God) and Hylobares (an initial skeptic). Because of the importance of this dialogue as a document in the development of philosophy of religion, I cite a sizable, central exchange:

> *Philotheus*: It is a great wonder to me that a person so ingenious as Hylobares, and so much conversant in philosophy, should at all doubt of the existence of the Deity, any more than he does of Philopolis's [another person in the text] existence or my own; for we cannot so audibly or intelligibly converse with him as God doth with a philosopher in the ordinary phenomena of nature. For tell me, O Hylobares, whether if so brief a treatise as that of *Archimedes de Sphaera and Cylindro* had been found by chance, with the delineations of all the figures suitable for the design, and short characters (such as they now use in Specious Arithmetic and Algebra) for the setting down of demonstrations of the orderly disposed propositions, could you or anyone else imagine that the delineating and fitting these things together was by chance, and not from a knowing and designing principle, I mean from a power intellectual?
>
> *Hylobares*: I must confess, I think it in a manner impossible that anyone that understood demonstrations should doubt, but that the description of them was by some intelligent being.
>
> *Philotheus*: But why do you think so, Hylobares?
>
> *Hylobares*: Because it is the property of that which is intelligent to lay several things together orderly and advantageously for a proposed design. Which is done so constantly and repeatedly in the treatise, and so methodically, that it is impossible to doubt but that it is the effect of some intellectual agent.

[31] Richard Ward, "The Life of the Learned and Pious Dr. Henry More," in *The Life of Henry More,* ed. Sarah Hutton et al. (Dordrecht: Kluwer, 2000), 101. To use terms Richard Rorty employs in "Cultural Politics and the Question of the Existence of God," the cultural politics of mid-seventeenth-century England invited More's combination of natural and revealed philosophical theology; see N. Frankenberry, ed., *Radical Interpretation in Religion* (Cambridge: Cambridge University Press, 2002).

Philotheus: Wherefore wherever we find frequent and repeated indications of pursuing skillfully a design, we must acknowledge some intelligent being the cause thereof.

Hylobares: We must so.

Philotheus: But what a small scroll and how few instances of pursuing a design is there in that treatise of Archimedes, in comparison of the whole volume of nature, wherein, as in Archimedes, every demonstration leading to the main upshot of all (which is the proportion betwixt the sphere and the cylinder) is a pledge of the wit and reason of the mathematician, so the several subordinate natures in the world (which are in a manner infinite) bear conspicuously in them a design for the best, and are a cloud of witnesses that there is a divine and intellectual principle under all.[32]

At least three points are worth noting in this exchange. First, More highlights the vital role of observation and the value of nature in understanding God. For More, the earlier ontological argument is bolstered by an appeal to the observation of (ostensible) purpose in nature.

Second, the argument works with an analogy – the resemblance of the cosmos to an object that we know has intelligent design. But, more fundamentally, the argument proceeds on the grounds that the mark of "intelligent being" is to bring about objects that are worthy of production. These objects have order, intelligibility, and fittingness. A principle is at work here, one that concerns the concept of intelligence, not just a concept of *human* intelligence. It is, by More's lights, a mark of intelligence to bring about valuable states of affairs. This thesis is not confined to anthropology and the perfection of merely human traits as though God is superhuman.

Third, in the dialogues, More's characters refer to what is impossible to doubt, not what is impossible to occur. Like the ashes spelling out words in the earlier analogy, it is *possible* that the treatise *Archimedes de Sphaera and Cylindro* was produced by brute chance or nonintentional forces, and it is likewise possible that the cosmos as a whole is shorn of intentional design. Yet this sheer possibility is not seen as a reason to doubt that both nature and the treatise are created by an intentional reality. In all, I suggest that the version of the design argument in play

---

[32] More, *Divine Dialogues* (1668), 20–22. Taken from the 1668 edition, published in London. More has an amusing description of the general character of the dialogue. He describes the characters as "All free spirits, mutually permitting one another the liberty of philosophizing without any breech of friendship."

in the dialogues is a form of argument to the best explanation or, more precisely, an argument from the best explanation. In other words, the format of the argument is that, given theism, the integrity and order of the cosmos is comprehensible and explainable, whereas this is not the case in a nontheistic framework. The point of the treatise analogy is similar: granted intelligent design, the treatise is intelligible and explainable, but matters are more puzzling or absurd otherwise. The importance of distinguishing an argument from design that is centered on analogies versus one that appeals to the best explanation will emerge later. [33]

In the course of arguing for theism from the apparent value of the cosmos, both Cudworth and More contend that theism offers a better account of the emergence of sentience and consciousness. How can matter in motion produce feeling and thought? In humanity's conscious action and reflection we see a powerful cognition and creative agency, whereas matter in motion is devoid of feeling, intention, and consciousness. Thus, according to Cudworth and More, it is more reasonable to attribute the emergence of consciousness in the cosmos to an overarching, supreme, conscious mind than to the atheist's account, which privileges matter. Whereas a divine mind with omnipotence, rationality, and intellect can account for the world, how is it that our world with its creatures of reason, intellect, and sensation can be accounted for by exclusively material causes? In his dialogues, More put great weight on what may be called the problem of emergence in a materialist philosophy. How can sensory, rational, intellectual life emerge from something with no sense, reason, or intellect?

More addresses the problem of evil in the *Divine Dialogues*, emphasizing the good of the cosmos taken as a whole and arguing that the material composition and stable condition of life prohibit God from constantly intervening in events to prevent harms.

More and Cudworth articulated their theistic arguments within a self-conscious historical setting. They believed that ancient pagan philosophy corroborated some Christian teaching, as it reflected the early revelation of God to Moses. Cudworth supposed that Pythagoras and others hinted at a teaching based on the revelation of the Triune nature of God. Although the hypothesis of a Mosaic perennial philosophy

---

[33] There is some reason to believe Hume drew on More's design argument in developing the *Dialogues Concerning Natural Religion*. See Elmer Sprague, "Hume, Henry More and the Design Argument," *Hume Studies* 14:2 (1988), and my discussion in Chapter 4.

behind Pythagoras may strike us today as absurd, it did signal a keen interest in the way in which historical inquiry can supplement and refine philosophical reflection.[34] Cudworth also did not limit his interest in the history of philosophy to work that heralded Christian philosophy. He paid great attention to the ways in which earlier philosophy by Democritus, Lucretius, and others prepared the way for nontheistic, alternative philosophies. Cudworth was intensely aware of the history of philosophy and the importance of seeing one's work in relation to whatever wisdom could be gained from ancient sources.

In surveying the arguments advanced by the Cambridge Platonists, one may see what amounts to an aesthetic fit between premises and conclusions. In other words, the Cambridge Platonists wrote as if there were something beautiful or aesthetically pleasing in the soul's apprehension of the idea, and then the reality, of God. More suggests this in his depiction of the way in which a person may be aroused to the idea of God:

> Suppose a skillful musician fallen asleep in the field upon the grass, during which time he shall not so much as dream anything concerning his musical faculty, so that in one sense there is no *actual skill* or notion, nor representation of anything musical in him; but his friend sitting by him, that cannot sing at all himself, jogs him and awakes him, and desires him to sing this or the other song, telling him two or three words of the beginning of the song, whereupon he presently takes it out of his mouth, and sings the whole song upon so slight and slender intimation. So the *mind* of man being jogged and awakened by the impulses of outward objects, is stirred up into a more full and clear conception of what was but imperfectly hinted to her [the soul] from external occasions; and this faculty I venture to call *actual knowledge*, in such a sense as the sleeping musician's skill might be called *actual skill* when he thought nothing of it.[35]

If theism is true, then evidence (or, by analogy, the song) makes sense (or is in harmony). If theism is false, our native-born ideas and perceptions of the world are absurd.

---

[34] A vast portion of Cudworth's *The True Intellectual System of the Universe* includes historical work. Both More and Cudworth defended the "Attic Moses," the idea that Moses influenced Plato. Cudworth refers to "a Divine or Mosaic Cabala" that had an impact on pre-Christian Greek philosophy.

[35] *An Antidote against Atheism*, 17.

Talk of aesthetics may suggest a facile subjectivity ("beauty is in the eye of the beholder"), but one must bear in mind that the quick and easy relativism of today's aesthetics had not yet taken shape. When Cudworth describes God as beauty, he affirms that it is right – fitting, warranted, justified – to take delight in God. Matters of beauty and evidence, like goodness itself, were not a matter of either human or divine will. As noted earlier, Cudworth took an unapologetic stance on the *Euthyphro*: God's love does not *make* things good; rather, God loves them *because they are* good. The beauty of a tree, or the soundness of an argument, is similarly not the result of God's pleasure or approval.

God's Light

To Cudworth and More, the reasoning employed in their defense of theism was, in itself, a muted form of communication with – or participation in – the life of God. In More's view, the exercise of human reason can become a communion with God: "The intellect of man is as it were a small compendious transcript of the divine intellect, and we feel in a manner in our own intellects the firmness and immutability of the divine, and of the eternal and immutable truths exhibited there."[36] Benjamin Whichcote celebrated reason in his widely circulated aphorisms: "To go against reason, is to go against God: it is the self same thing, to do that which the reason of the case does require; and that which God Himself does appoint: reason is the divine governor of man's life; it is the very voice of God."[37]

This view of reason was not uncontroversial. Whichcote's former teacher, Anthony Tuckney (1599–1670), argued that Whichcote and his students illegitimately subordinated Scripture to reason. Whichcote replied that there was no conflict; reason and Scripture are both derived from God, and each testifies to the other. The use of Scripture itself should be directed by reason: "Nothing without reason is to be

---

[36] *Annotations upon the Discourse of Truth* (London, 1862), 257–258. Culverwell: "Reason first danc'd and triumpht in those eternal Sun-beams, in the thoughts of God himself, who is the foundation and original of Reason," in *An Elegant and Learned Discourse*, ed. R. A. Greene and H. MacCallum (Toronto: University of Toronto Press, 1971), 97. See Frederick Beiser, *The Sovereignty of Reason: A Defense of Rationality in the English Enlightenment* (Princeton: Princeton University Press, 1996).

[37] Moral and Religious Aphorisms, n76. This may be found in a selection of aphorisms in Patrides, *The Cambridge Platonists*, 327.

proposed; nothing against reason is to be believed. Scripture is to be taken in a rational sense."[38] There is also no danger of impiety, so long as we do not intentionally subvert reason by vice, because "the Spirit of a Man is the Candle of the Lord; Lighted by God, and Lighting us to God."[39] Whichcote did not consider reason to be profane or secular, or in opposition to faith and spirituality; as he wrote: "I oppose not rational to spiritual, for spiritual is most rational."[40]

In *An Elegant and Learned Discourse of the Light of Nature*, Nathaniel Culverwell writes that faith is not "a bird of prey that comes to peck out the eyes of men; faith is no extinguisher to put out the candle of the Lord."[41] Throughout this discourse faith and reason are described in an abundance of positive images, including the romantic "Reason and faith may kiss each other."[42] For Culverwell, the relation between faith and reason is an amatory or romantic tale. The concord of our understanding and will with God's omniscience and goodness lies in creation. Our rational, cognitive powers are reliable because, as a fact of creation, they participate in God's provident care. "Now the spirit of man is the candle of the Lord. First, as ... a derivative light, a light from a light. Surely there's none can think that light is primitively and originally in the candle; but they must look upon that only as a weak participation of something that is more bright and glorious. All created excellency shines with borrowed beams, so that reason is but ... a breath of the divine breeze."[43] Our cognitive faculties derive their excellency from our maker.

The Cambridge Platonists on the whole embraced much of the new scientific rationality. More and Cudworth were both members of the Royal Society of London for the Promotion of Natural Knowledge

---

[38] Aphorism 880, in ibid., 334.

[39] Aphorism 916, in ibid., 334.

[40] Whichcote, "Whichcote's Third Letter," in *The Cambridge Platonists*, ed. G. R. Cragg (New York: Oxford University Press, 1968), 46. See Robert Greene's "Whichcote, the Candle of the Lord, and Synderesis," *Journal of the History of Ideas* 52:4 (1991).

[41] *An Elegant and Learned Discourse*, 14. Culverwell was more indebted to Aristotle than More, Cudworth, et al., but, for reasons laid out in *Cambridge Platonist Spirituality*, Alison Teply and I believe he should still be considered a Cambridge Platonist. He is standardly included in Cambridge Platonist collections (e.g., E. T. Compagnac's). See also D. W. Dockrill, "The Fathers and the Theology of the Cambridge Platonists," *Studia Patristica* 17:1 (1982): 427–439.

[42] *An Elegant and Learned Discourse*, 13.

[43] Ibid., 79.

and were apprised of Isaac Newton's (1642–1727) powerful new scientific developments.[44] Indeed, there is some evidence that More influenced Newton.[45] Some scholars credit More – whom Newton referred to as "the excellent Dr. More" – with introducing Newton to the works of Descartes and later promoting Newton's argument contra Descartes on the nature of space.[46] More argued for the existence of active powers in nature, a proposal that Newton took seriously in *Queries* and *Scholium Generale*. In the poem *Psychathanasia*, Henry More extols the merits of Copernicus's heliocentric view of the cosmos and the displacement of geocentricity. Still, natural science and reason, without concern for moral and spiritual development, ultimately place one in Plato's cave. More laments those naturalists who exult in the senses over an intellection that is open to ethical and religious values.

> Busying their brains in the mysterious toys of flitty motion, warie well
>   advize on 'ts inward principles and hid Entelechies:
> This is that awful cell where naturalists brood deep opinion, as they
>   themselves conceit; This errors den where in a magic mist men hatch
>   their own delusions and deceit, and grasp vain shows.[47]

This treatment of naturalism was not altogether out of step with some key contributors to modern science. Galileo, for example, lamented inquiry that promoted the senses over reason.[48]

---

[44] The Royal Society was the first scientific society in Great Britain.

[45] See F. E. Navel, *A Portrait of Isaac Newton* (Cambridge, Mass.: Harvard University Press, 1968), 38.

[46] See A. R. Hall, "Sir Isaac Newton's Notebook, 1661–65," in *Newton, His Friends and His Foes* (Aldershot: Ashgate, 1993), 243, and A. R. Hall, *Henry More: Magic, Religion and Experiment* (Oxford: Oxford University Press, 1990), 202. Although J. E. Power contends that More had a "marked influence" on Newton, he is more reluctant to see Newton following More on absolute space. See "More and Newton on Absolute Space," *Journal of the History of Ideas* 31:2 (1970).

[47] *Psychathanasia*, book I, canto I, stanza 16. See A. B. Grosart, ed., *The Complete Poems of Dr. Henry More* (Edinburgh: Edinburgh University Press, 1978). More's verse is in the style of Edmund Spenser's *Faerie Queene*. His "A Platonick Song of the Soul" is an extensive treatment of the origin, life, and immortality of the soul. For the Platonic strand in Spenser, see E. Bieman, *Plato Baptized* (Toronto: University of Toronto Press, 1988).

[48] See G. Santillana, ed., *Dialogue on the Great World Systems* (Chicago: University of Chicago Press, 1953), 341. Caution is in order, however, should one cast Galileo as a full-blooded Platonist. See T. R. Grills, "Galileo and Platonistic Methodology," *Journal of the History of Ideas* 31:4 (October–December 1970): 501–520. See also

The Cambridge Platonists opposed a religious life that would shun rational deliberation in favor of pure emotion. "Enthusiasm" was the term employed in the seventeenth through the mid-eighteenth century for what was presumed to be an ill-conceived, unwarranted claim of divine inspiration. More defined enthusiasm as "a misconceit of being inspired," while Dr. Johnson cast it as "a vain belief of private revelation; a vain confidence of divine favour or communication."[49] More, Cudworth, and the other Cambridge Platonists did not repudiate all recourse to emotion; however, they insisted that emotions and affection be in concert with reason. Their position here is very similar to Erasmus's and Thomas More's counsel of temperance and calm reflection.

Cambridge Platonists were not interested in the theory of knowledge or the concept of evidence for its own sake. Rather, they located reason, evidence, and inquiry in general within a comprehensive understanding of human beings as moral agents in an essentially good cosmos. Evidence and justification played a role within an extensive philosophical representation or philosophy of themselves as creatures in a good creation. Let us consider this larger philosophy in two respects: their understanding of the good of human nature and their understanding of God's relation to nature.

The Virtues of Human Nature

An exploration of Cambridge Platonist views about our nature confirms how they understood reason as an embedded faculty – a faculty whose natural, God-given functioning is tied to our individual and collective existence. I delimit here four areas of their philosophy of human nature in which reason functions, including human embodiment itself, human freedom, the compatibility of individual and collective well-being, and toleration.

The Concept of Embodiment

First, I note perhaps the most radical and central example of the way in which the Cambridge Platonists weave together reason and goodness

---

More's poem *Enthusiasmus Triumphatus* (1662; facsimile reprint, Los Angeles: University of California Press, 1966).

[49] More, *Enchiridion Ethicum*, sec. 2; Samuel Johnson, *A Dictionary of the English Language* (London: J. F. and C. Rivington, 1785).

in their philosophy of human nature. The interwoven picture is at odds with a great deal of subsequent philosophy of mind, which today does not (at least in the main) explicitly treat embodied human nature as good. Instead, most philosophy of mind addresses embodiment in terms of our causal constitution (how the brain works) and our powers of agency and sentience, which are customarily presented as elements of being human but without explicitly identifying humanity itself as good. Many philosophers of mind today are also materialists, dismissing those who distinguish mind (or soul) and body as propagators of a crippling, excessive dualism. The Cambridge Platonists are out of step on two counts: they explicitly maintained the goodness of embodiment, and they sought to integrate mind and body *without* collapsing the two into a single material reality.

The Cambridge Platonists may accurately be described in contemporary terminology as dualists, insofar as they held that the human mind – or soul, or spirit – is nonphysical, whereas the corporeal body is physical. It is important to appreciate, though, that the term "dualist" was not used in their philosophy of human nature. Probably the first use of "dualism" in English occurred in 1700, when it was used to describe Zoroastrianism, an Iranian religion that began in the seventh century B.C.E. and posited two opposing deities: one good and one evil. The dualism of the Cambridge Platonists did not pit good against evil, where the mind is good and the body is evil. Today, especially in theology, "dualism" commonly connotes disdain for the body, and the term itself is misleading in the context of a Cambridge Platonist view of human nature. Furthermore, although More argues for a distinction between mind and body, he resists what he considers an excessively sharp bifurcation of mind and body – rejecting Descartes' view (discussed in Chapter 2) in which the body is spatially extended but the mind is not. More held that *both* matter and spirit were spatially extended.[50]

The integrated nature of the mind-body relationship was secured due to matter's receptivity to spirit and the spirit's capacities of penetrability while maintaining its unity and the power of self-activity. More held that the spirit, unlike one's material body, is indivisible. Our identity is constituted by the unity of self as disclosed in self-awareness, and

---

[50] Spatial extension is sometimes taken to be a necessary and sufficient condition for being physical, but there are twentieth-century philosophers who treated sensory experiences ("sense data") as spatial but nonphysical. See, for example, Howard Robinson, *Perception* (London: Routledge, 1994).

our identity as embodied human beings is further articulated by sensation, reason, and agency. A human person is "a created Spirit endowed with sense and reason, and a power of organizing terrestrial matter into human shape by vital union therewith."[51] Cudworth described human embodiment as a soul "passionately present" in a body.[52] Strictly speaking, for both Cudworth and More, a person *is* the soul or spirit but, as a result of material embodiment, the person functions as a unified subject. Thus, when properly functioning and under normal conditions, it would be absurd to treat a person and her or his body as separate entities. In death such a demarcation makes sense but not under healthy, happier circumstances.

Like Cudworth, Whichcote, and other Cambridge Platonists, More held that moral virtue is intrinsic to human nature, for it flows from our very nature as rational beings. Our moral vocation begins in our human anatomy and basic mental faculties. Consequently, the aim of moral life is to bring our basic nature to fruition.

> Now a true feeling and possession of virtue, is also the conversion or bringing a man about, from what is contrary to his nature, to that which is conformable to it. For though all depravity be ... inbred, and connatural to brutes, yet in reality the same is quite contrary to human nature. *For to act according to nature or according to reason, is in a rational creature the same thing.* Wherefore all depravity is repugnant to human nature.[53]

Our physical, emotional, and spiritual health can be found in the affective acceptance of our identity.

> But that virtue is natural to human nature, and born to a twin therewith, is manifest, as well because man's soul is a rational being, as because righteousness or perfect virtue (as we are told *by Divine Revelation*) is immortal; and that it was sin only that brought death into the world. For since the state of innocence was to have been eternal, this plainly shows, that such a state was most perfect and most natural. And therefore

---

51 More, *The Immortality of the Soul*, book 1, chap. 8, in *Henry More* (Garland, 1978), 2:35. For a comparison of More's philosophy of mind with his contemporaries, see D. Garber, "Soul and Mind: Life and Thought in the Seventeenth Century," in *The Cambridge History of the Seventeenth-Century Philosophy*, ed. Garber et al., vol. 1 (Cambridge: Cambridge University Press, 1998).

52 *A Treatise Concerning Eternal and Immutable Morality*, 55.

53 *An Account of Virtue*, book III chap. 2. See the facsimile of the 1690 publication in *Henry More: Enchiridion Ethicum* (New York: Facsimile Text Society, 1930), 5–6.

that restitution unto such a state must be the most intrinsic and peculiar pleasure.[54]

The goodness and the completion of our nature is to be found in the exercise of our senses and other powers. Felicity, virtue, and human embodiment are thus bound together as a coherent whole, mirroring the supreme goodness of God. As Whichcote writes, "We are not men, so much by bodily shape; as by principles of reason and understanding."[55]

Our capacity to order our delights frees us to pursue the transcendent good of communion with God. "For while all other creatures have their senses tied down to the service of the body, or some particular delights; they can mount aloft, and are by a *liberty* in their *wills*, to shake off, or gradually destroy those ill desires, with which they are beset; and by the help of Heaven, to assert that liberty, which is most suitable to a creature made by God's image, and a partaker of divine sense."[56] Human embodiment, then, is conceived of as a good and comprises such goods as sensation, the proper functioning of bodily organs, agency, the capability to exercise reason as well as the successful exercise of reason in knowing ourselves and the world, and the affective acceptance of our nature as good and oriented to the divine.

The exercise of one's embodied life is teleological in the sense that it is intended by God to serve the good. Concord with the supernatural or divine is likewise cast as a natural fulfillment of our being rather than as an aberration to our nature.

Human Freedom

In Cudworth's view, our free agency and allegiance to goodness, like all things, does "not float without a head and governor . . . God."[57] Our

---

[54] Ibid., 6.

[55] Aphorism 1004, found in Patrides, *The Cambridge Platonists*, 335.

[56] *An Account of Virtue*, book III, chap. 1, in *Enchiridion Ethicum*, 175. In this section, I have referred to the "virtues of embodiment" in which "virtue" stands as nonmoral goods. See my article, "The Virtues of Embodiment," *Philosophy* 76:1 (2001). More might prefer to speak of the blessing of embodiment. For More's position on the interwoven character of embodiment and virtue, see *An Account of Virtue*, book III, especially chap. 9.

[57] *The True Intellectual System of the Universe*, 2 vols. (New York: Gould and Newman, 1837), 1:34.

freedom is a feature of our existence, as we were created in the image of God. This affirmation of freedom is pivotal to subsequent Cambridge Platonist views of goodness and toleration. Cudworth opens *A Treatise of Freewill* with this claim: "We seem clearly to be led by the *instincts of nature* to think that there is something . . . in nostra potestate, *in our own power* (though dependently upon God Almighty), and that we are not altogether passive in our actings, nor determined by inevitable necessity in whatever we do."[58] This power is one of the essential conditions for exercising moral agency. If all of our actions were predetermined, we could not be the proper bearers of praise or blame. Many of Cudworth's contemporaries were Puritan Reformers and staunchly committed to Calvinist predestination. Indeed, the audience of Cudworth's address to the House of Commons consisted largely of Presbyterian Reformers who embraced stringent views of God's providential role in history.[59] In opposition to this English Puritanism, Cudworth articulated human freedom in terms of "self-power," "self-determining power," and "single self-activity." This power required what he called an interior flexibility: creatures without freedom "have no self-power in them, no power to stop or excite, retard or accelerate themselves, no internal self-flexibility, but are mere swings and impetuosities of nature and have no internal self-flexibility in them."[60] The freedom of the self lies in its capacity to stand with some measure of independence from its own state and the causes that shape it. The self or soul is said to "reduplicate," to create itself by exercising the power of self-direction over against one's inclinations.[61]

---

[58] *A Treatise Concerning Eternal and Immutable Morality, with a Treatise on Freewill,* 155.

[59] For a good overview of the prevailing religious, philosophical, and political climate, see C. Webster, ed., *The Intellectual Revolution of the Seventeenth Century* (London: Routledge, 1974). Also see B. J. Shapiro, *Probability and Certainty in Seventeenth-Century England: A Study of the Relationships between Natural Science, Religion, History, Law, and Literature* (Princeton: Princeton University Press, 1983). J. A. I. Champion provides a useful overview of how philosophical and theological positions bore in on British religious life in his *The Pillars of Priestcraft Shaken: The Church of England and Its Enemies, 1660–1730* (Cambridge: Cambridge University Press, 1992).

[60] See Passmore, *Ralph Cudworth: An Interpretation,* 9.

[61] Ibid. Roland Hall has published three essays on the linguistic innovations of Cudworth. The first in particular notes Cudworth's use of "self-. . ." See Roland Hall, "New Worlds and Antedatings from Cudworth's 'Treatise on Free Will,'" *Notes and Queries* 205 (1960): 427–432; "Cudworth: More New Words," *Notes and Queries* 208 (1963):

Dispute over whether we possess such powers of self-transcendence emerges later in this book as we address the problem of evil. Cudworth, like More, clearly thought that the blame for our wrongful acts lies with us, not God. "We do not impute the evil of men's wicked activities to God the creator and *maker* of them, after the same manner as we do the faults of a clock or watch wholly to the watchmaker."[62]

The Compatibility of Individual and Collective Well-Being

A third feature of Cudworth's philosophy of human nature lies in his vision of concordant individual and collective flourishing grounded on a concept of the good. Cudworth's account of the goodness of our natural powers, as well as of the goodness of our civic and communal life, is bound up in the idea that God made us to flourish. Cudworth opposed the view that a sustained civil society could successfully be founded or administered on the basis of fear or secular self-interest.

> The right and authority of God himself is founded in justice; and of this is the civil sovereignty also a certain participation. It is not the mere creature of the people and of men's wills, and therefore annihilable again by their wills or pleasure; but hath a stamp of divinity upon it, as may partly appear from hence, because that "power of life and death" which civil sovereigns have was never lodged in singulars, before civil society; and therefore could not be conferred by them. Had not God and nature made a city, were there not a natural conciliation of all rational creatures and subjection of them to the Deity as their head (which is Cicero's "one city of gods and men"), had not God made "ruling and being ruled," superiority and subjection, with their chantment, nor yet by force, have made any firm cities or polities.[63]

Justice is the preeminent point of reference for Cudworth's political philosophy.

Cudworth's political and ethical views were also part of a broader philosophy of human nature. There is much to commend this link between political thought and philosophy of mind, for one can see a great

---

212–213; "Cudworth and His Contemporaries: New Words and Antedatings," *Notes and Queries* 220 (1975): 313–314.

[62] "On the Nature of Liberum Arbitrium," in the appendix to Rogers et al., *The Cambridge Platonists in Philosophical Context*, 220.

[63] Cudworth, "On Political Sovereignty," in Cragg, *The Cambridge Platonists*, 361.

deal of political theory in the early modern era stemming from philosophical accounts of reason, desire, needs, and so on.

Of all the Cambridge Platonists, Cudworth is the most extensive in his development of a philosophy of human nature that integrates a realist moral epistemology and a nonrelativist view of ethics. He advanced a natural-law account of the good, according to which acts and events are rightly deemed good or evil in relation to their fulfilling or harming human nature and the rest of creation. Cudworth upheld a unified view of the self with powers of speculative and practical reflection. The source of our conscious obligation to promote good and avoid evil lies in our rational, practical nature.[64]

Cudworth is often thought of as a forbearer of ethical rationalism, but I suggest that his Platonic Christianity amounted to envisaging a unified ethic, drawing on both rationality *and* natural affections. Henry More also explicitly invoked God's goodness in proposing an ethic that treated will, intellect, and desire in concord.

> This intellectual success therefore is from the Presence of God, who does (*kinein pos panta*) move all things in some sort or other, but residing in the undefiled Spirit moves it in the most excellent manner, inward, compendious, and comprehensive Presentation of Truth, ever antecedaneous to that Reason which in Theories of greatest importance approves it self afterwards, upon the exactest examination, to be most solid and perfect every way, and is truly that wisedome which is peculiarly styled the Gift of God, and hardly compitible to any but to persons of a pure and unspotted mind. Of so great concernment is it sincerely to endeavor to be holy and good.[65]

Divine sagacity incorporates intellect and desire.

Toleration

A fourth feature of the Cambridge Platonist philosophy of human nature involves toleration. It may seem odd to place such a political conviction under the category of a philosophy of human nature, but the Cambridge

---

[64] See Stephen Darwell in *The British Moralists and the Internal "Ought": 1640–1740* (Cambridge: Cambridge University Press, 1995), 120. Darwell's work is enhanced by his study of some unpublished manuscripts. Darwell singles out Cudworth as deserving much greater representation than he receives now in the history of ethics.

[65] "Preface General," *Philosophical Writings*, sec. 7. There is a facsimile of the 1662 volume in *Henry More* (Garland, 1978). The passage cited is on p. ix of vol. 1.

Platonists' case for increased liberty rested squarely upon their understanding of our humanity.

The twin convictions that we have free will and that reason is a God-given guide to life bolster the case for toleration advanced by the Cambridge Platonists. Whichcote proclaimed, "A man has as much right to use his own understanding in judging of truth as he has right to use his own eyes to see his way. Therefore it is no offense to another that any man uses his own right."[66] Such openness to dissent earned the Cambridge Platonists the label "latitudinarian," a term initially used in a derogatory sense, which later came to designate a constructive philosophy and politics of toleration.[67] The toleration advanced by the Cambridge Platonists was not absolute. More, for example, regrettably did not find atheism tolerable, but overall their case for toleration was an enormous advance for liberty considering the fractious social realities of the seventeenth century. Their substantial contribution to toleration may be measured, in part, by the criticism they endured. In *Some Observations upon the apologie of Dr. Henry More for his Mystery and Godliness*, Joseph Beaumont criticizes More for promoting "liberty of conscience."

Both Whichcote and Cudworth attended the Whitehall conference in 1655, which legally cleared the path for Jews to return to Britain. The conference annulled the legal authority of King Edward I's 1290 banishment order, but sadly the conference was less than fully successful in endorsing Jewish resettlement, largely due to worries from British "Merchants."[68] Still, the conference afforded the Cambridge Platonists

---

[66] Aphorism 40. Not printed in Patrides's text, but in Cragg's *The Cambridge Platonists*, 423. Whichcote may have influenced Locke on toleration. Locke was a member of Whichcote's church, St. Lawrence Jewry, from 1667 to 1675, and evidently appreciated Whichcote's sermons. See John Marshall's *John Locke: Resistance, Religion, and Responsibility* (Cambridge: Cambridge University Press, 1994), 78–79.

[67] See M. Griffin's *Latitudinarianism in the Seventeenth-Century Church of England* (Leiden: E. J. Brill, 1992). Perhaps it was the legacy of the broad churchmanship of the latitudinarians that earned this observation from Voltaire: "An Englishman, as a free man, goes to Heaven by whatever road he pleases" (*Philosophical Papers*, trans. and ed. E. Dilworth [Indianapolis: Bobbs-Merrill], p. 22). See John Gascoigne, "Cambridge and the Latitude-Men," in *Cambridge in the Age of the Enlightenment: Science, Religion and Politics from the Restoration to the French Revolution* (Cambridge: Cambridge University Press, 1989).

[68] See *A Narrative of the Late Proceeds at White-Hall, Concerning the Jews* (London: Chapman, 1656). For background, see I. Twersky and B. Septimus, eds., *Jewish Thought in the Seventeenth Century* (Cambridge, Mass.: Harvard University Press,

an opportunity to meet the esteemed Menasseh ben Israel (1604–1657), a leader of the Dutch Jewish community in which Spinoza (1632–1677) would later study. The Platonists may have promoted Anglo-Jewish relations through their scholarship – Cudworth was the Regius Professor of Hebrew, and More wrote appreciatively of the Kabbala strand of Jewish mysticism – but it is difficult to measure their impact.[69]

Like the vast majority of their contemporaries, the Cambridge Platonists were silent about the many barriers facing women in their time. The only exceptions involved Anne Viscountess Conway (a close friend of Henry More) and Lady Damaris Cudworth Masham (Ralph Cudworth's daughter). More's friendship with Lady Conway was rich in philosophy and affection. More confessed that "the greatest enjoyment the world offered [him]" was to be found in her company, and "there are evident signs of mutual influence in their philosophical work."[70] I discuss Conway's work in the next chapter as a response to Descartes' philosophy of God. Masham protested the inaccessibility of higher education for women. In her *Discourse on the Love of God* (1696), *Occasional Thoughts in Reference to a Virtuous or Christian Life* (1705), and her letters to Locke and Leibniz, one can see a firm allegiance to Cambridge Platonist themes as she asserts the goodness and unity of creation, as well as the indispensability of reason in religion. She advanced an understanding of proper devotion to God as centered on God's goodness rather than God's sheer power.[71]

The call for toleration and mutual religious forbearance by Cambridge Platonists should be understood not just against the backdrop of the English Civil War, but against the "Wars of Religion" that wracked Europe in the sixteenth century. Religious identity was often

1987), and Y. Kaplan et al., eds., *Menasseh Ben Israel and His World* (Leiden: Brill, 1989).

[69] See More's *The Defence of the Threefold Cabbala* (1662). Facsimile available in *Henry More* (Garland, 1978), vol. 2.

[70] See Sarah Hutton, ed., *The Conway Letters – the Correspondance of Anne Viscountess Conway, Henry More and Their Friends*, rev. ed. (Oxford: Oxford University Press, 1992), January 7, 1665/6 letter, 128. See also Marjorie Hope Nicolson's introduction.

[71] Lois Frankel comments: "Although by late 20th century standards Masham's brand of feminism is weak indeed, we must consider the extreme antifeminist times in which she lived"; see "Damaris Cudworth Masham: A Seventeenth Century Feminist Philosophy," *Hypatia* 4:1 (1989): 84. See Sarah Hutton's "Between Platonism and Enlightenment: Damaris Cudworth, Lady Masham," *British Journal for the History of Philosophy* 1 (1993).

a matter of dominant military and political power, a phenomenon that became formalized in the precept that the religion of the ruler is the religion of the people (*cuius regio, eius religio*). Although many nonreligious factors – commercial, territorial, and dynastic – contributed to the Thirty Years' War (1618–1648), it was infused with religious controversy even from its beginning, when the Protestant nobles of Austria and Bohemia resisted Ferdinand II's effort to impose Catholicism in 1618. Whichcote and the other Platonists did not advance their call for toleration on the basis of their own churchmanship or sectarian identity. In *The Development of Religious Toleration in England*, W. K. Jordan summarizes Whichcote's contribution: "Indeed, it may be that the calm and almost Olympian strictures which he [Whichcote] laid against religious coercion were more effective in persuading England of the iniquity of persecution than were the shrill cries of sectarian pleading. Whichcote added one more voice, and it was a powerful and respected voice, to the swelling chorus that demanded religious liberty in England."[72] This chorus demanded philosophical liberty as well.

In summary, I have underscored the ways in which the Cambridge Platonist view of human nature treated goodness as a central feature of embodiment. The Cambridge Platonists espoused an anti-determinist view of freedom; they believed in the concordant flourishing of individual

---

[72] *The Development of Religious Toleration in England, Attainment of the Theory and Accommodation in Thought and Institutions (1640–1660)* (Gloucester: Peter Smith, 1965), 108. The Cambridge Platonist case for tolerance was quite radical in its historical contexts. The Westphailian settlement in 1648 – which ended the Eight Year's War between the Dutch and the Spanish – rested on the thesis that you cannot achieve social unity without religious unity. Cambridge Platonist precepts about the goodness of human nature and reason can be seen as providing some grounds for envisioning a stable and reasonable religious pluralism. Given what I see as the role of Whichcote's personal integrity in his advancing a case for tolerance, consider this report on Whichcote and the Cambridge Platonists by Gilbert Burnet (1643–1715). "Whichcote... being disgusted with the dry systematical way of those times... studied to raise those who conversed with him to a nobler set of thoughts.... They declared against superstition on the one hand, and enthusiasm on the other. They loved the constitution of the Church, and the liturgy, and could well live under them; but they did not think it unlawful to live under another form. They wished that things might have been carried with more moderation. And they continued to keep a good correspondence with those who had differed from them in opinion, and allowed a great freedom both in philosophy and divinity; from whence they were called men of latitude. And upon this men of narrower thoughts and fiercer tempers fastened upon them the name of Latitudinarians." Cited by Stephen Neil, *Anglicanism* (New York: Oxford University Press, 1978), 160.

and collective human life, and they advocated political toleration. Their philosophy of human nature was fundamentally teleological, insofar as they felt that human nature constituted a valuable end (or good) in itself and served a greater end (or *telos*) in the cosmos. They believed their philosophy of human nature was not anti-scientific and that their theory accorded completely with modern science as it was understood at the inception of the Royal Society, whose charter describes its members as people "whose studies are to be applied to further promoting by the authority of experiments the sciences of natural things and of useful arts, to the glory of God the Creator, and the advantage of the human race."[73]

The Virtues of God's Presence

More and Cudworth were committed to articulating a coherent, non-fragmentary picture of the mind-body relationship alongside of a coherent portrait of God's relation to the cosmos. This broader picture of the cosmos was pivotal for them to secure their value-laden portrait of reason and human life. In order to achieve a properly teleological view of human nature, they needed a teleological view of nature as a whole. I add this brief section in an overview of Cambridge Platonism in order to emphasize that early modern philosophy of religion integrated the science and philosophy of nature. Religion *and science* were seen as valuable, mutually enhancing practices. But not just *any* science was seen as friendly to religion, and on this point Cudworth and More resisted a materialist science; that is, they opposed a science that left no room for mind as an independent source of agency.

The Cambridge Platonists faced the prospects of a mechanical science that construed the cosmos as a giant machine. The cosmos had a divine maker and sustainer, but a maker whose principle tools are matter, motion, mathematics, and geometry. The Cambridge Platonists worried about two undesirable alternatives. One is that God's sovereign, creative will overwhelms nature, ruling out free will. The other is that God retreats from nature and we have a universe that is essentially a self-perpetuating, impersonal machine. They sought to avoid these outcomes with a vital element, "Plastick Nature," which both protected the

---

[73] H. Schuman, *Scientists and Amateurs: A History of the Royal Society* (New York: H. Wolff, 1948), 6. For a more thorough history, see H. G. Lyons, *The Royal Society, 1660–1940* (New York: Greenwood, 1968).

existence of nature as an entity with its own (God-given) powers and yet welcomed God's creativity.

Both More and Cudworth posited the existence of this element between the material world as described in modern physics and God. Plastic nature is an incorporeal reality, enabling God's providential shaping of the cosmos and sustaining it in existence. In "The Digression Concerning the Plastic Life of Nature, or an Artificial, Orderly and Methodical Nature," Cudworth advances the case for plastic nature on the grounds of its superiority to two other claims:

> Unless there be such a thing admitted as a Plastic nature, that acts . . . *for the sake of something*, and *in order to ends*, regularly, artificially and methodically, it seems that one or other of these two things must be concluded. . . . that either in the efformation and organization of the bodies of animals, as well as the other phenomena, every thing comes to pass *fortuitously*, and happens to be as it is, without the guidance and direction of any *mind* or *understanding*; Or else, that God himself does all *immediately*, and as it were with his own hands, form the body of every gnat and fly, insect and mite, as of other animals in generations, all whose members have so much of contrivance in them, that *Galen* professed he could never enough admire that artifice which was in the leg of a fly, (and yet he would have admired the wisdom of nature more, had he been but acquainted with the use of microscopes).[74]

Cudworth did not assimilate nature to the Stoic's world soul, but he did attribute to it a receptivity and intelligibility that reflects God: "Nature is the stamp or impress of that infallibly omniscient art of the Divine."[75]

More posited plastic vital power *also* at the matrix of the unity of mind and body.

> Vital congruity [is] chiefly in the soul it self, it being the noblest principle of life; but is also in the matter, and is there nothing but such modification thereof as fits the plastic part of the soul, and tempts out that faculty into act. Not that there is any life in the matter with which this is the soul should sympathize and unite; but it is termed vital because it makes the matter a congruous subject for the soul to reside in, and exercise the functions of life. For that which has no life it self, may tie to it that which has. . . . Now as we see that the perceptive part of the soul is thus

---

[74] Cudworth, *The True Intellectual System of the Universe*, 1:209. The Cambridge Platonist desire to secure the integrity of nature without detracting from nature being a creation of God is similar to the scholastic rejection of occasionalism in favor of some form of concurrentism or secondary causality.

[75] Ibid., 220–221.

vitally affected with that which has no life in it, so it is reasonable that the plastic part thereof may be so too; That there may be an harmony betwixt matter thus and thus modified, and that power that we call Plastick, that is utterly devoid of all perception . . . ; that which ties the soul and this or that matter together, is an irresistible and imperceptible pleasure, if I may so call it, arising from the congruity of matter to the plastic faculty of the soul.[76]

God's creation and conservation of "Plastick" nature was bolstered, according to More, by the purposive character of the cosmos; it helped to account for such specific natural events as the axis of the earth and Robert Boyle's (1627–1691) experiments with the air pump. More and Cudworth sought to provide a unified foundational account of the interaction between God and the world, mind, and body.[77]

Culverwell, too, construed the world as an open system, like a musical instrument for God. By his lights, nature is constitutionally receptive to God's creative activity. "Thus God framed this great organ of the world, he tuned it, yet not so as that it could play upon it self, or make any music by virtue of this general composure . . . but that it might be fitted and prepared for the finger of God himself, and at the presence of his powerful touch might sound forth the praise of its Creator in a most sweet and harmonious manner."[78] Culverwell's reference to nature as an "organ" presages the debate between Leibniz and Clarke about whether nature is God's *sensorium* (see Chapter 3). Culverwell's depiction of nature is deeply steeped in his understanding of God's goodness: "All light is pleasant, 'tis the very smile of nature, the gloss of the world, the varnish of the Creation, a bright paraphrase upon bodies."[79]

This example of positing a divine organ, "Plastick" nature and so on, may strike contemporary readers as at best quaint. Such entities may seem little better than outdated theories like the nineteenth-century hypothesis that there is a substance, ether, filling all space. But the root motive behind the work of More, Cudworth, and Culverwell may be far more enduring. Their basic concern is whether human reasoning and value can find a place in the cosmos, which is through and through physical and explainable in mechanistic terms. If, for example, the ideal

---

[76] "The Immortality of the Soul" (London, 1712), 203.

[77] See W. Hunter's useful "The Seventeenth-Century Doctrine of Plastic Nature," *Harvard Theological Review* 43 (1950): 197–213. Boyle was not pleased by More's use of his *New Experiments Physics-Mechanical* (1660).

[78] *An Elegant and Learned Discourse of the Light of Nature*, 26.

[79] Ibid., 147.

explanation of your reasoning must exclude all appeal to beliefs and desires and only include nonconscious, non-intentional forces, can the activity of reasoning itself be preserved? Reasoning appears to involve apprehending how some beliefs entail (or make reasonable) other beliefs. If we set aside appeal to beliefs and purposes and supplant these with impersonal mechanisms, can there still remain what we recognize as reasoning? Perhaps something like "reasoning" can exist in a purely mechanical context, much in the way that a calculating machine may be said to undertake mathematical calculations, but the normativity of reason would be left out. My calculating machine does not see that $1 + 1 = 2$ is evident or justified, such that it responds 2 by virtue of grasping its entailment from $1 + 1$. In these comments, I am not commending the Cambridge Platonist hypothesis about "Plastick" nature! Like Boyle, I do not think one needs such an incorporeal entity to preserve purpose in nature. More modestly, I suggest that the questions that exercised the Cambridge Platonists about how human reason and value can be grounded in modern science are worthy, important, concerns. I return to this theme shortly when considering the scientific challenge to Cambridge Platonism.[80]

The Practice of Philosophy of Religion

Before turning to the obstacles facing the Cambridge Platonists, let us consider how they conducted their inquiry. Their writings suggest that philosophy was to be carried out in a context of moral virtue and an affective openness to the ways in which God may be revealed historically and in their experience.

As for the virtues, the Cambridge Platonists strove to follow Plato's advice. Consider Plato's seventh letter:

> It is barely possible for knowledge to be engendered of an object naturally good, in a man naturally good; but if his nature is defective, as is that of most men, for the acquisition of knowledge and the so-called virtues, and if the qualities he has have been corrupted, then not even Lynceus could make such a man see. In short, neither quickness of learning nor a good

---

[80] To secure the nonantiquarian status of these concerns, consult William Hasker, *The Emergent Self* (Ithaca: Cornell University Press, 1999). The problem of whether materialism can preserve mental causation and normative reasoning is one of the central concerns in philosophy of mind today. On this topic the Cambridge Platonists may be seen as quite contemporary.

memory can make a man see when his nature is not akin to the object, for this knowledge never takes root in an alien nature; so that no man who is not naturally inclined and akin to justice and all other forms of excellence, even though he may be quick at learning and remembering this and that and other things...will ever attain the truth that is attainable about virtue.[81]

All the Cambridge Platonists would agree.

As for affective openness, they counseled that inquiry into God's reality should be coupled with a genuine desire to find God. Cudworth believed that God is preeminently to be understood as loving. "Love is the supreme Deity and original of all things," which Cudworth then expands: "Eternal, self-originated, intellectual love, or essential and substantial goodness...having an infinite overflowing fullness and fecundity, dispenses itself uninvidiously, according to the best wisdom, sweetly governs all, without any force or violence (all things being naturally subject to its authority, and readily obeying its laws), and reconciles the whole world into harmony."[82] As the object of inquiry is a loving reality, it is appropriate to approach this reality as a lover seeks the beloved.

A distinction between two types of inquiry may be useful here: internal and external. In what may be called external inquiry, one need not have or seek to exemplify the property of the thing looked for: you do not have to be watery or even thirsty to seek water. The object sought is external to the search for it. But if you are inquiring into the nature of love, justice, goodness, and the like, it will not help if you are spiteful, unjust, and bent on ill will. For the Cambridge Platonists, the philosophical search for wisdom, beauty, goodness, and truth involved cultivating the virtue being sought. In this way, the search was internal as the inquirer into wisdom, for example, needed to seek to become wise herself or himself. Wisdom needs to be sought wisely.[83]

---

[81] *Plato's Epistles*, trans. G. R. Morrow (Indianapolis: Bobbs-Merrill, 1962), 240–241. The Cambridge Platonists, on the whole, held that it was vain to inflate the claims of reason. See J. Glanvill's *The Vanity of Dogmatizing*. There is a good facsimile edition published by Columbia University Press, 1931.

[82] Cudworth, *The True Intellectual System of the Universe*, 1:179–180.

[83] As an aside, the Cambridge Platonists did not hold that inquiry into vice was (in the terminology I suggest) internal. Thus, inquiry into foolishness is not helped by being foolish, anger is best not pursued irascibly, and so on. Perhaps having firsthand experience of vice may help one understand the vice, but one's inquiry into vice must be a virtuous one.

Whichcote contended that the awareness of God involved both moral and spiritual discipline: "We are absent from God; not by being other-wise, than He is; who is everywhere; but by being other-wise, than He is; who is all good: by a sensual life, a worldly mind, a wicked state."[84] A good life leads us to a good God.

The Cambridge Platonists view of reason and inquiry has been likened to a form of mysticism or the "nearly mystical."[85] Although I do not wish to employ such labels here, I do highlight the way in which, for the Cambridge Platonists, the proper exercise of reason secures one's identity. Being properly aware of yourself in a given en-vironment allows or constitutes (in part) your functioning in that en-vironment; however, if you are disoriented and your senses impaired, you may be incoherent or dysfunctional. The exercise of reason delim-its what ought to be believed, which, given their theism, reveals what ought to be the case. Recall More's ontological argument. For him, the perfection or fulfillment of reason brings one to an awareness of a – or the – divine reality that constitutes the definitive, all-important environment in which we are to live and function. The coordinated exercise of cognitive powers enables one to discover the divine, and this discovery reveals a God both transcendent and immanent, who is omnipresent in the cosmos.[86] Given the recognition that God actively calls one to the love of neighbor, it would not be impious to speak of God's local, proximate presence in a neighborhood of justice and compassion.

All in all, the Cambridge Platonists developed an extraordinary, in-tegrated system that forged what they took to be the perennial philos-ophy in the West and the great contribution of Hebrew and Christian revelation. They enabled later historians to refer to their movement as

---

[84] Aphorism 1118, in Patrides, *The Cambridge Platonists*, 336.

[85] See Edward Craig, *The Mind of God and the Works of Man* (Oxford: Clarendon, 1987), 67.

[86] Some contemporaries in philosophy of religion have focused on different symbols and imagery for inquiry, for example, Pamela Sue Anderson in *A Feminist Philosophy of Religion: The Rationality and Myths of Religious Belief* (Oxford: Blackwell, 1998). For the Cambridge Platonists, I do not think any specific imagery is salient (philoso-phy as a sea voyage or digging in a mine), but there is a prevalent supposition that attaining philosophical wisdom is akin to an awakening or proper discovery. See Peter Achinstein, "Who Really Discovered the Electron?" in *The Book of Evidence* (Oxford: Oxford University Press, 2001).

"modern Platonism."[87] To some theists, the age of Cambridge Platonism may seem to be the arcadia of philosophical theology. There is a close fit between the Cambridge Platonist view of grace and love and Shakespeare's world as revealed in the comedies.[88]

Let us now consider the enormous forces at work that threatened Cambridge Platonism and largely defined early modern philosophy of religion. I first take note of the role of science and then skepticism. Finally, I look at the challenge to specifically Christian theistic tradition, which included philosophical criticism but also expanded to historical disputes and the challenge of nontheistic traditions.

Three Challenges

Modern Science and God

Some modern science seemed tailor-made for religious purposes – Johannes Kepler (1571–1630) was looking for God's harmonies when he discovered the elliptical orbits. His work is easily read as replacing one belief about God's handiwork (circles) with another (ellipses). Arguably, an ellipse is no less "perfect" than a circle. Newton forged a powerful scientific portrait of the cosmos that, many argued, made God's reality evident in the world's design. Nonetheless the relation between science and religion was not always a happy one. In 1616 the Holy Office of the Roman Catholic Church rejected the hypothesis that the earth revolves around the sun. The following proposition was deemed foolish and absurd: "The earth is not the center of the world, nor immovable, but moves according to the whole of itself, also with a diurnal motion."[89] Kepler's *Epitome of the Copernican Astronomy* was banned

---

[87] See, for example, Henry Sidgwick, *Outlines of the History of Ethics* (London: Macmillan, 1949), 172.

[88] See chap. 6 of Ernst Cassirer, *The Platonic Renaissance in England*, trans. J. P. Pettegrove (New York: Guardian Press, 1970), especially 172–185. A Cambridge Platonist would equate radical skepticism with tragedy. There is something tragic about the skeptic's proposal that our best reasoning is never successful in establishing knowledge. By way of contrast, it is a proper relation to God that is the antidote to the tragic fracture of embodiment, poor reasoning, misuse of free will, the conflict between individual and collectives, and the tyranny of sheer power.

[89] Cited by Nicholas Wolterstorff, *Reason within the Bounds of Religion* (Grand Rapids: Eerdmans, 1976), 11.

by the Roman Catholic Church in 1621. The Inquisition coerced Galileo
into renouncing Copernicanism, in 1633. The development of the empirical experimental method by Francis Bacon (1561–1627) was not
against religion per se but against the view that the literal truth of the
Bible is a reliable guide to the physical structure of the universe. Even so,
Bacon's methodology seemed to pave the way for a secular treatment of
nature. It is not difficult to portray the modern era as relegating religious
convictions to the dark ages. Faith may be countenanced but merely as
a vessel – a "bark," to use Bacon's term – to guide us to heaven but
not as a guide to the observable heaven and earth disclosed by science.
(Galileo commended the Bible as a guide to get to heaven but not as a
guide to the nature of planets.) Contra Culverwell, in the seventeenth
century faith and reason were on uneasy terms and *not* always kissing.

Hobbes (1588–1679) was seen by the Cambridge Platonists as advancing a dangerous, scientific philosophy. He adopted a materialist
view of human life and employed a comprehensive view of the cosmos
that ruled out God as an incorporeal reality.

> What kind of attribute I pray you is *immaterial*, or *incorporeal substance*?
> Where do you find it in the Scripture? Whence came it hither, but from
> *Plato and Aristotle*, Heathens, who mistook those thin inhabitants of the
> brain they see in sleep, for so many *incorporeal* men; and yet they allow
> them motion, which is proper only to things *corporeal*. Do you think it an
> honor to God to be one of these? And would you learn Christianity from
> *Plato* and *Aristotle*? But seeing there is no such word in Scripture, how
> will you warrant it from natural reason? Neither *Plato* nor *Aristotle* did
> ever write or mention an *incorporeal Spirit*; for they could not conceive
> how a Spirit, which in their language was πνευμα (in ours *a Wind*)
> could be *incorporeal*. Do you understand the connection of *substance* and
> *incorporeal*? If you do, explain it in English; for the words are Latin.[90]

There was a widespread assumption in the seventeenth century that this
materialism amounted to atheism. There are strong reasons for thinking
that Hobbes was a theist, but for whatever that is worth, many readers of
Hobbes concluded that if materialism is in, God is out.[91] In *An Antidote
against Atheism*, Henry More claimed: "That saying is not less true
in politics, no bishop, no king, than this in metaphysics, no spirit, no

---

[90] Hobbes, *Considerations upon the Reputation, Loyalty, Manners and Religion of
Thomas Hobbes of Malmesbury* (London: 1680 for William Crooke, at the Green
Dragon without Temple-bar), 32–33.

[91] See Chapter 3 for Hobbes on religion.

God."[92] Just as the British nation overturned the ecclesiastical royalist bishops in 1644 and not long after the king was executed, the worry was that the case against the incorporeal would lead to a case against God. Shortly after Cudworth's address to the House of Commons, there was no king. Would "God" suffer the same fate?

The struggle to articulate the coherence of theism against a Hobbesian materialism was keenly felt. One can detect in Cudworth's work a recognition of the pressure that theism places on our ordinary use of terms. Cudworth carefully insists that God sees but without eyes, hears without ears, and while God lacks a brain and material body, God is wise and acts with understanding.[93] More resorts to what today would be called thought experiments involving parapsychology to secure the intelligibility of theism over against materialism in his *Antidote*.[94] Incidentally, it is More who is credited with first using the term "materialist" in English.[95]

The Cambridge Platonists worried not just about the fate of theism in light of a scientific materialism, but about the undermining of a humanistic understanding of persons as well. Once again, depending on your vantage point, Hobbes is either the protagonist or the bête noire. Hobbes depicted human thinking in terms of matter in motion. The Cambridge Platonists, especially More and Cudworth, were convinced that this jeopardized the claim that persons have any conscious thought whatsoever.

Should materialists be able to preserve *some* consciousness, the resultant life would be shorn of God, values, and freedom. This is More's assessment of a Hobbesian, materialist universe:

> That it is impossible there should be any God, or soul, or angel, good or bad; or any immortality, or life to come. That there is no religion, no piety nor impiety, no virtue nor vice, justice nor injustice, but what it pleases him that has the longest sword to call so. That there is no freedom

---

[92] *An Antidote against Atheism*, 142.

[93] See *The True Intellectual System of the Universe*, especially 1:507–572. The charge that theism violates ordinary language by speaking of God as a nonphysical intelligence is taken up in Chapter 8.

[94] The interest in the paranormal was not unusual for this era, and it was shared subsequently by some prominent philosophers including Henry Sidgwick, C. D. Broad, C. J. Ducasse, and William James. See, for example, H. L. Edge and J. M. O. Wheatley, eds., *Philosophical Dimensions of Parapsychology* (Springfield: Charles C. Thomas, 1976).

[95] See "Material," in *The Oxford Dictionary of English Etymology*, ed. C. T. Onions (Oxford: Clarendon, 1966).

of the will, nor consequently any rational remorse of conscience in any being whatsoever, but that all that is, is nothing but matter and corporeal motion; and that therefore every trace of man's life is as necessary as the tracts of lightning, and the falling of thunder, the blind impetus of the matter breaking through or being stopped everywhere, with as certain and determinate necessity as the course of a torrent after mighty storms and showers of rain.[96]

Hobbesian scientific atheism had what some philosophers took to be dangerous and radical political implications. If there is no God, what happens to the foundation of ethics? By the lights of the Cambridge Platonists, we should be good for goodness' sake, but in the absence of a just God to ensure that, in the end, good will overcome evil, world history may become irretrievably tragic. Atheism also appeared to remove the most promising grounds of hope for an afterlife. The belief that persons are annihilated with the death of their bodies was at radical odds with the Cambridge Platonist view of the inexhaustible goodness of persons; bodies may disintegrate but the soul should be rescued by its supremely good Creator and be reembodied, resurrected, and in communion with God. "The very nerves and sinews of religion," More wrote in the second part of his *Song of the Soul*, "is the hope of immortality."[97]

In taking account of the implications of Hobbes's modern, mechanical philosophy, one twentieth-century English philosopher credits Cudworth with foreshadowing a Nietzschean view of values. "There is a curious anticipation of Nietzsche here (the real precursor of Nietzsche in his period, or very shortly after it, was Mandeville); but he [Cudworth] saw that if a man was going to be an 'amoralist,' then he might well be so constituted as to like the 'war of all against all' which Hobbes thought would be the state of men without government."[98] A. N. Prior cites the "Nietzschean" Cudworth who reproaches Hobbes's counsel to bow to the presumed "laws of nature": "[The Hobbesian] laws of nature [are only] the laws of their own timorous and cowardly complexion; for they, who have courage and generosity in them . . . would never submit to such sneaking terms of equality and subjection, but venture for dominion; and resolve either to win the saddle or lose the horse."[99]

---

[96] *Immortality of the Soul* (London, 1712), 33.
[97] "Preface to the Reader," in *Psychathanasia*, book I (1647).
[98] A. N. Prior, *Logic and the Basis of Ethics* (Oxford: Clarendon, 1949), 23.
[99] Ibid., 22–23.

In Cudworth's view, Hobbes's strategy for restraining self-interest is infected with cowardly fear.

Most of the leading scientists and philosophers of the seventeenth century described themselves in terms of discovering and employing a more exact methodology – in mathematics, physics, and in the study of nature – than the ancients and the medieval schoolmen. Cambridge Platonist positing of "Plastick" nature would be tested and found wanting, deserving the same fate as Ptolemy's earth-centered cosmos, and would not survive in its seventeenth-century formulation. As R. A. Greene has observed, "Theories of an *anima mundi* or spirit of nature naturally flourish much more readily in the subtle illumination of Platonic myth and Spenserian allegory than in the dry light of experimental science."[100] More's contemporary, Robert Boyle, rejected "Plastick" nature on both scientific and theological grounds. Why should God require an intermediary agency in conserving and guiding the cosmos? Other, more nuanced portraits of biology and teleology would take its place and lay claim to serious reflection. In *Sources of the Self; The Making of the Modern Identity*, Charles Taylor offers a sympathetic portrait of the Cambridge Platonist treatment of love and the cosmos, but he aptly sees this at odds with future, mechanical science:

> This was a Platonism very influenced by Plotinus ... in which love played a central part; not only the ascending love of the lower for the higher, Plato's *eros*, but also a love of the higher which expressed itself in care for the lower, which could easily be identified with Christian *agape*. The two together make a vast circle of love through the universe. Nothing more at odds with the new mechanical philosophy can be conceived. In their natural science, Cudworth and his allies were fighting a rear-guard action against the future.[101]

Modern science in the seventeenth century revealed an increasingly unified, if imperfect, picture of the cosmos. For the medieval philosopher and scientist, the heavens were heavenly, with planets and stars moving in perfect circles. Kepler built a scientific case for seeing planetary orbits as ellipses. Galileo discovered other "imperfections" in the heavens with his observation of the sun, documenting the blemishes of sunspots.

---

[100] Greene, "Henry More and Robert Boyle on the Spirit of Nature," *Journal of the History of Ideas* 23:4 (October–December 1962): 453.

[101] *Sources of the Self: The Making of the Modern Identity* (Cambridge, Mass.: Harvard University Press, 1989), 250–251.

These and other findings led to a unified account of celestial and terrestrial motion. Newton, along with other prominent members of the Royal Society, such as Robert Boyle, Thomas Sprat, and John Wilkin, all believed (or professed to believe) in divine miracles and held that these miracles provided evidence of religious truths.[102] But, increasingly, the emphasis would be placed on God's design as a whole, not on God's special providence and the miraculous. The stage was also being set for seeing theism as a hypothesis, one among other possible explanations of the cosmos.[103]

Radical Skepticism and Faith

Skepticism in early modern philosophy was not ipso facto seen as either anti-scientific or anti-religious. Francis Bacon linked his experimental science with ancient skepticism. Bacon's science aimed at a middle course, keeping equal distance from a radical, absolute skepticism on the one hand and dogmatism on the other. Bacon tempered the self-confidence of the new method in empirical, natural science with an awareness of human fallibility. His castigation of presumptuous claims made on behalf of reason had a religious tone. Famously, he likened those who fall prey to unjustified convictions to those who are idolatrous.[104]

Robert Boyle and Joseph Glanvill (1636–1680), both members of the Royal Society, combined a modest skepticism about human faculties with modern scientific enterprises. Boyle published his *Sceptical Chemist* in 1661, while Glanvill published his *Scepsis Scientifica* (Confessed ignorance, the way to science) in 1665. As noted earlier, Henry More similarly embraced a fallibilist approach to human cognition; it is *possible* for us to be substantially wrong. As for religious uses of skepticism, Michel de Montaigne (1533–1592) and Pierre Bayle (1647–1706)

---

[102] See P. Harrison, "Newtonian Science, Miracles, and the Laws of Nature," *Journal of the History of Ideas* 56:4 (October 1995): 531–553.

[103] See Benjamin Carter, "Hypothesis of God: Methodological Problems of Theology in Intellectual History," lecture, St. Olaf College, 2004.

[104] For a nuanced look at Bacon's stance, see J. C. Briggs's "Bacon's Science and Religion," in *The Cambridge Companion to Bacon*, ed. M. Petonen (Cambridge: Cambridge University Press, 1996). Richard Popkin has ably argued that, historically, the opposite of skepticism is not disbelief in religion, but what he calls dogmatism. See R. H. Popkin, *The History of Skepticism, from Savonarola to Bayle* (Oxford: Oxford University Press, 2003).

are among the better-known critics of what they took to be the inflated claims of reason in the modern era, and each offered a modest defense of the legitimacy of religious convictions. Francisco Sanches, as well, contended that we cannot rule out, in principle, the failure of our cognitive faculties or reason. And yet, in *That Nothing Is Known* (1581), Sanches does not equate the unachievability of strict knowledge with the abandonment of religion.[105]

Skepticism over the use of reason was fed by religious fervor. Martin Luther (1483–1546) famously degraded the use of reason, likening it (in one colorful phrase) to a whore. Many of the Puritans who were contemporaries of the Cambridge Platonists were more at home with Tertullian (160–220) than with any sort of Christianized Plato. Tertullian's great rhetorical attack on natural philosophy is worth citing here:

> What indeed has Athens to do with Jerusalem? What concord's there between the Academy and the Church? What between heretics and Christians? . . . Away with all attempts to produce a mottled Christianity of Stoic, Platonic, and dialectical composition! We want no curious disputation after enjoying the gospel! With our faith, we desire no further belief. For once we believe this, there is nothing else that we ought to believe.[106]

But there was an uneasy peace at work here. Skepticism could as easily turn on religion as a whole as it did on dogmatism. E. M. Curley notes how seventeenth-century intellectual skepticism took root culturally, in part, because of the advent of modern science.

> To the average intelligent nonscientist, accustomed, as nonscientists generally are, to being guided by the consensus of the learned, the destruction of a scientific world view which had nearly universal acceptance for over a thousand years was deeply disturbing. It seemed to illustrate nothing so well as the skeptical position that for any given proposition counterarguments can be found as forceful as any of the arguments in its favor.[107]

Although some "believers" might see this counterbalance as making faith permissible, a more secular, stringent philosopher would see this as reason to suspend belief.

---

[105] There is a new translation of this: *That Nothing Is Known*, trans. D. F. S. Thomson (Cambridge: Cambridge University Press, 1988). The book ends with an amusing challenge to his opponents: "What?" Evidently, this is meant to invite a rejoinder.

[106] Tertullian, *Writings*, in *The Ante-Nicene Fathers*, ed. A. Roberts and J. Donaldson (Grand Rapids: Eerdmans, 1986), 3:246.

[107] *Descartes against Skeptics* (Cambridge, Mass.: Harvard University Press, 1978), 10.

Descartes rightly perceived the danger of a radical doubt of all the senses and appearances; the success of such doubt would sever our understanding of ourselves as embodied beings. As we observe in the next chapter, Descartes unleashed a radical thought experiment according to which we may not have any body at all. Unless such a severe possibility can be tamed, we seem to jeopardize what I earlier characterized as the Cambridge Platonist concept of the good of embodiment. Note the way Descartes' radical skeptical hypothesis seems to undermine all the virtues of embodiment outlined in the first part of the earlier section, "The Virtues of Human Nature."

> I will suppose therefore that not God, who is supremely good and the source of truth, but rather some malicious demon of the utmost power and cunning has employed all his energies in order to deceive me. I shall think that the sky, the air, the earth, colors, shapes, sounds and all external things are merely the delusions of dreams which he has devised to ensnare my judgment. I shall consider myself as not having hands or eyes, or flesh, or blood or senses, but as falsely believing that I have all these things. I shall stubbornly and firmly persist in this meditation; and, even if it is not in my power to know any truth, I shall at least do what is in my power, that is, resolutely guard against assenting to any falsehoods, so that the deceiver, however powerful and cunning he may be, will be unable to impose on me in the slightest degree. But this is an arduous undertaking, and a kind of laziness brings me back to normal life. I am like a prisoner who is enjoying an imaginary freedom while asleep; as he begins to suspect that he is asleep, he dreads being woken up, and goes along with the pleasant illusion as long as he can. In the same way, I happily slide back into my old opinions and dread being shaken out of them, for fear that my peaceful sleep may be followed by hard labor when I wake, and that I shall have to toil not in the light, but amid the inextricable darkness of the problems I have now raised.[108]

In the place of a confident, integrated embodiment, we have the prospect that (maybe) we are like prisoners, trapped in a cell while we merely *imagine* we are free agents in the world. Let us consider further the implications of Cartesian skepticism in the next chapter.

---

[108] *Meditations on First Philosophy*, in *The Philosophical Writings of Descartes*, trans. J. Cottingham, R. Stoothoff, and D. Murdoch (Cambridge: Cambridge University Press, 1984), 2:15.

Revelations and Religions

A dominant undertaking in early modern philosophy of religion is the articulation and justification or critique of theism. Much of the Cambridge Platonist literature was dedicated to combating atheism. The full title of Cudworth's major work is *The True Intellectual System of the Universe, Wherein All the Reason and Philosophy of Atheism is Confuted and its Impossibility Demonstrated*. More's *An Antidote against Atheism* was published in four editions.[109] This work was not all defensive or apologetic but constructive and exploratory. Cudworth wrote that "the idea of a perfect being is pregnant of many attributes."[110] The positive role of analyzing these attributes was significant, but so was the project of replying to nontheistic critics.

One attack on theism that exercised Cudworth and More was centered on the charge that, in the end, the theistic concept of God is largely negative. We may know that God is not a finite corporeal being like a mountain, but how might we achieve a positive concept of God's perfection? Hobbes and Margaret Cavendish (1623–1673) advanced what might be called an agnostic form of theism, or a theism that is much more restricted in terms than the bold, constructive philosophical projects like Cudworth's. Cavendish writes:

> No part of nature can or does conceive the essence of God, or what God is in himself; but it conceives only, that there is such a divine being which is supernatural: And therefore it cannot be said, that a natural figure can comprehend God: for it is not the comprehending of the substance of God, or its patterning out, (since God having not body, is all without figure) that makes the knowledge of God; but I do believe, that the knowledge of the existence of God, as I mentioned before, is innate, and inherent in nature and all her parts, as much as self knowledge is.[111]

So, while there may be innate knowledge that there is a God, God's being or nature is incomprehensible.

---

[109] For a collection of essays on the role of atheism in early modern philosophy, see M. Hunter and D. Wooton, eds., *Atheism from the Reformation to the Enlightenment* (Oxford: Clarendon, 1992).

[110] *The True Intellectual System of the Universe*, 2:558.

[111] Margaret Cavendish, Duchess of Newcastle, *Observations upon Experimental Philosophy*, ed. E. O'Neill (Cambridge: Cambridge University Press, 2001), 17. Cavendish, like Hobbes, endorses theism, but neither places stock in the kind of developed, constructive philosophical theology of Cudworth and his fellow Platonists.

Deism provided another threat to the Cambridge synthesis. "Deism" was a term first used synonymously with "theism," but in the seventeenth and eighteenth centuries it came to be distinguished from the classical Christian (as well as Jewish and Islamic) thesis that God provides a revelation historically, backed by miracles, attesting to truths of God that are not attainable through reason and reflection alone – that is, without God's special action in revelation. Deists acknowledged the existence of God but not the Bible as offering bona fide independent knowledge of God's will. Many deists allowed that the Bible contains truths and yet the authority for believing these truths does not come from the Bible but from reason and experience. Lord Herbert of Cherbury (1582/3–1648) was an important contributor to deism.[112] John Toland (1670–1722) and Matthew Tindal (1657–1733) are two later figures who similarly sought to limit the appeal to supernatural revelations testified to by miracles. These authors were often not hostile to Christianity; their work was largely spent on locating what they took to be the nonmysterious, rationally defensible core of the tradition. For the traditionalist, however, deistic Christianity appeared to be *Hamlet* without the prince, especially as classic teaching about the incarnation and trinity came to be either denied or reinterpreted in nonsupernatural terms (e.g., Christ may be thought of as divine insofar as he lived an exemplary, inspiring, compassionate life).

At the end of the seventeenth century, skepticism about the Bible's credibility began to ferment. Can we trust the Bible as an infallible, inerrant source of knowledge of faith in God? Are all parts of the Bible equally reliable? Just as Galileo had discovered imperfections in celestial bodies, were there analogous imperfections in Scripture? How does Christianity fare in contrast to other traditions that give center stage to claims of divine revelation like Judaism and Islam? Seventeenth-century Europeans encountered a diversity of religions in the Americas, as well as in the fertile, sophisticated context of Chinese Confucianism. Was Chinese wisdom the outcome of sacred revelation or unaided natural

---

[112] There is some debate whether Lord Herbert was himself a deist, but as noted in the Introduction I do not have the space allotted to sift through all the arguments here. See David Pailen's "Should Herbert of Cherbury Be Regarded as a Deist?" *Journal of Theological Studies* 51 (April 2000): 114–149. It is clear, however, that Cudworth was *not* a deist, contra his being described as a deist in J. Yolton, ed., *The Blackwell Companion to the Enlightenment* (Oxford: Blackwell, 1995), 447.

reason? Was it a mature, nontheistic religion? These questions called for philosophical reflection on the nature of history, the concept of evidence, the concept of miracles, and competing views of the laws of nature. Francis Bacon saw the divisions and plurality of religions as a direct challenge to Christian theism. The existence of many religions is identified by Bacon as the first cause for atheism. "The causes of atheism are: divisions in religion, if there be many; for any one main division addeth zeal to both sides, but many divisions introduce atheism."[113]

Doorways to Modern and Contemporary Philosophy

As I mention in the Introduction, I chose the Cambridge Platonists as the starting point for this book because they, like the keeper of doorways, Janus, looked to the past and to the future. Once inside the door of modern philosophy, there are many possible moves in a narrative history such as this one. I suggest we next look to Descartes. After Descartes, I survey extensive philosophical work, which would customarily be called empiricist and rationalist philosophy of religion. Francis Bacon offered this portrait of empiricists, rationalists, and those who attempt a middle path. "Those who have handled the sciences have been either Empiricists or Rationalists. Empiricists, like ants, merely collect things and use them. The Rationalists, like spiders, spin webs out of themselves. The middle way is that of the bee, which gathers its material from the flowers of the field, but then transforms and digests it by a power of its own."[114] If we retain the metaphor of doorways, one may

---

113 "Of Atheism," in *Essays or Counsels, Civil and Moral*, ed. B. Vikers (London: Folio Society, 2002), 57. Bacon's view in the end is that atheism is philosophically unacceptable. "It is true, that a little philosophy inclineth man's mind to atheism; but depth in philosophy bringeth men's minds about to religion" (ibid., 55).

114 Bacon, *Novum Organum*, trans. and ed. P. Urbach and J. Gibson (Chicago: Open Court, 1994), p. 105. In all, I see the Cambridge Platonists as closest to Bacon's bees, for they were in between the rationalists and empiricists, as well as in between some other rivals. I believe G. A. J. Rogers correctly locates the Cambridge Platonists in the history of ideas: "Occupying a territory that lies between the system of Descartes and that of Leibniz, between rationalism and empiricism, between ancient and modern science, between religion and philosophy, the Cambridge Platonists were at the heart of the formation of modern thought, and many of their questions are still our own, even if their solutions are no longer accepted" (Rogers et al., introduction to *The Cambridge Platonists in Philosophical Context*, ix).

get the impression that behind the doorway of Chapter 3 you will find a bewildering, haunted mansion of insects! The scope and fertility of the philosophy of religion is indeed immense and difficult to unify. But one trend that I seek to trace in subsequent thinkers is the metamorphosis of philosophical inquiry into something more impersonal and secular than we find in Cambridge Platonism.

✦

Cartesian Philosophy of Religion

Notwithstanding the immense goodness of God, the nature of man as a combination of mind and body is such that it is bound to mislead him from time to time.

Descartes[1]

Descartes and a Queen

On February 11, 1650, René Descartes, the person most often identified as the father of modern European philosophy, died in Sweden. The month before, he had written to a friend, "I am not in my element here."[2] Descartes, born in 1596 in southern France, was a celebrated philosopher at the time of his death, though also the subject of sustained criticism. He went to Stockholm at the request of Queen Christina (1626–1689) in order to tutor her in philosophy. They had corresponded on metaphysics and the nature and value of love. The fierce cold, a rigorous early morning schedule, and, in the end, pneumonia proved fatal.[3]

Descartes' short-lived but cordial relationship with the queen reflected his enthusiasm for philosophical dialogue with women at a time when women were still excluded from a formal, higher education. The first correspondence between Christina and Descartes involved themes

---

[1] *The Philosophical Writing of Descartes*, trans. J. Cottingham, R. Stoothoff, and D. Murdoch, 3 vols. (Cambridge: Cambridge University Press, 1984), 2:61 (hereafter CSM).

[2] CSM, 3:384.

[3] For an engaging biography, see Geneviève Rodis-Lewis, *Descartes: His Life and Thought*, trans. Jane Marie Todd (Ithaca: Cornell University Press, 1998). See also Susanna Akerman, "Kristina Wasa, Queen of Sweden," in *A History of Women Philosophers*, vol. 3, ed. M. E. Waithe (Dordrecht: Kluwer, 1991).

that were close to the heart of Cambridge Platonists. "The goodness of each thing," Descartes wrote in 1647, "can be considered in itself without reference to anything else, and in this sense it is evident that God is the supreme good, since he is incomparably more perfect than any creature."[4] Descartes went on to extol the goodness of freedom and the additional good of things in relation to greater goods. The year before his death, Descartes corresponded with another woman of philosophical training and insight, Princess Elizabeth (1618–1680), who intersects an aspect of the narrative of Cambridge Platonism presented in Chapter 1. King Charles I was the uncle of Elizabeth and Descartes wrote to console her upon learning of the king's execution. Elizabeth also proved to be an appreciative but important critic of Descartes' philosophy. Descartes dedicated *The Principles of Philosophy* (1644) to her, and a short treatise he wrote for her was the starting point for what would be his last book, *The Passions of the Soul* (1649).

While Descartes' time in Sweden was brief, it is fitting to appreciate his commitment to carrying out philosophy (including philosophy of religion) in one of the most dramatic, public settings in Northern European politics and culture. Queen Christina was renowned for her learning and her support of the arts (she was known as the Minerva of the North), her challenge to the conventional treatment of women, and her contribution to the Peace of Westphalia. Descartes was one of many scholars, musicians, and writers in her court. Philosophy was seen as one of several important contributors to cultural, religious, and political life.

Descartes Then and Now

Why highlight Descartes in a narrative history of philosophical reflection on religion? Many of his projects bear directly on central religious concerns: the knowledge of God, the essential role of reason in providing evidence for God's existence, the nature of the self, the possibility of an afterlife, and so on. Even more fundamentally, Descartes is credited (or blamed) for introducing what has come to be called a "foundationalist" treatment of knowledge. According to foundationalism, all our genuine claims to knowledge (whether these are claims to know God or to know that you are currently reading this book) are built on a

---

[4] CSM, 1:324.

foundation that is infallible (not subject to error). Subsequent versions of foundationalism vary in terms of the sturdiness of the foundational beliefs; a strong version of foundationalism like Descartes' insists on indubitable certainty; others insist that the foundational beliefs are simply justified or evident but not necessarily infallible. Descartes' methodology played an important role in understanding religious convictions philosophically. Descartes fueled a modern conviction that, in order to be rational, religious beliefs needed to be vindicated through rigorous philosophical investigation.

It is especially important, also, to study Descartes now because an enormous number of philosophers at large, and philosophers of religion in particular, blame Descartes for having a devastating effect on the history of ideas and even on the current intellectual climate. In many English-speaking philosophy departments and departments of religious studies and theological faculties today Descartes is public enemy number one. Some critics today as well as in his own time believe Descartes' goal to be unattainable, and thus a virtual guarantee of skepticism, both religious and secular. Descartes' world of severe intellectual demands was not (according to his major critics) inhabitable. He is also castigated for leaving us with a pernicious dualism between mind and body in which the mental and physical appear to be radically and unalterably distinct. Unlike More, who thought of the mind as an immaterial and yet spatially extended reality, Descartes held that the mind is not spatial at all. A host of subsequent philosophers and theologians sees this split as intolerable. Some of his contemporaries welcomed his mechanistic view of nature, but many environmental ethicists and animal rights philosophers in the twentieth and early twenty-first century take Descartes to task for his denial that nonhuman animals are conscious. (Cudworth, incidentally, opposed Descartes' view of animals.) Descartes' arguments for God's existence have never won wide support. Many critics of what is classified as the "modern era" begin with the articulation and critique of Descartes.[5]

---

[5] For a representative, caustic philosophical critique of Descartes, see Gilbert Ryle, *The Concept of Mind* (London: Hutchinson, 1949). While Ryle's criticism is mostly philosophical, it suggests analogous ethical and theological objections. Theological criticism has ranged from the supposition that Descartes was on the right track but simply failed in specifics to outright rejection of Descartes on all fronts. William Temple, mid-twentieth-century philosopher and Archbishop of Canterbury, referred to "The Cartesian 'Faux-Pas,'" in *Nature, Man and God* (New York: Macmillan, 1949), lecture III. Temple writes: "If I were asked what was the most disastrous moment in the

A Companion to Epistemology provides a useful representative judgment on Descartes that could easily be aligned with the judgment of many current theologians. "The power of Descartes' thinking is manifest; for a great part of the history of philosophy of our own century has been, in effect, a struggle to escape from Descartes' individualistic and autocratic perspective on the problems of knowledge and certainty – a perspective which, whether we like it or not, has become part of our conceptual heritage."[6] Descartes' method and worldview are typically seen as what we need to avoid at all costs.[7]

While I have stressed the criticism of Descartes, some philosophers of religion see him as still setting up the parameters of contemporary debate. Grace Jantzen writes in *Becoming Divine: Towards a Feminist Philosophy of Religion* that "Western Philosophy has struggled with and against Descartes in many ways. . . . Yet for all the arguments that have been raised, the subject, characterized by conscious rationality, has remained for centuries a stable platform of modernity; and . . . [it]

history of Europe, I should be strongly tempted to answer that it was that period of leisure when René Descartes, having no claims to meet, remained for a whole day 'shut up alone in a stove'" (57). The reference to a stove is to Descartes' solitary meditations by a stove in which he formulated his central philosophical ideas. For a look at some of the important responses to Descartes, see Nicholas Jolley, "The Reception of Descartes' Philosophy," in *The Cambridge Companion to Descartes*, ed. John Cottingham (Cambridge: Cambridge University Press, 1992). There is a very useful analysis of Descartes' followers and critics in T. M. Schmaltz, *Radical Cartesianism: The French Reception of Descartes* (Cambridge: Cambridge University Press, 2002).

[6] J. Cottingham, "Descartes," in *A Companion to Epistemology*, ed. J. Dancy and E. Sosa (Oxford: Blackwell, 1992), 96.

[7] This is D. Dennett's judgment in *Consciousness Explained* (Boston: Little, Brown, 1991) and elsewhere. Here is a typical line from Dennett on dualism: "Dualism . . . and vitalism [two theories which are in the Cambridge Platonist tradition] have been relegated to the trash heap of history, along with alchemy and astrology. Unless you are also prepared to declare that the world is flat and the sun is a fiery chariot pulled by winged horses – unless, in other words, your defiance of modern science is quite complete – you won't find any place to stand and fight for these obsolete ideas" (24). For a contemporary theological rejection of Descartes' dualism, see Sallie McFague, *The Body of God* (Minneapolis: Fortress Press, 1983). For a sustained theological attack on Descartes, see also Fergus Kerr, *Theology after Wittgenstein* (Oxford: Blackwell, 1986). This book might be subtitled *The Decline and Fall of Theological Cartesianism*. My own training in philosophy and theology in the 1970s and 1980s was thoroughly anti-Descartes. One of my college professors seriously advanced the thesis that Descartes was responsible for the Vietnam War.

is still hardly questioned in the philosophy of religion."[8] Given this influence, we do well to concentrate on Descartes in a self-conscious, critical fashion.

In this chapter, I present and assess some of Descartes' central contributions to philosophy of religion. Fortunately this will involve narrowing the scope of topics usually covered in more general studies of Descartes, though only barely because much of what he wrote had religious implications. Obviously Descartes' arguments about doubt and God are religiously significant, but his mind-body dualism also proves to be of religious importance. Descartes held that the immateriality of the soul was central to the religious conviction that the soul may (or *will*) survive the death of its material body. In the course of exploring Descartes' method, dualism, and so on, I at times challenge some of the criticism that has led to the pervasive dismissal of his work. My aim is therefore to encourage a reassessment of Descartes' work for contemporary philosophy of religion. After an exposition of his work, I consider several responses to Descartes: Anne Conway and Nicholas Malebranche are motivated to formulate what they see as a less fragmentary picture of God and the world, although they advance radically different proposals. Blaise Pascal is in radical opposition to Descartes' pursuit of philosophical certainty.

Cartesian Nature and Ambition

Unlike the Cambridge Platonists, who saw themselves as carrying on an older philosophical tradition, Descartes described himself as initiating a radically new project.[9] He set out to sweep away scholastic claims

---

[8] *Becoming Divine: Towards a Feminist Philosophy of Religion* (Bloomington: Indiana University Press, 1999), 33.

[9] The term "Cartesian," often used to describe Descartes' work and those influenced by it, is derived from the Latin version of the name Descartes. I am using the term "Cartesian" in this chapter in a broad fashion for the family of ideas Descartes advanced. Like the term "Platonism" in Chapter 1, a philosopher may still be called a Cartesian without adopting *all* of Descartes' views. As T. M. Lennon and Patricia Easton comment: "There was hardly a doctrine, view, or argument that was advanced by everyone thought to be Cartesian" (*The Cartesian Epistemology of François Bayle* [New York: Garland, 1992], 1). For Descartes' interest in ushering in fresh philosophical work, rather than working under earlier, scholastic frameworks, see rule 3 in *Rules for the Direction of the Mind* and Part One of his *Discourse on the Method*. The extent to which Descartes succeeded in breaking with medieval and ancient philosophy is in dispute. See, for example, Tom Sorrell, ed., *The Rise of Modern Philosophy: The*

to know about the universe that were (he thought) unfounded, if not unintelligible, and to replace these with proper, certain knowledge.[10] Henry More initially welcomed this project and may be credited as being one of Descartes' first British disciples. At one point, More described his own work as a blend of Cartesianism and Platonism. Cartesianism was said to constitute the body and Platonism the soul of his philosophical work up to 1662.[11] On reflection, however, More as well as Cudworth pulled away from Descartes, concluding that Cartesianism offers an excessive division between mind and matter, God and the world, and opposing some of his other convictions.

Descartes' credentials for being a *modern* philosopher lie, in part, in his approaching the world in mechanical terms. Earlier medieval philosophy of nature recognized efficient and material causes, but they also countenanced final causes (in which an object's behavior is accounted for in terms of its final purpose or state – the acorn's growth can be explained by virtue of its growing to become an oak tree), and they saw the world in terms of hylomorphism (in which a mental object has both form and matter).[12] This world of substantial forms and natural kinds differed from Descartes' nature, which privileged geometry and mathematics. "The only principles which I accept, or require, in physics are those of geometry and pure mathematics; these principles explain all natural phenomena, and enable us to provide quite certain demonstrations regarding them."[13] Descartes did not see the need to attribute to nature any quasi-vital dimension like plastic nature. God created a cosmos with regulative law and order.

Tension between the New and Traditional Philosophies from Machiavelli to Leibniz (Oxford: Clarendon, 1993) and Stephen Menn, *Descartes and Augustine* (Cambridge: Cambridge University Press, 1998).

[10] For example, some twentieth-century philosophers distinguished between weak and strong senses of the concept of knowledge in which weaker claims to know did not amount to strict, unmistakable certainty. Descartes allowed for some errors produced by our cognitive faculties, as noted in the passage cited at the outset of this chapter, but he looked for a foundation for knowledge that was indeed certain and not susceptible to error.

[11] See the preface general to More's *Collection of Several Philosophical Writings*, ed. Rene Welleck (New York: Garland, 1978), sec. 16.

[12] This account is too condensed given the riches and nuances of a medieval philosophy of nature. For an introduction to the complexities involved, see A. S. McGrade, ed., *The Cambridge Companion to Medieval Philosophy* (Cambridge: Cambridge University Press, 2003), chaps. 1, 6, 7, 8, 9.

[13] CSM, 1:247.

The twentieth-century philosopher and theologian Austin Farrer offers this telling portrait of nature that was part of modern philosophy. The goal was a uniform, mathematically analyzable nature.

> We can now see why "substantial forms" were the *bêtes noires* of the seventeenth century philosophers. It was because they turned nature into an unmanageable jungle, in which trees, bushes, and parasites of a thousand kinds wildly interlaced. There was nothing for it, if science was to proceed, but to clear the ground and replant with spruce in rows: to postulate a single uniform nature, of which there should be a single science. Now neither probatology nor cynology could hope to be universal – the world is not all sheep nor all dog: it would have to be hylology; for the world is, in its spatial aspect, all material. Let us say, then, that there is one uniform material nature of things, and that everything else consists in the arrangements of the basic material nature; as the show of towers and mountains in the sunset results simply from an arrangement of vapours. And let us suppose that the interactions of the parts of matter are all like those which we can observe in dead manipulable bodies – in mechanism, in fact. Such was the postulate of the new philosophers, and it yielded them results.[14]

Descartes' view of nature did not have final causes amid the "jungle" of Aristotelian natural kinds to accommodate. His conception of the human body and material bodies in general was more austere:

> By a body I understand whatever has a determinable shape and a definable location and can occupy a space in such a way as to exclude any other body; it can be perceived by touch, sight, hearing, taste or smell, and can be moved in various ways, not by itself but by whatever else comes into contact with it. For, according to my judgment, the power of self-movement, like the power of sensation or of thought, was quite foreign to the nature of a body; indeed, it was a source of wonder to me that certain bodies were found to contain faculties of this kind.[15]

Empirical study of these bodies had the promise of producing a unified, mechanical understanding of the physical world.

Descartes' early work, including the *Optics, Meteorology,* and *Geometry,* was in the sciences. In the course of his nearly fifty-four years, he made important contributions to the development of analytic

---

[14] Austin Farrer, introduction to *Theodicy,* by G. W. Leibniz (LaSalle: Open Court, 1990), 17–18.
[15] CSM, 2:17–18.

geometry; he also advanced substantial accounts of inertia and motion, and he is credited with discovering the law of refraction. The human body is described by Descartes as a machine, albeit one that is created by God and joined with a soul.[16] Descartes' modernity is also displayed in his pursuit of a unified philosophical foundation for all inquiry.

Although Descartes was at home with the methodology and findings of much of the science of his day, he was also keenly interested in the scope of doubt: What are the limits of doubt? What, if anything, is indisputable? In taking skepticism seriously, Descartes was a man of his era. In a host of important historical studies, Richard Popkin has brought to light the pervasive character of skepticism in modern times. "Modified skepticism has been a basic form of *modern* philosophy."[17] As I noted at the close of Chapter 1, a modified skepticism was a friendly companion to religious and scientific practice; however, more severe forms of skepticism threatened to overturn both.

Descartes held that for anyone who is not already religious through faith, religious faith needs justification through natural reason – that is, reason that is unaided by revelation. In his *Dedicatory Letter to the Sorbonne*, which introduces his *Meditations on First Philosophy*, Descartes wrote:

> For us who are believers, it is enough to accept on faith that the human soul does not die with the body, and that God exists; but in the case of unbelievers, it seems that there is no religion, and practically no moral virtue, that they can be persuaded to adopt until these two truths are proved to them by natural reason.... It is of course quite true that we must believe in the existence of God because it is a doctrine of Holy Scripture, and conversely, that we must believe Holy Scripture because it comes from God; for since faith is the gift of God, he who gives us grace to believe other things can also give us grace to believe that he exists. But this argument cannot be put to unbelievers because they would judge it to be circular.[18]

---

[16] CSM, 1:99. This view of soul and body was lampooned in the late twentieth century as positing a ghost in a machine.

[17] Popkin, "Scepticism in Modernity," in Sorrell, *The Rise of Modern Philosophy*, 15. While skepticism is a mark of modernity, it is also noted by Popkin to be a mark of much ancient philosophy. There is a similarity between Descartes' skeptical arguments and the work of Sextus Empiricus, the Greco-Roman skeptic.

[18] CSM, 2:3. See also Descartes' letter to Huygens (October 10, 1642): "However much we wish to believe and however much we think we do firmly believe that religion

Descartes, like the Cambridge Platonists, did not befriend an anti-intellectual religious faith. Moreover, in Descartes' great philosophical projects in which he employs his foundational methodology, he invites his readers to adopt the position of the "unbelievers" or at least the position of an inquirer who does not, at the outset, assume the truth of religious faith.

Descartes sought to use skepticism as a means of purifying beliefs. By his lights, the ability to withstand excoriating doubt is a mark of surety. What could not be doubted? In raising this question, Descartes carefully distinguished his aim from other skeptical projects.

> Reflecting especially upon the points in every subject which might make it suspect and give occasion for us to make mistakes, I kept uprooting from my mind any errors that might previously have slipped into it. In doing this I was not copying the sceptics, who doubt only for the sake of doubting and pretend to be always undecided; on the contrary, my whole aim was to reach certainty – to cast aside the loose earth and sand so as to come upon rock or clay.[19]

In his effort to reach rock-hard certainty Descartes famously entertained the possibility that his senses are systematically distortive so that the body he thinks he has is only apparent and not real.

In the *Meditations*, Descartes builds up to this skeptical nightmare by first asking us whether we can correctly and certainly distinguish between when we are awake and when we are dreaming that we are awake. If I cannot rule out the possibility that I am dreaming right now, my claim to know that I am awake is jeopardized. Descartes then places the dream argument to one side, for dreaming and waking life may have *some* distinguishable characteristics. The more radical hypothesis is that an all-powerful spirit has deceived us so that what we believe is the reliable perception of other people and the world around us is merely apparent. By giving the skeptic a virtually omnipotent ally, Descartes allows for the possibility of a massive, meticulous, and comprehensive illusion. Descartes has set up a test in which the cognitive sanctity of our beliefs should be tested by an adversary who has limitless resources.[20] Today, parallel Cartesian skeptical tests more often appeal

---

teaches, we are not usually so moved by it as to when we are convinced by very evident natural reasons" (CSM, 2:216).

[19] CSM, 1:125.

[20] This testing of our claims to knowledge is a heightened, perhaps maximum instance of what the Roman Catholic Church engaged in with its use of the so-called Devil's

to mad scientists than powerful demons. So, the late twentieth-century version of the Cartesian hypothesis is that you are not reading this book now in, say, a library, but that your brain has been removed from your body by mad scientists and placed in a tub of fluids where electrochemical stimulation is making you believe you are in the library.[21] The threat of Cartesian doubt is by no means a relic from the seventeenth century but alive and well in some contemporary philosophy departments.

The entertainment of such a severance between appearance and reality is a direct threat to the "virtues of embodiment" as described in Chapter 1. Can I rely on my senses? Agency? The proper functioning of my anatomy to support sustained conscious life? While the Cambridge Platonists attributed the coherence and goodness of embodiment to the intelligence and goodness of God, and Descartes will (eventually) make a similar recourse, he lingered over the skeptical hypothesis and entertained the possibility of a pernicious, godlike reality with greater concentration and weight than his contemporaries. The haunting nature of this doubt is brought out well in Grace Jantzen's comment: "Few students who descend his steps of doubt climb all the way back again."[22] It is worth underscoring that the kind of skepticism Descartes introduces is meant to test (and possibly undermine) our claims to knowledge as opposed to introducing contrary claims of knowledge. In this respect, Descartes is employing what some call *Pyrrhonian* as opposed to *Academic* skepticism. The latter – stemming from the third century B.C.E. – is more radical. An Academic skeptic may assert that nothing whatever is known by anyone (a view associated with Arcesilaus,

---

Advocate (*Advocatus Diaboli*). This was the popular name for someone (officially called the promoter of faith, or *promoter fidei*) whose role was to challenge the claim that a person was a saint.

[21] These thought experiments may be found in different versions in work by Peter Unger, Robert Nozick, Hilary Putnam, and others. Tom Carson has recently deployed a series of them designed to test our value judgments about making connections with each other and the external world. See Carson, *Value and the Good Life* (Notre Dame: University of Notre Dame Press, 2000). In *Consciousness Explained* Dennett protests that the scientific job of actually hooking up human brains in a fashion that would provide the hallucinatory simulation far surpasses human powers. In Descartes' case, this obstacle is bypassed. Recently, a popular movie series, beginning with *The Matrix*, is built on the conception of a three-dimensional "virtual world." A skeptical argument can now get off the ground by asking this question: how do you know you are not in the matrix?

[22] *Becoming Divine*, 33.

315–240 B.C.E.). In contrast, a follower of Pyrrho of Elis (365–275 B.C.E.) simply suspends judgment in all matters. Pyrrhonists do not claim to know that no one knows anything; perhaps there is a being who knows everything, perhaps not. Popkin offers this distinction: "Pyrrhonism is first distinguished from the negative dogmatism of Academic skepticism: the Pyrrhonists doubt and suspend judgments on all propositions, even that all is doubt. They oppose any assertion whatsoever, and their opposition, if successful, shows the opponent's ignorance; if unsuccessful, their own ignorance."[23] Back to Descartes' hypothesis: a Pyrrhonic suspension of the belief that you have a body will undermine the possibility of you knowingly acting in the world as an embodied person. Just as one cannot knowingly and deliberately checkmate someone without knowing the rules of chess, one must secure the knowledge of one's embodiment in order for one to act as a knowing agent in the world.[24]

Once he has conjured up the specter of radical skepticism, how does Descartes return to the convictions that he is embodied, that God does exist, and that the world is as it appears? In tracing Descartes' path back, let us pay close attention to Descartes' methodology. After this, it will be useful to follow the stages in Descartes' reasoning that he lays out in his *Meditations on First Philosophy*.[25] Descartes' next four steps are to secure that (1) at the very minimum he cannot doubt his own existence (Second Meditation), (2) he may be certain that God qua perfect being exists (Third and Fifth Meditations), and (3) this secures the reliability of his cognition – the appearance of the world is indeed trustworthy (Fourth and Fifth Meditations); and, finally, (4) the mind and body are distinct (Sixth Meditation).

---

[23] *The History of Skepticism from Erasmus to Spinoza* (Berkeley: University of California Press, 1979), 47.

[24] One reader of this chapter in manuscript form objected: "I can act as if I were a knowing agent in the world even if I think that the world might not be there (cf. *The Matrix* . . .)," but note the qualification "as if." My point is that you cannot know you are, say, shaking hands with someone unless you know that the person is actually there and so on. I explore the moral implications of skepticism about one's embodiment in "Imaginary Evil: A Skeptic's Wager," *Philosophia* 21:3–4 (1992).

[25] For a suggestive, interesting look at the dramatic, meditative character of this work, see Amélie Rorty's "The Structure of Descartes' *Meditations*" and Garry Hattfield's "The Senses and the Fleshless Eye: *The Meditations* as Cognitive Exercises," in *Essays on Descartes' Meditations*, ed. A. Rorty (Berkeley: University of California Press, 1986).

Cartesian Methodology

Descartes' concern for finding a reliable methodology is apparent in the titles of his work: *Rules for the Direction of the Mind* and *Discourse on the Method of Rightly Conducting One's Reason and Seeking the Truth in the Sciences.*

In Descartes' work one comes face to face with what is today called *the problem of the criterion.*[26] Consider this exchange between you and skeptic:

> *You*: I know that X (e.g., that I exist or any other propositions) is true.
> *Skeptic*: How do you know that?
> *You*: I know that X is true because I perceive X very clearly and distinctly. And because "whatever I perceive very clearly and distinctly is true," I conclude that X is true.[27]
> *Skeptic*: But how do you know that whatever you perceive very clearly and distinctly is true?
> *You*: I know it is true because I perceive that criterion about perception, clarity, and distinctness with clarity and distinction.
> *Skeptic*: You are appealing to the very criterion that I am calling into question. You have not really answered my first question.

At this stage, there seem to be at least two replies. The first one is simply to hold the line against the skeptic by claiming that one can indeed know something (e.g., that you exist) without relying on a method or criterion to provide further evidence or credence. Perhaps you may know something and not need to answer the skeptic's question in order for you to have bona fide knowledge. This approach to skepticism has been called *particularism* because the nonskeptic takes her stand with specific claims of knowledge.[28]

---

[26] For an overview, see the entry "Problem of the Criterion," in *A Companion to Epistemology,* ed. J. Dancy and E. Sosa (Oxford: Blackwell, 1992).

[27] CSM, 2:24.

[28] This was Roderick Chisholm's option. See his *The Problem of the Criterion* (Milwaukee: Marquette University Press, 1973). Some contemporary philosophers take refuge against skepticism by conceding that the skeptic reveals that one may not know that you know something but, for all that, it does not follow that you have no knowledge. Presumably children and nonhuman animals know things without knowing that they have such knowledge. For a good assessment of the surrounding issues, and some of the justification for Chisholm's stance, see "The Impossibility of the 'Theory of Knowledge,'" by Leonard Nelson, reprinted in *Empirical Knowledge,* ed. R. Chisholm and R. Swartz (Englewood Cliffs, N.J.: Prentice-Hall, 1973).

There is another reply, but it may be more problematic. Imagine that, rather than claiming simply to know X, you introduce a criterion (M) and then introduce yet another criterion (N) in order to justify your original claim to know X. This, however, seems to invite a vicious, infinite regress. On what grounds do you justify N? If you reply to the skeptic that you simply see that N is true, he will be unimpressed and charge you with begging the question. If you introduce another criterion, O, then you may be on the way to being compelled to introduce yet another criterion, P, and on and on.

Descartes may be read as inviting the problem of the criterion, especially if one gives exclusive attention to his *Rules for the Direction of the Mind*. In this text, he displays his tools of inquiry that involve *intuition* and *deduction*. Here is his rule 3: "Concerning objects proposed for study, we ought to investigate what we can clearly and evidently intuit or deduce with certainty, and not what other people have thought or what we ourselves conjecture. For knowledge can be attained in no other way."[29] Descartes then offers this picture of how intuition works.

> By "intuition" I do not mean the fluctuating testimony of the senses or the deceptive judgment of the imagination as it botches things together, but the conception of a clear and attentive mind, which is so easy and distinct that there can be no room for doubt about what we are understanding. Alternatively, and this comes to the same thing, intuition is the indubitable conception of a clear and attentive mind which proceeds solely from the light of reason. Because it is simpler, it is more certain than deduction, though deduction, as we noted above, is not something a man can perform wrongly. Thus everyone can mentally intuit that he exists, that he is thinking, that a triangle is bounded by just three lines, and a sphere by a single surface, and the like. Perceptions such as these are more numerous than most people realize, disdaining as they do to turn their minds to such simple matters.[30]

Although this setup invites the problem of the criterion, I believe that in the *Meditations* one may detect a different strategy against the skeptic. In the *Meditations*, I suggest that Descartes is a particularist.[31] He comes

---

[29] CSM, 1:13.

[30] CSM, 1:14.

[31] On this point, I commend James van Cleave's thesis: "In Descartes' philosophy, clear and distinct perception is a source of knowledge, but not (except in special cases) a ground for it. That is to say, attaining a state of clearly and distinctly perceiving a proposition p puts you in a state of directly (i.e., non-inferentially) knowing p. There

to see that something is true (that he exists), and Descartes *then* comes to investigate what marks such a bona fide claim of knowledge. In other words, rather than begin with a method, he begins with a particular knowledge-claim, something that is intuitively evident. Descartes uses a *method of doubt*, and, in the sequence of meditations, doubt comes first. But when he comes to what he cannot doubt (his own existence, to be discussed later), he does not know he exists by virtue of the fact that he cannot doubt this. In other words, his ground for knowledge is not the fact that his method of doubt was applied. Rather, he cannot doubt his existence because he knows it. The method of doubt was used by Descartes to discover what he knows, rather than the method of doubt being used to in some way constitute what he knows. His self-awareness is indubitable because he knows it and not vice versa.[32]

As there are several places in this book where claims about what we know are tested by thought experiments, let me add another analogy to bolster my proposal. Imagine your love for someone, Pat, is so strong that you conclude it is unconditional and unsurpassable (you could not love Pat anymore than you do). You then test your conclusion by considering a host of unwelcome possibilities. Would you still love Pat if (s)he hated you? Imagining further, you conclude after this method of testing that your love is indeed unconditional and unsurpassable. I suggest that the unsavory method of imagining awful states of affairs may have been vital in identifying the depth and parameter of your love, but what the thought experiment does is bring to the surface (or make clear) what you know directly: namely, you know you love Pat. It is because of your grasp of the strong character of your love that you

---

is no need to infer the truth of p from the higher order proposition that you do clearly and distinctly perceive it, or any need to have knowledge of that higher order proposition" (*Problems from Kant* [Oxford: Oxford University Press, 1999], 269). See his "Foundationalism, Epistemic Principles, and the Cartesian Circle," *Philosophical Review* 88 (1979). I defend a particularist epistemology with a Platonic metaphysics in "Taking Common Sense Seriously: The Philosophy of Roderick Chisholm," *Inquiry* 41 (Fall 1998).

[32] While I commend particularism, one may combine both particularism and methodism. I believe the method of doubt brings to the surface the fact that he knows he exists (it is by virtue of the fact that I know I exist that my existence is indubitable), but that does not rule out also arguing that one cannot doubt one's existence because you cannot deny one's existence without expressing a contradiction and that *any belief that cannot be denied without a contradiction* may be known to be true. Arguably, a proposition may be known to be true both through particularist grounds and by way of a criterion.

come to recite a familiar Shakespearean sonnet to Pat, proclaiming that because your love is true, it did not alter, notwithstanding foreseeable tempests and the like.

Let us next consider Descartes' reasoning and how he secures (or believes he secures) certainty about his own existence and *then* presses on to secure his criterion for knowledge.

A Substantial Self

In the *Meditations* Descartes uses his method of doubt until he comes to something known. He may be able to doubt successfully whether he is or has a body but he cannot doubt his existence. He tries to imagine that there is no world of bodies or the things he seems to observe. In the midst of this radical desolation, Descartes still finds the stubborn, undeniable fact of his own existence, which even the possibility of a malevolent powerful demon cannot shake.

> In that case am not I, at least, something? But I have just said that I have no senses and no body. This is the sticking point: what follows from this? Am I not so bound up with a body and with senses that I cannot exist without them? But I have convinced myself that there is absolutely nothing in the world, no sky, no earth, no minds, no bodies. Does it now follow that I too do not exist? No: if I convinced myself of something then I certainly existed. But there is a deceiver of supreme power and cunning who is deliberately and constantly deceiving me. In that case I too undoubtedly exist, if he is deceiving me; and let him deceive me as much as he can, he will never bring it about that I am nothing so long as I think that I am something. So after considering everything very thoroughly, I must finally conclude that this proposition, *I am, I exist*, is necessarily true whenever it is put forward by me or conceived in my mind.[33]

The strategy of taking a stand on the certitude of one's own reality is not entirely new; Augustine employed a similar line of reasoning against the skeptics of his day.[34] Still, Descartes' securing of self-knowledge is a pivotal move against skepticism in modern philosophy. Like many anti-skeptical moves it offers an ad hominem challenge. Doesn't the

---

[33] CSM, 2:16–17.

[34] Consider Augustine's claim: "Si fallor, sum" (If I am deceived, I exist). For some of the background to Descartes' work, see Stephen Mann and Jorge Secada, *Cartesian Metaphysics: The Scholastic Origins of Modern Philosophy* (Cambridge: Cambridge University Press, 2000).

skeptic have to renounce his or her skepticism to advance skepticism? Skeptics face the problem of self-refutation insofar as skeptics make any substantial claims about their own argument – for example, they must assert or assume their own existence. Skeptics are right to point out that Descartes' line of reasoning appears to beg the question. After all, if the project of doubting the existence of the (or any) self is to be advanced, the skeptic should only agree with Descartes that "there is thinking" or "there is doubting," not that *I*, the skeptic, am thinking and doubting. Still, Descartes' anti-skeptical argument lays out the difficulty of successfully articulating a subjectless philosophy.

Descartes' self is a substance, not a mode of some deeper underlying reality. "I am a thing which is real and which truly exists. But what kind of thing? As I have just said – a thinking thing."[35]

Descartes conceives of the mark of certainty in terms of clarity, distinctness, and light. "I now seem to be able to lay it down as a general rule that whatever I perceive very clearly and distinctly is true."[36] He displays this criterion in his further argument that God exists, to be considered in the next section. Before turning to his theism, I highlight three elements in Descartes' view of the individual that are at work in the early sections of the *Meditations*.

The Metaphysical Individual

Descartes thinks of the self as a *substance* and it is therefore worth pausing to reflect briefly on Descartes' notion of a thing or substance. For Descartes, the key defining characterization of a thing is its capacity to exist independently of other things. Preeminently it is the possibility of a substance existing alone. On this account, and given Descartes' theism in which no created thing can exist alone – that is, without God – it follows that no created thing is an individual substance, a position that Spinoza will develop (see Chapter 3). Because only God satisfies Descartes' strict concept of a substance, he holds that the term "substance" does not apply univocally to God and creatures. As applied to creatures, the term picks out things that require God in order to exist.[37]

Descartes' understanding of substance in terms of solitary existence suggests what may be called individualism. Descartes was by no means

[35] CSM, 2:18.
[36] CSM, 2:24.
[37] See CSM, 1:210.

unique in advancing his concept of substance and criterion of individuation. In the *Physics*, Aristotle writes: "For none of the categories except substance can exist independently."[38] And in the *Metaphysics*, Aristotle holds that "some things can exist independently and some cannot, the former one substances."[39] Such a principle of individuation seems in step with ordinary language (*running* cannot exist without a runner and it is thus not a substance), but Spinoza and nineteenth-century idealists will challenge this Cartesian-Aristotelian framework for its atomism and what they would see as a spurious individualism. More on this in later chapters.

The Individual and Ethics

Descartes' methodology is suffused with ethical admonitions. In the *Rules* he comments on how the individual *ought* to proceed with his or her inquiry, how one should order one's goals, and so on.[40] Descartes expressed an intention to write a systematic treatise on ethics, although he died before he could do so. But there is not in Descartes' extant publications the fuller Cambridge Platonist understanding of inquiry that is anchored in broader moral precepts, a tradition of inquiry that prizes reverent practice. In the depiction of his method of doubt in the *Discourse*, Descartes tells us that he decided (while suspending judgment about the existence of the world around him) to live in accord with prevailing customs:

> The first was to obey the laws and customs of my country, holding constantly to the religion in which by God's grace I had been instructed from my childhood, and governing myself in all other matters according to the most moderate and least extreme opinions – the opinions commonly accepted in practice by the most sensible of those with whom I should have to live. For I had begun at this time to count my own opinions as worthless, because I wished to submit them all to examination, and so I was sure I could do no better than follow those of the most sensible men. And although there may be men as sensible among the Persians or Chinese as among ourselves, I thought it would be most useful for me to be guided by those with whom I should have to live.[41]

---

[38] Aristotle, *Physics*, trans. P. H. Wickstead and F. M. Cornford (London: William Heinemann, 1957), 21.

[39] *Metaphysics*, ed. and trans. J. Warrington (London: J. M. Dent, 1956), 339.

[40] And in the *Discourse*, he admonishes himself toward self-mastery and discipline.

[41] CSM, 1:122.

This stance may (or may not) be admirable, but it does treat moral practice as a minor subsidiary in philosophical inquiry. There is even a line in part 3 of the *Discourse* where Descartes talks of the great advantage of *appearing* to be ethical while all along concentrating on something else: his search for a foundation for beliefs about the external world. "While appearing to live like those concerned only to lead an agreeable and blameless life, who take care to keep their pleasures free from vices, and who engage in every honest pastime in order to enjoy their leisure without boredom, I never stopped pursuing my project, and I made perhaps more progress in the knowledge of the truth than I would have if I had done nothing but read books or mix with men of letters."[42]

The Individual as a Knowing Agent

For Descartes, to grasp something successfully is akin to making contact with it or touching it. "To comprehend something is to embrace it in one's thought; to know something it is sufficient to touch it with one's thought."[43] The touch may not be complete or comprehensive; Descartes notes how touching a mountain or embracing a tree will inevitably be partial. Still, Descartes' portrait of the self is one that makes *contact* with that which it knows. This view of knowledge as a kind of touching or contact has been developed historically – perhaps the most faithful Cartesian articulation of this stance is found in Max Scheler's (1874–1928) view of philosophical reflection. "The 'ray' of reflection should try to touch only what is '*there*' in this closest and most living contact and only so far as it is there."[44] Successful philosophical study invites a metaphor of tactile contact, dismissing what turns out to be merely apparent objects of knowledge and thus what eludes our grasp or contact.

---

[42] CSM, 1:125–126. Descartes' treatment of moral values is not systematic. At one point he writes in a vein that echoes the Cambridge Platonist view of the good of embodiment. Descartes extols happiness stemming from the perfection of mind and body, but he does not develop this thesis extensively. For Descartes, the roots of philosophy are metaphysics, not morals, CSM, 1:186.

[43] Letter to Mersenne, 1630, in *Descartes: Philosophical Letters*, trans. A. Kenny (Minneapolis: University of Minnesota Press, 1970), 15.

[44] *Scheler: Selected Philosophical Essays*, trans. D. R. Lachterman (Evanston: Northwestern University Press, 1973), 138. See also work by Franz Brentanno, Adolf Reinach, Dietrich von Hildebrand, and F. Wenisch.

There is a further, related metaphor at work in Descartes' view of the knowing agent. Once you know something, it can be spoken of as a possession. "If you know something, it is completely yours."[45] You become enriched or, from the standpoint of cognition, enlarged through knowledge. This portrait gets developed by later philosophers. The twentieth-century Austrian philosopher, Dietrich von Hildebrand, in the spirit of Descartes, will come to speak of successful philosophical insights in terms of contemplative possessions.[46] For Descartes, philosophical maturity is a matter of the individual working toward enrichment and contact.

Theistic Arguments

In the *Meditations* Descartes offers two arguments for God's existence. Both employ the idea or concept of God as a perfect reality.

In the Third Meditation Descartes presents us with the idea of God. He then raises the question of the origin of this concept of God.

> By the word "God" I understand a substance that is infinite, [eternal, immutable,] independent, supremely intelligent, supremely powerful, and which created both myself and everything else (if anything else there be) that exists. All these attributes are such that, the more carefully I concentrate on them, the less possible it seems that they could have originated from me alone. So from what has been said it must be concluded that God necessarily exists.[47]

Descartes employs a causal principle to bolster the inference.

> Now it is manifest by the natural light that there must be at least as much [reality] in the efficient and total cause as in the effect of that cause. For where, I ask, could the effect get its reality from, if not from the cause? And how could the cause give it the effect unless it possessed it? It follows from this both that something cannot arise from nothing, and also that what is more perfect – that is, contains in itself more reality – cannot arise from what is less perfect. And this is transparently true not only in the case of effects which possess [what the philosophers call] actual or formal

[45] Letter to Beeckman, 1630, trans. Kenny, 17.

[46] Von Hildebrand, *What Is Philosophy?* (London: Routledge, 1960). "For the explorer taking cognizance as such is thematic. For us, however, the object and the contemplative possession of it are primary themes" (46).

[47] CSM, 2:31. See also 28–29.

reality, but also in the case of ideas, where one is considering only [what they call] objective reality.[48]

Alas, the precise interpretation of this argument is not obvious. It is easy to feel some sympathy with Bernard Williams in his commentary on the argument: "This is a piece of scholastic metaphysics, and it is one of the most striking indications of the historical gap that exists between Descartes' thought and our own, despite the modern reality of much else that he writes, that he can unblinkingly accept this unintuitive and barely comprehensible principle as self-evident in the light of reason."[49] I shall attempt to close the gap a bit and generate some sympathy for Descartes' line of reasoning. Here, as elsewhere, I write not as an apologist for the truth of Cartesianism but for the more modest goal of displaying what is fascinating about Descartes' work.

First, the argument seems to belie a contemporary, popular view of Descartes as one who has a view of the mind as self-enclosed with privileged, exclusive first-person awareness. It is true that Descartes thinks we may be more certain of our own existence than, say, the objects around us, but in the passages cited earlier he proposes that at least one idea that he possesses leads him to a reality beyond and greater than his own. By seeing (or believing he sees) this reality as omniscient, he presumably sets aside the notion that Descartes, the individual subject, has exclusive, privileged access to his own mental states. Some philosophers present "Cartesianism" as the view that the individual subject has exclusive certainty when he or she is in pain or other mental states.[50] If there is (or even could be) a God of all knowledge, then it is false that our awareness of our pain is necessarily privileged in the sense that no other being could know that we are in these states with equal certainty. Given that God exists, the *way* in which I know I am in pain will differ from God's knowledge of this, but I cannot claim to have greater certainty than an omniscient being. (Descartes

---

[48] CSM, 2:28.

[49] *Descartes: The Project of Pure Enquiry* (Middlesex: Penguin, 1979), 135.

[50] See, for example, Marcia Cavell, *The Psychoanalytic Mind* (Cambridge, Mass.: Harvard University Press, 1993). Due to Descartes' presumed internalism, Lynn Baker thinks that his dualism is refuted in light of the new externalist account of meaning. Without unpacking the technical moves here, I simply suggest that Descartes' understanding of the mind allows for an external bridge between the individual and the "external" world and so Baker's anti-Cartesian argument is unsuccessful. See her *Saving Belief* (Princeton: Princeton University Press, 1987). Be that as it may, many philosophers look back at what they see as Descartes' internal, exclusive view of self-awareness and see it as "the false prison" (to use David Pears's phrase).

and Cartesianism still retain a certain kind of "privileged access" to the subject, a kind of knowledge from the inside. When I am in pain, my mode or way of knowing is by my actually being in pain and, if God exists, God's knowing my pain would not have that kind of privileged mode. Still, Descartes' theism does not see the subjects' self-awareness as solitary – only I can be certain that I am in pain – or unrivaled in certainty. God's knowledge may be more exacting and excellent in many respects.)[51]

As for degrees of reality, Descartes writes in a reply to a critic about the differences between a substance and a mode, where the former has more reality than the latter. An example: a hand may be said to have more reality (or be more real or fundamental) than a fist, for the second is a mode of a hand. Insofar as Descartes' concept of God is of a being of unsurpassable power and the like, God would not be a mode of something else but a preeminent reality capable of generating all else that exists.[52] Perhaps in this context one may speak of reality in terms of degrees, highlighting that one thing is more basic than another. In Descartes' view, the concept of God and God's will is the primal, essential condition for there being a contingent world, but not vice versa, and thus, in a sense, God is more real.

On Descartes' imperfection: Descartes' case for his imperfection does not seem arduous. If Descartes were perfect, presumably Descartes would know this (possessing perfect knowledge), so that even being unsure whether he is perfect would be a good reason for him to deny his perfection.

The heart of the argument is a causal principle. It is as though Descartes treats the direction of causation the way water flows downhill. The sight of a waterfall is evidence that upstream and higher up there is a source of water. We are today readily aware of the claim that we human beings have invented the concept of a supreme, perfect being, which we then "project" onto reality due to wish fulfillment.[53] Reversing the waterfall example, think of a spring where the source of

---

51 See C. Taliaferro and M. Beaty, "God and Concept Empiricism," *Southwest Philosophy Review* 6 (July 1990): 97–105. I consider the impact of theism on the so-called privacy of the mental in *Consciousness and the Mind of God* (Cambridge: Cambridge University Press, 1994).

52 For Descartes, these include "eternal truths," for example, truths of mathematics. For other work that sympathetically articulates degrees of reality theistically, see G. Mavrodes, "Real and More Real," *International Philosophical Quarterly* 4 (1964), and James Ross, *Philosophical Theology* (New York: Bobbs-Merrill, 1969), chap. 6.

53 This is a topic for Chapter 6.

water ascends through the earth. Why, then, be tempted to think that
the source of the idea of God rests in God?

Descartes' description of God in terms of perfection, necessity, and
infinity offers a little help here. Can one generate (or explain) these ideas
by elements that are constructed by terrestrial, human elements? On the
thesis that the concept of God is a pure construct, one supposes that we
look to human traits like knowledge and power and then imagine them
to be unbounded or limitless, and we look to the trait of mortality and
imagine God to be immortal. But is the idea of divine perfection merely
the denial of our imperfection? In other words, is the claim that *God is
perfect* equivalent to *God is not imperfect*? The two are logically equivalent, but it may be argued that divine necessary perfection is a positive
attribute and not the absence or negation of a contingent, creaturely
attribute. In his correspondence and reply to Hobbes, Descartes insists
on the positive grasp of God's reality.

An analogy may prove useful. Take the (ostensibly) necessary truth
$1 + 1 = 2$. Arguably, to understand the proposition entails believing
it. After all, the proposition may be analyzed as the identity claim $1 +
1 = 1 + 1$. What if someone charged that the necessity of this propo-
sition was simply a projection, the result of wish fulfillment and the
fact that we live in a cosmos where one object and one object taken
together constitute two, but we can imagine things otherwise. The critic
further charges that the concept of necessity is simply the denial of
contingency. I believe one may well reply (with the twentieth-century
logician Gottlob Frege) that grasping the proposition is itself a positive
undertaking; one *sees* the necessity of the identity and thus *sees* that
$1 + 1 = 2$ is necessary. The necessity of the mathematical relation
is more certain than the probability that wish fulfillment has clouded
one's judgment; moreover, the necessity of the mathematics cannot be
accounted for by human conventions.[54] Analogously, neither can the
conception of God qua perfect being be an invention.[55]

---

[54] See Roderick Chisholm, *A Realistic Theory of Categories* (Cambridge: Cambridge
University Press, 1996), and Alvin Plantinga, *Essays in the Metaphysics of Modality*,
ed. M. Davidson (Oxford: Oxford University Press, 2003). Alas, Descartes would
not be able to adapt quite this defense, as he held that the eternal truths were God's
creations. My proposal here must therefore be seen as supporting a revised Cartesian
standpoint.

[55] For a different articulation and defense of Descartes' causal principle behind this
argument, see Geoffrey Gorham, "Causational Similarity in Descartes," in *New Essays
on the Rationalists*, ed. R. Gennaro and C. Huenemann (Oxford: Oxford University

Williams is right that some elements in Descartes' argument seem "scholastic." Thomas Aquinas (1225–1274) wrote of God in terms of maximal being or reality.[56] But the tradition of thinking of God as the most real being (*ens realissimum*) did not end with Descartes; it continued into the modern era with Leibniz and Kant, and it may yet reemerge in current philosophy of religion. Descartes' second argument for theism in the Fifth Meditation will be more readily recognized by those acquainted with contemporary work.

The second argument is an ontological one. Descartes contends that one "cannot think of God except as existing."[57]

> It is quite evident that existence can no more be separated from the essence of God than the fact that its three angles equal two right angles can be separated from the essence of a triangle, or than the idea of a mountain can be separated from the idea of a valley. Hence it is just as much of a contradiction to think of God (that is, a supremely perfect being) lacking existence (that is, lacking a perfection), as it is to think of a mountain without a valley.[58]

Descartes' argument was largely embraced by More and may be reconstructed along similar lines outlined in Chapter 1. Caterus, a contemporary of Descartes, contended that the argument only secured (if anything at all) that the idea of God is the idea of a being actually existing in the world, but Descartes fails to show the further point that God actually exists in the world. Descartes replied that Caterus did not sufficiently appreciate the uniqueness and character of the idea of God. With respect to indefinitely many ideas about things in the cosmos, in no case does the idea of a thing signify its necessity (that the *essence* of the thing entails its *existence*).

We shall revisit the ontological argument later – especially when we come to Kant – so I hold off here on further objections and replies.

Theism and Trust

Once Descartes secures theism, he believes he has good reason to trust his perceptual faculties about the world. He believes that some errors

Press, 1999), and Geoffrey Gorham, "Descartes' Dilemma of Eminent Containment," *Dialogue: Canadian Philosophical Review* 42 (2003).

[56] *Summa Theologiae* vol. I, q.2, a.3.

[57] CSM, 2:46.

[58] Ibid.

in our judgments should be regarded as inevitable, given the nature of our embodiment, but that on the whole a good God would have good reason to provide us with reliable cognitive faculties.

A problem arises here, similar to the problem of criterion that some critics call the "Cartesian Circle." Perhaps Descartes is in the following fix: He must trust his cognitive faculties in order to secure a belief in an all-good God, but in order to trust his cognitive faculties he needs the prior or antecedent belief in God's goodness. Is this a vicious circle? I suggest that it is not, although my proposal makes Descartes more committed to *coherence* as a mark of justification rather than systematic, sequential reasoning, which, like a chain, is only as strong as its weakest link. My proposal that follows goes beyond Descartes' argument about trust, but it does help to bolster the link between trust and theism that Descartes was trying to secure.

The development and functioning of our cognitive powers (perception, memory, etc.) require a world, social and structural, that is stable and trustworthy. A child would never learn a language if her caregivers were constantly acting in ways that were unpredictable and malignant. A child must begin by trusting her cognitive faculties, which, under happy circumstances, will in the end vindicate an understanding of her caregivers and environment as to some extent good or benign. The child's initial trust in her faculties is not built on an explicit trust in the goodness of her caregivers, but her coming to recognize the goodness of her caregivers makes overt or evident what enabled her trust at the beginning. By analogy, Descartes' use of cognition leads him to an understanding of the divine that is not just benign but supremely good. Descartes thereby winds up with a conception of his own reasoning and reality that is mutually supportive.[59] Imagine you believe you know X but lack any concept of how it is that you know X. Your coming to see how it is you know X may be seen as shoring up or vindicating your claim to know X. Arguably, an account of your developing cognition in a good environment would support the trustworthiness of your cognition, and – in far greater, more extensive terms – the wider, metaphysical account of the trustworthiness of all human cognition involving a divine mind would provide a greater, more encompassing support.

---

[59] For a juxtaposition between trusting God and three other forms of trust, see Marcel Sarot, "Why Trusting God Differs from All Other Forms of Trust," *Sophia* 35:1 (1996): especially 111–112.

This appeal to a greater, trustworthy environment introduces an appeal to coherence – the coherence of a "big picture," in which we grasp how it is that our faculties are indeed reliable – but I am not counseling a rampant "Cartesian" coherence theory of justification. To fill out my suggestion, consider the problem with adopting *only coherence* as a mark of justification, in which interdependent, mutually supportive beliefs count as evidence. The twentieth-century philosopher H. H. Price offers a good analysis of the problem. As Price raises a concern that arises later in this book, I cite him at length:

> Suppose we ask someone what he knows of Paris, and he replies "All I know of it is that it is the capital of France." We then ask him what he knows of France, and he says "All I know of France is that it is the country of which Paris is the capital." Clearly there is something wrong. A is described in terms of B, and B in terms of A. Sometimes the circle is less obvious because it is larger. France is described as the country which is west of Germany, and Germany as the country which has Belgium on the north-west side of it, and Belgium as the country which is south east of England across the sea. But if knowledge by description consisted just in "knowing one's way about" through such a system of interdependent descriptions it would not deserve the name of knowledge, not even of reasonable belief. It would have no relation to reality, to what actually exists or happens, or what has actually existed or happened. This whole conceptual structure of inter-connected descriptions floats in the air until some item in it is related to something which we know by acquaintance. To take a geographical example, if at a certain time I can know England by description as the country containing these objects I see or touch, I can escape from this *circulus in describendo*. And another person can escape from it if he knows France by description as the country containing the object which he sees or touches at a particular time.[60]

Using Price's imagery, I think Descartes is in a position where initially he thinks he has made bona fide contact (or touch) with himself. This contact (or confidence in the contact or touch) becomes more secure as he comes to realize (or know) that he is in contact with a divine reality that has empowered his very ability to make contact with himself, God, and the world about him. So (on my suggested rereading), Descartes may be seen in this section of the *Meditations* as offering a fuller account of what he is in contact with, and how it is that such contact is possible.

---

[60] *Belief* (London: George Allen and Unwin, 1969), 67–68.

Philosophical discussion of Descartes' view of trust is often limited to matters of cognition. But the need for trusting our cognition about ourselves and the world around us has implications for every area of our lives – from the sciences to politics to the conduct of personal relationships.[61] Indeed for Descartes, trusting in the goodness of God is the cement of the universe and the bonding in the mind-body relation. Given that the mind and body (or the mental and physical) are distinct, an untrustworthy or dysfunctional mind-body relation would leave one uncertain about when or if one's apparent intentional action was indeed one's action. Under such circumstances, could I trust my ostensible memories of the past? It was partly because the Cambridge Platonists appreciated the vital importance of securing a concordant mind-body relation that they were compelled to work out a philosophy of the virtues of human nature and to posit plastic nature. Descartes' appeal to God's goodness will seem comparatively more austere, given his greater enthusiasm for a mechanistic view of nature. Still, I suggest that Descartes and the Cambridge Platonists worked from an assumption that may be borne out in ordinary, common sense: the development of a coherent, reasonable use of cognition requires an overall good environment.[62]

I have suggested here that Descartes may take comfort in a commonsense approach to personal development or, more specifically, to childrearing. But it should be duly noted that Descartes himself did not appeal to childrearing.[63] And we do well to appreciate what many critics in the seventeenth century and today believe to be the tragic breakdown in Descartes' system. Descartes looked for a *foundation* upon which to build, order and regulate beliefs.

> Reason now leads me to think that I should hold back my assent from opinions which are not completely certain and indubitable just as carefully as I do from those which are patently false. So, for the purpose of rejecting

---

[61] For an interesting portrait of the interplay between trust and criticism, see Basil Mitchell, *Faith and Criticism* (Oxford: Clarendon, 1994).

[62] To complement this proposal, see Jonathan Bennett's "Truth and Stability in Descartes' Treatment of Skepticism," *Canadian Journal of Philosophy*, supp. vol. 16 (1990). In my (perhaps strained) defense of Descartes, I am not proposing that God should be thought of as *the environment*, but as the creator of, and provident presence within, creation.

[63] Against my effort to defend Descartes, it may also be argued that Descartes was not seeking an overall coherence in his metaphysics by appealing to God. Some commentators see him as arguing in a noncircular, deductive line of reasoning. Descartes is then faulted (typically) for getting things wrong at the outset or for inferring more than his premises allow him to.

all my opinions, it will be enough if I find in each of them at least some reason for doubt. And to do this I will not need to run through them all individually, which would be an endless task. Once the foundations of a building are undermined, anything built on them collapses of its own accord; so I will go straight for the basic principles on which all my former beliefs rested.[64]

The existence of the self, God, and now the trustworthiness of cognition were all supposed to comprise a sure response to skepticism. Descartes did not think our cognitive awareness of the world was impeccable – indeed, as I just mentioned, he thought the union of body and soul inevitably made us liable to some errors. But he required overall surety. Given high Cartesian standards for what counts as knowledge, if the theistic arguments fail, trouble ensues. Consider Bernard Williams's verdict:

> Descartes' arguments for the existence of God fail, and that fact is exceedingly important for his system and for its legacy. The road that Descartes constructed back from the extreme point of the Doubt, and from the world merely of first-personal mental existence which he hoped to have established in the *cogito*, essentially goes over a religious bridge. . . . The collapse of the religious bridge has meant that his most profound and most long-lasting influence has not been in the direction of the religious metaphysics which he himself accepted. Rather, philosophy after Descartes was driven to a search for alternative ways of getting back from the regions of skepticism and subjective idealism in which it was stranded when Cartesian enquiry lost the Cartesian road back.[65]

I am less convinced about *Descartes'* failure, but there was indeed a failure by many of his contemporaries and those who come afterward to find a secure bridge – be it religious or secular.

Descartes adopted a concept of reason that, like the Cambridge Platonist view of inquiry, had a divine element. "The human mind has within it a sort of spark of the divine, in which the first seeds of useful ways of thinking are sown, seeds which, however neglected and shifted by studies which impede them, often bear fruit of their own accord."[66] But for Descartes, belief in the divinity of the "spark" had to be earned through secular reflection – reflection that was neutral with respect to religious claims.

---

[64] CSM, 2:12.
[65] *Descartes: The Project of Pure Enquiry*, 162.
[66] *Rules for the Direction of the Mind*, in CSM, 1:17.

Dualist Arguments

As we saw in Chapter 1, arguments about human nature were central concerns in the Cambridge Platonist account of creation and linked to their conception of an afterlife. There was a fear that if human beings are the same thing as their material bodies, then the physical destruction or annihilation of their bodies entails the destruction or annihilation of the person. Physical death amounts to the complete, irrevocable end of a person's life. Descartes' case for dualism can stand independent of belief (or disbelief) in an afterlife, but he did see dualism and the afterlife as intertwined.[67] Descartes argued that he is not the same thing as his body. Extrapolating from his own case, he contends that all human beings are constituted by two elements, the person is a mind or soul that lacks spatial extension, whereas material bodies have (or consist of) spatial extension. Descartes certainly held that being human involves being embodied and, at various points in his writings, contended that we think of being a human being in terms of a singular unity. "We affirm that a human being is made up of body and soul, not by the mere presence or proximity of one or the other, but by a true substantial union."[68] And in one of his letters to Elizabeth, Descartes wrote: "It does not seem to me that the human mind is capable of conceiving at the same time the distinction and the union between body and soul, and because of this it is necessary to conceive them as a single thing and at the same time to conceive them as two things; and this is absurd."[69] In the end, Descartes sees the mind as unextended spatially albeit embodied in (or as) a spatially extended body. Still, he allowed that if one were to define "corporeal" in an extended sense to mean "anything which can in any way affect a body," he would call the mind corporeal.[70] Because Descartes held that material bodies are affected by the incorporeal (the

---

[67] The subtitle to the first edition (but not the second) of The *Meditations* advertises it as establishing the immortality of the soul. See CSM, 2:1. Also, see the reasoning at CSM, 2:10. While I concentrate on an argument for dualism from conceivability in what follows (as this is the most widely discussed), one can reconstruct a dualist argument on p. 10 of CSM involving the different identity conditions for mind and body. I consider a related argument from Butler at the end of Chapter 3. Descartes' contemporary Arnauld pointed out that the bare distinction of mind and body does not entail immortality (CSM, 2:204).

[68] Letter to Regius, 1642, trans. Kenny, 130.

[69] Letter to Elizabeth, 1643, trans. Kenny, 142. See also Descartes' letter to More, CSM, 3:375.

[70] Letter to Hyperaspistes, 1641, trans. Kenny, 112.

most radical case would be God's agency), he describes the mind as incorporeal.

There are at least two ways of interpreting Descartes' central, dualist argument. The first is, I think, inaccurate. It has been called the Argument from Doubt and it may be formulated as follows:

1. I cannot doubt I exist.
2. I can doubt that I have the body that I believe I do, in fact, I can doubt that there are any material bodies at all.
3. I am not the body I think I have nor am I any body whatever.

This is commonly held to be a fallacy because it does not respect a problem with referential terms. Consider the problem of the masked man: you may have observed a bank robbery and are certain that the bank was robbed by a masked man. Imagine you *cannot* doubt this, given what you saw. But you can doubt that your father robbed the bank. Regrettably this does not entitle you to conclude that your father did not rob the bank. Critics charge that Descartes failed to appreciate how our terms may be opaque or not sufficiently transparent to get at the thing doubted or believed. When I use the term "I" and the title "Heaviest person in the room," the two may refer to the same thing – me – even if I fiercely challenge the notion that I could be the heaviest person at hand.

Descartes, I believe, did not hold the Argument from Doubt and so is not subject to this objection. In the Second Meditation he *seems* to conclude that he is not his body on the grounds that he can doubt the existence of his body without doubting his own existence. "I am not that structure of limbs which is called a human body. I am not even some thin vapour which permeates the limbs – a wind, fire, air, breath, or whatever I depict in my imagination; for these are things which I have supposed to be nothing. Let the supposition stand; for all that I am still something."[71] But Descartes straightaway acknowledges that his reasoning is not secure yet, for he cannot at this point rule out that he (without knowing it) is identical with his body. "And yet may it not perhaps be the case that these very things which I am supposing to be nothing, because they are unknown to me, are, in reality, identical with the 'I' of which I am aware? I do not know, and for the moment I shall

---

[71] CSM, 2:18.

not argue the point, since I can make judgments only about things which are known to me."[72]

In the Sixth Meditation Descartes argues as follows:

> First, I know that everything which I clearly and distinctly understand is capable of being created by God so as to correspond exactly with my understanding of it. Hence the fact that I can clearly and distinctly understand one thing apart from another is enough to make me certain that the two things are distinct, since they are capable of being separated, at least by God. The question of what kind of power is required to bring about such a separation does not affect the judgement that the two things are distinct. Thus, simply by knowing that I exist and seeing at the same time that absolutely nothing else belongs to my nature or essence except that I am a thinking thing, I can infer correctly that my essence consists solely in the fact that I am a thinking thing. It is true that I may have (or, to anticipate, that I certainly have) a body that is very closely joined to me. But nevertheless, on the one hand I have a clear and distinct idea of myself, in so far as I am simply a thinking, non-extended thing; and on the other hand I have a distinct idea of body, in so far as this is simply an extended, non-thinking thing. And accordingly, it is certain that I am really distinct from my body, and can exist without it.[73]

Descartes is here advancing an argument that differs from the Argument from Doubt. He is arguing for the distinction of himself and his body on the grounds that it seems as though (or, more strongly, he sees that) one may exist without the other. If he has good grounds that he may exist without his body, he has reason to believe he is a substantive individual distinct from his body. The key move in the argument is the establishment that there is something true about himself but not true about his body.

The argument relies on a principle some call the "indiscernibility of identicals." In an identity relation – say, between *Cicero* and *Tully*, two names for the same Roman statesman-philosopher – then whatever is true of Cicero is true of Tully. If you were to see Cicero, you would see Tully. What the principle rules out is a proper identity where something is true of Cicero but not true of Tully. Consider the following formalization of a Cartesian argument for the distinction between oneself and one's body.

---

[72] Ibid. Descartes clarifies the point in his reply to Hobbes's second objection, 122–123.
[73] CSM, 2:54.

A. It is possible that I can exist and my body not exist. (Alternative claims: (i) I can exist without any physical body whatever or (ii) I could have a different body.)
B. It is not possible for my body to exist without my body. (Alternatively (iii) my body cannot exist without there being some body or (iv) my body cannot became an immaterial body.)
C. I am not my body.

Descartes seeks to secure a principle to the effect that whatever he clearly grasps to be possible is indeed possible. If this principle (or one that is closely related) is acceptable, then Descartes may be on his way to securing dualism.

This argument for dualism is often called the "modal argument" (as "modal" refers to possibility) but it is sometimes referred to as the "argument from separability" or the "argument from conceivability."

How might one secure Descartes' premises A and B? In the current nomenclature, this involves an appeal to *thought experiments*, narrative descriptions of states of affairs that seem to be possible. Many people now – as in the seventeenth century – believe that when they die, their body will be a corpse and not the person. Many also believe that they survive the destruction of their bodies. A Cartesian does not need an interlocutor to be convinced that these states of affairs actually occur; all she needs is the bare possibility of separability in order to secure the actual distinction of self and body.

In an effort to encourage further inquiry into the argument – in other words, to vie for the judgment that the argument is not *dead on arrival* – consider some brief objections and replies. As my goal is simply to make the argument interesting rather than to convince you of it, I am keeping the objection-reply format rather condensed.

Objection 1. Thought experiments may go horribly wrong. It may appear that you can exist without your body but you cannot. Antoine Arnauld (1612–1694) pointed out that someone can easily conceive of a triangle as right-angled yet not at all conceive of it as satisfying the Pythagorean theorem, or any other of the countless theorems that such figures satisfy. But that person would be wrong to infer that a right triangle could possibly not satisfy the theorem.[74]

Reply. I suggest this is a serious but not decisive objection. Someone *might* think there could be a triangle that does not satisfy the

---

[74] CSM, 2:141–143.

Pythagorean theorem. Even so, very elementary reflection reveals that any ostensible possibility here is not genuine. Descartes' claim is not simply that he can conceive of himself without conceiving of his body but that he can conceive of himself not having a body. The analogy in geometry would be the claim that one can conceive of a circle without four right angles rather than the more modest claim that one may conceive of a circle without conceiving of four right angles. Even so, if you consider a state of affairs and all the properties involved, and do not just fail to see it is incoherent but are able to imagine (picture, visualize, conceive of, see) its occurrence, I propose that is at least a prima facie reason to believe the state of affairs is possible. A moment's reflection reveals that the non-Pythagorean triangle could not exist, but the Cartesian thought experiments are more stubborn.[75]

Objection 2. The argument relies on a fallacy. Consider a disanalogy: George W. Bush is the forty-third president of the United States. But it is (or was) possible that Bush exists and there be no forty-third President (imagine the United States was taken over by Canada in 1812) and there could be a forty-third president but no Bush. The bare possibility of independent existence or separability does not secure a difference in objects.

Reply. The counter-example works only because "forty-third president of the United States" refers to a role that may be filled by any number of people. But the term "I" when I use it of myself does not refer to a role, nor does "my body." If we used the expression "forty-third president" in a strict referential way to refer to *that person* (Bush) rather than a role like the the *Chief Justice*, then (with that usage) you could not find Bush without finding the forty-third president.

Objection 3. The argument begs the question. If you were already a dualist, you would believe that you can exist without your body and vice versa. But surely no materialist would admit this. The argument is useless.

Reply. Surprisingly, many materialists have conceded that it appears as though one may exist without one's body. Here is one concession from the contemporary materialist D. M. Armstrong:

> But disembodied existence seems to be a perfectly intelligible supposition.... Consider the case where I am lying in bed at night

---

[75] I believe this first objection is the most serious. I offer a further reply to this objection in "Sensibility and Possibilia: A Defense of Thought Experiments," *Philosophia Christi* 3:2 (January 2002).

thinking. Surely it is logically possible that I might be having just the same experiences and yet not have a body at all. No doubt I am having certain somatic, that is to say, bodily sensations. But if I am lying still these will not be very detailed in nature, and I can see nothing self-contradictory in supposing that they do not correspond to anything in physical reality. Yet I need be in no doubt about my identity.[76]

The apparent separability of mind and body is conceded by a range of materialists as a problem. They, of course, think that there can be overriding reasons to dismiss whatever the evidential force of the thought experiment is while conceding that this is indeed an obstacle.

Objection 4. The thought experiment still presupposes what it seeks to establish. Recall the point made earlier about Descartes' methodology. You contended that it is because Descartes knows something (that he exists) that he cannot doubt it. Don't you have to know already that you and your body are distinct in order to know it is possible that there may be one without the other? Knowledge of distinctness is the ground or justification for accepting the thought or experiment, not vice versa. (The same follows for the earlier knowledge of your unconditional love for Pat.)

Reply. Cases arise frequently in philosophy in which modal thought experiments are pivotal in establishing a distinction of properties and objects. Imagine you and I are debating whether something is good if and only if it is pleasurable. At the outset we both might be unsure what to think. But then we consider a thought experiment in which there is great pleasure but there does not appear to be any goodness involved (perhaps we are imagining a creepy professor who takes pleasure in imagining the torture of students). The thought experiment may reveal to us that *being pleasurable* is distinct from *being good*. Perhaps there is some inchoate sense in which we grasped the distinctiveness prior to the thought experiment, but I suggest that thought experiments serve to vindicate or reveal the distinctness, for it seems evident that prior to the thought experiment one may not be at all sure of the distinction. Modal thought experiments have played a key role historically in the process of clarifying and identifying properties and things.[77]

---

[76] *A Materialist Theory of Mind* (London: Routledge, 1968), 19.

[77] In this and the other replies and for further articulation and defense of the points at issue, see my book *Consciousness and the Mind of God*. See also Taliaferro, "Possibilities in the Philosophy of Mind," *Philosophy and Phenomenological Research* 57:1 (1997); "Animals, Brains, and Spirits," *Faith and Philosophy* 12:4 (1995); and "Emergantism and Consciousness: Going Beyond Property Dualism," in *Soul, Body and Survival,*

Objection 5. All the argument establishes is that the concept of being a body is distinct from the concept of being a person (or *being me*). Perhaps, the only conclusion merited by the argument is that I am contingently related to my body. It could be that I am my material body and yet possibly distinct from it.

Reply. Arguably, this is too skeptical if taken to an extreme. If you seem to be able to conceive of the Empire State Building existing without Big Ben, isn't that a reason to believe the two are separate individuals? It would be too skeptical to conclude that one's conceiving one without the other only established that the concept of the Empire State Building is distinct from the concept of Big Ben. As for contingent identity, it is not at all clear how I might be identical at a given time with my body but possibly not identical at that time. If I am my body now, then its destruction entails my destruction. If it is possible now that I can survive its destruction and vice versa, then (contrary to the initial assumption) I am not the very same thing as my body. Recall that I am recommending a prima facie, not decisive reply. Someone may claim to be able to conceive of the morning star without the evening star and then conclude (falsely) that they are separate individuals instead of the same thing (the planet Venus). But the possibility of getting this wrong does not render the Cartesian argument developed here idle.

Objection 6. Henry More objected to Descartes on the grounds that the mind (self or person) is extended in space. Isn't talk of a person as *unextended* in violation of our experience and ordinary language?

Reply. One could still be a dualist (as More was) and yet argue that the self is a nonphysical spatially extended subject. From time to time, philosophers have treated spatially extended objects as nonphysical – sensory experiences of color, after-images, hallucinations, the sensory images that constitute dreams, and so on. To take an example Descartes uses: when your leg is amputated you may sometimes feel that you still have a leg spread out in space (a so-called phantom limb). A modal argument could be fashioned to the extent that one may imagine one's physical body perishing while you retain this extended field of sensations, a kind of phantom body.[78] In our ordinary language we do address each other as spatially extended and embodied, but our

---

    ed. K. Corcoran (Ithaca: Cornell University Press, 2001). For a critique, see Anthony Kenny, *Descartes: A Study of His Philosophy* (New York: Random House, 1968).

[78] A modal argument for dualism of this sort is articulated and defended by W. D. Hart in *The Engine of the Soul* (Cambridge: Cambridge University Press, 1988).

language is not thoroughly materialistic. It would be odd to think I can see, measure, and spatially locate your thoughts and emotions the way we see, measure, and spatially locate one's material processes, parts, or states. Also, a Cartesian can appeal to the way in which dualist language seems fitting in extraordinary but common enough cases such as when people die. Belief in an afterlife is too common across cultures and time to be somehow banned on the basis of violating "ordinary language."[79]

Even if all the above objections were accepted, a yet more sobering objection faces the Cartesian: how does one account for the interaction of something physical (the body) and nonphysical (the person, mind, or soul)?

Descartes seems to take up the position that they *simply do* interact and to offer the further proposal that the locus of interaction is a particular place in the body (the pineal gland) with the aid of "animal spirits." Descartes held that mind-body interaction involved no evident absurdity. He likened such interaction to God's causal relation to the cosmos. In correspondence with Henry More, Descartes writes:

> It is no disgrace for a philosopher to believe that God can move a body, even though he does not regard God as corporeal; so it so no more of a disgrace for him to think much the same of other incorporeal substances. Of course I do not think that any mode of action belongs univocally to both God and his creatures, but I must confess that the only idea I can find in my mind to represent the way in which God or an angel can move matter is the one which shows me the way in which I am conscious I can move my own body by my own thought.[80]

A common strategy among contemporary dualists is to hold that mind-body interaction is no more obscure or miraculous than interaction among physical objects.

> We may indeed admit that there is "something deeply mysterious about the interaction which Descartes' theory requires between two items of totally disparate natures, the immaterial soul, and the gland of any other part of an extended body" (B. Williams). But it is no more mysterious than

---

[79] Of course, despite such common usage, it is still possible that all beliefs about an afterlife that make their way into ordinary language (e.g., we can speak of burying someone's body while claiming that the person is in heaven or hell or reincarnated) involve conceptual confusion.

[80] CSM, 3:375.

many other things which we find in fact to be the case, and it is somewhat unfair for this reason to speak of "the obscurity of the idea that immaterial mind could move any physical thing" (Williams). "Obscurity" is a mildly reprobative term, and suggests that there is something which should be made plain. But there is a limit to explanation and a point where we just have to accept things as we find them to be. No explanation of ours is exhaustive, and if the world is in some ways very remarkable, we must accept that too.[81]

This may be a plausible conclusion but historically vast numbers of philosophers took the mind-body problem in other directions. We consider materialist approaches in the next chapter and elsewhere, noting the repercussions for philosophy of religion.

In the next section, let us consider Descartes' view of God's relation to the world. But before turning to this, and to his successors, I cite three elements of Descartes' work in philosophy of religion that may be gathered from the two preceding sections of this chapter and that are, I think, of perennial importance.

First, Descartes' use of thought experiments encourages philosophical work involving imagination. Philosophy involves more than empirical inquiry into the world; it raises questions of what might or might not be the case from the vantage point of a philosophy of science.[82] I noted in the Introduction that an attractive aspect of philosophy of religion is that it addresses embedded practices and not just abstract thought experiments. The point that needs to be made here is that there are religious *and* philosophical practices in which the imagination is employed, in which different possibilities are entertained about this life and the next. (I argue later, in Chapter 4, that imaginative thought experiments play a key role in the theistic arguments.)

Second, Descartes' approach to evidence may seem impersonal and regimented, but at its heart Descartes highlights the importance of trust in the goodness of another, external reality. The philosophical study of

---

[81] H. D. Lewis, *The Elusive Self* (Philadelphia: Westminster Press, 1982), 38. For a further defense of dualism, see my *Consciousness and the Mind of God*. Dualism is not without defenders today. See, for example, work by George Bealer, John Foster, Howard Robinson, W. D. Hart, W. Hasker, S. Goetz, and Richard Swinburne.

[82] For a study of how imaginative thought experiments may shape one's philosophy, see R. Sorenson, *Thought Experiments* (Oxford: Oxford University Press, 1992). I return to this in Chapter 8. For two good works on the imagination in philosophy, see Mary Warnock, *Imagination* (London: Farber and Farber, 1976), and *Imagination and Time* (Oxford: Blackwell, 1994).

trust has been piecemeal historically, but it is being taken up again in religious and secular contexts.[83] In an important essay, Annette Baier invokes Descartes' appeal to trust, arguing that some secular substitute is needed for Descartes' God.

> If God does not underwrite one's cognitive powers, what does? . . . I shall suggest that the secular equivalent of faith in God, which we need in morality as well as in science or knowledge acquisition, is faith in the human community and its evolving procedures – in the prospects for many cognitive ambitions and moral hopes. Descartes had deliberately shut himself away from other thinkers, distrusting the influence of his teachers and the tradition in which he had been trained. All alone, he found he could take no step beyond a sterile self-certainty. Some other mind must come to his aid before he could advance. Descartes sought an absolute assurance to replace the human reassurance he distrusted, and I suggest that we can reverse the procedure. If we distrust the theist's absolute assurance we can return to what Descartes spurned, the support of human tradition, of a cross-generational community.[84]

Although Baier explicitly rejects Descartes' preferred object of faith, she is still Cartesian insofar as she sees the need of the individual to seek external support in her or his development. Cartesianism is sometimes branded as anti-community, but its orientation toward a source of goodness transcending the individual challenges that label. Descartes saw persons as metaphysical individuals but not isolationists. (As a *Christian* theist Descartes saw God as triune and not without a difference of persons in the Godhead. God is not a solitary object for Descartes.)[85]

---

83 See Diego Gambetta, ed., *Trust: Making and Breaking Cooperative Relations* (Oxford: Blackwell, 1988).

84 "Secular Faith," in *Postures of the Mind* (Minneapolis: University of Minnesota Press, 1985), 292, 293. For another articulation of secular faith, see Wallace Murphee, "Faith for Atheists and Agnostics," *Sophia* 30:2–3 (1991).

85 A reader of an earlier version of this chapter raised this objection: "But Descartes does not trust others; as Baier points out, he trusts only God, and then only after arguing for God's entitlement to trust. So, at bottom, Descartes trusts only himself." I suggest instead that Descartes does not, at bottom, fully trust himself until he trusts God. His coming to recognize God's provident power and goodness is what establishes his final confidence in his faculties. The "sterile self-certainty" breaks open to a fertile recognition of the world, and the God in whom he trusts is a God that Descartes comes to see as revealed through traditions and a cross-generational community (the Christian Church).

A third element may seem in tension with my observation about trust. Although Descartes is not, I think, the supreme advocate of philosophical self-involvement, he does raise the challenge to individuals to use their own reasoning to test truth-claims. To some contemporary critics, Descartes here seems ahistorical, discounting his humble, physically embedded, political conditions. In his philosophical meditations, Descartes describes himself as sitting by a stove. Some feminist critics reply:

> But as feminists have asked, who lit the fire in Descartes' stove? The question is not intended only to draw attention to the taken-for-granted chores of the servant (girl?), and indeed all the domestic labour which supports and makes possible the intellectual work of "great" men, though it is that too. It is intended also to raise the question of the materiality and physicality that subtends consciousness itself: the physical world and Descartes' own body, without which he could never have developed consciousness and rationality. Descartes seems never to have asked himself how he became a conscious, rational subject, how he was born and brought up and nourished. At best he seems to have attributed his existence to God, the infinite subject. But even according to Christian thinking, God did not create Descartes full-grown out of thin air. His subjectivity, like everyone else's emerged out of his bodily development that had its origins in his mother's womb, was dependent on material sustenance, and learned to speak and to think within a symbolic order – a language and culture – which pre-existed him and within which his subjectivity was formed. Human subjectivity does not arrive, fully adult, into the world: it emerges, and it is not without pain or cost that conscious subjectivity develops out of the preconscious materiality and pre-existing discursive conditions of every human life.[86]

Is Descartes guilty as charged?

There are some mitigating circumstances. Yes, Descartes did think (in keeping with much Roman Catholic theology today) his soul was a creation by God, but rather than this amounting to a negation of the body, it may be seen as an elevation of human beings across gender and class and race. The soul of the servant girl or boy was no less a creation of God than his soul was. The problem with the wholesale endorsement of "materiality and physicality" as something wholesome and unproblematic misses the point that vast wealth and power was justified in Descartes' lifetime and beyond, largely in those terms: hereditary, monarchy, and

---

[86] Jantzen, *Becoming Divine*, 33.

inherited, dynastic wealth. A person's birth can privilege and safeguard a person' domination over others. Descartes' emphasis on consciousness and rationality rather than birthrights, lineage, and brute material strength can be seen as recognizing an individual's rightful ability to question the material status quo, including pre-existing political and religious claims of authority. In all, I think there is a dual legacy of Cartesianism to recognize: the importance of trust beyond the individual and yet the importance of questioning claims to authoritative control over oneself in light of privileged birth and material circumstances. It is interesting to note in this context that, shortly after Descartes' death, Queen Christina abdicated her crown.[87] It is also interesting that one of the first feminist modern philosophers, François Poulain de la Barre, was a Cartesian.[88]

In the next section let us reflect on Descartes' concept of God's relation to the world and then consider how two philosophers – Malebranche and Conway – sought a more unified picture of the God-world relation.

God and the World

Descartes and the Cartesian philosopher Malebranche (1638–1715) articulated their understanding of the world in thoroughly theistic terms. They conceived of God's creative will as an essential component of all worldly events. Unlike their contemporaries who attributed active powers to the world – whether these were held to be observable or hidden or "occult" – Descartes and Malebranche saw the material world as (in its own right) inert; its motion and its very being required God's creative power.[89] Part of the rationale for this conclusion is – in the broadest sense – scientific. Given my limits on space, I must recommend another source to unpack the details and simply note that here (again) is an early

---

[87] There is no evidence, however, that she did so as a result of Descartes' philosophy. See Susanna Akerman's study of Christina in chap. 2 of *A History of Women Philosophers*, ed. M. E. Waithe (Dordrecht: Kluwer, 1991). For the role of philosophy of mind in ethics, see the entry "Eighteenth Century Racism," in *The Columbia History of Western Philosophy*, ed. R. H. Popkin (New York: Columbia University Press, 1999). I note one way in which dualism may have an emancipatory, moral role in *Consciousness and the Mind of God*, 178–179.

[88] For an overview, see Siep Stuurman, "Social Cartesianism: François Poulain de la Barre and the Origins of the Enlightenment," *Journal of the History of Ideas* 58:4 (1977).

[89] For a general, philosophical study of motion and the concept of God, see M. J. Buckley, *Motion and Motion's God* (Princeton: Princeton University Press, 1971).

modern example of science being employed in the philosophy of God.[90] But there is space to note two interesting difficulties facing Descartes and Malebranche given their view of the proximate, radical dependency of the cosmos on God.

Let us consider Descartes first. Descartes held that the material world itself could not account for its own being.

> Indeed, when I examine the idea of a body, I perceive that a body has no power to create itself or maintain itself in existence; and I rightly conclude that necessary existence – and it is only necessary existence that is at issue here – no more belongs to the nature of a body, however perfect, than it belongs to the nature of a mountain to be without a valley, or to the nature of a triangle to have angles whose sum is greater than two right angles.[91]

On this front, Descartes is representing a classical theistic position one may see in Aquinas and others. But I believe he goes beyond the mainstream in the following portrait of his dependency on God's ongoing creativity.

> I do not escape the force of these arguments by supposing that I have always existed as I do now, as if it followed from this that there was no need to look for any author of my existence. For a lifespan can be divided into countless parts, each completely independent of the others, so that it does not follow from the fact that I existed a little while ago that I must exist now, unless there is some cause which as it were creates me afresh at this moment – that is, which preserves me. For it is quite clear to anyone who attentively considers the nature of time that the same power and action are needed to preserve anything at each individual moment of its duration as would be required to create that thing anew if it were not yet in existence. Hence the distinction between preservation and creation is only a conceptual one, and this is one of the things that are evident by the natural light.[92]

In one sense, Descartes is still in the classic theistic tradition by accepting a thesis "commonly accepted among theologians" that God now

[90] See D. Clarke, *Occult Powers and Hypotheses: Cartesian Natural Philosophy under Louis XIV* (Oxford: Clarendon, 1989); Gary Hatfield, "Force (God) in Descartes' Physics," *Studies in the History and Philosophy of Science* 10 (1979); and Geoffrey Gorham's "Mind-Body Dualism and the Harvey-Descartes Controversy," *Journal of the History of Ideas* 55:2 (1994).

[91] CSM 2:84.

[92] Ibid., 33.

preserves the world by the same action by which he creates it.[93] But in Descartes formulation I suspect there is a problem of not properly distinguishing a very real (not merely conceptual) distinction. Arguably, these are two profoundly different states of affairs: (A) I am preserved or conserved over time as the selfsame being, and (B) there is a new "me afresh" at each moment. The second state of affairs might look the same as the first – after all, God's creating a new book at each moment would look the same as God conserving the same book in being over time – but there would still be a dramatic difference between these states of affairs.[94]

Malebranche's challenge emerges in the course of his developing a radical account of the world depending on God's creativity. The world is external to God's being (or substance) but not to God's will insofar as God is the universal cause of the world and nothing can occur without his will.[95] This comprehensive radical claim is in tension with

---

[93] CSM, 1:133. In Aquinas, there is no serious distinction to be drawn between God bringing it about that something begins to exist and God bringing it about that it continues to exist. It was for this reason that when it comes to the notion of God as creator, it does not matter (for Aquinas) whether the cosmos began to exist. Either with or without a temporal beginning, God is the source of the "esse" of things.

[94] While I raise this as a difficulty, the matter may not be grave. Descartes may be read (or reread) as holding that the "same power and action" are at work in preservation and conservation. Descartes does recognize a conceptual distinction between the two. Malebranche does not collapse the concepts of creation and preservation, but he sees both as closely related from the standpoint of God's will for God's whole creation, and conservation of the cosmos is understood in terms of a single volition. "For the world certainly depends on the volitions of the Creator. If the world subsists, it is because God continues to will that the world exist. On the part of God, the conservation of creatures is simply their continued creation. I say, on the part of God who acts. For, on the part of creatures, there appears to be a difference since, in creation, they pass from nothing to being whereas, in conservation, they continue to be. But, in reality, creation does not pass away because, in God, conservation and creation are one and the same volition which consequently is necessarily followed by the same effects" (*Dialogues on Metaphysics*, trans. W. Doney [New York: Abaris Books, 1980], 153). For a theological assertion of God's creation that, I believe, threatens to undermine the continuity of objects over time, see Jonathan Edwards, *Doctrine of Original Sin* (1758). "God's upholding created substance, or causing its existence in each successive moment, is altogether equivalent to an immediate production out of nothing at each movement" (C. H. Faust and T. H. Johnson, eds., *Jonathan Edwards* [New York: American Book, 1935], part IV, chap. 2). See the analysis of this by R. Chisholm in *Person and Object* (LaSalle: Open Court, 1976), 138–144. See also P. Quinn, "Divine Creation, Continuous Creation, and Human Action," in *The Existence and Nature of God*, ed. A. J. Freddoso (Notre Dame: University of Notre Dame Press, 1983).

[95] *Dialogues on Metaphysics*, especially dialogues 9–13.

Malebranche's recognition of human free will. Moreover, it appears to make God accountable for human evil and ignorance.

Without trying to chart Malebranche's escape route in detail, I note that he does insist on human freedom (made evident by our inner sensation and reason as well as by revelation). But instead of construing the power to do evil as a positive power, he sees evil in terms of the mind settling on lesser goods or turning aside from God by serving a created good (like oneself) cut off from the God of all goods. In this way, God's conserving a cosmos in which there is evil – containing, for example, a vain prince – is partly the result of the prince failing to love others in God; this failure is not directly willed (approvingly) by God though God does will that the world contain free creatures, and thus God remains a universal cause without being morally responsible for the prince's failure.[96]

But how does God enter into the causal structure of the world? In *Dialogues on Metaphysics,* Malebranche construes what we might claim is the causal interaction between two bodies as the occasion that these bodies offer for God to alter the world.

> God communicates [*communiqué*] His power to creatures and unites them among themselves solely by virtue of the fact that He makes their modalities occasional causes of effects which He produces Himself – occasional causes, I say, which determine the efficacy of His volitions in consequence of general laws that He has prescribed for Himself to make His conduct bear the character of His attributes and spread throughout His work the uniformity of action necessary to bind together all the parts that compose it and to extricate if from the confusion and irregularity of a kind of chaos in which minds could never understand anything.[97]

Malebranche criticized the notion that causal powers somehow inhere in bodies. Malebranche's picture of the mind-body relation, then, features God as the principal author of the good of embodiment.

> He willed that I have certain sensations, certain emotions, when there are certain traces in my brain, certain movements of [animal] spirits. In short, He willed, and He wills unceasingly, that modalities of mind and body be reciprocal. This constitutes the union and natural dependence

---

[96] See E. J. Kramer, "Malebranche on Human Freedom," in *The Cambridge Companion to Malebranche,* ed. S. Nadler (Cambridge: Cambridge University Press, 2000).

[97] *Dialogues on Metaphysics,* 157–158. See P. Quinn's "Divine Creation, Secondary Causes, and Occasionalism," in *Divine and Human Action,* ed. T. V. Morris (Ithaca: Cornell University Press, 1988).

of the two parts of which we are composed. It consists exclusively in the mutual reciprocity of our modalities based on the unshakeable foundation of divine decrees, decrees which, by their efficacy, communicate to me the power that I have over my body and through it over others, decrees which, by their immutability, unite me to my body and through it to my friends, to my belongings, to everything surrounding me. I get nothing from my nature, nothing from that imaginary nature of the Philosophers; everything is from God and His decrees. God has joined all His works together, though He has not produced connecting entities in them. He has subordinated them among themselves without investing them with efficacious qualities...yes, it is He who exhales the air which He also made me breathe. It is He who, through my organs, produces the air's shocks and vibrations. It is He who propagates it externally and who forms the words by which I get to your mind and pour into your heart what cannot be contained in mine.[98]

Some of Malebranche's case against the observability of causation and some of his illustrations anticipate Hume's work, which we take up in Chapter 4.[99]

The guarantee of interplay (whether divinely mediated or direct) between physical objects did not appear to either Malebranche or Descartes to be absolute. The course of the cosmos seemed to be not un-like a political legislature which runs in a uniform fashion while allowing that its conduct might be subject to a veto from a sovereign power. (In other words, Malebranche allowed for, and believed in, miracles.)[100]

Malebranche and Descartes differed on the scope of God's power; Descartes held that God created eternal truths (e.g., truths of mathematics), whereas Malebranche (like Cudworth) held that eternal truths are beyond God's control. Although Malebranche's God is not as pervasive in creatively forging such necessary truth, Malebranche held that God is intimately involved in our perception of the world and each other. In *The Search after Truth* he writes:

> We should know...that through his presence God is in close union with our minds, such that He might be said to be the place of minds as space is,

---

[98] *Dialogues on Metaphysics*, 163–165.

[99] See C. J. McCracken, *Malebranche and British Philosophy* (Oxford: Clarendon, 1983), chap. 7. "That Hume was a thinker of great originality and power is obvious. What may be less obvious is the precise nature of his originality. Much in the *Treatise* is in fact borrowed; yet for all that, it remains a work of exceptional originality..." (255). For Malebranche's influence on Hume, see C. Hendel, *Studies in the Philosophy of David Hume* (Indianapolis: Bobbs-Merrill, 1963), 49–57.

[100] See *Dialogue* VIII.

in a sense, the place of bodies. Given these two things, the mind surely can see what in God represents created beings, since what in God represents created beings is very spiritual, intelligible, and present to the mind. Thus, the mind can see God's works in Him, provided that God wills to reveal to it what in Him represents them.[101]

In a sense, the correct grasping of an object cognitively involves our grasping a divine idea. The very functioning of our cognitive, perceptual faculties rests on God's provident care. This understanding of cognition anticipates Berkeley, who is discussed in Chapter 3.

Conway's Coherence

Anne Conway's (1631–1679) friendship with Henry More has already been noted. Their first correspondence was on Cartesianism, and they enjoyed a close philosophical rapport despite her ill health (she suffered from horrific headaches) and her conversion to the Society of Friends (Quakers) while More remained Anglican.[102] Her chief work, *Principles of the Most Ancient and Modern Philosophy*, was discovered after her death and published in Latin (1690) and then in English (1692). More coauthored a preface to the work and was probably its translator. This book is one of the most important philosophical works by an English woman to survive the seventeenth century. Many of the themes in the work align Conway with the Cambridge Platonists: love, toleration, free will, a rejection of the contemporary Calvinist view of divine retribution, opposition to tyranny, and a rejection of Hobbesian materialism. Still, she rejects both Descartes' and More's forms of dualism, and More's plastic nature. She prefers instead a more unified understanding of the cohesive nature of mind and body.

Conway underscored the problems besetting Cartesian interactionism, and she articulated in its stead a modified monism. Corporeality and incorporeality are distinguished, but they are seen as aspects of a continuum of creation. "This creation is one entity or substance in respect to its nature or essence . . . so that it varies according to its modes of existence, one of which is corporeality. There are many degrees of

---

[101] *The Search after Truth*, trans. and ed. T. Lennon and P. Olscamp, in *Nicholas Malebranche* (Columbus: Ohio State University, 1980), 230.

[102] For a fine treatment of this period, see Catherine Wilcox, *Theology and Women's Ministry in Seventeenth-Century English Quakerism* (Lewiston, N.Y.: Edwin Mellon Press, 1995).

this so that any thing can approach or recede more or less from the condition of a body or spirit."[103] Conway offers a picture of the cosmos suffused with affective, pervasive living elements.

> My third argument is drawn from that great love and desire which spirits or souls have for bodies, and especially for those bodies with which they are united and in which they dwell. Now, the basis of all love or desire, which brings one thing to another, is that they are of one nature and substance, or that they are like each other or of one mind, or that one has its being from another. We find examples of this among all animals which produce their own offspring in the same way as human beings.[104]

Conway thereby sought to replace Cartesian interaction with a universe of benevolent, organic unity.[105] While Conway's theology was unorthodox in terms of classic Christian theology, she upheld a high view of the mediating, cosmic role of Christ. Some historians see her as similar to Spinoza, who also linked his metaphysical monism with a high view of Christ. Leibniz and Conway corresponded, and some credit her with contributing to his monadology.[106]

Conway's legacy, I think, lies partly in her effort to achieve an overall coherence, a unified but religiously significant view of God and the cosmos. The evidence or justification behind her non-Cartesianism was its achievement (by her lights) of a more integrated view of the cosmos. The need for an integrated view of mind and body, God and world was not lost on subsequent dualist and theistic philosophers. Subsequent theistic dualists by and large did not accept Descartes' denial of nonhuman consciousness. Different theistic philosophers on through the twentieth century have understood God to be immanent and proximate to creation without adopting a monism like Conway's, but monism or a

---

[103] *Principles of the Most Ancient and Modern Philosophy*, trans. A. Coudert and T. Corse (Cambridge: Cambridge University Press, 1996), 41–42.

[104] Ibid., 46. For an appreciative defense of Conway, see Lois Frankel, "The Value of Harmony," in *Causation in Early Modern Philosophy*, ed. S. Nadler (University Park: Penn State University Press, 1993).

[105] Like the Cambridge Platonists, Conway was influenced by Plotinus and Neoplatonism. For further exposition of her thought as well as an excerpt from her principles, see the introduction and Conway entry in *Cambridge Platonist Spirituality*, ed. C. Taliaferro and Alison J. Teply (Mahwah, N.J.: Paulist Press, 2005).

[106] This is a matter of some dispute. See Carolyn Merchant's "The Vitalism of Anne Conway: Its Impact on Leibniz's Concept of the Monad," *Journal of the History of Philosophy* 17:3 (1979).

position in between theism and monism (process philosophy, discussed in Chapter 8) have significant defenders.

The Fragility of Philosophy of Religion

In another critique of Descartes, Blaise Pascal (1623–1662) charged that Descartes' God was religiously inadequate. Born in south-central France, Pascal, made important contributions to probability theory, physics, geometry, and mathematics. When nineteen years old, he invented the calculating machine, a precursor of the computer (earning the late twentieth-century honor of having a computer language named after him: PASCAL). He spent his early years in Rouen and then lived in Paris, where he participated as a layperson in the abbey community Port Royal, a center of the movement Jansenism. Named for Cornelius Jansen (1585–1638), Jansenism underscored the profundity of human weakness and evil on the one hand, and God's irresistible grace on the other.[107] Pascal inherited a straightforward view of human wickedness: "All men naturally hate one another."[108] And he testified in his own experience to the joy he believed he found in God's grace.

Pascal based his opposition to Cartesianism, in part, on his view that we are prone to inconstancy, self-interest, unreliable impulses, unguided imagination, eccentricity, credulity, pomposity, cleverness, and boredom rather than wisdom. Descartes had, or at least he implied, a more optimistic view of human nature. In Pascal's view, we lack the virtues that are essential to the philosophical quest for truths about the divine. "Man then is only disguise, falsehood, and hypocrisy in himself and towards others. He does not want to be told the truth; he avoids telling it to others; and all these tendencies, so far removed from right and reason, are naturally rooted in his heart."[109] Pascal also thought that Descartes' reasoning itself was marred. There is this brief entry by Pascal in the posthumous publication of his thoughts, the *Pensées*: "Descartes useless and uncertain."[110] Pascal lamented the aloofness and detachment of so-called metaphysical proofs of God's existence. "Metaphysical proofs of God are so remote from man's range of reason, and

---

[107] See Alexander Sedgwick's *Jansenism in Seventeenth-Century France* (Charlottesville: University Press of Virginia, 1997).

[108] *Pascal's Pensées*, trans. H. F. Stewart (London: Routledge, 1950), 89.

[109] Ibid., 79.

[110] Ibid., 161.

so involved that they fail to grip; and even if they were of service to some it would only be during the moment of demonstration; an hour afterwards men fear they have been wrong."[111] In Pascal one sees the spirit of Tertulian who warned against an easy peace between Jerusalem (faith) and Athens (philosophy).

Over the some 350 years since his death, Pascal has often been taken to be a reminder of the fragility of philosophy of religion. He calls us to reflect on the *humanity* of philosophy. "We always picture Plato and Aristotle clad in dons' gowns. They were honest folk, and like the rest cracked jokes with their friends."[112] We are not angelic, infallible, impartial inquirers into the good, the true, and the beautiful. Pascal laments our weaknesses while at the same time glorying in our bare capacity for thinking. "Man is but a reed, the weakest thing in nature; but a thinking reed, It does not need the universe to take up arms to crush him; a vapour, a drop of water, is enough to kill him. But though the universe should crush him, man would still be nobler than his destroyer, because he knows that he is dying, knows that the universe has got the better of him; the universe knows naught of that."[113] Pascal praises our capacity for reflection in the midst of caprice and turmoil.

While Pascal made contributions to what may be called a philosophy of grace and the debate over the compatibility of God's foreknowledge and free will, he is often singled out for *Pascal's Wager*, a pragmatic case for believing in God. The first thing to note about this wager is that it is located in a practical context. Pascal's interest lies in the "God of Abraham, God of Isaac, God of Jacob, not of the philosophers and the learned."[114] With respect to the God of Judeo-Christian tradition, Pascal asks us to consider two possibilities: either this being exists or not. "Let us examine this point and say "God is or is not." But which way shall we lean? Reason can settle nothing here; there is an infinite gulf between us. A game is on, at the other end of this infinite distance, and heads or

---

[111] Ibid., 5.

[112] Ibid., 157.

[113] Ibid., 83.

[114] Ibid., 363. This line is from what is called "The Memorial," a document he wrote after a religious experience, November 1654, which was sewn into the lining of his clothes. For one account of how the God of philosophers diverged from the God of religion in the modern era, see Etienne Gilson, *God and Philosophy* (Oxford: Oxford University Press, 1941).

tails will turn up."[115] Pascal elsewhere argues there are reasons in favor of Christian theism over against agnosticism, but in the key passages of Pascal's work where he develops the wager, the assumption is that from a purely intellectual point of view, the likelihood of God existing is equal to the likelihood of a coin coming up heads.

Pascal then insists on the inescapability of choice over God's existence. Here is the main text of the wager.

> Yes, but wager you must; there is no option, you have embarked on it. So which will you have. Come. Since you must choose, let us see what concerns you least. You have two things to lose: truth and good, and two things to stake: your reason and your will, your knowledge and your happiness. And your nature has two things to shun: error and misery. Your reason does not suffer by your choosing one more than the other, for you must choose. That is one point cleared. But your happiness? Let us weigh gain and loss in calling heads that God is. Reckon these two chances: if you win, you win all; if you lose, you lose naught. Then do not hesitate, wager that He is.[116]

Let us consider the merits of the wager against a few questions and objections.

Objection. Can one actually choose to believe or to disbelieve in God? Aren't beliefs involuntary?

Reply. Our beliefs may not be subject to our own immediate voluntary control, but perhaps one may cultivate some beliefs through sustained attention and action. Pascal commends participating in religious practices to develop religious beliefs.[117]

Objection. Surely agnosticism is a middle position, for it is not a denial that God exists but a suspension of belief or disbelief.

Reply. This is a plausible objection, but arguably agnosticism would count in one's life as a form of "atheism," a term that comes from the Latin for "without God"; thus, an agnostic's not embracing theism would leave her without God.[118] Even if agnosticism were a third choice,

---

[115] *Pascal's Pensées*, 117. In what follows, I develop only one of several interpretations of Pascal's Wager. For a good overview of relevant positions, see J. Jordan, ed., *Gambling on God: Essays on Pascal's Wager* (Lanham: Roman and Littlefield, 1994). See also Jordan's contribution "Pragmatic Arguments," in *A Companion to Philosophy of Religion*, ed. P. Quinn and C. Taliaferro (Oxford: Blackwell, 1997).

[116] *Pascal's Pensées*, 119.

[117] Ibid., 121.

[118] I address this worry and others in discussing William James's wager argument in Chapter 6.

Pascal's argument could be run as providing reasons for accepting theism rather than agnosticism or atheism.

Objection. Doesn't the wager appeal to self-interest and, in that respect, isn't it in conflict with religious virtues that are often cast as selfless and nonegoistic? Note the language of the wager: "If *you* win, *you* win all."

Reply. Yes, the wager may be articulated as a matter of self-interest. But it can be formulated in a fashion that is not. Imagine that acting on theistic convictions would involve expansive friendships, a deeper solidarity with the poor, a more strident allegiance to justice. If one may sketch positive values here that are not available (or less likely to be available) on the alternative schema, a wager argument will not be faulted on egoistic grounds.[119]

Objection. What about Pascal's talk of "infinity"? Does the concept of infinite happiness make sense? How can our standard concepts of rational wagering accommodate infinite utility?

Reply. Pascal is evidently referring to the afterlife, which he believes will involve indefinite or unending happiness. If such a life is extended indefinitely and happiness were a quantifiable matter, then perhaps there would be no time in the future when a person would attain an actual infinite number of "happiness units." But I suggest this is not a decisive worry. Pascal may simply talk in terms of unending rather than infinite happiness. A defender of Pascal may concede that the wager does not fit into the standard patterns of decision theory, but that is not the fault of either the wager or decision theory. Pascal's wager concerns a unique choice.

I submit that the case for and against Pascal's wager is not easily settled. A full assessment of its merit must take full stock of all the values and probabilities at stake. If one paints a grim portrait of theistic belief, in which acting on theistic belief is more likely to produce harm than good, then a wager argument may be formulated for atheism or agnosticism.[120]

---

[119] John Stuart Mill adapts a strategy like this in 1874. See R. Taylor, ed., *Theism* (Indianapolis: Bobbs-Merrill, 1957), 82. Mill is discussed in Chapter 6.

[120] For a sympathetic, fuller treatment of the relevant arguments, see Nicholas Rescher, *Pascal's Wager: A Study of Practical Reasoning in Philosophical Theology* (Notre Dame: University of Notre Dame Press, 1985). See also Ian Hacking, "The Logic of Pascal's Wager," *American Philosophical Quarterly* 9 (1972); D. Groothuis, "Wagering Belief: Examining Two Objections to Pascal's Wager," *Religious Studies* 30 (1994); Jordan's edited collection *Gambling on God*; W. Lycan and G. N. Schlesinger, "You Bet Your Life: Pascal's Wager Defended," in *Contemporary*

Whatever one makes over Pascal's wager, however, he invites us to question the autonomy and adequacy of reason when this is not governed by values. If we were to follow a purely intellectual rigor of Cartesian stripe, how far would we get in our beliefs and practices? If Pascal is right, we are not limited to abstract, purely intellectual reflection. "The heart has its own reasons which Reason does not know."[121] Pascal's portrait of humanity is not just a "thinking reed" but a passionate, thinking subject who may be as fragile as a reed and yet able to be in relation to the eternal God.

Measure for Measure

Chapter 1 displayed the great Cambridge Platonist synthesis in which reason as the candle of the Lord is duly at work providing evidence of God, God's provident care for creation, moral guidance, and the hope of immortality. Matters begin to look less settled as we take stock of subsequent figures. To be sure, the philosophers discussed in this chapter share many of the same religious convictions, but the foundation of these convictions is argued over with increased intensity. In particular, I have sought to exhibit in this chapter some of the specific arguments for God's existence, the appeal to Cartesian doubt, an argument for a soul or person-body dualism that allows for an afterlife, arguments over God's relation to the world, and (finally) Pascal's questioning the religious adequacy of philosophy.

The key figures in the next chapter are even bolder in their philosophical systems and methodology. They carry further the concern for

---

Perspectives on Religious Epistemology, ed. R. D. Geivett and B. Sweetman (Oxford: Oxford University Press, 1992); and T. V. Morris, *Making Sense of It All: Pascal and the Meaning of Life* (Grand Rapids: Eerdmans, 1992). For an interesting literary and philosophical study, see Nicholas Hammond, *Playing with Truth: Language and the Human Condition in Pascal's Pensées* (Oxford: Clarendon, 1994). Hammond concludes: "By playing with language and order, both dialectician and reader are continually reminded of man's flawed state. But the possibility of transcendence within the very concepts which indicate his fallenness points always to a God who is both stable and constant. Playing with shifting notions of truth becomes an eternal truth played through God" (228).

[121] *Pascal's Pensées,* 343. For a contemporary account of rationality that is friendly to Pascal's integration of values, emotions, and passion, see Robert Nozick, *The Nature of Rationality* (Princeton: Princeton University Press, 1993), especially chap. 3.

method that Francis Bacon identified as a central God-given task. In the *Novum Organon* Bacon urged his readers to be more concerned with following a sound method rather than pursuing apparent traditional goods. "All who have labored in learning from experience have from the outset fixed upon certain definite works, which they pursued with immoderate and premature eagerness, and have sought, as I say, fruit-bearing, not light-bearing, experiments. They have not followed the example of the order in which God on the first day created light alone and devoted a whole day to that. Nor on that day did He bring forth any material work, but descended to those things in the days that followed."[122]

Thomas Lennon has recently described the seventeenth century as the "belle *époque* of method."[123] He offers this portrait of methodology:

> Method was generally conceived of as a means to gain knowledge. However, to gain knowledge, one must start someplace, and where else but with what is known? Even to frame a question, something must be known if only in terms of the question in the acquisition of knowledge, the rabbinical apothegm holds true: It takes a pair of tongs to make a pair of tongs... the general situation is modeled by a jigsaw puzzle. One realizes that a piece is missing, a piece of a certain shape, and one looks for a piece of that shape, having found it, one then fits it into the empty space. The structure of knowledge is like the puzzle; method's two-step dynamic amounts to locating the missing piece and then fitting into its proper place.[124]

Building from this imagery, as we come to the eighteenth century, we have grave questions about whether the puzzle was made by design and a much less settled understanding of what the completed jigsaw puzzle will look like. The God of Spinoza has some striking differences from, for example, the God of John Locke. And the reasons behind their view of the divine differ radically.

As this chapter has tried to generate some sympathy for Descartes over against his philosophical and religious detractors, I add a closing observation in his defense before proceeding to John Locke in Chapter 3. Descartes' dualism and his skeptical inquiry are sometimes treated in

---

[122] *Novum Organum*, trans. and ed. P. Ubrach and J. Gibson (Chicago: Open Court, 1994), 12.

[123] T. Lennon, "Malebranche and Method," in Nadler, *The Cambridge Companion to Malebranche*, 8.

[124] Ibid., 10.

histories of philosophy as unique aberrations, historically distinguished mistakes.[125] I suggest "Cartesianism" has a wider appeal.

First, mind-body dualism was not unique to Descartes, nor to Plato before him. Dualism runs through a great many religious traditions across continents and cultures. Many of Descartes' critics, then and now, concede that dualism is (at least initially) a plausible starting point. Our mental life – our conscious subjectivity and feeling – seems to be different from our brain and other bodily parts and states. To entertain thoughts like "I am puzzled" appears to be very different from conceiving of brain events and vice versa; I may be sure I am puzzled but have no idea whatever about neurological events. To conceive of the puzzling ideas is not (or so it appears) the same thing as conceiving of the neurological states.[126] This disparity alone is not enough to establish two different objects (recall the fallacious argument from doubt), but it is a sign that there is more to us than our bodily states alone.[127] Added to this is the apparent contingency between ourselves and our bodies. Those religions which countenance reincarnation where a person (soul or mind) comes to have a different body seem committed to a person-body dualism. Because of this apparent distinction, the following contemporary materialists grant some prima facie credibility to dualism: Daniel Dennett, David Lewis, Thomas Nagel, Brian O'Shaughnessy, and J. J. C. Smart, among others.[128]

---

[125] Michael Williams, the contemporary epistemologist, advances this position.

[126] Consider this objection. Not knowing what is going on with me when I have thoughts does not mean that there is something going on with me of which I am unaware – for example, I may feel sick but have no idea as to the state of my body. Reply: But I suggest that there are all sorts of distinct properties at work in this example. There may be the properties of *being dizzy* or *being in pain*, for example, as well as being subject to lung disease. I believe that the apparent fact that one may conceive of *being in pain* without conceiving of any bodily states is prima facie reason for thinking these are distinct properties. Presumably, medical treatment of our sick subject identifies the various physical properties and events that account for the various mental properties and events. For an extended defense of the criterion I am employing to distinguish properties, see Roderick Chisholm, *A Realistic Theory of Categories* (Cambridge: Cambridge University Press, 1996).

[127] Recalling the examples in the Argument from Doubt earlier in this chapter, I believe that the properties *being a father* and *being a masked robber* are distinct, even if the same thing might have both properties. So, the considerations I raise here about independent conceivability of properties only shows a dualism of properties, not a dualism of concrete subjects.

[128] For bibliographical references, see *Consciousness and the Mind of God*, 26.

Second, I take note of two philosophers of very different sorts who bear an interesting relationship to Descartes: the Ethiopian philosopher Zera Yacob (1599–1692) and the Japanese Buddhist Nagarjuna (second century A.D.).

Yacob did not enter a small hut with a stove to develop his philosophical meditations. He entered a cave. Like Descartes, he sought a full-scale critical review of his convictions prompted by surrounding political, religious, and social conflict. Claude Summer, an Ethiopian philosophical historian, concedes that Yacob did not use Cartesian method of *universal* doubt, but he did employ a parallel critical investigation that ultimately led to the recognition of a good God of a good creation. His view of reason as a light given by God has Cartesian and Cambridge Platonist echoes.[129]

Nagarjuna was not a Cartesian with respect to believing in a substantial self and on many other fronts. Quite the opposite. He was keen to show that all putative metaphysical concepts (of the self et al.) entailed contradictions when affirmed. Anything else, he thought, would make Buddhism impossible. But in making his case for Buddhism there is an extended sense in which he, like Descartes, sought an indubitable, secure foundation to achieve a comprehensive metaphysics and epistemology. He concluded that there was none in the offing, and indeed this failure to settle on a foundation was a key to his doctrine of emptiness, a rich salvific goal. I cite him here, along with Yacob, and the more widespread appreciation of dualism, to challenge those who see Descartes' projects as altogether unique historically, isolated culturally to seventeenth-century Europe and those of us subsequently who have been influenced by Queen Christina's tutor.

---

[129] See Claude Summer, *Ethiopian Philosophy*, vol. 3 (Addis Ababa: Addis Ababa University, 1998).

✦

THREE

The Ascendancy of Rules of Evidence in Early Modern Philosophy of Religion

Light, true light in the mind is, or can be nothing else but the evidence of the truth of any proposition; and if it be not a self-evident proposition, all the light it has, or can have, is from the clearness and validity of those proofs upon which it is received.... Reason must be our last judge and guide in everything.

John Locke[1]

Locke's *Essay*

John Locke's *Essay Concerning Human Understanding* was published in 1689. His *Essay* places before us a salient case for governing our beliefs about ourselves, the world, and God by a fair-minded impartial weighing of evidence. John Locke began this work in 1670.

In the course of composing the *Essay*, Locke worked as secretary to the Earl of Shaftesbury (from 1667 to 1675), whose political career included vying for both sides in England's Civil War (first for the king, then for Parliament), playing an ambivalent role in Cromwell's government, and then acting as a commissioner who facilitated the restoration of the monarchy. He engaged in Anglo-European diplomacy, stood trial for treason, and went into exile in Holland. Locke's own life at the time of composing and publishing the essay was precarious. Locke was a Protestant like Shaftesbury, who favored the Protestant succession of the monarchy, along with parliamentary democracy and civil liberty. The reign of James II, a Roman Catholic, was an unstable period – socially, religiously, and politically – and this compelled Locke to seek refuge, like

---

[1] *An Essay Concerning Human Understanding*, ed. Alexander Fraser (New York: Dover, 1959), 4.19.14, 437–438.

his patron, in Holland. The English government branded him a traitor. In 1689, however, the threat vanished with the overthrowing of James II and the subsequent Glorious Revolution with the reign of William and Mary. In brief, Locke's *Essay* was not forged in a safe academic haven.

John Locke (1632–1704) begins the introduction to his essay with a call to inquire critically into the nature of understanding.

> Since it is the *understanding* that sets man above the rest of sensible beings, and gives him all the advantage and dominion which he has over them; it is certainly a subject, even for its nobleness, worth our labour to inquire into. The understanding, like the eye, whilst it makes us see and perceive all other things, takes no notice of itself; and it requires art and pains to set it at a distance and make it its own object. But whatever be the difficulties that are in the way of this inquiry; whatever it be that keeps us too much in the dark to ourselves; sure I am that all the light we can let in upon our minds, all the acquaintance we can make with our own understandings, will not only be very pleasant, but bring us great advantage, in directing our thoughts in the search of other things.[2]

Locke's essay calls readers to the noble, strenuous yet pleasant task of understanding our understanding. His optimistic plea for us to examine critically the scope of reason came at a time when, in his view, a great measure of harm resulted from misguided judgment.[3]

In Locke's work there is an intense, sustained movement to stabilize standards and expectations of reason and evidence in matters of religion. One may see this as part of a yet more general movement in the late seventeenth and early eighteenth centuries to arrive at a stable legal system. Many of the leading figures in early modern philosophy had legal training: Bacon, Leibniz (1646–1716), Hugo Grotius (1583–1645), and Samuel von Pufendorf (1632–1694). Locke's work was employed in one of the first British texts on legal evidence, Geoffrey Gilbert's *Law of Evidence* (1754), which was regarded as an authoritative work on evidence into the early nineteenth century. It begins with a reference to Locke:

> In the first Place, it has been observed by a very learned Man, that there are several Degrees from perfect Certainty and Demonstration, quite down

---

[2] Ibid., 25–26.

[3] For further background to the political and cultural setting of Locke's work, see Hans Aarsleff, "Locke's Influence," in *The Cambridge Companion to Locke*, ed. Vere Chappell (Cambridge: Cambridge University Press, 1994).

to Improbability and Unlikeliness, even to the Confines of Impossibility; and there are several Acts of the Mind proportion'd to these Degrees of Evidence, which may be called the Degrees of Assent, from full Assurance and Confidence, quite down to Conjecture, Doubt, Distrust and Disbelief.[4]

Gilbert then goes on to articulate different rules of evidence that bolster judicial decisions. We are in a legal world of deliberation that is freed from the trappings of feudal law, which permitted trial by ordeal and combat and the horrors of witch trials. It was time to abandon the practices of witch poking, floating, and tear tests (supposedly, a witch would not shed tears when hearing about the passion and crucifixion of Christ), and to develop responsible views on the credibility of witnesses, the difference between fact and interpretations, a formalized treatment of burdens of proof, and so on.[5]

Still, for better or for worse, Locke is not without some rapport with the philosophical school of Cambridge Platonism outlined in Chapter 1. He thought the light of reason did disclose the existence of God, argued against the unbridled sovereignty of the state, advanced the case for social and political toleration of dissent, and argued for the reasonability of Christian faith. He even warmly commended the homilies of Whichcote.[6]

---

[4] W. Twining, *Rethinking Evidence: Exploratory Essays* (Oxford: Basil Blackwell 1990), 36. See also Twining's *Theories of Evidence* (London: Weidenfeld & Nicolson, 1985).

[5] More and Cudworth defended the coherence of the concept of witches and other paranormal entities but this was largely part of their case for the coherence of immaterial intelligence and agency. See More's *Antidote against Atheism*, especially the latter sections, and Cudworth's *The True Intellectual System of the World*. More contributed to the expansion of the posthumous editions of Glanvill's *Saducismus Triumphatus; or, A Full and Plain Evidence Concerning Witches and Apparitions*. Glanvill's work on witches was extensive. For a good overview, see "Witchcraft," in Barbara Shapiro's *Probability and Certainty in Seventeenth Century England* (Princeton: Princeton University Press, 1983).

[6] See John Marshall's *John Locke: Resistance, Religion and Responsibility* (Cambridge: Cambridge University Press, 1994), 179, and Maurice Cranston, *John Locke: A Biography* (New York: Macmillan, 1957). Locke's ties with the Cambridge Platonists were intertwined and intimate. As noted in Chapter 1, Damaris Cudworth Masham, daughter of Ralph Cudworth and a committed Cambridge Platonist, was a close companion. See chap. 16 of Cranston's biography. Lady Masham was with Locke at his death. See John Head, "The Life of the Author," in *The Works of John Locke* (London: Rivington Press, 1824), xxviii–xxxix. Nicholas Wolterstorff has done important work on Locke, especially in *John Locke and the Ethics of Belief* (Cambridge: Cambridge University Press, 1996) and "John Locke's Epistemological Piety: 'Reason Is the Candle

In order to locate Locke in this narrative of modern philosophy of religion, I backtrack by considering Hobbes's work. I then turn to Locke, followed by overviews of two "empiricists" (Berkeley, Edwards), some early American philosophers, and then two "rationalists" (Leibniz, Spinoza).[7] I then describe a British philosopher who was in between the empiricists and rationalists (Butler) and take note of philosophy's relation to tradition in the early modern era. The theme of this chapter is the ascendancy of a concern for evidence in the philosophical assessment of religion, and the interesting ways in which this evidence is construed in terms of our relation to the world as either independent of mind or thoroughly dependent on a divine mind. Philosophy of religion during this period was carried out in tandem with a philosophical investigation into the structure of the cosmos with a profound concern for the value of human nature and the possibility of life after death.

Hobbes's Challenge

Hobbes's philosophical views of religion have been – and still are – a hotbed of competing interpretations. He has been cast as an atheist and a skeptic in ethics, as well as a devoted Christian theist and a staunch defender of a scientific, realist view of ethics and civil duty.

Hobbes was born in Westport, England, in 1588. Educated at Oxford, he traveled extensively on the European continent. He served as a secretary to Francis Bacon, enjoyed the patronage of English aristocracy, and became embroiled in scientific, political, and religious

of the Lord,'" *Faith and Philosophy* 11:4 (October 1994). But Wolterstorff neglects the Cambridge Platonist background to Locke; this seems like an oversight especially given that "The Candle of the Lord" was *the* central motif of the movement. Wolterstorff casts Locke's piety as "an eccentric version of Protestant piety" on these grounds: "In classic Protestantism, the governing metaphors are auditory: speaking and listening. Though Locke does, on a few occasions, speak about listening to the voice of Reason, his governing metaphors are overwhelmingly visual" ("John Locke's Epistemological Piety," 591). I am not sure where Wolterstorff draws the line between *classic* and *eccentric* Prostestantism, but Locke was not out of step with Whichcote, Cudworth, More, Smith, Culverwell, Norris, and the like, as well as many continental reformers. See R. Colie, *Light and Enlightenment: A Study of the Cambridge Platonists and the Dutch Arminians* (Cambridge: Cambridge University Press, 1957).

[7] I place these terms in quotations only because they can be misleading without qualification. Shunning any highly technical usage of these terms, I suggest that those typically labeled empiricists give more scope and evidentiary weight to sensory experience than those who are labeled rationalists.

controversy. His best known book, *Leviathan*, published in 1651, is a classical work on political sovereignty that is founded on a comprehensive account of human nature and morality.[8] On this point, Hobbes shared with the Cambridge Platonists the conviction that political theory rests upon a philosophy of human nature.

Hobbes's key reference point is scientific knowledge, an understanding of the world based on empirical experience and yet refined by precision of language, and theoretical accounts of causal explanation. Scientific knowledge, then, concerns knowing the causes and effects of events in the world. Sense perception is a key component in our knowledge of the world because it is inextricably defined by causal relations involving the world. Hobbes is not tempted by Cartesian worries about whether he can infer the external world from the world of appearances; he was more concerned with containing real malignant political tyranny than he was with addressing Descartes' imaginary evil demon. For Hobbes, scientific knowledge encompasses both natural events and the creation of such artifacts as the commonwealth or state.

Hobbes's science reveals a fundamentally materialistic view of nature, including human nature.

> The world (I mean not the earth only, that denominates lovers of it *worldly men*, but the *universe*, that is, the whole mass of all things that are), is corporeal, that is to say, body, and hath the dimensions of magnitude, namely, length, breadth, and depth: also every part of the body, is likewise body, and hath the like dimensions; and consequently every part of the universe, is body, and that which is not body, is no part of the universe; and because the universe is all, that which is no part of it, is *nothing*; and consequently *no where*.[9]

God is described by Hobbes in material terms. "To his Lordship's question here: *What I leave God to be?* I answer, I leave him to be a most pure, simple, invisible spirit corporeal."[10] God is not finite, nor confined to a place. Hobbes held that there can be no incorporeal bodies; he assimilated the thesis that God is incorporeal to atheism. Hobbes attestation to God's corporeal reality can be found

---

[8] For a good biography, see A. P. Martinich, *Hobbes* (Cambridge: Cambridge University Press, 1997). For an older but still accessible and clear text, see A. E. Taylor, *Thomas Hobbes* (New York: Dodge, 1948).

[9] *Leviathan*, in *English Works*, ed. J. Green (New York: Harper and Brothers, 1929), 3: XLVI, 672.

[10] *An Answer to Bishop Bramhall*, in *English Works*, 4:313.

in *An Historical Narration Concerning Heresy and the Punishment Thereof.*[11]

Hobbes allows for the special creation of humanity by God but he upholds a materialist, quasi-evolutionary account of the emergence of life. "It is true that the earth produced the first living creatures of all sorts but man . . . so it is evident that God gave unto the earth that virtue. Which virtue must needs consist in motion, because all generation is motion."[12]

Hobbes's work is shot through with enormous attention to biblical authority and theological convictions.[13] In my own reading of Hobbes, I find it very difficult to believe that his stated allegiance to theological tenants is entirely ironic or strategic. As Richard Popkin puts its, "Hobbes may have lived, eaten and drunk among French sceptics, but no influence appears in his works."[14] Still, Hobbes was skeptical about how much we may know about God.

Hobbes endorses a version of a first cause or cosmological argument. The powers of nature are best accounted for by a divine cause.

> And forasmuch as God Almighty is incomprehensible it followeth, that we can have no conception or image of the Deity . . . excepting only this, that there is a God: for the effects we acknowledge naturally, do include a power of their producing, before they were produced; and that power presupposeth something existent that hath such power: and the thing so existing with power to produce, if it were not eternal, must needs have been produced by somewhat before that, till we come to an eternal, that is to say, the first power of all powers, and first cause of all causes: and that is it which all men conceive by the name of God.[15]

---

[11] See A. P. Martinich, *Hobbes: A Biography* (Cambridge: Cambridge University Press, 1999). For an overview of recent scholarship on Hobbes's religious views, see Patricia Springborg, "Hobbes on Religion," in *The Cambridge Companion to Hobbes,* ed. T. Sorell (Cambridge: Cambridge University Press, 1996). A seminal, polemical essay on this topic is Peter Geach's "The Religion of Thomas Hobbes," *Religious Studies* 17 (1981): 549–558.

[12] *English Works,* 7:176.

[13] The magnitude of biblical references in Hobbes's work is difficult to miss. It is calculated that biblical passages are cited more than six hundred times in *Leviathan* and over double that in his six other political books. See "A Biblical Culture," in Christopher Hill, *The English Bible and the Seventeenth-Century Revolution* (London: Penguin Press, 1993).

[14] "Hobbes and Scepticism I," in *The Third Force in Seventeenth-Century Thought* (Leiden: Brill, 1992), 20. See also Ronald Hepburn "Hobbes on the Knowledge of God," in *Hobbes and Rousseau,* ed. R. S. Peters (New York: Anchor Books, 1972).

[15] *Human Nature* (1650), chap. 11.

Because Hobbes thought we could achieve very little further content to the idea of the divine than as a first, eternal power, he challenged Descartes' claim that we possess a positive idea of God.

> It is the same way with the most holy name of God; we have no image, no idea corresponding to it. Hence we are forbidden to worship God in the form of an image, lest we should think we could conceive Him who is inconceivable. Hence it appears that we have no idea of God. But just as one born blind who has frequently been brought close to a fire and has felt himself growing warm, recognizes that there is something which made him warm, and, if he hears it called fire, concludes that fire exists, though he has no acquaintance with its shape or colour, and has no idea of fire nor image that he can discover in his mind; so a man, recognizing that there must be some cause of his images and ideas, and another previous cause of this cause and so on continuously, is finally carried on to a conclusion, or to the supposition of some eternal cause, which, never having begun to be, can have no cause prior to it; and hence he necessarily concludes that something necessarily exists. But nevertheless he has no idea that he can assert to be that of this eternal being, and he merely gives a name to the object of his faith or reasoning and calls it God.[16]

Hobbes advanced a strictly empirical study of human nature and his *Leviathan* proposes a scientific foundation for politics, but there is no parallel empirical or scientific study of God.

Despite Hobbes's agnostic stance on God's nature, he advanced a strong conception of God's power and its entitlements. "The power of God alone without other help is sufficient justification of any action he does.... That which he does, is made just by his doing it.... Power irresistible justifies all actions, really and properly in whomsoever it be found; less power does not, and because such power is in God only, he must needs be just in all actions."[17]

This stringent view of omnipotence fed Hobbes's theodicy.

> If God be omnipotent, he is irresistible; if so, just in all his actions, though we, who have as much capacity to measure the justice of God's actions as a man born blind to judge of colors, haply may not discern it. What then need any man trouble his head, whether he be predestined or not? Let him live justly and honestly according to the religion of his country,

16 *The Philosophical Writings of Descartes*, trans. J. Cottingham, R. Stoothoff, and D. Murdoch, 3 vols. (Cambridge: Cambridge University Press, 1984), 2:127.
17 Hobbes, cited by Martinich, *Hobbes*, 204.

and refer himself to God for the rest, since he is the potter, and may do what he please with the vessel.[18]

Hobbes appears to be the mirror opposite of Cudworth.

In Chapter 1 it was noted that Cudworth's philosophy of God's sovereignty related to his conception of the sovereignty of the state. For Hobbes, the state had a power that was not entirely different from Descartes' conception of God's power to fashion eternal truths. Hobbes embraced a view of civil authority that allowed the sovereign to determine for its subjects what counts as good or bad reasoning.

> It is needful therefore, as oft as any controversy ariseth in these matters contrary to the public good and common peace, that there be somebody to judge of the reasoning, that is to say, whether that which is inferred, be rightly inferred or not; that so the controversy may be ended. But there are no rules given by Christ to this purpose, neither came he into the world to teach *logic*. It remains therefore that the judges of such controversies, be the same with those whom God by nature had instituted before, namely, those who in each city are constituted by the sovereign. Moreover, if a controversy be raised of the accurate and proper signification, that is the definition of those names or appellations which are commonly used; insomuch as it is needful for the peace of the city, or the distribution of right to be determined; the determination will belong to the city. For men, by reasoning, do search out such kind of definitions in their observation of diverse conceptions, for the signification whereof those appellations were used at diverse times and for diverse causes. But the decision of the question, whether a man do reason rightly, belongs to the city [*sic*]. For example, if a woman bring forth a child of unwonted shape, and the law forbid to kill a man; the question is whether the child be a man. It is demanded therefore, what a man is. No man doubts but the city shall judge it, and that without taking an account of Aristotle's definition that man is a rational creature. And these things, namely, *right, policy*, and *natural sciences*, are subjects concerning which Christ denies that it belongs to his office to give any precepts, or teach any thing beside this only, that in all controversies about them, every single subject should obey the laws and determinations of his city.[19]

---

[18] Ibid., 196.

[19] From *De Cive* (chap. 17, part XII). Richard H. Popkin may have overstated the extent to which Hobbes relegated truth to the sovereign. For a modification on this reading, see Leiser Madanes, "Hobbes on Peace and Truth," in *Skepticism in the History of Philosophy*, ed. R. H. Popkin (Dordrecht: Kluwer, 1996).

This account of reasoning implies that matters of political expediency can shape what is deemed legitimate belief, and also, it seems, what is deemed valid or legitimate reasoning, so logic becomes conventional, which is a radical claim indeed. Although such passages horrified Cambridge Platonists, two points may soften the apparent sharp division between the Hobbesian and Platonist: Hobbes offers here what may be considered (in part) a description of how political communities actually function. Magistrates do in fact determine what is considered right reason. The Platonist would reply that magistrates may reason badly and yet note that, in practice, what is socially accepted as right reasoning has political authority behind it.[20] Second, Platonists can concede that at least some matters of right reason should be determined by civil authority. The case Hobbes chooses here (the decision over who is to count as a human being) may be too radical, but decisions over the parameters of a commonwealth, the right stewardship over surplus agriculture, and so on are another matter.

It must also be borne in mind that, in one sense, Hobbes shared with the Platonists from Cambridge a well-justified apprehension (or, to be less formal, *fear*) of political powers that inflict violence and rapacious policies. Hobbes translated Thucydides' *History of the Peloponnesian War*, published in 1628. There are different interpretations of Thucydides' work, but one theme Hobbes highlights is the danger of democracy. Athens was a democracy, but that was not incompatible with its having an empire and engaging in brutal, disastrous campaigns. Thucydides enshrines, at the heart of the history, the famous Melian dialogue in which the Athenians' reasoning is founded on an undisguised appeal to power. Here is the key reason that the Athenians offer to the people of the island of Melos to encourage their joining Athens in the war against Sparta or face annihilation: "It is for the good of our own empire" and to provide "evidence of our power."[21] This kind of *evidence* is what really matters; all other rhetoric is placed to one side.

The Council of the Melians replied as follows:

> No one can object to each of us putting forward our own views in a calm atmosphere. That is perfectly reasonable. What is scarcely consistent with such a proposal is the present threat, indeed the certainty, of your making

---

[20] Readers acquainted with Nietzsche and Foucault will see this as vital in their critique of "the Enlightenment."

[21] *History of the Peloponnesian War*, trans. R. Warner (London: Penguin, 1972), 402.

war on us. We see that you have come prepared to judge the argument yourselves, and that the likely end of it all will be either war, if we prove that we are in the right, and so refuse to surrender, or else slavery.

Athenians: If you are going to spend the time in enumerating your suspicions about the future, or if you have met here for any other reason except to look the facts in the face and on the basis of these facts to consider how you can save your city from destruction, there is no point in our going on with this discussion. If, however, you will do as we suggest, then we will speak on.

Melians: It is natural and understandable that people who are placed as we are should have recourse to all kinds of arguments and different points of view. However, you are right in saying that we are met together here to discuss the safety of our country and, if you will have it so, the discussion shall proceed on the lines that you have laid down.[22]

At the end of the dialogue, Thucydides summarizes the outcome.

Siege operations [by the Athenians] were now carried on vigorously and, as there was also some treachery from inside, the Melians surrendered unconditionally to the Athenians, who put to death all the men of military age whom they took, and sold the women and children as slaves. Melos itself they took over for themselves, sending out later a colony of 500 men.[23]

The conquest of the Melians by the Athenians in the Peloponnesian War is one of the most vivid, deliberate exercises of "might makes right." Part of what motivates Hobbes's desire for a principled sovereign power was to block such capricious slaughter and premature, violent death. His treatment of reason and evidence is based on the assumption that a person does, naturally, seek self-preservation and his aim is to establish a society in which a rational order under a sovereign power will secure prudent safeguards. Hobbes's enemy was the same enemy as Thucydides: unenlightened self-interest.[24] Statecraft can be rational or irrational in reference to the evident ways in which regimes contribute to, or compromise, universal self-interest.

---

[22] Ibid., 401.

[23] Ibid., 408.

[24] For similarities and differences between Hobbes and Thucydides, see Laurie Johnson, *Thucydides, Hobbes, and the Interpretation of Realism* (Dekalb: Northern Illinois University Press, 1993). Hobbes saw Thucydides as the perfect aristocratic antidote to the English attraction to Greek and Roman republicanism. He favored Thucydides rather than Aristotle and Cicero.

While Hobbes appears as a shadow eclipsing the Good from the standpoint of Cambridge Platonism, he may also be seen as a defender of the role of theistic belief in securing civil governance and of the compatibility of materialistic mechanism and religion. Anyone interested in the relation between science and religion in the early modern era needs to take Hobbes seriously.[25]

Lockean Strictures and Toleration

Locke's methodology takes rational reflection on experience to be pivotal. He opposed the appeal to innate ideas made by the Cambridge Platonists, insisting instead that without sense experience our minds are like a blank slate.

> Let us then suppose that the mind to be, as we say, white paper, void of all characters, without any ideas: – How comes it to be furnished? Whence comes it by that vast store which the busy and boundless fancy of man has painted on it with an almost endless variety? Whence has it all the materials of reason and knowledge? To this I answer, in one word, from EXPERIENCE. In that all our knowledge is founded; and from that it ultimately derives itself. Our observation employed either, about external sensible objects, or about the internal operations of our minds perceived and reflected on by ourselves, is that which supplies our understanding with all the materials of thinking. These two are the foundation of knowledge, from which all the ideas we have, or can naturally have, do spring.[26]

Locke did not, then, believe that we have within us an idea of God that philosophers are to make explicit. The idea of God, like all other beliefs,

---

[25] There is much to learn in comparing Hobbes and Cudworth. Samuel Mintz describes Cudworth as Hobbes's "most intellectually formidable opponent" (*The Hunting of Leviathan* [Cambridge: Cambridge University Press, 1962], 50). But there is also this regret. Notwithstanding the Cambridge Platonist reputation for tolerance, Cudworth signed the expulsion order of the Hobbist Daniel Scargill, fellow of Corpus Christi, in 1688. After recanting, Scargill was readmitted to the university. Perhaps on Cudworth's behalf one should take note of Hobbes's condemnation of the classical education of his time. Hobbes thought the universities were seditious as they promoted democratic principles. See Lawrence Stone, *The Causes of the English Revolution, 1529–1642* (New York: Harper and Row, 1972), 96.

[26] *Essay*, 2.1.2.121–122. For an excellent record of twentieth-century scholarship on Locke, see R. Hall and R. Woolhouse, *80 Years of Locke Scholarship* (Edinburgh: Edinburgh University Press, 1983).

needs to be articulated with an experiential base. For Locke, an inbuilt disposition to certain beliefs or a found persistent conviction did not amount to evidence.

> The strength of our persuasions are no evidence at all of their own rectitude; crooked things may be as still and inflexible as straight; and men may be as positive and peremptory in error as in truth. How come else the untractable zealots in different and opposite parties? For if the light, which everyone thinks he has in mind, which in this case is nothing but the strength of his own persuasion, be an evidence that it is from God, contrary opinions may have the same title to be inspirations; and God will not only be the Father of lights but of opposite and contradictory lights, leading men contrary ways; and contradictory propositions will be divine truths, if an ungrounded strength of assurance be an evidence, that any proposition is a divine relation.[27]

Locke, like Descartes, insists on the importance of evidentially grounded beliefs. So convictions about God, the good, and the afterlife need to be earned through evidence.

Locke distinguished three types of propositions.

> 1. According to reason are such propositions, whose truth we can discover, by examining and tracing those ideas we have from sensation and reflection; and by natural deduction, find to be true or probable. 2. Above reason are such propositions, whose truth or probability we cannot derive from those principles. 3. Contrary to reason are such propositions, as are inconsistent or irreconcilable to our clear and distinct ideas. Thus the existence of God is according to reason; the existence of more than one God contrary to reason; the resurrection of the dead, above reason.[28]

Locke thereby stands against a form of fideism, which would permit belief against reason (fideism is the view that religious belief is not based on reason but on faith). The truths of religion therefore need to be garnished from the first category or, with the help of indirect evidence provided by miracles, the second.[29]

In Locke's view, the existence of God can be made evident to reason. In the chapter "Our Knowledge of the Existence of God" of the *Essay*, Locke develops a cosmological argument for God as "an eternal, most powerful, and most knowing Being." God is the Creator of all. Locke's

---

[27] *Essay*, 4.19.11.

[28] *Essay*, 4.13.23.

[29] For an overview, see T. Penelhum, *God and Skepticism* (Dordrecht: Reidel, 1987).

design argument is similar to Cudworth's.[30] Locke does not support an ontological argument. Revelation claims backed by miracles give us the further evidence of God as a redeemer, acting through the messiah Jesus Christ, and the promise of an afterlife.

Locke's work has fed what some historians see as a fundamentally Protestant individualism. In an insightful recent study, *Canon and Criterion in Christian Theology*, William Abraham writes: "The very notion of the Church as an extended historic community, bound in some sense by its canonical history, is replaced by a vision of the Church as a voluntary association of individuals held together by their own independent judgment concerning the correctness of the doctrine of justification by faith as established from the Scriptures."[31] In a Lockean religion the individual takes on a higher, more solitary role than in, say, the religion of the Cambridge Platonists. As Abraham correctly argues, the Lockean code of ethics in the governance of belief is a profound shift from earlier medieval treatments of tradition and reason. Locke's insistence on the individual's duty to scrutinize beliefs is uncompromising. Locke writes:

> Faith is nothing but a firm assent of the mind: which if it be regulated, as is our duty, cannot be afforded to anything, but upon good reason; and so cannot be opposite to it. He that believes, without having any reason for believing, may be in love with his own fancies; but neither seeks truth as he ought, nor pays the obedience due his maker, who would have him use those discerning faculties he has given him, to keep him out of mistake and error. He that does not this to the best of his power, however he sometimes lights on the truth, is in the right but by chance; and I know not whether the luckiness of the accident will excuse the irregularity of his proceeding. This at least is certain, that he must be accountable for

---

[30] Michael Ayers, *Locke*, vol. 2 (London: Routledge, 1991), 182.

[31] W. Abraham, *Canon and Criterion in Christian Theology* (Oxford: Clarendon, 1998), 227. In Locke's time, churches were becoming voluntary organizations, much as they are today in liberal democracies. See Locke's *First Letter of Toleration*. Also see William Babcok, "A Changing of the Christian God: The Doctrine of the Trinity in the Seventeenth Century," *Interpretation* 45 (1991), and John Redwood, *Reason, Ridicule and Religion* (London: Thames and Hudson, 1970), chap. 7. As for Locke's overall influence, Wolterstorff sees Locke's normative epistemology as culturally more significant than Descartes' work. "Descartes' project is much more the continuation of the medieval project of scientia than the anticipation of Locke's proposal for governing the understanding" (*John Locke and the Ethics of Belief*, 181). Wolterstorff believes that book 4 of Locke's essay is the "center of gravity" for the work.

whatever mistakes he runs into: whereas he that makes use of the light and faculties God has given him, and seeks sincerely to discover truth, by those helps and abilities he has, may have this satisfaction in doing his duty as a rational creature, that though he should miss truth, he will not miss the reward of it. For he governs his assent right, and places it as he should, who in any case or matter whatsoever, believes or disbelieves, according as reason directs him. He that does otherwise, transgresses against his own light, and misuses those faculties, which were given him to no other end, but to search and follow the clearer evidence, and greater probability.[32]

The moral framework of Locke's proposal is fueled, in part, by his acquaintance with the way ungrounded beliefs may lead to shameful, dishonorable political tyranny and religious persecution.[33] For Locke, an irrational faith would be flawed or imperfect as religious faith; proper, mature faith, by contrast, is informed by reason. The relationship between "Faith and Reason" for Locke was not, at best, opposing elements.

While Locke shared with Cambridge Platonists and Descartes a dualism of mind and body, he nonetheless left the door open as to whether our fundamental nature is physical or nonphysical.

We have the ideas of *matter* and *thinking*, but possibly shall never be able to know whether any mere material being thinks or no: it being impossible for us, by the contemplation of our own *ideas*, without revelation, to discover whether Omnipotency has not given to some system of matter, fitly disposed, a power to perceive and think, or else joined and fixed to matter, so disposed, a thinking immaterial substance: it being, in respect of our notions, not much more remote from our comprehension to conceive that God can, if he pleases, superadd to matter a faculty of thinking, than that he should superadd to it another substance with a faculty of thinking; since we know not wherein thinking consists, nor to what sort of substances the Almighty has been pleased to give that power, which cannot be in any created being, but merely by the good pleasure and bounty of the Creator.[34]

Locke's invitation to a materialist account of human nature puts him in the midst of the same religiously controversial waters as Hobbes. If we

---

[32] *Essay*, 4.17.24, 413–414.

[33] I follow Wolterstorff in seeing Locke as a socially and politically engaged thinker. See the preface to *John Locke and the Ethics of Belief*.

[34] *Essay*, 4.3.6.

are composed entirely of matter, and death involves the destruction of our bodies, how can we be united with God in life after death?

There were several options open to Locke. He appears to have accepted the thesis that we are or contain an immaterial soul that survives the destruction of the body. In the seventeenth century another tradition, sometimes called mortalism, became prominent. On this account, human persons are their material bodies, they perish at death and are re-created at the resurrection. This fit well with then current interpretations of Christian Scripture and creed.[35]

Locke's openness to a materialist account of human beings involves an appeal to God's power that is quite different from Descartes' use of theism in his case for dualism. Descartes argued for dualism on the grounds that God could create and sustain Descartes in existence and not his body (or any material body). Locke argues instead that we should not rule out or restrict our conception of God's power; for all we know, God can make matter think. Locke's appeal to God's freedom here displays a feature of early modern scientific philosophy – namely, that to discover the nature of the world involves empirical inquiry. One cannot rely on conceptual analysis or the study of ideas alone in order to discover how God created and structured the cosmos.

Locke is especially well known for his *Letter Concerning Toleration* and then *An Essay Concerning Toleration*, which argue for the liberties

---

[35] For a recent exchange on Locke's neutral position on whether matter can think, see Clifford Williams "Christian Materialism and the Parity Thesis," *Religious Studies* 39 (February 1996), defending Christian materialism, and for a reply, see J. P. Moreland's "Locke's Parity Thesis about Thinking Matter," *Religious Studies* 34 (1998); see also his paper on topic neutrality in *Religious Studies* 37 (2001). For an important historical work, see John Yolton's *Thinking Matter: Materialism in Eighteenth-Century Britain* (Minneapolis: University of Minnesota Press, 1983). For those interested in tracing this debate today, the following literature is a good start. On the materialist side, see Lynne Baker's "Need a Christian Be a Mind/Body Dualist," *Faith and Philosophy* 12 (1995); Trenton Merrick's "The Resurrection of the Body and Life Everlasting," in *Reason for the Hope Within,* ed. M. Murray (Grand Rapids: Eerdmans, 1999); Peter van Inwagen's *Material Beings* (Ithaca: Cornell Univeristy Press, 1990). Each argues for the compatibility of a materialist view of human persons and belief in an afterlife, an incorporeal God, and other Christian convictions. On the dualist side, see John Cooper, *Body, Soul, and Life Everlasting* (Grand Rapids: Eerdmans, 1989); J. P. Moreland and Scott Rea, *Body and Soul* (Downers Grove, Ill.: InterVarsity Press, 2000); William Hasker, *The Emergent Self* (Ithaca: Cornell University Press, 1999); John Foster, *The Immaterial Self* (London: Routledge, 1991); Richard Swinburne, *The Evolution of the Soul* (Oxford: Oxford University Press, 1997).

of dissent in civil society. Locke objected to religious persecution on several grounds. Religious beliefs cannot by their nature be enforced.

> The care of Souls cannot belong to the Civil Magistrate, because his Power consists only in outward force; but true and saving Religion consists in the inward perswasion of the Mind, without which nothing can be acceptable to God. And such is the nature of the Understanding, that it cannot be compell'd to the belief of any thing by outward force. Confiscation of Estate, Imprisonment, Torments, nothing of that nature can have any such Efficacy as to make Men change the inward Judgment that they have framed of things.[36]

State-sponsored religious formation also leaves citizens subject to caprice, which threatens their salvation.

> The care of the Salvation of Mens Souls cannot belong to the Magistrate; because, though the rigour of Laws and the force of Penalties were capable to convince and change Mens minds, yet would not that help at all to the Salvation of their Souls. For there being but one Truth, one way to Heaven; what Hopes is there that more Men would be led into it, if they had no Rule but the Religion of the Court, and were put under a necessity to quit the Light of their own Reason, and oppose the Dictates of their own Consciences, and blindly to resign up themselves to the Will of their Governors, and to the Religion, which either Ignorance, Ambition, or Superstition had chanced to establish in the Countries where they were born? In the variety and contradiction of Opinions in Religion, wherein the Princes of the World are as much divided as in their Secular Interests, the narrow way would be much straitned; one Country alone would be in the right, and all the rest of the World put under an obligation of following their Princes in the ways that lead to Destruction; and that which heightens the absurdity, and very ill suits the Notion of a Deity, Men would owe their eternal Happiness or Misery to the places of their Nativity.

In short, Locke saw that the end or goal of religious life (salvation, love of God, redemption) could not be met with threats of force that men and women would, by nature, hate and fear.

Locke tolerates Jews and Muslims, but not Roman Catholics. Chiefly this is because he contends that Roman Catholics have sworn allegiance to a foreign prince. He also does not think atheists should hold public office. This is because of their presumed disbelief in God as an

---

[36] *A Letter Concerning Toleration*, ed. J. H. Tully (Bloomington: Hackett, 1983), 27.

all-powerful, just sovereign force who will expose all wrongdoing and bring about rectitude in the next life. To put matters succinctly: you can't trust the oath of an atheist for he or she has no reason to think he or she will be punished by certain judgment. In *The Reasonableness of Christianity*, Locke wrote of the need for belief in the afterlife for proper moral motivation.

> The philosophers, indeed, shewed the beauty of virtue: they set her off so as drew men's eyes and approbation to her; but leaving her unendowed, very few were willing to espouse her....But now there being put into the scales, on her side, "an exceeding and immortal weight of glory," interest is come about to her; and virtue now is visibly the most enriching purchase, and by much the best bargain....The view of heaven and hell will cast a slight upon the short pleasures and pains of this present state, and give attractions and encouragements to virtue, which reason and interest, and the care of ourselves, cannot but allow and prefer. Upon this foundation, and upon this only, morality stands firm, and may defy all competition.[37]

This was not an anomalous conviction in Locke's time but widely assumed. Hobbes held this stance, and it was not until Mill (to be discussed in Chapter 6) made his case for tolerance in the nineteenth century that it was challenged in a sustained fashion.[38]

Locke shared with Hobbes a social contract account of human political life and a moral psychology that is based on the desire for pleasure and revulsion to pain. Locke's account of property had strong religious implications. Like Hobbes and a vast number of theists historically (spanning Jewish, Christian, and Islamic sources), Locke also held that the creation belongs to God. But unlike some theologians who used divine sovereignty to confer absolute sovereignty to political rulers, Locke argued that each person is given ownership of themselves and their bodies by God. There is a strong theistic strand running through Locke's understanding of the propriety and limits of self-governance:

> The *State of Nature* has a Law of Nature to govern it, which obliges every one: And Reason, which is that Law, teaches all Mankind, who will but

---

[37] *The Reasonableness of Christianity*, ed. I. T. Ramsey (Stanford: Stanford University Press, 1958), 70.
[38] Even the anti-clerical Voltaire insisted on the important utility of the belief in divine rectitude.

consult it, that being all equal and independent, no one ought to harm another in his Life, Health, Liberty, or Possessions. For Men being all the Workmanship of one Omnipotent, and infinitely wise Maker: All the Servants of one Sovereign Master, sent into the World by his order and about his business, they are his Property, whose Workmanship they are, made to last during his, not one anothers, Pleasure. And being furnished with like Faculties, sharing all in one Community of Nature, there cannot be supposed any such *Subordination* among us, that may Authorize us to destroy one another, as if we were made for one anothers uses, as the inferior ranks of Creatures are for ours. Every one as he is *bound to preserve himself,* and not to quit his Station wilfully; so by the like reason when his own Preservation comes not in competition, ought he, as much as he can. *To preserve the rest of Mankind,* and may not unless it be to do Justice on an Offender, take away, or impair the life, or what tends to the Preservation of the Life, Liberty, Health, Limb or Goods of another.[39]

While some historians play down the role of Locke's religious beliefs in his political theory, there are notable exceptions. John Dunn writes: "Jesus Christ (and Saint Paul) may not appear in person in the text of the *Two Treatises* but their presence can hardly be missed when we come upon the normative creaturely equality of all men in virtue of their shared species membership."[40] Recently it has been argued by Jeremy Waldron that such a religious background may be crucial to a contemporary Lockean political theory. "I actually don't think it is clear that we – now – *can* shape and defend an adequate conception of basic human equality apart from some religious foundation."[41] Locke's theism is further testified to in his apologetic work, *On the Reasonableness of Christianity*. Locke's Christianity was not deistic, for he made a case for Jesus' messiahship based, in part, on the miraculous. Still, Locke treated

[39] *The Second Treatise of Government*, book II, chaps. 2, 6, as found in *Two Treatises of Government*, ed. P. Laslett (New York: New American Library, 1963), 311. For a contemporary defense of Locke's view of property, see Baruch Brody, "Morality and Religion Reconsidered," in *Readings in Philosophy of Religion*, ed. B. A. Brody (Englewood Cliffs, N.J.: Prentice-Hall, 1974), and C. Taliaferro, "God's Estate," *Journal of Religious Ethics* 20 (1992). For criticism, see Mark C. Murphy, *An Essay on Divine Authority* (Ithaca: Cornell University Press, 2002).

[40] John Dunn, *Political Thought by John Locke* (Cambridge: Cambridge University Press, 1969), 99.

[41] Jeremy Waldron, *God, Locke and Equality* (Cambridge: Cambridge University Press, 2003), 13.

belief in the *Trinity* and the teaching that Jesus is both God and man as not central to salvation.[42]

Locke has been taken to task in the late twentieth century on many grounds. His treatment of property has been blamed for promoting a possessive individualism and castigated for providing the underpinnings of European claims on property in the British colonies. Native American entitlements to land were challenged on the Lockean grounds that bona fide property was a reflection of invested labor. Some European Americans held that Native Americans did not put the land to industrious use and thus were not entitled to the land they inhabited as property.[43] Although Locke's philosophy has been put to ill use politically, his ethical values were articulated in terms of the universal pursuit of happiness and avoidance of misery.

1. Happiness and misery are the two great springs of humane actions and through the different ways we finde men so busy in the world they all aime at happynesse and desire to avoid misery as it appears to them in different places and shapes.

2. I doe not remember that I have heard of any nation of men who have not acknowledged that there has been right and wrong in mens actions as well as truth and falshood in their sayings. Some measures there have been every where owned though very different some rules and boundarys to mens actions by which they were judged to be good or bad, nor is there I thinke any people amongst whome there is noe distinction between virtue and vice. Some kinde of morality is to be found every where received I will not say perfect and exact but yet enough to let us know that the notion of it is more or lesse every where and that even where politique societys and magistrates are silent men yet are under some laws to which they owe obedience.[44]

Locke's political views helped bolster the American rebellion against the British monarch and parliament.

In summary, apart from Locke's contribution to religious ethics, his case for tolerance, and the religious significance of his view of mind and

---

[42] For a further work on Locke's philosophy of religion, I highly recommend W. M. Spellman, *John Locke* (London: Macmillan, 1997). For a specific study, see Spellman, *John Locke and the Problem of Depravity* (Oxford: Clarendon, 1988).

[43] See D. T. Goldberg, *Racist Culture* (Oxford: Blackwell, 1993).

[44] "Of Ethics in General," in the valuable collection, John Locke, *Writings on Religion*, ed. Victor Nuovo (Oxford: Clarendon, 2002), 9.

matter, Locke is preemimently someone who contended that evidence is an essential justificatory element in religious belief. This plea for evidential grounding seems based both on a recognition of an intellectual duty as well as an ethic that takes stock of the harm that can result from ungrounded beliefs. Although Locke's conclusions were not secular, his methodology lacked the prominence given to cultivating religious, affective virtues in the course of inquiry.[45]

The Mind of God in Anglo-American Idealism

Berkeley was born in Ireland, educated at Trinity College, University of Dublin, traveled through continental Europe, spent a year in Rhode Island in North America, and sought to establish a school in Bermuda. He was a bishop in the Anglican Church and wrote extensively in philosophy and theology.[46] It will be useful to begin by noting how Berkeley departed from Locke.

In the preceding section I omitted Locke's view of perception because it does not directly bear on his philosophy of religion. For Berkeley, however, perception is key to his thinking of God, so it is necessary here to begin with a brief description of Locke's philosophy of perception.

Locke was a proponent of the new science and accepted a form of atomism and mechanical explanation over against the "jungle" of Aristotelian final causes. He, like Galileo, held that material objects had two kinds of properties: primary and secondary qualities. Primary qualities (shape, mass, volume) resemble the qualities of the object, whereas secondary qualities (color, taste, visual appearance) do not resemble the qualities in the object. They are features attributable to objects, but by virtue of how they appear or affect human beings. There were several reasons for this demarcation, one of which is that the color, taste, and appearance of objects vary radically depending upon the person interacting

---

[45] If we use the terminology of Chapter 1, Locke's methodology was more extrinsic than intrinsic. In an intrinsic inquiry into the nature of God, for example, one would cultivate godliness or an affective openness to God – as found in the Cambridge Platonist works. In "Natural Reason and the Trinity: Some Lessons from the Cambridge Platonists," in *The Trinity: The Beginning of East-West Dialogue,* ed. Melville Stewart (Dordrecht: Reidel, forthcoming), I propose that it was Locke's more secular method that led him away from belief in the Trinity.

[46] For a life of Berkeley, see John Wild, *George Berkeley: A Study of His Life and Philosophy* (Cambridge, Mass.: Harvard University Press, 1936).

with them, but there is no such change for the primary qualities. Locke's view of material substances themselves is subject to dispute, but in this context we can take note of a plausible interpretation of Locke: a substance is a substratum supporting the primary and secondary qualities. In observing a material object, for example, a desk, one is seeing the properties of this substratum.

Consider now Berkeley's rejoinder. In *Of the Principles of Human Knowledge*, Berkeley adopts a view of knowledge that resembles Locke's.

> It is evident to any one who takes a survey of the *objects of human knowledge,* that they are either *ideas* actually imprinted on the senses; or else such as are perceived by attending to the passions and operations of the mind; or lastly, *ideas* formed by help of memory and imagination – either compounding, dividing, or barely representing those originally perceived in the aforesaid ways. By sight I have the ideas of light and colours, with their several degrees and variations. By touch I perceive hard and soft, heat and cold, motion and resistance; and of all these more and less either as to quantity or degree. Smelling furnishes me with odours; the palate with tastes; and hearing conveys sounds to the mind in all their variety of tone and composition.[47]

In addition to these sensible ideas Berkeley affirms the existence of the self.

> That neither our thoughts, nor passions, nor ideas formed by the imagination, exist without the mind is what everybody will allow. And to me it seems no less evident that the various sensations or ideas imprinted on the Sense, however blended or combined together (that is, whatever objects they compose), cannot exist otherwise than in a mind perceiving them. I think an intuitive knowledge may be obtained of this, by any one that shall attend to what is meant by the term *exist* when applied to sensible things.[48]

But beyond the self and sensible ideas, Berkeley hesitates.

> The table I write on I say exists; that is, I see and feel it: and if I were out of my study I should say it existed; meaning thereby that if I was in my study I might perceive it, or that some other spirit actually does perceive it. There was an odour, that is, it was smelt; there was a sound, that is, it was heard; a colour or figure, and it was perceived by

---

[47] *Berkeley's Complete Works,* ed. A. C. Fraser (Oxford: Clarendon, 1901), 1:257.
[48] Ibid., 259.

sight and touch. This is all that I can understand by these and the like expressions. For as to what is said of the *absolute* existence of unthinking things, without any relation to their being perceived, that is to me perfectly unintelligible. Their *esse* is *percepi*; nor is it possible they should have any existence out of the minds or thinking things which perceive them.[49]

Berkeley countered that Locke's fundamental distinction between primary and secondary qualities was ungrounded. The very same reasons given for claiming that the so-called secondary qualities are mind-dependent may be offered in arguing that primary qualities are mind-dependent. The relativity of perception appears to afflict primary qualities. There is the further challenge of being able to conceive of something not already implicating a mind. The full title of one of Berkeley's elegant and most important works is *Three Dialogues Between Hylas and Philonous The Design of which is plainly to Demonstrate the reality and perfection of Human Knowledge, the Incorporeal Nature of the Soul and the Immediate Providence of a Deity in Opposition to Sceptics and Atheists; Also to open a Method for Rendering the Sciences more easy, useful, and compendious.* Philonous (literally, the love of mind) embodies Berkeley's position, whereas Hylas (derived from Greek for matter) represents a Lockean position.

Philonous works with a highly restricted view of what is perceivable, arguing that we have no perceptual acquaintance with Lockean material substances.

I say it is nothing to the purpose. Our discourse proceeded altogether concerning sensible things, which you defined to be, *the things we immediately perceive by our senses.* Whatever other qualities, therefore, you speak of, as distinct from these, I know nothing of them, neither do they at all belong to the point in dispute. You may, indeed, pretend to have discovered certain qualities which you do not perceive, and assert those insensible qualities exist in fire and sugar. But what use can be made of this to your present purpose, I am at a loss to conceive. Tell me then once more, do you acknowledge that heat and cold, sweetness and bitterness (meaning those qualities which are perceived by the senses), do not exist without the mind?[50]

[49] Ibid.
[50] Ibid., 389–390.

Philonous argues that the Lockean concept of matter is either conceptually empty or confused. Berkeley avoids skepticism as he argues that there is a Divine Mind in which all qualities reside.

> I deny that I agreed with you in those notions that led to Scepticism. You indeed said the *reality* of sensible things consisted in an *absolute existence out of the minds of spirits,* or distinct from their being perceived. And pursuant to this notion of reality, *you* are obliged to deny sensible things any real existence: that is, according to your own definition, you profess yourself a sceptic. But I neither said nor thought the reality of sensible things was to be defined after that manner. To me it is evident, for the reasons you allow of, that sensible things cannot exist otherwise than in a mind or spirit. Whence I conclude, not that they have no real existence, but that, seeing they depend not on my thought, and I have an existence distinct from being perceived by me, *there must be some other Mind wherein they exist.* As sure, therefore, as the sensible world really exists, so sure is there an infinite omnipresent Spirit who contains and supports it.[51]

Berkeley argues that he goes one better than Locke, Hobbes, et al. who acknowledge God as seeing the cosmos but do not see this divine perception as explanatory.

> But neither do we agree in the same opinion. For philosophers, though they acknowledge all corporeal beings to be perceived by God, yet they attribute to them an absolute subsistence distinct from their being perceived by any mind whatever; which I do not. Besides, is there no difference between saying, *There is a God, therefore He perceives all things;* and saying, *Sensible things do really exist; and, if they really exist, they are necessarily perceived by an infinite Mind: therefore there is an infinite Mind, or God?* This furnishes you with a direct and immediate demonstration, from a most evident principle, of the *being of a God.* Divines and philosophers had proved beyond all controversy, from the beauty and usefulness of the several parts of the creation, that it was the workmanship of God. But that – setting aside all help of astronomy and natural philosophy, all contemplation of the contrivance, order, and adjustment of things – an infinite Mind should be necessarily inferred from the bare *existence of the sensible world,* is an advantage to them only who have made this easy reflection: That the sensible world is that which we perceive by our several senses; and that nothing is perceived by the senses beside ideas; and that no idea or archetype of an idea can exist otherwise than in a mind. You may now, without any laborious search into the sciences, without

---

[51] Ibid., 424.

any subtlety of reason, or tedious length of discourse, oppose and baffle the most strenuous advocate for Atheism.[52]

Jonathan Edwards (1703–1758) held a similar, Berkeleyan account of the relationship between God and creation.

Edwards dedicated most of his life to being a pastor in Northampton, Massachusetts, and a missionary to Native Americans. He became president of the College of New Jersey (now named Princeton) in the final weeks of his life. He is perhaps best know in early American literature for his extraordinary sermon, "Sinners in the Hands of an Angry God" (1741), a classic text during the religious revival in the British American colonies called the Great Awakening. It is regrettable that this sermon is the most widely published of his work, for it can overshadow the subtlety and sophistication of his philosophy and his meditations on God, community, virtue, and beauty.[53] Edwards undertook some scientific projects (on insects, light, and in what today would be called psychology). Philosophically he is noted for his case against free agency of the kind described in Chapter 1. Cudworth's concept of human freedom takes away from the sovereignty of God. In ethics, Edwards's account of virtue is similar to Henry More's. He studied both More and Locke closely, and when it came to God's relation to the world, he sided with Berkeley.

> When we say that the world, i.e., the material universe, exists nowhere but in the mind, we have got to such a degree of strictness and abstraction that we must be exceedingly careful that we do not confound and lose ourselves by misapprehension. That is impossible, that it should be meant that all the world is contained in the narrow compass of a few inches of space, in little ideas in the place of the brain; for that would be a contradiction. For we are to remember that the human body and the brain itself exist only mentally, in the same sense that other things do. And so that which we call place is an idea too. Therefore things are truly in those places, for what we mean when we say so is only that this mode of our idea of place appertains to such an idea. We would not, therefore, be understood to deny that things are where they seem to be, for the principles we lay down, if they are narrowly looked into, do not infer that. Nor will it be found that they at all make void natural philosophy, or the science of the causes

---

[52] Ibid., 425.

[53] In *America's God* (Oxford: Oxford University Press, 2002), Mark Noll ably summarizes Edwards's more positive orientation as a thinker: "The unifying center of Edwards' theology was the glory of God depicted as an active, harmonious, ever-unfolding source of absolutely perfect Being marked by supernal beauty and love" (23).

or reasons of corporeal changes; for to find out the reasons of things in natural philosophy is only to find out the proportion of God's acting. And the case is the same, as to such proportions, whether we suppose the world only mental in our sense, or no.[54]

Edwards's world of nature is shot through with beauty. Indeed, Edwards was at home with the preeminence of beauty in the Christian Platonic view of God. The beauty of the natural world and of Scripture were taken by Edwards as evidence of God.

Edwards, more so than Locke and Berkeley, advocated a model of inquiry that was not secular; moral and religious values were of preeminent importance and were to be revered in the practice of philosophy. In a fascinating reconstruction of Edwards's work, William Wainwright offers this portrait:

> Two features of Edwards's position are especially significant. First, the epistemic virtues are not merely negative; they involve more than the exclusion of the passions and selfish partialities that subvert reason. Nor are the epistemic virtues confined to noncontroversial excellences such as the love of truth. They include properly ordered natural affections such as gratitude and a love of being in general that God infuses into the hearts of His elect. These affections not only cast out others that adversely affect reasoning; they also affect it themselves. Under their influence, we reason differently and more accurately.[55]

Edwards upholds the vital importance of sufficient evidence for religious belief. (He may be described as both an evidentialist and a foundationalist.) But Edwards thinks that seeing the evidence requires repudiation of self-interest and the cultivation of benevolence.

A few observations on idealist philosophy of religion: As we have seen, starting in Chapter 1, modern mechanistic science seemed to jeopardize the independence and freedom of the human mind. It raised the specter that the mind was explainable as the outcome of deterministic bodily forces. It also seemed to place the divine mind at some distance from the world causally (God as creator of a machine world that functions on its own) and cognitively (God must be inferred). For Berkeley-Edwards idealists, God was also inferred and yet

---

[54] Jonathan Edwards, *Scientific and Philosophical Writings*, ed. W. E. Anderson (New Haven: Yale University Press, 1980), 353. The passage quoted is from Edwards's work "The Mind" in which he cites favorably Cudworth's *Intellectual System*. See the introduction by Anderson for a helpful overview.

[55] *Reason and the Heart: A Prolegomenon to a Critique of Passional Reason* (Ithaca: Cornell University Press, 1995), 51.

the whole of nature was seen as constituted by God, God's activity, and created minds. The idealists sought to shift the burden of proof onto those who give the mind (whether divine or human) only secondary, marginal status. Berkeley's theistic idealism has defenders today (Howard Robinson, John Foster).[56] Even those who are not theists have had recourse to Berkeley's notion that our language about material objects may be analyzed in terms of sense experience (R. Firth, C. I. Lewis, A. J. Ayer).

Perhaps his more enduring challenge in philosophy at large – and not only his philosophical reflection on religious beliefs – is the insistence upon the primacy of the mental (whether this be phrased in terms of sensory experience, concepts, the understanding, or consciousness). In late twentieth-century philosophy of mind, a position emerged that sought to eliminate the mental from a theory of what exists – a stance that has appropriately been called "eliminativism." Paul and Patricia Churchland, Willard Van Orman Quine, D. Dennett, S. Stitch, and others have, to varying degrees, sought to eliminate beliefs and other mental states from their final account of reality. The Berkeleyan reminds us of how difficult it is to remove the mental, for however sophisticated our science, it seems that science and its theories will involve mental items like concepts, beliefs, knowledge.[57] More on the clash between idealism and materialism in the philosophy of religion in Chapter 6.[58]

Before turning to Leibniz, Spinoza, and Butler, some observations on philosophy of religion in North America are fitting.

Early American Philosophy of Religion

Philosophical work, even including acquaintance with indigenous American religions, was itself primitive, at best, in early modern

---

[56] See, for example, John Foster, *The Case for Idealism* (London: Routledge and Kegan Paul, 1982).

[57] See Hasker, *The Emergent Self*. Securing a stable philosophical role for mental life is important for religious traditions that assume the existence of beliefs, desires, sensations, thinking, meditation, and so on.

[58] For a recent, helpful study, see George Pappas, *Berkeley's Thought* (Ithaca: Cornell University, 2000). Berkeley is not always recognized in today's canon of philosophy of religion literature, but he is taken seriously by J. L. Mackie and others. Berkeley's future may lie, to some extent, in cross-cultural philosophy of religion. See Jay Garfield, "Western Idealism through Indian Eyes: A Cittamatra Reading of Berkeley, Kant and Schopenhauer," *Sophia* 37:1 (1998).

philosophy in North America. Native cultures were brutally assaulted by European powers shortly after Columbus crossed the Atlantic in 1492. The utter annihilation of many of the people of the Caribbean by the Spanish in the sixteenth century led to the conquest of the Aztecs, Incas, Mayas, and so on. Regrettably, the outcry against Spanish, Portuguese, and then other European powers was only gradual among the philosophers studied here.[59] John Locke famously (and I think inconsistently) thought slavery was permissible. Berkeley's trip to the New World was motivated by the project of converting Native Americans. Only recently have philosophers of religion taken seriously the contributions of Native American religions.[60]

In the British colonies, two of the most widely read authorities were Locke and Newton. The Cambridge Platonists achieved a foothold through the writings of Henry More and the training of many Cambridge men who migrated to the colonies, where they developed a Platonic Puritanism.[61] H. G. Gates offers this overview: "A kind of naive Platonism was the common possession of colonial settlers."[62] The Cambridge Platonists have been credited with establishing a foundation for recognizing the basic goodness of native peoples in the highly authorative history, *The Problem of Slavery in Western Culture*. David Brion Davis writes:

> For beneath a superficial diversity of cultures one might find a universal capacity for happiness and contentment, so long as man's natural faculties had not been perverted by error and artificial desire. We must look to primitive man, said Benjamin Whichcote, if we would seek man's moral sense in its pristine state. Natural law, said Nathaniel Culverwel, is truly recognized and practiced only by men who have escaped the corruptions of civilization. If traditionalists objected that savages were ignorant of the Gospel, the answer was that heathen might carry within them the true

---

[59] See D. Eltis, *The Rise of African Slavery in the Americas* (Cambridge: Cambridge University Press, 2000).

[60] A refreshing contribution is the philosopher of religion Jerry Gill, *Native American Worldviews* (New York: Humanity Books, 2002).

[61] A classic history, well worth consulting is Perry Miller, *The New England Mind* (Cambridge, Mass.: Harvard University Press, 1939).

[62] *Philosophical Ideas in the United States* (New York: American Book, 1934), 91. For a good overview of the American intellectual climate, see Noll, *America's God*. Noll rightly underscores the extensive influence of the Scottish Enlightenment with Thomas Ried et al.

spirit of Christ, and hence be better Christians than hypocrites who knew and professed all the articles of faith.[63]

Much early colonial theology emphasized God as a provident director of history. At its best (in John Winthrop's famous sermon in 1630, "A Model of Christian Charity") there was an ethic of "brotherly affection."[64]

In the previous section of this chapter I emphasize an Anglo-American idealism. But materialism, or accounts of the cosmos that border on materialism, were also present. The philosophy of God and the philosophy of nature were profoundly interwoven.

In *The Principles of Action in Matter*, Cadwallader Colden (1688–1776) prepared the way for a more positive conception of matter than Locke or Newton allowed (and certainly more than Descartes and Malebranche). Working from within a Newtonian framework, and in sympathy with Hobbes, Colden developed a conception of matter sufficiently powerful so that it might, *in theory*, account for much more than Newton and Locke had supposed. Colden construed matter in positive, potent terms; matter was not something that was identified principally in terms of geometry and resistance but as a causally active source that could provide a rich explanatory framework for describing and explaining the world. Although Colden stopped short of a thoroughgoing materialism, he did go quite far in that direction. He conceded the contingency of the present cosmos but was less sure about whether there was ever a time when there was no physical world.

Other materialist elements entered the American scene by way of Joseph Priestly (1733–1804). Much admired by Thomas Jefferson (1743–1826), Priestly earned his scientific and intellectual reputation by discovering oxygen and sought refuge in America to escape prosecution for his more radical antireligious polemics. Priestly identified the mind with the body and denied the existence of an afterlife. Thomas Cooper, Priestly's son-in-law, carried on the case for materialism in his *View of the Metaphysical and Physiological Arguments in Favor of Materialism*. He, too, denied the credibility of believing

---

[63] D. Davis, *The Problem of Slavery in Western Culture* (Ithaca: Cornell University Press, 1966), 351.

[64] I offer an overview of early theology and philosophy in this period in "Land, Labor, and God in American Colonial Thought," in *The Agrarian Roots of Pragmatism*, ed. P. B. Thompson and T. C. Hilde (Nashville: Vanderbilt University Press, 2000).

that there is an afterlife on the grounds that the mind and body are identical.

Benjamin Rush (1746–1813) sought out a material explanation of human character and moral decision making. In *Influence of Physical Causes upon the Moral Faculty*, Rush argued for the physical under-pinnings of the mind and the importance of empirical inquiry into the root causes of our moral activity. Joseph Buchanan (1785–1829) also sought to develop a scientific, material account of human thought and action in his *Philosophy of Human Nature*, a physical scientific account of human thought and action. Like Priestly, Cooper, and others drawn to a materialist view of human nature, he denied individual immortality.

The Christian Philosopher by Cotton Mather (1681–1724) is not a materialist document, but it displays early American mixing of theology and natural science (or, more accurately for Mather, an ecstatic celebra-tion of the natural world). One of my favorite lines: "Even the most *noxious* and most *abject* of the Vegetables, how useful they are!"[65]

While some of the philosophers cited here court a secular worldview, they retained a general theistic or deistic framework. It was not un-usual for early American philosophers to invoke a God's eye view of the cosmos. Alan Heimert and Andrew Delbanco summarize the Puritan outlook, and I suggest their depiction holds up for many non-Puritan Europeans settlers: "If the Catholic question had been 'what shall I do to be saved?' and the question of the Reformers became 'how shall I know if I am saved?' perhaps the American Puritans asked, more eventually, 'what am I in the eyes of God?'"[66]

Leibniz's Idealism: The Good and the Evident

Gottfried Wilhelm Leibniz (1646–1716) was a German philosopher of extraordinary breadth; he contributed to metaphysics, epistemology, ethics, physics, mathematics, political theory, history, and diplomacy. There was considerable debate in his lifetime over who discovered differential calculus: Newton or Leibniz. (There is reason to believe Newton was the first but Leibniz was the first to publish it.) In 1666 he was made a doctor of laws at Altdorf, Nuremberg. Religious con-cerns were at the center of Leibniz's work. Like Berkeley, he was not

---

[65] *The Christian Philosopher* (Urbana: University of Illinois Press, 1994), 137.
[66] A. Heimert and A. Delbanco, eds., *The Puritans in America* (Cambridge, Mass.: Harvard University Press, 1985), 15.

persuaded by Locke's (and others') attempt to distinguish primary and secondary qualities. He shared with Berkeley an idealist conception of reality.

His philosophy of God, like Cambridge Platonist theism, gives centrality to the good and perfection. His *Discourse on Metaphysics* begins: "The conception of God which is the most common and the most full of meaning is expressed well enough in the words: God is an absolutely perfect being."[67] He uses the divine attribute of perfection as part of his case for God's existence and many of his major tenets about nature.

Leibniz's ontological argument, like Anselm's, Descartes' and More's, moves fundamentally from two key premises: one that casts God's key attribute in terms of an excellence that involves necessary existence, and another premise that secures that this being is possible. By his lights, if one can establish the possibility of God, one may infer God is not impossible and is therefore necessary. Leibniz does not assume from the outset that God's existence is possible. He acknowledges that we may think we are conceiving of something that is possible but which turns out to be confused or conceptually faulty. "It must be, they say, that I have an idea of God, or of a perfect being, since I think of him and we cannot think without having ideas; now the idea of this being includes all perfections and since existence is one of these perfections, it follows that he exists. But I reply, inasmuch as we often think of impossible chimeras, for example of the highest degree of swiftness, of the greatest number, such reasoning is not sufficient."[68]

Leibniz argues for the possibility of divine existence on several grounds.[69] One argument for the possibility of God's existence involves an appeal to the cosmological argument. If one can secure the thesis that the existence of a contingent world would not be explainable without the action of a necessary being, then from the belief in the existence of our contingent world and the reasonability of believing this world is explainable, one may infer a necessary being. This way of supporting a belief in the possibility of God may seem beside the point. After all, if you have established the actual existence of God, inferring God's possibility is fairly unexciting. (Everything that is actual is possible.) But

---

[67] In *Leibniz: Discourse on Metaphysics; Correspondence with Arnauld and Monadology*, trans. G. R. Montgomery (LaSalle: Open Court, 1945).

[68] Ibid., 40.

[69] For an exposition of the arguments, see R. M. Adams, *Leibniz: Determinist, Theist, Idealist* (Oxford: Oxford University Press, 1994).

matters change if one were to appeal to a less than decisive cosmological argument. Imagine that the cosmological argument gives you *some* reason to believe there is a God. In that case, you have *some* reason to think God's existence is possible, and the ontological argument looks more interesting.[70] Consider an analogy in philosophy of mind. Imagine a debate over Descartes' case for dualism where the disputants disagree over whether a mind or person can exist without a body. Imagine that the Cartesian then presents a strong case from parapsychology and reports of out-of-the-body experiences to the conclusion that minds do persist after bodily death. Such an argument might fail to persuade the non-Cartesian that minds do persist, and yet the argument might move the interlocutor closer to the conclusion that it is at least possible for there to be disembodied minds.[71]

Leibniz was not as strident as Locke in pressing for each individual's governance of belief with respect to evidence. In *New Essays on Human Understanding* he addresses Locke on faith.

> If you take faith to be only what rests on *rational grounds for belief*, and separate it from the inward grace which immediately endows the mind with faith, everything you say, sir, is beyond dispute. For it must be acknowledged that many judgments are more evident than the ones which depend on these rational grounds. Some people have advanced further towards the latter than others have; and indeed plenty of people, far from having weighed up such reasons, have never known them and consequently do not even have what could count as *grounds for probability*. But the inward grace of the Holy Spirit makes up for this immediately and supernaturally, and it is this that creates what theologians strictly call "divine faith." God, it is true, never bestows this faith unless what he is making one believe is grounded in reason – otherwise he would subvert our capacity to recognize truth, and open the door to enthusiasm – but it is not necessary that all who possess this divine faith should know those reasons, and still less that they should have them perpetually before their eyes. Otherwise none of the unsophisticated or of the feeble-minded – now at least – would have the true faith, and the most enlightened people might not have it when they most needed it, since no one can always remember his reasons for believing.[72]

---

[70] Clement Dore, "Examination of an Ontological Argument," *Philosophical Studies* 28 (1975).

[71] See Chapter 1, n27.

[72] P. Remnant and J. Bennett, eds., *New Essays on Human Understanding* (Cambridge: Cambridge University Press, 1981), 497.

Leibniz thereby offers a mediating position on faith and reason. Faith is still treated along evidentialist lines (it is good for religious beliefs to be evidentially justified), but it is relaxed insofar as not everyone who has religious faith has a duty to grasp the reasons for faith.

Leibniz held that nature is a composite of discrete objects without parts, called monads. We ourselves are fundamentally noncomposite simple substances who are subject to the immediate agency of God.

> In the strictly metaphysical sense no external cause acts upon us excepting God alone, and he is in immediate relation with us only by virtue of our continual dependence upon him. Whence it follows that there is absolutely no other external object which comes into contact with our souls and directly excites perceptions in us. We have in our souls ideas of everything, only because of the continual action of God upon us, that is to say, because every effect expresses its cause and therefore the essences of our souls are certain expressions, imitations or images of the divine essence, divine thought and divine will, including all the ideas which are there contained. We may say, therefore, that God is for us the only immediate external object, and that we see things through him. For example, when we see the sun or the stars, it is God who gives to us and preserves in us the ideas and whenever our senses are affected according to his own laws in a certain manner, it is he, who by his continual concurrence, determines our thinking. God is the sun and the light of souls.[73]

Leibniz holds that the cosmos is suffused with divine power and divine agency. Each fundamental component of the cosmos, each monad, is designed to harmonize with other monads in a rational order. In this work as with Berkeley, Locke, and so may early modern philosophers, we see Leibniz's philosophy of nature as an integral part of his philosophy of God and religion.

A published exchange of letters between Leibniz and Samuel Clarke (1675–1729) over eleven years (1705–1716) is a rich resource of debate over God's relation to the world. The correspondence also contains illuminating work on Newton's view of space, gravity, vacuums in nature, the miraculous, and the principle of sufficient reason. I highlight two areas of contention: God's awareness of the world, and the view of God as a designer. This exchange further documents the way in which philosophers of religion sought to articulate God's relation to the world. I simply reproduce part of the exchange here with modest observations

---

[73] Ibid., 47.

rather than throw my lot in with either camp. My goal here is primarily to display the way in which the philosophy of God was debated.

God's Awareness of the World

In *The Opticks* (end of Query 28), Newton assimilated space to God's sensorium;

> Does it not appear from phenomena that there is a Being incorporeal, living, intelligent, omnipresent, who in infinite space, as it were in his sensory, sees the things themselves intimately, and thoroughly perceives them, and comprehends them wholly by their immediate presence to himself: of which things the images only carried through the organs of sense into our little sensoriums, are there seen and beheld by that which in us perceives and thinks. And tho' every step made in this philosophy brings us not immediately to the knowledge of the first cause, yet it brings us nearer to it, and on that account is to be highly valued.[74]

"Our little sensoriums" are the effective epicenters of our sensation: they are the machination that collects the data of the sensory organs and allows us to interpret the data as we do. God's sensorium works on a separate level from ours in that his sensorium senses the things themselves whereas ours only sense the images. Leibniz objected that making space essential to God's omniscience removed creation's dependence on God. In Newton's defense, Clarke writes:

> Sir Isaac Newton doth not say, that space is the organ which God makes use of to perceive things by; nor that he has need of any medium at all, whereby to perceive things: but on the contrary, that he, being omnipresent, perceives all things by his immediate presence to them, in all space whereever they are, without the intervention or assistance of any organ or medium whatsoever. In order to make this more intelligible, he illustrates it by a similitude: that as the mind of man, by its immediate presence to the pictures or images of things, form'd in the brain by the means of the organs of sensation, sees those pictures as if they were the things themselves; so God sees all things, by his immediate presence to them; he being actually present to the things themselves, to all things in the universe; as the mind of man is present to all the pictures of things formed in his brain. Sir Issac Newton considers the brain and

---

[74] Newton in *The Leibniz-Clarke Correspondence Together with Extracts from Newton's Principia and Opticks*, ed. H. G. Alexander (New York: Philosophy Library, 1956), 174.

organs of sensation, as the means by which those pictures are formed: but not as the means by which the mind sees or perceives those pictures, when they are so formed. And in the universe, he doth not consider things as if they were pictures, formed by certain means, or organs; but as real things, form'd by God himself, and seen by him in all places wherever they are, without the intervention of any medium at all. And this similitude is all that he means, when he supposes infinite space to be (as it were) the *sensorium* of the Omnipresent Being.[75]

There are at least three points to notice in this exchange. First, both philosophers are committed to viewing the divine attributes in a coherent fashion. Second, Newton and Clark appeal to an analogy from human nature to help fill out our grasp of the divine attribute of omniscience. So, divine seeing is elucidated with respect to our seeing. But, third, Newton, Clark, and Leibniz were firmly opposed to an anthropomorphic view of God. God's perfection and transcendent excellence needed to be secure. In this fashion, each philosopher could appeal to human analogies in their case for a coherent theism, but such appeal needed to be limited, lest one diminish God's transcendence.

God as Creator

Leibniz thought Newton's God had to intervene continually with the cosmos to keep it in order. Newton's God had to prevent the stars from collapsing, and the solar system needed adjusting (see Opticks, Query 28 and 31). Leibniz holds that this is an unworthy, imperfect philosophy of God.

> Sir Isaac Newton, and his followers, have also a very odd opinion concerning the work of God. According to their doctrine, God Almighty wants to wind up his watch from time to time: otherwise it would cease to move. He had not, it seems, sufficient foresight to make it a perpetual motion. Nay, the machine of God's making, is so imperfect, according to these gentlemen that he is obliged to clean it now and then by an extraordinary concourse, and even to mend it, as a clockmaker mends his work; who must consequently be so much the more unskillful a workman, as he is oftener obliged to mend his work and to set it right. According to my opinion, the same force and vigour remains always in the world, and only passes from one part of matter to another, agreeably to the laws of nature, and the beautiful pre-established order. And I hold, that when

---

[75] Ibid., 12–13.

God works miracles, he does not do it in order to supply the wants of nature, but those of grace. Whoever thinks otherwise, must needs have a very mean notion of the wisdom and power of God.[76]

Again, one can see here the commitment to coherence, the use of analogy, and a resistance to anthropomorphism. Clarke replies:

The word *correction*, or *amendment*, is to be understood, not with regard to God, but to us only. The present frame of the solar system (for instance), according to the present laws of motion, will in time fall into confusion; and perhaps, after that, will be amended or put into a new form. But this amendment is only relative, with regard to our conceptions. In reality, and with regard to God; the present frame, and the consequent disorder, and the following renovation, are all equally parts of the design framed in God's original perfect idea. 'Tis in the frame of the world, as in the frame of man's body: the wisdom of God does not consist, in making the present frame of either of them eternal, but to last so long as he thought fit.

The wisdom and foresight of God, do not consist in providing originally remedies, which shall of themselves cure the disorders of nature. For in truth and strictness, with regard to God, there are no disorders, and consequently no remedies, and indeed no powers of nature at all, that can do any thing of themselves, (as weights and springs work of themselves with regard to men); but the wisdom and foresight of God, consist (as has been said) in contriving at once, what his power and government is continually putting in actual execution.[77]

Clarke's reply construes God's "corrections" as not genuine shifts or unanticipated divine maneuvers. The anthropomorphic view of God as a bad clockmaker is resisted on the grounds that a created cosmos is the creation of something which does not itself have divine perfection and invulnerability to decay.[78]

Leibniz's most famous work in philosophy of religion is probably *Theodicy* in which Leibniz confronts the problem of evil. If there is an all-good, all-knowing, all-powerful God, why is there evil? Several

---

[76] Ibid., 11–12.

[77] Ibid., 22–23. For an analysis of this exchange, see Ezio Vailati, *Leibniz and Clarke* (Oxford: Oxford University Press, 1997). For Leibniz's other correspondence, see especially his letters with Arnauld on freedom and omniscience.

[78] For early modern debate over the decay of nature, see Victory Harris, *All Coherence Gone* (Chicago: University of Chicago Press, 1949). See also John Donne's poem "An Anatomie of the World."

features of that work are important to consider. First, it locates the problem of evil as part of an overall theistic philosophy, which includes positive arguments for the existence of God. I cite a compact passage of *Theodicy* at length.

> *God is the first reason of things:* for such things as are bounded, as all that which we see and experience, are contingent and have nothing in them to render their existence necessary, it being plain that time, space and matter, united and uniform in themselves and indifferent to everything, might have received entirely other motions and shapes, and in another order. Therefore one must seek the reason for the existence of the world, which is the whole assemblage of *contingent* things, and seek it in the substance which carries with it the reason for its existence, and which in consequence is *necessary* and eternal. Moreover, this cause must be intelligent: for this existing world being contingent and an infinity of other worlds being equally possible, and holding, so to say, equal claim to existence with it, the cause of the world must needs have had regard or reference to all these possible worlds in order to fix upon one of them. This regard or relation of an existent substance to simple possibilities can be nothing other than the *understanding* which has the ideas of them, while to fix upon one of them can be nothing other than the act of the *will* which chooses. It is the *power* of this substance that renders its will efficacious. Power relates to *being*, wisdom or understanding to *truth*, and will to *good*. And this intelligent cause ought to be infinite in all ways, and absolutely perfect in *power*, in *wisdom* and in *goodness*, since it relates to all that which is possible. Furthermore, since all is connected together, there is no ground for admitting more than *one*. Its understanding is the source of *essences*, and its will is the origin of *existences*. There in few words is the proof of one only God with his perfections, and through him of the origin of things.[79]

The problem of evil is thereby addressed in the context of cosmology. It is also addressed within a framework that attributes to God unsurpassable knowledge of all possibilities and a commitment to there being a sufficient reason for every feature of the world. Leibniz elsewhere formulates this principle: "Nothing happens without a reason why it

---

[79] *Theodicy*, 127. Robert Sleigh comments: "It may be said with only the mildest exaggeration that Leibniz never met a purported proof of the existence of God that he didn't like." See "Remarks on Leibniz's Treatment of the Problem of Evil," in *The Problem of God in Early Modern Philosophy*, ed. E. J. Kremer and M. J. Latzer (Toronto: University of Toronto Press, 2001), 167.

should be so, rather than otherwise."[80] By virtue of this demand for explanation, Leibniz believes a full account of the cosmos must transcend the cosmos. But it is also due to this demand that the gravity of the problem of evil is intensified. There must be a sufficient reason for the evils of the world. Leibniz contends that God has chosen, in creating, the best possible world. If there were no such world, there would have been no creation.

> Now, this supreme wisdom, united to a goodness that is no less infinite, cannot but have chosen the best. For as a lesser evil is a kind of good, even so a lesser good is a kind of evil if it stands in the way of a greater good; and there would be something to correct in the actions of God if it were possible to do better. As in mathematics, when there is no maximum nor minimum, in short nothing distinguished, everything is done equally, or when that is not possible nothing at all is done: so it may be said likewise in respect of perfect wisdom, which is no less orderly than mathematics, that if there were not the best (*optimum*) among all possible worlds, God would not have produced any. I call "World" the whole succession and the whole agglomeration of all existent things, lest it be said that several worlds could have existed in different times and different places. For they must needs be reckoned all together as one world or, if you will, as one Universe. And even though one should fill all times and all places, it still remains true that one might have filled them in innumerable ways, and that there is an infinitude of possible worlds among which God must needs have chosen the best, since he does nothing without acting in accordance with supreme reason.[81]

Another point to observe about Leibniz's theodicy is that he appeals to greater goods, according to which the evils that exist are allowed by God in order to create the best.

> It is true that one may imagine possible worlds without sin and without unhappiness, and one could make some like Utopian . . . romances: but these same worlds again would be very inferior to ours in goodness. I cannot show you this in detail. For can I know and can I present infinites to you and compare them together? But you must judge with me *ab effectu*, since God has chosen this world as it is. We know, moreover, that often an evil brings forth a good whereto one would not have attained without that evil. Often indeed two evils have made one great good.[82]

---

[80] Ibid., 2nd letter.
[81] Ibid., 128.
[82] Ibid., 129.

Leibniz's theodicy famously became the target of Votaire's satire *Candide* (1759) in which its hero, the gentle and honest Candide, encounters the horrors of war, homicide, massive earthquake, and so on. His tutor, Dr. Pangloss, a follower of Leibniz, instructs Candide that despite all such hardship "all is for the best in this best of all possible worlds."

A full-scale evaluation of Leibniz's theodicy is impossible in a book of this size, but a few further comments are in order. Contemporary philosophy of religion has challenged the coherence of a best possible world, charging that it is as absurd as the concept of a greatest number. Arguably, any world you imagine as great (a trillion happy people) may be surpassed (two trillion happy people). R. M. Adams has argued that God's grace allows for the creation of worlds like ours where we are less than perfect. Prior to this contemporary critique, Aquinas rejected the possibility of a best possible world. Still, Leibniz's view of God's perfection has defenders among both atheists, theists, and agnostics today. And if one does address the problem of evil over against Leibniz's concept of perfection and the best, one is taking on the problem of evil under the most stringent conditions. As such, a Leibnizian theodicy, if successful, would be a greater achievement than if one were to argue successfully that it is permissible for an all-good God to create and allow the continuation of our cosmos.[83]

Other general themes to appreciate in Leibniz's theodicy include his combination of resignation and determination: his peaceful resignation toward past ills and his moral determination to prevent future ills. One of the dangers of a theodicy is that if one secures the view that past harms were permissible (it is not incompatible with the goodness of God for God to have permitted them) then one may not be as prone to prevent future harm. On this front, Leibniz insists on our moral fortitude in seeking the good.

> In order to act in accordance with the love of God, it is not sufficient to force ourselves to be patient; rather, we must truly be satisfied with everything that has come to us according to his will. I mean this acquiescence

---

[83] In other words, Leibniz's goal is not merely establishing that it is rationally permissible to believe in the goodness of God notwithstanding evil. Many theists today take the comparatively more modest role of arguing that atheist arguments are not compelling. Critics of a best possible world theodicy include R. M. Adams, G. Schlesinger, and B. Reichenbach. For a defense of Leibniz, see David Blumenfeld, "Is the Best Possible World Possible?" *Philosophical Review* 84 (1975). For a critique, see R. M. Adam, "Must God Create the Best?" *Philosophical Review* 81 (1972).

with respect to the past. As for the future, we must not be *quietists* and stand ridiculously with arms folded, awaiting that which God will do, according to the sophism that the ancients called *logon aergon*, the lazy argument. But we must act in accordance with *the presumptive will of God*, insofar as we can judge it, trying to contribute with all our power to the general good and especially to the embellishment and perfection of that which affects us, or that which is near us and, so to speak, in our grasp.[84]

There is also another mitigating point on Leibniz's behalf. Leibniz may be read as offering grounds for a hope in the prevailing power of goodness. If one despairs of the primacy of good and achievability of justice, one may be just as brave and resilient in seeking goodness and justice. And yet there is also a tendency to yield to forces that one judges to be inevitably overpowering and disastrous.[85] Insofar as Leibnizian hope can have an amelioratory, galvanizing impact, strengthening the resolve of moral action, Leibniz's theodicy may be seen more as an instrument of justice than an accommodation of injustice. Terry Pinkard has recently offered the following modest reply to Voltaire's dismissal of Leibniz:

> The great Lisbon earthquake [which occurred on November 1, All Saint's Day, in 1755, killing 30,000] that ... spurred Voltaire into lampooning the whole matter [of Leibniz's theodicy] in his novel, *Candide*, and it became more and more difficult after that point to maintain that everything in the world was in the order it was supposed to be. There was, however, more to [Leibniz's] line of thought than mere smug assertions that the world was as it should be. Seeking God's perfection in the world meant reflecting on God's *love* for the world, which, in turn, gradually began to undermine the gloomy picture of human nature presented by some Christian thinkers (particularly, the Calvinists) in favor of a view that held the world's imperfections were capable of a sort of redemption in the here and now, not some afterlife.[86]

---

[84] Cited by Donald Rutherford in his illuminating essay "Leibniz and the Stoics," in *The Problem of Evil in Early Modern Philosophy*, ed. E. J. Kremer and M. J. Latzer (Toronto: University of Toronto Press, 2001), 154.

[85] It would be difficult to document this, other than anecdotally – for example, by comparing two patients with the same illness where one despairs and the other hopes for recovery. I return to this matter in Chapter 5 in the context of Kant's moral argument.

[86] Terry Pinkard, *German Philosophy, 1760–1860* (Cambridge: Cambridge University Press, 2002), 9.

That justice, political reconciliation, and toleration were among Leibniz's key aims is the judgment of one contemporary, prominent Leibniz scholar. Nicholas Rescher, in *The Philosophy of Leibniz*, writes:

> Leibniz eagerly wanted to persuade his readers (usually his correspondents), not in order to win personal disciples in high places, but to secure effective adherents to implement a vision of truths which he felt capable of healing the theological strifes and political discords in Europe of his day. Had fame been his prime goal he would have written more books and fewer letters. What Leibniz wanted was not public acclaim, but influential converts who could implement in the sphere of action his reconciling insights in the sphere of thought. It is always risky to speculate on motives, but in my own mind there is no doubt that the aspirations which actuated him were, in the main, not those of selfishness but of public spirit.[87]

Leibniz's work on Chinese philosophy supports the estimation of Leibniz's expansive, universalist tendencies.[88] I return to the expansion of philosophy of religion in Chapter 7.

During Leibniz's lifetime, there was heated dispute over the status of Chinese philosophy and religion. Jesuit missionaries to China offered a positive conception of Confucianism, seeing it in a similar light to early Platonism and Aristotelianism, as pre-Christian but virtuous paganism. Some Jesuits even saw Confucius's work as based on divine revelation. Other missionaries, especially the Franciscans and Dominicans, saw Confucianism as debased; they succeeded in persuading the church to prohibit Chinese Catholics from Confucian practices of venerating ancestors.[89] The debate among these parties came to be known as the Rites Controversy. Leibniz sided with the Jesuits (by and large) and saw in Chinese thought many of the same tenets of his own philosophy. In this matter, he may have failed to consider the distinctive, non-Leibnizian case of Chinese thought, but it has been persuasively

---

[87] *The Philosophy of Leibniz* (Englewood Cliffs, N.J.: Prentice-Hall, 1967), 160.

[88] See Leibniz, *Writings on China*, trans. D. J. Cook and H. Rosemont (Chicago: Open Court, 1994); David Mungello, *Leibniz and Confucianism: The Search for Accord* (Honolulu: University Press of Hawaii, 1977); and Adolf Reichwein, *China and Europe: Intellectual and Artistic Contacts in the Eighteenth Century* (New York: Barnes and Noble, 1968).

[89] This proved to be disastrous from the standpoint of the church as it effectively excluded Catholic Chinese from holding political office.

argued that his goal in analyzing Chinese thought was, in part, to advance the cause of toleration in Europe. D. J. Cook and H. Rosement offer this account of Leibniz:

> He wished to reconcile Catholics and Protestants, and to halt the internecine strife plaguing the European states of his day. He believed that China could assist in achieving this goal, his writings displaying the following pattern of reasoning: my philosophy is fully compatible with those elements of Christian theology on which there is a large measure of agreement between Catholics and Protestants; my philosophy is fully compatible with (early) basic beliefs of the Chinese; therefore Chinese basic beliefs are fully compatible with those basic beliefs shared by Catholics and Protestants, and therefore in turn those Christian doctrines in dispute between Catholics and Protestants should be seen as relatively unimportant in the larger scheme of things, and can be adjudicated to the satisfaction of all on the basis of reason – with a resultant international peace and harmony among and between all the world's peoples.[90]

Spinoza's Anti-Supernaturalism

Benedict de Spinoza (1632–1677) advanced a substantial challenge to theistic philosophy of religion. He articulated a monist philosophy according to which there is one only substance: God. "Besides God no substance can exist or be conceived."[91] He relegated all the features of the world to attributes of God. At the heart of Spinoza's system is a firm adherence to principles of rationality and explanation at odds with the claims of revealed religions and traditional religious beliefs about miracles.

Spinoza was born in Amsterdam, attended Jewish schools, studied under Rabbi Manasseh ben Israel (who met with Cudworth and Whichote in the Whitehall conference), and produced work of enormous controversy. His *Tractatus Theologico-Politicus* (1670) is a naturalistic reading of the Bible, a case for freedom of speech, and a differentiation between philosophy and theology. Spinoza assimilates religious faith to an acknowledgment of God as a Supreme, omnipresent, good being.

---

[90] *Writings on China*, 3.

[91] *Ethics*, trans. and ed. G. H. R. Parkinson (Oxford: Oxford University Press, 2000), 85.

The right relation to God is justice, charity, love of neighbor, and forgiveness. Further analysis of the being of God is left for philosophy.

> The aim of philosophy is, quite simply, truth, while the aim of faith, as we have abundantly shown, is nothing other than obedience and piety. Again, philosophy rests on the basis of universally valid axioms, and must be constructed by studying Nature alone, whereas faith is based on history and language, and must be derived only from Scripture and revelation.... So faith allows to every man the utmost freedom to philosophize, and he may hold whatever opinions he pleases on any subjects whatsoever without imputation of evil. It condemns as heretics and schismatics only those who teach such beliefs as promote obstinacy, hatred, strife and anger, while it regards as the faithful only those who promote justice and charity to the best of their intellectual powers and capacity.[92]

Spinoza offers an ontological argument whereby he secures his monism. God's absolute infinity precludes the existence of any competing nature. He rejects libertarian freedom and favors a principle of explanation that rules out chance. "There is in mind no absolute, i.e. no free will, but the mind is determined to will this or that by a cause, which is again determined by another, and that again by another, and so on to infinity."[93] Spinoza's metaphysics has an important place in the development of early modern philosophy of religion, for it inserts a nontheistic, religiously satisfying (if Spinoza is right) understanding of God compatible with rational arguments. For our purpose here, Spinoza's distinctive contribution may also be found in his case against the traditional reading of Jewish and Christian Scripture. Spinoza, followed by Hume (discussed in the next chapter), offers what may be considered a naturalist critique of miracles. He allows that it might be reasonable for "men of old" to accept miracles but all events must ultimately achieve an explanation in scientific terms known by "the natural light of reason."

Spinoza's place in the history of Jewish thought is of great interest. Steven Nadler argues that Spinoza's chief failing from the standpoint of the Jewish Amsterdam of his day was his denial of the afterlife of the individual person.[94] Spinoza's denial of immortality was related to

---

[92] *Theological-Political Treatise*, trans. S. Shirley (Indianapolis: Hackett, 1998), 169.

[93] *Ethics*, 155.

[94] See Nadler, *Spinoza's Heresy; Immortality and the Jewish Mind* (Oxford: Clarendon, 2001). See also Nadler's *Spinoza: A Life* (Cambridge: Cambridge University Press, 1999). J. Samuel Preus articulates Spinoza's anti-supernaturalism in *Spinoza and the*

his rejection of dualism. He was highly critical of Descartes' view of mind-body interaction.

> What, I ask, does he understand by the union of mind and body? What clear and distinct conception does he have of thought that is very closely united to some tiny portion or quantity? I certainly wish that he had explained this union by its proximate cause. But he conceived of the mind to be so distinct from the body that he could not assign any particular cause either for this union or for the mind itself, but it was necessary for him to have recourse to the cause of the whole universe, that is, to God.[95]

In this exchange over Descartes' dualism, one can readily see the appeal behind a monist philosophy such as materialism: there is no need to explain the relationship between disparate entities. Spinoza's denial of an afterlife and nontheistic view of the divine earned him a reputation for atheism.[96]

Spinoza did depart from a classical theistic model of God, according to which God acts purposely in creating and conserving the cosmos. Spinoza wrote of God as nature.

> Nature does not act for an end; for the external and infinite entity that we call God, i.e. Nature, acts by the same necessity as that by which he exists. . . . Therefore, the reason, i.e. the cause, why God or in other words Nature acts, and the reason why he exists, is one and the same. Therefore, just as he does not exist for the sake of any purpose, neither does he act for the sake of any purpose, but just as he has no principle or end of existing, so he has no principle or end of acting. What is called a "final cause" is simply human appetite, in so far as it is conceived as if it were a principle, i.e. a primary cause of some thing."[97]

While Spinoza's portrait of God as nature has been interpreted as mechanistic naturalism in religious clothing, I believe this is misleading. Spinoza's God may be shorn of passion ("strictly speaking God loves no one and hates no one"), but we are beckoned to the love of God.[98] "The person who understands himself and his emotions clearly and

---

Irrelevance of Biblical Authority (Cambridge: Cambridge University Press, 2001). For Spinoza's relationship to Christianisty, see G. Hunter, "Spinoza: A Radical Protestant?" in Kremer and Latzer, *The Problem of Evil in Early Modern Philosophy.*

[95] *Ethics*, 289.

[96] This charge is noted by Hume in *A Treatise of Human Nature*, 1.4.5.

[97] *Ethics*, 226.

[98] Ibid., 299.

distinctly loves God, and the more so, the more he understands himself and his emotions.... this love for God must occupy the mind most of all."[99] Spinoza's repeated underscoring of the love of God makes his philosophy (in my view) a profoundly religious work.[100]

Under the heading of "anti-supernaturalism," a brief word is due on a philosopher (as well as dramatist) influenced by Spinoza, Gotthold Ephraim Lessing (1729–1781). Lessing was accused of unorthodoxy by aligning himself with Spinoza's concept of God. Lessing popularized Spinoza's misgivings about grounding universal religious convictions on contingent, historical events and narratives. In the *Tractus Theologico-Politicus* Spinoza writes:

> Natural divine law ... does not depend on the truth of any historical narrative whatever, for inasmuch as this natural divine law is comprehended solely by consideration of human nature, it is plain that we can conceive it as existing as well in Adam as in any other man.... The truth of a historical narrative (*fides historiarum*), however assured, cannot give us the knowledge or, consequently, the love of God, for love of God springs from knowledge of him, and knowledge of him should be derived from general ideas, in themselves certain and known, so that the truth of a historical narrative is far from being a necessary requisite for our highest good.[101]

Lessing dramatically represented the gap between reason and historical revelation as an "ugly broad ditch which I cannot get across, however often and however earnestly I have tried to make the leap."[102] For Lessing, the key difficulty is that relying on historical testimony will involve indirect, nonimmediate evidence of events very remote from his own time. Lessing lives "in the eighteenth century, when miracles no longer occur."[103]

> If I had lived at the time of Christ, then of course the prophecies fulfilled in his person would have made me pay great attention to him. If I had actually seen him perform miracles, if I had had no cause to doubt that true miracles existed, then in a worker of miracles who had been marked

---

[99] Ibid., 298–299.

[100] See H. Rawen and Lenn Goodman, eds., *Jewish Themes in Spinoza's Philosophy*, (Albany: SUNY Press, 2002), especially Goodman's essay "What Does Spinoza's *Ethics* Contribute to Jewish Philosophy?"

[101] Ibid., 60.

[102] Lessing, cited by Toshimasa Yasukata in *Lessing's Philosophy of Religion and the German Enlightenment* (Oxford: Oxford University Press, 2002), 56.

[103] Ibid., 58.

out so long before, I would have gained so much confidence that I would willingly have submitted my intellect to his, and I would have believed him in all things in which equally indisputable experience did not tell against him. The problem is that reports of fulfilled prophecies are not fulfilled prophecies, that reports of miracles are not miracles. *These*, the prophecies fulfilled before my eyes, the miracles that occur before my eyes, are *immediate* in their effect. But *those* – the reports of fulfilled prophecies and miracles – have to work through a *medium* that takes away all their force.[104]

Several of these themes are taken up in the next chapter. David Hume will develop an argument against the credibility of accepting reported miracles. As for the distinction between immediate and mediated awareness, Chapter 4 includes Hume's proposal that even our awareness of other people's thoughts and the external world is not immediate. But two observations are important here. First, in Lessing and some of his contemporaries there is a universalist, more impersonal concept of the divine than in the Christian and Jewish tradition in which God acts providentially to liberate or redeem creation. Historical narratives seem to be indispensable mediums whereby someone today can have cognition of, and religious access to, some earlier event in which God redeemed or emancipated people. If historical narratives are set to one side, one seems to rule out the possibility that God can redeem or liberate people through a historical event that is afterward credibly relied upon. Second, one can detect in Lessing and others a harder or firmer concept of nature as a realm that may itself be divine (as we see with Spinoza) but excludes what may be called "the Supernatural," where the supernatural refers to that which is beyond nature.[105]

Probability as the Guide to a Supernatural Life

Joseph Butler (1692–1752) was educated at Oxford, appointed Bishop of Durham in the Church of England, and made important contributions to moral theory and the philosophical exploration of theism. While Butler was influenced by Locke, Clarke, and Leibniz, he may also be seen in the Cambridge Platonist tradition.

---

[104] Ibid., 58.

[105] The first entry for "supernatural" in Johnson's dictionary is "Being above the powers of nature."

Butler once claimed "Probability is the very guide of life."[106] In Butler one may see a continuation of the project initiated by Locke to arrive at rules of evidence.

> From these things it follows, that in questions of difficulty, or such as are thought so, where more satisfactory evidence cannot be had, or is not seen; if the result of examination be, that there appears upon the whole, any the lowest presumption on one side, and none on the other, or a greater presumption on one side, though in the lowest degree greater; this determines the question, even in matters of speculation; and in matter of practice, will lay us under an absolute and formal obligation, in point of prudence and of interest, to act upon that presumption or low probability, though it be so low as to leave the mind in very great doubt which is the truth. For surely a man is as really bound in prudence to do what upon the whole appears, according to the best of his judgment, to be for his happiness, as what he certainly knows to be so.[107]

What I wish to highlight in Butler's work is an awareness that probabilistic reasoning need not be carried out in a piecemeal, secular fashion. Butler assumes the coherence of theism, the possibility and desirability of the miraculous and the deliverance of our natural affections. He is interesting to consider here in contrast to Hume in the next chapter. For Hume, the supernatural God (if there is a God) is a remote invisible power that may be inferred only tenuously. For Butler, there is no need for an irrational leap to belief in God, the afterlife, and the good life now, to which God calls us to through conscience. A broadly theistic philosophy is justified through reflection on nature, both our own nature and creation at large.

To illustrate Butler's holistic approach to philosophy and probability, consider his assessment of the case for or against belief in an individual afterlife.

Is the observation of a person's bodily death the observation of the extinction or annihilation of the person? Is the observation of bodily death even evidence that the person has ceased to be? Butler thinks the answer is not a clear yes.

> [A]s we are greatly in the dark, upon what the exercise of our living powers...themselves depend upon; the powers themselves as distinguished, not only from their actual exercise, but also from the present

---

[106] *The Analogy of Religion* (Oxford: Clarendon Press, 1896), 5.
[107] Ibid., 6.

capacity of exercising them; and as opposed to their destruction: for sleep, or however a swoon, shows us, not only that these powers exist when they are not exercised, as the passive power of motion does in inanimate matter; but shows also that they exist, when there is no present capacity of exercising them: or that the capacities of exercising them for the present, as well as the actual exercise of them, may be suspended, and yet the powers themselves remain undestroyed. Since then we know not at all upon what the existence of our living powers depends, this shows further, there can no probability be collected from the reason of the thing, that death will be their destruction: because their existence may depend upon somewhat in no degree affected by death.[108]

He thinks mind-body dualism is coherent and contends that it is possible for a person to exist without his or her body. "It is as easy to conceive, that we may exist out of bodies, as in them; that we might have animated bodies of any other organs and senses wholly different from these now given us, and that we may hereafter animate these same or new bodies variously modified and organized; as to conceive how we can animate such bodies as our present."[109] We distinguish mind and body, in part, by noting the different identity conditions of each. He contends that "[w]e have several times over lost a great part or perhaps the whole of our body, according to certain common established laws of nature; yet we remain the same living agents: when we shall lose as great a part, or the whole, by another common established law of nature, death; why may we not also remain the same?"[110]

Because of the apparent dissimilarity between person and body, and our agnosticism over what sustains us in existence, merely to observe the evident dissolution of the body is not ipso facto to observe the evident perishing of the person

Butler's positive case for immortality rests on an assumption that objects remain in existence until there is a cause for their nonexistence. It may not be very impressive as an argument, although in the next chapter on Hume I suggest how a Butlerian argument for immortality might gain ground. The point of discussing immortality here is that the assessment of probability must take seriously such background assumptions as these: Is it reasonable to conclude that person and body are identical? If they are not identical, how probable is it that the existence of the person

[108] Ibid., 25.
[109] Ibid., 29.
[110] Ibid., 32.

(not just the activity of the person) depends essentially and exclusively upon the body?[111]

Butler achieved great praise for his work on conscience and moral psychology. Prominent ethicists such as Richard Price, Thomas Reid, and Henry Sidgwick credited Butler with overturning simple, reductive approaches to moral motivation. Butler was pitted against what he took to be Hobbes's psychology of self-interest.[112]

Philosophers and Traditions: The Battle of the Books

The work of Spinoza and his followers brings to the fore a central topic in modern philosophy: the credibility of tradition. Early modern philosophers like Descartes cast themselves as undertaking a radically new project: they could put tradition on hold and await its justification through their principles of philosophy. Spinoza undertook a related task insofar as he did not see himself as beholden to a prior or independent religious identity. The philosophers of this chapter (Hobbes, Locke, Berkeley, Edwards, some of the early colonial thinkers, Leibniz, Spinoza) may be seen as laying different claims on the limits of tradition. Some embraced Christian tradition on the basis of evidence; some did not. The bewildering but fascinating development of new philosophies grew out of what some have called the battle of the books, in which philosophies that celebrate mechanical explanation, mathematics, and geometry, are in radical tension with Platonic, Aristotelian, and medieval view of nature.[113]

In an effort to complete the portrait of philosophy of religion in this chapter and earlier work, I refer to Jean-Jacques Rousseau's famous essay "A Savoyard Vicar." Rousseau is a fascinating figure who repays close study, but given limitations of space, I highlight only one of his essays as it provides an interesting juxtaposition to some of the other

---

[111] See Terence Penelhum, *Butler* (London: Routledge, 1985). In general, I have a higher view of Butler's case for immortality then Penelhum; see my paper "The Virtues of Immortality," Wheaton College Conference, Philosophy of Mind, Wheaton, Ill., 2001.

[112] For a sound and enthusiastic assessment of Butler's moral psychology, see C. D. Broad, *Five Types of Ethical Theory* (London: Routledge, 1956), chap. 3. For a good overview, placing Bulter in the history of philosophy and theology, see E. C. Mossner, *Bishop Butler and the Age of Reason* (New York: Macmillan, 1936).

[113] See R. F. Jones, *Ancients and Moderns: A Study of the Background of the Battle of the Books* (St. Louis: Washington University Press, 1936).

work in this chapter.[114] In this essay, Rousseau (1712–1778) highlights the themes of this and the previous chapter. He engages in Cartesian doubt:

> I was in that state of doubt and uncertainty in which Descartes requires the mind to be involved, in order to enable it to investigate truth. This disposition of mind, however, is too disquieting to long continue, its duration so corrupt as to seek fresh indulgence; and nothing preserves so well the habit of reflection as to be more content with ourselves than with our fortune.
>
> I reflected, therefore, on the unhappy lot of mortals floating always on the ocean of human opinions, without compass or rudder – left to the mercy of their tempestuous passions, with no other guide than an inexperienced pilot, ignorant of his course, as well as from whence he came, and whither he is going. I often said to myself: I love the truth – I seek, yet cannot find it. Let any one show it to me and I will readily embrace it. Why doth it hide its charms from a heart formed to adore them?[115]

Here we see the predicament of early modern philosophers of religion, in search of a foundation. How are we to measure the evidential backing of traditions?

> I conceived that the weakness of the human understanding was the first cause of the prodigious variety I found in their sentiments, and that pride was the second. We have no standard with which to measure this immense machine; we cannot calculate its various relations; we neither know the first cause nor the final effects; we are ignorant even of ourselves; we neither know our own nature nor principle of actions; nay, we hardly know whether a man be simple or compound being. Impenetrable mysteries surround us on every side; they extend beyond the region of sense; we imagine ourselves possessed of understanding to penetrate them, and we have only imagination. Every one strikes out a way of his own across this imaginary world; but no one knows whether it will lead him to the point he aims at.[116]

In the end, Rousseau employs natural reason and an "inner light" to establish a belief in a provident, good God, the soul, and the afterlife.

---

[114] For a fuller exploration of the religious elements in Rousseau's work, see R. Grimsley, *Rousseau and the Religious Quest* (Oxford: Clarendon, 1968).

[115] From E. W. Eliot, ed., *French and English Philosophers*, Harvard Classics, vol. 34 (New York: P. F. Collier and Son, 1910), 247.

[116] Ibid., 248.

Rousseau, for better or worse, rests with this general portrait and leaves to one side the traditional belief in miracles, special divine acts, and the incarnation. Philosophical defenses of these more specific convictions were plentiful at Rousseau's time, but there is an evident opposition or more qualified philosophy of religion that is in play in the eighteenth century. Moreover, not everyone wanted to follow an "inner light" when there were secular rules of evidence to deploy in the testing of religious beliefs and practices. It is still good to pause to consider Rousseau, in order to appreciate the intellectual chaos and indecisiveness for some philosophers at this time period. While Rousseau is sometimes described as thoroughly optimistic about human nature, more recent scholars have unearthed his ambivalence. Mark Cladis offers this portrait: "Rousseau, like Janus, gazed in two directions at the same time, or at least in rapid succession. In one direction, he beheld humans as naturally innocent and able to be content; in the other, he perceived humans as inevitably destructive and destined for immense suffering."[117]

[117] "Rousseau's Soteriology: Deliverance at the Crossroads," *Religious Studies* 32 (1996): 90.

✦

FOUR

Humean Philosophy of Religion

Every enquiry, which regards religion, is of the utmost importance.

David Hume[1]

Life and Death in 1776

David Hume's (1711–1776) health began to fail in 1772. Despite the growing hardships of fever, internal hemorrhages, and weight loss (he dropped seventy pounds in a year), he remained in possession of his powers and mild tempered, certain that he would die soon. Hume wrote an account of his life that included the following portrait.

> In spring 1775, I was struck with a disorder.... I now reckon upon a speedy dissolution. I have suffered very little pain from my disorder; and what is more strange, have, notwithstanding the great decline of my person, never suffered a moment's abatement of my spirits; insomuch, that were I to name the period of my life, which I should most choose to pass over again, I might be tempted to point to this later period. I possess the same ardour as ever in study, and the same gaiety in company. I consider, besides, that a man of sixty-five, by dying, cuts off only a few years of infirmities; and though I see many symptoms of my literary reputation's breaking out at last with additional luster, I knew that I could have but a few years to enjoy it. It is difficult to be more detached from life than I am at present.[2]

---

[1] *The Natural History of Religion*, in *David Hume: Writings on Religion*, ed. A. Flew (LaSalle: Open Court, 2000), 107.

[2] "My Own Life," in *An Enquiry Concerning Human Understanding*, ed. A. Flew (LaSalle: Open Court, 1988), 10. Routledge has recently published a very useful introduction: David O'Connor, *Hume on Religion* (London: Routledge, 2001). For an overview of Hume, there is the "classic" Norman Kemp Smith, *The Philosophy of*

Hume's detachment did not lead him to neglect reading the first volume of Edward Gibbon's *History of the Decline and Fall of the Roman Empire* and Adam Smith's *Wealth of Nations*, published in 1776. In his final days Hume made arrangements for the publication of his *Dialogues Concerning Natural Reason*, a text that is central to this chapter.

Hume's death was famous. He had argued against the reasonability of belief in an afterlife and against belief in miracles. The Scottish writer James Boswell (who would later, in 1791, publish the famous *The Life of Samuel Johnson*) visited Hume on Sunday, July 7, 1776. Boswell evidently wished to see if Hume would relent, in the end, and profess Christian belief. After all, Hume never explicitly renounced his baptism. Boswell got the topic of immortality into the conversation and made this report afterward.

> He said he never had entertained any belief in Religion since he began to read Locke and Clarke. I asked him if he was not religious when he was young. He said he was. . . . He then said flatly that the Morality of every Religion was bad, and, I really thought, was not jocular when he said "that when he heard a man was religious, he concluded he was a rascal, though he had known some instances of very good men being religious." . . . I had a strong curiosity to be satisfied if he persisted in disbelieving a future state even when he had death before his eyes. I was persuaded from what he now said, and from his manner of saying it, that he did persist. I asked him if it was not possible that there might be a future state. He answered It was possible that a piece of coal put upon the fire would not burn; and he added that it was a most unreasonable fancy that we should exist for ever. . . . I asked him if the thought of Annihilation never gave him any uneasiness. He said not the least. . . . I tried him . . . , saying that a future state was surely a pleasing idea. He said No, for that it was always seen through a gloomy medium; there was always a Phlegethon or a Hell. "But," said I, "would it not be agreeable to have hopes of seeing our friends again?" and I mentioned three Men lately deceased, for whom I knew he had a high value: Ambassadour Keith, Lord Alemoor, and Baron Muir. He owned it would be agreeable, but added that none of them entertained such a notion. I believe he said, such a foolish, or such an absurd, notion; for he was indecently and impolitely

David Hume (London: Macmillan, 1941), and the more recent D. F. Norton, *David Hume: Common Sense Moralist, Skeptical Metaphysician* (Princeton: Princeton University Press, 1982), and T. Penelhum, *David Hume: An Introduction to His Philosophical System* (West Lafayette: Purdue University Press, 1992). The secondary literature on Hume is huge; the journal *Hume Studies* is a good place to start any research.

positive in incredulity. "Yes," said I, "Lord Alemoor was a believer." David acknowledged that *he* had *some* belief....

The truth is that Mr. Hume's pleasantry was such that there was no solemnity in the scene; and Death for the time did not seem dismal. It surprised me to find him talking of different matters with a tranquility of mind and a clearness of head, which few men possess at any time. Two particulars I remember: Smith's *Wealth of Nations*, which he recommended much, and Monboddo's *Origin of Language*, which he treated contemptuously. I said, "If I were you, I should regret Annihilation. Had I written such an admirable History, I should be sorry to leave it." He said, "I shall leave that history, of which you are pleased to speak so favourably, as perfect as I can."... He said he had no pain, but was wasting away.[3]

To us today, the scene of a dying man or woman expressing disbelief in an afterlife may seem unsurprising and perhaps a commonplace. But at the time, to live and die without fear of annihilation and hope for immortality was radical. "I am left," Boswell writes, "with impressions which disturbed me for some time."[4]

Most of the philosophers discussed thus far, with the notable exception of Spinoza, professed a belief in an afterlife for individuals, or at least they did not deny this belief in an afterlife was probably an important source of solace, and not just an element in moral motivation, for at the time the average life expectancy was under forty, a third of the children died before the age of five, and there were many diseases not treatable by medicine – diphtheria, typhoid, typhus, and smallpox among others.[5] Hume's facing his own death with no thought of any survival was exceptional.

David Hume is often described as a skeptic, for he doubted the philosophical credibility of theistic arguments, as well as miracles and the afterlife; the substantiality of the self; the rational foundation of ethics; the rational trustworthiness of our beliefs about the future; and even the reliability of our access to the world around us. Hume described himself as a skeptic, and so this term does no violence to his stated self-understanding. Still, in addition to his skepticism is his belief (or at least endorsement) of a sweeping form of naturalism, according to which

---

[3] From *Boswell Papers*, cited in E. C. Mossner, *The Life of David Hume* (Austin: University of Texas Press, 1954), 597–598.

[4] Ibid., 598.

[5] See "Death," in *The Blackwell Companion to the Enlightenment*, ed. John Yolton et al. (Oxford: Blackwell, 1995).

human beings are closely linked to our fellow animals on an earth that is lacking clear evidence of a provident God.

Hume was born in Scotland, educated at the University of Edinburgh, and employed in a variety of professional capacities, from being a librarian in the Advocates Library in Edinburgh to the British chargé d'affaires in Paris. All of these occupations pale compared with his extraordinary literary and philosophical achievement. Philosophical reflection on religion may be found in much of his work but especially in *A Treatise of Human Nature* (1739–1740), *An Enquiry Concerning Human Understanding* (1748), *The Natural History of Religion* (1757), *Dialogues Concerning Natural Religion* (1779), and several essays. A leading scholar on Hume today rightly observes that Hume "wrote more about religion than about any other single philosophical subject," and so there is more than enough material here for a book, let alone a chapter.[6] Because Hume's philosophy of religion is closely related to his overriding methodology and his view of the nature and limits of human experience, let us first consider some general features of Hume's philosophy.

Hume's World and Self

Hume, in his life and work, is generally thought of as the culmination of British empiricism, bringing to a natural refinement the work of Bacon, Hobbes, Locke, and Berkeley. There is some truth in this. Bacon and those who followed him gave pride of place to the natural sciences and empirical inquiry. On this front Hume is impeccable. "There is no question of importance, whose decision is not compriz'd in the science of man; and there is none, which can be decided with any certainty, before we become acquainted with that science. In pretending therefore to explain the principles of human nature, we in effect propose a complete system of the sciences, built on a foundation almost entirely new, and the only one upon which they can stand with any security."[7] Hume is often (and I think correctly) described as an "evidentialist," insofar as he holds that beliefs are rational only if sufficiently supported by evidence. The evolution of empiricism may be seen in terms of the gradual sweeping

---

[6] J. C. A. Gaskin, *Hume's Philosophy of Religion* (Atlantic Highlands, N.J.: Humanities Press International, 1988), 1. Gaskin's own work is in great sympathy with Hume. He and Antony Flew have developed one of the best, contemporary versions of Hume's critical treatment of religion.

[7] *A Treatise of Human Nature*, ed. L. A. Selby-Bigge (Oxford: Clarendon, 1978), xvi.

away of philosophical paraphernalia not grounded in experience. Like
Locke, Hume thought the mind-body relation was open to empirical
inquiry.[8] Like Berkeley, he questioned Locke's distinction of primary and
secondary qualities. Hume insists that, from the standpoint of rational,
philosophical reflection (as opposed to common sense), we do not have
unmediated access to a world independent of us.

> [T]he slightest philosophy . . . teaches us, that nothing can ever be present
> to the mind but an image or perception, and that the senses are only the
> inlets, through which these images are conveyed, without being able to
> produce any immediate intercourse between the mind and the object. The
> table, which we see, seems to diminish, as we remove farther from it: but
> the real table, which exists independent of us, suffers no alteration: it was,
> therefore, nothing but its image, which was present to the mind.[9]

He employed an account of meaning, according to which meaningful
terms are derived from our experience, both sensory and the impressions
of reflection. The failure to *achieve* the relevant experience or impression
undermines the tenability or intelligibility of a term. Thus, he challenged
terms supposedly referring to a substantive, concrete self, "causation,"
and Platonic views of the good.

Descartes had argued for the indubitibility of the self. Hume acknowledges the Cartesian claim. "There are some philosophers, who imagine
we are every moment intimately conscious of what we call our self; that
we feel its existence and its continuance in existence; and are certain,
beyond the evidence of a demonstration, both of its perfect identity
and simplicity. . . . [N]or is there any thing, of which we can be certain,
if we doubt of this."[10] But Hume does doubt the self as described by
Descartes. "For my part, when I enter most intimately into what I call
myself, I always stumble on some particular perception or other, of
heat or cold, light or shade, love or hatred, pain or pleasure. I never
can catch *myself* at any time without a perception, and never can observe any thing but the perception. When my perceptions are remov'd
for any time, as by sound sleep; so long am I insensible of *myself*, and
may truly be said not to exist."[11] By Hume's lights, Descartes courts a
fiction. We *posit* a substantial self; the self is not discovered. Of course,

---

[8] Though Hume did not follow Locke in rejecting all innate ideas; see ibid., 648.
[9] *Enquiries Concerning Human Understanding and Concerning the Principles of Morals*, ed. L. A. Selby-Bigge (Oxford: Clarendon, 1966), 152.
[10] *A Treatise*, 251.
[11] Ibid., 252.

if the concept of the self is posited, it does not follow that the self is ipso facto a fiction. Still, according to Hume, the Cartesian hypothesis of such a substantial self behind experience does not help account for our personal identity and, at the end of the day, Hume casts the Cartesian view of the self as an evident absurdity. There can be no content given to the concept of a self that is underneath our sensory ideas or is having sensory impression, nor

> Have we any idea of *self*, after the manner it is here explain'd. For from what impression cou'd this idea be deriv'd? This question 'tis impossible to answer without a manifest contradiction and absurdity; and yet 'tis a question, which must necessarially be answer'd, if we wou'd have the idea of self pass for clear and intelligible. It must be some one impression, that gives rise to every real idea. But self or person is not any one impression, but that to which our several impressions and ideas are suppos'd to have a reference.[12]

Hume instead characterized himself and other persons in terms of bundles of impressions. Hume's view of the self as a bundle, "a kind of theatre," a "heap or collection," "a system of different perceptions," is philosophically interesting for its own sake, and it is a topic that will be considered near the end of this chapter.[13]

Hume is widely celebrated for his critical work on causation. Like Malebranche as well as Bayle, Hume contended that we do not observe causal powers at work in the world, "We have no other notion of cause and effect, but that of certain objects, which have been *always conjoin'd* together, and which in all past instances have been found inseparable."[14] To seek necessary connections between cause and effect is vain. "Upon the whole, necessity is something, that exists in the mind, not in objects; nor is it possible for us ever to form the most distinct idea of it, consider'd as a quality in bodies. Either we have no idea of necessity, or necessity is nothing but that determination of the thought to pass from causes to effects and from effects to causes, according to their experienc'd union."[15] Causal relations are therefore identified without positing unobservable connections. In Hume's famous phrase, "experience only teaches us, how one event constantly follows another;

---

[12] Ibid., 251.
[13] See ibid., 261.
[14] Ibid., 93.
[15] Ibid., 165.

without instructing us in the secret connexion, which binds them together, and renders them inseparable."[16]

Scholars differ on how far Hume went in his skepticism. I believe he
did leave the self, causation, and a mind-independent world in precarious shape from the standpoint of reason. For example, when discussing
a mind-independent world, he says,

> It is a question of fact, whether the perceptions of the senses be pro-
> duced by external objects, resembling them; how shall this question be
> determined? By experience surely; as all other questions of a like nature.
> But here experience is, and must be entirely silent. The mind has never
> anything present to it but the perceptions, and cannot possibly reach any
> experience of their connexion with objects. The supposition of such a
> connexion is, therefore, without any foundation in reasoning.[17]

And yet Hume does not thereby relinquish self-reference, talk of causation, the external world, and the like. He rather locates the basis for
all such references not in reason but in our animal nature. Hume does
not think that nature (or God) has made us capable of a pure governance of our beliefs so that each of them is rationally compelled. In
a famous passage in the *Treatise* Hume declares: " 'Tis happy, therefore, that nature breaks the force of all sceptical arguments in time,
and keeps them from having any considerable influence on the understanding."[18] In the end, Hume does wish to secure some skepticism of some religious convictions, but he does not wish to leave us
altogether in skeptical paralysis in terms of daily, practical life, and
certainly not in scientific practice. I follow commentator Ira Singer in
thinking of Hume as a "problematic naturalist."[19] He clearly rejects a
supernaturalism of miracles and many traditional religious convictions,
but on the other hand Hume believed that many of his own philosophical tenets were defective (see the appendix to the *Treatise*). And
"Hume's naturalism is troubled and troubling, precisely because the natural process of belief-formation itself operates haltingly or unreliably,

---

[16] *An Enquiry*, 66.

[17] Ibid., 153.

[18] *A Treatise*, 187.

[19] Ira Singer, "Nature Breaks Down: Hume's Problematic Naturalism in Treatise I iv,"
Hume Studies 26:2 (2000). I should add that Singer's interpretation is open to dispute
and not orthodox. Norman Kemp Smith is a key Humean scholar who is responsible
for reading Hume as more of a naturalist rather than a skeptic.

with nature itself subverting ... or disappointing our most modest cognitive hopes."[20]

Hume's commitment to a criterion of observation was radical. He allowed that propositions are intelligible if they involve abstract relations of ideas, but he certainly accepted no principles that Descartes and Leibniz advanced about truths of reason that generated metaphysical results.

> It seems to me, that the only objects of the abstract sciences or of demonstration are quantity and number.... All other enquiries of men regard only matter of fact and existence.... When we run over libraries, persuaded of these principles, what havoc must we make? If we take in our hand any volume; of divinity or school metaphysics, for instance; let us ask, *Does it contain any abstract reasoning concerning quantity or number?* No. *Does it contain any experimental reasoning concerning matter of fact and existence?* No. Commit it then to the flames; for it can contain nothing but sophistry and illusion.[21]

Note the severity of Hume's condemnation. He judged that work not based on experimental reasoning or reflection on quantity or number "can contain nothing but – illusion." In other words, such work is not merely unjustified, and thus possibly true but simply not grounded on sufficient evidence. Rather, the very intelligibility of claims that transcend empirical inquiry and the relation of ideas is suspect and should be (from a philosophical perspective) annihilated.

I propose we consider the merits of Hume's philosophy of religion under a series of headings: Against the Design Argument; A Cosmological Argument; Design Again; History and Miracles in the Realm of Nature; and Annihilation and Suicide. This chapter is entitled "Humean Philosophy of Religion" as opposed to "Hume's Philosophy of Religion" so a further section considers Hume's ethics along with an extension of that ethic by Adam Smith into what may be called an ideal observer theory. I believe that Smith's development of Hume's treatment of impartiality and benevolence suggests one way in which there can be a fruitful overlap between secular and religious ethics. While Hume's philosophy has been aptly described as "militantly secular," under the heading of an ideal observer theory I suggest that some Humean principles

[20] Ibid., 226.
[21] *An Enquiry*, 163.

(as interpreted and developed by Smith) may be viewed as not exclusively secular.[22]

A significant amount of Hume's work on theistic arguments is found in his *Dialogues Concerning Natural Religion,* a debate between three key characters: Cleanthes (a theist who believes God may be known through observation and reason), Philo (a critic who opposes Cleanthes' project and yet comes to a deistic conclusion), and Demea (who also opposes Cleanthes but does so from the standpoint of a mystical theist).[23] Hume's *Dialogues* are probably modeled on Cicero's work *Concerning the Nature of the Gods* and *Concerning Divinity,* although a case can be made for Hume's reliance on Henry More's *Divine Dialogues.*[24] Complex moves in the dialogue have kept commentators busy for more than two hundred years wrestling with the question, Which character most closely represents Hume? Philo is probably the majority view, though this is complicated by the dialogue's framework in which two additional figures (Pamphilus and Hermippus) survey the exchange and Pamphilus pronounces Cleanthes the winner. In this context, I highlight some of the major arguments and refer to some of the secondary interpretive literature for further work.[25]

Against the Design Argument

Cleanthes introduces a design argument as follows:

> Look around the world: Contemplate the whole and every part of it: You will find it to be nothing but one great machine, subdivided into an infinite

[22] See Antony Flew's depiction of Hume's militant secular philosophy in "The Impossibility of the Miraculous," in *Hume's Philosophy of Religion* (Winston-Salem: Wake Forrest University Press, 1986).

[23] Hume's polemic against theism may be seen in much of his work. Edward Craig writes that Hume aimed at "the destruction of the image of God, and substituted for it an anthropology which looked not to the divine but to the natural world for its comparisons, and to the sciences for its methods" (*The Mind of God and the Works of Man* [Oxford: Clarendon, 1987], 70).

[24] See Chapter 1. Also see Peter Dendle, "Hume's Dialogues and *Paradise Lost,*" *Journal of the History of Ideas* 6:2 (1999).

[25] My focus is largely on Cleanthes and Philo, though I do look at Demea's cosmological argument and his view of evil. For a further look at Demea, see Dames Dye, "A Word on Behalf of Demea," *Hume Studies* 15:1 (1989). For a sustained, critical study of Hume's major work on religion, see Keith Yandell, *Hume's "Inexplicable Mystery"* (Philadelphia: Temple University Press, 1990). For a new treatment of the dialogues as philosophy and literature, see W. L. Session, *Reading Hume's Dialogues: A Veneration for True Religion* (Bloomington: Indiana University Press, 2002).

number of lesser machines, which again admit of subdivisions, to a degree beyond what human senses and faculties can trace and explain. All these various machines, and even their most minute parts, are adjusted to each other with an accuracy, which ravishes into admiration all men, who have ever contemplated them. The curious adapting of means to ends, throughout all nature, resembles exactly, though it much exceeds, the productions of human contrivance; of human design, thought, wisdom, and intelligence. Since therefore the effects resemble each other, we are led to infer, by all the rules of analogy, that the causes also resemble; and that the Author of Nature is somewhat similar to the mind of man; though possessed of much larger faculties, proportioned to the grandeur of the work, which he has executed. By this argument *a posteriori*, and by this argument alone, do we prove at once the existence of a Deity, and his similarity to human mind and intelligence.[26]

Consider a formalized version of the argument. I reproduce Derk Pereboom's schema:

(1) Nature is a great machine, composed of lesser machines, all of which exhibit order (especially adaptation of means to ends). (*premise*)
(2) Machines caused by human minds exhibit order (especially adaptation of means to ends). (*premise*)
(3) Nature resembles machines caused by human minds. (1, 2)
(4) If effects resemble each other, their causes do as well. (*premise*)
(5) The cause of nature resembles human minds. (3, 4)
(6) Greater effects demand greater causes (causes adequate to the effects). (*premise*)
(7) Nature is much greater than machines caused by human minds. (*premise*)
(8) The cause of nature resembles but is much greater than human minds. (5, 6, 7)
(9) The cause of nature is God. (8)
(10) Therefore, God exists. (9)[27]

The argument is crafted to provide a bridge from our firsthand acquaintance with intelligence and design to the positing of an intelligent, designing God. It is an argument from analogy or resemblance. The argument is a posteriori as it is based on contingent matters of fact that, in this case, we may observe.

---

[26] *Dialogues Concerning Natural Religion*, ed. Stanely Tweyman (London: Routledge, 1991), 109.

[27] From "Early Modern Philosophical Theology," in *A Companion to Philosophy of Religion*, ed. P. Quinn and C. Taliaferro (Oxford: Blackwell, 1997), 108.

In all, the objections to the design argument include what may be called the problem of dissimilitude (or the lack of resemblance between the cosmos and human artifacts), the uniqueness objection, the objection from alternative nontheistic hypotheses, the problem of anthropomorphism, and the problem of evil. In this section I exhibit some of the key passages where Hume's Philo advances each objection. Later in the chapter, I assess each of these objections both in the context of the *Dialogues* and subsequent philosophical responses to Hume.

The Problem of Dissimilitude. Philo warns Cleanthes that the ambitious scope of his argument places enormous pressure on his analogies. The case of inquiring into the nature of a cosmos is very different from inquiry into terrestrial matters,

> That a stone will fall, that fire will burn, that the earth has solidity, we have observed a thousand and a thousand times; and when any new instance of this nature is presented, we draw without hesitation the accustomed inference. The exact similarity of the cases gives us a perfect assurance of a similar event; and a stronger evidence is never desired nor sought after. But wherever you depart, in the least, from the similarity of the cases, you diminish proportionably the evidence; and may at last bring it to a very weak analogy, which is confessedly liable to error and uncertainty.[28]

Philo, in particular, notes how different the cosmos appears than from an artifact like a house.

> If we see a house, Cleanthes, we conclude, with the greatest certainty, that it had an architect or builder; because this is precisely that species of effect, which we have experienced to proceed from that species of cause. But surely you will not affirm, that the universe bears such a resemblance to a house, that we can with the same certainty infer a similar cause, or that the analogy is here entire and perfect. The dissimilitude is so striking, that the utmost you can here pretend to is a guess, a conjecture, a presumption concerning a similar cause;[29]

The Uniqueness Objection. This objection builds on the last one. Not only is the cosmos profoundly different from houses and other known,

---

[28] *Dialogues*, 109–110.
[29] Ibid., 110.

human artifacts, the cosmos is unique. As such, we are reasoning about something well beyond our experience.

> But how this [design] argument can have place, where the objects, as in the present case, are single, individual, without parallel or specific resemblance, may be difficult to explain. And will any man tell me with a serious countenance, that an orderly universe must arise from some thought and art, like the human; because we have experience of it? To ascertain this reasoning, it were requisite, that we had experience of the origin of worlds; and it is not sufficient surely, that we have seen ships and cities arise from human art and contrivance.[30]

The Objection from Alternative Possibilities. This objection has two sides. First, Philo offers a diminished, modest view of the nature of thought or mind. Philo suggests there is something parochial about using reason, design, and thought in explaining the cosmos as a whole. "Why select so minute, so weak, so bounded a principle as the reason and design of animals...found to be upon this planet? What peculiar privilege has this little agitation of the brain which we call thought, that we must thus make it the model of the whole universe? Our partiality in our own favour does indeed present it on all occasions: But sound philosophy ought carefully to guard against so natural an illusion."[31] Philo goes on to place before Cleanthes a host of alternative causes that are no worse than theism (or as equally good as theism) in accounting for cosmic order. Philo takes special interest in an explanation of the cosmos in terms of vegetation and generation, a biological account that foreshadows Darwin's theory of evolution. Philo outlines to Demea a multitude of possible nontheistic accounts.

> But what is this vegetation and generation, of which you talk, said DEMEA? Can you explain their operations, and anatomize that fine internal structure, on which they depend?
>
> In as much, at least, replied PHILO as CLEANTHES can explain the operations of reason, or anatomize that internal structure, on which *it* depends. But without any such elaborate disquisitions, when I see an animal, I infer, that it sprang from generation; and what with as great certainty as you conclude a house to have been reared by design. These words, *generation, reason*, mark only certain powers and energies in nature, whose effects are known, but whose essence is incomprehensible; and one of these

---

[30] Ibid., 11.
[31] Ibid., 113.

principles, more than the other, has no privilege for being made a standard to the whole of nature.[32]

In reality, DEMEA, it may reasonably be expected, that the larger the views are which we take of things, the better will they conduct us in our conclusions concerning such extraordinary and such magnificent subjects. In this little corner of the world alone, there are four principles, *reason, instinct, generation, vegetation*, which are similar to each other, and are cause of similar effects. What a number of other principles may we naturally suppose in the immense extent and variety of the universe, could we travel from planet to planet and from system to system, in order to examine each part of this mighty fabric? Any one of these four principles above mentioned (and a hundred others, which lie open to our conjecture) may afford us a theory, by which to judge of the origin of the world; and it is a palpable and egregious partiality to confine our view entirely to that principle, by which our own minds operate. Were this principle more intelligible on that account, such a partiality, might be somewhat excusable: But reason, in its internal fabric and structure, is really as little known to us as instinct or vegetation; and perhaps even that vague, indeterminate word, nature, to which the vulgar refer every thing, is not at the bottom more inexplicable. The effects of these principles are all known to us from experience: But the principles themselves, and their manner of operation are totally unknown: Nor is it less intelligible, or less conformable to experience to say, that the world arose by vegetation from a seed shed by another world, than to say that it arose from a divine reason or contrivance, according to the sense in which CLEANTHES understands it.[33]

By Philo's lights, the plausibility of alternative, nontheistic accounts defeats Cleanthes' argument. Philo's thesis is that Cleanthes' theistic hypothesis is no more reasonable than speculative, nontheistic alternatives. Philo advances not only alternative nonreligious hypotheses, but he considers the possibility of multiple gods rather than a single deity,

> And what shadow of an argument, continued Philo, can you produce, from your hypothesis, to prove the unity of the Deity? A great number of men join in building a house or ship, in rearing a city, in framing a commonwealth: Why not several deities combine in contriving and framing a world? This is only so much greater similarity to human affairs. By sharing the work among several, we may so much farther limit the

[32] Ibid., 133.
[33] Ibid., 139–140.

attributes of each, and get rid of that extensive power and knowledge, which must be supposed to one deity, and which, according to you, can only serve to weaken the proof of his existence. And if such foolish, such vicious creatures as man can yet often unite in framing and executing one plan; how much more those deities or demons, whom we may suppose several degrees more perfect?[34]

More radical still, is Philo's hypothesis that matter itself has no external cause for its order. The world, perhaps, is innately intelligible. "For ought we can know *a priori*, matter may contain the source or spring of order originally, within itself, as well as mind does; and there is no more difficulty in conceiving, that the several elements, from an internal unknown cause, fall into that arrangement, than to conceive that their ideas, in the great, universal mind, from a like internal, unknown cause, fall into that arrangement."[35]

The Problem of Anthropomorphism. In the *Dialogues* this charge is developed in two ways. First, there is the worry that an appeal to analogies with human creators will import into the concept of God unworthy, base elements.

> All the sentiments of the human mind, gratitude, resentment, love, friendship, approbation, blame, pity, emulation, envy, have a plain reference to the state and situation of man, and are calculated for preserving the existence, and promoting the activity of such a being in such circumstances. It seems therefore unreasonable to transfer such sentiments to a supreme existence, or to suppose him actuated by them; and the phenomena, besides, of the universe will not support us in such a theory. All our ideas, derived from the senses, are confessedly false and illusive; and cannot, therefore, be supposed to have place in a supreme intelligence.[36]

The other worry is that if you are going to employ human analogies, why not assume that the creator has a human body? Philo has formulated a slippery slope argument. "And why not become a perfect anthropomorphite? Why not assert the deity or deities to be corporeal, and to have eyes, a nose, mouth, ears, etc. Epicurus maintained, that not man had ever seen reason but in a human figure; therefore the gods must have a human figure. And this argument, which

[34] Ibid., 130.
[35] Ibid., 111–112.
[36] Ibid., 121.

is deservedly so much ridiculed by Cicero, becomes, according to you, solid and philosophical."[37] This outcome would presumably reduce Cleanthes' empirical philosophy of God to absurdity. Recall in Chapter 3 the central importance of resisting anthropomorphic views of God.

The Problem of Evil. The treatment of the problem of evil in the *Dialogues* is quite interesting as it falls to the mystical theist, Demea, to raise the reality of evil as a cause for religious devotion.

> It is my opinion, I own, replied DEMEA, that each man feels, in a manner, the truth of religion within his own breast; and from a consciousness of his imbecility and misery, rather than from any reasoning, is led to seek protection from that Being, on whom he and all nature is dependent. So anxious or so tedious are even the best scenes of life, that futurity is still the object of all our hopes and fears. We incessantly look forward and endeavor, by prayers, adoration, and sacrifice, to appease those unknown powers, whom we find, by experience, so able to afflict and oppress us. Wretched creatures that we are! What resource for us amidst the innumerable ills of life, did not religion suggest some methods of atonement, and appease those terrors with which we are incessantly agitated and tormented?[38]

Philo builds on Demea's delimination of life's ills:

> Observe too, says PHILO, the curious artifices of nature in order to imbitter the life of every living being. The stronger prey upon the weaker, and keep them in perpetual terror and anxiety. The weaker too, in their turn, often prey upon the stronger, and vex and molest them without relaxation. Consider that innumerable race of insects, which either are bred on the body of each animal, or flying about infix their stings in him. These insects have others still less than themselves, which torment them. And thus on each hand, before and behind, above and below, every animal is surrounded with enemies, which incessantly seek his misery and destruction.[39]

Philo contends that Cleanthes' account of God in terms of mercy, benevolence, and other moral attributes is unjustified. Whatever

---

[37] Ibid., 131.
[38] Ibid., 152.
[39] Ibid., 153.

benevolence God has must be radically dissimilar from the benevolence as we find it among humans.

> And it is possible, CLEANTHES, said PHILO, that after all these reflections, and infinitely more, which might be suggested, you can still persevere in your anthropomorphism, and assert the moral attributes of the Deity, his justice, benevolence, mercy, and rectitude, to be of the same nature with these virtues in human creatures? His power we allow infinite: Whatever he wills is executed: But neither man nor any other animal are happy: Therefore he does not will their happiness. His wisdom is infinite: He is never mistaken in choosing the means to any end: But the course of nature tends not to human or animal felicity: Therefore it is not established for that purpose. Through the whole compass of human knowledge, there are no inferences more certain and infallible than these. In what respect, then, do his benevolence and mercy resemble the benevolence and mercy of men?[40]

Despite the vigorous, negative verdict on theism, Philo delimits two approaches to evil. If one already has a belief in an all-good God, the evil of the cosmos will not ipso facto undermine belief. That is, it is possible that the evils of the world serve a worthy, greater good such that less evil in the cosmos would create more evil. But this approach differs from the point of view of someone who does not have a prior conception of the creator of the cosmos.

> Did I show you a house or palace, where there was not one apartment convenient or agreeable; where the windows, doors, fires, passages, stairs, and the whole economy of the building were the source of noise, confusion, fatigue, darkness, and the extremes of heat and cold; you would certainly blame the contrivance, without any farther examination. The architect would in vain display his subtlety, and prove to you, that if this door or that window were altered, greater ills would ensue. *What he says, may be strictly true: The alteration of one particular, while the other parts of the building remain, may only augment the inconveniences.* But still you would assert, in general, that, if the architect had had skill and good intentions, he might have formed such a plan of the whole, and might have adjusted the parts in such a manner, as would have remedied all or most of these inconveniences. His ignorance, or even your own ignorance of such a plan, will never convince you of the impossibility of it. If you find many inconveniences and deformities in the building, you will always, without entering into any detail, condemn the architect.

[40] Ibid., 156–157.

In short, I repeat the question: Is the world, considered in general, and as it appears to us in this life, different from what a man or such a limited being would, *beforehand*, expect from a very powerful, wise, and benevolent Deity? It must be strange prejudice to assert the contrary. And from thence I conclude, that, however consistent the world may be, allowing certain suppositions and conjectures, with the idea of such a Deity, it can never afford us an inference concerning his existence. The consistence is not absolutely denied, only the inference. Conjectures, especially where infinity is excluded from the divine attributes, may, perhaps, be sufficient to prove a consistence; but can never be foundations for any inference.[41]

I offer an analysis of the strength and weakness of Hume's assault later in the chapter, but let us first consider the case for and against a cosmological argument.

A Cosmological Argument

In the *Dialogues*, Hume splits up the defense of the design and cosmological arguments, rather than follow the tradition of linking the two.[42] Hume has Demea advance the cosmological argument and Cleanthes attack it. I suggest that splitting the two up provides an overall weaker case for theism than if taken together, but if the argument fails due to Cleanthes' objections the matter is of little consequence.[43]

First, we consider Demea's cosmological argument:

The argument, replied DEMEA, which I would insist on is the common one. Whatever exists must have a cause or reason of its existence; it being absolutely impossible for any thing to produce itself, or be the cause of its own existence. In mounting up, therefore, from effects to causes, we must either go on in tracing an infinite sucession, without any ultimate cause at all, or must at last have recourse to some ultimate cause, that is necessarily existent: Now that the first supposition is absurd may be thus proved. In the infinite chain or succession of causes and effects, each single effect is determined to exist by the power and efficacy of that cause,

---

[41] Ibid., 162–163.

[42] Although Thomas Aquinas did not use the terms "cosmological and design arguments," he did develop complementary theistic arguments that appealed to contingency and purpose.

[43] One implication of the divide worth considering, however, is that it does align Cleanthes with Hume as Cleanthes' objections match Hume's own views expressed elsewhere. It thus bolsters the cause for commentators who argue that, in the end, Hume is closer in sympathy to Cleanthes rather than Philo.

which immediately preceeded; but the whole external chain or succession, taken together, is not determined or caused by any thing: And yet it is evident that it requires a cause or reason, as much as any particular object, which begins to exist in time. The question is still reasonable, why this particular succession of causes existed from eternity, and not any other succession, or no succession at all. If there be no necessarily existent Being, any supposition, which can be formed, is equally possible; nor is there any more absurdity in nothing's having existed from eternity, than there is in that succession of causes, which constitutes the universe. What was it then, which determined something to exist rather than nothing, and bestowed being on a particular possibility, exclusive of the rest? *External causes* there are none. *Chance* is a word without a meaning. Was it *nothing*? But that can never produce any thing. We must, therefore, have recourse to a necessarily existent Being, who carries the REASON of his existence in himself; and who cannot be supposed not to exist without an express contradiction. There is consequently such a Being, that is, there is a Deity.[44]

I hope to bring out the merits of the argument in the course of citing and then considering replies to Cleanthes' three Humean objections: the problem of necessity, the parity objection, and the objection from parts and wholes.

The Problem of Necessity

Cleanthes' objection is thoroughly Humean.

I shall begin with observing, that there is an evident absurdity in pretending to demonstrate a matter of fact, or to prove it by any arguments *a priori*. Nothing is demonstrable, unless the contrary implies a contradiction. Nothing, that is distinctly conceivable, implies a contradiction. Whatever we conceive as existent, we can also conceive as non-existent. There is no Being, therefore, whose non-existence implies a contradiction. Consequently there is no Being, whose existence is demonstrable. I propose this argument as entirely decisive, and am willing to rest the whole controversy upon it.

It is pretended, that the Deity is a necessarily existent Being and this necessity of his existence is attempted to be explained by asserting, that, if we knew his whole essence or nature, we should perceive it to be as impossible for him not to exist as for twice two not to be four. But it is evident, that this can never happen, while our faculties remain the same as

[44] *Dialogues*, 148–149.

at present: It will still be possible for us, at any time, to conceive the non-existence of what we formerly conceived to exist; nor can the mind ever lie under a necessity of supposing any object to remain always in being; in the same manner as we lie under a necessity of always conceiving twice two to be four. The words, therefore, *necessary existence* have no meaning; or which is the same thing, none that is consistent.[45]

Cleanthes' thereby distinguishes his view of God from the theism found in More, Descartes, Leibniz (and, before them, Anselm and Aquinas) in which God's existence is seen as unconditionally necessary. (Cleanthes also differs from Spinoza's view of divine necessity.) Cleanthes has advanced an ambitious objection for, if successful, it would demonstrate the falsehood or unfounded nature of classical and early modern philosophical theism.[46]

Is the objection successful? If Hume is right that matters of necessity can only apply to the relations of ideas, then it cannot apply to an existing being.[47] But some philosophers think that Hume has not demonstrated that thesis.[48] In fact, his very concept of demonstration is problematic. Hume writes "nothing is demonstrable, unless the contrary implies a contradiction." Is the contrary of Hume's thesis a contradiction? It has been argued that there is no evident contradiction in the claim that there is one (or more) necessarily existing being(s). Hume grants $2 + 2 = 4$ is necessary, so the concept of "necessary" is meaningful, by his lights. Consider the claim that the necessity of $2 + 2 = 4$ is not due to the relation of ideas. Arguably, $2 + 2 = 4$ would still be necessarily true even if there were no human-Humean ideas. Because of the apparent necessity of mathematical and other truths (A is A) not dependent on any mind, some philosophers claim there are necessarily existing, unconditional, matters of fact. Is such a philosophical claim contradictory? If there is no *contradiction*, or at least no evident one, why rule out the possibility of Demea's concept of a necessarily existing being?[49]

---

[45] Ibid., 149.

[46] For a more recent argument in the Humean tradition, see J. N. Findlay, "Can God's Existence Be Disproved?" *Mind* 57 (1948).

[47] Hume's view seems to be that it is necessarily the case that necessity only applies to the relation of ideas.

[48] The replies to Hume that follow have been developed by a range of philosophers, for example, James Ross, Alvin Plantinga, R. M. Adams, and others cited later.

[49] For a recent non-Humean treatment of necessity, see M. J. Loux, *Metaphysics* (London: Routledge, 1998). There is a useful analysis of some theistic alternatives in Anthony

Hume contends, "Whatever we conceive of as existent, we can also conceive of as non-existent." But if the strategy in the preceding paragraph makes headway, one can point to ostensibly necessarily existing propositions that cannot not exist, and thus any claim to conceive of them ceasing to be or not existing would not be the successful entertaining of a bona fide possibility. Arguably, one can conceive of the necessary *matter of fact* (not relation of my ideas) $2 + 2 = 4$ and yet not conceive of it as either nonexistent or false. It may be objected that this begs the question against Hume for he does not grant that $2 + 2 = 4$ is a necessary matter of fact. It is not begging the question, however, to raise the question of why we ought to embrace Hume's framework at this point.[50]

What of the claim to conceive of God's nonexistence? R. M. Adams and some other philosophers have argued that this is not as easy as it may appear.[51] In earlier chapters, we have covered versions of the ontological argument in which philosophers claimed that to conceive of a perfect or maximally excellent being is to conceive of a being that necessarily exists (or whose nonexistence is impossible). Has Hume given us good reason to believe that he can imagine the genuine possibility of *that being not existing or existing at one time and then failing to exist*? Successful thought experiments (discussed in Chapter 2) depend upon properly grasping the relevant properties. Demea (or a defender of the cosmological argument) could challenge the Humean Cleanthes to demonstrate that he can successfully conceive of a maximally excellent

Kenny, "God and Necessity," in *British Analytic Philosophy*, ed. B. Williams (London: Routledge, 1966).

[50] Robert Koons has recently argued that Hume's position that necessary existence is impossible is self-defeating. "The Humean principle ... is self-defeating. Is it supposed to be true by definition that only logical or definitory truths are necessary? Surely in saying this, Hume, Russell, and others intended to be saying something informative. How could such a principle be contingent? What sort of contingent facts about the actual world make it the case that there are no non-logical necessities? What empirical justification have the anti-essentialists provided for their claim? In response, the objector must simply deny that he can make any sense of this notion of modality, except insofar as it is replaced by the clear and well-behaved notion of logical consistency. This sweeping denial of modality is simply obscurantist, undermining fruitful philosophical research into the nature of natural law, epistemology, decision, action and responsibility, and a host of other applications" (*Realism Regained* [Oxford: Oxford University Press, 2000], 115).

[51] See R. M. Adams, "Has It Been Proved That All Real Existence Is Contingent?" in *The Virtue of Faith* (Oxford: Oxford University Press, 1987).

being possessing only contingent, not necessary existence. The fact, if it is one, that Hume can secure the possible nonexistence of empirical objects and states of affairs does not secure the possible nonexistence of a nonempirical reality such as God.[52] Cleanthes' claim is that it is possible "for us, at any time, to conceive of the non-existence of what we formerly conceived to exist." This is a stronger claim than simply holding that you can conceive of X existing and you can also not conceive of X existing. (This would seem to be true of any X, for when you are unconscious you are presumably not conceiving of anything whatever.) Cleanthes may rightly claim not to conceive of a maximally excellent and therefore necessary existing being, but that falls short of successfully conceiving that such a being is a demonstrable impossibility.[53]

The Parity Objection

Cleanthes charges that, if we allow that there can be, or there must be, a necessarily existing being, this being may turn out to be the universe itself. In other words there is just as much reason to see the material world as necessary as a transcendent cause such as God.

> But farther; why may not the material universe be the necessarily existent Being, according to this pretended explication of necessity? We dare not affirm that we know all the qualities of matter; and for aught we can determine, it may contain some qualities, which, were they known, would make its non-existence appear as great a contradiction as that twice two is five. I find only one argument employed to prove, that the material world is not the necessarily existent Being; and this argument is derived from the contingency both of the matter and the form of the world. "Any particle of matter," it is said, "may be *conceived* to be annihilated; and any form may be *conceived* to be altered. Such an annihilation or alteration, therefore, is not impossible." But it seems a great partiality not to perceive, that the same arguments extends equally to the Deity, so far as we have any conception of him; and that the mind can at least imagine him to be non-existent, or his attributes to be altered. It must be some unknown, inconceivable qualities, which can make his non-existence appear impossible, or his attributes unalterable: And no reason can be assigned, why

---

[52] See George E. Hughes, "Has God's Existence Been Disproved?" *Mind* 58 (1949).

[53] See the discussion of Hume in C. Hartshorne, *Anselm's Discovery* (LaSalle: Open Court, 1965). On the difficulty of conceiving of God's nonexistence, see also Laura Garcia, "A Response to the Modal Problem of Evil," *Faith and Philosophy* 1 (1989).

these qualities may not belong to matter. As they are altogether unknown and inconceivable, they can never be proved incompatible with it.[54]

Philo goes on to indicate why, in a choice between God or the world, we should see the reason for the world's existence as internal to the world itself and not lying in something transcendent.

> Why not stop at the material world? How can we satisfy ourselves without going on *in finitum*? And after all, what satisfaction is there in that infinite progression? Let us remember the story of the *Indian* philosopher and his elephant. It was never more applicable than to the present subject. If the material world rests upon a similar ideal world, this ideal world must rest upon some other; and so on, without end. It were better, therefore, never to look beyond the present material world. By supposing it to contain the principle of its order within itself, we really assert it to be God; and the sooner we arrive at that divine Being, so much the better. When you go one step beyond the mundane system, you only excite an inquisitive humour, which it is impossible ever to satisfy.[55]

Typically, subsequent defenders of the cosmological argument build on the point made earlier about the difference between conceiving of the nonexistence of God versus the nonexistence of the cosmos.[56] The difficulty with stopping with the material world is its apparent contingency. The world does not seem to carry the reason for its existence in itself. We can positively conceive of the material world's nonexistence. How far must Demea go in claiming to positively conceive of a creator whose nonexistence is impossible? I am not sure that a successful cosmological argument must secure a positive conception of divine necessity; it may suffice instead to argue that there must be such a being if we are to account for a contingent cosmos.[57] If there is some reason to believe (as Butler and his contemporaries thought) that the cosmos is contingent and yet requires a necessarily existing cause, then one has some reason to believe there is a necessarily existing cause transcending the cosmos even if we cannot form a positive conception of that necessary being.

[54] Ibid., 149–150.

[55] Ibid., 125.

[56] See, for example, Richard Taylor, *Metaphysics* (Englewood Cliffs, N.J.: Prentice-Hall, 1992).

[57] Many defenders of cosmological arguments have not defended an ontological argument on the grounds that while God's necessary existence or self-existence is self-evident to those who understand the divine nature, it is not evident to ordinary human cognition. This was Aquinas's position.

Further reasons are cited for not stopping at the material world in the subsequent section on design.

The Objection from Parts and Wholes

Cleanthes contends that if we can explain the existence of any (and thus every) part of the cosmos in terms of other parts of the cosmos, there is no reason to go beyond the cosmos to explain it.

> In such a chain or succession of objects, each part is caused by that which preceded it, and causes that which succeeds it. Where then is the difficulty? But the WHOLE, you say, wants a cause. I answer that the uniting of these parts into a whole, like the uniting of several distinct countries into one kingdom, or several distinct members into one body, is performed merely by an arbitrary act of the mind, and has no influence on the nature of things. Did I show you the particular causes of each individual in a collection of twenty particles of matter, I should think it very unreasonable, should you afterwards ask me, what was the cause of the whole twenty.[58]

In reply, it has been argued that Demea rightly seeks for a reason why the cosmos as a whole exists even if each of its parts is explained with reference to other parts. If each individual, contingent thing among twenty had an account, we would still want to know why any of them existed at all, or why there weren't different sorts of individual, contingent things. Moreover, it has been argued that the need for an overall explanation is still in play even if we entertain a cosmos that is infinite or without beginning. Hume's appeal to the sufficiency of explanations exclusively within the cosmos has its defenders (Paul Edwards, Bertrand Russell) but also a range of critics (W. Rowe, B. Riechenbach, R. Purtill). An amusing reply to Hume and Edwards was advanced by Alexander Pruss. He imagines a bizarre world of chickens and eggs.

> Consider a possible world in which there is an infinite sequence of chickens (of both sexes) and eggs, stretching infinitely far back in time. The chicken lay eggs, and the eggs hatch into chickens. The [state of affairs to be explained] consists of all the chickens and eggs. Now, each chicken is explained by the egg from which it had hatched, and each egg is explained in terms of the chicken which had laid it. Therefore each individual . . . had

---

[58] *Dialogues*, 150.

been explained, and the [Humean] principle implies that we have explained the whole chicken-and-eggs sequence.[59]

Pruss concludes that we would still have only a circular, and thus unsatisfying, explanation. I do not claim here that the cosmological argument is or is not invulnerable to Hume's and other's objections. My aim is only to sketch the different, historically significant replies.[60]

Design Again

As we return to the design argument, it should be noted that while Philo subjects the argument to severe criticism, Hume represents Philo, in the end, as embracing a modest deistic or theistic conclusion (sometimes called "thin theism").

> If the whole of Natural Theology, as some people seem to maintain, resolves itself into one simple, though somewhat ambiguous, at least undefined proposition, *That the cause or causes of order in the universe probably bear some remote analogy to human intelligence:* If this proposition be not capable of extension, variation, or more particular explication: If it affords no inference that affects human life, or can be the source of any action or forbearance: And if the analogy, imperfect as it is, can be carried no farther than to the human intelligence; and cannot be transferred, with any appearance of probability, to the qualities of the mind: If this really

---

[59] A. Pruss, "The Hume-Edwards Principle and the Cosmological Argument," *International Journal for Philosophy of Religion* 43 (1998): 154. For two other replies to Hume, see Louis Leahy, "Contingency in the Cosmological Argument," *Religious Studies* 12 (1976), and Richard Swinburne, "Whole and Part in Cosmological Arguments," *Philosophy* 44 (1969).

[60] I discuss the cosmological argument again in Chapter 5. Obviously other objections need addressing to have a successful argument. See, for example, G. E. M. Anscombe, " 'Whatever Has a Beginning Must Have a Cause': Hume's Argument Exposed," *Analysis* 3 (1971); Bruce Reichenbach, *The Cosmological Argument* (Springfield: Charles C. Thomas Publishers, 1972); William Rowe, *The Cosmological Argument* (Princeton: Princeton University Press, 1975); Richard Swinburne, *The Existence of God* (Oxford: Clarendon, 1991); also, Taylor, *Metaphysics*. Paul Edward's defense of Hume is in "The Cosmological Argument," reprinted in the fine collection, *The Cosmological Argument*, ed. D. R. Burrill (Garden City: Anchor Books, 1967). In *Theism, Atheism and Big Bang Cosmology* (Oxford: Clarendon, 1993), cosmological arguments are debated by W. L. Craig (defending) and Quentin Smith (attacking). For a powerful defense of the cosmological argument, see Philip Quinn, "Creation, Conservation, and the Big Bang," in *Philosophical Problems of the Internal and External Worlds*, ed. J. Earman et al. (Pittsburgh: University of Pittsburgh Press, 1993).

be the case, what can the most inquisitive, contemplative, and religious man do more than give a plain, philosophical assent to the proposition, as often as it occurs; and believe that the arguments, on which it is established, exceed the objections, which lie against it? Some astonishment indeed will naturally arise from the greatness of the object: Some melancholy from its obscurity: Some contempt of human reason, that it can give no solution more satisfactory with regard to so extraordinary and magnificent a question. But believe me, CLEANTHES, the most natural sentiment which a well-disposed mind will feel on this occasion, is a longing desire and expectation, that heaven would be pleased to dissipate, at least alleviate, this profound ignorance, by affording some particular revelation to mankind, and making discoveries of the nature, attributes, and operations of the divine object of our faith. A person, seasoned with a just sense of the imperfections of natural reason, will fly to revealed truth with the greatest avidity: While the haughty Dogmatist, persuaded, that he can erect a complete system of Theology by the mere help of philosophy, disdains any farther aid, and rejects this adventitious instructor. To be a philosophical Skeptic is, in a man of letters, the first and most essential step towards being a sound, believing Christian.[61]

These and other passages have been subject to speculative accounts of how far Hume went in his positive appraisal of religion.[62]

In assessing the overall debate between naturalism and theism in the *Dialogues*, I suggest that we need to delimit two closely related, distinct methodologies. The first is a strict inductive, inferential method from effect to cause. "When we infer any particular cause from an effect, we must proportion the one to the other, and can never be allowed to ascribe to the cause any qualities, but what exactly is sufficient to produce the effect."[63] And: "If the cause be known only by the effect, we never ought to ascribe to it any qualities, beyond what are precisely requisite to produce the effect: nor can we, by any rules of just reasoning, return back from the cause, and infer other effects from it, beyond those by which alone it is known to us."[64] This inductive, inferential methodology implies that two philosophical inquirers (Philo and Cleanthes) share a common understanding of the effects but then disagree about what

---

[61] *Dialogues*, 284–285.

[62] See, for example, John Immerwahr, "Hume's Aesthetic Theism," *Hume Studies* 22:2 (1996); Beryl Logan, "Why Hume Wasn't an Atheist," *Hume Studies* 22 (1996); and D. T. Siebert, "Hume on Idolatry and Incarnation," *Journal of the History of Ideas* 45:3 (1984).

[63] *An Enquiry*, 170.

[64] Ibid., 171.

one should conclude about the cause. However, this outlook does not seem to match certain maneuvers in the *Dialogues*, and there are some independent reasons to consider an alternative schema that we may refer to as the method of comprehensive explanations.[65] On this schema, a naturalist may reason that, given naturalism, the cosmos and human life are accounted for – and, in fact, better accounted for – than in the best, competing frameworks. The theist, on the other hand, proposes that it makes more sense (and it is better justified) to see the cosmos theistically.

Reference to different ways of seeing the cosmos emerges in the *Dialogues* in connection with the problem of evil. Cleanthes *sees* the world as designed for the good, whereas Philo suggests it makes more sense to see it as poorly designed or designed by creator(s) indifferent to human welfare or simply not designed at all. Recall More's design argument in Chapter 1 according to which he sees letters among the ashes and the skeptic merely sees ashes. The two agree that there are such and such shapes and matter, but "the believer" sees meaningful communication and presumably goes on to offer reasons why this apparent perception should be accepted as genuine, whereas the skeptic sees a random, meaningless configuration. In Hume's *Dialogues*, Cleanthes begins with the analogical version of the design argument cited earlier, but then he shifts to what he calls an "irregular argument," even though it has enormous force.

Some beauties in writing we may meet with, which seem contrary to rules, and which gain the affections, and animate the imagination, in opposition to all precepts of criticism and to the authority of the established masters of art. And if the argument for theism be, as you pretend, contradictory to the principles of logic; its universal, its irresistible influence proves clearly, that there may be arguments of a like irregular nature. Whatever cavils may be urged; an orderly world, as well as a coherent, articulate speech, will still be received as an incontestable proof of design and intention.[66]

Cleanthes' reference to "articulate speech" stems from this analogy:

Suppose, therefore, that an articulate voice were heard in the clouds, much louder and more melodious than any which human art could ever reach:

[65] See B. L. Clarke, "The Argument from Design – A Piece of Abductive Reasoning," *International Journal of Philosophy of Religion* 5 (1974), and R. Hambourger "The Argument from Design," in *Intentions and Intentionality*, ed. Cora Diamond (Ithaca: Cornell University Press, 1979).

[66] *Dialogues*, 119.

Suppose, that this voice were extended in the same instant over all nations, and spoke to each nation in its own language and dialect: Suppose, that the words delivered not only contain a just sense and meaning, but convey some instruction altogether worthy of a benevolent Being, superior to mankind: Could you possibly hesitate a moment concerning the cause of this voice? And must you not instantly ascribe it to some design or purpose? Yet I cannot see but all the same objections (if they merit that appellation) which lie against the system of theism, may also be produced against this inference.[67]

What is happening here, I suggest, is a shift from a narrowly conceived analogical argument to one assessing theism and its alternates in light of the coherence and evidential justification of their overall view of the cosmos (the method of comprehensive explanations). Cleanthes may be seen as arguing that if one views the cosmos theistically, it makes more sense, and is in fact more reasonable, to see the cosmos in this way rather than in nontheistic terms (the cosmos is uncreated, undesigned, etc.). As it happens, Philo attacks both the regular and "irregular" argument, but there is some textual support that Philo comes to his tentative theistic conclusion on the basis of the irregular version. The shift from an inferential, inductive method to one emphasizing comprehensive explanations can help account for Philo's otherwise surprisingly conciliatory conclusion.[68]

This alternative approach to the arguments under debate does not beg the question against naturalism or provide by itself any concrete support for theism. All Hume's objections still come into play. But this alternative allows one to detect interconnections between arguments and to see how an overall case can be made for a way of seeing the cosmos. I also believe this alternative does greater justice to the general role of theistic and naturalistic reasoning in modern philosophy of religion, a role that has tended to be comprehensive and cumulative in argumentation.[69] Also, consider how matters of design and teleology (purposiveness) function in typical, nonphilosophical contexts. C. D. Broad once claimed: "Teleology is an observable characteristic."[70] In

---

[67] Ibid., 117.

[68] See Beryl Logan, "The Irregular Argument in Hume's Dialogues," *Hume Studies* 18:2 (1992). See also Leon Pearl's "Hume Criticism of the Argument from Design," *Monist* 54 (1970).

[69] See Chapters 8 and 9.

[70] C. D. Broad, *The Mind and Its Place in Nature* (Paterson, N.J.: Littlefield, 1960), 81.

other words, ordinarily one may be said to observe purposive behavior or design. I suggest that some religious believers observe the world as designed, whereas others do not, and the philosophical debate then ensues about whether the observations of design are in fact reliable or are merely apparent and much like a mirage that disappears when you look at it from a different angle.[71] (One may reverse this picture: the debate may proceed on the grounds that a naturalist sees the cosmos as undesigned and then the argument is over whether *that* observation is reasonable.)

My suggestion may seem merely a matter of rephrasing the terms of debate, but Hume's inferential, inductive method does seem to offer a highly restricted view of reason. Hume's stricture, cited earlier, would seem to rule out ordinary, nonproblematic reasoning and fundamental science. Hume writes, "If the cause be known only by the effect, we never ought to ascribe to it any qualities beyond what are precisely requisite to produce the effect: nor can we, by any rules of just reasoning, return back from the cause, and infer other effects from it, beyond those by which alone it is known to us." Consider the following trivial case of ordinary reasoning: we can imagine circumstances when I see broken glass, and, on the basis of other observation, along with other evidence, I infer that juvenile delinquents broke the glass. The following subsequent reasoning from the posited cause to effect seems perfectly reasonable: other things being equal, if there are such juveniles about, and conditions remain constant, it is likely that tomorrow there will be more broken glass. If I were restricted to minimal inferences from effect to cause, my inferences may be unduly restricted – for example, I may only infer a single act of juvenile delinquency and be rigorously agnostic about any subsequent repercussions. The point is that we routinely consider overall hypotheses (in this case, theories about criminal behavior, neighborhoods, juvenile life) rather than work with strict induction from effect to a posited minimal cause necessary to produce the effect. Similarly, scientific theorizing is often constituted by positing effects given such and such hypothetical causes as outlined in comprehensive theorizing.[72]

---

[71] See Del Ratzsche, "Perceiving Design," in *God and Design*, ed. N. A. Manson (London: Routledge, 2003).

[72] On this front, I think Richard Swinburne successfully outlines comprehensive argumentation in *The Existence of God* (Oxford: Clarendon Press, 1979). For a contrary position, see D. H. Mellor, "God and Probability," *Religious Studies* 3 (1969).

In concluding these observations about methodology, I cite one further, famous passage in which Hume idealizes proper inferential reasoning.

> A body of ten ounces raised in any scale may serve as a proof, that the counterbalancing weight exceeds ten ounces; but can never afford a reason that it exceeds a hundred. If the cause, assigned for any effect, be not sufficient to produce it, we must either reject that cause, or add to it such qualities as will give it a just proportion to the effect. But if we ascribe to it farther qualities, or affirm it capable of producing other effects, we can only indulge the license of conjecture, and arbitrarily suppose the existence of qualities and energies, without reason or authority.... No one, merely from the sight of one of Zeuxis's pictures could know, that he was also a statuary or architect, and was an artist no less skilful in stone and marble than in colours. The talents and taste, displayed in the particular work before us; these we may safely conclude the workman to be possessed of. The cause must be proportioned to the effect; and if we exactly and precisely proportion it, we shall never find in it any qualities, that point farther, or afford an inference concerning any other design or performance. Such qualities must be somewhat beyond what is merely requisite for producing the effect, which we examine.[73]

My suggestion in response is that such scale-based or metered reasoning is rare. On the contrary, I think that our reasoning often takes place on the basis of proposed, comprehensive beliefs (or assumptions) about ourselves and the world, and that the evidence for such comprehensive beliefs is diverse and cumulative. I further suggest that the kind of reasoning Hume describes in this passage of checking scales itself takes place within a more comprehensive view of the cosmos – for example, a scientific or economic worldview that supports or provides a framework for quantification, weights, scales, and measurements.

Here are some additional rejoinders to Philo's objections, developed in the *Dialogues* or in subsequent replies to Hume.

Reply to the Problem of Dissimilitude. I think Cleanthes' reply to Philo has much to commend it. "It would surely be very ill received, replied CLEANTHES; and I should be deservedly blamed and detested, did I allow, that the proofs of a Deity amounted to no more than a guess or conjecture. But is the whole adjustment of means to ends

---

[73] *An Enquiry*, 170–171.

in a house and in the universe so slight a resemblance? The economy of final causes? The order, proportion, and arrangement of every part?"[74] Cleanthes charges that Philo's skepticism would involve a rejection of what most would conclude is clearly a matter of design and intelligence. Cleanthes' comparison of the cosmos to articulate speech (cited earlier) is, I think, a powerful analogy.[75] Assimilating the cosmos to a voice conjures up the early modern idea that nature is like a book.[76]

Reply to the Problem of Uniqueness. It has been argued that contemporary astrophysics would not be carried out if Hume's objection were taken seriously. Big Bang cosmology seems undeterred by the fact that our universe is the only one we experience; moreover, there seems to be little worry about the scientific use of analogies or the appeal to resemblance when it comes to referring to the cosmos as a whole. Richard Swinburne counters the uniqueness objection as follows.

> From time to time various writers have told us that we cannot reach any conclusions about the origin or development of the universe, since it is (whether by logic or just in fact) a unique object, the only one of its kind, and rational inquiry can only reach the conclusions about objects which belong to kinds, e.g. it can reach a conclusion about what will happen to this bit of iron, because there are other bits of iron, the behaviour of which can be studied. This objection of course has the surprising, and to most of these writers unwelcome, consequence, that physical cosmology cannot reach justified conclusions about such matters as the size, age, rate of expansion, and density of the universe as a whole (because it is a unique object); and also that physical anthropology cannot reach conclusion about the origin and development of the human race (because, as far as our knowledge goes, it is the only one of its kind). The implausibility of these consequences leads us to doubt the original objection, which is indeed totally misguided.[77]

---

[74] *Dialogues*, 109.

[75] Ibid., 117. For two interesting discussions of analogies, which press for the primacy of seeing the cosmos as more like a work of art than a machine, see A. E. Taylor, "The Present-Day Relevance of Hume's *Dialogues Concerning Natural Religion*," *Proceedings of the Aristotelian Society* 18 (1939), and R. H. Hurlbutt, *Hume, Newton and the Design Argument* (Lincoln: University of Nebraska Press, 1965).

[76] In the early modern era, the knowledge of God was thought (by some) to be grounded on nature – which functioned as a book of God – and on the book of revealed Scripture.

[77] Swinburne, *The Existence of God*.

Reply to the Problem of Alternative Possibilities. At least two lines of reasoning are worth pursuing. The first involves building up a fuller picture of the design hypothesis, highlighting its radical distinction from cosmologies not involving design. Cleanthes might simplify the design hypothesis by referring to explanations in terms of a divine (or very powerful) intentional being. Intentional explanations have the merit of accounting for some state of affairs in light of perceived goodness – for example, the explanation behind your writing a book is because you believe this to be good. Moreover, intentions are not merely (in Hume's phrase) a "little agitation of the brain." This is partially because they are not physical (or so it may be argued). Hume himself holds that volition is not physical. But "agitations" are not, under ordinary conditions, intentions or intentional. There is also something odd in Philo's describing thought (reason and design) as "so minute, so weak," and "so bounded." Is there anything intrinsically so minute about thought or thinking? Perhaps human and animal thought is fleeting, weak, limited, and episodic, but in hypothesizing about the possible cause or explanation of the cosmos why believe that a supremely great intentional or thinking agency would be minute, weak, or bounded in its intentionality or thought? Arguably, although biology may enable our thinking (as Hume thought), it is also (as Hume thought) what limits or threatens our thinking (see Hume on annihilation later in the chapter). A being transcending biology and the physical structure of the cosmos may (for all we know) have boundless powers of thought, reason, and design. What Philo does not appreciate is that an intentional account of the cosmos is one in which the goodness of the cosmos counts as one of the reasons for why it exists.[78] An appeal to intentionality in explaining states of affairs is not merely one explanation among others. Rather, it stands out as an account rooted in perceived value and, as such, differs profoundly from explanations involving Hume's other candidates. Hume writes:

> Thought, design, intelligence, such as we discover in men and other animals, is no more than one of the springs and principles of the universe, as well as heat or cold, attraction or repulsion, and a hundred others, which fall under daily observation. It is an active cause, by which some particular parts of nature, we find, produce alterations on other parts. But can a conclusion, with any propriety, be transferred from parts to the whole?

[78] See Mark Wynn, *God and Goodness* (London: Routledge, 1999).

Does not the great disproportion bar all comparison and inference? From observing the growth of a hair, can we learn any thing concerning generation of a man? Would the manner of a leaf's blowing, even though perfectly known, afford us any instruction concerning the vegetation of a tree?[79]

But note the difference between an intentional explanation (a tree was planted by a gardener intent on making a garden) versus explanations limited to heat, cold, attraction, or repulsion.[80] Hume's other list of causes – "reason, instinct, generation, vegetation" – may be seen as reducible to two kinds of explanation. If we assume that an appeal to instinct is merely a mechanistic, largely biological affair, the explanations are either intentional (involving reason and purpose) or nonintentional.

A second line of reasoning to develop involves a closer inspection of Hume's analogies to the effect that the universe resembles a giant vegetable or a cosmic animal.

Now if we survey the universe, so far as it falls under our knowledge, it bears a great resemblance to an animal or organized body, and seems actuated with a like principle of life and motion. A continual circulation of matter in it produces no disorder: A continual waste in every part is incessantly repaired: The closest sympathy is perceived throughout the entire system: And each part or member, in performing its proper offices, operates both to its own preservation and to that of the whole. The world, therefore, I infer, is an animal, and the Deity is the SOUL of the world, actuating it, and actuated by it.[81]

I address the appeal to a divine soul in the next set of replies. Here it has been suggested that Cleanthes might argue that the best account of a giant vegetable universe or cosmic animal is an overriding intentional reality.[82] Presumably the existence of Hume's gigantic animal world would be good, and an intentional explanation of that world can make

[79] Ibid., 208.

[80] As for Hume's specific case of hair and leaves, today through DNA testing we can tell quite a bit from a single hair, and a leaf may also give us a host of information about the tree.

[81] Wynn, *God and Goodness*, 232.

[82] See Alvin Plantinga, *God and Other Minds* (Ithaca: Cornell University Press, 1967). Compare with Wesley Salmon, "Religion and Science, a New Look at Hume's *Dialogues*," *Philosophical Studies* 33 (1978). Also useful is George Schlesinger, "Probabilistic Arguments for Divine Design," *Philosophia* 3 (1973).

that goodness one of the reasons why it was created and is sustained in being.[83]

I believe one of Cleanthes' best replies to Philo on cosmic order is his appeal to a natural library.

> Suppose, therefore, that you enter into your library, thus peopled by natural volumes, containing the most refind reason and most exquisite beauty: Could you possibly open one of them, and doubt, that its original cause bore the strongest analogy to mind and intelligence? When it reasons and discourses; when it expostulates, argues, and enforces its views and topics; when it applies sometimes to the pure intellect, sometimes to the affections; when it collects, disposes, and adorns every consideration suited to the subject: Could you persist in asserting, that all this, at the bottom, had really no meaning and that the first formation of this volume in the loins of its original parent proceeded not from thought and design? Your obstinacy, I know, reaches not that degree of firmness: Even your skeptical play and wantonness would be abashed at so glaring an absurdity.[84]

If the analogy holds between our cosmos and such a library, I suggest that Cleanthes' appeal to intentionality carries weight. The library analogy does, however, invite Demea to press home the charge of anthropomorphism.

> Your instance, Cleanthes, said he, drawn from books and language, being familiar, has, I confess, so much more force on that account but is there

---

[83] Portraying the universe as an animal god recalls the practice of theriomorphism, attributing animal characteristics to nonanimals. Ancient religions in Egypt, for example, saw the gods in animal form. The gist of the reply to Hume that I am sketching here may be reworked as a response to Richard Dawkins on the design argument. Dawkins develops this Humean objection: "To invoke a supernatural Designer is to explain precisely nothing, for it leaves unexplained the origin of the Designer. You have to say something like "God was always there" and if you allow yourself that kind of lazy way out, you might as well just say 'DNA was always there,' or 'Life was always there' and be done with it" (*The Blind Watchmaker* [New York: W. W. Norton, 1996], 28). Apart from observing points made earlier about the apparent contingency of the cosmos (DNA, life, etc.) versus entertaining the supposition that, if there is a God, God exists necessarily, "a supernatural Designer" is able to offer something that is not available to naturalistic accounts. On theism, the good of there being DNA and life can be the reason why DNA and life exist – they were created by God because they are good – whereas the naturalist cannot make recourse to such an overriding meaningful course. I return to the design argument in Chapters 5, 6, and 9.

[84] Ibid., 118.

not some danger too in this very circumstance, and may it not render us presumptuous, by making us imagine we comprehended the Deity, and have some adequate idea of his nature and attributes? When, I read a volume, I enter into the mind and intention of the author: I become him, in a manner, for the instant; and have an immediate feeling and conception of those ideas, which revolved in his imagination, while employed in that composition. But so near an approach we never surely can make to the Diety. His ways are not our ways. His attributes are perfect, but incomprehensible. And this volume of nature contains a great and inexplicable riddle, more than any intelligible discourse or reasoning.[85]

Let us consider this objection straightaway.

Reply to the Problem of Anthropomorphism. Demea's objection, just cited, seems peculiar as classical theism allows (or, rather, it teaches) that God does know the cosmos thoroughly. This will be an important element in discussing Adam Smith's development of Hume's ethic near the end of this chapter. As for whether Cleanthes' theism fails because it attributes to God gratitude, resentment, love, friendship, approbation, blame, pity, emulation, and envy, matters are not easily settled. Perhaps this predicament can be addressed successfully if, on the basis of revelation, religious experience, a successful argument from morality, or an ontological argument, one may establish God's essential goodness. This would allow one to set aside envy, resentment, blame, and pity as unworthy of God while preserving or refining love, just approbation and disapprobation, and other divine attributes like being merciful.[86] As for God being physical, one may either appeal to Hume's own view of the mental as nonphysical, or, should one bring the cosmological argument in as a support for the design argument, one could deny the world is God or God's body on the grounds of its contingency.[87]

The Problem of Evil. Because the problem of evil is addressed at several places later in this book (Chapters 6 and 9), I only briefly raise three points here. First, Cleanthes own reply is that Philo has exaggerated the extent of evil and suffering. In Cleanthes' judgment, pleasure outweighs

---

[85] Ibid., 120.

[86] I develop a strategy like this in "The Vanity of God," *Faith and Philosophy* 6:2 (1989).

[87] See Leon Pearl, "Hume's Criticism of the Argument from Design," *Monist* 54 (1970), and A. E. Taylor, *Does God Exist?* (London: Macmillan, 1945), chap. 4.

pain.[88] There is an interesting alliance in the dialogue between Demea and Philo, as both affirm the preponderance of suffering in this life. Demea does not share Philo's despair, however, as he holds that there is an afterlife. (Both Philo and Cleanthes put to one side considerations of an afterlife.)[89] The *Dialogues* thereby raise an important question of the role of an afterlife in assessing the problem of evil.

Second, the problem of evil is intensified in a Humean framework, as Hume accepts a form of determinism. Theists have traditionally appealed to the freedom of creatures as part of their account of the origin and nature of freedom.

Third, Hume's addressing the problem of evil contains an admirable, explicit treatment of both the scope of human reason and values. So, Hume records debate about whether our experience of the cosmos is like the experience of a porch of a great and better building. Hume's care in setting up the problem of evil by differentiating the way in which evil is assessed given different background assumptions is highly useful. As discussed in Chapter 9, current debate on the problem of evil makes great use of the ways in which evil can and cannot carry evidential weight for theism.

History and Miracles in the Realm of Nature

Hume's argument against the rationality of belief in miracles has occasioned a great deal of literature, not just about its validity and soundness but about its interpretation. I accept a mainline understanding of Hume's line of reasoning, offering some secondary literature, comments, and questions.[90]

---

[88] It has been argued that on this point, Hume's own views may be closer to Cleanthes than Philo. See Corliss Swain, "Ancient Skepticism Meets Modern Science" (St. Olaf College, unpublished paper, 2004).

[89] See Jerry Walls's interesting analysis of this in *Heaven* (Oxford: Oxford University Press, 2002), chap. 1.

[90] The critical literature on Hume's view of miracles is massive. Recent books include D. Johnson, *Hume, Holism, and Miracles* (Ithaca: Cornell University Press, 1999); John Earman's aggressively titled *Hume's Abject Failure: The Argument against Miracles* (Oxford: Oxford University Press, 2000); Robert Larmer's more festively titled *Water into Wine?* (Montreal: McGill-Queen's Universtiy Press, 1988); and R. D. Geivett and G. R. Habermas, eds., *In Defense of Miracles* (Downers Grove, Ill.: Intervarsity, 1997). Strong advocates of Hume's argument against miracles include: A. Flew, M. Martin, J. C. A. Gaskin, J. L. Mackie, and M. Baggar. For a contemporary version of Hume's case against miracles, see Gaskin, *Hume's Philosophy of Religion*, and

Hume defines a miracle as follows:

> A miracle may be accurately defined, *a transgression of a law of nature by particular volition of the Deity, or by the interposition of some invisible agent*. A miracle may either be discoverable by men or not. This alters not its nature and essence. The raising of a house or ship into the air is a visible miracle. The raising of a feather, when the wind wants ever so little of a force requisite for that purpose, is as real a miracle, though not so sensible with regard to us.[91]

Not surprisingly, the definition is not free of controversy: by describing a miracle as a *transgression*, Hume suggests there is a violation involved in God's miraculous action. Older treatments of miracles – Augustine's, for example – did not suppose that God's special actions in nature were *violations* or *transgressions*. For Augustine, it is not a law of nature that God should not act in nature for special purposes. God would do no violence to the laws of motion by elevating houses without the aid of terrestrial or lawfully well-behaved cosmic intermediaries. On theistic grounds the laws of motion are themselves reflections of God's intentional creativity. A miracle would then be God simply *acting differently* or in *particular ways* as distinct from God's general comprehensive sustaining of the cosmos.[92] The second peculiarity to notice in Hume's concept of a miracle is that traditional accounts of miracles see them as constituents in an overriding divine plan or intention. Miracles are not, then, peculiar events unattached to religious contexts. Hume makes no mention of this in his definition. A Humean miracle could be God causing a violation of nature's laws in an isolated, eccentric context – for example, God moving a feather two inches on a remote, unobserved, deserted island. Hume's conception of miracles seems too capacious and dislodged from religious contexts.

These are not as yet deep problems with Hume's account. Some theists are happy with the idea of a miracle involving the violation or suspension of a law of nature. The crucial element (most disputants seem to agree) is that in a reported miracle (Jesus rising to life after being dead three days) God is believed to have brought about an event that otherwise would not have occurred.

Robert J. Fogelin, *A Defense of Hume on Miracles* (Princeton: Princeton University Press, 2003).

[91] *An Enquiry*, 149.

[92] Johnson's dictionary depicts a miracle as an event "effected by power more than natural."

Hume's argument works from an evidentialist perspective.

> A wise man, therefore, proportions his belief to the evidence. In such con-
> clusions as are founded on an infallible experience, he expects the event
> with the last degree of assurance, and regards his past experience as a full
> *proof* of the future existence of that event. In other cases, he proceeds
> with more caution: He weighs the opposite experiments: to that side he
> inclines, with doubt and hesitation; and when at last he fixes his judgment,
> the evidence exceeds not what we properly call *probability*. All probabil-
> ity, then, supposes an opposition of experiments and observations, where
> the one side is found to overbalance the other, and to produce a degree of
> evidence, proportioned to the superiority. A hundred instances or exper-
> iments on one side, and fifty on another, afford a doubtful expectation
> of any event; though a hundred uniform experiments, with only one that
> is contradictory, reasonably beget a pretty strong degree of assurance. In
> all cases, we must balance the opposite experiments, where they are op-
> posite, and deduct the smaller number from the greater, in order to know
> the exact force of the superior evidence.[93]

Hume's numbering instances may seem puzzling, but I believe the main
point should be relatively clear. One ought to believe the preponderance of evidence; when a belief has more evidence than its denial or
suspension, one should accept the belief. (Presumably reasonable belief
involves not just the slight advantage of a belief over its negation; the
belief would have to be more reasonable than suspending judgment.)

Here, at some length, is a decisive passage in Hume's argument.

> A miracle is a violation of the laws of nature; and as a firm and unalter-
> able experience has established these laws, the proof against a miracle,
> from the very nature of the fact, is as entire as any argument from expe-
> rience can possibly be imagined. Why is it more than probable, that all
> men must die; that lead cannot, of itself, remain suspended in the air; that
> fire consumes wood, and is extinguished by water; unless it be, that these
> events are found agreeable to the laws of nature, and there is required
> a violation of these laws, or in other words, a miracle to prevent them?
> Nothing is esteemed a miracle, if it ever happen in the common course of
> nature. It is no miracle that a man, seemingly in good health, should die
> on a sudden: because such a kind of death, though more unusual than any
> other, has yet been frequently observed to happen. But it is a miracle, that
> a dead man should come to life; because that has never been observed
> in any age or country. There must, therefore, be a uniform experience

[93] *An Enquiry*, 144–145.

against every miraculous event, otherwise the event would not merit that appellation. And as a uniform experience amounts to a proof, there is here a direct and full *proof,* from the nature of the fact, against the existence of any miracle; nor can such a proof be destroyed, or the miracle rendered credible, but by an opposite proof, which is superior.[94]

The reason why some of Hume's critics have thought his argument here begs the question is that Hume appears simply to assume no one has observed a miracle – more specifically, no one has observed a resurrection. Christians of Hume's day believed that a resurrection has indeed been witnessed and so would not accept that a resurrection "has never been observed in any age or country."

To avoid the charge of begging the question (as well as to adopt a charitable reading of the text), Hume's argument is best seen as advancing this thesis: the evidence that supports a report of a miracle will always be outweighed by the evidence against it. This is true, so Hume argues, because we may easily explain why reports of miracles should be made and have widespread currency; the belief in miracles is prompted by vanity, ignorance, fear, and a love for the marvelous and extraordinary. So understood, Hume's case against miracles does not beg the question but for it to be persuasive (or more persuasive), I believe that Hume's overriding naturalist outlook needs to be made more explicit. I develop this suggestion briefly.

If one emerged from prior philosophical reflection with a classical form of theism – according to which God is all-powerful, all-knowing, supremely good – then one would be more open to recognizing miracles than if one thought instead that theism is probably false. If theism is a live, plausible hypothesis (as it was for Hume's contemporary, Butler), one may argue further that a good God would have some reason to be revealed miraculously in history. This might be advanced on the grounds that a relationship with God is good, or that a divine redemption is needed, and so on. The way Hume sets up his argument against miracles, theism is allowed very little room in explaining events of any kind. Consider this example Hume uses in which an extraordinary event occurs but is presumed *not* to admit of a theistic explanation.

For I own, that otherwise, there may possibly be miracles, or violations of the usual course of nature, of such a kind as to admit of proof from human testimony; though, perhaps, it will be impossible to find any such in all

---

[94] Ibid., 148.

the records of history. Thus, suppose, all authors, in all languages, agree, that, from the first of January 1600, there was a total darkness over the whole earth for eight days: suppose that the tradition of this extraordinary event is still strong and lively among the people: that all travellers, who return from foreign countries, bring us accounts of the same tradition, without the least variation or contradiction: it is evident, that our present philosophers, instead of doubting the fact, ought to receive it as certain, and ought to search for the causes whence it might be derived. The decay, corruption, and dissolution of nature, is an event rendered probable by so many analogies, that any phenomenon, which seems to have a tendency towards that catastrophe, comes within the reach of human testimony, if that testimony be very extensive and uniform.[95]

The event, as described, gives one no clue as to how it might serve a divine end. The total darkness (perhaps a symbol of superstition?) seems ripe for naturalistic interpretation as the event, from a theistic point of view, seems ad hoc and pointless. Elsewhere Hume does offer a description of a healing – and that is more plausible as a traditional miracle narrative – but mere extraordinary events such as a spectacular eclipse for no apparent reason would be religious anomalies. Narratives of Christ's crucifixion and resurrection include extraordinary events (Matthew 27:51–53), but these are best read as part of a narrative that has a moral and religious value – that is, the events are not for the sake of entertainment or scientific challenges but for redemption.

My suggestion that Hume's case against the supernatural is best read as a constituent part of his overall case for naturalism can be a sign not of the weakness but the strength of his position. I believe that assessing Hume's views on other matters – doubts about an afterlife and suicide – are similarly strengthened when seen as part of a comprehensive naturalism.[96]

---

[95] Ibid., 165.

[96] Elsewhere, Anders Hendrickson and I argue there is an interesting parallel between Hume's argument about miracles and his case for white supremacy over blacks. See "Hume's Racism and the Case against Miracles," *Philosophia Christi* 4:2 (winter 2003). Hume held that there was a uniform and constant association of whites and superior intelligence, and blacks and inferior intelligence. He acknowledged reports of black intelligence (as he acknowledged reports of miracles), but he dismissed such reports in light of his view of the regular, uniform, exceptionless character of nature. He is so convinced of this that he offers an explanation of ostensible anomalies. Hume holds that it is more probable that blacks merely simulate intelligence, the way a bird may merely simulate language, without being intelligent; presumably both may be accounted for within the bounds of Hume's conception of the laws of nature.

Hume's work *The Natural History of Religion* begins with describing early human religion as exceptionless polytheism. "It is a matter of fact incontestable, that about 1,700 years ago all mankind were polytheists."[97] The evidence for this includes our "present experience concerning the principles and opinions of barbarous nations. The savage tribes of America, Africa, and Asia are all idolaters."[98] We also have "the fables" or early polytheistic narratives of Europe. But equally important, Hume argues, we have reason to think that polytheism would appear more evident than monotheism.

While some "works of nature" suggest a single author, observations of "the various events of human life necessarily lead to polytheism."[99] Many creators are supposed, due to the frequent absence of a singular organizing principle in nature. Hume also proposes that the chief reason for early, polytheistic religion is fear and hope, a fear of the unknown and hope for refuge.

As I mentioned at the outset of this chapter, Hume was familiar with Gibbon's famous work, *History of the Decline and Fall of the Roman Empire*. Gibbon, like Hume, vied against the credibility of early Christian historical writing. In Gibbon's highly controversial chapter "The Triumph of Barbarism and Religion," Hume would have found support for his own analysis. The crucial thesis that Gibbon (and Hume) wished to secure was that the emergence and sustained force of religion could be accounted for on terms other than the religion being actually true.

Throughout his *Natural History* and in several other sources, Hume singles out God's attribute of being "invisible." God is an "invisible, intelligent power"; "we trace the footsteps of invisible power." Elsewhere Hume refers to "the invisible regions or world of spirits" and the "Invisibility and Incomprehensibility of the Deity." This link between

---

Hendrickson and I argue that antecedently held values and philosophical convictions prevented Hume from giving proper weight to reports of both black intelligence and miracles. We do *not* argue that his case against miracles should be rejected because he was a racist. Arguments about miracles and race may be easily separated. Nonetheless, their parallel formulation in Hume's work is (we think) philosophically interesting. For a good overview of Hume's and his contemporaries' racism, see R. H. Popkin, "Eighteenth-Century Racism," in *The Columbia History of Western Philosophy*, ed. Popkin (New York: Columbia University Press, 1999).

[97] *The Natural History of Religion*, in *David Hume: Writings on Religion*, 109.

[98] Ibid., 109–110.

[99] Ibid., 113.

invisibility and incomprehensibility may suggest Hume is advancing an ancillary argument against theism – namely, the concept of an invisible, intelligence or power is nonsense. But for Hume the conceivability of there being objects that are nonspatial and thus not visible was no bare possibility. In the *Treatise* Hume writes:

> This maxim is *that an object may exist, and yet be no where*: and I assert, that this is not only possible, but that the greatest part of beings do and must exist after this manner. An object may be said to be no where, when its parts are not so situated with respect to each other, as to form any figure or quantity; not the whole with respect to other bodies so as to answer to our notions of contiguity or distance. Now this is evidently the case with all our perceptions and objects, except those of the sight and feeling. A moral reflection cannot be plac'd on the right or on the left hand of a passion, nor can a smell or sound be either of a circular or a square figure.[100]

Hume thought that desires, passions, tastes, sounds, and so on were mental, invisible realities. So, in speaking of the *invisible*, Hume was not (at least explicitly and consistently) proposing that the concept of God is nonsense – as some do later (see Chapter 8).

Annihilation and Suicide

As Boswell observed, Hume did not believe in an afterlife. Nor did Hume think suicide is morally impermissible under all circumstances. A person may, under certain conditions, take his or her own life.

In the essay "Of the Immortality of the Soul," Hume claims that abstract a priori reasoning about the person or the soul cannot settle questions about personal survival. From a moral point of view, Hume contends that the desire for an afterlife is sometimes the outcome of unworthy desires and fears (of punishment and reward), whereas the parameters of this life are a sufficient forum for our desires. "The powers of men are no more superior to their wants, considered merely in this life, than those of foxes and hares are, compared to their wants and to their period of existence."[101] The key argument for mortality is based on the evident dependency of the mind on the body. "Where any two objects are so closely connected that all alterations which we have ever

---

[100] *A Treatise*, 235–236.
[101] *David Hume: Writings on Religion*, 32.

seen in the one are attended with proportionable alterations in the other, we ought to conclude, by all rules of analogy, that, when there are still greater alterations produced in the former, and it is totally dissolved, there follows a total dissolution of the latter."[102] This depiction draws on a central feature of causation, according to Hume, in which the cause and effect are always conjoined. Hume's argument culminates in the following picture of mind-body dependency:

> Judging by the usual analogy of nature, no form can continue, when transferred to a condition of life very different from the original one, in which it was placed. Trees perish in the water; fishes in the air; animals in the earth. Even so small a difference as that of climate is often fatal. What reason then to imagine that an immense alteration, such as is made on the soul by the dissolution of its body and all its organs of thought and sensation, can be effected without the dissolution of the whole? Everything is in common between soul and body. The organs of the one are all of them the organs of the other. The existence therefore of the one must be dependent on that of the other.[103]

How does Hume's argument fare alongside Butler's?

Very well, I think, if we assume it is part of an overall case for naturalism. Butler's position is not absurd, though, if one's assessment of naturalism shifts. Imagine one has *some* reason to believe there is an all-good God who desires the welfare and flourishing of persons. If we assume a dualist position (whether from Butler or Hume) according to which the mind is contingently dependent on the body – that is, the dissolution of the body does not *entail* the perishing of the mind – then to see a person's body perish is not, ipso facto, to see the mind perish. Consider an analogy. Imagine you are being physically supported by two persons, myself and your strong, caring sister who, for one reason or another, we can't see. I lose my grip and leave the scene. Are you likely to fall? Only if we believe that your sister doesn't really care, or she thinks your falling would be good, or she lacks the strength to hold you, and so on. Hume's case for perishing has cogency to the extent that one does not presume there is an analogous divine sister in the picture.

The sister analogy may be contrasted with Hume's view of Charon. Near his death, Adam Smith reported Hume's playful reflection on the

---

[102] Ibid., 35.
[103] Ibid., 36.

mythological ferryman Charon, whose job it is to transport the shades of the dead to the lower world. Smith records Hume's ruminations.

> "I could not well imagine," said he, "what excuse I could make to Charon in order to obtain a little delay. I have done every thing of consequence which I ever meant to do, and I could at no time expect to leave my relations and friends in a better situation than that in which I am now likely to leave them; I, therefore, have all reason to die contented." He then diverted himself with inventing several jocular excuses, which he supposed he might make to Charon, and with imagining the very surly answers which it might suit the character of Charon to return to them. "Upon further consideration," said he, "I thought I might say to him, 'Good Charon, I have been correcting my works for a new edition. Allow me a little time, that I may see how the Public receives the alterations.' But Charon would answer, 'When you have seen the effect of these, you will be for making other alterations. There will be no end of such excuses; so, honest friend, please step into the boat.' But I might still urge, 'Have a little patience, good Charon, I have been endeavouring to open the eyes of the Public. If I live a few years longer, I may have the satisfaction of seeing the downfall of some of the prevailing systems of superstitions.' But Charon would then lose all temper and decency. 'You loitering rogue, that will not happen these many hundred years. Do you fancy I will grant you a lease for so long a term? Get into the boat this instant, you lazy loitering rogue.'"[104]

If one's background assumption is that the timing and consequence of one's death is being managed by an irascible, impatient, unsympathetic overseer, one would be led naturally to a different conclusion than if one posits a caring, patient, all-powerful alternative.

Hume's essay "Of Suicide" is, in part, a reply to Locke but also to some traditional arguments against suicide going back to Plato. Hume's argument does not presuppose atheism but a God of only general provident design. As God is interested in the comprehensive structure of the cosmos, God gives to creatures sufficient authority and autonomy to determine their own ends.

> What is the meaning, then, of that principle, that a man, who, tired of life, and hunted by pain and misery, bravely overcomes all the natural terrors of death, and makes his escape from this cruel scene; that such a man, I say, has incurred the indignation of his creator by encroaching on the office of divine providence and disturbing the order of the universe?

---

[104] From *An Enquiry*, 23.

Shall we assert, that the Almighty has reserved to himself, in any peculiar manner, the disposal of the lives of men, and has not submitted that event, in common with others, to the general laws by which the universe is governed? This is plainly false. The lives of men depend upon the same laws as the lives of all other animals; and these are subjected to the general laws of matter and motion. The fall of a tower or the infusion of a poison will destroy a man equally with the meanest creature: An inundation sweeps away everything without distinction that comes within the reach of its fury. Since therefore the lives of men are for ever dependent on the general laws of matter and motion, is a man's disposing of his life criminal, because, in every case, it is criminal to encroach upon these laws or disturb their operation? But this seems absurd. All animals are entrusted to their own prudence and skill for their conduct in the world, and have full authority, as far as their power extends, to alter all the operations of nature. Without the exercise of this authority, they could not subsist a moment. Every action, every motion of a man innovates in the order of some parts of matter, and diverts, from their ordinary course, the general laws of motion. Putting together, therefore, these conclusions, we find *that* human life depends upon the general laws of matter and motion, and *that* 'tis no encroachment on the office of providence to disturb or alter these general laws.[105]

So, by Hume's lights, a person may judiciously take his own life under some circumstances without encroaching on God's sovereign providence. (Note the related ways in which Hume opposed *encroaching* on God as well as on God *violating* nature.) Like the case against immortality, the background assumption is key. Hume's assessment of the background gives little solace to someone looking for God's special providence. And there is little comfort in looking to the universe itself, given the assumption that oysters are of little value: "The life of man is of no greater importance to the universe than that of an oyster."[106]

Before moving to Humean ethics and Smith's ideal observer theory, I note two features of Hume's work that may provide very modest support for an afterlife. Hume's view of causation allows that there can be no a priori case against an afterlife. At the end of the *Enquiry* Hume notes that we cannot rule out as impossible even quite dramatic possibilities; "If we reason *a priori*, anything may appear to produce anything. The falling of a pebble may, for aught we know, extinguish the sun; or the

---

[105] *David Hume: Writings on Religion*, 43.
[106] Ibid., 44.

wish of a man control the planets in their orbits."[107] A defender of an afterlife might rejoin: for aught we know, physical death may mark a persons' passage to heaven or reincarnation rather than annihilation. In the exchange with Boswell cited at the outset of this chapter, Hume likened the possibility of an afterlife to the possibility that coal wouldn't burn when placed in a fire. Hume, famously, thought we cannot rule out such a possibility in the future. It is interesting to note in this context the biblical narrative in Daniel, chapter 3, of God's miraculous salvation whereby God's prophets are not burned by fire.

A second point where Hume offers help would be specifically for a dualistic view of the afterlife. Recall the Cartesian modal argument for dualism that moves from the possibility of there being a person and no body or a body and no person to the conclusion that the person is not identical with his or her body (see Chapter 2). As we have seen earlier, Hume supports a very strong principle of conceivability: "[W]hatever we *conceive* is possible."[108] If we can conceive of mind-body separation, then by Hume's lights this would provide evidence that such a separation as a bona fide possibility. (Of course, in discussing the cosmological argument earlier in this chapter I raised some reservation about appealing to conceivability without great care.)

An Ideal Observer

Hume's morality does not appeal to divine commands and power, or to a human sovereign's power backed by sanctions (Hobbes), or to Cudworth's idea that human morality is a reflection of the immutable, eternal nature of reality.[109] Consistent with his naturalism, Hume locates the root of ethics in our feelings of enjoyment and aversion, our sentiments of praise and approval on the one hand, and blame and disapproval on the other. Reason alone does not motivate us toward moral awareness or practice. We must instead begin with the desires and feelings we actually have and then refine them through reasonable reflection. To some critics, Hume's proposal seemed hopelessly unstable

---

[107] *An Enquiry*, 194.

[108] See Chapter 1, note 27.

[109] There is a helpful essay juxtaposing Hume's ethics with Cudworth's and others in D. F. Norton, "Hume, Human Nature, and the Foundations of Morality" in *The Cambridge Companion to Hume,* ed. Norton (Cambridge: Cambridge University Press, 1993). See also E. C. Mossner, *The Life of David Hume* (Oxford: Oxford University Press, 1980).

because the life of feelings is inconsistent, malleable, and untrustworthy. Hume paints a different picture. Outlining the human tendency toward uniform, coordinated feelings of aversion, resentment, desire, and amiability, Hume specifically highlights the role of sympathy.[110]

Hume's work set the stage for what has come to be known as the ideal observer theory, as this was worked out by Adam Smith in *The Theory of Moral Sentiments* (1759), and in *The Methods of Ethics* (1874) by Henry Sidgewick (1838–1900) and by others.[111]

Smith developed his Humean ethic on the grounds of our natural ability to sympathize with others.

> How selfish soever man may be supposed, there are evidently some principles in his nature, which interest him in the fortune of others, and render their happiness necessary to him, though he derives nothing from it except the pleasure of seeing it. Of this kind is pity or compassion, the emotion which we feel for the misery of others, when we either see it, or are made to conceive it in a very lively manner. That we often derive sorrow from the sorrow of others, is a matter of fact too obvious to require any instances to prove it; for this sentiment, like all the other original passions of human nature, is by no means confined to the virtuous and humane, though they perhaps may feel it with the most exquisite sensibility. The greatest ruffian, the most hardened violator of the laws of society, is not altogether without it.[112]

Moral reflection begins with a sympathy for others that becomes refined in the course of our imaginative identification or empathy with them.

> As we have no immediate experience of what other men feel, we can form no idea of the manner in which they are affected, but by conceiving what we ourselves should feel in the like situation. Though our brother is upon the rack, as long as we ourselves are at our ease, our sense will never inform us of what he suffers. They never did, and never can, carry us beyond our own person, and it is by the imagination only that we can

---

[110] *An Enquiry Concerning the Principles of Morals*, sec. II, part I.

[111] Two influential twentieth-century contributions to this school of ethics include Roderick Firth, "Ethical Absolutism and the Ideal Observer," *Philosophy and Phenomenological Research* 12 (1952), and R. B. Brandt, *Ethical Theory* (Englewood Cliffs, N.J.: Prentice-Hall, 1959). I defend an ideal observer theory in "A God's Eye View," in *Faith and Analysis*, ed. H. A. Harris and C. I. Insole (Farnborough: Ashgate, forthcoming).

[112] *The Theory of Moral Sentiments*, ed. D. D. Raphael and A. L. Macfie (Oxford: Clarendon, 1976), 9.

form any conception of what are his sensations. Neither can that faculty help us to this any other way, than by representing to us what would be our own, if we were in his case. It is the impressions of our own sense only, not those of his, which our imaginations copy. By the imagination we place ourselves in his situation, we conceive ourselves enduring all the same torments, we enter as it were into his body, and become in some measure the same person with him, and thence from some idea of his sensation, and even feel something which, though weaker in degree, is not altogether unlike them. His agonies, when they are thus brought home to ourselves, when we have thus adopted and made them our own, begin at least to affect us, and we then tremble and shudder at the thought of what he feels. For as to be in pain or distress of any kind excites the most excessive sorrow, so to conceive or to imagine that we are in it, excites some degree of the same emotion, in proportion to the vivacity or dullness of the conception.[113]

In this fashion, Smith sought to offer a moral psychology (or a philosophy of sentiments) that would fill out what Hume called a general point of view from which we form judgments.[114]

Smith goes on to point out how the intensity and stability of one's judgments can vary significantly depending upon the refinement of one's imaginative powers, the degree of one's self-concern, and the accuracy of our beliefs about others.

Let us suppose that the great empire of China, with all its myriads of inhabitants, was suddenly swallowed up by an earthquake, and let us consider how a man of humanity in Europe, who had no sort of connexion with that part of the world, would be affected upon receiving intelligence of this dreadful calamity. He would, I imagine, first of all, express very strongly his sorrow for the misfortune of that unhappy people, he would make many melancholy reflections upon the precariousness of human life, and the vanity of all the labours of man, which could thus be annihilated in a moment. He would too, perhaps, if he was a man of speculation, enter into many reasonings concerning the effects which this disaster might produce upon the commerce of Europe, and the trade and business of the world in general. And when all this fine philosophy was over, when all these humane sentiments had been once fairly expressed, he would pursue his business or his pleasure, take his repose or his diversion, with

---

[113] Ibid.

[114] On the relation of Smith and Hume, see the introduction to *An Enquiry Concerning the Principles of Morals,* ed. T. L Beauchamp (Oxford: Clarendon, 1998). On Hume's "general point of view," see Christine Korsgaard "The General Point of View: Love and Moral Approval in Hume's Ethics," *Hume Studies* 25:1–2 (1999).

the same ease and tranquility, as if no such accident had happened. The most frivolous disaster which could befall himself would occasion a more real disturbance.[115]

What this passage exhibits is the distance between ourselves as prudential, self-concerned subjects and the viewpoint we may take up when we truly seek to be (or view the world from the standpoint of) an impartial, fully informed sympathetic spectator.

I offer here an overview of an ideal observer theory, bringing out some of its intuitive appeal by highlighting commonplace features of moral argumentation; I then bring out the implications of an ideal observer theory for philosophy of religion.

Imagine you and I are debating the moral permissibility of suicide or, to use a term that avoids some of the moral content built into the word "suicide," the permissibility of a terminally ill person taking his own life when there are no cures and great anguish.[116] Would our debate consist merely in my display of aversion while you, for example, felt appeasement and acceptance? Arguably other factors would enter in, starting with an inquiry into whether the patient is actually suffering and the degree of suffering. We might then debate the probability that a cure might be found or, failing that, the likelihood that the pain can be managed. We might further investigate whether the person has made promises he could still fulfill, the impact of his death on others, and the method of killing including the use of other persons who may otherwise be averse to it; finally, we may also consider whether there is a provident God who will use nature itself (rather than act through the person's deliberations) to bring about death at the best time. This inquiry would concern the facts that form the basis or ground of our disagreement. Agreement on these facts alone might suffice to settle much moral disagreement. The facts at issue may be called nonmoral facts in that they refer to states of affairs which may be conceived without thereby conceiving the moral rightness or wrongness, goodness or evil involved. After this inquiry there would be at least two other goals in our moral inquiry involving impartiality and sympathy.

Moral reflection – whether rudimentary or quite theoretical – is often in tension with an undue partiality. For example, imagine that the person in the preceding example is my enemy. Perhaps my aversion to

---

[115] *The Theory of Moral Sentiments*, 136.

[116] This alternative avoids the problem that, for some, "suicide" simply means self-murder.

euthanasia in this case is due to the fact that I wish him to suffer. Presumably some appeal to impartiality is an essential ingredient in the fairness of moral reasoning. It would be fair to ask me this: would you still oppose euthanasia if the roles were reversed and you were the one suffering? This practice of putting yourself in the other person's shoes seems basic to the golden rule.

The next feature is Hume's favorite: sympathy. Perhaps shared understanding of the facts at hand and impartiality are not enough. Ethical disputes often involve the appeal to the affective awareness of *what it is like to* suffer from such and such cause, or to have one's life cut short, and so on. Debating, say, capital punishment or famine relief often involves an affective dimension so that debaters are impaired if they have no idea of what it is like to await execution or no idea of the experience of hunger.[117]

The import of this portrait of moral reflection is that it sketches an ideal vantage point from which to assess matters. In moral debate, my judgment that X is right may be understood as the judgment that X would be approved of by a person (an *ideal observer*) who truly grasped all the relevant facts, was truly impartial, and was affectively apprised of the points of view of all involved parties.[118] This may be described as seeking a God's-eye point of view.

Of course, God, as traditionally conceived, is more than such an ideal observer (God is omnipotent, the Creator, etc.) and some theistic traditions may attribute partiality to God (God has a *chosen* people). But the majority of Jewish, Christian, and Islamic philosophers understand God as upholding fairness and, given that the goods of the cosmos are unevenly distributed, theists often see this as serving an overall good. God's omniscience would represent an ideal case of awareness of the happiness or sadness of all parties to any moral dispute. The way I have articulated the appeal to an ideal observer does not require that the person making such an appeal thinks that there actually is an ideal observer. Indeed, while Smith sees God as a supreme judge, he contends that God has "made man ... the immediate judge of mankind."[119] And Hume was highly motivated not to rely on divinely revealed precepts in

---

[117] See P. C. Mercer, *Sympathy and Ethics* (Oxford: Clarendon, 1972), and the magnificent work by Max Scheler, *The Nature of Sympathy*, trans. P. L. Heath (London: Routledge, 1954).

[118] See my "Relativizing the Ideal Observer Theory," *Philosophy and Phenomenological Research* 49:1 (1988).

[119] *Moral Sentiments*, 130.

his morality. His principle aim may be seen as showing that God is *not* necessary for moral beliefs and practice. Still, if one extrapolates the features that Hume and then Smith developed (impartiality, accurate grasp of relevant facts, sympathy with involved parties), in the end, one winds up with an idealized portrait of a God's-eye point of view.[120] In the very development of the ideal-observer theory, one can trace efforts by Smith and then Sidgwick to achieve a comprehensive moral point of view.

Smith's clearest account of the ideal-observer theory is in his *Theory of Moral Sentiments*. But one can see in Smith a tension between the ethics that comes from ideal, benevolent reflection and the self-interest that makes up our economic life. It is revealing that while Smith condemned slavery morally, his case against slavery in *The Wealth of Nations* was more effective, where the reasons to oppose slavery are that it impedes industry and is not a prudent use of property.[121] Achieving a "God's-eye point of view" may not be incompatible with endorsing Smith's view of free markets, but one can trace the respects in which (for Smith) the sympathetic observer's point of view hints at something overarching and, as it were, transcending self-interest. The ideal-observer theory has a bearing on philosophy or religion, for it conceives of a moral point of view compatible between some secular and religious ethics. Both religious and secular ethicists can see themselves as seeking out the same goal – a God's-eye point of view – even if only one of them thinks there really is a God who has such a view.[122]

There are various objections to seeing ethical reflection as seeking out an ideal observer's or God's-eye point of view. Consider three difficulties.

The Problem of Relativity. Ideal observers (IOs) may disagree. This establishes the insufficiency of the theory as a coherent understanding of moral reflection.

Reply. The easiest reply is to concede that while the conditions for being an IO (possessing ideal knowledge, impartiality, and affective appraisal) are indeed not sufficient, they are still necessary. Failure to aim

---

[120] This portrait is idealized. Tom Carson developed an IO theory that allowed for multiple, alternative points of view that were ideal only relative to particular persons.

[121] See D. B. Davis, *The Problem of Slavery in the Age of Revolution, 1770–1823* (Ithaca: Cornell University Press, 1975).

[122] See *Contemporary Philosophy of Religion*, chap. 6, and my "The Ideal Observer's Philosophy of Religion," in *The Proceedings of the Twentieth World Congress of Philosophy*, Philosophy Documentation Center, vol. 4 (Bowling Green: Bowling Green State University, 1999).

at these ideals still counts as a defect of moral inquiry.[123] The following predicament seems on the face of it to be absurd: I approve of X (euthanasia or whatever) and yet I at the same time hold that if I truly knew all the facts and I was impartial and truly acquainted with the affective dimension of all involved, I would disapprove of X. Rather, I suggest that a serious moral claim to approve of something is to believe that such approval would be vindicated on the highest level. Other replies are possible. If IOs would disagree about, say, the approval of an act, perhaps either the act or its omission is permissible. Alternatively, one may deny that there are any plausible grounds for supposing IOs would disagree. Arguably, any detailed description of the disagreement would involve focusing on a feature that would be captured by both IOs and thus form grounds for uniformity in IO approval or disapproval.

A Religious Objection. The concept of God invoked by the ideal-observer theory is religiously unacceptable. Consider Demea's objection to Cleanthes' anthropomorphic God. Demea objected to God's immediate awareness of other's feelings.

Reply. Here it seems that Demea may be doing more to advance an imperfect rather than perfect view of the divine. Compare two beings who share all the classical theistic attributes but one is omniciencent and knows all the ideas, minds, and intentions of all creatures whereas the other does not. Arguably, omniscience would be an excellent power that the first being has, whereas the other is diminished in excellence; the first being can have compassion, for example, whereas the second does not have the grounds essential for compassion.

There may, however, be another point behind the religious objection. If the ideal observer is imagined to *sympathize* with all involved parties, does that not court impiety as well as morally corrupt reflection? In assessing the moral status of serial killing, must I *sympathize* with a serial killer? Surely not in the sense that I endorse or advocate his action. But it might be essential for me to be affectively apprised of his point of view, grasping what led him to the action, understanding why he thought his action was justified. This may all be essential not only in terms of achieving a comprehensive understanding of the person's identity but also in terms of law (Was he fully responsible for his actions? What sorts of punishments would effectively change the killer's point of view?).

---

[123] Our aim, though, is not so much at omniscience but at sufficiently justified beliefs that we would wager that our beliefs are compatible with an omniscient vantage point.

The Problem of Skepticism. Invoking a God's-eye point of view is to invoke skepticism. A God's-eye point of view is not achievable by human beings.

Reply. The ideal-observer theory is compatible with skepticism; this may be seen as a virtue. Accepting the theory does not, by itself, beg the question against some forms of skepticism. But none of its key advocates historically have been skeptics. Take an extreme example of a well-entrenched moral judgment: it is wrong to skin and salt children. Why assume that a truly impartial, fully informed ideal point of view of the affective dimensions involved would leave one apoplectic at such a thought?

I suggest that much of religious ethics in different traditions involves the invocation of such an ideal vantage point. The bare fact that the golden rule is so pervasive secures one route toward seeking an ideal where one imagines that appropriate moral action should involve transcending narrow self-interest and seeking a higher vantage point. In England, at the time of Hume and Smith, one can see the case against slavery gain ground in religious *and* secular circles by appeal to facts, impartiality, and affective appraisal. Consider this provocation by John Wesley to captains of slave ships: "No you never *feel* another's pain? Have you no sympathy? . . . No pity for the miserable? When you saw the flowing eyes, the heaving breasts, or the bleeding sides of tortured limbs of your fellow-creatures, was you a stone, or a brute? . . . Did not one tear drop from your eyes?"[124] Atheist or theist, Christian or Hindu, all can see the force of this dimension to moral reasoning.

One way to connect the IO theory with the material in Chapter 3 is to revisit the travesty Hobbes sought to avoid: atrocities such as the Athenian conquest of Melos. If the Athenians truly engaged in impartial reflection, imaginatively grasping the point of view of the people of Melos, and grasped all the relevant facts, would they have condemned their threats and, eventually, their pillaging, killing, and enslaving? I do not attempt to answer this but only make a suggestion. Euripides' play *The Trojan Women* presented to the people of Athens a portrait of what it is like from the standpoint of the victims to be bereaved and enslaved. It is difficult to measure the impact of the play at the time and its role in Athenian moral political reflection, especially given the fact that Athens

---

[124] Wesley, *Thoughts upon Slavery* (Philadelphia, 1774), 10–14, 52. I believe had Hume developed his understanding of beneficence and sympathy along ideal, impartial lines he would have abandoned his view of blacks.

was facing the possibility that Sparta might do unto Athens what Athens did unto Melos. (This was not a matter of thought experiments and abstract speculation involving the golden rule.) Whatever its role then, it is difficult to read the play today while remaining sanguine about war policies that slaughter male prisoners, enslave women, and so on. Arguably, the IO theory may be coupled with using testimony, literature, and other arts to shape moral reflection.

Admittedly, the IO theory is hardly the whole of ethics. Indeed, I see it as demarcating the beginning or only one element of ethical reflection. Still, the theory is able to bridge some religions and secular moral inquiry.

The Virtues of Inquiry

Hume's writing, especially on religion, is shot through with warnings about gloomy, melancholy dispositions, fear, pride, enthusiasm, ignorance, depression, hypocrisy, ambition, revenge, a persecuting spirit, love of wonder, and so on. He also applauds gentleness, moderation, benevolence, and proportioning one's belief to the evidence when possible. I read him as a deeply *humane* philosopher, aware of the need for, and dangers of, passion in philosophical reflection.[125]

One way to locate Hume in the history of philosophy of religion is to take note of his balance between theoretical detachment and the attachment to practice. On the one hand, he challenges the religious believer to step back from zealous faith and to consider the history of religion and its philosophical credibility. Hume's eighteenth century was only slightly more secular than the seventeenth century of Chapter 1. "Seventeenth-century thought was God-ridden. Whenever a man took up his pen and attempted to write about the weather, the seasons, the structure of the earth, and constitution of the heavens, the nature of political society, the organization of the Church, social morality or ethics, he was by definition taking up his pen to write about God."[126] While counseling a detachment from God-ridden thought, Hume is still aware that removing oneself from the feelings and practices that define one's life may be dangerous. Hume is staunchly opposed to an

---

[125] I therefore see Hume's racism as a complete aberration, given his other values.

[126] John Redwood, *Reason, Ridicule and Religion: The Age of Enlightenment in England, 1660–1750* (London: Thames and Hudson, 1976), 9.

excessive detachment that courts a skepticism that would undermine practical living. Like Descartes, Hume seems to have grasped how skepticism may shatter what, in Chapter 1, may be called the virtues of embodiment. He thought that reason alone may lead one to a crippling, dead end.

> This *intense* view of these manifold contradictions and imperfections in human reason has so wrought upon me, and heated my brain, that I am ready to reject all belief and reasoning, and can look upon no opinion even as more probable or likely than another. Where am I, or what? From what causes do I derive my existence, and to what condition shall I return? Whose favour shall I court, and whose anger must I dread? What beings surround me? on whom have I any influence, or who have any influence on me? I am confounded with all of these questions, and begin to fancy myself in the most deplorable condition imaginable, inviron'd with the deepest darkness, and utterly depriv'd of the use of every member and faculty.[127]

Excessive skeptical detachment would be devastating, and he argues too that an ethic built on pure reason, abstracted from feeling, would not survive. So, while he is wary of unreflective action, he also seeks a balance.

Hume's critique of religion has important representatives today, some of which will come to the fore in subsequent chapters. In his time and in the early nineteenth century some of his more prominent critics like Thomas Reid (1710–1796) took exception to his starting points. According to Reid many of the modern philosophers we have discussed so far lead us to Hume's fragmented view of the self and experience.

> If [my mind] is, indeed, what the *Treatise of Human Nature* makes it, I find I have been only in an enchanted castle, imposed upon by specters and apparitions.... I see myself, and the whole frame of Nature, shrink into fleeting ideas, which, like Epicurus's atoms, dance about in emptiness.... Descartes no sooner began to dig in this mine than skepticism was ready to break in upon him. He did what he could to shut it out. Malebranche and Locke, who dug deeper, found the difficulty of keeping out this enemy still to increase; but they laboured honestly in the design. Then Berkeley, who carried on the work, despairing of securing all, bethought himself on an expedient. By giving up the material world,

---

[127] *A Treatise*, 1–4.

which he thought might be spared without loss, and even with advantage, he hoped by an impregnable partition to secure the world of spirits. But, alas! *The Treatise of Human Nature* wantonly sapped the foundation of this partition, and drowned all in one universal deluge.[128]

Reid's antidote to Hume was to challenge Hume's starting point. Why limit our experiential awareness to sensible ideas or sensations? Consider the case of self-observation. Is it the case that I never observe or experientially grasp myself but only some sensation of heat or color or taste and so on? Reid and his followers have argued that in the course of such sensory states, we actually do grasp ourselves. I do not merely experience heat; I experience myself as hot, as seeing green, as tasting something salty, and the like.[129]

Later philosophers will object that Hume has unduly circumscribed our concept of "observation."[130] Can't we experience values? What about the possibility of perceiving God? Can this be ruled out a priori? (These concerns are taken up in Chapter 8.)

Humean philosophical inquiry is staunchly opposed to "enthusiasm," as this has been described in Chapters 1 and 3. But it is worth noting that there were philosophers, contemporary and just prior to Hume, who defended a philosophical method that took seriously a broad range of experiences in shaping the philosophy of nature and God. The Earl of Shaftsbury, Anthony Ashley Cooper (1671–1713), for example, recommended a "noble enthusiasm" – which could include a sense of beauty, the sublime, and even a sense of the divine presence.[131]

---

[128] *An Inquiry into the Human Mind*, ed. W. Hamilton (Edinburgh, 1846), 103.

[129] For a recent defense of Reid's notion of self-observation, see Roderick Chisholm, *Person and Object* (LaSalle: Open Court, 1976).

[130] See Dale Tuggy, "Reid's Philosophy of Religion," in *The Cambridge Companion to Reid*, ed. Terence Cuneo et al. (Cambridge: Cambridge University Press, 2003).

[131] Shaftsbury developed an interesting philosophy of love and God that was deliberately in between the theistic mysticism and the "rational religion" of the philosophers. For an interesting overview including a comparison between Hume and Shaftsbury, see Stanley Grean, *Shaftesbury's Philosophy of Religion: A Study in Enthusiasm* (Athens: Ohio University Press, 1967).

✦

FIVE

Kantian Philosophy of Religion

Two things fill the mind with ever new and increasing admiration and awe, the more often and steadily we reflect upon them; *the starry heavens above me and the moral law within me*. I do not seek or conjecture either of them as if they were veiled obscurities or extravagances beyond the horizon of my vision; I see them before me and connect them immediately with the consciousness of my existence. The first starts at the place that I occupy in the external world of the senses, and extends the connection in which I stand into the limitless magnitude of worlds upon worlds, systems upon systems, as well as into the boundless times of their periodic motion, their beginning and continuation. The second begins with my invisible self, my personality, and displays to me a world that has true infinity, but which can only be detected through the understanding, and with which . . . I know myself to be in not, as in the first case, merely contingent, but universal and necessary connection.

Immanuel Kant[1]

A Friendship in the Enlightenment

In the late seventeenth and in the eighteenth century in Europe, one may find a movement often referred to as the Enlightenment (in French, *Siècle de lumières*; in German, *Aufklärung*). Kant's motto for this period is bold. "*Enlightenment is man's emergence from his self-imposed immaturity. Immaturity* is the inability to use one's understanding without guidance from another. This immaturity is *self-imposed* when its cause lies not in lack of understanding, but in lack of resolve and courage to use it without guidance from another. *Sapere Aude!* 'Have courage to

---

[1] *Critique of Practical Reason*, trans. and ed. Mary Gregor (Cambridge: Cambridge University Press, 1997), 5:161–162.

use your own understanding!' – that is the motto of enlightenment."[2] In different ways we have seen philosophers – Locke and Hume, for example – make similar claims about reason, evidence, and our duties to undertake philosophical inquiry. Some philosophers, like Kant, had faith that humanity would indeed find the courage to throw off the fetters of cowardly self-constraint and unjustified traditions. While Kant discouraged *tutelage*, he did not discourage seeking guidance and inspiration from an inward apprehension of the moral law, and the contemplation of the grandeur, complexity, and structure of the cosmos. Nor did he discourage friendship.

In 1777 the German Jewish philosopher Moses Mendelssohn (1729–1786) visited Kant in Königsberg. Kant confided to a correspondent:

> Today Mr. Mendelssohn, your worthy friend and mine (for so I flatter myself), is departing. To have a man like him in Königsberg on a permanent basis, as an intimate acquaintance, a man of such gentle temperament, good spirits, and Enlightenment – how that would give my soul the nourishment it has lacked so completely here, a nourishment I miss more and more as I grow older! I could not arrange, however, to take full advantage of this unique opportunity to enjoy so rare a man, partly from fear lest I might disturb him . . . in the business he had to attend to locally. Yesterday he did me the honor of being present at two of my lectures, *a la fortune du pot*, as one might say, since the table was not prepared for such a distinguished guest. . . . I beg you to keep for me the friendship of this worthy man in the future.[3]

At the time of their meeting, Mendelssohn was the more recognized philosopher. In a philosophy essay contest in 1762, Mendelssohn won first prize over Kant's contribution.

Mendelssohn contributed to aesthetics and literary theory as well as to philosophy of religion. He defended the evidential, rational legitimacy of theistic belief and the concept of beauty as sensible perfection, and he argued that Jews should have civil rights while promoting general religious tolerance. Mendelssohn's *Phaedo or On the Immortality of the Soul* (1769) was hailed by his contemporaries as a Platonic defense of life after death.

---

[2] *Foundations of the Metaphysics of Morals and What Is Enlightenment*, trans. L. W. Beck (Indianapolis: Bobbs-Merrill, 1959), 85. The motto Kant cites is from Horace and was adopted in Berlin in 1736 by a Society of the Friends of Truth.

[3] Cited by Manfred Kuehn, *Kant: A Biography* (Cambridge: Cambridge University Press, 2001), 230.

In the 1780s Mendelssohn was embroiled in controversy over the religious implications of the work of another friend, Gotthold Ephraim Lessing (as discussed in relation to Spinoza in Chapter 3). Kant defended Mendelssohn, albeit in a fashion that did not preserve Mendelssohn's case for religious belief. Kant would present a different case, to be articulated later, but as we begin to make our way into Kant's work, it is worth looking at two passages in Kant's essay on behalf of Mendelssohn. The essay is called "What Does It Mean to Orient Oneself in Thinking?" Kant in the end offers this high view of the role of reason.

> Friends of the human race and of what is holiest to it! Accept what appears to you most worthy of belief after careful and sincere examination, whether of facts or rational grounds; only do not dispute that prerogative of reason which makes it the highest good on earth, the prerogative of being the final touchstone of truth. Failing here, you will become unworthy of this freedom, and you will surely forfeit too; and besides that you will bring the same misfortune down on the heads of other, innocent parties who would otherwise have been well disposed and would have used their freedom *lawfully* and hence in a way which is conducive to what is best for the world![4]

As we shall see, however, the "reason" to which Kant appeals involves more than pure reason – values and practice are also seen as key. There is a hint of the riches of reason in an earlier passage in the essay as Kant places stock in an interior, subjective grounding.

> In the proper meaning of the word, to *orient* oneself means to use a given direction (when we divide the horizon into four of them) in order to find the others – literally, to find the *sunrise*. Now if I see the sun in the sky and know it is now midday, then I know how to find south, west, north, and east. For this, however, I also need the feeling of a difference in my own subject, namely, the difference between my right and left hands. I call this a *feeling* because these two sides outwardly display no designatable difference in intuition. If I did not have this faculty of distinguishing, with the need of any difference in the objects, between moving from left to right and right to left and moving in the opposite direction and thereby determining *a priori* a difference in the position of the objects, then in describing a circle I would not know whether west was right or left of the southernmost point of the horizon, or whether I should complete the circle by moving north

---

[4] From A. Wood and G. D. Giovanni, eds., *Religion and Rational Theology: A Collection of Kant's Texts* (Cambridge: Cambridge University Press, 2001), 18.

and east and thus back to south. Thus even with all the objective data of the sky, I orient myself *geographically* only through a *subjective* ground of differentiation; and if all the constellations, though keeping the same shape and position relative to one another, were one day by a miracle to be reversed in their direction, so that what was east now became west, no human eye would notice the slightest alteration on the next bright starlit night, and even the astronomer – if he pays attention only to what he sees and not at the same time to what he feels – would inevitably become *disoriented*.[5]

Kant's new orientation will take some of the main themes in philosophy of religion we have seen in the earlier chapters and recast them in thought and practice. Chapter 1 started with philosophers whose understanding of God and religion privileged the good, the true, and the beautiful. In Kant we may also see a deep concern with this trinity: his *Critique of Pure Reason* concerns what we may know to be true, his *Critique of Practical Reason* involves what we may know and practice concerning the good, and his *Critique of Judgment* involves the beautiful. Kant's central place of the good, true, and beautiful has led one scholar to treat him as a Platonist, but this classification would need strenuous qualifications.[6] Kant leaves us with a body of work that is a great distance from his Platonic friend Mendelssohn, who, in the year before he died, wrote *Morning Lessons,* a book that defends Leibniz's theism. Still, Kant sought to ground belief in theism, ethics, and our search for truth on a firm foundation.

In brief, Kant's philosophy of religion proves vital to our consideration for at least four reasons: he is credited, along with Hume, for dismantling classic theistic arguments; he has shifted the case for religion from a preoccupation with metaphysical truths to morality; he has made valuable philosophical recoveries of such theological concepts as sin and salvation; and his cosmopolitan view of history raises important questions for the role of religious faith in a global republicanism. While Kant clearly does not see himself as bound or answerable to tradition and its "guidance from another," he has had an important impact on philosophical religious tradition.

---

[5] Ibid., 8–9.

[6] See T. K. Seung, *Kant's Platonic Revolution in Moral and Political Philosophy* (Baltimore: Johns Hopkins University Press, 1994).

Volcanic Philosophy of Religion

Kant was born in 1724 and lived most of his life in Königsberg, in eastern Prussia. His family and early education were marked by Pietism, a German, Lutheran reform movement that emphasized humanity's inability to completely resist evil, the need for redemption through spiritual rebirth, and the primacy of religious practice over theory and speculative theology. Until 1770 Kant's work espoused a mixture of a broadly conceived rationalism and modest skepticism about the scope of metaphysics. During the 1770s, the "silent years," Kant devoted himself to developing what one scholar has called "a philosophical volcano the likes of which the world has rarely seen."[7] At age fifty-seven, Kant published the *Critique of Pure Reason* (1781; a revision was published in 1787), which established him as a preeminent philosopher of his time. This work was also sufficient to secure Kant a key place in the history of modern philosophy of religion. We begin by considering the central project of Kant's first *Critique* and then in subsequent sections survey his famous objections to theistic arguments, his view of the relationship between morality and religion, his understanding of the atonement, and finally his international cosmopolitanism. At the end of the chapter I consider the response to Kant that took shape in what some scholars call the romantic movement.

Kant's work may be described as volcanic, in that, while he preserved necessary and universal knowledge, promoted modern science, and (eventually) secured morality and religious faith, he did so by denying our cognitive access to a world independent of our minds. The objects we observe are not to be presumed to exist in some objective, mind-independent manner.

> All our intuition is nothing but the representation of appearance; that the things that we intuit are not in themselves what we intuit them to be, nor are their relations so constituted in themselves as they appear to us; and that if we remove our own subject or even only the subjective constitution of the senses in general, then all the constitution, all relations of objects in space and time, indeed space and time themselves would disappear, and as appearances they cannot exist in themselves, but only in us. What may be the case with objects in themselves and abstracted from all this receptivity

---

[7] Paul Guyer, *The Cambridge Companion to Kant* (Cambridge: Cambridge University Press, 1992), 4.

of our sensibility remains entirely unknown to us. We are acquainted with nothing except our way of perceiving them, which is peculiar to us, and which therefore does not necessarily pertain to every being, though to be sure it pertains to every human being.[8]

We are naturally prone to see and to think of the world as it appears to us as a realistic fact. The way the world is may or may not be exactly as it appears, but there is *a way things are in the world*, quite independent of our cognition. Similarly, Kant grants that it is natural (or at least customary) to think that the investigation into God's existence must be a theoretical inquiry to establish the best reasons to believe there is (or is not) a God. But this is, according to Kant, an illusion.

Kant's first critique is concerned with *pure* reason because he develops an account of cognition involving a priori or purely theoretical arguments without depending on specific, empirical experiences. He outlines what he takes to be the necessary conditions for any experience whatsoever. This part of the work is the *transcendental deductions*. "I call all cognition *transcendental* that is occupied not so much with objects but rather with our *a priori* concepts of objects in general."[9] Kant did not deny that we know certain features of the world and ourselves as we experience them. We grasp necessary mathematical relations and truths of geometry and of space and time. How is this possible? Kant locates the reason in our very modes of cognition. We simply cannot experience or be aware of things differently. Our experience is always formatted, reflecting basic categories of cause and effect, time and possibility, substance and attribute.

> All appearances as possible experiences, therefore, lie *a priori* in the understanding, and receive their formal possibility from it, just as they lie in the sensibility as mere intuitions, and are only possible through the latter as far as their form is concerned. Thus as exaggerated and contradictory as it may sound to say that the understanding is itself the source of the laws of nature, and thus of the formal unity of nature, such an assertion is nevertheless correct and appropriate to the object, namely experience. To be sure, empirical laws, as such, can by no means derive their origin from the pure understanding, just as the immeasurable manifoldness of the appearances cannot be adequately conceived through the pure form of sensible intuition. But all empirical laws are only particular

---

[8] *Critique of Pure Reason*, trans. and ed. Paul Guyer and A. W. Wood (Cambridge: Cambridge University Press, 1998), A42.

[9] Ibid., A11.

determinations of the pure laws of the understanding, under which and in accordance with whose norm they are first possible, and the appearances assume a lawful form, just as, regardless of the variety of their empirical form, all appearances must nevertheless always be in accord with the pure form of sensibility.[10]

Kant's thesis may be cast as the claim that all the categories we use in our experience of the world reflect our own framework. As Kant puts his thesis in the short but powerful *Prolegomena to Any Future Metaphysics*: "[T]he understanding does not derive its laws from, but prescribes them to nature."[11] Kant's position is thereby considered transcendental in two respects: first, he goes underneath the data of experience to identify the condition necessary to account for the data; and, second, he identifies those conditions as universal and necessary structures of experience rather than contingent, peculiar features of experience.

Kant thereby seeks to safeguard and guarantee our claims to know necessary truths while at the same time placing to one side metaphysical questions about a reality that extends beyond our representations.

> Observation and analysis of the appearances penetrate into what is inner in nature, and one cannot know how far this will go in time. Those transcendental questions, however, that go beyond nature, we will never be able to answer, even if all of nature is revealed to us, since it is never given to us to observe our own mind with any other intuition than that of our inner sense. For in that lies the mystery of the origin of our sensibility. Its relation to an object, and what might be the transcendental ground of this unity, undoubtedly lie too deeply hidden for us, who know even ourselves only through inner sense, thus as appearance, to be able to use such an unsuitable tool of investigation to find out anything except always more appearances, even though we would gladly investigate their non-sensible cause.[12]

This paradoxical position is not something accidental to reason or some eccentric feature of our nature. Our desire to seek independent metaphysical knowledge is both natural and impossible to fulfill. In the preface to the first edition of *The Critique of Pure Reason,* Kant writes: "Human reason has the peculiar fate in one species of its cognitions that it is burdened with questions which it cannot dismiss, since they

---

[10] Ibid., A127–128.

[11] *Prolegomena*, trans. L. W. Beck (New York, 1950), 67.

[12] *Critique of Pure Reason*, A277.

are given to it as problems by the nature of reason itself, but which it also cannot answer, since they transcend every capacity of human reason."[13]

In a famous passage in his preface to the *Critique of Pure Reason*, Kant casts his proposal as a revolution analogous to Copernicus's celebrated overturning of an earth-centered view of the sun and planets.

> Up to now it has been assumed that all our cognition must conform to the objects; but all attempts to find out something about them *a priori* through concepts that would extend our cognition have, on this presupposition, come to nothing. Hence let us once try whether we do not get farther with the problems of metaphysics by assuming that the objects must conform to our cognition, which would agree better with the requested possibility of an *a priori* cognition of them, which is to establish something about objects before they are given to us. This would be just like the first thoughts of Copernicus, who, when he did not make good progress in the explanation of the celestial motions if he assumed that the entire celestial host revolves around the observer, tried to see if he might not have greater success if he made the observer revolve and left the stars at rest. Now in metaphysics we can try in a similar way regarding the intuition of objects. If intuition has to conform to the constitution of the objects, then I do not see how we can know anything of them *a priori*; but if the object (as an object of the senses) conforms to the constitution of our faculty of intuition, then I can very well represent this possibility to myself.[14]

Just as Copernicus could explain and then overturn our tendency to think the sun travels round the earth, Kant could explain and overturn our tendency toward the traditional metaphysical investigation of the world in itself.

A full-scale assessment of Kant's arguments in the *Critique* is, of course, impossible here. Some of the reasons for siding with Kant rest on his arguing for the inadequacies of the alternatives. He also argued that reason generates contradictory conclusions and may thereby be seen to be discredited as a guide to metaphysics. Some of these arguments are considered later. Let us consider first the negative critique of theistic arguments, described by Mendelssohn as "world-crushing."[15]

---

[13] Ibid., Aviii.

[14] Preface to the second edition, *Critique of Pure Reason*, Bxvi–xvii.

[15] Cited in Wood and DiGiovanni, *Religion and Rational Theology*, xxiv.

Kant on Three Classic Theistic Arguments

Kant holds that the concept of God is the concept of "the original being...the highest being...the being of all beings," supreme in intelligence, power, and knowledge, personal, absolutely necessary, and unconditional – that is, not derived from any deeper reality.[16] Kant construes this theistic ideal as natural and fitting to common sense. The concept of God as "an all-encompassing perfection" emerges in our considered reflection on nature and its cause.

> One sees things alter, arise, and perish; therefore they, or at least their state, must have a cause. About every cause, however, that may be given in experience, the same thing may once again be asked. Now where could we more appropriately locate the supreme causality than right where the highest causality is, i.e., in that being, originally containing within itself what is sufficient for the possible effect, whose concept also comes about very easily through the single trait of an all-encompassing perfection. This highest cause we then take to be absolutely necessary, because we find it absolutely necessary to ascend to it and no ground for going still further beyond it. Therefore even through the blindest polytheism in all peoples we see shimmering a few sparks of monotheism, to which they have been led not by reflection and deep speculation, but only in accordance with a natural course of common understanding becoming gradually more intelligible.[17]

Part of the success of Kant's overall project rests on the failure of the alternative, traditional philosophical case for religious belief. If, say, the Cambridge Platonist, Cartesian, Lockean, or Leibnizian case for recognizing God's existence is successful, then there is no need to look at the categories of cognition to constitute our knowledge claims. A successful theistic argument (or a successful argument against God's existence from, say, Hume's Philo) would show that human reason was capable of revealing the structure of reality. Initially, in his "pre-critical period," Kant adopted the traditional route, publishing a text with the brazen title *The Only Possible Argument in Support of a Demonstration of the Existence of God.*[18] In the *Critique of Pure Reason* (section 3 through 6 in the chapter "Ideal of Pure Reason"), Kant seeks to undermine

---

[16] *Critique of Pure Reason*, A579.

[17] Ibid., A590.

[18] This has been translated by Ralf Meerbote in *Immanuel Kant: Theological Philosophy, 1775–1770* (Cambridge: Cambridge University Press, 1992). For a reconstruction of

traditional theistic metaphysics. A magisterial portrait of God is pivotal to his critique, for a chief complaint he raises against the cosmological and design arguments is that neither one succeeds in reaching a high, exalted monotheism. As Allen Wood observes: "Kant himself always thought that a theology which fell short of establishing the supreme ontological perfection of the divine being would be a complete failure."[19] In some respects, this outlook is very much like the Humean analysis of the design argument: even if some features of the world are evidence of intelligent design, this does not establish omnipotence, goodness, and other divine attributes.

Kant thinks that of the three main theistic arguments, the ontological is the most promising (or dangerous) in its justifying monotheism. Because of this, he concentrates most of his critical acumen on that argument. One of Kant's critical objections is that the very concept of a metaphysically necessary being is not intelligible or at least not known to be intelligible.

> Now a nominal definition of this concept is quite easy, namely that it is something whose non-being is impossible; but through this one becomes no wiser in regard to the conditions that make it necessary to regard the non-being of a thing as absolutely unthinkable, and that are really what one wants to know, namely whether or not through this concept we are thinking anything at all. For by means of the word unconditional to reject all the conditions that the understanding always needs in order to regard something as necessary, is far from enough to make intelligible to myself whether through a concept of an unconditionally necessary being I am still thinking something or perhaps nothing at all.[20]

This may seem like an odd line of attack, as Kant's work has been cast as providing a philosophical guarantee for necessity, but Kant thinks that all such necessity (the necessity of a triangle having three sides) is a function of our judgments. "All the alleged examples [of necessity] are without exception taken only from judgments but not from things and their existence."[21]

Kant develops a case against belief in God as a necessary being in the context of a commonplace version of the "oversubtle" ontological

Kant's argument, see R. M. Adams, "God, Possibility, and Kant," *Faith and Philosophy* 17:4 (October 2000).

[19] *Kant's Rational Theology* (Ithaca: Cornell University Press, 1978), 99.
[20] *Critique of Pure Reason*, A593.
[21] Ibid., A594.

argument, vestiges of which may be found in More, Descartes, and Leibniz. The argument is designed to secure the possibility of God as a necessarily existing being and then demonstrate that it is contradictory to claim there is no God. According to Kant, ontological arguments wind up treating existence as a real, determining predicate. When someone attributes "existence" or "being" to God, have they attributed some property in addition to other properties – predicates like goodness, omnipotence, omnipresence?

> Being is obviously not a real predicate, i.e., a concept of something that could add to the concept of a thing. It is merely the positing of a thing or of certain determinations in themselves. In the logical use it is merely the copula of a judgment. The proposition God is omnipotent contains two concepts that have their objects. God and omnipotence; the little word "is" is not a predicate in it, but only that which posits the predicate in relation to the subject. Now if I take the subject (God) together with all his predicates (among which omnipotence belongs), and say God is, or there is a God, then I add no new predicate to the concept of God, but only posit the subject in itself with all its predicates, and indeed posit the object in relation to my concept.[22]

Kant dramatically offers this judgment: "Thus the famous ontological (Cartesian) proof of the existence of a highest being from concepts is only so much trouble and labor lost, and a human being can no more become richer in insight from mere ideas than a merchant could in resources if he wanted to improve his financial state by adding a few zeros to his cash balance."[23] Ontological arguments therefore rest on a conceptual or grammatical mistake. It is an error to derive existence from the concept of God, for the concept of God does not contain existence.[24]

Did Kant succeed in his critique of the ontological argument? Many philosophers, but not all, in the nineteenth and twentieth century think he did. Still, reservations about Kant's success came from various quarters. Some defenders of the ontological argument take aim at Kant's whole project of locating the source of necessity in our forms of cognition. Why believe that *that* necessity is any less mysterious than the necessary relations and properties posited by Platonists? Or, more

---

[22] Ibid., A596–599.

[23] Ibid., A602.

[24] Kant speaks of real, determinate predicates as enlarging concepts. Cf. Cudwarth's claim that "the idea of a perfect being is pregnant of many attributes" (see Chapter 1).

specifically, why is it less mysterious than necessity so employed by Leibniz or, to invoke a more recent figure who was cited in the preceding chapter, the logician Frege?[25] In fact, a range of philosophers think Kant has not so much rescued or secured necessary relations as undermined them. An objection originally raised by Bertrand Russell, once an advocate of an ontological argument, has been restated as follows:

> According to Kant, the necessary truths of arithmetic and geometry owe their necessity to our cognitive constitutions – for example, to the fact that we can only apprehend cubes as being eight-cornered. But it is contingent that we have the constitution we do – our nature might change, or it might have been different originally even if for some necessity after all – if our constitution had been different, those laws would have been false and other laws would have held in their place. But that is absurd, as Kant should be among the first to acknowledge.[26]

Russell's friend, G. E. Moore, leveled the following criticism at Kant's whole schema of locating our grasp of essential relations in our cognition:

> This proposition, that our minds are so constituted as always to produce the same appearances, is itself a universal synthetic proposition... but how can any of us know this? Obviously, it is a question which requires an answer just as much as any of those which Kant set out to answer; and yet he never even attempts to answer it: it never seems to have occurred to him to ask how we can know that *all* men's minds are so constituted as *always* to act in a certain way. And once this question is raised, I think the whole plausibility of his argument disappears.[27]

---

[25] As Frege writes in "The Thought: A Logical Inquiry," the thought "which we express in the Pythagorean theorem is timelessly true, true independently of whether anyone takes it to be true. It needs no bearer. It is not true for the first time when it is discovered, but is like a planet, already before anyone has seen it, has been in interaction with other planets," cited in E. D. Wlemke, *Essays on Frege* (Urbana: University of Illinois Press, 1968), 523. In a similar, anti-Kantian spirit, G. H. Hardy writes "317 is a prime, not because we think it is so, or because our minds are shaped in one way rather than another, but *because it is so*, because mathematical reality is built that way;" see *A Mathematician's Apology* (Cambridge: Cambridge University Press, 1941), 47. As it happens, Frege did not accept the ontological argument. See J. W. Forgie, "Frege's Objections to the Ontological Argument," *Nous* 6 (1972).

[26] J. van Cleve, *Problems from Kant* (Oxford: Oxford University Press, 1999), 38.

[27] G. E. Moore, *Some Main Problems of Philosophy* (New York: Collier Books, 1962), 171.

Obviously, the debate over Kant's whole transcendental framework goes well beyond debating Kant's critique of theistic arguments. Still, if one rejects as inadequate the claim that necessary truths like $1 + 1 + 1 = 3$ are mind-dependent, then one may be on the road to recognizing properties like "contingent existence" and "necessary existence." For example, one may take the property "being the number seven" as having the property of "being necessary" while this book has the property of "being contingent." One may also think of necessity as a property had, not just by judgments but by states of affairs. While the judgment "$1 + 1 + 1 = 3$" may be necessary, isn't this because the state of affairs "$1 + 1 + 1 = 3$" necessarily obtains? Such a state of affairs is necessary because it could not but obtain. Arguably, it has the property of "being such that it necessarily obtains." Assertions about the concept of God as the concept of a being who exists necessarily do not (to some critics) seem akin to Kant's merchant.[28]

It is not my intent here to completely overturn Kant's attack to establish an ontological argument. I only suggest the argument may not have met its final end in *The Critique of Pure Reason*, chapter 3, section 4.

---

[28] Note the shift in images in the literature. In his criticism of the argument, Kant refers to a befuddled merchant, whereas Descartes used the metaphor of a mountain and valley. Hegel is cited in the next chapter defending a version of the ontological argument. For twentieth-century defenders, see N. Malcolm, A. Plantinga, J. Ross, C. Dore, S. T. Davis, C. Hartshorne, and R. M. Adams. I sketch what I take to be a defensible version of the ontological argument in *Contemporary Philosophy of Religion* (Oxford: Blackwell, 1998), chap. 10. The most sustained critical treatment of the argument is Graham Oppy, *Ontological Arguments and Belief in God* (Cambridge: Cambridge University Press, 1995). In 1948, John Findley advanced a famous "disproof" of God based on the ontological argument. He contended that if God exists, God exists necessarily. But "necessity" does not apply to objects, only to propositions. See "Can God's Existence Be Disproved?" *Mind* 57 (1948). Recall Hume's distinction between relations of ideas on the one hand and matters of fact on the other. Matters of fact, for Hume, all turn out to be contingent and this puts in jeopardy the supposition that God's existence could be a necessary fact. As I note in the preceding chapter, the most common objection has been that this Humean and Findleyan distinction is unwarranted; there are truths that are necessary (e.g., everything is itself, $1 + 1 = 2$) even if no minds existed. Given that there are such necessary truths (or necessarily true propositions, as Findley grants), why rule out other realities as candidates for necessary existence, such as properties, relations, and God? Findlay later revised his "disproof" and developed an elaborate philosophical theology in the spirit of Plotinus. For further discussion of necessary existence, see A. Plantinga, *The Nature of Necessity* (Oxford: Clarendon, 1974), and J. Hoffman and G. Rosendkrantz, *The Divine Attributes* (Oxford: Blackwell, 2002).

As for the cosmological argument, Kant takes it to be "at least natural" and acknowledges that it "has been the most persuasive... not only for the common but also for the speculative understanding."[29] Kant's central objection is that the cosmological argument rests on the ontological argument. I cite the key passage at length:

> In order to ground itself securely, this proof gets a footing in experience, and thereby gives itself the reputation that it is distinct from the ontological proof, which puts its whole trust solely in pure concepts *a priori*. But the cosmological proof avails itself of this experience only to make a single step, namely to the existence of a necessary being in general. What this being might have in the way of properties, the empirical ground of proof cannot teach; rather, here reason says farewell to it entirely and turns its inquiry back to mere concepts: namely being would have to have, i.e., which among all possible things contains within itself the required conditions (*requisita*) for an absolute necessity. Now reason believes it meets with these requisites solely and uniquely in the concept of a most real being, and so it infers: that is the absolutely necessary being. But it is clear that here one presupposes that the concept of a being of the highest reality completely suffices for the concept of an absolute necessity in existence, i.e., that from the former the latter may be inferred – a proposition the ontological proof asserted, which one thus assumes in the cosmological proof and takes as one's ground, although one had wanted to avoid it. For absolute necessity is an existence from mere concepts. Now if I say: the concept of the *ens realissimum* is a concept, and indeed the one single concept, that fits necessary existence and is adequate to it, then I must admit that the latter could be concluded from it. Thus it is really only the ontological proof from mere concepts that contains all the force of proof in the so-called cosmological proof; and the supposed experience is quite superfluous – perhaps leading us only to the concept of a necessary being, but not so as to establish this concept in any determinate thing.[30]

At first, the criticism here may seem less severe than against the ontological argument, for Kant seems to allow that the cosmological argument could well bring us to *a necessary being*. This may simply be a strategic concession, however, as the more substantial thesis is that the belief in a necessary being as generated by the cosmological argument would still not suffice to ground the God of monotheism philosophically. Essentially, the cosmological argument faces two problems: the problem of elucidating the nature of necessity when it comes to a metaphysical

---

[29] *Critique of Pure Reason*, A604.
[30] Ibid., A604–607.

being or cause, and the problem of establishing that the necessary being is God.

As I noted earlier, Kant's complaints about the intelligibility of a necessary being are open to challenge. Second, if one allows that there can be a necessary being that truly answers the cosmological line of reasoning, one may adopt the modest position that it offers *some* evidence for theism, even if that evidence is not by itself sufficient. Given a theistic portrait of God, one would have some reason to believe there would be a contingent cosmos. Perhaps, from the mere existence of such a contingent cosmos one cannot reason *to* theism, for it would also be true that given the existence of a necessary cosmic cause (having some but lacking other divine attributes) one would also expect a contingent cosmos. Still, even an attenuated cosmological argument to a cause that transcends the cosmos would displease a strict naturalist.[31] Kant's discontent with anything less than a fully monotheistic conclusion comes into focus in his analogous criticism of the design argument.

Kant clearly finds the last of the three classic arguments the most authoritative. "This proof always deserves to be named with respect. It is the oldest, clearest and the most appropriate to common human reason."[32] Kant's version of the argument is memorable and deserves a full citation.

> The present world discloses to us such an immeasurable showplace of manifoldness, order, purposiveness, and beauty, whether one pursues these in the infinity of space or in the unlimited division of it, that in accordance with even the knowledge about it that our weak understanding can acquire, all speech concerning so many and such unfathomable wonders must lose its power to express, all numbers their power to measure, and even our thoughts lack boundaries, so that our judgment upon the whole must resolve itself into a speechless, but nonetheless eloquent, astonishment. Everywhere we see a chain of effects and causes, of ends and means, regularity in coming to be and perishing, and because nothing has entered by itself into the state in which it finds itself, this state always refers further to another thing as its cause, which makes necessary just the same further inquiry, so that in such a way the entire whole would have to sink into the abyss of nothingness if one did not assume something subsisting for itself originally and independently outside this infinite

---

[31] Kant held that the cosmological argument presupposes the ontological argument, but one may move from a successful cosmological argument to an ontological argument. See Michael Tooley, "Does the Cosmological Argument Entail the Ontological Argument?" *Monist* 54 (July 1970).

[32] *Critique of Pure Reason*, A623.

contingency, which supports it and at the same time, as the cause of its existence, secures its continuation. This highest cause (in regard to all things of the world) – how great should one think it is? We are not acquainted with the world in its whole content, still less do we know how to estimate its magnitude by comparison with everything possible. But since in respect to causality we need an ultimate and supreme being, what hinders us from at the same time positing in it a degree of perfection exceeding everything else that is possible? This we can easily effect, though to be sure only through the fragile outline of an abstract concept, if we represent all possible perfection united in it as a single substance – which concept is favorable to our reason in its parsimony of principles, not subject to any contradictions, and even salutary for the extension of the use of our reason within experience, through the guidance such an idea gives to order and purposiveness, but is nowhere contrary to experience in any decisive way.[33]

Despite his evident sympathy with this evidence of design, Kant contends that at most the argument establishes a very great architect of the cosmos, not a being of omnipotence, omniscience, and perfection.

The proof could at most establish a highest architect of the world, who would always be limited by the suitability of the material on which he works, but not a creator of the world, to whose idea everything is subject, which is far from sufficient for the great aim that one has in view, namely that of proving an all-sufficient original being. If we wanted to prove the contingency of matter itself, then we would have to take refuge in a transcendental argument, which, however, is exactly what was supposed to be avoided here.[34]

I cannot help observing that this conclusion is still quite dramatic. As Allen Woods writes: "It is hard to deny that if there is a necessarily existent cause of the world and intelligent author of its order, the result would have considerable philosophical interest, even if it could not be shown that this being is *ens realissimum*."[35] I return to Kant on design in this chapter in discussing his view of history.

Kant offers a fascinating set of arguments call the Antinomies (literally, "conflict of laws") to secure his thesis that traditional metaphysics fails. Let us consider these in the next section.

---

[33] Ibid., A622.

[34] Ibid., A627.

[35] *Kant's Rational Theology*, 99. See also Thomas McPherson, *The Argument from Design* (London: Macmillan, 1972), chap. 6.

Reason and Contradictions

Kant contends that reason generates the following pairs of propositions which he labels in terms of a thesis and antithesis. The result is a set of four antinomies or demonstrations of a proposition and its denial. Traditional (sometimes called transcendental realism) metaphysics is seen here as hopelessly generating opposite conclusions. In rejecting transcendental realism, he seeks to establish transcendental idealism.

Thesis: The world has a beginning in time, and in space it is also enclosed in boundaries.

Antithesis: The world has no beginning and no bounds in space, but is infinite with regard to both time and space.

Thesis: Every composite substance in the world consists of simple parts, and nothing exists anywhere except the simple or what is composed of simples

Antithesis: No composite thing in the world consists of simple parts, and nowhere in it does there exist anything simple.

Thesis: Causality in accordance with laws of nature is not the only one from which all the appearances of the world can be derived. It is also necessary to assume another causality through freedom in order to explain them.

Antithesis: There is no freedom, but everything in the world happens solely in accordance with laws of nature.

Thesis: To the world there belongs something that, either as a part of it or as its cause, is an absolutely necessary being.

Antithesis: There is no absolutely necessary being existing anywhere, either in the world or outside the world as its cause.[36]

Each antinomy has some relevance to philosophical work on religious belief. The first, third, and fourth antinomies bear on theism. The first concerns theistic claims over *creatio ex nihilo*. Some theists hold that the cosmos had a beginning while other theists and naturalists have denied this. The third antinomy ties in with debate over free will, clearly an important factor in debating the problem of evil, the compatibility of freedom and divine foreknowledge, and God's providence. The fourth touches on the cosmological argument and involves questioning whether the cosmos was created. The second does not directly bear on theism, although it does have an impact on two philosophies of God described earlier (Conway's in Chapter 2, Leibniz's in Chapter 3).

[36] See *Critique of Pure Reason*, A406–565.

Kant used the antinomies to expose what he saw as the problem of traditional metaphysics with its project of describing and explaining things in themselves. So, concerning the first antinomy, Kant holds that the world in itself is neither finite nor infinite as a whole. We are not privileged to have access to the world in itself but only to the phenomenal world that is formed by our own cognition. So, with respect to the first antinomy, Kant proposes that both thesis and antithesis should be rejected. We cannot cognitively get to the world in itself but only our forms of cognition. Kant gave pride of place to the antinomies as the driving force behind his critique of traditional metaphysics. "It was not the investigation of the existence of God, immortality, and so on, but rather the antimony of pure reason – 'the world has a beginning; it has no beginning, and so on,' right up to the fourth: 'There is freedom in man, versus there is no freedom, only the necessity of nature' – that is what first aroused me from my dogmatic slumber and drove me to the critique of reason itself, in order to resolve the scandal of ostensible contradiction of reason with itself."[37]

Kant's antinomies embody a more widespread worry about philosophy itself. At the end of the day, does philosophy generate incompatible but equally plausible convictions? The antinomies of Kant are not easily dismissed: there are contemporary philosophers who would defend each thesis, while others just as vigorously defend the antithesis. Several options are available in response. One may enter the fray and simply argue, as some have done, for the superiority of one thesis over the other. To consider one of Cudworth's projects, a defender of incompatible libertarianism (a nondeterministic view of freedom) may introduce a concept of agent causation to secure the thesis that human persons are not completely determined.[38] Kant, as it happens, does contend that we are free, and not thoroughly determined, though he locates this freedom on a transcendent, noumenal level.

In our day it is rare that a case for any of the theses or antitheses be made that purports to be a *demonstration*. So, for example, a philosopher like William Craig who accepts the first thesis (he thinks the cosmos had a beginning), while denying the antithesis, provides arguments for his position, but these are not presented with apodictic certainty. It is

---

[37] From *Kant's Perpetual Peace and Other Essays*, trans. T. Humphrey (Indianapolis: Hackett, 1983), 15.

[38] More recent defenders of libertarian freedom include R. Chisholm, P. Van Inwagen, and S. Goetz.

thus rare to discover self-advertised arguments of water-tight certainty in the metaphysics for a thesis and antithesis.

The use of antinomies is not limited to Kant's time. Two recent cases involve Anthony Kenny and Paul Draper. Kenny has defended what he thinks is a good case for theism (argument from design) and an equally good case against it (from the problem of positing nonphysical agency). Draper has defended theism also with a design argument and atheism based on the problem of evil.[39]

Under such circumstances, there are several options. One can suspend judgment and be agnostic.[40] Alternatively, one may locate other reasons for opting for one thesis rather than the other, in the tradition of Pascal. Kant's antinomies are all highly theoretical as opposed to morally pressing, but bringing in more concrete cases may help illustrate the role of a Pascalian wager. Imagine you are in the grips of a conflict: you possess strong moral reasons to support capital punishment (which Kant did) and equally strong reasons to oppose it. Under these conditions there may still be an overriding practical consideration leading you to oppose the death penalty – for example, the burden of proof should always be on any case for homicide because of the danger of killing the innocent.[41] There may be other factors that can help guide someone either to the thesis or antithesis (see the discussion of William James, at the end of Chapter 6).

What if Kant is correct that the antinomies establish that we cannot pursue a metaphysic of the world as it is (Are we free? Did the cosmos have a beginning?) but must restrict ourselves to the analysis of our own cognition and representations? A worry arises that some of the same reasons that afflict the traditional metaphysician afflict the Kantian. In other words, if Kant is right that reasoning about the

---

[39] See Draper, "Cosmic Fine-Tuning and Terrestrial Suffering: Parallel Problems for Naturalism and Theism," *American Philosophical Quarterly* 41:4 (2004).

[40] There is a long-standing controversy in epistemology over cases in which the evidence for the truth of some proposition, X, is just as strong as the evidence for the falsehood of the proposition, not-X. Followers of the ancient skeptic, Sextus Empiricus, conclude that in such cases one ought to suspend judgment. More generous epistemologists contend that in some such cases, believing either is permissible (believing X under such circumstances is not ipso facto intellectually negligent or wrong).

[41] T. Penelhum has two interesting texts on belief and evidence that speak to these issues, *God and Skepticism* (Dordrecht: Reidel, 1983), and *Reason and Religious Faith* (Boulder: Westview, 1995). See also R. Geivett and B. Sweetman, eds., *Contemporary Perspectives in Religious Epistemology* (Oxford: Oxford University Press, 1992).

world itself will generate incompatible results, doesn't the same incompatibility arise in the world of representations? If some state of affairs involves a contradiction (e.g., *there are only simple parts and there is nothing simple*), that contradiction is just as problematic as a state of affairs in the world as it is in the world of representation or cognition. Consider the following: can there be a square circle in the world? No. This would involve there being an object with four right angles and not having four right angles at the same time. Can one conceive of, or represent, a square circle? Although we may well believe contradictory states of affairs when these involve either highly abstract matters or extended moral quandaries (perhaps I often believe my brother to be a criminal, but I also often believe he is innocent), it is more problematic to suppose one can consciously embrace incompatible propositions at the same time. Can you at once believe something is both a square and a circle? Arguably, this is just as problematic as holding that there actually is a square circle "in the world." So, the problems Kant raises for the traditional metaphysical philosopher may still afflict Kant's alternative view of cognition and representation.[42]

Moral Faith

The starry heavens above (or our representation of them) may not secure God, immortality, and human freedom, but the moral law within is another story. Kant's critique of metaphysics was not just a critique of theism but of atheism as well. For Kant, any traditional metaphysic of

---

[42] There is a further difficulty for those who wish to deny meaningful inquiry into how things are "in themselves." Kant presents an analysis of our representation of the world, as distinct from how the world is in itself. But if we make bona fide claims about our cognition (or our representations of the world or our understanding) must these not stand as genuine claims about *the-way-things-are* or *what exists*? If someone claims "there are only conceptual frameworks," isn't that person committed to claiming that it is true, and not merely a matter of conceptual frameworks, that there are indeed conceptual frameworks? Realism seems (at least to some philosophers) to be built into meaningful discourse. For a contemporary realist, "traditional" reply to Kant, see Michael Loux, *Metaphysics* (London: Routledge, 2002). For two good, contrary positions on realism, see Hilary Putnam, *Representation and Reality* (Cambridge, Mass.: MIT Press, 1989), and William Alston, *A Realist Conception of Truth* (Ithaca: Cornell University Press, 1995). From the standpoint of philosophy of religion, Michael Dummett is an interesting figure for he has advocated nonrealism as well as a traditional Roman Catholic faith.

reality is in error. He felt the need to bracket metaphysics to clear the ground for something else.

> I cannot even assume God, freedom and immortality for the sake of the necessary practical use of my reason unless I simultaneously deprive speculative reason of its pretension to extravagant insights; because in order to attain to such insights, speculative reason would have to help itself to principles that in fact reach only to objects of possible experience, and which, if they were to be applied to what cannot be an object of experience, then they would always actually transform it into an appearance, and thus declare all practical extension of pure reason to be impossible. Thus I had to deny knowledge in order to make room for faith; and the dogmatism of metaphysics, i.e., the prejudice that without criticism reason can make progress in metaphysics, is the true source of all unbelief conflicting with morality, which unbelief is always very dogmatic.[43]

Kant makes room for faith in the *Groundwork for the Metaphysics of Morals* (1785) and *Critique of Practical Reason* (1788).

Kant argued for this moral faith on the grounds of our duty to the highest good. Kant held that we have categorical or unconditional moral duties (some of which are noted in the later section "Cosmopolitanism and Religion"). These are not conditioned by the desires we happen to have; therefore I may have a duty not to lie even if I have no desire whatever about not lying. The rational and ideal end that a moral agent ought to will is the highest good. Anything less would be a reflection of some imperfection or a less than rational or moral will. The highest perfect good, in Kant's view, is an ideal of happiness and virtue. There is something absurd or tragic, from a moral point of view, about a cosmos in which vice brings happiness and virtue is the advent of unhappiness. Kant then reasons that if we ought to will something, the object of our will must be possible. There would be no point in willing what is impossible: if we ought to will something we must be able to will it. Kant adopted a principle that may be abbreviated as "ought implies can." If I ought to do X, it must be that *I can do X*; if I can't do it, it is not my duty to do it. The completely good goal of my will (concord of happiness and virtue) is only possible if there is an all-powerful, just God of the natural world who will indeed bring about this ideal end. God can make it the case that our moral, rational ideal is intelligible. Therefore, Kant argues, a rational, moral agent should postulate

---

[43] *Critique of Pure Reason*, Bxxx.

that there is a just, all-powerful God who will harmonize virtue and happiness.

Kant develops this argument along with an argument for postulating an afterlife. An afterlife is essential for the concord of felicity and virtue, as well as the achievement of (the progress toward) a holy will or perfect goodness. Kant's portrait of an afterlife involves a progressive movement toward holiness, a movement that is unending.

Kant's moral argument does not make morality rest on God's arbitrary use of power. To refer back to Cudworth's deployment of the Euthyphro dilemma (from Chapter 1), Kant, like Cudworth, considers a thing's goodness to be a quality independent of God's love. Similarly, it is not God's love or power that lends rightness to one's duty. Yet without postulating a God, and thus without a guarantee that there is a moral order to the cosmos, our moral agency is not fully intelligible; the world, from the standpoint of a moral agent, would be absurd and irrational. If we assume that moral agency is rational and not fantastic, we are led to postulate theism. This move is not, however, tantamount to a reassertion of the theism of Kant's precritical days. Kant still sees us as not equipped to refer to God as a reality independent of our conceptual schemes, God is affirmed, I believe, but as a *noumenal* reality. The noumenal world is not an extension of our empirical world; it is not knowable by us and thus may be characterized as a transcendental reality. Kant thereby places his theology more in the realm of practice than metaphysics.

> It was a duty for us to promote the highest good; hence there is in us not merely the warrant but also the necessity, as a need connected with duty, to presuppose the possibility of this highest good, which, since it is possible only under the condition of the existence of God, connects the presupposition of the existence of God inseparably with duty; that is, it is morally necessary to assume the existence of God.... It is well to note here that this moral necessity is subjective, that is, a need and not objective, that is, itself a duty; for, there can be no duty to assume the existence of anything (since this concerns only the theoretical use of reason). Moreover, it is not to be understood by this that it is necessary to assume the existence of God as a ground of all obligation in general (for this rests, as has been sufficiently shown, solely on the autonomy of reason itself). What belongs to duty here is only the striving to produce and promote the highest good in the world, the possibility of which can therefore be postulated, while our reason finds this thinkable only on the presupposition of a supreme intelligence; to assume the existence of this supreme intelligence is thus connected with the consciousness of our

duty, although this assumption itself belongs to a theoretical reason; with respect to theoretical alone, as a ground of explanation, it can be called hypothesis; but in relation to the intelligibility of an object given us by the moral law (the highest good), and consequently if a need for practical purposes, it can be called belief and, indeed, a pure rational belief since pure reason alone (in its theoretical as well as in its practical use) is the source from which it springs.[44]

There are ardent defenders and opponents of Kant's moral argument today.[45]

To bring out some of the intuitive appeal for a Kantian style moral argument, I offer a classic description of the cosmos without God by Bertrand Russell.

That man is the product of causes which had no prevision of the end they were achieving; that his origin, his growth, his hopes and fears, his loves and his beliefs are but the outcome of accidental collections of atoms; that no fire, no heroism, no intensity of thought and feeling, can preserve an individual life beyond the grave; that all the labors of the ages, all the devotion, all the inspiration, all the noonday brightness of human genius, are destined to extinction in the vast death of the solar system, and that the whole temple of man's achievement must inevitably be buried beneath the debris of a universe in ruins – all these things, if not quite beyond dispute, are yet so nearly certain that no philosophy which rejects them can hope to stand. Only within the scaffolding of these truths, only on the firm foundation of unyielding despair, can the soul's habitation henceforth be safely built.[46]

Russell commends moral action (his views are discussed in Chapter 9); indeed, he wrote vigorously to advance causes he thought were just, even serving in jail to protest a war. But Russell's view of the fate of

---

[44] *Critique of Practical Reason in Practical Philosophy* 5:125–126. For a good overview of Kant's moral theology and its successors, see Peter Byrne, *The Moral Interpretation of Religion* (Grand Rapids: Eerdmans, 1998).

[45] For a defense, see John Hare, *The Moral Gap: Kantian Ethics, Human Limits and God's Assistance* (Oxford: Oxford University Press, 1996), and work by G. Mavrodes, L. Zagzebski, and R. M. Adams. For a critique, see J. L. Mackie's *The Miracle of Theism* (Oxford: Clarendon, 1982), and work by M. Martin, K. Nielson, and P. Grim.

[46] Russell, "A Free Man's Worship," in *Mysticism and Logic* (New York: Barnes and Noble, 1917), 47–48. George Mavrodes employs Russell's "vision" as part of theistic moral argument that resembles Kant. See his "Religion and the Queerness of Morality," in *Rationality, Religious Belief and Moral Commitment,* ed. R. Audi and W. Wainwright (Ithaca: Cornell University Press, 1986).

humanity may be seen (by some philosophers) as rendering tenuous, or even undermining, the motive to pursue justice and compassion. It has been argued that theism provides a context, whereas naturalism does not, for the intelligibility of moral agency. Of course, a fuller development of the argument would need to consider objections such as the counterclaim that a nontheistic, Buddhist system of Karma would provide an equally good (or better) framework for the intelligibility of morality. Some theists have used Kantian considerations to argue that one should hope that God exists.[47] There is also the reply to a Kantian argument that reverses the conclusion; in the twentieth century Albert Camus will contend that because theism is false, traditional morality is absurd.

Before moving on to Kant's view of evil, it is useful to cite one of Kant's strongest testimonies to his proposed moral faith.

> Moral theism is of course critical, since it pursues all the speculative proofs for the existence of God step by step, and recognizes them to be insufficient; indeed, the moral theist asserts absolutely that it is impossible for speculative reason to demonstrate the existence of such a being with apodictic certainty; but he is nevertheless firmly convinced of the existence of this being, and he has a faith beyond all doubt on practical grounds. The foundation on which he builds his faith is unshakable and it can never be overthrown, not even if all human beings united to undermine it. It is a fortress in which the moral human being can find refuge with no fear of being driven from it, because every attack on it will come to nothing. Hence his faith in God built on this foundation is as certain as a mathematical demonstration. This foundation is *morals*, the whole system of duties, which is cognized *a priori* with apodictic certainty through pure reason. This absolutely necessary morality of actions flows from the idea of a freely acting rational being and from the nature of actions themselves. Hence nothing firmer or more certain can be thought in any science than our obligation to moral actions. Reason would have to cease to be if it could in any way deny this obligation.... now the human being has a secure foundation on which he can build his faith in God; for although his virtue must be without any selfishness, even after denying the many claims of seductive temptations he still feels in himself a drive to hope for a lasting happiness.[48]

---

[47] See Louis P. Pojman, "Faith without Belief?" *Faith and Philosophy* 3 (1996): 157–176.

[48] *Lectures on the Philosophical Doctrine of Religion*, in Wood and Giovanni, *Religion and Rational Theology*, 28:1011. For a twentieth-century moral argument for theism with some Kantian elements but without Kant's reservations about metaphysics, see A. E. Taylor's "Theism" in the *Encyclopedia of Religion and Ethics*, ed. J. Hastings

A Mysterious Grace

Kant held that human beings are fundamentally predisposed to the good. We possess animal instincts for self-preservation, a desire for society, and the like. We also have a predisposition to exercise practical reason in respecting our own and others' humanity. Notwithstanding our orientation to the good, Kant also holds that we have a propensity toward evil. His account of how we came to have this propensity involves the key components of his philosophy, in which the noumenal realm of the self (God and freedom) is distinguished from the phenomenal realm. He holds that we came to possess this disposition to evil through noumenal, libertarian freedom. As Philip Quinn writes:

> He tells us that, though the propensity to evil can be represented as innate, it should not be represented as merely innate, for it should also be represented as brought by humans upon themselves. It can be represented as innate because, as the underlying ground of all morally evil actions in their lives, it is to be thought of as present in its possessors antecedent to all such actions and so represented temporally as present in them as far back as birth. It should be represented as brought by its possessors upon themselves because, being morally evil, it has to be a product of libertarian freedom for which its possessors can be held morally accountable. And it can be represented as brought by its possessors upon themselves, Kant thinks, because it can be thought of as, and actually is, the product of an atemporal act of noumenal libertarian freedom on the part of each of its possessors.[49]

While this explanation of our responsibility for evil dispositions may seem odd, Kant is more plausible in simply claiming that we often, at base, embrace "the evil maxim" of privileging our happiness over others. "This evil is *radical*, since it corrupts the ground of all maxims."[50]

In the face of our succumbing to, and entrenchment in, evil, a radical change of heart is essential. We come to realize the need for such a conversion through what Kant described as an archetype or original

---

(New York: Charles Scribner, 1951): "Love, with no limitations, if it is clear-sighted, for us at least must be an amor ascendens, and as it has its source in good (for real love is always formed with good, not formed with evil in its object), so unless it can at last rest in the supreme Good, which is good altogether, it must remain unsatisfied" (12:286).

[49] "Sin and Original Sin," in *A Companion to Philosophy of Religion*, ed. P. Quinn and C. Taliaferro (Cambridge: Blackwell, 1997), 546.

[50] *Religion within the Boundaries of Mere Reason*, in Wood and Giovanni, *Religion and Rational Theology*, 6:37.

idea of moral perfection. God's grace through the archetype enables a person to undergo a *revolution* by which they turn to the good (or the good maxim) and then display practical *reform* in their action. Salvation is achieved by human agency and divine grace.

> Granted that some supernatural cooperation is also needed to his [man's] becoming good or better, whether this cooperation only consist in the diminution of obstacles or be also a positive assistance, the human being must nonetheless make himself antecedently worthy of receiving it; and he must accept this help (which is no small matter), i.e. he must incorporate this positive increase of force unto his maxim: in this way alone it is possible that the good be imputed to him, and that he be acknowledged a good human being.[51]

Kant's understanding of grace allows him to modify and reinterpret some central Christian tenets. So, the historical Jesus can function as the saving archetype. We may even think of Jesus as "God incarnate" if that means that the person, Jesus, is seen to be holy. From a religious point of view, our moral life may be seen in thoroughly theistic terms, "*Religion* is (subjectively considered) the recognition of all our duties as divine commands."[52] But Kant, like Lessing, does not see salvation as resting primarily in a historic event (Christ's atonement) that gives rise to credible divine revelation attested to by miracles. No historical doctrine is essential for salvation. Moreover, the inner nature of faith, for Kant, is individual and not a matter for public profession.[53]

> Investigation into all forms of faith that relate to religion invariably runs across a *mystery* behind their inner nature, i.e. something *holy*, which can indeed be *cognized* by every individual, yet cannot be *professed* publicly, i.e. cannot be communicated universally. As something *holy* it must be a moral object, hence an object of reason and one capable of being sufficiently recognized internally for practical use; yet, as something *mysterious*, not for theoretical use, for then it would have to be communicable to everyone and hence also capable of being externally and publicly professed.[54]

Kant pictures religion as two concentric circles. In the inside circle is the pure religion of moral faith and God's saving grace or aid. In the outer

---

[51] Ibid., 6:44.
[52] Ibid., 6:154.
[53] Ibid., 6:119.
[54] Ibid., 6:137.

circle, there is historical, religious tradition. As a rational philosopher, one should be committed to the inner circle. If one is at the same time committed to historical revelation, one needs to be able to show how the two cohere, without any compromise to the inner, pure circle.

Cosmopolitanism and Religion

Kant's principle aim in much of his celebrated, later work is a universal understanding of history and political authority. In *Idea for a Universal History with a Cosmopolitan Intent* (1784) and *To Perpetual Peace: A Philosophical Sketch* (1795), Kant sought to identify rational, evident principles that would prohibit war between nations. It has been objected that Kant's work has had little impact politically. Witness Karl Marx's judgment:

> While the French bourgeoisie, by means of the most colossal revolution that history has ever known, was achieving domination and conquering the continent of Europe, while the already emancipated English bourgeoisie was revolutionizing industry and subjugating India politically and all the rest of the world commercially, the impotent German burghers did not get any farther than "good will".... Kant's good will fully corresponds to the impotence, depression and wretchedness of the German burghers, whose petty interests were never capable of developing into the common interests of a class but had their counterpart in their cosmopolitan swollen-headedness.[55]

Marx was surely off the mark as far as Kant is concerned. Kant's concept of a federation of nations influenced the twenty-eighth president of the United States, Woodrow Wilson, who advocated the League of Nations at the Paris Peace Conference following World War I. Kant's global federalism and international republicanism may be seen as one (among many) inspirations behind the eventual founding of the United Nations.[56]

Kant's case for perpetual peace includes strictures on warfare, national sovereignty, immigration, and prohibitions against economic exploitation and intimidation. Kant's political philosophy and moral

---

[55] From Marx's *The German Ideology*, cited by R. C. Solomon, *Continental Philosophy since 1750* (Oxford: Oxford University Press, 1988), 25.

[56] See Rawls, *The Law of Peoples* (Cambridge, Mass.: Harvard University Press, 1999). See also Rawls's treatment of the ideal observer theory in *A Theory of Justice* (Cambridge, Mass.: Harvard University Press, 1971), beginning on p. 184.

faith thereby led him to see philosophy as having an important, public role.

> That kings should be philosophers, or philosophers kings is neither to be expected nor to be desired, for the possession of power inevitably corrupts reason's free judgment. However, that kings or sovereign peoples (who rule themselves by laws of equality) should not allow the class of philosophers to disappear or to be silent, but should permit them to speak publicly is indispensible to the enlightenment of their affairs. And because this class is by nature incapable of sedition and of forming cliques, it cannot be suspected of being the formulator of *propaganda*.[57]

In this bid for global justice, does religion have a role? I suggest that Kant saw religion, when it is rational, as a key driving force in the establishment of international justice. Pure rational religious faith consists principally in living a morally good life as God commands. Because of his separation of historical faith and pure rational religion, Kant should not be seen as holding that historic Christianity was essential to his global, republican federalism. Moreover, Kant's reinterpretation of revelation claims would seem both to block the imposition of a religion on a people and to set aside political claims to land and authority by an appeal to divine providence. But in light of his moral faith, Kant holds that mature moral motivation includes willing and working for the concord of virtue and happiness, and this would, presumably, involve either a theistic framework or possibly a karmic system of justice.[58] Kant's faith in a cosmopolitan concordance of nations suggests, I believe, that Kant saw nature itself as designed or structured for this end.

> Perpetual peace is *insured* (guaranteed) by nothing less than that great artist *nature*...whose mechanical process makes her purposiveness... visibly manifest, permitting harmony to emerge among men through their discord, even against their wills. If we regard this design as a compulsion resulting from one of her causes whose laws of operation are unknown to us, we call it *fate*, while, if we reflect on nature's purposiveness in the flow of world events, and regard it to be the underlying wisdom of a higher cause that directs the human race toward its objective goal

---

[57] Kant's *Perpetual Peace and Other Essays*, 126.

[58] There are many accounts of Karma and rebirth, some of which are friendly to Kant's understanding of moral rectitude, for example, retribution and purgation. See W. D. O'Flaherty, ed., *Karma and Rebirth in Classical Indian Traditions* (Berkeley: University of California Press, 1980).

and predetermines the world's course, we call it *providence*. We cannot actually have *cognitive* knowledge of these intricate designs in nature, nor can we *infer* their actual existence from it, but (as with all relations between the forms of things and purposes in general) we can and must *attribute* them to objects only in thought...so as to conceive of their possibility on an analogy with mankind's productive activities...[59]

This language of design is also attested to in Kant's *Critique of Judgment*. After reflecting on humanity's place in nature, Kant comments: "It proves no more than this, that by constitution of our cognitive faculties, and, therefore, in bringing experience into touch with the highest principles of reason, we are absolutely incapable of forming any conception of the possibility of such a world [as ours] unless we imagine a highest cause operating designedly."[60] Kant may have kept these observations closely tethered, lest they herald a return to traditional metaphysics. Nonetheless, Kant commends a teleological understanding of nature and history.[61]

Kant's ethic of respect has had a role in religious ethics. In the next chapter, we take note of utilitarians (both religious and secular), some of whom were not at all enthusiastic about the concept of human rights. (Bentham characterized human rights as nonsense on stilts.) Kant valued persons for their own sake, enjoining us to consider a nonutilitarian ethic: "So act to treat humanity, whether in your own person or in that of any other, in every case as an end in itself, never as a means only."[62] Kant's ethic is founded on a respect for rational individuals for their own sake, thus inhibiting an ethic grounded principally in comparing better and worse utilities. The main world religions have sought in different

---

[59] Ibid., 120.

[60] *Critique of Judgment*, trans. J. C. Meredith (Oxford: Oxford University Press, 1921), 399. See also Bernard M. G. Reardon, "Teleology," in *Kant as Philosophical Theologian* (Basingstoke: Macmillan, 1988). As an aside, Alvin Plantinga takes Kant to be wrong in his critique of metaphysics, but I suggest that Kant's view of nature in the *Critique of Judgment* and of cosmopolitan internationalism would fit Plantinga's reformed epistemology. If our faculties function properly (so Kant seems to argue), we will (given grace, moral revolution, and reform through some maxims) have an international, pacific republic. See Plantinga on Kant in *Christian Warrant* (Oxford: Oxford University Press, 2000).

[61] See especially Kant's "Idea for a Universal History with a Cosmopolitan Intent."

[62] *Metaphysics of Morals*, ed. Mary Gregor (Cambridge: Cambridge University Press, 1991).

ways to address and respect human dignity.[63] Kant's legacy, in part, is the challenge to restrain religion within the limits of a framework of fundamental human rights.[64] (The topic of religion in a liberal society is discussed in Chapter 9.)

This chapter began with notes on a friendship between Kant and Mendelssohn. Kant's picture of friendship in his lectures on *Ethics* may seem rather cool; he counsels caution in sharing intimacy, a respectful distance so as to avoid rash exchanges, and so on. But there is also praise of openhearted love, the reciprocal possession of a person and his friend, common thinking and feeling, which is profoundly attractive. Kant's political philosophy may also be seen as proposing the deeply appealing ideal of a friendship among people across nations. Religion's role lies in the deliberate, devoted, rational practice of respecting other persons. Kant's idea of the philosopher is not the medieval notion that a philosopher is a friend of God where that involves the soul seeking a unitive experience of the divine. The philosopher's role does, however, include using reason in the cause of peace and, ultimately, in contributing to friendship among people.[65]

Reason and Romance

Kant's work is so extensive in scope and detail that it has been compared to a great empire that no single successor could adopt and rule as a whole. Not surprisingly, a philosopher may be described (historically and today) as a Kantian even if she only adheres to a segment of Kant's teaching. In this concluding section, I briefly highlight several philosophically minded theologians (or philosophical theologians) who either modified or rejected Kant.

---

[63] See, for example, L. Rouner, ed., *Human Rights and the World's Religions* (Notre Dame: University of Notre Dame Press, 1988), and A. Swidler, ed., *Human Rights in Religious Traditions* (New York: Pilgrim's Press, 1982).

[64] See Paul Mojzes, ed., *Religion and the War in Bosnia* (Atlanta: Scholars Press, 1998).

[65] I think a Kantian would happily approve of the goal of education as outlined in the African National Congress Constitution: "Education shall be directed towards the development of the human personality and a sense of personal dignity, and shall aim at strengthening respect for human rights and fundamental freedoms and promoting understanding, tolerance and friendship amongst South Africans and between nations." Cited by Martha Nussbaum, *Cultivating Humanity* (Cambridge, Mass.: Harvard University Press, 1997), 66.

Kant's work was often seen as a preeminent work of rational criticism. In the preface to the first edition of *The Critique of Pure Reason*, Kant wrote: "Our age is the genuine age of criticism, to which everything must submit. Religion through its holiness and legislation through its majesty commonly seek to exempt themselves from it. But in this way they excite a just suspicion against themselves, and cannot lay claim to that unfeigned respect which has been able to withstand its free and public examination."[66] Johann Georg Hamann (1730–1788) responded to Kant by criticizing Kant's critical tools. Specifically, he argued that Kant's formal view of reason – in which reason and experience may be separated and the a priori and a posteriori demarcated – was untenable. Hamann is one of several thinkers who have been considered part of the romantic movement. He and others argued that Kant (and many Enlightenment thinkers) wrongly sequestered religious and poetic feelings and experience.

A close friend of Hamann, Friedrich Heinrich Jacobi (1743–1819) extended this critical response to Kant, arguing that faith and feeling can be legitimate grounds for religious belief. Religion does not need to be within the bounds of reason alone. Indeed, he contended that the Enlightenment conception of reason was dehumanizing. (It is interesting to note that Jacobi used Hume as an ally against Kant's formulism.)[67] Samuel Coleridge (1772–1834) should also be recognized here as reaffirming metaphysically defined, traditional religious faith in light of a more expanded concept of "reason" that included feelings and imagination.[68]

Perhaps the most influential in this "romantic" response to Kant is the German theologian Friedrich Schleiermacher (1768–1834). He was influenced by Kant early in life, but rejected the noumenal-phenomenal divide and, in the end, propounded a view of religion that privileged the immediate consciousness of the finite, temporal things of this world

---

[66] *Critique of Pure Reason*, Axi–xii.

[67] Debate over the cultural and moral implications of Kant's work continues. Hamann's and Jacobi's critique raises issues which bear a family resemblance to some of the concerns in Robin May Schott, ed., *Feminist Interpretations of Immanuel Kant* (University Park: Penn State University, 1997).

[68] In his very fine work, *Coleridge, Philosophy and Religion* (Cambridge: Cambridge University Press, 2000), Douglas Hedley brings to light the strong links between Coleridge and the Cambridge Platonists. Coleridge is especially interesting to consider in light of his opposition to Kant on the limits of experience. Coleridge held that we may have a "living communion with the Universal Spirit" (Hedley, 248).

existing through and in the Infinite and Eternal. Schleiermacher was profoundly opposed to Kant's conception of religion within the limits of reason. In *On Religion: Speeches to Its Cultural Despisers*, Schleiermacher offers this intuitive, experiential portrait:

> Religion's essence is neither thinking nor acting, but intuition and feeling. It wishes to intuit the universe, wishes devoutly to overhear the universe's own manifestations and actions, longs to be grasped and filled by the universe's immediate influences in childlike passivity.... Religion maintains its own sphere and its own character only by completely removing itself from the sphere and character of speculation as well as from that of praxis.[69]

Schleiermacher saw the imagination as essential to religion. "You will not consider it blasphemy, I hope, that belief in God depends on the direction of the imagination. You will know that imagination is the highest and most original element in us, and that everything besides it is merely reflection upon it; you will know that it is our imagination that creates the world for you, and that you can have no God without the world."[70] While the imagination plays an essential religious role, religion remains a cognitive enterprise, a way of apprehending the divine. In Schleiermacher's view, Kant, and rationalism in general, missed the whole point of the religious life with its imagination, intuition, and distinctive human feelings.

To his followers, Schleiermacher stands as a strong opponent to eighteenth-century moralism, rationalism, and Kantianism. But his alternative picture of religious faith has seemed to some both too uncritical and cut off from a defining reference point for religion: sacred, revealed Scriptures. The object or deliverance of Schleiermacher's religious experience appears severely limited.

> Intuition is and always remains something individual, set apart, the immediate perception, nothing more. To bind it and to incorporate it into a whole is once more the business not of sense but of abstract thought. The same is true of religion; it stops with the immediate experiences of the existence and action of the universe, with the individual intuitions and feelings; each of these is a self-contained work without connections with others or dependence upon them; it knows nothing about derivation and connection, for among all things religion can encounter, that is what its

---

[69] *On Religion* (Cambridge: Cambridge University Press, 1996), 22–23.
[70] Ibid., 53.

nature most opposes. Not only an individual fact or deed that one could call original or first, but everything in religion is immediate and true for itself.[71]

There are elements of Spinoza's concepts of God just below the surface of some of Schleiermacher's writing.

In the next chapter we consider nineteenth-century debate over evidence, different views of faith, and the object of faith. We also come to see (in Chapter 7) how this rift between rational inquiry and what I described under the heading of the romantic movement has given rise to two distinct movements in philosophy of religion.

[71] Ibid., 26.

SIX

✦

Religion and the Philosophical
Gods and Giants

Stranger: What we shall see is something like a battle of gods and giants
going on between them over their quarrel about reality.

Theaetetus: How so?

Stranger: One party is trying to drag everything down to earth out of
heaven and the unseen, literally grasping rocks and trees in their hands,
for they lay hold upon every stock and stone and strenuously affirm that
real existence belongs only to that which can be handled and offers resistance to the touch. They define reality as the same thing as body, and as
soon as one of the opposite party asserts that anything without a body is
real, they are utterly contemptuous and will not listen to another word.

Theaetetus: The people you describe are certainly a formidable crew. I
have met quite a number of them before now.

Stranger: Yes, and accordingly their adversaries are very wary in defending their position somewhere in the heights of the unseen, maintaining
with all their force that true reality consists in certain intelligible and
bodiless forms. In the clash of argument they shatter and pulverize those
bodies which their opponents wield, and what those others allege to
be true reality they call, not real being, but a sort of moving process
of becoming. On this issue an interminable battle is always going on
between the two camps.

Plato[1]

Intelligence, Evidence, and Happiness

In Plato's dialogue, *The Sophist*, the philosophical battle over the world
is depicted as warfare between the giants and the gods. The giants

---

[1] *The Sophist* 246 a–c, in *The Collected Dialogues of Plato*, ed. E. Hamilton and H.
Cairns (Princeton: Princeton University Press, 1961).

248

privilege the material world, whereas the gods favor intelligence and transcendent immaterial forms. In this framework, one may readily see that those in the middle – who prize both matter and immaterial intelligence – find themselves in the awkward position of being attacked from both sides.[2] This chapter highlights the nineteenth-century struggle over the evidence of intelligence in and transcending the cosmos. After Kant, a pivotal debate unfolded between naturalists and idealists. The division between these camps is more complex than an affirmation or denial of material bodies but, in general, the idealists gave greater priority to mind (intelligence, meaning, purpose) in the cosmos than the naturalists, and one's philosophical priority here had important religious implications. The major idealist philosophies in the nineteenth century were not completely at odds with naturalism; indeed, these movements shared significant convictions. And yet idealists tended to give primacy to mind and reason as defining the very structure of the cosmos, whereas many naturalists highlighted impersonal, causal, and mechanical explanations.[3] This debate raised fundamental issues concerning the normativity of rules of evidence and the philosophical assessment of religious beliefs. The chapter concludes with pragmatism, a movement that falls somewhere between the gods and giants and also seems to carry on the Kantian concern for moral faith.

In keeping with the practice of beginning most chapters with a brief portrait of an event or a milieu, I offer the following sketch of the nineteenth-century debate over the evidence for and against religious belief. Jeremy Bentham (1748–1832) is, overall, in the camp of the giants, whereas William Paley (1743–1805) and Richard Whatley (1787–1863) are with the gods.[4] Each philosopher offered an interesting combination

---

[2] For an interesting historical and philosophical analysis of Plato's imagery, see T. M. Lennon, *The Battle of the Gods and Giants: The Legacies of Descartes and Gassendi, 1655–1715* (Princeton: Princeton University Press, 1993). Lennon writes: "The Cambridge Platonists, whom one would have expected ranged among the gods against the giants, in fact occupy a corner distinct from both" (52).

[3] I do not want to put too much emphasis on the terms "naturalism" and "idealism." If "naturalism" includes nontheistic, nonmaterialist, but scientific views of the cosmos, some German idealists may be considered naturalists. See "The Enlightenment and Idealism," by F. Beiser in *The Cambridge Companion to German Idealism*, ed. Karl Ameriks (Cambridge: Cambridge University Press, 2000).

[4] By invoking Plato's metaphors, I pay homage to the perennial, ongoing nature of this philosophical debate. I also highlight the *Sophist*, as the dialogue considers threats to the very basis of reasoning. A major factor in the nineteenth-century debates was over which philosophy provided a sound treatment of reason itself.

of a strong commitment for basing beliefs on evidence and for advancing social justice.

Jeremy Bentham went to Oxford University in 1760 when only twelve years old. As a student, he was required to subscribe to the Thirty-nine Articles of the Anglican Church, which testify to the Trinity, the Incarnation, and Churchmanship. The pressure to endorse the articles, and the prevailing religious culture of the time, were factors that fueled his subsequent philosophical case against religion and theism. Bentham wrote extensively on the topics of evidence and happiness, arguing for the importance of adjusting belief to evidence and for the fundamental good of happiness. To Bentham, religion seemed completely at odds with the available evidence and an impediment to the greatest happiness for the greatest number of people. Bentham's reputation as a secular rationalist and a champion of utilitarianism is well known. Less widely recognized, though, is that his theistic predecessors were also ardently committed to a hedonistic view of values, as well as to proportioning belief to evidence.

William Paley was a leading authority on evidence and happiness. His two key works on evidence are *The View of the Evidences of Christianity* (1794) and *The Natural Theology* (1802). Written after Hume's *Dialogues*, Paley's work focused largely on a design argument, although he was also wont to note religion's contribution to moral practice and the felt, natural concord of the soul in relation to God. He, like many fellow theistic utilitarians, held that God made us for happiness. Paley's ethic of rules and rights, regulated by God, had radical implications. Paley, for example, opposed slavery before this was popular, and he protested the vast inequalities of wealth in his society.[5]

Bentham was also an advocate for social reform; after Oxford he pursued law, working on the High Court, King's Bench division. The extent of Bentham's critical writing on religion has been greatly overlooked, largely due to the selective editing of his works posthumously.[6] Almost all of his philosophy of religion is a sustained attack, marshaled with a lawyer's attention to the rules of evidence. During this period of

---

[5] See his analogy of the pigeons in "Of Property" in book III of Paley's *Moral and Political Philosophy*. For studies of theological utilitarians, see W. E. H. Lecky, *History of European Morals from Augustine to Charlemagne*, 2 vols. (London, 1869); E. Albee, *A History of English Utilitarians* (London, 1901); and James Grimmin, *Secular Utilitarianism* (Oxford: Clarendon, 1990).

[6] See Grimmin's *Secular Utilitarianism*. For further background, see also Grimmin, "John Brown and the Theological Tradition of Utilitarian Ethics," *History of Political Thought* 4:3 (1983).

philosophical exchange, the tools of debate intersected with the emerging modern judiciary in which evidence laws are key. There is a tenor to the arguments and counterarguments reminiscent of the impersonal rule-following of legal arbitration. A contemporary theologian described Bentham as "an attorney general," albeit he did not think Bentham conducted his case with the cool evenhandedness one would expect from a court committed to the fair and impartial application of rules of evidence.[7]

In addition to Bentham and Paley, Richard Whatley may be singled out as one who forcefully argued for the exploration of religion from an evidentiary standpoint. One of his books, *Elements of Rhetoric: Comprising an Analysis of the Laws of Moral Evidence and of Persuasion, with Rules for Argumentative Composition and Elocution* (1828), made an important contribution to the theory of evidence. Although I do not discuss Whatley in the main body of the chapter that follows, I cite him here at the outset as another outstanding example of a philosopher who combined a high view of the importance of evidence in religion with social reform. He opposed Britain's exportation of prisoners to Australia, he sought to reconcile Catholic and Protestant communities, and he advocated improved agriculture rather than workhouses in Ireland. Like Bentham and Paley, he articulated a philosophy of religion that took social justice *and* evidence seriously. He was critical of arguments both for and against theism, although he developed his own cumulative case for theism.[8]

In the next three sections, I consider naturalistic treatments of religion, starting with a philosopher who was very much indebted to Bentham.

Naturalism in Philosophy of Religion

In 1822 John Stuart Mill (1806–1873) read Bentham's work on scientific legislation with great admiration. Perhaps Mill was initially drawn to Bentham's work due to Mill's own thoroughly secular and (more or

---

[7] See Grimmin's *Secular Utilitarianism*. For a prime example of Bentham's *legal* critique of religion, see his *Not Paul, but Jesus* (Cambridge, 1823).

[8] Whatley served as the Anglican Archbishop of Dublin. He wrote an amusing text early in his life arguing that some of the skeptical arguments used against Scripture would lead us to doubt evident history such as the existence of Napoleon. See *Historic Doubts Relative to Napoleon Bonaparte* (1819; Berkeley: Scolar, 1985). For a good overview of Paley and Whatley, see William Sweet, "Paley, Whatley, and 'Enlightenment Evidentialism,'" *International Journal for Philosophy of Religion* 45 (June 1999): 143–167.

less) Humean upbringing. In his *Autobiography*, Mill reports his father's conviction that "the manner in which the world came into existence was a subject on which nothing was known: that the question 'Who made me?' cannot be answered, because we have no experience or authentic information from which to answer it; and that any answer only throws the difficulty a step further back, since the question immediately presents itself, Who made God?"[9] Mill himself characterized his secular upbringing as highly unusual: "I am thus one of very few examples, in this country, of one who has, not thrown off religious belief, but never had it."[10] Mill refined Bentham's utilitarianism as well as his critique of the supernatural, although Mill opposed Hume's case against believing in the miraculous.

Mill's key arguments against theism include the problem of evil and the inadequacy of positive theistic arguments. Mill contended that classical theism, according to which God is omnipotent and just, would not permit the kind of undeserved and pointless suffering that is often found in the world.

> If the law of all creation were justice and the Creator omnipotent, then in whatever amount suffering and happiness might be dispensed to the world, each person's share of them would be exactly proportioned to that person' good or evil deeds; no human being would have a worse lot than another, without worse deserts; accident or favouritism would have no part in such a world, but every human life would be the playing out of a drama constructed like a perfect moral tale. No one is able to blind himself to the fact that the world we live in is totally different from this; insomuch that the necessity of redressing the balance has been deemed one of the strongest arguments for another life after death, which amounts to an admission that the order of things in this life is often an example of injustice, not justice. If it be said that God does not take sufficient account of pleasure and pain to make them the reward or punishment of the good or the wicked, but that virtue is itself the greatest good and vice the greatest evil, then these at least ought to be dispensed to all according to what they have done to deserve them; instead of which, every kind of moral depravity is entailed upon multitudes by the fatality of their birth; through the fault of their parents, of society, or of uncontrollable circumstances, certainly through no fault of their own. Not even on the most distorted and contracted theory of good which ever was framed by

---

[9] Mill, *Autobiography and Literary Essays*, ed. J. M. Robson and J. Stillinger (London: Routledge, 1982), 45.
[10] Ibid., 45.

religious or philosophical fanaticism, can the government of Nature be made to resemble the work of a being at once good and omnipotent.[11]

Mill takes a pivotal claim used by theists to argue for an afterlife (the world, taken alone, is unjust, so an all-good God would insure an afterlife) and uses it to condemn classical theism. (There is an echo here of Philo using Demea's view of the cosmos against Demea's own theism.) One implication of Mill's view of the cosmos is that nature should be condemned – not in the sense that Mill *blames* nature for its character and laws but that he thinks of nature as (at least at times) equal in repugnance to human wickedness.

> In sober truth, nearly all the things which men are hanged or imprisoned for doing to one another, are nature's every day performances. Killing, the most criminal act recognized by human laws, Nature does once to every being that lives; and in a large proportion of cases, after protracted tortures such as only the greatest monsters whom we read of ever purposely inflicted on their living fellow-creatures.... Nature impales men, breaks them as if on the wheel, casts them to be devoured by wild beasts, burns them to death, crushes them with stones like the first Christian martyr, starves them with hunger, freezes them with cold, poisons them by the quick or slow venom of her exhalations, and has hundreds of other hideous deaths in reserve, such as the ingenious cruelty of a Nabis or a Domitian never surpassed. All this, Nature does with the most supercilious disregard both of mercy and of justice, emptying her shafts upon the best and noblest indifferently with the meanest and worst; upon those who are engaged in the highest and worthiest enterprises, and often as the direct consequence of the noblest acts; and it might almost be imagined as a punishment for them. She mows down those on whose existence hangs the well-being of a whole people, perhaps the prospects of the human race for generations to come, with as little compunction as those whose death is a relief to themselves, or a blessing to those under their noxious influence. Such are Nature's dealings with life. Even when she does not intend to kill, she inflicts the same tortures in apparent wantonness.[12]

I offer three observations. First, Mill's view of nature was bolstered by the picture of suffering and struggle that Charles Darwin documented. Darwinian evolution provided only partial support for Mill, however, for ethical reasons that are noted later. The problem, in part, lies in Mill's

[11] From *Three Essays on Religion*, printed in *Essays on Ethics, Religion and Society* (London: Routledge, 1969), 389.

[12] Ibid., 385.

awkward position in "blaming" nature for evil while also believing that we ourselves – with our capacity for moral judgment and cognition – are the result of nature. If nature is a mass-murdering tormentor, why expect "her" to have given us any goodness or the capacity for such condemnation?[13]

Second, nature, in Mill's account, can in no way serve as a source of moral instruction. Given his portrait of nature, one should probably be relieved that he did *not* use nature as a moral teacher. Still, in Chapter 9 I discuss some contemporary ecology that offers a more positive conception of the good of nature.

Third, we may wonder why Mill set the bar for theism at such a great height. Must an all-good creator govern the world in such a way that there is an *exact* proportion of virtue and happiness (a "perfect moral tale")? If creatures are given genuine freedom and codependency, whereby one person's welfare depends upon others' responsibilities, it is difficult to imagine that God should fix or determine the outcome of every action without continuous miracles, a perpetual state of rescue that would seem to undermine the idea of a stable, natural world. (More on this problem in Chapter 9.)

Mill is not entirely detached from the vestiges of the religion of his age. Part of his sympathy for religion may stem from his appreciation of Wordsworth and Coleridge. Mill, in the end, took up a position that was more conciliatory than Bentham's. He concedes that, while belief in an afterlife is not an essential feature for moral motivation, its truth is desirable at least for some.[14] He also thought atheism was unjustified

---

[13] Some philosophers have defended theism on the grounds that, if it were not for theism, there would be no proper grounding of moral judgments nor a reasonable expectation that moral agents would exist at all. See, for example, David Freeman, "On God and Evil," in *God and the Good*, ed. Clifton Orlebeke and L. Smedes (Grand Rapids: Eerdmans, 1975). For a clever reply on how and why an evil power would create morally perceptive creatures, see S. M. Cahn "Cacodaemony," *Analysis* 37 (1977). See also John King-Farlo, "Cacodaemony and Devilish Isomorphism," *Analysis* 38 (1978). Mill's use of the female gender for nature provides an opportunity to point out that he was in support of women's equality politically and a close friend and advocate for Mary Wollstonecraft (1759–1797), author of *A Vindication of the Rights of Woman* (1792). For a sympathetic portrait of Wollstonecraft's religious beliefs, see Mitzi Auchterloinie, "Equal Citizens in a Heavenly Jerusalem: The Influence of Religion on the Feminism of Mary Wollstonecraft" (M.A. thesis, University of Exeter, 1993).

[14] Mill does not go as far as Bernard Williams in "The Makropulus Case: Reflections on the Tedium of Immortality," in *Problems of the Self* (Cambridge: Cambridge University Press, 1973). Grace Jantzen presents a similar view in "Do We Need

by the evidence, given that there was some evidence of cosmic design. It is worth citing his summary of his study of theism. Note the somewhat legal tone of the writing:

> From the result of the preceding examination of the evidences of Theism, and (theism being presupposed) of the evidences of a Revelation, it follows that the rational attitude of a thinking mind towards the supernatural, whether in natural or in revealed religion, is that of skepticism as distinguished from belief on the one hand, and from atheism on the other: including, in the present case, under atheism, the negative as well as the positive form of disbelief in a God, viz., not only the dogmatic denial of his existence, but the denial that there is any evidence on either side, which for most practical purposes amounts to the same thing as if the existence of a God had been disproved. If we are right in the conclusions to which we have been led by the preceding inquiry there is evidence, but insufficient for proof, and amounting only to one of the lower degrees of probability. The indication given by such evidence as there is, points to the creation, not indeed of the universe, but of the present order of it by an Intelligent Mind, whose power over the materials was not absolute, whose love for his creatures was not his sole actuating inducement, but who nevertheless desired their good. The notion of a providential government by an omnipotent Being for the good of his creatures must be entirely dismissed. Even of the continued existence of the Creator we have no other guarantee than that he cannot be subject to the law of death which affects terrestrial beings, since the conditions that produce this liability wherever it is known to exist are of his creating. That this Being, not being omnipotent, may have produced a machinery falling short of his intentions, and which may require the occasional interposition of the Maker's hand, is a supposition not in itself absurd nor impossible, though in none of the cases in which such interposition is believed to have occurred is the evidence such as could possibly prove it; it remains a simple possibility, which those may dwell on to whom it yields comfort to suppose that blessings which ordinary human power is inadequate to attain, may come not from extra-ordinary human power, but from the bounty of an intelligence beyond the human, and which continuously cares for man. The possibility of a life after death rests on the same footing – of a boon which this powerful Being who wishes well to man, may have the power to grant, and which if the message alleged to have been sent by him was really sent, he has actually promised. The whole domain of

Immortality?" *Modern Theology* 1 (1984), to which I reply in "Why We Need Immortality," *Modern Theology* 6 (1990). Mill seems to take a middle position, that for some people an afterlife is desirable.

the supernatural is thus removed from the region of Belief into that of simple Hope; and in that, for anything we can see, it is likely always to remain; for we can hardly anticipate either that any positive evidence will be acquired of the direct agency of Divine Benevolence in human destiny, or that any reason will be discovered for considering the realization of human hopes on that subject as beyond the pale of possibility.[15]

With Mill, as with Bentham, we find a formal inquiry into religion analogous to a tribunal. Mill assesses the practice of supernatural government much as one might assess the practice of some magistrate governing a nation. Although Mill's evidence-based philosophy retained the possibility of a mild, deistic notion of God, further nineteenth-century science would chip away at this position.

Before turning to science and religion, I briefly note Mill's misgivings about Hume on miracles. Mill thought that Hume begged the question against the believer in miracles. In *A System of Logic*, Mill points out the pivotal role of background assumptions in weighing evidence.

> All, therefore, which Hume has made out, and this he must be considered to have made out, is that (at least in the imperfect state of our knowledge of natural agencies, which leaves it always possible that some of the physical antecedents may have been hidden from us) no evidence can prove a miracle to anyone who did not previously believe the existence of a being or beings with supernatural power, or who believes himself to have full proof that the character of the Being whom he recognizes is inconsistent with his having seen fit to interfere on the occasion in question. If we do not already believe in supernatural agencies, no miracle can prove to us their existence. The miracle itself, considered merely as an extraordinary fact, may be satisfactorily certified by our senses or by testimony; but nothing can ever prove that it is a miracle: there is still another hypothesis – that of its being the result of some unknown natural cause; and this possibility cannot be so completely shut out as to leave no alternative but that of admitting the existence and intervention of a Being superior to nature. Those, however, who already believe in such a Being, have two hypotheses to choose from, a supernatural and an unknown natural agency; and they have to judge which of the two is the most probable in the particular case. In forming this judgment an important element of the question will be the conformity of the result to the laws of the supposed agent, that is, to the character of the Deity as they conceive it.[16]

---

[15] *Three Essays on Religion*, 482–483.

[16] Mill, *A System of Logic*, book III, chap. XXV, included in *Historical Selections in the Philosophy of Religion*, ed. Ninian Smart (New York: Harper and Row, 1962), 344.

I believe Mill's observations here partly vindicate the suggestion in Chapters 3 and 4 about the importance of assessing naturalism and philosophies of God in light of a comprehensive or cumulative case. Mill was not a defender of supernatural miracles; he only thought that the case against the miraculous needed to be worked out as part of an overall articulation and defense of naturalism.

Biology and Theology

Current scholarship in the history of science paints a complex picture of the relationship between religion and science. It is no longer an unargued assumption that they are at odds.[17] Be that as it may, there are prominent examples in the nineteenth century of some philosophers who thought that a more scientific orientation would exclude religious ideals. Some nineteenth-century science did not appear to conflict with religion as much as it challenged religion's necessity. Darwinian evolution is a good example of the latter, although it certainly challenged a literal reading of Genesis and provided further evidence for Mill's assessment of nature as cruel and not governed by providence.

Charles Darwin's *On the Origin of Species* (1859) offered a picture of natural development that seemed to be in conflict with a prevalent religious conviction that species, including the human species, are created separately by God. Darwin held that life evolved or descended from a common ancestor, a view he further articulated in *The Descent of Man* (1871). Certainly the belief in the natural development of life with modifications was held earlier. One may see it hinted at in

---

[17] I return to this topic in Chapter 9. Scholars have long debated the extent to which science and religion are or can be complementary or in essential conflict. Two classic, nineteenth-century texts that popularized a picture of conflict are John William Draper, *History of the Conflict between Religion and Science* (1874), and Andrew Dickson White, *A History of the Warfare of Science with Theology in Christendom* (1896). A more complementary portrait was developed by William Whewell in his *History of the Inductive Sciences* (1847) and *Astronomy and General Physics* (1852–1856). E. A. Burt argued for the positive theological contribution to science in *Metaphysical Foundation of Modern Physical Science* (1924), and Alfred North Whitehead argued that modern science rested on prior theistic convictions; see his *Science and the Modern World* (1926). See also Reijer Hooykaas, *Natural Law and Divine Miracle* (1959) and *Religion and the Rise of Modern Science* (1972); and Maurice Mandelbaum, *History, Man and Reason* (1971). Stephen Jay Gould rejects a simple view of science and religion in conflict in *Ever Since Darwin* (1977).

ancient Greece (Thales, Anaxamander), in the medieval era (Gregory of Nyssa, Augustine), and among moderns (Leibniz, probably Hume). Jean Baptiste Lamark (1744–1829) developed the theory biologically but without identifying the proper means or mechanism of descent. But in Darwin's work, the biology is better, and evolution achieved (or began to achieve) substantial, intellectual credibility.

There was some reason to read Darwin's work as compatible with theistic faith. After all, Darwin himself contended that the laws he identified show us God's mode of creation. There is even an attenuated, utilitarian theodicy at play in his biology in which "death, famine, rapine, and the concealed war of nature" contribute to "the highest good, which we can conceive, the creation of the higher animals.... The existence of such laws should exalt our notion of the power of the omniscient Creator."[18] The word "creation" is used widely throughout *Origins of Species*, more than a hundred times. The book also begins with a passage from Francis Bacon extolling the study of God's works, along with another theistic passage. Some prominent Anglicans and others welcomed Darwin's work as revealing God's broader, ongoing creative work (Charles Kingsley, Aubrey Moore, and Frederick Temple, Archbishop of Canterbury).

But Darwin's work did promote a picture of nature that involved red teeth and claws. Is nature truly the creation of an all-good God? Given evolution, it is harder to posit the origin of evil as an aboriginal, free turning away from God by the first humans. Also, Darwin's work was largely taken to challenge the argument from design. Paley held that the constitution and functions of nature were evidence of God, much the way a watch is evidence of a watchmaker.[19] Darwin's account of biological change did not seem to require God's specific engineering. Darwin himself gradually gave up on theism and adopted agnosticism.[20] Two prominent philosophers who supported Darwin's work were also self-described agnostics: Herbert Spencer (1820–1903), who coined the phrase "the survival of the fittest," and Thomas Huxley (1825–1895),

---

[18] Darwin, *The Foundations of the Origin of Species: Two Essays Written in 1842 and 1844*, ed. Francis Darwin (Cambridge: Cambridge University Press, 1909), 51–52.

[19] See Paley's *Natural Theology; or, Evidences of the Existence and Attributes of the Deity*, 11th ed. (London: R. Faulder and Son, 1807); his *Evidences of Christianity* (London: J. F. Dove, 1794) is more concerned with the credibility of Christianity as a revealed religion.

[20] See *The Evolution of Darwin's Religious Views* (Macon: Mercer University Press, 1986).

who earned the title of "Darwin's bulldog" because of his polemical, popular defense of Darwin. In a sense, Darwin provided the biology to back up Hume's proposal of the nontheistic evolution of life in the *Dialogues* (Chapter 4). Richard Dawkins, a contemporary Darwinarian, summarizes Darwin's significance: "Darwin made it possible to be an intellectually fulfilled atheist."[21]

Darwin's ascent or descent (depending on your viewpoint) to agnosticism is narrated in his biography. His rejection of miracles was part of his overall position that the laws of nature are uniform throughout time and world history. This thesis, called "uniformitarianism," gained ground from Lyell's *Principles of Geology* and was repeatedly asserted by Darwin, sometimes in dicta like "Nature makes no jumps" and "Nature has no gaps." By linking human history with the mammalian stock from which we evolved, Darwinism raises questions about our alleged superiority to nonhuman animals, the foundation of ethics, and even the reliability of our reasoning. The latter emerges on the following grounds: if evolution is the outcome of chance (mutations), sexual selection, and impersonal, or nonintentional natural causes (in other words, causes that have no prevision about some good to be achieved), can we trust our own thinking which is itself the result of evolution? Darwin himself raised this concern: "The horrid doubt always arises whether the convictions of man's mind, which has been developed from the mind of the lower animals, are of any value or at all trustworthy. Would any one trust in the convictions of a monkey's mind, if there are any convictions in such a mind?"[22]

Some philosophers today think this is a deep problem with evolution specifically or, more broadly, with scientific naturalism. If we posit an impersonal cosmic starting point, how do we accommodate the emergence of thought, reasoning, and moral and epistemological norms? The contemporary naturalist Paul Churchland sees the landscape here with clarity: "Most scientists and philosophers would cite the presumed fact that humans have their origins in 4.5 billion years of purely chemical and biological evolution as a weighty consideration in favor of expecting mental phenomena to be nothing but a particularly exquisite articulation of the basic properties of matter and energy."[23] Some naturalists

---

[21] Richard Dawkins, *The Blind Watchmaker* (New York: Norton, 1987), 6.

[22] Letter to William Graham, July 3, 1851, in *The Life and Letters of Charles Darwin*, ed. Francis Darwin, vol. 1 (London: John Murray, 1887), 315–316.

[23] Churchland, *The Engine of the Soul* (Cambridge, Mass.: MIT Press, 1995).

have taken Churchland's strategy of eliminating the mental (denying the existence of belief and desires), but others have held that consciousness and reasoning are emergent features of natural evolution, and then either take these features as nonphysical properties or identify them as biological phenomena. The temptation to elimination is great, however, given the cosmic background Churchland highlights. In *Darwin's Dangerous Idea*, Daniel Dennett sees Darwin as paving the way for explaining consciousness, reasoning, and intelligence in terms of nonconscious, nonintelligent forces.

> Aristotle called God the Unmoved Mover, the source of all motion in the universe, and Locke's version of Aristotelian doctrine...identifies this God as Mind, turning the Unmoved Mover into the Unmeant Meaner, the source of all Intentionality. Locke took himself to be proving deductively what the tradition already took to be obvious: original intentionality springs from the Mind of God; we are God's creatures, and derive our intentionality from Him. Darwin turned this doctrine upside down: intentionality doesn't come from on high; it percolates up from below, for the initially mindless and pointless algorithmic processes that gradually acquire meaning and intelligence as they develop. And perfectly following the pattern of all Darwinian thinking, we see that the first meaning is not full-fledged meaning; it certainly fails to manifest all the "essential" Properties of *real* meaning (whatever you may take those properties to be). It is mere quasi-meaning, or semi-semantics.[24]

As I mentioned, some advocates of evolution see intentionality and consciousness as genuine emergent states. But Dennett does not, in the end, and the direction he counsels eliminates intentionality as a distinct causal force.[25] Dennett sees intentionality as something that must

---

[24] *Darwin's Dangerous Idea* (New York: Simon and Schuster, 1995), 205.

[25] I consider Dennett's views at length in *Consciousness and the Mind of God* (Cambridge: Cambridge University Press, 1994). For a superb collection of work on the implications of eliminativism and other naturalist strategies, see J. Beilby, ed., *Naturalism Defeated?* (Ithaca: Cornell University Press, 2002), with contributions by Plantinga, Sosa, Fodor, et al. For further reading on evolution versus design, probably the best collection of papers is W. Dembski and M. Ruse, eds., *Debating Design: From Darwin to DNA* (Cambridge: Cambridge University Press, 2004). See also N. A. Manson, ed., *God and Design* (London: Routledge, 2003). There is a good collection which is largely anti-design: R. T. Pennock, ed., *Intelligent Design; Creationism and Its Critics* (Cambridge, Mass.: MIT Press, 2001). See the review by Jeffrey Koperski, *American Catholic Philosophical Quarterly*, forthcoming. J. P. Moreland, ed., *The Creation Hypothesis* (Grand Rapids: Inter Varsity, 1998), and Michael Ruse, *Can a Darwinian Be a Christian?* (Cambridge: Cambridge University Press, 2001) are also good.

ultimately be explained by the nonintentional. "The account of intelligence required of psychology must not of course be question-begging. It must not explain intelligence in terms of intelligence, for instance by assigning responsibility for the existence of intelligence in creatures to the munificence of an intelligent creator."[26] Whereas the theist does appeal to the intelligence and intentionality of God, Dennett ultimately must appeal to the nonintentional, nonconscious cosmos. "Any ultimate explanation of mental phenomena will have to be in *non*-mental terms, else it won't be an *explanation* of it. There might be explanations of some mental phenomena in terms of others – perhaps *hope* in terms of *belief* and *desire* – but if we are to provide an explanation of all mental phenomena, we would in turn have to explain such mentalistic explainers until finally we reached entirely non-mental terms."[27] Nonmental terms do not involve reasons, however. The worry is that by explaining the normativity of reason (I accept a conclusion by virtue of grasping the evidential force of the premises) in nonnormative terms, we explain away (or eliminate) normativity. Some philosophers see this cost as too high or altogether unwarranted. "When we hear of some new attempt to explain reasoning...naturalistically," writes Peter Geach, "we ought to react as if we were told that someone has squared the circle or proved the square root of 2 to be rational."[28] There are a variety of naturalistic projects that seek to address this challenge.[29]

---

[26] Dennett, *Brainstorms* (Cambridge, Mass.: MIT Press, 1978), 83.

[27] Dennett, *Consciousness Explained* (Cambridge, Mass.: MIT Press, 1991), 454.

[28] Peter Geach, *The Virtues* (Cambridge: Cambridge University Press, 1977), 52. See V. Reppert's "Eliminative Materialism, Cognitive Suicide, and Begging the Question," *Metaphilosophy* 23 (1992), and W. Hasker, *The Emergent Self* (Ithaca: Cornell University Press, 1999), 1–26. See also Thomas Nagel, *The Last Word* (Oxford: Oxford University Press, 1997), 127–143.

[29] The challenge facing naturalism may be articulated using a distinction introduced by Peter Strawson: according to "hard naturalism," the mental is eliminated because it is not describable in the language of physics, whereas "soft naturalism" allows that there are subjective experiences, moral attitudes, and so on. The problem at hand is whether one can retain a soft stance between hard naturalism and some nonnaturalist metaphysic. For an important treatment of this concern, see Gary Hatfield, *The Natural and the Normative* (Cambridge, Mass.: MIT Press, 1990). Hatfield takes note of the culturally embedded nature of epistemic, normative practices. He thereby seeks to preserve a noneliminative, normative philosophy without "a normative metaphysics on which to ground it" (270). Further reflection would take us to a debate over whether the emergence and normativity of our cultural practices is best explained by a normative or nonnormative metaphysic.

Some philosophers have drawn on evolution in order to launch a new way of conceiving of the theory of knowledge: *evolutionary epistemology*. Debate has seized on such questions as: Are true beliefs essentially favored in natural selection? Because religious beliefs have had a remarkable longevity, is their perpetuation and (ostensible) aid to survival evidence of their truth? The next section takes up naturalist arguments that support a negative answer.

Sociological, Political, Psychological Naturalism

A case for secular naturalism is bolstered by the work of Ludwig Feuerbach (1804–1872), Karl Marx (1818–1883), Max Weber (1864–1920), and Sigmund Freud (1856–1939).

Feuerbach was a student of Hegel for two years at Berlin, but he came to reject Hegel's idealism in favor of materialism.[30] Feuerbach famously argued that the concept of God is a projection, by use of which humans lose sight of their actual relationship to one another. We start with properties that we have (power and knowledge); then we remove their finite limits; then we project their unlimited versions (omnipotence and omniscience). In *The Essence of Christianity* (1841), translated by the novelist George Eliot, Feuerbach claims:

> Religion is the dream of the human mind. But even in dreams we do not find ourselves in emptiness or in heaven, but on earth in the realm of reality; we only see real things in the entrancing splendor of imagination and caprice instead of seeing them in the simple daylight of reality and necessity. Hence I do nothing more to religion – and to speculative philosophy and theology as well – than to open its eyes...i.e., I change the object as it is in the imagination into the object as it is in reality.[31]

[30] For Feuerbach's debt to Hegel, see "The Legacy of Idealism in the Philosophy of Feuerbach, Marx, and Kierkegaard," by K. Ameriks in Ameriks, *The Cambridge Companion to German Idealism.*

[31] *The Essence of Christianity* trans. George Eliot (New York: Harper and Brothers, 1957), xxxix. George Eliot (pseudonym of Mary Ann Cross), the Victorian novelist, had evident sympathy with Feuerbach's view of religion. Consider this reported conversation with her: "Taking as her text the three words which have been used so often as the inspiring trumpet calls of man – the words of God, Immortality, Duty – she pronounced with terrible earnestness, how inconceivable was the first, how unbelievable the second, and yet how peremptory and absolute the third." Cited by John Passmore, *A Hundred Years of Philosophy* (New York: Basic Books, 1966), 32.

Feuerbach contended that we must abandon the search for God and the hope of immortality and emphasize instead our concrete, lived experience.

Feuerbach's work is remarkable in that it identifies a cause or instrument whereby the religious concept of God is forged, and then capitalizes on this discovery by advancing a kind of religious anthropology. He valorized anthropology as part of a humanistic theology.

> The true sense of Theology is Anthropology. . . . I by no means say (that were an easy task!): God is nothing, the Trinity is nothing, the Word of God is nothing, &c. I only show that they are not *that* which the illusions of theology make them, – not foreign, that religion takes the apparent, the superficial in Nature and humanity for the essential, and hence conceives their true essence as a separate, special existence: that consequently, religion, in the definitions which it gives of God, *e.g.*, of the Word of God, – at least in those definitions which are not negative in the sense above alluded to, – only defines or makes objective the true nature of the human word. The reproach that according to my book religion is an absurdity, a nullity, a pure illusion, would be well founded only if, according to it that into which I resolve religion, which I prove to be its true object and substance, namely, *man*, – *anthropology*, were an absurdity, a nullity, a pure illusion. But so far from giving a trivial or even a subordinate significance to anthropology, – a significance which it and in opposition to it, – I, on the contrary, while reducing theology to anthropology, exalt anthropology into theology, very much like Christianity, while lowering God into man, made man into God; though, it is true, this human God was by a further process made a transcendental, imaginary God, remote from man.[32]

In Feuerbach, one finds what may be called a theology of immanence without transcendence. Feuerbach takes the classic, Christian concern for the sacred and holy, and redirects this attention to the sacredness or holiness of human life itself.

> Eating and drinking is the mystery of the Lord's Supper; – eating and drinking is, in fact, in itself a religious act; at least, it ought to be so. Think, therefore, with every morsel of bread which relieves thee from the pain of hunger, with every draught of wine which cheers thy heart, of the god who confers these beneficent gifts upon thee, – think of man! But in thy gratitude towards man forget not gratitude towards holy Nature! Forget not that wine is the blood of plants, and flour the flesh of plants, which

---

[32] *The Essence of Christianity*, xxxviii.

are sacrificed for thy well-being! Forget not that the plant typifies to thee the essence of Nature, which lovingly surrenders itself for thy enjoyment! Therefore forget not the gratitude which thou owest to the natural qualities of bread and wine! And if thou art inclined to smile that I call eating and drinking religious acts, because they are common everyday acts, and are therefore performed by multitudes without thought, without emotion; reflect that the Lord's Supper is to multitudes a thoughtless, emotionless act, because it takes place often; and, for the sake of comprehending the religious significance of bread and wine, place thyself in a position where the daily act is unnaturally, violently interrupted.[33]

In such passages, Feuerbach displays a deep appreciation for the value of natural experiences. "The purpose of my lectures...is to transform...lovers of God into lovers of man."[34] The eclipse of God as a transcendent power shows us a way to become reacquainted with the sensuous and aesthetic of this world.[35]

Karl Marx warmly commended Feuerbach as essentially correct on religion. While Marx's early writings betray some sympathy for religion, the bulk of his mature work is a substantial critique. There are at least two factors to note in this critique; first, like Hume and others, Marx offers a *moral* objection against the theistic religious tradition. Marx objected to the way religion has been used to placate the working class and the vulnerable. Second, Marx's overall account of human development, historical materialism, purports to explain the emergence of religion and all human institutions in economic terms. Thus, Marx's account of history is one more instance of an account of religion that does not assume the truth of religion.

In philosophy of religion, the most vital debate over Marxism in the late twentieth century has focused on the compatibility of Marxism with different world religions. The movement called liberation theology, which began in post–World War II Latin America, forced theologians to consider the overlap and tension between Christianity and

---

[33] Ibid., 277. See also Feuerbach's collection, *Thoughts on Death and Immortality*, trans. and ed. J. A. Massey (Berkeley: University of California Press, 1980). This contains some of Feuerbach's poetry and aphorisms.

[34] *The Essence of Christianity*, 23.

[35] Although I have placed Feuerbach among the naturalists, he (as well as Marx) could be discussed in relation to Hegel. For a discussion of Feuerbach's relation to idealism and materialism, see Eugene Kamenka, *The Philosophy of Ludwig Feuerbach* (New York: Praeger, 1970).

Marxism.[36] Theologians and philosophers have questioned whether Marxism is necessarily a rival to traditional religion – perhaps it may even function as a religion itself.

Max Weber has a bearing on philosophy of religion because of his influential promotion of a "value-free" but naturalistic sociology of religion. Weber is especially important for his analysis of the modern conception of the cosmos as lacking any meaning or value in itself. We now live in a mechanistic age in which control and manipulation are paramount. The world Weber presents is no longer a manifestation of God or gods, or inherently divine, and finding the meaning of events is no longer analogous to reading texts. Charles Taylor effectively contrasts an older conception of the self – in which one's identity is meaningfully shaped through alignment with transcendent values – with the modern world Weber documents. "Manipulability of the world confirms the new self-defining identity, as it were: the proper relation of man to a meaningful order is to put himself into tune with it; by contrast nothing sets the seal more clearly on the rejection of this vision than successfully treating the world as object of control. Manipulation both proves and as it were celebrates the vision of things as 'disenchanted' to use Max Weber's famous phrase."[37] In Weber's sociology, religions that see the cosmos as informed by overall purpose and meaning are premodern.

Weber's sociology of religion is too rich to outline in detail. He produced a fascinating study of different religious offices (e.g., the role of prophets) and, while his most famous book was on European Protestantism, he began a study of Hinduism, Buddhism, Confucianism, and Taoism.[38] Weber secured the importance of studying religion for sociology and economics. He also further advanced a naturalistic account, according to which religious formation was not the outcome of natural reason or credible revelation but the result of indoctrination into communities built around entrenched, ceremonial practices and charismatic leaders (prophets, priests) presumed to have magical powers.

Several of Freud's works address the credibility of religion, especially *Totem and Taboo* (1913), *The Future of an Illusion* (1927), *Civilization and Its Discontents* (1930), and *Moses and Monotheism* (1939).

---

[36] See D. Turner, *Marxism and Christianity* (Oxford: Blackwell, 1983), and Rosino Gibellini, *The Liberation Theology Debate* (London: SCM Press, 1987).

[37] Charles Taylor, *Hegel* (Cambridge: Cambridge University Press, 1975), 8.

[38] See Weber, *The Sociology of Religion* (Boston: Beacon Press, 1964).

Running throughout his work is the thesis that our conscious experience is heavily shaped by underlying causes of which we may be unaware.

> In psycho-analysis there is no choice for us but to assert that mental processes are in themselves unconscious, and to liken the perception of them by means of consciousness to the perception of the external world by means of the sense-organs.... Just as Kant warned us not to overlook the fact that our perceptions are subjectively conditioned and must not be regarded as identical with what is perceived though unknowable, so psycho-analysis warns us not to equate perceptions by means of consciousness with the unconscious mental processes which are their object. Like the physical, the psychical is not necessarily in reality what it appears to us to be.[39]

If Freud is right, then the root cause of religious experience may be altogether secular – perhaps the result of disordered, conflicting desires, unresolved guilt, wish fulfillment, and so on.[40] Freud's psychoanalytic investigation into the root causes of religious belief may be considered an "unmasking explanation," insofar as Freud endeavors to reveal the true grounds of a belief. I borrow the term from Barry Stroud:

> The philosophical project understood in this way might seem at first glance to differ only in its greater generality from what we recognize as a very natural and familiar task. I will call an explanation that explains away the appearance of something, or explains the belief in it without having to suppose that the belief is true, an "unmasking" explanation. It reveals the basis or source of a belief as not connected in the right way with its truth. It thereby unmasks or exposes a belief or appearance for what it is – an illusion, a false belief, or a mere appearance.[41]

Of course, unmasking explanations can be a double-edged sword, for religious psychoanalysts could propose that the real motive behind secularism involves fear, narcissism, vanity, wish fulfillment, and so

---

[39] *The Essentials of Psychoanalysis*, ed. A. Freud, trans. James Strachey (Harmondsworth: Penguin, 1986), 147.

[40] Freud, like Darwin, also worried about the nature of reason given his naturalism. See P. Ricoeur, *Freud and Philosophy*, trans. D. Savage (New Haven: Yale University Press, 1970). Another work that forwarded the naturalist analysis of religion should be mentioned: Sir James George Frazer, *The Golden Bough: A Study of Magic and Religion*, ed. Robert Frazer (London: Oxford University Press, 1994). Frazer saw religion and magic as primitive, early stages of human thought which will ultimately give way to science.

[41] Barry Stroud, *The Quest for Reality* (Oxford: Oxford University Press, 2000), 75.

on.[42] Another aspect to Freud's work may also cause difficulties for a pure, thoroughgoing naturalism, for it turns out that Freud's explanations involve intentionality, purpose, and mental states not reducible to mere behavior.[43]

The work of Freud, Weber, Marx, and Feuerbach may be seen as building a case for a suspicion of tradition and what appeared at the time to be commonsense interpretations of experience. It is fitting to end this section with William Kingdom Clifford (1845–1879), a British philosopher and mathematician. He advanced the case for an evidence-based critique of religion. Clifford held that "it is wrong always, everywhere, and for anyone to believe anything upon insufficient evidence."[44] Of course, determining what counts as "sufficient" can be hard to settle in a general philosophy of evidence, but Clifford illustrated his stance with the example of a shipowner who fails to inspect and secure his vessel properly. Even if the ship's subsequent voyage is safe, the failure to heed the relevant evidence is wrong. The case of the shipowner is worth citing as a parable.

A shipowner was about to send to sea an emigrant ship. He knew that she was old, and not overwell built at the first; that she had seen many seas and climes, and often had needed repairs. Doubts had been suggested to him that possibly she was not seaworthy. These doubts preyed upon his mind, and made him unhappy; he thought that perhaps he ought to have her thoroughly overhauled and refitted, even though this should put him to great expense. Before the ship sailed, however, he succeeded in overcoming the melancholy reflections. He said to himself that she had gone safely through so many voyages and weathered so many storms, that it was idle to suppose that she would not come safely home from this trip also. He would put his trust in Providence, which could hardly fail to protect all these unhappy families that were leaving their fatherland

---

[42] Compare a contemporary Freudian critique – Adolf Grünbaum, "Psychoanalysis and Theism," *Monist* 79 (1987) – with a reply by William Alston, "Psychoanalytic Theory and Theistic Belief," in *Faith and the Philosophers*, ed. J. Hick (London: Macmillan, 1964). See also William Wainwright, "Natural Explanations and Religious Experience," *Ratio* 15 (1973).

[43] Because of this, some "hard nosed" naturalists like B. F. Skinner rejected any Freudian appeal to "hidden" causes and motives. For a recent effort to employ Freudian insight into religion, see Kirk A. Bingman, *Freud and Faith* (Albany: SUNY Press, 2003).

[44] W. K. Clifford, "The Ethics of Belief," in *Lectures and Essays* (London: Macmillan, 1879). This is widely anthologized. See, for example, C. Taliaferro and P. Griffiths, eds., *Philosophy of Religion: An Anthology* (Oxford: Blackwell, 2003), 199.

to seek for better times elsewhere. He would dismiss from his mind all ungenerous suspicions about the honesty of builders and contractors. In such ways he acquired a sincere and comfortable conviction that his vessel was thoroughly safe and seaworthy; he watched her departure with a light heart, and benevolent wishes for the success of the exiles in their strange new home that was to be; and he got his insurance money when she went down in mid-ocean and told no tales.

Let us return to this case at the end of this chapter when considering a rejoinder by William James. In brief, Clifford's zeal for ensuring we have no unjustified beliefs is unprecedented.

> Whoso would deserve well of his fellows in this matter will guard the purity of his belief with a very fanaticism of jealous care, lest at any time it should rest on an unworthy object, and catch a stain which can never be wiped away.... If a belief has been accepted on insufficient evidence, the pleasure is a stolen one. Not only does it deceive ourselves by giving us a sense of power which we do not really possess, but it is sinful, because it is stolen in defiance of our duty to mankind. That duty is to guard ourselves from such beliefs as from a pestilence, which may shortly master our body and spread to the rest of the town.[45]

Hegelian Idealism

In the nineteenth century we meet a form of idealism in the work of Georg Wilhelm Friedrich Hegel (1770–1831) that differs from the idealistic philosophical theology of Berkeley and Edwards (Chapter 3). In Berkeley's and Edwards's world, the individual subject and her psychology are prominent, and the world is constituted by God's perception; there is a real distinction between God and the created soul. For Hegel, God is not theistic. Moreover, Hegel seeks to offer a transcendent level of consciousness that will encompass and account for individual subjectivity. He understands individual, concrete things and history itself as dimensions of a complex Spirit. "Spirit is thus a self-supporting, absolute, real being. All previous shapes of consciousness are abstract forms of it. They result from Spirit analyzing itself, distinguishing its moments, and dwelling for a while with each."[46]

---

[45] "The Ethics of Belief," 196, 198.
[46] *Phenomenology of Spirit*, trans. A. V. Miller (Oxford: Oxford University Press, 1977), 264.

Hegel was born in Stuttgart, studied classics and then theology, and after several posts, including being a tutor and editor, became a professor of philosophy at the University of Berlin.[47] A simple summary of Hegel's extraordinary philosophy is impossible. This is partly due to its scope. Hegel had distinctive views on epistemology, metaphysics, the role of the nation-state, freedom and individuality, world religion and culture, history, and art. Sören Kierkegaard (to be discussed in Chapter 7) paid tribute to the magnitude of Hegel's work by satirizing those who claim to have gone "beyond Hegel." "Those who have gone beyond Hegel are like country people who must always give their address *via* a larger city; thus the address in this case must read – John Doe *via* Hegel."[48] In addition to its scope, Hegel's work has been subject to widely divergent interpretations, beginning in his lifetime. According to the Left or left-wing Hegelians, Hegel was an atheist, hostile to Christianity. Feuerbach and Marx are in this camp. The so-called Right or right-wing Hegelians construe Hegel as he professed himself to be: an orthodox Lutheran. Hegel's philosophy has been especially subject to fierce debate in the mid-twentieth century, when it was accused of fostering a despotic sub-jugation of the individual to the state. The chapter on Hegel in Bertrand Russell's *A History of Western Philosophy* famously takes Hegel to task on grounds of philosophical obscurity and eclipsing the individual per-son.[49] As with Descartes in Chapter 2, here I defend Hegel against some of these charges.

Hegel believed that the object of philosophy and religion were the same.

> Philosophy misses an advantage enjoyed by the other sciences. It cannot like them rest the existence of its objects on the natural admission of consciousness, nor can it assume that its method of cognition, either for starting or for continuing, is one already accepted. The objects of phi-losophy, it is true, are upon the whole the same as those of religion. In

[47] Terry Pinkard has written an outstanding life of Hegel, *Hegel: A Biography* (Cambridge: Cambridge University Press, 2000).

[48] *Søren Kierkegaard's Journals and Papers*, trans. H. V. Hong and E. Hong, 7 vols. (Bloomington: Indiana University Press, 1967–1978), 1:1571.

[49] *A History of Western Philosophy* (New York: Simon and Schuster, 1945), chap. 22. Dan Robinson (Oxford) has said that you can almost hear the bombs exploding in the background as Russell wrote on Hegel during the German bombardment of Britain. A related, influential, hostile treatment of Hegel can be found in K. R. Popper, *The Open Society and Its Enemies*, vol. 2 (London: Routledge and Kegan Paul, 1945), which is titled "The High Tide of Prophecy: Hegel, Marx, and the Aftermath."

both the object is Truth, in that supreme sense in which God and God only is the Truth. Both in like manner go on to treat of the finite worlds of Nature and the human Mind, with their relation to each other and to their truth in God.[50]

Both philosophy and religion are to use reason; Hegel was not part of the romantic movement, although he did have close friendships and sympathies with members of this movement.[51]

Hegel was not a foundationalist nor did he seek out infallible certitude like Descartes. He employed reason to overcome Kant's split between God, the self, and freedom in the noumenal world and human thought and experience (forms of human subjectivity) in the phenomenal realm. Hegel, as well as many of his contemporaries like F. W. J. Schelling (1775–1854) and Johann Gottlieb Fichte (1762–1814), found Kant's dualism itself problematic; the notions of a noumenal God and free self not conceivable in spatiotemporal terms made no sense. Moreover, Hegel faults Kant for an ahistorical, detached view of reason. In a telling passage, in his *Lectures on the History of Philosophy* Hegel writes of the good of reason and its vindication in an all-encompassing understanding of God:

> We have already remarked upon the first manifestations of this principle, the principle of our own human thought, our own knowing, its activity, its right, its trust in itself. It is the principle of finding satisfaction in our own activity, reason, imagination, and so forth, of taking pleasure in our products and our work and deeming it permissible and justifiable to do so, indeed, regarding our own work as something in which we may and should essentially invest our interest.... This validation of the subjective domain now needed a higher – indeed, the highest – confirmation in order to be completely legitimated and to become even the absolute duty. To attain to this level it had to be grasped in its purest shape. The highest confirmation of this principle is the religious confirmation, when this principle of our own spirituality and our own autonomy is recognized in our relation with God and to God... This, then, is the great principle of [the Reformation], that all externality disappears at the point of the absolute relationship to God. All self-estrangement, with its consequent dependence and servitude... disappears. This principle of subjectivity became a moment of religion itself and thereby attained to its absolute recognition.[52]

---

[50] *Hegel's Logic*, trans. W. Wallace (Oxford: Clarendon, 1975), 1.

[51] See Pinkard's biography of Hegel for background.

[52] *Lectures on the History of Philosophy*, vol. 3, *Medieval and Modern Philosophy*, ed. Robert F. Brown, trans. Robert F. Brown and J. M. Stewart with H. S. Harris (Berkeley:

Hegel seeks to identify the tension between different, compelling ideas (like the thesis and antithesis of Kant's antinomies) and to bring to light how they lead to a higher idea in a synthesis. The drive toward a synthesis is fueled by the refusal to settle for contradictions. To retain a dualism like Descartes', however, would be to settle for "unhappy consciousness." Hegel goes on to resolve these dualities in an overriding idea, God.

"The True is the whole," Hegel insists, and it is from the standpoint of the whole of reality that human knowledge, the sciences, and history make sense.[53] Hegel's conception of "the whole" has, at its base, the *absolute* or God. Hegel adopts a version of the ontological argument. We cannot but conceive of God as existing. The category of being belongs to the concept of God. Contra Kant, the concept of being is not added to the concept of God in the same way that a merchant would add zeroes to some price.

> It is well to remember, when we speak of God, that we have an object of another kind than any hundred sovereigns, and unlike any one particular notion, representation, or however else it may be styled. It is in fact this and this alone which marks everything finite: its being in time and space is discrepant from its notion. God, on the contrary, expressly has to be what can only be "thought as existing"; his notion involves being. It is this unity of the notion and being that constitutes the notion of God.
>
> If this were all, we should have only a formal expression of the divine nature which would not really go beyond a statement of the nature of the notion itself. And that the notion, in its most abstract terms, involves being is plain. For the notion, whatever other determination it may receive, is at least reference back on itself, which results by abolishing the intermediation, and thus is immediate. And what is that reference to self, but being? Certainly it would be strange if the notion, the very inmost of mind, if even the "Ego," or above all the concrete totality we call God, were not rich enough to include so poor a category as being, the very poorest and most abstract of all.[54]

But unlike More, Descartes, and others, Hegel holds that God is not distinguishable from history or the world. Thus, Hegel seeks to use the concept of an existing God, absolute, to unfold and construct an understanding of all reality. By his lights, the absolute – to be the

University of California Press, 1990), 94–102. See Wolterstorff, *John Locke and the Ethics of Belief* (Cambridge: Cambridge University Press, 1996), last chapter.

[53] Preface to *Phenomenology of Spirit*, 11.

[54] *Hegel's Logic*, 85.

absolute – must be manifested in the phenomenal world and in human knowledge. A full understanding of the absolute turns out to be the outcome of a sustained inquiry into all history. The absolute, taken alone and apart from such fuller inquiry, is philosophically (and religiously) inadequate.

In Hegel's view, the unfolding of world history is the unfolding of God, the Absolute or Spirit. Hegel's philosophy is one of progress and optimism; his broad concept of world history may be read as a theodicy. In *Introduction to the Philosophy of History*, Hegel writes:

> For some time, it was customary to admire God's wisdom at work in animals, in plants, and in the destinies of individuals. If we grant that providence reveals itself in such objects and materials, then why not also in world history? Here, the material seems too great. Yet the divine wisdom, i.e. Reason, is one and the same on the large scale and on the small, and we must not consider God to be too weak to apply His wisdom on a large scale. In our knowledge, we aim for the insight that whatever was intended by the Eternal Wisdom has come to fulfillment – as in the realm of nature, so in the realm of spirit that is active and actual in world. To that extent our approach is a theodicy, a justification of the ways of God.[55]

The individual human being's life must be understood, in the end, in relation to history and the greater reality of which we are a part. But Hegel should not be thought of as seeing human history as happy; he casts history as a "slaughter-bench" involving "monstrous sacrifices."[56]

Philosophy of religion, in Hegel, achieves a global historical setting. Regrettably, Hegel held that the East or the "Oriental World" (Persia, India, and China) is only an initial, imperfect stage of universal history where only the ruler is taken to be free. History then displays increased freedom, first in Roman civilization and then the Christian-Germanic world. Hegel shares with other deistic philosophers an antipathy for a religious faith based on miracles, although he was far more appreciative of the role of religion in satisfying human needs. So Hegel defended popular religion (a healthy *Volksreligion* or folk religion) involving three elements:

I. Its doctrines must be grounded on universal Reason.
II. Fancy, heart, and sensibility must not thereby go empty away.

[55] *Introduction to the History of Philosophy*, trans. L. Rauch (Indianapolis: Hackett, 1988), 18.
[56] Ibid., 24.

III. It must be so constituted that all the needs of life – the public affairs of the State – are tied in with it.[57]

The result is a philosophy of religion that appreciates that religion is more than a matter of embracing a hypothesis or science.

> It is inherent in the concept of religion that it is not mere science of God, of his attributes, of our relation and the relations of the world to him and of the enduring survival of our souls – all of this might be admitted by mere Reason, or known to us in some other way – but religion is not a merely historical or rational knowledge, it is a concern of the heart, it has an influence on our feelings and on the determination of our will – partly because our duties and the laws make a stronger impression on us when they are presented to us as the laws of God; and partly because the image (*Vorstellung*) of the sublimity and the goodness of God towards us fills our hearts with wonder and with a sense of humility and gratitude.[58]

But religion will inevitably approach the absolute with a kind of picture – thinking, conceiving of the divine in theistic or polytheistic terms – whereas philosophy more adequately offers insight into God as unrestricted by such dualistic imagery. Proper religion, for Hegel, may usefully draw on myths or narratives to bolster morality.

> The general principle to be laid down as a foundation for all judgments on the varying modifications, forms, and spirit of the Christian religion is this – that the aim and essence of all true religion, our religion included, is human morality, and that all the more detailed doctrines of Christianity, all means of propagating them, and all its obligations (whether obligations to believe or obligations to perform actions in themselves otherwise arbitrary) have their worth and their sanctity appraised according to their close or distant connection with that aim.[59]

But to get to a fuller view of God requires philosophical, nonimaginistic thinking.

> God is universal, concrete, full of content, [by which it is implied] that God is One only, and not one as contrasted with many Gods, but that there is only the One, that is, God. . . . God in His universality, this Universal, in which there is no limitation, no finiteness, no particularity, is the absolute

[57] Hegel cited by R. K. Williamson, *Introduction to Hegel's Philosophy of Religion* (Albany: SUNY Press, 1984), 16.

[58] Ibid., 15.

[59] Ibid., 26.

Self-subsisting Being, and the only Self-subsisting Being; and what subsists has its root, its subsistence, in this One alone.

God is the absolute Substance, the only true reality. All else, which is real, is not real in itself, has no real existence of itself; the one absolute reality is God alone, and thus He is the absolute Substance.[60]

Hegel was criticized for subordinating the individual to the whole, and there is, I think, some merit in this characterization. Still, his system explicitly works to minimize abstractions. Individual persons must be seen in nonabstract terms. "It is not Man that exists," writes Hegel, "but the specific individual."[61] Moreover, Hegel recognized the way in which, concretely, a person's identity is shaped by other persons. One of Hegel's most famous examples of the development of identity involves a master and slave. They do not exist separately but are related as oppressor or oppressed. Hegel notes how the slave may achieve liberation through the development of self-consciousness in the course of the slave's work, while the master remains dependent on his perception of himself as a master. Liberation comes about, according to Hegel, when we see others as ends in themselves, as proper subjects.[62] Hegel's work here may be seen as filling out and anchoring Kant's categorical imperative in concrete, historical terms.

Charles Taylor, in an important study of Hegel, highlights two features of Hegel's work (among others), which I single out in concluding this section.

First, Taylor offers this summation of Hegel's view of the divine that I believe captures the nuances and complexity of his position.

Hegel's spirit, or *Geist*, although he is often called "God," and although Hegel claimed to be clarifying Christian theology, is not the God of traditional theism; he is not a God who could exist quite independently of

---

[60] Ibid., 196.

[61] *Introduction to the History of Philosophy*, 27.

[62] The section of the *Phenomenology of Spirit* that addresses self-consciousness, lordship, and bondage is philosophically fascinating. Hegel articulates the following idea: "Self-consciousness exists in and for itself when, and by the fact that, it so exists for another; that is, it exists only in being acknowledged" (111). Given the dependency of one self-consciousness upon the recognition of others, Hegel proposes that there is a natural desire either to destroy or to control others. The religious implications of this view of self-consciousness are addressed in the next chapter in reference to Sartre, Beauvoir, and Buber. Ultimately, Hegel sets forth an ideal interaction of self and others in mutual recognition and respect.

men, even if men did not exist, as the God of Abraham, Isaac and Jacob before the creation. On the contrary, he is a spirit who lives only through men. They are the vehicles, and the indispensable vehicles, of his spiritual existence, as consciousness, rationality, will. But at the same time *Geist* is not reducible to man, he is not identical with the human spirit, since he is also the spiritual reality underlying the universe as a whole, and as a spiritual being he has purposes and he realizes ends which cannot be attributed to finite spirits qua finite, but on the contrary which finite spirits serve. For the mature Hegel, man comes to himself in the end when he sees himself as a vehicle of a larger spirit.[63]

In this framework, Hegel avoids the theological anthropology of Feuerbach without resorting to classical theism.

In a second, astute passage, Taylor locates Hegel aptly in relation to mechanistic naturalism. "Like the theist view, he wants to see the world as designed, as existing in order to fulfill a certain prospectus, the requirements of embodiment for Geist. But like naturalists, he cannot allow a God who could design this world from the outside, who could exist before and independently of the world."[64] Hegel articulated the departure from theism as the death of God, but this signaled a transformation of the concept of God to an immanent reality, rather than the absence of God. Hegel dramatically described the concept of God in terms of crucifixion and then as an Easter return. In Hegel's mature philosophy, teleology, reason, and purpose are seen as fundamental features of reality.[65] His systematic view of nature, as defined by reason and purpose, counts as a challenge to forms of naturalism that either eliminate or marginalize reason and purpose.[66]

Idealism after Hegel

This section surveys, in compact terms, a host of philosophers who were, broadly speaking, in the idealist tradition. I highlight just a few aspects of their work bearing on the themes of evidence and religious faith, noting the way the philosophers that follow differ from their naturalistic

---

[63] *Hegel*, 44–45.

[64] Ibid., 101.

[65] See D. Anderson, "The Death of God and Hegel's System of Philosophy," *Sophia* 35:1 (1996).

[66] While Hegel's philosophy is a challenge at this juncture to certain forms of materialism, his work was (famously) recast in the service of dialectical materialism by Karl Marx.

contemporaries. Two of the more famous post-Hegelian idealists were the British philosophers Francis Herbert Bradley (1846–1924) and John Ellis McTaggart (1866–1925).

Bradley distinguished his work from both Hegel and Kant. His most famous work, *Appearance and Reality*, was a critical affirmation of reality as a single, nonpluralistic whole.

> The way of taking the world which I have found most tenable is to regard it as a single Experience, superior to relations and containing in the fullest sense everything which is. Whether there is any particular matter in this whole which falls outside of any finite centre of feeling, I cannot certainly decide; but the contrary seems perhaps more probable. We have then the Absolute Reality appearing in and to finite centres and uniting them in one experience. We can, I think, understand more or less what, in order for this to be done, such an experience must be. But to comprehend it otherwise is beyond us and even beyond all intelligence.... Those for whom philosophy has to explain everything need therefore not trouble themselves with my views.[67]

The ultimate, singular Absolute is, for Bradley, what subsumes and unifies all dimensions of reality. At the end of *Appearance and Reality* he summarizes and endorses the essential teaching of Hegel: "Outside of Spirit there is not, and there cannot be, any reality, and the more that anything is spiritual, so much more is it veritably real."[68]

McTaggart upheld an atheistic idealism that was built around a community of subjects. Although an atheist, he yet believed in (or allowed for) life after death. Curiously, in philosophy of religion today, his work is most often used in debate over God's relation to time. McTaggart, famously, distinguished two views of time, what he called the A and the B series. In the A series, time is divided into a past, present, and future. In the B series, there is precedence, simultaneity, and subsequent. He argued that the A series creates irresolvable paradoxes. Our experience of the temporal moment as *now* cannot be part of a definitive, final account of time. Here is a version of his argument against recognizing the reality of an event as now.

> Past, present, and future are incompatible determinations. Every event must be one or the other, but no event can be more than one. If I say that any event is past, that implies that it is neither present nor future,

---

[67] *Appearance and Reality* (London: Allen and Unwin, 1969), 245.
[68] Ibid., 489.

and so with the others. And this exclusiveness is essential to change, and therefore to time. For the only change we can get is from future to present, and from present to past.

The characteristics, therefore, are incompatible. But every event has them all. If M is past, it has been present and future. If it is future, it will be present and past. If it is present, it has been future and will be past. Thus all the three characteristics belong to each event. How is this consistent with their being incompatible?[69]

McTaggart concludes: "I believe that nothing that exists can be temporal, and that therefore time is unreal."[70] The reason why McTaggart's work comes into the philosophy of God is because some conceive of God's existence as atemporally eternal. By their lights, God does not experience the creation in terms of now and then. God's omniscience would, rather, be more aligned with the B series in which God eternally (timelessly) grasps the temporal relations holding between events. In addition to the God and time debate, McTaggart is an ally of those of us who privilege love in their metaphysics. His magisterial work, *The Nature of Existence,* concludes with praise of "a timeless and endless state of love – love so direct, so intimate and so powerful that even the deepest mystic rapture gives us but a foretaste of its perfection."[71]

There were scores of other idealists in the nineteenth and twentieth centuries who developed different, constructive treatments of religion. These included Bernard Bosanquet (1848–1923) and Andrew Pringle-Patterson (1856–1931).[72] Many, but by no means all, of the philosophical theists in the nineteenth and early twentieth centuries drew on or subscribed to idealism. These include T. H. Green (1836–1882), Josiah Royce (1855–1916), William Sorley (1855–1935), J. H. Muirhead (1855–1940), Hastings Rashdall (1858–1924), C. C. J. Webb (1865–1954), A. E. Taylor (1869–1945), William Temple (1881–1944), and C. A. Campbell (1897–1974).[73] For some, such as A. E. Taylor, religion

---

[69] *The Nature of Existence*, vol. 2 (Cambridge: Cambridge University Press, 1927), book 5, chap. 33.

[70] Ibid.

[71] Ibid., 913.

[72] For a good overview, see G. Watts Cunningham, *The Idealistic Argument in Recent British and American Philosophy* (New York: Century, 1933).

[73] For a sampling of this literature, see Royce's two-volume work, *The World and the Individual* (New York: Macmillan, 1983), as well as his *The Sources of Religious Insight* (New York: Charles Scribner's Sons, 1912). See also Royce, *The Problem of Christianity* (New York: Macmillan, 1913); Sorley, *Moral Values and the Idea of God*

was a central concern. Taylor offered a sustained defense of historical revelation in his Gifford Lectures.[74]

A cluster of philosophers emerged in the United States who forcefully combined idealism and theism; they became known as "personalists" or sometimes "Boston personalists," as they flourished at Boston University. In order of succession, three of the better known personalists are Borden Parker Bowne (1847–1910), Edgar Sheffield Brightman (1884–1932), and Peter Bertocci (1910–1989). Martin Luther King Jr. (1929–1968), a graduate of Boston University, was partly influenced by these theistic idealists who gave center stage in ethics and metaphysics to the concept of a person. The Boston personalists resembled the Cambridge Platonists in their resistance to modern materialism. Instead of attacking Hobbes, however, Bowne critiqued Herbert Spencer's naturalism. Bowne held that, given naturalism, the emergence of consciousness was absurd, but "assume a controlling purpose and all becomes luminous."[75] As his followers Brightman and Bertocci would also argue later, "a mechanical motion of a brain-molecule is no explanation of thought."[76] Brightman and Bertocci did not accept all the attributes of classic theism, and their philosophy of God bears some resemblance to process philosophy (to be discussed in Chapter 8). Thus, in their view, God was not omnipotent or in possession of limitless agency.

(Cambridge: Cambridge University Press, 1918); Rashdall's two-volume work, *The Theory of Good and Evil* (Oxford: Oxford University Press, 1907), *Philosophy and Religion* (London: Duckworth, 1909), and *The Problem of Evil* (Manchester, 1912); Temple, *Nature, Man and God* (New York: Macmillan, 1934); Taylor, *The Faith of a Moralist* (London: Macmillan, 1930) and *Does God Exist?* (London: Macmillan, 1945); Campbell, *On Selfhood and Goodhood* (London: Allen and Unwin, 1952) and *Defense of Free Will* (London: Allen and Unwin, 1967); Webb, *Studies in the History of Natural Theology* (Oxford: Clarendon, 1915) and *God and Personality* (Aberdeen University Studies, 1919). Each of these works contains rich material for philosophy of religion; I especially commend Taylor and Campbell. Taylor offered an impressive version of a theistic moral argument. Campbell proposed one of the best arguments (in my view) for libertarian free will.

[74] See his *Natural Theology and the Positive Religions* (London: Macmillan, 1930), 43–108.

[75] Bowne, *The Philosophy of Herbert Spencer* (New York: Nelson and Phillips, 1874), 254.

[76] Ibid., 276. For a good overview, see Brightman, *Person and Reality*, ed. P. Bertocci (New York: Ronald Press, 1958), and A. C. Knudsen, *The Philosophy of Personalism* (Boston: Boston University Press, 1949).

The traditional debate between theism and atheism continued in the style and substance of Cleanthes versus Philo and Paley versus Bentham. There was a series of Bridgewater treatises defending theism (1833–1836). Probably the most prominent respondent to naturalism and to the naturalist critique of the design argument was F. R. Tennant (1866–1957), whose two-volume work, *Philosophical Theology*, still repays close study. Tennant's work (published in 1928 and 1930) is probably the most sustained and forceful restatement of a theistic argument from design in the first half of the twentieth century. Tennant's argument is comprehensive and cumulative but gives pride of place to the emergence of life in the cosmos.[77]

There was some shift in ground as the debate over religious experience became more prominent in late nineteenth- and early twentieth-century philosophy. Two leading contributors to this surge of interest are Rudolf Otto (1869–1937) and Evelyn Underhill (1875–1941).

Otto offered a sympathetic analysis of religious experience.

> The feeling of it [the holy] may at times come sweeping like a gentle tide, pervading the mind with a tranquil mood of deepest worship. It may pass over into a more set and lasting attitude of the soul, continuing, as it were, thrillingly vibrant and resonant, until at last it dies away and the soul resumes its "profane," non-religious mood of everyday experience. It may burst in sudden eruption up from the depths of the soul with spasms and convulsions, or lead to the strangest excitements, to intoxicated frenzy, to transport, and to ecstasy. It has its wild and demonic forms and can sink to an almost grisly horror and shuddering. It has its crude, barbaric antecedents and early manifestations, and again it may be developed into something beautiful and pure and glorious. It may become the hushed, trembling, and speechless humility of the creature in the presence of – whom or what? In the presence of that which is a *mystery* inexpressible and above all creatures.[78]

In Otto's work, virtually all religion is informed by an experience of mystery, awe, and fascination (*mysterium tremendum fascinans*). Unlike Freud and Weber, Otto saw this experience as genuinely disclosing a transcendent (nominous) reality. In Otto's view, the sense of the holy had as much force and meaning as our apprehension of moral imperatives.

---

[77] Tennant, *Philosophical Theology*, vol. 2 (Cambridge: Cambridge University Press, 1930). See especially chap. 4.

[78] *The Idea of the Holy*, trans. J. W. Harvey (New York: Oxford University Press, 1958), 12, 13.

His study of religion was genuinely cross-cultural (see his *Mysticism East and West,* published in 1926). In Marburg, Germany, he founded a museum for the comparative study of religion.

Evelyn Underhill did not consider herself a philosopher, although she wrote on philosophy and is included in *A History of Women Philosophers,* where Underhill's classic study of *Mysticism* (1911) is said to remain "one of the fundamental analyses of mysticism."[79] *Mysticism* and her other works did much to arouse scholarly (as well as popular) interest in constructive, cognitive interpretations of religious experience.

With the advent of idealism came a deeper appreciation for Hindu and Buddhist philosophy. At first this was the result of European thinkers being influenced by the East. So, Arthur Schopenhauer (1788–1860), an opponent of Hegel but fellow idealist, claimed that the foundation of his work was the Hindu Scriptures, the Vedas, along with Plato and Kant. His ethics extols a Buddhist form of renunciation.

W. T. Stace (1886–1967) defended the legitimacy of mystical experience across many religions. (Stace was aided in his acquaintance with Hinduism and Buddhism, as he spent his early adulthood in the British civil service in Ceylon.) Stace challenged the sufficiency of a mechanistic science.

> Religion has generally been associated with teleology, science with mechanism. Hence another contrast between the medieval and the modern minds is that by the former teleology was stressed, by the later mechanism is stressed. It is an important characteristic of the modern mind, which it derived from science, that its outlook is almost wholly mechanistic, and that it has thrust a teleological view of the world into the background, even if it does not deny teleology altogether. Most biologists are mechanists, and tend to frown upon explanations even of the behavior of living beings by purposes. And in psychology the same dislike of teleology is common, and the introduction of the notion of purpose is often considered unscientific.... It is true that water boils at a certain temperature. Perhaps a mechanical explanation of this can be give in terms of molecules, atoms, or electrons. But however far we proceed in such a scientific way, we shall only be saying, in greater or less detail, what happens, not why anything happens. The world will still be a brute fact world, which just is what it is, without any rhyme or reason having been given for it. The molecules or electrons behave in this way and not in that

---

[79] M. E. Waithe, ed., *A History of Women Philosophers* (Dordrecht: Kluwer, 1995), 328. Underhill is the first woman lecturer to be listed at Oxford University (337).

way. Only if we could see the ultimate purpose of things, if we could see all things in the light of "the form of the good," should we understand. Only then would the world be intelligible. A world seen without this vision of an ultimate plan is nothing but a mass of senseless and unintelligible "facts."[80]

In place of a reductive science, Stace defended a capacious view of the mystical.[81]

In the 1920s and 1930s the Indian philosopher Radhakrishnan became an important representative of philosophical Hinduism. Though influenced by Shankara's Advaita Vedanta tradition, Radhakrishnan did not treat the world of appearances and phenomena as illusion (*maya*). The world as we experience it is real, but it is dependent, temporal, and imperfect in relation to the Supreme reality. "'Maya' has a standing in the world of reality...it is not so much a veil as the dress of God."[82] Radhakrishnan familiarized westerners with the doctrine of Karma, outlining a philosophy of justice and the divine not indebted to Hebrew or Christian sources. Radhakrishnan saw religious experience as providing some grounds for rejecting naturalism.

> The possibility of the experience [of God] constitutes the most conclusive proof of the reality of God. God is "given," and is the factual content of the spiritual experience. All other proofs are descriptions of God, matters of definition, and language. The fact of God does not depend on mere human authority or evidence from alleged miraculous events. The authority of scripture, the traditions of the Church...may not carry conviction to many of us who are the children of science and reason, but we must submit to the fact of spiritual experience, which is primary and positive. We may dispute theologies, but cannot deny facts. The fire of life in its visible burning compels assent, though not the fumbling speculations of smokers sitting around the fire.[83]

---

[80] W. T. Stace, *Religion and the Modern Mind* (Philadelphia: J. B. Lippincott, 1960), 25, 31. One of Stace's most important books on religious experience is *Mysticism and Philosophy* (Philadelphia: J. B. Lippincott, 1960). For a reply, see Ninian Smart, "Mystical Experience," *Sophia* 1 (1962).

[81] Max Muller (1823–1900) was another inspiration for expanding philosophy of religion to include Asian thought. He was one of Kant's early translators into English. He also translated many Hindu and Buddhist texts.

[82] Radhakrishnan, *The Brahma Sutra* (London: Allen and Unwin, 1960), 157.

[83] *Eastern Religions and Western Thought* (Oxford: Oxford University Press, 1959), 22–23.

The problem with naturalism, for Radhakrishnan, was its denial of evident spiritual principles, ethical as well as religious. He diagnosed a Darwinian materialism succinctly: "In a closed world governed by uniform laws, no spiritual principle can interfere."[84]

At this stage it is worth emphasizing the two very different, prevalent positions taken on religious experience in the late nineteenth and early twentieth centuries. Darwin is representative of the naturalist who acknowledges the argument from religious experience. "At the present day the most usual argument for the existence of an intelligent God is drawn from the deep inward conviction and feelings which are experienced by most persons."[85] But, by Darwin's lights, these experiences do not have any evidential significance. "It may be truly said that I am like a man who has become colour-blind, and the universal belief by men of the existence of redness makes my present loss of perception of not the least value as evidence. The argument would be a valid one if all men of all races had the same inward conviction of the existence of one God; but we know that this is very far from being the case. Therefore I cannot see that such inward convictions and feelings are of any weight as evidence of what really exists."[86] Shortly after Darwin's death, however, some philosophers challenged the demand that in order to qualify as evidence it was necessary that "all men of all races" testify to "the existence of one God." It is not obvious that "all men of all races" testify to the existence of the same moral truths, but that alone does not undermine the evidential value of an individual's moral experience. (Imagine you experience the evil or wrongness of slavery in a society where slavery is deemed justified. Would your experience have no value whatever as even prima facie evidence that slavery is wrong?) Second, studies such as Otto's *Idea of the Holy* and Underhill's *Mysticism* provided

---

[84] *An Idealist View of Life* (London: George Allen, 1957), 24. Another philosopher who may be noted here as contributing to a nonnaturalist philosophy of religion is John Henry Newman, who defended the existence of an "illative sense" of truth whereby we are able to infer God's existence. See his *An Essay in Aid of a Grammar of Assent* (London: Longmans, Green, 1903). See especially his response to Gibons. Wainwright offers a good analysis of Newman in *Reason and the Heart* (Ithaca: Cornell University Press, 1995). The common "opponent" of most of the philosophers of this section is today called scientism. See Michael Stenmark, *Scientism* (Aldershot: Ashgate, 2001).

[85] *The Autobiography of Charles Darwin*, ed. Nora Barlow (New York: W. W. Norton, 1969), 90.

[86] Ibid., 91.

comprehensive accounts of the existence and character of religious experiences, offering reasons as to why not everyone would have such experiences (e.g., an antecedent commitment against the possibility of such experience) while at the same time arguing that positive reports of religious experience should be taken seriously as evidence that challenges naturalism.

Pragmatism in Philosophy of Religion

"Pragmatism" is sometimes touted as America's first philosophy and seminal contribution to world philosophy. Pragmatism is today undergoing a renaissance, and so it is important to pause over its bearing on philosophy of religion. Each of its three main representatives, Charles Sanders Peirce (1839–1914), William James (1842–1910), and John Dewey (1859–1952), addressed religion.

The term "pragmatism" is derived from the Greek *pragmata*, meaning "business," "affairs," "acts." Pierce advanced pragmatism as an account of meaning, according to which "the rational purport of a word or other expression, lies exclusively in its conceivable bearing upon the conduct of life."[87] Pierce, James, and Dewey each cast their appreciation and criticism of religion in terms of human conduct and values.

Pierce emphasized the practical side of religion as a loving way of life and not an abstract mental exercise. "It is absurd to say that Religion is a mere belief. You might as well call society a belief, or politics a belief or civilization a belief. Religion is a life and can be identified with a belief only provided that belief be a living belief."[88] Although he did not develop an argument from religious experience, evidently he thought that experience could correctly yield religious convictions. "As to God, Open your eyes – and your heart, which is also a perceptive organ – and you see him."[89] In a somewhat Platonic spirit, Pierce's concept of truth was intrinsically linked with the concept of the good. "Truth, the conditions of which the logician endeavours to analyze, and which is the goal of the reasoner's aspirations, is nothing

---

[87] Pierce, *Selected Writing*, ed. P. P. Wiener (New York: Dover, 1966), 183.

[88] *Collected Papers* (Cambridge, Mass.: Harvard University Press, 1931–1968), 6:439.

[89] Ibid., 267. See D. R. Anderson, "An American Argument for Belief in the Reality of God," *International Journal for Philosophy of Religion* 26 (1989).

but a phrase of the *Summum bonum* which forms the subject of pure Ethics."[90]

James privileged *practice* or *use* in his case for religion, developing a wager argument for theism. For James, the "cash value" of an idea is paramount and, for him, the cash value of theistic convictions was sufficient for faith.

> You see that pragmatism can be called religious, if you allow that religion can be pluralistic or merely melioristic in type. But whether you will finally put up with that type of religion or not is a question that only you yourself can decide. Pragmatism has to postpone dogmatic answer, for we do not yet know certainly which type of religion is going to work best in the long run. The various overbeliefs of men, their several faith ventures, are in fact what are needed to bring the evidence in. You will probably make your own ventures severally. If radically tough, the hurly-burly of the sensible facts of nature will be enough for you, and you will need no religion at all. If radically tender, you will take up with the more monistic form of religion: the pluralistic form, with its reliance on possibilities that are not necessities, will not seem to afford you security enough.
>
> But if you are neither tough nor tender in an extreme and radical sense, but mixed as most of us are, it may seem to you that the type of pluralistic and moralistic religion that I have offered is as good a religious synthesis as you are likely to find. Between the two extremes of crude naturalism on the one hand and transcendental absolutism on the other, you may find that what I take the liberty of calling the pragmatic or melioristic type of theism is exactly what you require.[91]

James's most sustained treatment of religion is in his Gifford Lectures, 1901–1902, published with the title *The Varieties of Religious Experience*. James characterizes the religious life in five respects:

1. That the visible world is part of a more spiritual universe from which it draws its chief significance;
2. That union or harmonious relation with that higher universe is our true end;
3. That prayer or inner communion with the spirit thereof – be that spirit "God" or "law" – is a process wherein work is really done, and spiritual energy flows in and produces effects, psychological or material, within the phenomenal world.

[90] *Collected Papers*, 1: entry 576.
[91] James, *Pragmatism and the Meaning of Truth* (Cambridge, Mass.: Harvard University Press, 1978), 144.

Religion includes also the following psychological characteristics:

4. A new zest that adds itself like a gift to life and takes the form either of lyrical enchantment or of appeal to earnestness and heroism.
5. An assurance of safety and a temper of peace, and, in relation to others, a preponderance of loving affections.[92]

James's conclusions in this work are tentative and not unambiguous. The language is often theistic but James also refers to God in terms of the highest part of the universe.

Like Pascal (discussed in Chapter 2) James held that some convictions can be held, and may be permissible and good to hold, even if the evidence is not decisive. In his celebrated essay "The Will to Believe," James set up a framework for such convictions. He asks us to consider two incompatible "live" hypotheses, a concept for which he provides the following definition: "A live hypothesis, is one which appeals as a real possibility to him to whom it is proposed."[93] His example of two live hypotheses are agnosticism versus religious, specifically Christian belief. And his target is Clifford's claim (cited earlier) that "It is wrong always, everywhere, and for everyone, to believe anything upon insufficient evidence." Against Clifford, he advances the following: "Our passional nature not only lawfully may, but must decide an option between propositions, whenever it is a genuine option that cannot by its nature be decided on intellectual grounds; for to say, under such circumstances, 'Do not decide, but leave the question open,' is itself a passional decision, – just like deciding yes or no, – and attended with the same risk of losing the truth."[94] The fear – or the almost pathological phobia that James attributes to Clifford – about embracing error should not prevent one from accepting and acting on a hypothesis that may be true.

James's case for his more latitudinarian approach to belief involves highlighting the essential role of our "passional nature" (what he sometimes calls passionate desire, affirmation, volition, tendency, or simply faith) in virtually all cognition.[95]

---

[92] *The Varieties of Religious Experience* (New York: Modern Library, 1929), 475, 476.
[93] *The Will to Believe: Human Immortality and Other Essays on Popular Philosophy* (New York: Dover Publications, 1956), 2.
[94] Ibid., 11.
[95] Ibid., 13.

You believe in objective evidence, and I do. Of some things we feel that we are certain: we know, and we know that we do know. There is something that gives a click inside of us, a bell that strikes twelve, when the hands of our mental clock have swept the dial and meet over the meridian hour. . . . Objective evidence and certitude are doubtless very fine ideals to play with, but where on this moon lit and dream-visited planet are they found? . . . I live, to be sure, by the practical faith that we must go on experiencing and thinking over our experience, for only thus can our opinions grow more true; but to hold any one of them – I absolutely do not care which – as if it never could be reinterpretable or corrigible, I believe to be a tremendously mistaken attitude, and I think that the whole history of philosophy will bear me out. There is but one indefectibly certain truth, and that is the truth that pyrrhonistic skepticism itself leaves standing, – the truth that the present phenomenon of consciousness exists. That, however, is the bare starting point of knowledge, the mere admission of a stuff to be philosophized about.

No concrete test of what is really true has ever been agreed upon. Some make the criterion external to the moment of perception, putting it either in revelation, the *consensus gentium*, the instincts of the heart, or the systematized experience of the race. Others make the perceptive moment its own test, – Descartes, for instance, with his clear and distinct ideas guaranteed by the veracity of God; Reid with his "common sense"; and Kant with his forms of synthetic judgment *a priori*. The inconceivability of the opposite; the capacity to be verified by sense; the possession of complete organic unity or self-relation, realized when a thing is its own other, – are standards which, in turn, have been used. The much lauded objective evidence is never triumphantly there. . . . Practically one's conviction that the evidence one goes by is of the real objective brand, is only one more subjective opinion added to the lot. For what a contradictory array of opinions have objective evidence and absolute certitude been claimed![96]

James's specific case for wagering on the truth of religion as opposed to adapting agnosticism rests on his securing that the religious hypothesis is indeed "alive" and that the choice between either religion or agnosticism is momentous and forced.[97]

We cannot escape the issue by remaining skeptical and waiting for more light, because, although we do avoid error in that way *if religion be untrue*, we lose the good, *if it be true*, just as certainly as if we positively chose to disbelieve. It is as if a man should hesitate indefinitely to ask a certain

[96] Ibid., 13–16.
[97] Ibid., 26.

woman to marry him because he was not perfectly sure that she would prove an angel after he brought her home. Would he not cut himself off from that particular angel-possibility as decisively as if he went and married someone else? Skepticism, then, is not avoidance of option; it is option of a certain particular kind of risk. *Better risk loss of truth than chance of error*, – that is your faith-vetoer's exact position.[98]

Clifford's strongest point rests in concrete examples where the nature of "sufficient evidence" is easily determined in practical ways – for example, Do not set sail on a ship when you have not checked whether it leaks. But in matters of comprehensive philosophies of the cosmos (theism vs. naturalism vs. monism), "sufficient evidence" seems more malleable or at least less exact.

What should be made of James's work? Clifford's subsequent followers have sought to argue that religious beliefs are not live, so James's case cannot get off the ground in the first place. There have also been arguments that religious beliefs are in fact harmful, and so there are good moral arguments to wager against them. Even more in keeping with Clifford's original stance, it has been argued that to bring in matters of welfare, human-flourishing, and goodness is a different enterprise from assessing hypotheses from the standpoint of epistemology or knowledge. It has been asked whether it is even possible for us to passionately believe and act on hypotheses without sufficient evidence. On the other hand, followers of James receive support from some developments that are displayed in subsequent chapters involving an expanded treatment of methodology in philosophy of religion (Chapter 7), the attack on an empiricism much like Clifford's (Chapter 8), and some new work in the philosophy of science (Chapter 9).[99]

I believe that one of James's lasting contributions to philosophy of religion was his breadth, his defense of alternative hypotheses in light of modern science. So, for example, in his famous Ingersoll Lecture at Harvard University, James did not argue positively that there was an afterlife. Rather he assumed a reigning naturalistic treatment of human nature according to which thought is a function of the brain and then

---

[98] Ibid.

[99] For a provocative example of James's style of arguing, see especially his essays "Is Life Worth Living?" and "The Dilemma of Determinism"; both appear in *The Will to Believe*. For a recent defense of James's fundamental argument, see L. S. Betty, "Going beyond James: A Pragmatic Argument for God's Existence," *International Journal for Philosophy of Religion* 49:2 (2001).

went on to speculatively conceive of how this would not rule out the possibility of an afterlife.[100]

The third pragmatist in this section, Dewey, did not ignore religion, though philosophy of religion was not one of his major concerns. Dewey was clearly committed to an anti-supernatural outlook. He nonetheless reserved the term "religious" as a positive, highly valued category naming a defining, unifying attitude toward life. "The religious is 'morality touched by emotion' only when the ends of moral conviction arouse emotions that are not only intense but are actuated and supported by ends so inclusive that they unify the self. The inclusiveness of the end in relation to both self and the 'universe' to which an inclusive self is related is indispensable."[101] The result was a philosophy of religion that goes considerably beyond matters of institutional tradition.

> The adjective "religious" denotes nothing in the way of a specifiable entity, either institutional or as a system of beliefs. It does not denote anything to which one can specifically point as one can point to this and that historic religion or existing church. For it does not denote anything that can exist by itself or that can be organized into a particular and distinctive form of existence. It denotes attitudes that may be taken toward every object and every proposed end or ideal.[102]

Dewey was anti-Platonic insofar as he eschewed transcendental, eternal ideals to which he owed loyalty and love, but he conceived of the individual's highest development in terms of a value-based integration of the self and the universe. "The self is always directed toward something beyond itself and so its own unification depends upon the idea of the integration of the shifting scenes of the world into that imaginative totality we call the Universe."[103]

A surprising but I believe quite useful place to look for a Deweyan philosophy of religion involves his work in aesthetics.[104] In *Art as Experience*, Dewey writes of the way in which our experiences can be defined by values. We do not see merely sensory shapes and colors; we see, rather, the fight in the street or the romance on a ship. Leaving

---

[100] See "Human Immortality; Two Supposed Objections to the Doctrine," reprinted in *The Will to Believe*.

[101] *A Common Faith* (New Haven: Yale University Press, 1944), 22, 23.

[102] Ibid., 9.

[103] Ibid.

[104] See William M. Shea, "Qualitative Wholes: Aesthetic and Religious Experience in the Work of John Dewey," *Journal of Religion* 60:1 (1980).

to one side the details of just how Dewey develops his value-laden concept of experience in his treatment of art, I take note of how Dewey appreciated the experiential evidence of values. "The undefined pervasive quality of an experience is that which binds together all the defined elements, the objects of which we are focally aware, making them a whole. The best evidence that such is the case is our constant sense of things as belonging or not belonging, of relevancy, a sense which is immediate."[105] In his work on aesthetics, Dewey leaves the door open for an experiential study of the values that are ingredients in religion – whether this be the traditional use of the term "religion" or the more extensive use Dewey proposed. Dewey writes: "I have had occasion to speak more than once of a quality of an intense aesthetic experience that is so immediate as to be ineffable and mystical.... All direct experience is qualitative, and qualities are what make life-experience itself directly precious.... A work of art may certainly convey the essence of a multitude of experiences, and sometimes, in a remarkably condensed and striking way."[106] If one may prize such experiences in works of art, perhaps one might prize a host of valued, qualitative experiences in religion as well.

Dewey's pragmatism has sometimes been interpreted as profoundly anti-tradition – whether this be religious or secular. His philosophy of education prizes democracy and coordinated individual experimentation, unfettered by sectarian and parochial constraints. But Dewey's work does not counsel an uncritical rejection of what passes as tradition. In light of contemporary individual experimentation, John Herman Randall summarizes Dewey's position: "The great traditions and 'present realities' – they are equally indispensable materials for philosophic reflection, in our present or in any past present; and the philosophic task, ever old and ever new, is to bring them together significantly and fruitfully."[107] In an essay "Whither Mankind," Dewey offers this overview of the place of tradition for philosophers:

A philosopher who would relate his thinking to present civilization in its predominantly technological and industrial character, cannot ignore any of these movements [eighteenth-century rationalism, German idealism, the religious and philosophical traditions of Europe] any more than he can

---

[105] *Art as Experience* (New York: Perigee Books, 1980), 194.
[106] Ibid., 293.
[107] "Interpretation of History of Philosophy," in *The Philosophy of John Dewey*, ed. P. A. Schilpp (Evanston: Northwestern University, 1939), 95.

dispense with consideration of the underlying classic tradition formed in Greece and the Middle Ages. If he ignores traditions, his thoughts become thin and empty. But they are something to be employed, not just treated with respect or dressed out in a new vocabulary. Moreover, industrial civilization itself has now sufficiently developed to form its own tradition.... if philosophy declines to observe and interpret the new and characteristic scene, it may achieve scholarship; it may erect a well equipped gymnasium wherein to engage in dialectical exercises; it may clothe itself in fine literary art. But it will not afford illumination or direction to our confused civilization. These can proceed only from the spirit that is interested in present realities and that faces them frankly and sympathetically.[108]

The result, as far as philosophy of religion is concerned, is an approach to evidence and religious faith that takes seriously both tradition and contemporary experience and practice.

[108] Cited by Randall, ibid., 94–95.

✦

SEVEN

Continental and Feminist Philosophy of Religion

The wise man as astronomer: As long as you feel the stars to be "above" you, you do not gaze as one who has insight.

Friedrich Nietzsche[1]

Two Rivers

The category "continental philosopher" is the popular term for many of the figures covered in this chapter. In a way, the roots of continental philosophy stretch back to the rift described at the end of Chapter 5 between those thinkers who are loosely associated with the romantic movement and those associated with Kant. Intellectuals such as Jacobi rejected the Enlightenment dream of a critical philosophy founded on reason. Frederick Beiser effectively states the process of how an Enlightenment ideal devolved.

> The context of German philosophy toward the close of the eighteenth century was dominated by one long-standing cultural crisis: the decline of the *Aufklärung*, the German Enlightenment. This crisis threw into question its main article of faith: the sovereignty of reason. The *Aufklärung* was the German "age of reason," or, since reason was conceived as a critical power, "the age of criticism." The *Aufklärung* gave reason complete sovereignty because it claimed that reason could criticize all of our beliefs, accepting or rejecting them strictly according to whether there is sufficient evidence for them ... such was the bold programme – and dream – of the *Aufklärung*. Tragically, though, it carried the seeds of its own destruction. Simply to state its principle of the sovereignty of reason is to

---

[1] *Aphorisms*, in *Essays in Philosophy*, ed. H. Peterson (New York: Washington Square Press, 1969), 217.

raise grave questions about it. For if reason must criticize everything on heaven and earth, must it not also criticize itself? And, if it does so, how does it prevent its self-criticism from becoming scepticism? A nightmare looms: that the self-criticism of reason ends in nihilism, doubt about the existence of everything. That fear was the sum and substance of the crisis of the *Aufklärung*.[2]

"Continental philosophers" share a suspicion of Kantian critical philosophy, Descartes' foundationalism, the empiricist and rationalist appeal to evidence, and certainly the way religion was debated by the likes of Paley and Mill. The two figures I address at the outset, Kierkegaard and Nietzsche, railed against the great system building of Hegel and some of the other idealists described in Chapter 6.

While continental philosophy may be seen as stemming from a revolt against rationalism in the nineteenth century, its outlook should not in any way be cast in terms of a lessened concern for evidence. For the phenomenologists (Husserl and Heidegger especially), providing evidence was necessary for justifying any view. But, for them, evidence is understood more broadly than argumentation as we find it in Kant, Hume, Locke, et al. Moods, for example, are key sources of evidence for understanding human nature. Anxiety, as we will see in Heidegger, is the evidence of our orientation to our death ("being-towards-death"). Many of the continental figures that follow were rigorous investigators into the character and philosophical implications of experience. Although the continental tradition largely opposed a Kantian rationalism, there is a sense in which many early continental thinkers see themselves as continuing Kant's transcendental psychology, his setting aside inquiry into the noumenal or mind-transcendent world and focusing instead on the structure of consciousness and the meaningful structure of experience.

Another way to demarcate continental thinkers is to view them in opposition to *analytic philosophy*, in which conceptual and linguistic analysis is paramount. An analytic philosopher may devote all of his or her energy to analyzing the concept of knowledge, identifying the necessary and sufficient conditions for a person to know some proposition. By contrast, continental thinkers may privilege at the outset our

---

[2] F. Beiser, "Post-Kantian Philosophy," in *A Companion to Continental Philosophy*, ed. S. Critchley and W. R. Schroeder (Oxford: Blackwell, 1998), 22. See also Critchley, *Continental Philosophy* (Oxford: Oxford University Press, 2001), chap. 2. Critchley links continental philosophy to the romantic rebellion against the Enlightenment.

experience of knowing. The "continent" refers to Europe, but this term can be somewhat misleading, for many self-described analytic thinkers opposed to continental philosophy were (and are) European.[3]

In the second half of the twentieth century, there was philosophical and professional tension between continental and analytic philosophers. This produced a lamentable, almost comic intellectual climate, captured in John Passmore's influential A Hundred Years of Philosophy:

> The fact we have to live with, then, is that if most British philoso-phers are convinced that Continental metaphysics is arbitrary, preten-tious, and mind-destroying, Continental philosophers are no less confi-dent that British empiricism is philistine, pedestrian, and soul-destroying. Even when existentialism reflects certain aspects of British empiricism – as in its emphasis on contingency – it does so in the manner of the distort-ing mirrors in a Fun Fair; what seemed eminently rational and ordinary suddenly looks grotesque.[4]

The British philosopher Michael Dummett famously compared a primary analytic philosopher (Frege) and a continental philosopher (Husserl) to the Rhine River and the Danube River, respectively, for they "arise quite close to each other and for a time pursue roughly par-allel paths, only to diverge in utterly different directions and flow into separate seas."[5]

I believe that the partisanship between continental philosophy of re-ligion and its analytic counterpart is regrettable and that there are wor-thy, important projects incorporating both. But rather than bemoan or celebrate fractious academic competition, I turn first to Kierkegaard.

---

[3] For those who like neat labels for schools of thought, there is now the so-called American continental philosophy; see the anthology with that title, edited by W. Brogan and J. Risser (Bloomington: Indiana University Press, 2000).

[4] J. Passmore, A Hundred Years of Philosophy (New York: Basic Books, 1966), 477.

[5] M. Dummett, Origins of Analytic Philosophy (London: Duckworth, 1993), 26. For an overview, see David Brown's Continental Philosophy and Modern Theology (Oxford: Blackwell, 1987). Unfortunately, the limitation of space has meant my not covering several figures of distinction. Henri-Louis Bergson (1859–1941) did important work on the concept of time and ethics. For a starting point in exploring his philosophy of religion, see his The Two Sources of Morality and Religion, trans. R. A. Audra et al. (London: Macmillan, 1935). Another extraordinary thinker I cannot address is the Dutch philosopher Herman Dooyeweerd (1884–1977). He argued for a religious foundation for ontology and epistemology. His multivolume masterpiece is A New Critique of Theoretical Thought (Philadelphia: Presbyterian and Reformed Publishing, 1953–1958).

Continental philosophers (generally) trace their lineage to Kierkegaard, Nietzsche, Husserl, or Heidegger, either building on or opposing these philosophers. There are serious interconnections – philosophical and personal – among most of the continental figures to be discussed here.[6] The chapter concludes with feminist philosophy of religion, for while some feminists are analytic philosophers, many feminists have been influenced by – and contribute to – continental thought.

Subjectivity in Philosophy of Religion

Søren Kierkegaard (1813–1855) was born in Copenhagen. He studied philosophy in Berlin as well as in Copenhagen and distinguished himself as a prolific writer, authoring twenty-one books in twelve years.[7] His writing is variegated in style, ranging from comforting and pastoral to incisive and brazenly ironic. He frequently employed pseudonyms as a method of indirect communication with the reader – adding layers of meaning and difficulties of interpretation.[8] He was highly critical of Hegelianism and the established Danish church. Although any of Kierkegaard's works could serve as the centerpiece of a philosophy of religion, space limitations compel me to highlight only a few aspects of his work, beginning with his view of faith and evidence.[9]

Kierkegaard is perhaps best known for his critique of "objectivity." For Kierkegaard, the kind of objectivity found in systems like Hegel's was inhumane and damaging. In his view, belief and doubt were not matters of cognition. "Belief and doubt are not two forms of knowledge, determinable in continuity with one another, for neither

---

[6] Consider just one example of the personal connections. Levinas organized Husserl's 1929 visit to Paris to give his "Paris Lectures" (later developed into the "Cartesian Meditations"); he knew Sartre and Beauvoir in Paris; he attended the monthly Saturday evening soirées of Marcel in the early 1930s; he was a friendly critic of Buber; he was Derrida's teacher; his funeral oration was delivered by Derrida, and so on. Of course, Kierkegaard and Nietzsche did not *interact* with each other (though in his correspondence of 1888 Nietzsche records his desire to read Kierkegaard).

[7] For a good biography of Kierkegaard, see Alastair Hannay, *Kierkegaard* (Cambridge: Cambridge University Press, 2001).

[8] See L. Machey, *Kierkegaard: A Kind of Poet* (Philadelphia: University of Pennsylvania Press, 1971).

[9] For a good introduction to Kierkegaard through a single work, see C. Stephen Evans, *Passionate Reason: Making Sense of Kierkegaard's Philosophical Fragments* (Bloomington: Indiana University Press, 1992).

of them is a cognitive act; they are opposite passions."[10] The key for Kierkegaard is the individual's passionate, subjective relation to eternal truth.

> Subjectivity is the truth. By virtue of the relationship subsisting between the eternal truth and the existing individual, the paradox came into being. Let us now go further, let us suppose that the eternal essential truth is itself a paradox. How does the paradox come into being? By putting the eternal essential truth into juxtaposition with existence. Hence when we posit such a conjunction within the truth itself, the truth becomes a paradox. The eternal truth has come into being in time: this is the paradox.[11]

Coming to terms with eternal truth could involve some recourse to reason, but reason cannot settle the matter. "There has been said much that is strange, much that is deplorable, much that is revolting about Christianity; but the most stupid thing ever said about it is that it is to a certain degree true."[12]

Kierkegaard's critique of "objectivity" is linked to his fight to secure the centrality of the individual person, rather than lose the individual in a Hegelian system. He likened his case for the individual to the famous battle at Thermopylae, where the ancient Greeks temporarily managed to stave off the overwhelming Persian invasion. "'The individual' is the category through which, in a religious aspect, this age, all history, the human race as a whole, must pass. And he who stood at Thermopylae was not so secure in his position as I who have stood in defense of this narrow defile, 'the individual,' with the intent at least of making people take notice of it."[13] An individual can lose himself or herself through philosophical self-deception, constructing uninhabitable systems cut off from their own lives. "In relation to their systems most systemizers are like a man who builds an enormous castle and lives in a shack close by; they do not live in their own enormous systematic buildings."[14] By

---

[10] *Philosophical Fragments*, trans. D. F. Swenson (Princeton: Princeton University Press, 1967), 105.

[11] *Concluding Unscientific Postscript*, trans. D. F. Swenson and W. Lowrie (Princeton: Princeton University Press, 1941), 187.

[12] Ibid., 205.

[13] *The Point of View of My Work as an Author*, trans. W. Lowrie (New York: Oxford University Press, 1939), 128.

[14] *The Journals of Søren Kierkegaard*, trans. Alexander Dru (New York: Oxford University Press, 1938), 156.

supplanting objectivity with subjectivity, Kierkegaard gives primacy to the individual's relation to the truth.

> When the question of truth is raised in an objective manner, reflection is directed objectively to the truth, as an object to which the knower is related. Reflection is not focused upon the relationship, however, but upon the question of whether it is the truth to which the knower is related. If only the object to which he is related is the truth, the subject is accounted to be in the truth. When the question of the truth is raised subjectively, reflection is directed subjectively to the nature of the individual's relationship; if only the mode of this relationship is in the truth, the individual is in the truth even if he should happen to be thus related to what is not true.[15]

Kierkegaard locates Christianity firmly in subjectivity: "It is subjectivity that Christianity is concerned with, and it is only in subjectivity that its truth exists, if it exists at all; objectively, Christianity has absolutely no existence."[16]

Kierkegaard's valorization of subjectivity raises the question of whether his Christianity involves renouncing the claim that it is true at all. I believe that interpretation is a misreading of the rhetorical force of his attack against what seemed to him an arid, detached notion of truth and God. Consider a parallel case involving Meister Eckhart, the fourteenth-century mystic and scholastic. If one reads only the following passage, it appears Eckhart has collapsed the distinction between God and soul, and that the existence of "God" depends on the soul's attention: "Know, then, that God is present at all times in good people and that there is a Something in the soul in which God dwells. There is also a Something by which the soul lives in God, but when the soul is intent on external things that Something dies, and therefore God dies."[17] But then Eckhart goes on to clarify that the death of God pertains to the point of view and concerns of the soul. And to ensure that he is not misunderstood, he adds: "Of course, God himself does not die. He continues very much alive to himself."[18] Like Eckhart, I suspect that Kierkegaard combined a belief in the radical transcendence of God and a robust view of the inward need of the soul to be in relation to God. For

---

[15] *Concluding Unscientific Postscript*, 178.

[16] Ibid., 116.

[17] R. B. Blakney, *Meister Eckhart: A Modern Translation* (New York: Harper and Row, 1941), 133.

[18] Ibid.

Kierkegaard, it is largely the transcendence of God that explains why our relationship with God must be a matter of faith and subjectivity, rather than sheer rational belief. "The paradox in Christian truth is invariably due to the fact that it is truth as it exists for God. The standard of measure and the end is super-human; and there is only one relationship possible: faith."[19]

Kierkegaard held that religious faith had to arise (or be undertaken) amid uncertainty and anxiety.

> Without risk there is no faith. Faith is precisely the contradiction between the infinite passion of the individual's inwardness and the objective uncertainty. If I am capable of grasping God objectively, I do not believe, but precisely because I cannot do this I must believe. If I wish to preserve myself in faith I must constantly be intent upon holding fast to the objective uncertainty, so as to remain out upon the deep, over seventy thousand fathoms of water, still preserving my faith.[20]

Kierkegaard disdained the traditional enterprise of attempting to prove or disprove God's existence. Moreover, he did not think authentic religious faith could be built solely on historical evidence. (Recall Lessing's ditch in Chapter 3.) Kierkegaard proposed that religious belief must be seen as a passionate venture. The presence of risk makes possible the good of faith. "There is nothing to be said ... except that it is the good which is attained by venturing everything absolutely."[21] The "objective" uncertainty of God's existence is the setting for a good leap of faith.[22]

Probably the most haunting philosophical meditation that Kierkegaard advanced involves the narrative in Genesis in which Abraham appears to be called by God to sacrifice his son Isaac. What should he do? In *Fear and Trembling*, we are left with the dilemma of

---

[19] *The Journals of Søren Kierkegaard*, 376. See C. Stephen Evans, "Is Kierkegaard an Irrationalist? Reason, Paradox, and Faith," *Religious Studies* 25 (1989), and L. P. Pojman, *The Logic of Subjectivity* (Tuscaloosa: University of Alabama Press, 1984). For a relevant, interesting account of religious faith in objectively true or false narratives, see Hugo Meynell, "Faith, Objectivity, and Historical Falsifiability," in *Language, Meaning and God*, ed. B. Davies (London: Geoffrey Chapman, 1987).

[20] *Concluding Unscientific Postscript*, 182.

[21] Ibid., 382.

[22] For a good analysis of the structure of Kierkegaard's treatment of faith, see R. M. Adam, "Kierkegaard's Arguments against Objective Reasoning in Religion," reprinted in Adam, *The Virtue of Faith* (Oxford: Oxford University Press, 1987).

balancing our universal ethical duty with the absolute, direct command of God.[23] Kierkegaard's meditation is perhaps the greatest literary engagement with the question of whether God's commands can make some action a duty, when that action would otherwise be a violation of human ethics. However one interprets Kierkegaard's ethics or his account of faith and knowledge, it is clear that he saw himself as asserting the vitality and value of the individual over and against an impersonal, system-centered ethos. "Each age has its own characteristic depravity. Ours is perhaps not pleasure or indulgence or sensuality, but rather a dissolute pantheistic contempt for the individual man."[24] As evidence of his success, consider Simone de Beauvoir's (1908–1986) recourse to Kierkegaard's defense of the individual against Hegelian speculation:

> I went on reading Hegel, and was now beginning to understand him rather better. His amplitude of detail dazzled me, and his System as a whole made me feel giddy. It was indeed tempting to abolish one's individual self and merge with Universal Being, to observe one's own life in the perspective of Historical Necessity. . . . But the least flutter of my heart gave such speculations the lie. Hate, anger, expectation of misery would assert themselves against all my efforts to by-pass them, and this "flight into the Universal" merely formed one further episode in my private development. I turned back to Kierkegaard, and began to read him with passionate interest. . . . Neither History, nor the Hegelian System could, any more than the Devil in person, upset the living certainty of "I am, I exist, here and now, I am myself."[25]

As we shall see later, this Kierkegaardian emphasis on the contingent, passionate individual is a key theme for Beauvoir and many of the other continental figures.

---

[23] As I believe Kierkegaard leaves us a dilemma that he does not resolve, I will not try to resolve matters here! Many philosophers have addressed Kierkegaard's *Fear and Trembling*. See, for example, work by R. M. Adam, C. Stephen Evans, Anthony Rudd, Philip Quinn, and Gordon Marino. For a recent, novel reading of Kierkegaard's dilemma, see James Rissler, "A Psychological Constraint on Obedience to God's Commands," *Religious Studies* 38 (2002). For an illuminating, comprehensive account of Kierkegaard's view of ethics, see Anthony Rudd, *Kierkegaard and the Limits of the Ethical* (Oxford: Clarendon, 1993).

[24] *Concluding Unscientific Postscript*, 317.

[25] Cited by Roger Poole, "The Unknown Kierkegaard: Twentieth Century Receptions," in *The Cambridge Companion to Kierkegaard*, ed. A. Hannay and G. Marino (Cambridge: Cambridge University Press, 1998), 55.

Genealogical Philosophy of Religion

Friedrich Nietzsche (1844–1900), born in Prussia, was a professor of philology at the University of Basel. His failing health compelled his resignation in 1879, and he spent his remaining years traveling, writing and, near the end, enduring a protracted illness. His works are among the most brilliant, fierce, and passionate in philosophy.

Nietzsche was adamantly opposed to the dispassionate inquiry of a philosophy that invokes timeless universals. In *Human, All Too Human*, Nietzsche underscored the concrete goal of philosophical inquiry in historical contexts.

> All philosophers have the common failing of starting out from man as he is now and thinking they can reach their goal through an analysis of him. They involuntarily think of "man" as an *aeterna veritas*, as something that remains constant in the midst of all flux, as a sure measure of things. Everything the philosopher has declared about man is, however, at bottom no more than a testimony as to the man of a *very limited* period of time. Lack of historical sense is the family failing of all philosophers.[26]

In his extended early essay *The Use and Abuse of History,* Nietzsche distinguished between different sorts of inquiry: the antiquarian, the monumental, and the critical. For Nietzsche, the role of history is not principally a search for objective truth but for that which is life-affirming. The study of the past for its own sake (antiquarianism), for moral guidance and inspiration (the monumental), or for an accurate, analytic disclosure of what occurred (the critical) may be good or bad depending upon whether it enhances or strengthens our lives today. Like Kierkegaard, Nietzsche shuns "objective truth" divorced from real life. Nietzsche had little patience for the evidentialism of Bentham and Mill and their mathematical, utilitarian formulas for maximizing happiness. Moreover, although at first he appreciated Schopenhauer's idealism and his resignation to seeing life as interminable suffering, he came to spurn pessimistic, pacific values. His famous feud with the composer Richard Wagner (1813–1883), with whom he had once shared a close friendship, arose partly due to Nietzsche's assertion of the goodness of life over and against Wagner's operatic display of the pessimism of Schopenhauer.

---

[26] *Human, All Too Human*, trans. R. J. Hollingdale (Cambridge: Cambridge University Press, 1986), 321.

Nietzsche adopted a view of truth that was not based on the correspondence of belief and facts, arguing that a true belief does not necessarily correspond to worldly facts. In the essay, "On Truth and Lie in
an Extra-Moral Sense," he writes:

> What then is truth? A mobile army of metaphors, metonyms, and
> anthropomorphisms – in short, a sum of human relations, which have
> been enhanced, transposed, embellished poetically and rhetorically, and
> which after long use seem firm, canonical, and obligatory to a people:
> truths are illusions about which one has forgotten that this is what they
> are; metaphors which are worn out and without sensuous power; coins
> which have lost their pictures and now matter only as metal, no longer
> as coins.[27]

For Nietzsche, truth is largely a matter of perspective. Nietzsche conceives of a true belief as that which is seen to be the case from a given perspective. The contrary position, and the one to which Nietzsche brings
all his rhetorical skills to destroy, is the inheritance of a form of Platonic
Christianity. "To speak of spirit and the good as Plato did meant standing truth on her head and denying *perspective* itself, the basic condition
of all life."[28] Nietzsche famously described Christianity as Platonism
for the people and traced the fault of European cultural decay to the
Platonic Christian claim to grasp eternal truths.[29]

> Henceforth, my dear philosophers, let us be on guard against the danger-
> ous old conceptual fiction that posited a "pure, will-less, painless, timeless
> knowing subject"; let us guard against the snares of such contradictory
> concepts as "pure reason," "absolute spirituality," "knowledge in itself":
> these always demand that we should think of an eye that is completely
> unthinkable, an eye turned in no particular direction, in which the ac-
> tive and interpreting forces, through which alone seeing becomes seeing
> *something*, are supposed to be lacking; these always demand of the eye
> an absurdity and a nonsense. There is *only* a perspective seeing, *only* a
> perspective "knowing"; and the *more* eyes, different eyes, we can use to
> observe one thing, the more complete will our "concept" of this thing,
> our "objectivity," be.[30]

---

[27] "Of Truth and Lie in an Extra-Moral Sense," in *The Portable Nietzsche*, trans.
W. Kaufman (New York: Viking Press, 1965), 46.

[28] *Beyond Good and Evil*, trans. R. J. Hollingdale (Middlesex: Penguin, 1973), 14.

[29] Ibid.

[30] *On the Genealogy of Morals*, trans. W. Kaufman and R. J. Hollingdale (New York:
Vintage Books, 1967), e.iii, 5.12.

In this passage, Nietzsche grants a partial foothold to "objectivity," but just barely.[31]

In Nietzsche's view, we are limited to our human perspective, one that privileges sensory experience. "All credibility, all good conscience, all evidence of truth comes only from the senses."[32] Nietzsche links his opposition to "a higher being with 'absolute knowledge'" with his opposition to the traditional metaphysical inquiry into the "true reality" – or the way things are in themselves.

> The intellect cannot criticize itself, simply because it cannot be compared with other species of intellect and because its capacity to know would be revealed only in the presence of "true reality," i.e., because in order to criticize the intellect we should have to be a higher being with "absolute

---

[31] Indeed, it is difficult (in my view) to completely abandon recourse to a realist notion of truth, according to which truth is independent of (or not dependent on) human perspectives. When Nietzsche writes, "There is only perspective seeing," isn't he committed to the realist claim that *there are such things as perspectives*, and that *the existence of such perspectives is not itself dependent on Nietzsche's realization that there are perspectives*? The problem here may be illustrated by the contemporary philosopher Hilary Putnam's claim that, from a God's-eye point of view, there are no truths, to which he adds the paradoxical caveat that we must resist making such a claim. Once you assert that there are no truths from a God's-eye point of view, critics will want to know about your own point of view, asking whether your assertion is true exclusively from *your* perspective and not from others.

There are at least two replies to consider. The first would be to weaken the Nietzschean claim to one about *justification* or *evidence* as opposed to truth. One may well hold that, for any person's belief that something is true (*there is a God* or *there is no God*), her supporting evidence or justification will always come from her point of view. (This claim may seem obviously true but in Chapter 9 we consider alternative accounts of justification.) In passing, I note that a realist view of truth with a perspective-based (or *perspectival*) view of evidence can fit into Leibniz's concept of perceptual fecundity. See Christia Mercer, *Leibniz's Metaphysics: Its Origin and Development* (Cambridge: Cambridge University Press, 2002), 218–219. Alternatively, one may appeal to an idealist argument to oppose a realist view of "objective truth." Arguably, all *our* talk of truth will be from our perspectives. An argument can be mustered here to the effect that any talk of truth *beyond our perspective* is absurd, as we shall always be working from within a human perspective. This form of argument is closely related to idealist arguments about the mind dependency of the world. See A. C. Ewing, *Idealism: A Critical Study* (London: Methuen, 1933). For reasons Ewing identifies, I find the case against realism here unpersuasive. For further realist arguments, see Roger Trigg, *Reality at Risk: A Defense of Realism in Philosophy and the Sciences*, 2nd ed. (London: Harvester Wheatsheaf, 1989), and *Rationality and Science* (Oxford: Blackwell, 1993).

[32] *Beyond Good and Evil*, 82.

knowledge." This presupposes that, distinct from every perspective kind of outlook or sensual-spiritual appropriation, something exists, an "in-itself." – But the psychological derivation of the belief in things forbids us to speak of "things-in-themselves."[33]

This link between realism and theism has received some positive support of late. Putnam has proposed that, "The whole content of realism lies in the claim that it makes sense to talk of a God's eye point of view."[34] If one assumes traditional theism, God sees and knows the cosmos as it is. A God's-eye point of view would be the ideal case of knowledge *and* thus (if one assumes realism) of truth. Denying such a case of ideal knowledge and truth seems to go hand in hand with opposing traditional theism.

Because Nietzsche was against formalizing a system of philosophy, his influence in philosophy of religion is often seen in terms of a provocation and subterfuge rather than as spearheading a new systematic account of religion.[35] He is widely recognized for his critique of Christianity as a religion rooted in resentment and an impotent hatred of the strong. He held that Christianity's ethic of compassion is motivated by the vengeful effort of the weak as they try to bind the strong. Nietzsche vied for the reversal of Christian values, which he saw principally in terms of submissiveness, servility, and self-effacement, and a sacrifice of the intellect to faith. Nietzsche's own values, or rather, value, was stated succinctly: "There is nothing to life that has value, except the degree of power."[36] For Nietzsche, power may be understood in terms of health, vitality, and the affirmation of the body and eros. In his view, Christianity opposes all of these. "God is a conjecture: but who could drink all the bitterness of this conjecture without dying?"[37] Nietzsche is

---

[33] *The Will to Power*, trans. W. Kaufman and R. J. Hollingdale (New York: Vintage Books, 1968), 263.

[34] *Realism with a Human Face* (Cambridge, Mass.: Harvard University Press, 1990), 23. See also M. Jay, *Downcast Eyes* (Berkeley: University of California Press, 1993).

[35] So, for example, Merold Westphal has used Nietzsche's critique of Christianity as a means of refining Christian faith; see his *Suspicion and Faith* (New York: Fordham University, 1998). I believe one of the best critical replies to Nietzsche is Max Scheler's *Ressentiment*, ed. L. A. Coser and trans. W. W. Holdheim (New York: Schocken Books, 1976). In this book, Scheler (1874–1928) produces a subtle moral psychology that directly bears on religious practice.

[36] *The Will to Power*, 37.

[37] *Thus Spake Zarathustra*, in *The Philosophy of Nietzsche*, ed. W. H. Wright (New York: Modern Library, 1927), 91.

also known for his proclamation that, from a cultural and intellectual point of view, the concept of God is moribund.

> Have you not heard of that madman who lit a lantern in the bright morning hours, ran to the market place, and cried incessantly: "I seek God! I seek God!... Whither is God?" he cried; I will tell you. *We have killed him* – you and I. All of us are his murderers. But how did we do this?... Who gave us the sponge to wipe away the entire horizon?... God is dead. God remains dead. And we have killed him.... There has never been a greater deed; and whoever is born after us – for the sake of this deed he will belong to a higher history than all history hitherto.[38]

Nietzsche is not exact in his recommendation for God's replacement; his work on the will, Dionysian passion, and the role of art and tragedy continues to exercise scholars. In *Redeeming Nietzsche: On the Piety of Unbelief*, Giles Fraser puts forward the following hypothesis:

> Nietzsche approaches "the question of God" with the instincts of his Lutheran Pietistic upbringing.... from this perspective the "first question" of theology is not "Does God exist?" but rather something like "how are we saved?" Indeed... Nietzsche is obsessed with the question of salvation and much of his work is driven by an attempt to expose the pathologies of Christian soteriology and re-invent a very different soteriological scheme which, unlike its Christian parent, leads to genuine joy.[39]

This stress on genuine joy seems plausible.[40]

Nietzsche might be considered a friend of naturalism, given his antagonism to supernaturalist Christianity. But his view of truth and perspectives does not generate a purely realistic, naturalistic view of science. "We have arranged for ourselves a world in which we can live – by positing bodies, lines, planes, causes and effects, motion and rest, form and content; without these articles of faith nobody now could endure life. But that does not prove them. Life is no argument. The conditions of life might include error."[41] I believe Nietzsche is an important

---

[38] *The Gay Science*, trans. W. Kaufman (New York: Random House, 1974), sec. 125.

[39] *Redeeming Nietzsche: On the Piety of Unbelief* (London: Routledge, 2002).

[40] One should also register here that both Nietzsche and Kierkegaard wrote with humor, as well as sober prose. Their imagery is sometimes fantastic, for example, "We are not thinking frogs, nor objectifying and registering machines with their innards removed" (Nietzsche, *The Gay Science*, sec. 3).

[41] *Beyond Good and Evil*, 70.

inspiration to those who seek to locate the historical grounding and causes of our fallible ideals, whether these are natural or supernatural. Along with Freud and Feuerbach, he questions the motives that *really* lie behind our endeavors. To borrow a term from Barry Stroud, which I used in Chapter 6, Nietzsche advances an " 'unmasking' explanation" of faith. Because of Nietzsche's strategy of unmasking, I see him as a proponent of a *genealogical* philosophy of religion, one that is focused on the psychology that shapes our philosophical and religious convictions. Nietzsche's work is an especially rich source for exploring moral psychology, an important focus of recent religious and secular ethics. Witness this succinct way in which self-deception is described: " 'I have done that,' says memory. 'I cannot have done that' – says my pride, and remains adamant. At last, memory yields."[42]

Regrettably, this chapter must include some mention of Nazism (Heidegger was a member of the Nazi Party). Adolf Hitler professed approval of Nietzsche's philosophy, and some have worried whether Nietzsche's exaltation of the strong and his critique of pity and compassion made some contribution to Nazi ideology. But Nietzsche clearly and firmly opposed tyrannical state power.[43] He explicitly repudiated German imperialism, lamenting the effect of the German victory in the Franco-Prussian War. In 1888 he wrote: "Nowadays the Germans are bored with intellect, the Germans mistrust intellect, politics devours all seriousness for really intellectual things – *Deutschland, Deutschland, Deutschland über alles* was, I fear, the end of German philosophy."[44]

Heidegger, Sartre, Camus, Beauvoir

These four continental philosophers are typically referred to as "phenomenologists," a term derived from the Greek word *phainomenon* (appearance) and *logos* (knowledge of). Phenomenology is focused on the study of appearances or what is presented to us in experience. Edmund Husserl (1859–1938) spearheaded early phenomenology, but because philosophy of religion was not a major concern in his published writing, I do not address him here. I will also bracket further use of

---

[42] Ibid., 72.

[43] See the chapter "The New Idol" in *Thus Spake Zarathustra*.

[44] Cited by Hollingdale in the commentary, *Beyond Good and Evil*, 233. There is a good treatment of both Nietzsche and Wagner on such matters in B. Magee, *The Tristan Chord* (New York: Henry Holt, 2000), chap. 17 and the appendix.

terminology like "phenomenology." One can debate the extent to which Heidegger was a phenomenologist, but the debate over such labels is distracting in the current context.

Martin Heidegger (1884–1976) gained tremendous prominence before the Second World War and afterward, although more recently there have been grave misgivings over his work because of his membership, however brief, in the Nazi Party.[45] His largest, most sustained, and influential work, *Being and Time* (1927), records an analysis of humanity in our finitude and mortality. Heidegger links this analysis to an overriding concern with the nature and reality of being. We humans are the ones who raise the question, What is being? and so an investigation into being is linked to an investigation of human life.

For Heidegger, Western philosophy – including philosophy of religion – has faltered because of its focus on objects: *beings* as opposed to *being*. Heidegger calls us to a seemingly more primordial task: we must reorient our philosophy toward being and reclaim human agency and authenticity in light of the inevitability of death. Heidegger led many philosophers of religion to rethink the concept of God as *a* being and encouraged a theological focus on the value of being and authenticity. Despite the *massive* gap between Heidegger's thought and traditional Thomistic philosophy, there was one point at which theologians were receptive to some of Heidegger's philosophy: Aquinas also saw God as *Being*, rather than a concrete, circumscribable entity. Heidegger's call to take *being* seriously resonated with several leading Roman Catholic theologians, especially Karl Rahner (1904–1984). Theologians from many traditions – including Rudolf Bultmann (1884–1976), Paul Tillich (1886–1965), and John Macquarrie (b. 1919) – were influenced or engaged by Heidegger's thought.[46]

Two of Heidegger's early essays, "Phenomenology and Theology" and "The Onto-Theo-Logical Constitution of Metaphysics," have been republished recently. "Onto-theological" refers to the conception of God as an entity; both essays underscore Heidegger's repudiation of

---

[45] See Victor Farias, *Heidegger and Nazism*, ed. J. Margolis and T. Rockmore, trans. P. Burrell et al. (Philadelphia: Temple University Press, 1987), and Hugo Ott, *Martin Heidegger: A Political Life* (New York: Basic Books, 1993). Heidegger supported the Nazi cause for ten months when he served in the rectorship of the University of Freiburg.

[46] For a theological engagement with Heidegger, see John Caputo's two books: *The Mystical Element in Heidegger's Thought* (Athens: Ohio University Press, 1977) and *Heidegger and Aquinas* (New York: Fordham University Press, 1982).

a theistic God as one entity or being among others.[47] John Caputo summarizes the core message of these two essays: "If Kant sought to put an end to ontotheological speculation and to replace it with ethics, Heidegger wanted to open the door, not to a new round of speculation, to be sure, but to a new meditation upon God after, or at the limits of, onto-theo-logic, a God who would emerge from a meditative experience of the upsurge of Being as emergence into unconcealment."[48] Heidegger likened the search for truth in religion to the pursuit of (or a receptivity to) a *revealing* or *disclosing*, as opposed to the verification or falsification of propositions. Heidegger saw himself as rediscovering an ancient notion of truth, which, in Greek (*aletheia*), meant "unhiddenness" or "unconcealment." The result, which surfaced in his mature, later thought, was a view of philosophy that was more meditative or contemplative than argumentative. For Heidegger, this meant the recovery of a form of philosophy more primordial than Plato's. In Plato, one begins to see truth as "correctness" (in Greek, *orthotes*) rather than as "unconcealedness." Heidegger held that Plato's concern for the correctness of belief, exemplified in his arguments with the giants and gods (materialists and nonmaterialists) of his day, resulted in a departure from philosophy's original vocation.[49]

Heidegger's renunciation of the dominant concern for logical analysis and evidence in propositions is apparent in much of his work, especially in his "Letter on Humanism":

> Being, as the element of thinking, is abandoned by the technical interpretation of thinking. "Logic," beginning with the Sophists and Plato, sanctions this explanation. Thinking it is judged by a standard that does not measure up to it. Such judgment may be compared to the procedure of trying to evaluate the nature and powers of a fish by seeing how long it can live on dry land. For a long time now, all too long, thinking has been

---

[47] The term "onto-theology" comes from Kant, *Critique of Pure Reason*, A632 = B660. Kant used the term for the philosophical task of arguing for the existence of God by means of concepts rather than experience. Various uses of the term "onto-theology" are described by Merold Westphal in his *Overcoming Onto-theology* (New York: Fordham, 2001). Westphal writes: "Onto-theology, as Heidegger understands it, is the project of rendering the whole of being intelligible to human understanding. Since it has no room for that which overflows comprehension, it distorts our understanding of God (as well as of ourselves and the world of nature)" (265).

[48] Caputo, *The Religious* (Oxford: Blackwell, 2002), 4.

[49] See John Caputo's "Aletheia and the Myth of Being," in *Demythologizing Heidegger* (Bloomington: Indiana University Press, 1993).

stranded on dry land. . . . Such names as "logic," "ethics," and "physics" begin to flourish only when original thinking has come to an end. During the time of their greatness the Greeks thought without such headings. They did not even call thinking "philosophy." Thinking comes to an end when it slips out of its element.[50]

Proper philosophy receives its inspiration in a kind of poetic orientation toward being.[51]

Sketching Heidegger's more constructive picture of philosophy is difficult. He bases his case in favor of the contemplation of being, in part, on his critique of traditional metaphysics. He believes that Western philosophy as a whole is destined for *nihilism*, a denial of binding norms.[52] What if Heidegger was wrong regarding the inevitability of nihilism but right in his conviction that we should live and think in orientation to being? In other words, can Heidegger's work be seen as an additional contribution to, for example, a successful form of naturalism or idealism? One reason why followers of Heidegger would resist such a synthesis is the enormous amount of damage done by traditional, Western metaphysics. In Heidegger's view, it caused our forgetfulness of being as well as our objectification of the world. Moreover, modern projects like Descartes' had hideously and unsuccessfully set up the human inquirer as a detached, disinterested subject. Rather, according to Heidegger, we *are* beings in the world and it is superfluous for the philosopher to attempt to justify a belief in our existence. Like Kierkegaard and Nietzsche, Heidegger laments the legacy of an epistemology that seems to privilege a spectator's approach to the world. To give Heidegger the last word, and also to offer a further sample of his style of writing, consider this plea at the conclusion of an essay on pre-Platonic philosophy. Note the way Heidegger frames his preferred

---

[50] "Letter on Humanism," in *Basic Writings*, ed. D. Krell (London: Routledge, 1993), 195.

[51] See "Why Poets?" in *Martin Heidegger: Off the Beaten Track*, ed. and trans. J. Young and K. Haynes (Cambridge: Cambridge University Press, 2002). Heidegger's thoroughgoing atheism is the central theme of L. P. Hemming, *Heidegger's Atheism* (Notre Dame: University of Notre Dame Press, 2002). For a fascinating look at how Heidegger has been rethought over the years, see Caputo, *Demythologizing Heidegger*. See also D. O. Dahlstrom, *Heidegger's Concept of Truth* (Cambridge: Cambridge University Press, 2001), especially 5.5.

[52] See "Nietzsche's Word: 'God is Dead,'" in Young and Haynes, *Martin Heidegger: Off the Beaten Track*.

approach to being over against a rapacious philosophy of domination. His case for a philosophy (or poetry) of being is partly ethical.

> Man is about to hurl himself upon the entire earth and its atmosphere, to arrogate to himself the hidden working of nature in the form of energy, and to subordinate the course of history to the plans and orderings of a world government. This same defiant man is incapable of saying simply what *is*; of saying *what* this is, that a thing *is*.
>
> The totality of beings is the single object of a singular will to conquer. The simplicity of being is buried under a singular oblivion.
>
> What mortal can fathom the abyss of this confusion? In the face of this abyss one can try to shut one's eyes. One can erect one illusion after another. The abyss does not retreat.
>
> Theories of nature, doctrines about history, do not remove the confusion. They further confuse things until they are unrecognizable, since they themselves are nourished by the confusion which surrounds the difference between beings and being.
>
> Is there any rescue? It comes first and only when the danger *is*. The danger *is* when being itself reaches its extremity and when the oblivion which issues from being itself turns about.
>
> But what being, in its essence, *needs to use* [*braucht*] the essence of man? What if the essence of man rests in thinking the truth of being?
>
> Then thinking must poeticize on the enigma of being. It brings the dawn of thought into proximity to that which is to be thought.[53]

Philosophy, for the later Hiedegger, has a therapeutic or emancipating role in realigning us toward being.[54]

---

[53] Ibid., 280–281.

[54] Two other resources should be noted for further exploration of Heidegger on religion. Scholarship is divided on how to interpret both, and I will simply cite these without comment. The first is an interview published after his death in "Only a God Can Save Us: The Spiegel Interview," *Précis* 1966, reprinted in *Heidegger: The Man and the Thinker*, ed. T. Sheehan (Chicago: Precedent Publisher, 1981), 57, in which Heidegger says: "Philosophy will not be able to effect any direct transformation of the present state of the world. This is true not only of philosophy but of any simply human contemplation and striving. Only a god can save us now. We can only through thinking and writing prepare to be prepared for the manifestation of God, or for the absence of God as things go downhill all the way." The meaning of this statement is hotly debated. Another resource is Heidegger's extensive discussion of God in the *Beitrage*, published in English as *Contributions to Philosophy (From Ewing)*, trans. P. Emad and K. May (Bloomington: Indiana University Press, 1999). See the section "The Last God." The *Beitrage* is a book he was working on in the mid-1930s and is considered his second major work (along with *Being and Time*). It was only published in Germany in 1989.

The three remaining continental thinkers in this section were influenced by Heidegger. All three worked out their philosophy from an explicit (but not always enthusiastic) secular atheism. The nonexistence of God was, for them, philosophically and morally important. Jean Paul Sartre (1905–1980) offers this conclusion in his chief philosophical work, *Being and Nothingness*: "The passion of man is the reverse of that of Christ, for man loses himself as man in order that God may be born. But the idea of God is contradictory and we lose ourselves in vain. Man is a useless passion."[55] Sartre and Albert Camus (1913–1960) hold that theism involves an anthropomorphic projection (much like Feuerbach contended), and the failure of this projection generates a sense of the absurdity of life. "Man stands face to face with the irrational," writes Camus. "He feels within him his longing for happiness and reason. The absurd is born of this confrontation between human need and the unreasonable silence of the world."[56] Sartre, Camus, and Simone de Beauvoir each held that the absence of God places upon us a profound responsibility to shape our values. In *The Rebel*, Camus writes: "When the throne of God is overturned, the rebel realizes that it is now his own responsibility to create the justice, order, and unity that he sought in vain within his own condition, and in this way to justify the fall of God. Then begins the desperate effort to create, at the price of crime and murder if necessary, the dominion of man. This will not come about without terrible consequences, of which we are so far only aware of a few."[57]

Each of these thinkers articulated a cosmos – philosophically and artistically – that was radically contingent. In the novel *Nausea*, Sartre offers a telling portrait of life's absurd contingency.

> And without formulating anything clearly, I understood that I had found that key to Existence, the key to my Nausea, to my own life. In fact, all that I was able to grasp afterwards comes down to this fundamental absurdity. . . . The world of explanations and reasons is not that of existence. . . . The essential thing is contingency. I mean that, by definition, existence is not a necessity. To exist is simply *to be there*; what exists

---

Scholarship on Heidegger continues to evolve, and much of the current work will need reassessment once all the Heidegger archives are finally opened and accessible.

[55] *Being and Nothingness*, trans. M. E. Barner (New York: Philosophical Library, 1956), 784.

[56] *Myth of the Sisyphus*, trans. J. O'Brien (New York: Vintage, 1955), 34.

[57] *The Rebel*, trans. H. Read (New York: Vintage, 1956), 25.

appears, lets itself be *encountered*, but you can never *deduce* it. There are people, I believe, who have understood that. Only they have tried to overcome this contingency by inventing a necessary causal being. But no necessary being can explain existence: contingency is not an illusion, an appearance which can be dissipated; it is absolute, and consequently perfect gratuitousness. Everything is gratuitous, that park, this town, and myself. When you realize that, it turns your stomach over and everything starts floating about.[58]

This felt contingency of life is central to Sartre's (and Camus' and Beauvoir's) *existentialism*. Existentialism was summarized by Sartre in the phrase "existence precedes essence." The Platonist privileges essences (forms, ideals, goods), whereas the existentialist affirms existences and leaves to human freedom the task of defining values.

Another significant contribution to philosophy of religion comes especially from Sartre and Beauvoir. Both wrote on the ways in which the gaze or regard of another person can threaten one's subjectivity. Sartre specifically saw the roots of our feeling of guilt in another's look – which is why in his play, *No Exit*, he proclaims, "Hell is other people."[59] In *Being and Nothingness* Sartre writes:

> It is before the Other that I am *guilty*. I am guilty first when beneath the Other's look I experience my alienation and my nakedness as a fall from grace which I must assume. This is the meaning of the famous line from Scripture: "They knew that they were naked"... and as an instrument, and I cause him to experience that same alienation which he must now assume. Thus original sin is my upsurge in a world where there are others; and whatever may be my further relations with others, these relations will be only variations on the original theme of my guilt.[60]

This passage bears on theistic accounts of God's omniscience. Does the conception of God as an ideal observer threaten one's subjectivity? Beauvoir writes on how an appeal to "the eye of God" can serve to humiliate men and subdue women.[61] There is a fatalistic pessimism, I believe, in Sartre's and Beauvoir's concept of personal relations and love. Sartre contends that the ability to understand or conceive of another person cognitively is always trumped by the person's subjective freedom. If

---

[58] *Nausea*, trans. L. Alexander (Norfolk: New Directions, 1949), 393.

[59] *No Exit* (New York: Vintage International, 1989).

[60] *Being and Nothingness*, 531.

[61] *The Second Sex*, trans. H. M. Parshley (New York: Alfred A. Knopf, 1971), 621–622.

you think you have captured another person's identity, you have transformed them into a mere object. And this problem of knowing another person seems to block our full interaction with others, for good or for ill.

> The Other escapes me. I should like to act upon his freedom, to appropriate it, or at least, to make the Other's freedom recognize my freedom. But this freedom is death; it is no longer absolutely *in the world* in which I encounter the Other-as-object, for his characteristic is to be transcendent to the world. To be sure, I can *grasp* the Other, grab hold of him, knock him down.... But everything happens as if I wished to get hold of a man who runs away and leaves only his coat in my hands. It is the coat, it is the outer shell which I possess.... I can make the Other beg for mercy or ask my pardon, but I shall always be ignorant of what this submission means for and in the Other's freedom.[62]

Sartre does, however, hint that his analysis of the other's gaze may break down under unusual, "radical" circumstances. After setting up his dark view of the gaze of others, Sartre adds this footnote: "These considerations do not exclude the possibility of an ethics of deliverance and salvation. But this can be achieved only after a radical conversion which we can not discuss here."[63] (Fortunately some of the philosophers discussed in the next section do present an alternative framework in which to understand love and personal encounters.)[64]

Finally, it is important to recognize Beauvoir's "unmasking" of sexism. In *The Second Sex*, Beauvoir exposes and criticizes sexism across cultures, religious and secular, demonstrating the many ways women have been oppressed. She shows the ways in which men's (and sometimes women's) appeal to reason, impartiality, and evidence can mask an oppressive political and psychological agenda. Beauvoir argues for the development of a philosophy of women by women. "The most sympathetic of men never fully comprehend woman's concrete situation.... We know the feminine world more intimately than do the men because we have our roots in it, we grasp more immediately than do men what it means to a human being to be feminine and we are more concerned

---

[62] Ibid., 393. For Beauvoir's analysis of intersubjectivity, see her novel *She Came to Stay*, published in 1943, the same year as *Being and Nothingness*. Some scholars speculate that Beauvoir developed an account of the objectifying gaze and intersubjectivity prior to Sartre.

[63] *Being and Nothingness*, 534.

[64] See Richard Creel, "Atheism and Freedom: A Response to Sartre and Baier," *Religious Studies* 25 (1989).

with such knowledge."[65] Because the primary voice in philosophy, religion, and the like has been male, women "have no past, no history, no religion of their own." Beauvoir does not simply argue for the political or philosophical equality of men and women.

> People have tirelessly sought to prove that woman is superior, inferior, or equal to man. Some say that, having been created after Adam, she is evidently a secondary being; others say on the contrary that Adam was only a rough draft and that God succeeded in producing the human being in perfection when He created Eve. Woman's brain is smaller; yes, but it is relatively larger. Christ was made a man; yes, but perhaps for his greater humility. Each argument at once suggests its opposite, and both are often fallacious. If we are to gain understanding, we must get out of these ruts; we must discard the vague notions of superiority, inferiority, equality which have hitherto corrupted every discussion of the subject and start afresh.[66]

Contemporary feminist philosophy of religion (to be discussed later) may be seen as part of this fresh start, exposing past harms and developing projects that speak from and to women.

Weil, Buber, Levinas, Marcel

These four continental thinkers were contemporaries of the four philosophers just discussed, though for the most part they were not as well known at the outset. They share with Heidegger and the others a concern for the philosophical exploration of experience and emotions. Their philosophies are driven by a central concern for values. Unlike the first group, each of these philosophers advanced a more constructive view of (at least some aspects of) religious life. Buber and Levinas were Jews who contributed to Judaism; Marcel was a Roman Catholic, and Weil was a Jew deeply drawn to Catholic Christianity but who deliberately, as a matter of conscience, refused baptism.

Simone Weil (1909–1943) studied philosophy in Paris (she was one of the first women to attend Ecole Normale) and went on to spend her life in political activism and writing. In 1933 she participated in the March of Miners in France over the loss of wages and employment. In solidarity with workers, she took several factory jobs. During the

---

[65] *The Second Sex*, xxvi–xxviii.
[66] Ibid., xxvii.

Spanish Civil War she was part of an anarchist-syndicalist group. In the early part of World War II she worked for the French Resistance, stationed in England (the Resistance did not allow her to parachute into occupied France, as she desired to do.)[67] She was insistent upon an ethic of compassionate solidarity with the oppressed. She died after a hunger strike that she carried out in an act of solidarity with the French who were suffering under German occupation.

Weil's philosophy of religion overlapped with her political philosophy. In both, she opposed the brutal, dehumanizing use of power. In *Gravity and Grace,* she counsels disciplined, humane service, and a zealous restraint of the use of power. She criticized the historical exultation of political power in Western civilization, referring to the Roman Empire as the "great beast."[68] In place of a philosophy and politics of centralized power, Weil argued the vital importance of a humane, "rooted" concept of individual identity in a just community. In *The Need for Roots* she writes:

> To be rooted is perhaps the most important and least recognized need of the human soul. It is one of the hardest to define. A human being has roots by virtue of his real, active and natural participation in the life of a community which preserves in living shape certain particular treasures of the past and certain particular expectations for the future. This participation is a natural one, in the sense that it is automatically brought about by place, conditions of birth, profession and social surroundings. Every human being needs to have multiple roots. It is necessary for him to draw well nigh the whole of his moral, intellectual and spiritual life by way of the environment of which he forms a natural part.[69]

Her ethics and philosophy of religion emphasized tolerance, collaboration, and especially the limited good of self-interest.

Weil's emphasis on restraint and limit gave rise to an almost mystical view of evidence. She writes: "Limitation is the evidence that God loves us."[70] By her lights, through the renunciation of power and self-will one

---

[67] See Weil, "Spiritual Autobiography," in *The Simone Weil Reader,* ed. G. A. Panichas (New York: D. McKay, 1977).

[68] See Weil, *Oppression and Liberty* (London: Ark Paperbacks, 1988). For an appreciative interpretation of her work, see Peter Winch, *Simone Weil: The Just Balance* (Cambridge: Cambridge University Press, 1989).

[69] S. Weil, *The Need for Roots,* trans. A. F. Wills (London: Routledge, 1997), 41.

[70] Simone Weil, *Gravity and Grave,* trans. A. Wills (New York: Octagon Books, 1979), 158.

may endure a void, but this can make room for grace. She contrasts her position with that of Thucydides:

> [Thucydides writes:] "Tradition teaches us in regard to the gods, and experience shows us, as regards men, that by a necessity of nature, every being invariably exercises all the power of which it is capable." ... Like a gas, the soul tends to fill the entire space which is given it. A gas which contracted, leaving a vacuum, this would be contrary to the law of entropy. It is not so with the God of the Christians. He is a supernatural God....
>
> Not to exercise all the power at one's disposal is to endure the void. This is contrary to all the laws of nature. Grace alone can do it.
>
> Grace fills empty spaces, but it can only enter where there is a void to receive it, and it is grace itself which makes this void.[71]

In addition to these themes, Weil adhered to a view of God's beauty that is at the core of Christian Platonism. Weil writes: "In everything which gives us the pure authentic feeling of beauty there is really the presence of God. There is, as it were, an incarnation of God in the world, and it is indicated by beauty.... The beautiful is the experimental proof that the incarnation is possible."[72] Weil's theological aesthetics is more of an experiential testimony than the fruit of a sequential philosophical argument.[73]

---

[71] Ibid., 55.

[72] Ibid., 207.

[73] Very briefly, I suggest that there is a coherent way to articulate her position philosophically. Given classical Platonic theism, according to which God is beautiful and the Creator of the cosmos, any beauty in the cosmos may be seen as participating in the life of God. Such "participation" may be considered in terms of volition, knowledge, and desire or pleasure. Imagine God creates a cosmos in which there is some beauty (e.g., a beautiful friendship), and God wills this friendship to flourish and takes pleasure in it. The beautiful friendship would not thereby be an incarnation (God entering into the flesh), but it would be an instance of God's affective delight in the terrestrial world. The term "participation" is broad and has had different philosophical uses. If we follow a broadly Platonic usage, the beautiful friendship may be said to *participate* in the life of God insofar as God is an essential reality that (in part) forms or makes possible the friendship. Given a strong view of God's conservation of the cosmos (*creatio continua*), the beautiful friendship may be said to reflect God's presence. More would have to be said to fill out this picture; I only suggest that more *can* be said fruitfully to fill out Weil's outlook. As for her reference to "experimental proof," I think that would have to be part of an overall argument from religious experience (e.g., a vindication of the claim that one may see in Dante and Beatrice's relationship a reflection of God's love).

Martin Buber (1878–1965), highlighted the difference between personal and impersonal relations, what may be called I-You (or I-Thou) and I-it relations. Although his work was not crafted as a reply to Sartre's and Beauvoir's analysis of intersubjectivity, it may fruitfully be seen as a radical alternative to such an account of the threat of *the gaze*. His ethic is grounded on a keen awareness of the essential subjectivity of persons. To destroy or eclipse a person's subjectivity is to destroy or eclipse the person herself. To treat someone as a person is to be open to a subject that resists strict categorization. Buber thought of God as an "Absolute Person," but Buber was not party to traditional metaphysics and the classical theistic view of God. In his book, *I-Thou*, he wrote about how God may be addressed (in prayer, for example) but not described. As in Weil, there is an experiential dimension to his philosophy of religion. "My philosophy . . . does not serve a series of repeated propositions . . . but an experienced, perceived attitude that it has been established to make communicable."[74]

Although Buber's philosophy was informed by Kant, Kierkegaard, Nietzsche, and Dostoyevsky, Hasidism and the broader Jewish tradition provided a key influence and setting for Buber's work.[75] Buber's view of subjectivity prevented him from being a strict traditionalist, however. For example, his emphasis on the authentic encounter between the self and God in tradition fell short of what Franz Rosensweig (1886–1929) saw as affirming the universality of divine law. Buber resisted seeing religious faith as "faith in a proposition" rather than trust.[76] In *The Two Types of Faith*, Buber writes: "The Torah of God is understood as God's

[74] Buber in *The Philosophy of Martin Buber*, ed. P. A Friedman and M. S Friedman (LaSalle: Open Court, 1967), 690. *I and Thou*, trans. R. G. Smith, 2nd ed. (New York: Charles Scribner's Sons, 1958), is probably Buber's most famous work, but see also *Between Man and Man*, trans. R. Smith (London: K. Paul, 1947); *Eclipse of God* (New York: Harper, 1957); and *Pointing the Way* (Buffalo, N.Y.: Prometheus Books, 1990). Maurice Friedman has written extensively on Buber, including a three-volume study outlining Buber's early, middle, and later years (published by E. P. Dutton, 1981–1983). As noted earlier, one might find in Buber a reply to Sartre's and Beauvoir's view of *the gaze* of other persons. Another place to look is *God Still Matters* by Herbert McCabe, ed. B. Davies (London: Continuum, 2002).

[75] For a fuller treatment of the Jewish background, see Oliver Leaman, "Jewish Existentialism: Rosenzweig, Buber, and Soloveitchik," in *History of Jewish Philosophy*, ed. D. H. Frank and O. Leaman (London: Routledge, 1997).

[76] Cited in Maurice Friedman, *Martin Buber: The Life of Dialogue*, 4th ed. (London: Routledge, 2002), 315.

instruction in His way and therefore not as a separate *Objectivum*. It includes laws, and laws are indeed its most vigorous objectivizations, but the Torah itself is essentially not law. A vestige of the actual speaking always adheres to the commanding word, the directing voice is always present or at least its sound is heard fading away."[77] Buber's allegiance is to the voice and personal disclosure as opposed to a codified, philosophical theology.

Emmanuel Levinas (1905–1995) was a professor of philosophy in Paris who, like Buber, was a Jewish philosopher who privileged ethics over the analytic and positivist pursuit of scientific truth (to be discussed in the next chapter). Much of his work may be read as a response to the Holocaust. He advanced a radical critique of totalitarian regimes and egocentric ethics. His philosophical study of face-to-face encounters is a fascinating continuation of Buber's work. Levinas explains the experience of facing another person in the following interview:

> *Interviewer*: In the face of the Other you say there is an "elevation," a "height." The Other is higher than I am. What do you mean by that?
>
> *E. L.*: The first word of the face is the "Thou shalt not Kill." It is an order. [Again the other is given a God-like attribute.] There is a commandment in the appearance of the face, as if a master spoke to me. However, at the same time, the face of the Other is destitute; it is the poor for whom I can do all and to whom I owe all. And me, whoever I may be, but as a "first person," I am he who finds the resources to respond to the call.
>
> *Interviewer*: One is tempted to say to you: yes, in certain cases. But in other cases, to the contrary, the encounter with the Other occurs in the mode of violence, hate and disdain.
>
> *E. L.*: To be sure. But I think that whatever the motivation which explains this inversion, the analysis of the face such as I have just made, with the master of the Other and his poverty, with my submission and my wealth, is primary. It is the presupposed in all human relationships. If it were not that, we would not even say, before an open door, "after you, sir!" It is an original "After you, sir!" that I have tried to describe.[78]

---

[77] Ibid., 315.

[78] Cited by H. Putnam, "Levinas and Judaism," in *The Cambridge Companion to Levinas*, ed. S. Critchley (Cambridge: Cambridge University Press, 2002), 45.

For Levinas, it is in the face-to-face encounter that one may realize one's responsibility for and obligation to another person. Self-interest becomes subordinate to a concern for the other. His philosophy of religion does not involve Buber's experience of God as a "you" who is present. Obedience to God is thoroughly a matter of just, respectful practices. The collection, *Of God Who Comes to Mind*, elucidates some of Levinas's thought on God, though *Totality and Infinity* is probably his most influential work.[79]

The work of Buber and Levinas illustrates the idea that philosophy may be carried out either inside or outside of the same religious tradition. I suggest Buber is plausibly read as a Jewish philosopher, committed to philosophically articulating, defending, and interpreting aspects of Judaism in light of contemporary experience. Levinas, a practicing Jew, drew on talmudic and biblical sources yet did not see himself as a Jewish philosopher: "I am not a Jewish thinker. I am just a thinker."[80]

Gabriel Marcel (1889–1973) shares with Buber and Levinas an overriding sense of the supreme value of human persons, as well as an ethic of openness and availability to others. Like Weil, Marcel vigorously opposed all dehumanizing, mechanistic views of persons. He maintained that the mystery of *Being* evades analytic description. Marcel focused his work on a study of hope and fidelity. Although Marcel was not a systematic thinker, his meditations and speculative arguments have proved valuable.[81]

These four continental thinkers, like the four earlier philosophers, did not give primary consideration to Cartesian doubts about the existence of the external world. Unlike the foundationalists, they did not concern themselves with building a case for the external world based upon empirical data or explanatory coherence.[82] Although their conception

---

[79] See especially E. Levinas, "God and Philosophy," in *Of God Who Comes to Mind* (Stanford: Stanford University Press, 1986).

[80] Cited by Simon Critchley in his introduction to *The Cambridge Companion to Levinas*, 23.

[81] To see the gentleness of his writing, see the end of *Mystery of Being*, vol. 2, trans. René Hahue (Chicago: Gateway Edition, 1960).

[82] Still, it should be noted that while they did not adhere to Cartesian foundationalism, there were Cartesian aspects to continental philosophy and some sought a philosophical foundation for science. See *Cartesian Meditations* by Edmund Husserl, trans. D. Cairns (The Hague: Nijhoff, 1960).

of other persons was widely divergent (compare Sartre and Buber), they all insisted on the indisputable existence of "the other." Marcel championed this kind of assuredness about existence in relation to others:

> Not only do we have a right to assert that others exist, but I should be inclined to contend that existence can be attributed only to others, and in virtue of their otherness, and that I cannot think of myself as existing except in so far as I conceive of myself as not being the others: and so as other than them. I would go so far as to say that it is of the essence of the Other that he exists. I cannot think of him as other without thinking of him as existing. Doubt only arises when his otherness is, so to say, expunged from my mind.[83]

Gadamer, Ricoeur, Derrida, Foucault

Each of these continental philosophers contributed to the study of philosophy of religion. Their work is so complex and diverse that it is difficult to address all four philosophers in relation to a common theme. Notwithstanding the danger of oversimplification, I suggest they each address the meaning of personal identity in relation to religion.[84] Arguably, the meaning of one's life (i.e., one's being a scholar or a pilot or an agnostic, etc.) or one's identity is shaped by traditions, narrations, and institutions, as well as by biology and all the relevant ecology. The British philosopher Austin Farrer offers this artful picture of individual identity, which helps set the stage for thinking about these four philosophers:

> Our humanity is itself a cultural heritage; the talking animal is talked into talk by those who talk at him.... his mind is not at first his own, but the echo of his elders. The echo turns into a voice, the painted portrait steps down from the frame, and each of us becomes himself. Yet by the time we are aware of our independence, we are what others have made us. We

---

[83] *Being and Having*, 104.

[84] If this chapter is more defined by listing personal names rather than stating themes or problems, it is partly a reflection of the fact that, as Richard Rorty once observed, continental philosophy – as opposed to analytic philosophy – is more centered on personal names than problems. (See Rorty reference in Critchley, *Continental Philosophy*, 55.) In continental philosophy of religion, one is very likely to see a title that includes a personal name, like "The Question of God in the Thought of Levinas," than one that does not.

can never unweave the web to the very bottom. . . . Nor is it only parental impresses of which we are the helpless victims. How many persons, how many conditions have made us what we are; and, in making us so, may have undone us.[85]

The philosophers discussed in this section develop competing views of the cultural heritage, the language and conventions, that shape our identity, including our religious identity.

Hans-Georg Gadamer (1900–2002) was born in Germany and taught philosophy in different universities, including the Universities of Marburg, Leibzig, Frankfurt, and Heidelberg. He repudiates what he sees as the Enlightenment appraisal of disinterested reason. In its stead, he invites a new appreciation for tradition.

> The fundamental prejudice of the Enlightenment is the prejudice against prejudice itself, which denies tradition its power. . . . The overcoming of all prejudices, this global demand of the Enlightenment, will itself prove to be a prejudice, and removing it opens the way to an appropriate understanding of the finitude which dominates not only our humanity but also our historical consciousness. . . . *the prejudices of the individual, far more than his judgments, constitute the historical reality of his being.*[86]

Gadamer's methodology, then, does not endeavor toward an "ideal observer" point of view or a purging of one's historical setting. "Prejudices are not necessarily unjustified and erroneous, so that they inevitably distort the truth. In fact, the historicity of our existence entails that prejudices, in the literal sense of the word [prejudgments], constitute the initial directedness of our whole ability to experience. Prejudices are biases of our openness to the world. They are simply conditions whereby we experience something."[87] Gadamer's defense of this new orientation toward tradition is, in part, the impossibility of an alternative.

---

[85] Cited by Fred Lawrence in "Gadamer, the Hermeneutic Revolution, and Theology," in *The Cambridge Companion to Gadamer*, ed. R. J. Dostal (Cambridge: Cambridge University Press, 2002), 185.

[86] Gadamer, *Truth and Method*, 2nd ed., trans. J. Weinsheimer and D. C. Marshall (New York: Crossroad, 1991), 270, 276–277.

[87] Gadamer, *Philosophical Hermeneutics*, trans. D. E. Linge (Berkeley: University of California Press, 1976), 9.

Contrary to some popular misconceptions of his work, Gadamer does not simply valorize prejudice and tradition.

> The idea that authority and tradition are something one can appeal to for validation is a pure misunderstanding [of authority and tradition]. Whoever appeals to authority and tradition will have no authority. Period. The same goes for prejudgments. Anyone who simply appeals to prejudices is not someone you can talk with. Indeed, a person who is not ready to put his or her own prejudices in question is also someone to whom there is no point in talking.[88]

Gadamer's point about the importance of tradition and context is simply that one's reasoning begins in the world where prejudgment is an essential condition, a condition that may yield good or ill. Merold Westphal writes: "The prejudices Gadamer seeks to rehabilitate are not ugly attitudes toward people who are different from ourselves, but the preunderstandings presupposed by every understanding. Just as embodiment is a condition for being either Jack the Ripper or Mother Teresa, so prejudgment is a condition for seeing those who are different from me either as inferior or as my sisters and brothers."[89] Gadamer's further point is that traditions do need to be vindicated philosophically. He is aware, however, of the limitation of resources that may be available to each member of a tradition; for those not aware of all the evidence for or against a tradition, belief in the tradition may still be "an act of reason itself which, aware of its own limitations, trusts to the better insight of others.[90]

Gadamer's treatment of meaning and language has had an impact on philosophy of religion. His understanding of language and meaning is based on a humane, value-laden concept of personal exchange.

> Mutual understanding happens by the fact that talk stands up against talk, but does not remain static. Instead, in talking to each other we pass over into the imaginative world of the other, we as it were open ourselves up to them, and they do so to us. So we play into each other until the game of giving and taking, the conversation proper, begins. No one can deny that in such real conversation there is something of chance, the favor

---

[88] Richard Palmer, ed., *Gadamer in Conversation* (New Haven: Yale University Press, 2001), 44.

[89] Merold Westphal, "Hermeneutics as Epistemology," in *The Blackwell Guide to Epistemology*, ed. J. Greco and E. Sosa (Oxford: Blackwell, 1999), 427.

[90] *Truth and Method*, 279.

of surprise, finally also of lightness, yes, even of elevation, which pertains to the nature of game-play. And truly the elevation of conversation is experienced not as a loss of self-possession, but, even without ourselves actually attending to it, as an enrichment of ourselves.[91]

Gadamer's prime focus has been hermeneutics (from the Greek *hermeneuein,* "to interpret, translate, make intelligible") or the theory of interpretation. By his lights, the interpretation and meaning of texts are not matters of acquiring evidence of an author's original intent but rather of engaging in a virtual dialogue with the text.

> Whoever wants to understand a text always performs a projection. We project a meaning of the whole, as soon as a first meaning is manifest in the text. Such a meaning in turn only becomes manifest because one is already reading the text with certain expectations of a determinate meaning. Understanding what is there to be understood consists in working out such a projection which of course is constantly revised by what emerges in penetrating its meaning further.... [A]ny revision of the projection exists in virtue of the possibility of casting up a new projection; ... rival projections towards the elaboration can be generated one after the other, until the unity of sense is fixed unequivocally; ... the interpretation is initiated with anticipatory notions that are replaced by more adequate ones.[92]

According to Gadamer, when we learn from a text such as the Bible, we learn something about ourselves here and now. In religious tradition, the believer wants to know not what the Gospels had to teach to a first-century Christian but what they have to teach us in the present. Interpreting a sacred text is thereby linked to the practical application of the text in the life of the believer.[93] Gadamer's work has inspired a philosophy of religion that privileges narratives and (to use a favorite

---

[91] *Philosophical Hermeneutics,* 56–57.

[92] Cited by Lawrence, "Gadamer, the Hermaneutic Revolution, and Theology," 189. Lawrence's essay on Gadamer's contribution to theology is well informed and engaging. He concludes: "In making manifest the ever mysterious nature of human self-understanding in time, Gadamer opens up philosophy to theology, and challenges theology to be philosophical" (193).

[93] By Gadamer's lights, "The Gospel message is freely proffered and only becomes the good news for one who accepts it.... If the Christian message does represent such a freely made offer, a free promise, which is directed at each of us though we have no claim on it, the task of proclaiming is implied in our acceptance of it"; see *The Relevance of the Beautiful and Other Essays,* ed. Robert Bernasoni, trans. N. Walker (Cambridge: Cambridge University Press, 1986), 148. Also see David Vessey, "The Unique Alterity of Faith in Gadamer's Hermeneutics" (unpublished manuscript, 2003).

term of his) compares "horizons of interpretation" – balancing reason and tradition, for example.

Paul Ricoeur (b. 1913) was born in France and taught philosophy at the University of Paris and the University of Chicago. Like Gadamer, Ricoeur has made important contributions to hermeneutics. He has sought to make explicit the different meanings of texts as well as to articulate what he sees as the narratives that constitute (in part) our lives.

> Philosophy remains hermeneutics, that is, a reading of the hidden meaning inside the text of the apparent meaning. It is the task of hermeneutics to show that existence arrives at expression, at meaning, and at reflection only through the continual exegesis of all the significations that come to light in the world of culture. Existence becomes a self only by appropriating this meaning which first resides "outside," in works, institutions and cultural monuments in which the life of the spirit is objectified.[94]

According to Ricoeur, our identity is not immediately apparent or self-evident. It is achieved through the development of a narrative in which our ethical and religious (or secular) actions have meaning.

Because of his appreciation for diversity in narratives and symbols, Ricoeur's work is capacious, ranging from a fascinating study of evil (*The Symbolism of Evil*, 1960) to Freud (*Freud and Philosophy*, 1970) and metaphor (*The Rule of Metaphor*, 1975). Richard Kearney offers this useful description of Ricoeur's work in relation to Heidegger and Gadamer:

> Together with Heidegger and Gadamer, Ricoeur considers interpretation not on the basis of a psychological self-consciousness, but against the historical horizon of a finite being-in-the-world. But while Heidegger takes the "short route" to Being, where interpretation culminates, Ricoeur and Gadamer opt for the "long route" which examines the various inevitable detours which interpretation undergoes through language, myth, ideology, the unconscious and so on – before it arrives at the ultimate limit of Being. Man's final project is indeed a being-towards-death whose fundamental encounter with "nothingness" provokes the question of Being. But between birth and death, human understanding is compelled to

---

[94] Ricoeur, *The Conflict of Interpretations: Essays In Hermeneutics*, trans. D. Savage (New Haven: Yale University Press, 1974).

traverse a range of hermeneutic fields, where meaning is dispersed, hidden, withheld or deferred.[95]

Because of his deep sensitivity and appreciation for the different layers of meaning that make up our lives, Ricoeur's work stands in sharp contrast to a reductive scientific naturalism. Ricoeur laments the nihilism that he sees as a result of a scientific-technical ideology.

> And this cultural configuration is that of nihilism. The scientific illusion and the retreat of the sacred into its own particular phantoms together belong to the forgetfulness of our roots. In two different yet convergent manners the desert is spreading. And what we are in the midst of discovering, contrary to the scientific-technical ideology, which is also the military-industrial ideology, is that humanity is simply not possible without the sacred.[96]

One way to appreciate Ricoeur's commitment to meaningful religious narratives is to consider him in contrast to the Algerian-French philosopher Jacques Derrida (b. 1930).

In the 1960s, Derrida introduced a practice of deconstruction. To deconstruct an institution, text, religion, or society is to critique it from the inside, bringing to the surface internal contradictions and instability, thus overturning the idea that it rests on clear, dominant, fixed meaning. In his early work, Derrida argued that Plato's concepts of the subject, substance, existence, and essence are not proper, fundamental elements of reality, but merely illusions. Even "Platonism" as a philosophy has an illusory, abstract identity; while there may be some legitimacy to speaking of "Platonism," it will be in tension with the Platonic text.

> Platonism would mean, in these conditions, a thesis or the theme which one has extracted by artifice, misprision, and abstraction from the text, torn out of the written fiction of "Plato." Once this abstraction has been supercharged and deployed, it will be extended over all the folds of the text, of its ruses, overdeterminations, and reserves, which the abstraction will come to cover up and dissimulate. This will be called Platonism, or the philosophy of Plato, which is neither arbitrary nor illegitimate, since a certain force of thetic abstraction at work in the heterogeneous text of

---

[95] Kearney, *Modern Movements in European Philosophy* (Manchester: Manchester University Press, 1986), 100.

[96] Ricoeur, "Manifestations and Proclamations," in *Figuring the Sacred: Religion, Narrative, and Imagination*, ed. M. Wallace, trans. D. Pellauer (Minneapolis: Fortress Press, 1995), 64.

Plato can recommend one to do so. . . . "Platonism" is thus certainly one of the effects of the text signed by Plato, for a long time, and for necessary reasons, the dominant effect, but this effect always turned back against the text.[97]

In philosophy of religion, Derrida's work has fueled a critique of what are called *ontotheology* and a *theology of presence*. These theologies presume that we may metaphysically think and refer to the reality of God (e.g., God is thought of as essentially good, powerful, knowing, loving, and so on.)

Derrida has represented himself as an atheist, exploring "faith without religion" and without dogmatic claims of historical, messianic redemption. Derrida instead proposes a universal "structure of messianicity." He illustrates this structure as follows:

Each time I open my mouth, I am promising something. When I speak to you, I am telling you that I promise to tell you something, to tell you the truth. Even if I lie, the condition of my lie is that I promise to tell you the truth. So the promise is not just one speech act among others; every speech act is fundamentally a promise. This universal structure of the promise, of the expectation of the future, for the coming, and the fact that this explanation of the coming has to do with justice – this is what I call the messianic structure.[98]

Derrida sees such promising as akin to a divine immanence. His nonhistorical, messianic philosophy is understood in terms of "the gift" for which we expect and long but which is ultimately impossible. The nonreality of "the gift" prevents his structure of messianism from collapsing into traditional monotheism or some other nontheistic metaphysic. Once the gift is understood as a historical person or event, "you reduce the messianic structure to messianism, then you are reducing the universality and this has important political consequences. Then you are accrediting one tradition among others and a notion of an elected people, or a given literal language, a given fundamentalism."[99] Given the problem of historical messianism, Derrida commends a paradoxical posture of longing and waiting: we wait and long for something that cannot be given.

---

[97] Derrida, *On the Name*, ed. T. DuToit, trans. D. Wood et al. (Stanford: Stanford University Press, 1995), 119–120.

[98] Derrida in J. D. Caputo, *Deconstruction in a Nutshell: A Conversation with Jacques Derrida* (New York: Fordham University Press, 1997), 22–23.

[99] Ibid., 23.

What is the function of "the gift" or anything that is "totally foreign to the horizon of economy, ontology, knowledge, constantive statements, and theoretical determination and judgment"?[100] I believe Derrida is counseling or commending an openness to a religious life in which this is understood partly in terms of a noneconomic, nontheorizing, non-self-conscious giving and openness to the *tout autre*. The noncalculating character of what Derrida calls "the gift" is essential to its standing outside our practices of manipulation and control.

> A gift is something that is beyond the circle of reappropriation, beyond the circle of gratitude. A gift should not even be acknowledged as such. As soon as I know I give myself something...I just cancelled the gift. I congratulate myself or thank myself for giving something and then the circle has already started to cancel the gift.... If the gift is given, then it should not even appear to the one who gives it or to the one who receives it, not appear as such. That is paradoxical, but that is the condition for a gift to be given.... That is the condition the gift shares with justice. A justice that could appear as such, that could be calculated, a calculation of what is just and what is not just, saying what has to be given in order to be just – that is not justice. That is social security, economics. Justice and gift should go beyond calculation.[101]

By retaining a universal messianic structure and refusing to settle on a specific criteria of justice, Derrida advances what in mystical theology is called the *via negativa* or the apophatic.

Derrida's work has won great attention from theologians as of this writing, along with Jean-Luc Marion's work, which has also been linked with the apophatic tradition, especially after the mystic Dionysius the Areopagite. In brief, Marion puts to one side any philosophical affirmation or denial of God's existence in metaphysics. Such a metaphysical God is an idol, and thus Nietzsche's pronouncement of the death of God may be seen as emancipatory. For Marion, the God of philosophical theism is religiously as well as philosophically inadequate. In this passage from *God without Being*, Marion develops this critique, relying on Heidegger.

> In thinking "God" as *causa sui* [self-caused], metaphysics gives itself a concept of "God" that at once marks the indisputable experience of him

---

[100] J. Caputo and M. Scanlon, "On the Gift: A Discussion between Jacques Derrida and Postmodernism," in *God, the Gift and Postmodernism*, ed. Caputo and Scanlon (Bloomington: Indiana University Press, 1999), 59.

[101] *Deconstruction in a Nutshell*, 18–19.

and his equally incontestable limitation; by thinking "God" as an efficiency so absolutely and universally foundational that it can be conceived
only starting from the foundation, and hence finally as the withdrawal
of the foundation into itself, metaphysics indeed constructs for itself an
apprehension of the transcendence of God, but under the figure simply of
efficiency, of the cause, and of the foundation. Such an apprehension can
claim legitimacy only on condition of also recognizing its limit. Heidegger
draws out this limit very exactly: "Man can neither pray nor sacrifice to
this God. Before the *causa sui*, man can neither fall to his knees in awe
nor can he play music and dance before this god."[102]

The result does seem puzzling from the standpoint of classical and
early modern philosophy. Consider, for example, Marion's translator,
Thomas Carlsen's account.

> At this point within Marion's theological project, the "death of God" an-
> nounced by Friedrich Nietzsche (1844–1900) comes to play a productive
> role. If the godless thinking to which Heidegger appeals might open a
> path to some more divine God, then the "death of God," by destroying
> all metaphysical concepts of God, might hold real theological promise.
> A confrontation with the death of God, Marion suggests, can help us to
> take seriously "that the 'God' of ontotheology is strictly equivalent to an
> idol, one that presents the Being of beings as the latter are thought meta-
> physically." And if God can "begin to grab hold of us" only to the degree
> that "we claim to advance outside of ontotheology," then Nietzsche's cri-
> tique of metaphysics, by pointing beyond ontotheology, may open us to
> the hold of God.[103]

From a more traditional vantage point, it seems that a God that does not
exist (or is without being) may have difficulty getting a hold on anything,
but Marion's point is to challenge such "ontotheological" tradition.

Before returning to Ricoeur, I note the difficulty for Derrida's invocation of the ineffable and the impossibility of the appearance of justice.
Richard Kearney writes:

> If *tout autre* is indeed *tout autre*, what is to prevent us saying yes to an evil
> alien as much as to a transcendent God who comes to save and liberate? Is
> there really no way for deconstruction to discriminate between true and
> false prophets, between bringers of good and bringers of evil, between

---

[102] *God without Being*, trans. T. A. Carlson (Chicago: University of Chicago Press,
1991), 35.

[103] T. A. Carlson, "Postmetaphysical Theology," in *Postmodern Theology*, ed. K. J.
Vanhoozer (Cambridge: Cambridge University Press, 2003), 61–62.

holy spirits and unholy ones? How do we tell the difference, even if it's only more or less? How do we decide – even if we can never *know* (for certain), or *see* (for sure), or *have* (a definite set of criteria)? Blindness is all very well for luminary painters and writers, for Homer and Rembrandt, but don't most of the rest of us need just a *little* moral insight, just a few ethical handrails as we grope through the dark night of postmodern spectrality and simulacritude toward the "absolute other," before we say "yes," "come," "thy will be done"? Is there really no difference, in short, between a living God and a dead one, between Elijah and his "phantom," between messiahs and monsters?[104]

As Linda MacCammon comments, "Derrida's claim that justice and the gift never appear in history places the source of hope solely in the idea of gift, the *idea* of justice."[105]

Ricoeur and Derrida make an interesting contrast. Ricoeur acknowledges the profound difficulties facing traditional religious language. On this front, he even charges that the concept of "God" is not philosophical. He does not go as far as Derrida, but he does share *some* of Derrida's skepticism about ontotheology. Even so, he construes biblical narratives as meaningful texts that may be used to articulate an understanding of God.

> The [Divine] name works on the schema or model by making it move, by making it dynamic, by inverting it into an opposed image. (Thus God assumes all the positions in the figures of the family: father, mother, spouse, brother, and finally Son of Man.) Just as, according to Kant, the Idea requires the surpassing of not only the image but also the concept, in the demand to "think more," the Name subverts every model, but only through them.[106]

I suggest that Ricoeur's understanding of meaning may well stand as a challenging alternative to Derrida's messianism, for those developing a continental philosophy of religion today.

Brief notice should be taken of Michel Foucault (1926–1984). Formally trained as a philosopher, Foucault's major interest was historical, critical sociology. He addressed religious concerns in several books,

---

[104] Kearney, "Desire of God," in Caputo and Scanlon, *God, the Gift, and Postmodernism*, 127.

[105] L. M. MacCammon, "Jacques Derrida, Paul Ricoeur, and the Marginalization of Christianity," in *Paul Ricoeur and Contemporary Moral Thought*, ed. J. Wall et al. (London: Routledge, 2002), 196.

[106] Ricoeur, "Naming God," in *Figuring the Sacred*, 233.

noting how the church conceived of, and administered to, those deemed insane, uncovering the way religion has been employed to shape human sexuality, and so on. He is significant in philosophy of religion for his anti-Enlightenment critique of reason and his analysis of overt and covert institutional control over people. He continued, in a systematic way, Nietzsche's genealogical philosophy of religion. Foucault has an influential argument about the rise of the confessional as a tool for the construction of the modern understanding of the self. He argues that our contemporary practice of discursive introspection has religious roots.[107]

Feminist Philosophy of Religion

Feminist philosophers who engage in religion and religious themes have roots in many different areas of philosophy, one of which is continental. I mentioned how Nietzsche and Foucault have been seen as helpful allies in raising incisive questions about the roots of philosophical and theological ideals and methods.[108] Another influential contributor is the Belgian-French feminist and psychoanalyst Luce Irigaray (b. 1930). Irigaray is highly suspicious of claims to objectivity that are shorn of historical context. "Every piece of knowledge is produced by subjects in a given historical context. Even if that knowledge aims to be objective, even if its techniques are designed to ensure objectivity, science always displays certain choices, certain exclusions, and these are particularly determined by the sex of the scholars involved."[109] Irigaray claims that the gender of scholars has damaged philosophical scholarship on religion, among other areas.

Feminists vary between asserting that there is no gender-neutral "objectivity" and a more qualified claim that there are objective truths

---

[107] See Foucault, *The History of Sexuality*, vol. 1, trans. Robert Hurley (London: Penguin, 1990), 58–70. In the introduction to the second volume in this series, Foucault mentions a book (which would have been *The History of Sexuality*, vol. 4) called *Confessions of the Flesh* that is known to have been written but is being kept from publication according to his wishes.

[108] See, for example, Anne Hunter's use of Foucault's *Discipline and Punish: The Birth of the Prison* in her "Numbering the Hairs of Our Heads: Male Social Control and the All-Seeing Male God," *Journal of Feminist Studies in Religion* 8:2 (1992).

[109] "A Chance for Life: Limits to the Concept of the Neuter and the Universal in Science and Other Disciplines," in *Sexes and Genealogies*, trans. Gillian Gill (New York: Columbia University Press, 1993), 204.

but that our grasp of these truths (and thus our evidence for them) are from specific, gendered vantage points. One difficulty some feminists find with repudiating *all* claims about objective truth is that this seems to render nonsense claims about blind injustice and oppression – that is, unjust oppressive societies that believe that they are acting rightly. Imagine a society that is sexist and racist, but no one recognizes this. Intuitively, at least many would say that such a society is possible (or, more accurately, many believe that most societies are now or have in the past engaged in blind sexism and racism) and that it is wrong in its practices, regardless of whether anyone is aware of this.

Some feminists hold that there is an essential feminine nature that gives women a special, privileged, or at least independent moral, social, and religious insight. On this view, there is a distinctive women's way of knowing that is either unavailable to men or at least different from a distinctive men's way of knowing.[110] Irigaray offers a portrait of female sexual development, from puberty to menopause, that gives women a vital moral vantage point. "But every stage in this development has its own temporality, which is possibly cyclic and linked to cosmic rhythms. If women have felt so terribly threatened by the accident at Chernobyl, that is because of the irreducible relation of their bodies to the universe."[111] An appeal to female anatomy is not the only basis for rethinking philosophy of religion in light of feminism and women's experiences. Grace Jantzen writes of women's experience as providing a key resource:

> The feminist movement as a whole is deeply grounded in women's experience: both the experience of oppression, and the experience of possibilities of liberation arising out of a sense of sisterhood or community among women working together for change. Although there has been little systematic analysis of it specific to the philosophy of religion, it can be seen that this dual experience of oppression and liberating sisterhood is also taken by feminists as the primary source of religious knowledge.[112]

---

[110] To borrow the term from Mary Belenky et al., *Women's Ways of Knowing: The Development of Self, Voice and Mind* (New York: Basic Books, 1986).

[111] Ibid., 200.

[112] "Feminism in the Philosophy of Religion," in *Companion Encyclopedia of Theology*, ed. P. Bryne and L. Houlden (London: Routledge, 1995), 494.

One result of the advent of feminism has been an expansion of the methods employed in philosophy of religion. Jantzen, for example, proposes "a wider understanding of reason which includes sensitivity and attentiveness, well-trained intuition and discernment, creative imagination, and lateral as well as linear thinking."[113] Unpacking this expanded method in precise, analytic terms may be against the spirit of her work, but it can readily be said that, for Jantzen, philosophy of religion needs to give a preeminent role to the values which are at stake. For example, in considering the classical, theistic conception of God, she asks: "Are the characteristics thus projected really the ones that will best facilitate human becoming? Or are they partial, distorting or inimical to the flourishing of some groups of people?"[114] While she has critiqued what she sees as woefully absent in a male-oriented philosophy of religion, she has also constructively enlarged the parameters of the field to include fresh philosophical work on the imagination, desire, and birth. She has also promoted a heightened spirit of self-questioning in which a philosopher (male or female but especially male) does not unquestioningly assume that his or her viewpoint is neutral and objective.[115]

In *A Feminist Philosophy of Religion* and elsewhere, Pamela Sue Anderson also proposes an expanded methodology, which takes seriously concerns with gender, race, ethnicity, and class. She is not content with a philosophical method that places values to one side. "If a coherent unity is what defines reason and what justifies a philosophical argument, then should the question be asked: Whose coherence is this? Who set that particular limit which makes possible that particular coherence?"[116] Anderson maintains that feminist philosophers of

---

[113] *Becoming Divine: Towards a Feminist Philosophy of Religion* (Manchester: Manchester University Press, 1998), 69, 202.

[114] Ibid., 89.

[115] See the exchange between Paul Helm and Jantzen in "The Indispensability of Belief to Religion" by Helm and "What Price Neutrality? A Reply to Paul Helm" by Jantzen, both in *Religious Studies* 37:1 (2001): 87–92.

[116] *A Feminist Philosophy of Religion: The Rationality and Myths of Religious Belief* (Oxford: Blackwell, 1998), 10–11. I note here three additional statements by feminist philosophers of religion on their methodology. Mary Daly, in *Beyond God the Father* (Boston: Beacon, 1973), 21: "In my thinking, the specific criterion which implies a mandate to reject certain forms of God-talk is expressed in the question: Does this language hinder human becoming by reinforcing sex-role socialization? Expressed positively . . . the question is: Does it *encourage* human becoming toward psychological and social fulfillment, towards an androgynous mode of living, toward transcendence?" Sallie McFague: "The main criterion for a 'true' theology

religion should not restrict their attention to traditional Christian or other religious narratives. She endeavors instead to subvert what she sees as patriarchal myths. As some feminists reconceive of narratives, others have sought to bring feminist insights into religious rites.[117] Of course, one of the salient points of focus has been the use of male imagery and language of God with feminists either offering a more inclusive spectrum or rejecting all male imagery and advancing instead distinctive female imagery and language.[118]

The contribution of feminism to philosophy of religion is very much in its ascendancy, with diverse development – Jantzen and Anderson, for example, differ on some substantial terrain about ethics and the value of analytical philosophy of religion.[119] One tendency among some feminist philosophers of religion has been to challenge concepts of God that seem

is pragmatic, preferring those models of God that are most helpful in the praxis of bringing about fulfillment for living beings," in *Models of God* (Philadelphia: Fortress Press, 1987), 196. Rosemary Radford Ruether: "Our criterion for what is truthful is, finally, what is most ethically redemptive," in "Imago Dei, Christian Tradition and Feminist Hermeneutics," in *Image of God and Gender Models*, ed. W. E. Børrensen (Oslo: Solum Forlag, 1991), 277. Compare with Peter Bryne's "Omnipotence, Feminism and God," *International Journal for Philosophy of Religion* 37:3 (1995): 145–165. Some (but by no means all) feminist philosophy takes the route of postmodernism and relativism. In the introduction to the collection *Women Philosophers* (London: J. M. Dent, 1996), Mary Warnock writes: "This relativism [of Derrida, Foucault], generally known as postmodernism, has had an obfuscating effect not only on epistemology but, more notoriously, on history, theology, and above all, literary criticism. But there are signs that, at least among philosophers, there is a growing tendency to fight back, and women have played an important role in this renaissance, as well as the other" (xlvi).

[117] See Amy Hollywood, "Towards a Feminist Philosophy of Ritual and Bodily Practice," in *Difference in Philosophy of Religion*, ed. P. Goodchild (Aldershot: Ashgate, 2003).

[118] Probably the key publication in contemporary literature criticizing masculine pictures of God is Daly, *Beyond God the Father*. See also Rosemary Ruether, *Sexism and God-Talk* (London: SCM, 1983), and J. Soskice, "Can a Feminist Call God Father?" in *Women's Voices: Essays in Contemporary Theology*, ed. Theresa Elwes (London: Marshall Pickering, 1992).

[119] Jantzen, for example, largely dismisses contemporary analytical philosophy of religion, whereas Anderson seeks to build a bridge between her own post-Ricoeurian Kantianism and a form of analytical philosophy of religion. Her views are too rich to summarize easily here, but I note her project of mediating between what she depicts as passion and intellect, desire and reason; her not advancing a concept of essential female desire that should be treated with preeminence over essential male desire; and her development of a form of feminist standpoint epistemology. For a development of this outlook, see Anderson's "'Standpoint': Its Rightful Place in a Realist Epistemology," *Journal of Philosophical Research* 16 (2001).

to reflect "masculine" preoccupations with control and the scope of power. Sarah Coakley laments a one-sided preoccupation with power: "What is palpably missing is a sustained or positive reflection on the nurturing and all-encompassing dimensions of divine love – gendered metaphors that have well-known instantiations in the history of Christian theology and spirituality (e.g., Anselm, Julian of Norwich), but do not characteristically leap to the forefront of the analytic philosopher's imagination."[120] Jantzen offers this critique of classical theism at the heart of much philosophy of religion:

> The concept of God, on which so much energy is spent in the philosophy of religion, is a concept which needs thorough investigation from a feminist perspective, not because of some puzzles about omnipotence or about the coherence of theism or the compatibility of omniscience with human freedom, but because it is a concept which is regularly used in ways that are oppressive of women, which perpetuates economic and racial injustice, and which imperils the earth.[121]

Some feminist philosophers of religion work within the Christian, theistic tradition, seeking to correct sexist abuse from within (e.g., Pamela Johnson, Rosemary Ruether, Janet Soskice), whereas others seek to develop a more proximate view of God and cosmos (pantheism or the world is *in* God) or a denial of the divine as in any way independent of human, female consciousness and aspiration.[122] In response to feminist criticism of earlier (and some contemporary) philosophy of religion, I offer three brief observations.

First, I suggest that a substantial amount of traditional and modern philosophy of religion has been very keen to emphasize the *good* and *just* rather than sheer power and knowledge (that was the starting point of this book in Chapter 1). The Cambridge Platonist emphasis on divine goodness – political and theological – rather than upon bare

---

[120] "Feminism," in *A Companion to Philosophy of Religion*, ed. P. Quinn and C. Taliaferro (Oxford: Blackwell, 1997), 603.

[121] "Feminism in the Philosophy of Religion," in *Companion Encyclopedia of Philosophy*, ed. Peter Byrne and Leslie Houlden (New York: Routledge, 1995), 497.

[122] A leading journal of feminist scholarship is *Hypatia*, named after an Egyptian Neoplatonist who made important contributions to mathematics and philosophy; she authored an influential commentary on Ptolemy. Tragically, she was murdered in Alexandria (d. 415) by a fanatical mob of Nitrian monks. See M. E. Waithe, "Hypatia of Alexandria," in *A History of Women Philosophers*, ed. Waithe, vol. 1 (Dordrecht: Martinus Nijhoff Publishers, 1987).

supernatural power and knowledge was not a matter of dabbling in academic "puzzles about omnipotence." I doubt that Cudworth, More, Conway, Leibniz, Paley, and others would disagree with the following contemporary charge by Dorothee Soelle. In fact, I think they would enthusiastically agree with Soelle's stance. "As a woman I have to ask why it is that human beings honor a God whose most important attribute is power, whose prime need is to subjugate, whose greatest fear is equality.... why should we honor and love a being that does not transcend but only reaffirms the moral level of our present male dominated culture? Why should we honor and love this being... if this being is in fact no more than an outsized man?"[123] Jantzen offers an important challenge about the political, social, and cultural implications of this concept of God. I simply suggest that modern philosophers of religion have engaged in this project (e.g., Hume, Feuerbach, Nietzsche, Scheler, Freud, and Marx).

Second, building on the preceding point, I suggest that feminist concerns about injustice need not result in the abandonment of the traditional enterprise of theological and philosophical inquiry (i.e., concern for the coherence of theism, the origin of the cosmos, the adequacy of naturalism – religious or secular – and so on). Jantzen, in the following passage, suggests there is something suspicious about the philosophical debate over divine attributes: "In fact, feminists are suspicious that the energy spent in arguing about the finer points of the puzzles surrounding the concept of the God of Christendom is actually a way of colluding with the injustices perpetuated in 'his' name, or at the very least, that making such a debate central to the agenda of the philosophy of religion deflects attention from the weightier issues of how that concept of God is related to practices of injustice."[124] Philosophical debate on the divine attributes *can be* distracting. But is a concern for such things as the compatibility of omniscience and freedom ipso facto distracting from the concern of justice? These debates historically have often taken place when the value of human freedom has come under fire politically. Leibniz, for example, was keenly concerned with the dignity and compatibility of human freedom and God's providence, yet his concern for political peace in his time was beyond reproach. Or consider again the Cambridge Platonist case for freedom and God's sovereignty; both, I

---

[123] *The Strength of the Weak: Toward a Christian Feminist Identity*, trans. R. Kimker (Philadelphia: Westminster, 1984), 97.

[124] Ibid., 497–499.

think, went hand in hand with their case for political tolerance and charity. I suggest that other twentieth-century theistic liberation movements that have emerged from (or been shaped by) Christianity have made an important use of divine attributes.[125]

As I argued in Chapters 1 and 2, the locus of some debate over the nature of evidence and faith is philosophy of mind. I proposed that if the skeptic can convince us that we may not be embodied, or that the world around us is an unknowable "external world," our agency and concept of the good of embodiment is impaired. In some feminist philosophy of religion the ground shifts: skepticism that the person (soul or mind or the mental in general) is nonphysical is grounded on the goodness of female embodiment. Moreover, the next step has been to argue that with the demise of mind-body dualism, the breakdown of theism is soon to follow. (This precisely follows Henry More's prediction.) Here is a representative claim from Grace Jantzen. She refers at the outset to a book, *God's World, God's Body*, in which she defends the view that the cosmos is God's body.

> For example, I argued in *God's World, God's Body* that cosmic dualism, the idea that God and the world are utterly different and separate, is a large-scale version of mind-body dualism; and if the latter is philosophically and theologically dubious then so must be the former. At the time, I did not appreciate that both of these dualisms also mirror the male-female dualism: men have from Plato onwards been associated with mind and spirit and transcendence, while women have been linked with the body, reproduction, and the material world. These connections have been clearly demonstrated by several writers, notably Rosemary Ruether and Sallie McFague. Whether because of male anxiety deriving from the need of a boy child to separate from his mother to achieve male identity, as Freud and his followers suggest, or whether there is some other cause, male-dominated Western religion and philosophy demonstrate a discomfort with sexuality, the body, and the material world, and have

---

[125] Granted, when Martin Luther King Jr. invoked God's love and power in the fight against black oppression, or Desmond Tutu spoke of God's hatred of injustice in South African apartheid, or José Miguez Bonino referred to God as a liberator in the historical struggle to overcome oppression, they were not writing papers for periodicals like The *International Journal for Philosophy of Religion*, and they were not engaged in philosophical analysis. Still, divine attributes were involved and a study of them is therefore not irrelevant. Some of the leading contributors to the literature on divine attributes are women. Jantzen references the freedom and omniscience debate. Probably Linda Zaszebski is the most important current contributor to that literature.

often sought other-worldly alternatives. As Luce Irigaray puts it: "the patriarchal order is based upon worlds of the beyond: worlds of before birth and especially of the afterlife, other planets to be discovered and exploited for survival, etc. It doesn't appreciate the real value of the world we have and draws up its often bankrupt blueprints on the basis of hypothetical worlds."[126]

Jantzen's use of the term "dualism" here may not mean the bare belief that a human person has physical and nonphysical (or immaterial) attributes or parts. Perhaps "dualism" is being used to name a view of mind-body separateness in which the body is seen as reproductive, female, and subordinate to the male spirit. If so, then, dualism is clearly sexist. But I suggest that many feminists are "dualists" insofar as they maintain that thinking, feeling, sensing, emotion, and intentionality are embodied in – but are not identical to – our bodily states and processes. The idea that the mental *is* the physical can be formulated as the claim that the mental is, or will be, fully described and explained in an ideal physics. To some philosophers (to be discussed in Chapters 8 and 9) this claim seems false; there is a subjectivity or experiential character of the mental not able to be captured in physics. Regardless of the merits of their counterarguments, I suggest the case for and against materialism (and the possibility of an afterlife) need not reflect a "male-dominated" scale of values. To those who are not materialists and recognize some aspects of human life as nonphysical, the sexuality to which Jantzen refers would be seen as an interplay of the mental and physical, a psychological-physical event in which there is felt desire, pleasure, and not just physical contact but *experienced* physical contact.[127] Perhaps some term other than "dualism" should be used here to name the thesis that there is more to a human person than the physical parts and processes.[128]

---

[126] "Feminism in the Philosophy of Religion," 504.

[127] See the philosophical account developed in *Sexual Desire: A Moral Philosophy of the Erotic* by Roger Scruton (New York: Free Press, 1986). Note especially Scruton's comments on the incarnation, on p. 128 and elsewhere. I believe a similar observation about the interplay of the physical and mental needs to be highlighted in an account of reproduction (which Jantzen references) and not just sexuality. Human reproduction, in religious tradition, is the object of many rites that (I believe) resist a material account of persons.

[128] Because materialism is *monistic* insofar as it asserts that reality is completely and exhaustively physical, the denial of this position could be called *pluralism*. Although "pluralism" already has a fixed meaning in the study of culture, it would carry less negative meaning in philosophy and theology than "dualism."

As part of this overall response to Jantzen's treatment of dualism, I add the suggestion that the "traditionalist" interest in philosophy of religion with "otherworldly alternatives" may be seen as stemming from the lure of *this* world, not a shunning of it. One can see in the Cambridge Platonists, in Leibniz, Locke, and Berkeley, and in the exchange between Hume and Boswell, and so on, a hope that physical dissolution is not the annihilation of persons, because the ongoing existence and flourishing of persons is good, not because men need to separate from their mothers or they don't appreciate the value of this world. Having made this suggestion, Jantzen's critique may still be cogent and vital insofar as attention to an afterlife obscures or delays the pursuit of justice and goodness in this life. Jantzen's important contributions to philosophy of religion compel one to consider well the impact of a philosopher's work on gender, race, culture, and politics.

Feminist philosophy of religion is diverse, as I noted earlier, and no serious philosopher of religion can afford to bypass this engaging, vibrant movement. The next chapter examines five other twentieth-century developments within philosophy of religion.

EIGHT

✦

Five Major Moves

For my own part, I think that if one were looking for a single phrase to capture the stage to which philosophy has progressed, "the study of evidence" would be a better choice than "the study of language." ... The study of evidence goes further, inasmuch as it does not limit us, as "the study of language" appears to do, to elucidating the content of our beliefs, but also raises the question of our warrant for holding them; and this is surely a philosophical question when it is conceived in sufficient general terms.... We can give "the study of evidence" a broad enough interpretation to make it cover two questions which have returned into the forefront of philosophical interest. What are we justified in taking there to be? And how far is what there is of our own making?

A. J. Ayer[1]

What light kindling your lamp of life
Brings you here to the world?
Rabindranath Tagore[2]

Lunch and Mystical Poetry

In the early 1920s a group of scientifically oriented intellectuals began meeting in Vienna, Austria. The Vienna Circle, as it came to be called, was made up at first of a mathematician, a sociologist, and a physicist, but it soon attracted philosophers of considerable power and influence, many of whom had a strong grounding in mathematics and science. The

---

[1] A. J. Ayer, *Philosophy in the Twentieth Century* (New York: Random House, 1982), 18.

[2] *Song Offerings*, trans. J. Winter (London: Anvil Press Poetry, 2000), 80.

circle achieved its highest level of stature and activity under the guidance of Moritz Schlick (1882–1936), the chair of the history and theory of the inductive sciences at the University of Vienna. Schlick had important ties to a scientific community that included Albert Einstein. The circle promoted the unity of science in a spirit of international cooperation and came to have vast philosophical influence after the World War II.[3]

Schlick and others in the circle were profoundly impressed by an Austrian philosopher who was trained at Cambridge University, Ludwig Wittgenstein (1898–1951). The circle, drawn to what it perceived as Wittgenstein's strict adherence to a scientific worldview, studied closely his famous *Tractatus Logico-Philosophicus* (1921).

> The correct method in philosophy would really be the following: to say nothing except what can be said, i.e. propositions of natural science – i.e. something that has nothing to do with philosophy – and then, whenever someone else wanted to say something metaphysical, to demonstrate to him that he had failed to give a meaning to certain signs in his propositions. Although it would not be satisfying to the other person – he would not have the feeling that we were teaching him philosophy – *this* method would be the only strictly correct one.[4]

This radical stricture on method rendered odious what the circle saw as the pretentious nonsense of idealism, the work of Martin Heidegger, and traditional theology.

In 1927 Schlick arranged a lunch meeting with Wittgenstein. Schlick is reported to have approached Wittgenstein with "the reverential attitude of a pilgrim."[5] Schlick's wife reported that "he returned in an ecstatic state, saying little, and I felt I should not ask questions." A meeting with circle members soon followed, but the result was baffling to Schlick. Wittgenstein refused to engage in the philosophy of the *Tractatus*. Instead, he read them the poetry of Rabindranath Tagore (1861–1941), a Bengali mystic.

This chapter looks at the critique of religion developed by the Vienna Circle and the movement positivism, sometimes called "*logical*

---

[3] See Victor Kraft, *The Vienna Circle*, trans. Arthur Pap (New York: Philosophical Library 1953).

[4] *Tractatus Logico-Philosophicus*, trans. D. Pears and B. F. McGinness (London: Routledge, 1974), 6.53.

[5] This and passages cited in this paragraph are taken from A. Janik and S. Toulmin, *Wittgenstein's Vienna* (New York: Simon and Schuster, 1973), chap. 7. This is a superb book.

positivism" or "*verificationism.*" The term "positivism" was first used for a critical, scientific methodology and view of the world by French philosophers Claude-Henri Saint-Simon (1760–1825) and Auguste Comte (1789–1857). In what follows, I am concerned with positivism as we find it in Austrian and Anglo-American contexts without tracing French forebears.[6] After considering the reply to positivism (a critique of its critique of religion), let us turn to a powerful philosophy of religion inspired by Wittgenstein. I then take note of the prospect of a renaissance in philosophy of religion, before plunging into a twentieth-century, revised, constructive philosophy of religious tradition and the advent of pluralistic philosophy of religion. In all, this chapter considers five developments: the move toward and then against positivism; a move to a philosophy of religion inspired by Wittgenstein; a move to a favorable philosophical conception of religious tradition; and then a move to take on board a plurality of religious tradition.[7]

In the preceding chapter I employed the imagery of philosophy as two distinct rivers, because (regrettably) a range of philosophers has understood themselves to be operating in two ostensibly incompatible frameworks: continental and analytic. Closer inspection, however, reveals that philosophy of religion in the second half of the twentieth century is more like a network of rivers or, if we consider the breadth of literature and themes, a number of oceans with different, sometimes conflicting currents. In the last section of this chapter, I am especially keen not to oversimplify the (almost bewildering) extensiveness of contemporary philosophy of religion.

Positivism and Philosophy of Religion

In addition to Schlick, the Vienna Circle included Otto Neurath (1882–1945), Herbert Feigl (1902–1988), Rudolf Carnap (1891–1970), Kurt Gödel (1906–1978), Friedrich Waisman (1896–1959), and Hans Reichenbach (1891–1953). A. J. Ayer (1910–1989) became one of its

---

[6] Comte is especially interesting for philosophers of religion as he explicitly advances a view of science in religious terms. For Comte, the belief in science and humanity involves something akin to religious belief and love.

[7] Two recent histories published by Kluwer bear on material in this and the next chapter. I recommend E. T. Long, *Twentieth-Century Western Philosophy of Religion* (Dordrecht: Kluwer, 2001), and James Harris, *Analytic Philosophy of Religion* (Dordrecht: Kluwer, 2000). For an overview, see also M. W. F. Stone, "Philosophy of Religion," in *Philosophy 2*, ed. A. C. Grayling (Oxford: Oxford University Press, 1998).

foremost advocates in the English-speaking world. The positivist philosophy of the circle came to have great influence, in part, because of the diaspora of its members due to the rise of National Socialism: Carnap wound up at the University of Chicago after time spent elsewhere, Feigle went to the University of Minnesota, Waisman went to Oxford, Gödel to Princeton, and Reichenbach – by way of Turkey – made his way to the University of California. There are considerable differences between these figures – Gödel, for example, held that there are reasons to believe individuals survive death – but their biggest impact on philosophy of religion was to challenge the *meaningfulness* of religious language.[8] In saying that "God exists," does one really assert an intelligible proposition that theists and atheists can debate? Or, rather, is "God exists" a pseudoproposition, without content? Consider Ayer's formulation of the positivist critique.

Ayer divided all propositions into two fundamental categories.

> Like Hume, I divide all genuine propositions into two classes: those which, in his terminology, concern "relations of ideas," and those which concern "matters of fact." The former class comprises the *a priori* propositions of logic and pure mathematics, and these I allow to be necessary and certain only because they are analytic. That is, I maintain that the reason why these propositions cannot be confuted in experience is that they do not make any assertion about the empirical world, but simply record our determination to use symbols in a certain fashion.[9]

Meaningful discourse, for Ayer, is tied to abstract, conceptual relations as we find them in mathematics and logic or, if the discourse concerns matters of fact, it must involve (in principle) verifiable procedures under empirical conditions.

> The criterion which we use to test the genuineness of apparent statements of fact is the criterion of verifiability. We say that a sentence is factually significant to any given person, if and only if, he knows how to verify the proposition which it purports to express – that is, if he knows what observations would lead him, under certain conditions, to accept the proposition as being true, or reject it as being false. If, on the other hand, the putative proposition is of such a character that the assumption of its truth, or falsehood, is consistent with any assumption whatsoever concerning the nature of his future experience, then, as far as

---

[8] Not *all* those who were part of this circle advanced this critique, but, through Ayer, this outcome became part of the circle's legacy.

[9] *Language, Truth and Logic* (London: Victor Gollancz, 1936), 11.

he is concerned, it is if not a tautology, a mere pseudo-proposition. The sentence expressing it may be emotionally significant to him; but it is not literally significant.... To make our position clearer, we may formulate it in another way. Let us call a proposition which records an actual or possible observation an experiential proposition. Then we may say that it is the mark of a genuine factual proposition, not that it should be equivalent to an experiential proposition, or any finite number of experiential propositions, but simply that some experiential propositions can be deduced from it in conjunction with certain other premises without being deducible from those other premises alone.[10]

Empirical hypotheses with detectable, observable implications are cognitively meaningful. Ayer's schema does not rule out other uses of language. Commands and moral judgments are legitimate uses of language, but they do not provide bona fide propositions – statements that are either true or false. There are no experiential propositions that would confirm or falsify moral values, for example.

Ayer, Carnap, and others held that the assertion "God exists" or those like them ("God is loving, just..." etc.) fail to be meaningful, proper assertions because they cannot be verified or falsified. Language about God may *look* syntactically intelligible, but this is a mere appearance.

Here is a central passage in *Language, Truth, and Logic* in which Ayer contends that theistic language is meaningless:

What is not so generally recognised is that there can be no way of proving that the existence of a god, such as the God of Christianity, is even probable. Yet this also is easily shown. For if the existence of such a god were probable, then the proposition that he existed would be an empirical hypothesis. And in that case it would be possible to deduce from it, and other empirical hypotheses, certain experiential propositions which were not deducible from those other hypotheses alone. But in fact this is not possible. It is sometimes claimed, indeed, that the existence of a certain sort of regularity in nature constitutes sufficient evidence for the existence of a god. But if the sentence "God exists" entails no more than that certain types of phenomena occur in certain sequences, then to assert the existence of a god will be simply equivalent to asserting that there is the requisite regularity in nature; and no religious man would admit that this was all he intended to assert in asserting the existence of a god. He would say that in talking about God, he was talking about a transcendent being who might be known through certain empirical manifestations, but certainly could not be defined in terms of those manifestations. But in

[10] Ibid., 19–20, 26.

that case the term "god" is a metaphysical term. And if "god" is a meta-physical term, then it cannot be even probable that a god exits. For to say that "God exists" is to make a metaphysical utterance which cannot be either true or false. And by the same criterion, no sentence which pur-ports to describe the nature of a transcendent god can possess any literal significance.[11]

Ayer's conclusion works with equal force against any nontheistic reli-gious language in which there are metaphysical claims. The Hindu thesis that "Atman is Brahman" is in the same boat as any classical theistic conviction.

While the positivists were especially interested in a critique of tradi-tional metaphysics, they also took aim at some continental philosophers, especially Heidegger. Here is the setup of Carnap's attack on Heidegger in which he charged that, although Heidegger's language conforms to some syntactical rules, it is logical nonsense.

> Let us now take a look at some examples of metaphysical pseudo-statements of a kind where the violation of logical syntax is especially obvious, though they accord with historical-grammerical syntax. We se-lect a few sentences from that metaphysical school which at present ex-erts the strongest influence in Germany. [The following passages are from Heidegger's work.]
>
>   "What is to be investigated is being only and – *nothing* else; being alone and further – *nothing*; solely being, and beyond being – *nothing*. *What about this Nothing? . . . Does the Nothing exist only because the Not, i.e. the Negation, exists?* Or is it the other way around? *Does Negation and the Not exist only because the Nothing exists? . . .* We assert: *the Nothing is prior to the Not and the Negation. . . .* Where do we seek the Nothing? How do we find the Nothing . . . we know the Nothing . . . *Anxiety re-veals the nothing. . . .* That for which and because of which we were anx-ious, was "really" – nothing. Indeed: the Nothing itself – as such – was present. . . . *What about this Nothing? – The Nothing itself nothings.*"[12]

The positivists lampooned Heidegger's project. One unsympathetic jest was to liken Heidegger's concept of Being to breathing: being is like breathing, only quieter.[13]

[11] Ibid., 173–174.

[12] Rudolf Carnap, "The Elimination of Metaphysics," in *Logical Positivism*, ed. A. J. Ayer (Glencoe, Ill.: Free Press, 1959), 69.

[13] There is a good discussion of the Heidegger-Carnap clash in Simon Critchley, *Conti-nental Philosophy* (Oxford: Oxford University Press, 2001), chap. 6.

Debates with theists often amounted to comparing assertions or narratives about God with some evident nonsense. Carnap wrote about a peculiar property he called "teavy" and "toovy," while Ayer spoke about a "drogulus" as in "There's a drogulus over there."[14] A drogulus was a nonsensical, invisible being that escapes detection as well as coherent description. The case for the meaninglessness of religious language became, then, an argument from analogy. "God" seemed no more intelligible than teavy, toovy, drogulus or, in a famous debate, an invisible gardener. Antony Flew developed the following narrative:

> Once upon a time two explorers came upon a clearing in the jungle. In the clearing were growing many flowers and many weeds. One explorer says, "Some gardener must tend this plot." The other disagrees, "There is no gardener." So they pitch their tents and set a watch. No gardener is ever seen. "But perhaps he is an invisible gardener." So they set up a barbed-wire fence. They electrify it. They patrol it with bloodhounds. (For they remember how H. G. Wells' *The Invisible Man* could be both smelt and touched though he could not be seen.) But no shrieks ever suggested that some intruder has received a shock. No movements of the wire ever betray an invisible climber. The bloodhounds never give cry. Yet still the Believer is not convinced. "But there is a gardener, invisible, intangible, insensible to electric shocks, a gardener who has no scent and makes no sound, a gardener who comes secretly to look after the garden which he loves." At last the Skeptic despairs, "But what remains of your original assertion? Just how does what you call in invisible, intangible, eternally elusive gardener differ from an imaginary gardener or even from no gardener at all?[15]

Flew's critique of theism here is that no evidence is allowed to count against it. The claim that there is a God, like the claim that there is an invisible gardener, dies the death of a thousand qualifications.

---

[14] See Carnap, "The Elimination of Metaphysics," and A. J. Ayer in debate with Frederick Copleston, "Logical Positivism – A Debate," Third Program, BBC (June 13, 1949). This is reprinted in several places, including Paul Edwards and Arthur Pap, eds., *A Modern Introduction to Philosophy*, 2nd ed. (New York: Free Press, 1957). Paul Edwards shares the positivist critique of religious language. See, for example, his "Being – Itself and Irreducible Metaphors," in *Religious Language and the Problem of Religious Knowledge*, ed. R. E. Santoni (Bloomington: Indiana University Press, 1968).

[15] "Theology and Falsification: A Symposium," in *The Philosophy of Religion*, ed. B. Mitchell (Oxford: Oxford University Press, 1971), 13. Flew adopted this thought experiment from John Wisdom's work.

The parable of the invisible gardener hints at an objection to theism that would be amplified later by Flew and others. Does it make sense even to think there could be an invisible gardener? Is the concept of nonphysical gardener or God no more coherent than the concept of a square with no right angles? Flew, Kai Nielsen, Anthony Kenny, and Paul Edwards each argued that the concept of being a person and our concepts of knowledge, action, justice, and the like are inextricably bound up with *embodied, material* life. To suppose that there could be something immaterial or nonpyhysical that was yet a person or person-like would be an evident absurdity. Paul Edwards put the objection as follows:

> I have no doubt that when most people think about God and his alleged activities, here or in the hereafter, they vaguely think of him as possessing some kind of rather large body. Now if we are told that there is a God who is, say, just and good and kind and loving and powerful and wise and if, (a) it is made clear that these words are used in one of their ordinary senses, and (b) God is not asserted to be a disembodied mind; then it seems plain to me that *to that extent* a series of meaningful assertions has been made. And this is so whether we are told that God's justice, mercy, etc., are "limitless" or merely that God is superior to all human beings in these respects. However, it seems to me that all these words lose their meaning if we are told that God does not possess a body. Anyone who thinks otherwise without realizing this I think is supplying a body in the background of his images. For what would it be like to be, say, just without a body? To be just, a person has to *act* justly – he has to behave in certain ways. This is not reductive materialism. It is a simple empirical truth about what we mean by "just." But how is it possible to perform these acts, to behave in the required ways without a body? Similar remarks apply to the other divine attributes.[16]

---

[16] Edwards, "Some Notes on Anthropomorphic Theology," in *Religious Experience and Truth*, ed. S. Hook (New York: New York University Press, 1961), 242–243. For other contributions to this literature, see M. Diamond and T. Litzenburg, eds., *The Logic of God: Theology and Verification* (Indianapolis: Bobbs-Merrill, 1975). For Kenny's worry about nonphysical agency, see his autobiography *A Path from Rome* (Oxford: Oxford University Press, 1986), 147. This book is a wonderfully written portrait of twentieth-century philosophy documenting Kenny's intellectual development. Antony Flew develops a case against the meaningfulness of discourse about God as an incorporeal reality in *God and Philosophy* (New York: Dell, 1966), chap. 2. Flew contends that to describe God as a wise, intentional agent (and so on) is to take terms that have meaning among corporeal, human animals and then to apply these terms in a context where the meaning is lost. Theistic terms to describe God are "so distinctively

This line of criticism is by no means antiquarian. Kai Nielsen advances it in his recent *Naturalism and Religion* where he argues that there can be no evidence for God's existence. Even if the stars in the sky were to spell out "God exists," this would not be evidence for theism.

> We are no better off with the stars in the heavens spelling out GOD EXISTS than with their spelling out PROCRASTINATION DRINKS MELANCHOLY. We know that something has shaken our world, but we know not what; we know – or think we know, how could we tell which it was in such a circumstance? – that we heard a voice coming out of the sky and we know – or again think that we know – that the stars rearranged themselves right before our eyes and on several occasions to spell out GOD EXISTS. But are we wiser by observing this about what "god" refers to or what a pure disembodied spirit transcendent to the universe is or could be? At most we might think that maybe those religious people have something – something we know not what – going for them. But we also might think it was some kind of big trick or some mass delusion. The point is that we wouldn't know what to think.[17]

Nielsen seems right on this point: if "God exists" fails to be intelligible, then no empirical evidence will make it evident.[18]

The (ostensibly) nonempirical nature of theism is explained in the entry "supernatural" in the *Blackwell Dictionary of Philosophy* (1996).

> Supernatural beings exist above or beyond nature, where "nature" is to be understood in a wide sense, to take in all of space and time and

personal, they cannot, without losing all their original meaning, be thus uprooted from their peculiarly human habitat and transferred to a context so totally different. Being an agent, showing willpower, displaying wisdom are so much prerogatives of people, they refer so entirely and particularly to human transactions and human experience, that it becomes more and more forced and unnatural to apply the relevant expressions the further you go down the evolutionary scale. To try to apply them to something which is not an animal at all cannot but result in a complete cutting of the lines of communication" (37).

[17] Nielsen, *Naturalism and Religion* (Amherst, N.Y.: Prometheus Books, 2001), 279.

[18] Nielsen has advanced his critique of religion in many places, for example, *Contemporary Critiques of Religion* (New York: Herder and Herder, 1971); "Empiricism, Theoretical Constructs and God," *Journal of Religion* 54 (July 1974); "God and Verification Again," *Canadian Journal of Philosophy* 11 (April 1965); *Reason and Practice* (New York: Harper and Row, 1971); *Scepticism* (London: Macmillan, 1973); *An Introduction to Philosophy of Religion* (New York: St. Martin's Press, 1982); and "God, Disembodied Existence and Incoherence," *Sophia* 26:3 (October 1987). Grace Jantzen expresses some sympathy with Nielsen's critique of God as a nonphysical reality in her *God's World, God's Body* (Philadelphia: Westminster, 1984).

everything existing within that framework, i.e. the whole of the physical universe. It is especially in the context of religious belief that the concept of the supernatural has been used. If scientists (or non-scientists) discover a new type of wave, a new force, a strange phenomenon in a remote galaxy, the very fact that it was there to be discovered makes it a natural phenomenon which may in due course be described in science textbooks. Supernatural beings run no risk of having their existence disclosed by scientific or everyday observation.

The next object of interest would be to ask whether supernatural beings run the risk of being disclosed at all. The outlook in the preceding entry compliments the objection that by positing some reality outside the physical cosmos one has ceased to make sense. R. W. Hepburn raised this worry:

> Compare these sentences – "Outside my room a sparrow is chirping", "Outside the city the speed limit ends," "Outside the earth's atmosphere meteors do not burn out" and finally "God is outside the universe, outside space and time". What of this last statement? The word "outside" gets its central meaning from relation item to item *within* the universe. It . . . is being stretched to the breaking-point in being applied to the whole universe as related to some being that is not-the-universe: its sense is being extended to the point where we may easily come to speak nonsense without noticing it.[19]

This worry about meaning, in its turn, compliments an assumption that the causal explanations in the cosmos must remain closed, involving only the physical world. Consider this entry for "God" from *The Oxford Companion to Philosophy* (1995):

> There is also the problem of how a purely spiritual being could be contacted, and how he (or she or it) could interfere in the universe. Suppose I suffer from an inoperable brain tumour and pray to God for a cure. If God is physical he might hear my prayer and send healing rays, unavailable to earthly physicians, that would break up the tumour. But how could a disembodied mind hear me in the first place, and, if he could, how could he, not being physical, apply the force that would send the rays into my brain? More basically, how could a pure mind create the physical universe, or for that matter how could he create anything at all?

Today the Nielsen-Kenny-Edwards objection to theism is often articulated in terms of objecting to the concept of a "bodiless person."

---

[19] *Christianity and Paradox* (London: Watts, 1958), 5.

D. Z. Phillips – whose work is discussed later in this chapter – also endorses this objection.

Due to the work of logical positivists and related critics, the immediate post–World War II intellectual climate was hostile to any metaphysic that strayed from what is confirmable in the natural sciences. In 1951 Austin Farrer offered this description of the plight of metaphysics.

> To many people now alive metaphysics means a body of wild and meaningless assertions resting on spurious argument. A professor of metaphysics may nowadays be held to deal handsomely with the duties of his chair if he is prepared to handle metaphysical statements at all, though it be only for the purpose of getting rid of them, by showing them up as confused forms of something else. A chair in metaphysical philosophy becomes analogous to a chair in tropical diseases: what is taught from it is not the propagation but the cure.[20]

Indeed, Hans Reichenbach was even reluctant to endorse the study of past, diseased metaphysics. "Those who work in the new [scientific] philosophy do not look back; their work would not profit from historical considerations."[21] The "dialogue" between religion and science consisted of the elimination of religion; "the belief in science has replaced, in large measure, the belief in God."[22]

Even Peter Strawson, who sought a modest revival of metaphysics, albeit one that was hedged by lots of Kantian strictures, remarked with dismay: "It is with very moderate enthusiasm that a twentieth-century philosopher enters the field of philosophical theology, even to follow Kant's exposure of its illusions."[23]

For an important "classic" statement of this broadly anti-metaphysical, or at least anti-theological, method, see the ending to Bertrand Russell's *A History of Western Philosophy*. This constitutes a radical denial of the philosophy of religion raised in Chapter 1, Cambridge Platonism. I cite this at length as it will be instructive later.

> Philosophy, throughout its history, has consisted of two parts inharmoniously blended: on the one hand a theory as to the nature of the world, on the other an ethical or political doctrine as to the best way of living. The failure to separate these two with sufficient clarity has been a

---

[20] Editor's introduction to Leibniz, *Theodicy* (La Salle: Open Court, 1990), 7.
[21] *The Rise of Scientific Philosophy* (Berkeley: University of California Press, 1951), 325.
[22] Ibid., 44.
[23] *The Bounds of Sense* (London: Methuen, 1966), 207.

source of much confused thinking. Philosophers, from Plato to William James, have allowed their opinions as to the constitution of the universe to be influenced by the desire for edification: knowing, as they supposed, what beliefs would make men virtuous. They have invented arguments, often very sophistical, to prove that these beliefs are true. For my part I reprobate this kind of bias, both on moral and on intellectual grounds.

All this is rejected by the philosophers who make logical analysis the main business of philosophy. They confess frankly that the human intellect is unable to find conclusive answers to many questions of profound importance to mankind, but they refuse to believe that there is some "higher" way of knowing, by which we can discover truths hidden from science and the intellect. For this renunciation they have been rewarded by the discovery that many questions, formerly obscured by the fog of metaphysics, can be answered with precision, and by objective methods which introduce nothing of the philosopher's temperament except the desire to understand. Take such questions as: What is number? What are space and time? What is mind, and what is matter? I do not say that we can here and now give definitive answers to all these ancient questions, but I do say that a method has been discovered by which, as in science, we can make successive approximations to the truth, in which each new stage results from an improvement, not a rejection, of what has gone before.

In the welter of conflicting fanaticisms, one of the few unifying forces is scientific truthfulness, by which I mean the habit of basing our beliefs upon observations and inferences as impersonal, and as much divested of local and temperamental bias, as is possible for human beings. To have insisted upon the introduction of this virtue into philosophy, and to have invented a powerful method by which it can be rendered fruitful, are the chief merits of the philosophical school of which I am a member. The habit of careful veracity acquired in the practice of this philosophical method can be extended to the whole sphere of human activity, producing, wherever it exists, a lessening of fanaticism with an increasing capacity of sympathy and mutual understanding. In abandoning a part of its dogmatic pretensions, philosophy does not cease to suggest and inspire a way of life.[24]

Contra Positivism

There are some philosophers of religion who flourished during the high-water mark of positivism, and now who would not dispute the findings

---

[24] *A History of Western Philosophy* (New York: Simon and Schuster, 1945), 834–836.

of positivism. For them, the role of religious language is not referential; that is, religious talk about God is not first and foremost to be understood as referring to a being transcending the cosmos. By their lights, religious language is about something else – a certain way of living or valuing the world. In response to Flew, R. M. Hare suggested that religious beliefs were more like unfalsifiable attitudes. R. B. Braithwaite proposed that religious language was principally ethical, prescribing *agape*, the unconditional love for one's neighbor.[25] Some theologians adopted this position with enthusiasm. Don Cupitt, for example, offered the following understanding of Christianity: "Belief in the God of Christian faith is an expression of allegiance to a particular set of values, and the experience of the God of Christian faith is the experience of the impact of those values on one's life."[26] Later in this chapter, when discussing Wittgenstein, we will return to consider this option.

The problem with positivism is that it seemed to jeopardize scientific and commonsense statements. If you demand that propositions be decisively verifiable or falisifiable, it seems there are legitimate statements about the past (15 billion years ago the universe emerged from a state of temperature T, density D, as described in the Big Bang model) or generalizations about the future (some day there will be a swan weighing 500 pounds) that do not meet that standard.[27] Bas van Fraassen writes, "Do the concepts of the Trinity [and] the soul . . . baffle you? They pale besides the unimaginable otherness of closed space-times, event horizons,

---

[25] See R. B. Braithwaite, *An Empiricist's View of the Nature of Religious Belief* (Cambridge: Cambridge University Press, 1955), and R. M. Hare, "Theology and Falsification," in *New Essays in Philosophical Theology*, ed. A. Flew and A. MacIntyre (New York: Macmillan, 1955).

[26] *Taking Leave of God*, 69.

[27] Billions of years of not seeing such a swan would not decisively falsify this claim and billions of years of seeing swans less than 500 pounds would not verify the statement that all swans weigh less than 500 pounds. See Carl Hempel, "Problems and Changes in the Empiricist Criterion of Meaning," in *Semantics and the Philosophy of Language*, ed. L. Linsky (Urbana: University of Illinois Press, 1952). Probably the best-known and most influential reply in the philosophy of religion to the verification challenges was Alvin Plantinga, *God and Other Minds* (Ithaca: Cornell University Press, 1967). Richard Swinburne, *The Coherence of Theism*, 2nd ed. (Oxford: Clarendon, 1993), was also a significant contribution. The case against verification is by no means over. For a defense of verificationism, see Michael Martin, *Atheism* (Philadelphia: Temple University Press, 1990).

EPR correlations, and bootstrap models."[28] There is also the perennial appeal of skepticism. Ayer, Schlick, and the others wanted to rule out what is untestable, partly because they were opposed to radical skepticism. A comprehensive Cartesian skepticism advances (at least initially) the possibility that one's sensory experiences may all be systematically mistaken, and there is no way to detect this. For the positivists, the demon hypotheses (or brain in vat scenarios) are to be rejected for they are not verifiable.[29] Still, philosophers over the ages have found it nearly impossible to rule out the possibility of massive, systematic error. Back to Descartes' worry in Chapters 1 and 2, can you be absolutely certain that you are in the circumstances you take yourself to be in? Isn't it *possible* that you are being electro-chemically stimulated merely to appear to be awake and so on?[30] To insist on verifiability as a requirement for meaning seems to rule out meaningful narratives of how one might be systematically and irrevocably deceived.

The very intelligibility of positivism came under attack. Is the statement about what is meaningful (e.g., Ayer's claim reproduced earlier in this chapter) itself meaningful? Philosophers like George Mavrodes concluded that positivism could at most be a recommendation for what is to count as meaningful, or as a summary of what is in common with claims that are widely recognized as meaningful. But this strategy faces two problems: first, it seems to beg the question against theists and other religious believers. Why should they begin at the outset with the assumption that theistic or monistic propositions are spurious or under threat? Why shouldn't their statements be treated

---

[28] "Empiricism in the Philosophy of Science," in *Images of Science*, ed. P. Churchland and C. Hooker (Chicago: University of Chicago Press, 1985), 258.

[29] See Chapter 2, note 21.

[30] There have been many attempts to tame skepticism in the years after World War II. In the early 1980s Hillary Putnam tried to rule out the possibility of systematic, Cartesian doubt on the basis of a philosophy of reference. The problem is that we, or many of us, seem to be able to imagine being subject to systematic sensory and cognitive stimulation (as depicted in the movie *The Matrix*) while (falsely) drawing the conclusion that Putnam has established that we are not being so deceived. Insofar as positivist principles treat unverifiable hypotheses as meaningless, they will face the problem that some ostensibly meaningful skeptical scenarios make the true nature of reality unverifiable, at least by us. See H. H. Price, "Be Mad in Order to Be Wise," in *Belief* (London: George Allen & Unwin, 1969), 228–231. The objection from skepticism is especially appropriate, as Ayer himself conceded the coherence of skepticism about the external world in *The Foundations of Empirical Knowledge* (London: Macmillan, 1940).

with a presumption of meaning (á la the principle of charity) until proven otherwise?[31] Second, it was argued that meaning was prior to verification; you have first to grasp the meaning of a proposition before grasping what conditions would confirm or disconfirm it. This line of reasoning was designed to pry apart the positivist charge that meaning and verifiability were somehow conceptually unified.[32]

Positivism also underwent criticism on the grounds that it rendered ethics nonsense. Ayer, for example, held that ethical judgments were the equivalent of expressing feelings like saying "boo" or "hurrah" in response to cruelty or happiness. Russell and Carnap, like Ayer, also held that morality was merely a matter of expressing wishes. Many, *but not all*, philosophers came to believe that Carnap, Ayer, and Russell did not do justice to the apparent content and intelligibility of moral language and experience. John Findlay and others argued that we *experience* values. Findlay replied to the attempted separation of fact and values. He frames his objection against Hume. "It is easy to defeat Hume, that worst of phenomenological observers, phenomenologically: in experience fact and value come before us as married and not isolated, and in many cases they come before us as logically, necessarily married, not brought together by an arbitrary link of taste or decision."[33]

Moral arguments may be (and have been) advanced with an appeal to principles and experience. Since the late 1960s there has been a massive growth of work in value theory that seems to attest to the cognitive, meaningful content in moral discourse.[34] Russell's comment in *The Philosophy of Bertrand Russell* is representative of the difficulty of holding out for a complete dismissal of the cognitive meaningfulness of ethics:

> I am accused of inconsistency, perhaps justly, because, although I hold ultimate ethical valuations to be subjective, I nevertheless allow myself emphatic opinions on ethical questions. If there is an inconsistency, it is

---

[31] See F. Copleston, *Studies of Logical Positivism* (London: Burns and Oates, 1956), and Keneth Konyndyk, "Verificationism and Dogmatism," *International Journal for Philosophy of Religion* 8 (1977).

[32] See George Mavrodes, "God and Verification," *Canadian Journal of Theology* 10 (July 1964): 182–191.

[33] Findlay, *The Transcendence of the Cave* (London: George Allen & Unwin, 1967), 61.

[34] Witness, for example, the enormous work now being carried out in applied ethics. See *The Encyclopedia of Applied Ethics*, ed. Ruth Chadwick (San Diego: Academic Press, 1998).

one that I cannot get rid of without insincerity; moreover, an inconsistent system may well contain less falsehood than a consistent one.... In the first place, I am not prepared to forego my right to feel and express ethical passions; no amount of logic, even though it be my own, will persuade me that I ought to do so. There are some men whom I admire, and others whom I think vile; some political systems seem to me tolerable, others an abomination. Pleasure in the spectacle of cruelty horrifies me, and I am not ashamed of the fact that it does. I am no more prepared to give up all this than I am to give up the multiplication table.[35]

It was largely because of appreciating the depth and authority of our "stubborn" judgments about what is tolerable that many contemporaries of Russell and Ayer adopted a realist, cognitive view of ethics. C. D. Broad, for example, argued, "In any possible world it would be fitting to feel gratitude towards one's benefactors and unfitting to feel pleasure at the undeserved suffering of another."[36] The dismissal of ethics as meaningless also created a problem for Ayer, who spoke of knowledge claims in terms of rights as in the *right to certainty*. If one can have rights in terms of knowledge why not in ethics proper?[37] There is a similar tension in Russell's philosophy.

Return to the model of inquiry Russell presents at the end of his *History* that repudiates the convergence of theoretical, scientific inquiry and ethical concern for the "best way of living." Russell's preferred "impersonal" methodology of "scientific truthfulness" is advanced not just on intellectual but on "moral grounds." Isn't Russell himself advancing a philosophical "way of life" that he takes to be "edifying"? For Russell, the philosopher's temperament ought to be nondogmatic, nonfanatic, careful, sympathetic, and committed to "mutual understanding." This illustrates the difficulty of ruling out *moral values* while retaining intellectual values. Even in the passage from Russell's work cited earlier, he acknowledged that a criticism of his subjectivism may have been "justly" articulated and that he has a "right" to certain feelings and expressions. If one retains intellectual rights, why not moral rights?

---

[35] P. A. Schilpp, ed., *The Philosophy of Bertrand Russell* (Chicago: Northwestern University Press, 1944), 720.

[36] C. D. Broad, *Five Types of Ethical Theory* (London: Routledge, 1956), 282.

[37] Ayer later conceded that his account of ethics in *Language, Truth and Logic* was inadequate.

Apart from these worries, positivists faced the rejoinder that theistic claims do have empirical implications about the world.[38] If there is a God of omnipotent love, then there are certain expectations one *should* indeed see. This approach took the problem of evil seriously, with some philosophers arguing that the cosmos is in fact fundamentally good or, if not good, it is not such that a God of omnipotent love should never have created it. According to Basil Mitchell, William Wainwright, and others, we can approach the world with an eye to assessing its good or ill and assess how this bears on the credibility of different religious beliefs.[39] This reply to positivism connects twentieth-century debate with the classic and early modern debate over the problem of evil (Cleanthes vs. Philo, Leibniz *contra mundum*, Mill vs. Paley, and so on). I provide an overview of the current literature on the problem of evil in Chapter 9.

Some of the debate over verification took seriously not just this life but a possible afterlife. John Hick offered this account of how one might verify theistic beliefs.

> Two men are traveling together along a road. One of them believes that it leads to a Celestial City, the other that it leads nowhere; but since this is the only road there is, both men must travel it. Neither has been this way before, and therefore neither is able to say what they will find around each next corner. During the journey they meet both with moments of refreshment and delight, and with moments of hardship and danger. All the time one of them thinks of his journey as a pilgrimage to the Celestial City and interprets the pleasant parts as encouragements and the obstacles as trials of his purpose and lessons in endurance, prepared by the king of the city and designed to make of him a worthy citizen of the place when at last he arrives there. The other, however, believes none of this and sees their journey – only the road itself and the luck of the road in good weather and in bad.
>
> During the course of the journey the issue between them is not an experimental one. They do not entertain different expectations about the coming details of the road, but only about its ultimate destination. And

---

[38] Basil Mitchell offered an interesting reply to Flew, where he assimilated religious belief to the belief, in wartime, of someone's loyalty where the evidence is murky. See Mitchell, "Theology and Verification," reprinted (along with Flew's essay) in Mitchell, *The Philosophy of Religion*.

[39] See William Wainwright, "The Presence of Evil and the Falsification of Theistic Assertions," *Religious Studies* 4 (April 1969).

yet when they do turn the last corner it will be apparent that one of them has been right all the time and the other wrong. Thus, although the issue between them has not been experimental, it has nevertheless from the start been a real issue. They have not merely felt differently about the road; for one was feeling appropriately and the other inappropriately in relation to the actual state of affairs. Their opposed interpretations of the road constituted genuinely rival assertions, though assertions whose status has the peculiar characteristic of being guaranteed retrospectively by a future crux.[40]

The case may seem quite bizarre, but some of the positivists allowed for the bare possibility of an afterlife, and A. J. Ayer, to his dismay, near the end of his life actually had a so-called near-death experience. One of Ayer's last essays was entitled "What I Saw When I Was Dead."[41]

Two other replies to positivism were developed that need to be considered.

First, it was argued that the assumption made by Ayer and others about what counts as observation seemed too narrow. There were seismic disputes over whether all our knowledge – claims about the world – could come down to propositions backed by simple, empirical experiences. Ayer himself allowed (in principle) for mystical experiences to count as the grounds for meaningful propositions.

> For his part, the mystic may protest that his intuition does reveal truths to
> him, even though he cannot explain to others what these truths are; and

---

[40] Hick's parable raises this question, What if there is no last corner and the road never ends? Imagine both travelers endlessly move down the road and no Celestial City appears. It would still be the case that, at any time in the journey, there would be no definitive falsification that a Celestial City exists. Still, I think the whole concept of a pilgrimage in theistic religions involves there being an intended destination that the pilgrim will (by the grace of God) attain. On this view, an endless road without there ever being a sighting of the Celestial City would count as a reason to abandon the pilgrimage. Hick's own view is that there is an afterlife that will provide an occasion for entering the "Celestial City." See his *Death and the Afterlife*, rev. ed. (New York: Harper and Row, 1987). For some important clarifications on his use of the Celestial City parable, see Hick, "Eschatological Verification Reconsidered," *Religious Studies* 13 (1977).

[41] See Ayer's "What I Saw When I Was Dead," *Sunday Telegraph* (August 28, 1988), reprinted in Ayer, *The Meaning of Life and Other Essays* (London: Weidenfeld and Nicholson, 1990). See G. S. Karka, "Eschatological Falsification," *Religious Studies* 12 (June 1976), and the collection S. T. Davis, ed., *Death and Afterlife* (New York: St. Martin's Press, 1989).

that we who do not possess this faculty of intuition can have no ground for denying that it is a cognitive faculty. For we can hardly maintain *a priori* that there are no ways of discovering true propositions except those which we ourselves employ. The answer is that we set no limit to the number of ways in which one may come to formulate a true proposition. We do not in any way deny that a synthetic truth may be discovered by purely intuitive methods as well as by the rational method of induction. But we do say that every synthetic proposition, however it may have been arrived at, must be subject to the test of actual experience. We do not deny *a priori* that the mystic is able to discover truths by his own special methods. We wait to hear what are the propositions which embody his discoveries, in order to see whether they are verified or confuted by our empirical observations.[42]

Ayer allows for mystical "intuition" as a vehicle in which "to discover truths." He goes on to insist that these truths then be "verified or confuted by our empirical observations," but why can't the mystic's experience itself count as an experiential verification? So long as "empirical" is understood with sufficient breadth, why rule out a priori the mystical? In his defense of religious experiences, H. H. Price notes how a person might attain certain experiences that warrant religious belief. In *Belief*, H. H. Price writes:

What we call "a spiritual person" (a repulsive phrase, but it is hard to find another) is not, of course, just a person who knows things which others do not. Nevertheless, according to the assumption we are discussing, he *is* a person who has experiences which unspiritual persons do not have; and though these experiences are not purely and simply cognitive, it is held that they provide him with evidence for certain important propositions, evidence which unspiritual persons are not able to obtain. On the Theistic view, it is evidence concerning the existence and attributes of God, and especially for the proposition that God loves us. Furthermore, it would be claimed that a spiritual person's experiences provide him with a better understanding of the Theistic world-outlook itself: he understands, better than the rest of us, what is *meant* by saying that there is a God who created the universe, and that he loves each one of us, including those of us who deny that he exists, or think it nonsensical to say He does.[43]

---

[42] *Language, Thought, and Logic*, 180–181.
[43] H. H. Price, *Belief* (London: George Allen, 1969), 474–475.

Price's reply to Ayer's secular empiricism could take this form: Ayer advances "the empiricism of one who has had little experience."[44] Part of the seductive appeal of Flew's gardener, Ayer's drogulus, and Nielsen's nonphysical star-speller is that they are so bizarre and without purpose. Compare them to Rudolf Otto's portrait of religious experience noted in Chapter 6. A fuller, more sympathetic description of religious experience and belief helped to counter the positivist critique.

Second, consider the objection about disembodiment described earlier. Forms of materialism that have been popular in the twentieth century have eliminated mental life or rendered it as an exclusively physical state or activity. But this view has not achieved hegemony. The first respondents to positivism were not materialists; they defended the reality of consciousness as something nonphysical and thus not open to the kind of public inspection required by a verificationist. These philosophers included H. D. Lewis, A. C. Ewing, C. A. Campbell, J. Harrison, R. Swinburne, and J. R. Lucas.[45] Their arguments took various forms, but a popular device was to employ thought experiments of

---

[44] This was Mill's objection to Bentham, cited by Passmore in *A Hundred Years of Philosophy* (New York: Macmillan, 1957), 13. See, for example, William Alston, *Perceiving God* (Ithaca: Cornell University Press, 1991); Caroline Frank, *The Evidential Force of Religious Experience* (Oxford: Clarendon Press, 1989); Jerome Gellman, *Experience of God and the Rationality of Theistic Belief* (Ithaca: Cornell University Press, 1997); Gary Gutting, *Religious Belief and Religious Skepticism* (Notre Dame: University of Notre Dame Press, 1983); Richard Swinburne, *The Existence of God*, rev. ed. (Oxford: Oxford University Press, 1991); William Wainwright, *Mysticism: A Study of Its Nature, Cognitive Value, and Moral Implications* (Madison: University of Wisconsin, 1981); Keith Yandell, *The Epistemology of Religious Experience* (Cambridge: Cambridge University Press, 1993); H. D. Lewis, *Our Experience of God* (New York: Macmillan, 1959); and Nelson Pike, *Mystic Union* (Ithaca: Cornell University Press, 1992). I believe the best, systematic criticism of this revival of constructive, sympathetic treatments of religious experience is Matthew Bagger, *Religious Experience, Justification, and History* (Cambridge: Cambridge University Press, 1999). See also Martin, *Atheism*; William Rowe, "Religious Experience and the Principle of Credulity," *International Journal for Philosophy of Religion* 13 (1982); Wayne Proudfoot, *Religious Experience* (Berkeley: University of California Press, 1985); and A. O'Hear, *Experience, Explanation and Faith* (London: Routledge, 1984). Richard Gale has some important critical essays; "The Overall Argument of Alston's Perceiving God," *Religious Studies* 30 (1994), is representative.

[45] See, for example, H. D. Lewis, *The Elusive Mind* (London: Allen and Unwin, 1969); J. R. Lucas, *The Freedom of the Will* (Oxford: Clarendon, 1970); C. A. Campbell, *On Selfhood and Godhood* (London: Allen and Unwin, 1957); and A. C. Ewing, *The Fundamental Questions of Philosophy* (London: Routledge, 1951).

the Cartesian sort discussed in Chapter 2. Swinburne advanced a narrative of an embodied person who gradually loses his body. Insofar as his
description seemed intelligible, Flew's invisible gardener looked less and
less like a contradiction in terms. Here is Swinburne's extensive thought
experiment:

> Imagine yourself, for example, gradually ceasing to be affected by alcohol
> or drugs, your thinking being equally coherent however men mess about
> with your brain. Imagine too that you cease to feel any pains, aches, and
> thrills, although you remain aware of what is going on in what has been
> called your body. You gradually find yourself aware of what is going on
> in bodies other than your own and other material objects at any place
> in space – at any rate to the extent of being able to give invariably true
> answers to questions about these things, an ability which proves unaf-
> fected by men interfering with lines of communication, e.g. turning off
> lights so that agents which rely on sight cannot see, shutting things in
> rooms so that agents which rely on hands to feel things cannot do so.
> You also come to see things from any point of view which you choose,
> possibly simultaneously, possibly not. You remain able to talk and wave
> your hands about, but find yourself able to move directly anything which
> you choose, including the hands of other people (although if you do move
> someone else's hands, he will normally himself deny responsibility for
> these movements). You also find yourself able to utter words which can
> be heard anywhere, without moving any material objects. However, al-
> though you find yourself gaining these strange powers, you remain other-
> wise the same – capable of thinking, reasoning, and wanting, hoping and
> fearing. It might be said that you would have nothing to want, hope, or
> fear – but that is false. You might hope that these strange powers would
> remain yours or fear that men would dislike you. Even if you could control
> their thoughts you might want them to like you spontaneously without
> being forced to do so by you, and you might fear that this want would
> not be fulfilled. Your hopes would be natural aspirations uttered to your-
> self, and shown by feelings of joy and relief when they were fulfilled, and
> sorrow when they were not realized. You would think and reason as men
> often do in words uttered to yourself. Surely anyone can thus conceive
> of himself becoming an omnipresent spirit. So it seems logically possible
> that there be such a being. If an opponent still cannot make sense of this
> description, it should be clear to many a proponent how it could be spelt
> out more fully.[46]

[46] See *The Coherence of Theism* (Oxford: Oxford University Press, 1977), 104–105. See
also Jonathan Harrison, "The Embodiment of Mind, or What Use Is Having a Body?"
Proceedings of the Aristotelian Society 74 (1973–1974). For a survey of the massive

Swinburne rightly describes his narrative thought experiment as "strange," and one might add *conceptually bizarre*, but if it is logically possible, then the objection of Kai Nielsen and others has been met.

Once one grants the conceptual possibility of a person not being necessarily identical to a material object (such that a person could not exist without being a body), one can see a way of replying to Hepburn's objection (cited earlier) about the coherence of supposing God is "outside the universe." In theism, God is *not* believed to be spatially outside the universe; God is believed to be *omnipresent*, present everywhere, but not identical to the universe. On this view, God is not identical to any meteor, room, or bird (Hepburn's examples), but God creatively conserves them in existence, knows them, and so on. As for the assumption that a nonphysical being cannot act (cited earlier), why assume this is any more plausible than the occasionalist thesis (Chapter 2) according to which there is no direct causal relation between material bodies? In a limited fashion, the theist might make use of Hume's more capacious approach to causation, which a priori does not rule out such connections.[47]

There is a more recent group of philosophers, less radical than dualists like Swinburne, who also argue for the reality of consciousness as something that is not easily identified with physical, bodily life. Galen Strawson, Thomas Nagel, Colin McGinn, and Frank Jackson have all opposed a simpleminded materialism that would automatically render theism as incoherent.[48] Nagel, a nontheist, goes so far as to claim: "No doubt [conscious experience] occurs in countless forms totally unimaginable to us, on other planets in other solar systems throughout

---

use of thought experiments in philosophy of mind, see T. Schick and L. Vaughn, eds., *Doing Philosophy: An Introduction through Thought Experiments* (Chicago: McGraw-Hill Higher Education, 2003). See also my *Consciousness and the Mind of God* (Cambridge: Cambridge University Press, 1994). For a defense of the coherence of nonphysical intelligence, see also J. Hoffman and G. S. Rosenkrantz, *Substance: Its Nature and Existence* (London: Routledge, 1997). For a critical treatment of disembodiment, see Terence Penelhum, *Survival and Disembodied Existence* (New York: Humanities Press, 1970).

[47] Hume wanted spatial contiguity with material causation, but as a dualist he allowed for hopes, desires qua nonspatial elements to have causal roles. See William Hasker, *The Emergent Self* (Ithaca: Cornell University Press, 1999), for arguments against the causal closure of the physical world.

[48] See, for example, Galen Strawson, *Mental Reality* (Cambridge, Mass.: MIT Press, 1994), and Colin McGinn, *The Mysterious Flame* (New York: Basic Books, 1999).

the universe."[49] Perhaps Nagel is wrong about the actual distribution of consciousness. Still, the openness to different nonhuman forms of intelligence is at odds with more restrictive views of Flew and Nielsen.[50] In summary, Kai Nielsen's attack on theism as incoherent seems to be a minority position today with most of the prominent atheists (e.g., J. L. Mackie) arguing that, while theism is coherent, it is false. The review of Nielsen's last book in the *Times Literary Supplement* was under the title "A Genial Solitude" as his position is now a minor one in the field: "As one puts the book down, one realizes that Nielsen occupies a rather lonely position as a philosopher."[51] Despite his own attraction to the positivist critique, Ronald Hepburn summarizes a widely held conviction: "There can be no short-cut in the philosophy of religion past the painstaking examination and re-examination of problems in the entire field.... No single, decisive verification test, no solemn Declaration of Meaninglessness, can relieve us of the labor."[52]

In various chapters I have highlighted the importance of taking on comprehensive views of the arguments in philosophy of religion. In this context, it is worth citing a similar judgment about the nature of

---

[49] *Mortal Questions* (Cambridge: Cambridge University Press, 1979), 166. Ayer came to reject physicalism in "Our Knowledge of Other Minds," reprinted in Ayer's *Philosophical Essays* (London: Macmillan, 1963).

[50] James van Cleve uses the existence of what he calls "sensa" to argue that meaningful claims can be made that transcend and are independent of evidence: "[L]et us stipulate that sensa are entities that do not exist unless someone senses them, so they are mind-body dependent. But the following facts are at least evidence-transcendent (i.e., there could not be conclusive evidence for them) and arguably also evidence-independent (i.e. they could obtain in the absence of evidence sufficient for knowledge). A certain sensum occurs fourteen billion years after the Big Bang. A red sensum of mine is contemporaneous with a green sensum of yours. Given the round, pinkish sensa that are occurring now, if biting-sensa were to occur also, pomegranatey-tasting sensa would follow. There is a mental history containing an infinite sequence of sensa in which each red is followed by a blue and each blue by a red. Sensa of winning at Wimbledon once occurred in a dream that was never reported and is now irrecoverable in memory." *Problems from Kant* (Oxford: Oxford University Press, 1999), 14.

[51] *TLS*, January 18, 2002; the reviewer is A. Kenny. Part of the burden of Nielsen's reasoning is that he needs to establish not just the improbability of nonphysical agency but its impossibility. I assess some of these arguments in "The Possibility of God," in *The Rationality of Theism*, ed. P. Copan and P. Moser (London: Routledge, 2003).

[52] Hepburn, "From World to God," *Mind* 72 (1963): 50.

meaning by Carl Hempel in 1958.

> But no matter how one might reasonably delimit the class of sentences
> qualified to introduce empirically significant terms, this new approach [by
> the positivists] seems to me to lead to the realization that cognitive signifi-
> cance cannot well be construed as a characteristic of individual sentences,
> but only of more or less comprehensive systems of sentences (correspond-
> ing roughly to scientific theories). A closer study of this point suggests
> strongly that . . . the idea of cognitive significance, with its suggestion of
> a sharp distinction between significant and non-significant sentences or
> systems of such, has lost its promise and fertility . . . and that it had better
> be replaced by certain concepts which admit of differences in degree, such
> as the formal simplicity of a system; its explanatory and predictive power;
> and its degree of confirmation relative to available evidence. The analysis
> and theoretical reconstruction of these concepts seems to offer the most
> promising way of advancing further the clarification of the issues implicit
> in the idea of cognitive significance.[53]

If Hempel is right, the project initiated by Ayer had to be qualified, taking
into account larger theoretical frameworks. Theistic and nontheistic
religious philosophies could not be ruled out at the start but could be
allowed a hearing with their competing views of cognitive significance.

The debate over positivism gave a major impetus for philosophers of
religion to study more closely the nature of religious language and the
interwoven way in which religious language does and does not count
as part of an explanatory system. There has been a massive amount
of fruitful work at the intersection of philosophy of religion and the
philosophy of language.[54] The movement described in the next section

---

[53] Carl Hempel, "The Empiricist Criterion of Meaning," in *Logical Positivism*, ed. A. J.
Ayer (Glencoe, Ill.: Free Press, 1959), 129. Hempel is still in the empirical tradition,
but he allows for theoretical constructs that go beyond observation predicates.

[54] See William Alston, *Divine Nature and Human Language* (Ithaca: Cornell University Press, 1989); David Burrell, *Analogy and Philosophical Language* (New Haven:
Yale University Press, 1973); Frederick Ferré, *Language, Logic and God* (New York:
Harper and Brothers, 1961); John Macquarrie, *God Talk* (New York: Harper and Row,
1967); Sallie McFague, *Metaphorical Theology* (Philadelphia: Fortress Press, 1982);
Ralph McInerny, *The Logic of Analogy* (Notre Dame: University of Notre Dame Press,
1961); James Ross, *Portraying Analogy* (Cambridge: Cambridge University Press,
1982); Janet Soskice, *Metaphor and Religious Language* (Oxford: Clarendon, 1985);
I. M. Crombie, "The Possibility of Theological Statements," in *Faith and Logic*, ed.
Basil Mitchell (Boston: Beacon Press, 1957); Michael Durrant, *The Logical Status of
God* (New York: St. Martin's, 1973).

places the meaning of religious language at the forefront of philosophy of religion.

Wittgenstein and Philosophy of Religion

Wittgenstein's early work, especially the *Tractatus*, did not constitute a major contribution to philosophy of religion except to reinsert in philosophical discourse what appeared to be a quasi-religious sense of the mystical. Several key passages in the *Tractatus* suggest a non-positivist outlook that allows for a religious quietude. Consider these propositions:

> 6.44 It is not *how* things are in the world that is mystical, but *that* it exists.
>
> 6.45 To view the world *sub specie aeterni* is to view it as a whole – a limited whole. Feeling the world is a limited whole – it is this that is mystical.
>
> 6.522 There are, indeed, things that cannot be put into words. They *make themselves manifest*. They are what is mystical.

The end of the *Tractatus* is the dramatic claim that his work is, in some sense, nonsense.

> 6.54 My propositions serve as elucidations in the following way: anyone who understands me eventually recognizes them as nonsensical, when he has used them – as steps – to climb up beyond them. (He must, so to speak, throw away the ladder after he has climbed up it.)
>
> He must transcend these propositions, and then he will see the world aright.
>
> What we cannot speak about we must pass over in silence.

Neither is the result clearly theistic, nor does Wittgenstein's early work fit easily into a traditional religious mold. (Some philosophers see Schopenhauer's view of the self and the world in the *Tractatus*.) If Wittgenstein's early work had only a modest impact, quite the opposite is true of his later work.

The reasons behind Wittgenstein's departure from what appeared (at first) to be hospitable to positivism are complex. To seize upon only one strand in his rich, powerful thinking, Wittgenstein renounced what may be called "a picture theory of meaning" in which one measures the truth and falsehood of a proposition with its corresponding reality (the way one might compare a picture of a dog with a dog). In its stead, Wittgenstein focused on the *use* of language and especially on the ordinary use of language prior to philosophical reflection. "But I did not get my picture of the world by satisfying myself of its correctness; nor do I have it because I am satisfied of its correctness. No: it is the inherited background against which I distinguish between true and false."[55] Wittgenstein rejected (or sought to resist) the "traditional" goals of philosophy to seek the essence of reality, to argue for or against the existence of God to solve the mind-body problem, to formulate comprehensive ethical theories, and so on.

Our prephilosophical language has its home in what Wittgenstein referred to as "a form of life," a socially embedded way of being in the world.[56] Wittgenstein did not assume that this social context was thoroughly secular. Praying, like forming and testing a hypothesis or telling a joke, may well have a place in a form of life, and its language constitutes what Wittgenstein referred to as a language game.[57] Philosophical problems arise when we confuse language games – when we assimilate the language game of prayer with physics, for example – and when we pursue philosophy as if it were a science with the job of offering "deep" explanations of reality. "We must do away with all explanation, and description alone must take its place. . . . Philosophy is a battle against the bewitchment of our intelligence by means of language."[58] Wittgenstein had an optimistic view of the wisdom of our ordinary, non-philosophical discourse. Philosophy's role is not to challenge ordinary language. "Philosophy may in no way interfere with the actual use of language; it can in the end only describe it. . . . Since everything lies open to view there is nothing to explain. For what is hidden, for example, is of no interest to us."[59] While this outlook seems to leave little room for a *philosophical* theist or a Buddhist arguing for a no-self theory of the self, it also seems to leave theistic and Buddhist practices, forms of life and language games, intact.

In his *Lectures on Religious Belief*, Wittgenstein places to one side the relevance of evidence when it comes to understanding religious beliefs.

> Suppose that someone believed in the Last Judgment, and I don't. Does this mean that I believe the opposite to him, just that there won't be such a thing? I would say: "Not at all, or not always."

---

[55] *On Certainty*, ed. G. E. M. Anscombe and G. H. von Wright (New York: Harper, 1969), 94.

[56] *Philosophical Investigations*, trans. G. E. M. Anscombe (Oxford: Blackwell, 1953), 18.

[57] Ibid., 23.

[58] Ibid., 109.

[59] Ibid., 124–126.

> Suppose I say that the body will rot, and another says "No. Particles
> will rejoin in a thousand years, and there will be a Resurrection of you."
>   If some said: "Wittgenstein, do you believe in this?" I'd say: "No."
> "Do you contradict the man?" I'd say: "No."[60]

Wittgenstein did not seem to believe that religious convictions can be
assessed in terms of predictions and confirmation.

> If I even vaguely remember what I was taught about God, I might say:
> "Whatever believing in God may be, it can't be believing in something
> we can test, or find means of testing." You might say: "This is nonsense,
> because people say they believe on *evidence* or say they believe on religious
> experiences." I would say: "The mere fact that someone says they believe
> on evidence doesn't tell me enough for me to be able to say now whether
> I can say of a sentence "God exists" that your evidence is unsatisfactory
> or insufficient."[61]

I suggest that one of his devout admirers and friends, Norman Malcolm,
has come close to accurately describing Wittgenstein's stance in *A
Memoir*:

> I believe that Wittgenstein was prepared by his own character and expe-
> rience to comprehend the idea of a judging and redeeming God. But any
> cosmological conception of a Deity, derived from the notions of cause or
> of infinity, would be repugnant to him. He was impatient with "proofs"
> of the existence of God, with attempts to give religion a *rational* founda-
> tion. When I once quoted to him a remark of Kierkegaard's to this effect:
> "How can it be that Christ does not exist, since I know that He has
> saved me?" Wittgenstein exclaimed: "You see! It isn't a question of *prov-
> ing* anything!" He revered the writings of St. Augustine. . . . I do not wish
> to give the impression that Wittgenstein accepted any religious faith –
> he certainly did not – or that he was a religious person. But I think that
> there was in him, in some sense the *possibility* of religion. I believe that he
> looked on religion as a "form of life". . . . in which he did not participate,
> but with which he was sympathetic and which greatly interested him.[62]

Wittgenstein had a significant impact on Elizabeth Anscombe and
Peter Geach, who retained a traditional Roman Catholic theology.
Anthony Kenney, under the influence of Wittgenstein, relinquished

---

[60] Cyril Barrett, ed., *Wittgenstein: Lectures and Conversations* (Los Angeles: University
   of California Press, 1967), 60.

[61] Ibid.

[62] N. Malcolm, *Ludwig Wittgenstein: A Memoir* (Oxford: Oxford University Press),
   71–72.

religious faith.[63] The biggest impact of Wittgenstein's later philosophy is seen in the work of British philosophers of religion, including Rush Rhees, Cyril Barrett, D. Z. Phillips, B. R. Tilgham, Peter Winch, Fergus Kerr, and F. R. Holland. I shall offer a tentative sketch of Phillips's outlook after commenting on two aspects of Wittgenstein's place in twentieth-century philosophy.

First, Wittgenstein's later philosophy came on the scene when the prevailing analytical philosophy of G. E. Moore and Bertrand Russell was beginning to look sterile. Moore was an exemplary philosopher on many fronts, especially in his close analytical scrutiny of moral and perceptual judgments. But he also seemed to leave us without a systematic horizon or satisfactory framework. Gilbert Ryle offered this portrait:

> Like Socrates, Moore was apt to suppose that his analytic operations would terminate, if ever successful, in some analyses or definitions of composite concepts. But, like Socrates, he produced very few such analyses. Nor does what we have learned from him consist in a repertoire of such analyses. He taught us to try to assess and how to assess the forces the expressions on which philosophical issues hinge. It is a not very important accident that, with many of his critics and champions, he did not fully realize that, before these forces have been assessed, definitions can do no good, and after they have been assessed, there is no more good for them to do, save the little good that mnemonics do. In his "Autobiography" Moore announces gladly and unenviously the drastic reorientation that Wittgenstein was giving to philosophical enquiries and methods. He realized, without any resentment, that the tide of interest was ebbing from the estuaries in which he had so pertinaciously dredged. He does not mention, and probably never mentioned it himself, how much Wittgenstein's sails needed the keel and the ballast that Moore provided.[64]

Moreover, Moore's work labored over terrain (philosophical analysis) that struck Wittgenstein as confused.

[63] See *A Path from Rome*, 147. Probably the most eccentric but clever implementation of Wittgenstein's work on behalf of traditional theism was carried out by O. K. Bouwsma. See his *Philosophical Essays* (Lincoln: University of Nebraska Press, 1965), *Without Proof or Evidence* (Lincoln: University of Nebraska Press, 1984), and *Wittgenstein: Conversations, 1949–51* (Indianapolis: Hackett, 1986).

[64] Ryle, *Collected Papers* (London: Hutchinson, 1971), 270. Wittgenstein's popularity at Cambridge would eclipse Moore and diminish C. D. Broad's prominence. See P. A. Schilpp's biography of Broad in the series: *The Library of Living Philosophers* (New York: Tudor Publishing, 1959).

I mention one other aspect of Wittgenstein's impact with some hesitation, although I am not the first to do so. Wittgenstein evidently had a profound, charismatic, personal affect on many of those who knew him. Although the philosophy of the period was comparatively less exciting, Wittgenstein the person was fascinating. Malcolm testifies to this in his memoir. Consider this fuller description of Wittgenstein at the Vienna Circle meeting that begins this chapter. Carnap writes:

> When I met Wittgenstein, I saw that Schlick's warnings were fully justified. But his behavior was not caused by any arrogance. In general, he was of a sympathetic temperament and very kind; but he was hypersensitive and easily irritated. Whatever he said was always interesting and stimulating. . . . His point of view and his attitude toward people and problems, even theoretical problems, were much more similar to those of a creative artist than to a scientist; one might almost say, similar to those of a religious prophet or seer. When he started to formulate his view on some specific problem, we often felt the internal struggle that occurred in him at that very moment, a struggle by which he tried to penetrate from darkness to light under an intensive and painful strain, which was even visible on his most expressive face. When finally, sometimes after a prolonged arduous effort, his answer came forth, his statement stood before us like a newly created piece of art or a divine revelation. . . . The impression he made on us was as if insight came to him as through a divine inspiration, so that we could not help feeling that any sober rational comment or analysis of it would be a profanation.[65]

Wittgenstein's life has been the subject of a controversial biography and a host of studies.[66]

D. Z. Phillips is perhaps the most prominent representative of a philosophy of religion inspired by Wittgenstein. He shares Wittgenstein's model of philosophy as *not* involving explanation – as in philosophical inquiry into the nature and cause of the cosmos. Philosophy is (or should be) principally a contemplative activity.[67] He does employ philosophy to argue that certain conceptions of God are incoherent, so it is not completely idle when it comes to the critique of religion.[68] But a primary task for him seems to be in opposition to traditional

---

[65] Cited by Avrum Stroll, *Twentieth-Century Analytic Philosophy* (New York: Columbia University Press, 2000), 76–77.

[66] See R. Monk, *Ludwig Wittgenstein: The Duty of Genius* (London: Cape, 1990).

[67] *Philosophy's Cool Place* (Ithaca: Cornell University Press, 1999).

[68] Phillips thinks it is incoherent to suppose that God is a person without a body.

philosophical conceptions of God that we find in Descartes and other metaphysicians. He surveys many models of God and offers some simple advice:

> God as the Archimedean point in Descartes' thought; God as the source of a reality conceived as the most general of all subjects of which everything else can be predicated, including the concepts in terms of which we make true and false judgments; God as a reality in Kant's noumenal realm; God as the author of psychological laws which govern the formation of our original and acquired perceptions; God as the designer of our faculties; God as an assumption which explains the harmony between "mind" and "experience"; God as a person without a body; God as pure consciousness. I have suggested that these exercises in metaphysical realism distort the realities; for God's sake, it is important to turn aside from them. To see why we have been tempted by them is to see, at the same time, why God himself can't tell us anything about them.[69]

In terms of what Phillips advocates, rather than opposes, he seems to want philosophers to attend to the practice of religious persons and communities. Whereas some philosophers see these communities as forthrightly committed to such claims as "God exists," Phillips sees this interpretation as misleading, for religious "believers" do not think God's existence is akin to empirically detectable realities like mountains and rivers. Here is Phillips's reply to the charge that religious believers think God existed before humanity:

> Within religion, things are said about God of a time which precedes man's existence. That does not mean God existed before men in the sense in which mountains, rainbows or rivers did. These are all empirical phenomena and my beliefs concerning their prior existence allow me to ask questions about what they looked like, how long they had existed, whether some of these empirical phenomena have ceased to exist, and so on. Nothing of this sort makes any sense where God's reality is concerned.[70]

Although this break from the modern philosophy we find with David Hume is profound, there is a very remote resemblance to Kant. One of Hume's best advocates and commentators today, J. C. A. Gaskin,

---

[69] Phillips, " 'What God Himself Cannot Tell Us': Realism versus Metaphysical Realism," *Faith and Philosophy* 18:4 (2001): 498.

[70] "On Really Believing," in *Is God Real?*, ed. Joseph Runzo (New York: St. Martin's, 1993), 17.

describes Hume as treating religion "as a public, inspectable phenomenon. Its beliefs can be examined and its practices observed. There is no hint that he ever views religion as a way of life, a metaphysics of existence, a worthwhile thing to which total commitment is possible."[71] Phillips is very much on the other side. But there is a sense in which Kant is a distant ally insofar as Kant also repudiated traditional metaphysics and sought to emphasize the primacy of practice, specifically *moral* practice. Some philosophers read Phillips as an atheist and others as a pious theist. In a recent study, Randy Ramal argues that "as a philosopher, Phillips cannot be looked at as either an atheist or theist; what he believes in his personal life is not something he discusses in his work, and it would be confused to read his works as presupposing atheism or belief."[72] I suspect Ramal is correct. If so, what is the province of philosophy of religion? It may be described as *apophatic* (or the *via negativa*), outlining what cannot be said about the divine. Phillips is skeptical about the constructive theistic projects surveyed in Chapter 9. But on the *cataphatic (via positiva)* side, Phillips commends a philosophy of religion that keeps its focus firmly on religion itself.

> To see what is meant by the reality of God, we must take note of the concept formation by which the notion of the divine is rooted in the reactions of praise and worship. This is why, in *The Concept of Prayer*, I argued against the philosophical tradition which assumes that one ought to determine first whether God exists before considering the grammar of worship. From *The Concept of Prayer* to *Religion without Explanation* I have denied that philosophy can determine *whether* there is a God. On the other hand, I have also emphasized the futility of thinking that we can see what is meant by the reality of God in isolation from the context of worship and praise.[73]

This approach recognizes a role of religious practice that is profoundly different from the positivist disdain for religious life.[74]

---

[71] *Hume's Philosophy of Religion* (London: Macmillan, 1978), 230.

[72] See Randy Ramal, " 'Reference' to D. Z. Phillips," *International Journal for Philosophy of Religion* 48 (2000): 35–56.

[73] *Belief, Change and Forms of Life* (Atlantic Highlands: Humanities Press, 1986), 25.

[74] For additional philosophy of religion inspired by Wittgenstein, see Rush Rhees, *Without Answers* (1969); F. Kerr, *Theology after Wittgenstein* (Oxford: Blackwell, 1986); and B. R. Tilghman, *An Introduction to Philosophy of Religion* (Oxford: Blackwell, 1994). See also replies to Wittgenstein and Phillips in William Alston, "The Christian

A recurrent theme among philosophers of religion inspired by Wittgenstein is to highlight the values that are at stake in religion rather than to focus on evidence, testing or hypothesizing about the structure of reality. Rush Rhees prefers to think of God in relation to beauty rather than a cosmological power:

> Suppose you had to explain to someone who had no idea at all of religion of what a belief in God was. Could you do it in this way? – By proving to him that there must be a first cause – a Someone – and that this something is more powerful (whatever this means) than anything else: so that you would not have been conceived or born at all but for the operation of Something and Something might wipe out the existence of everything at any given time? Would this give him any sense of the wonder and glory of God? Would he not be justified if he answered, "what a horrible idea! Like a Frankenstein without limits, so that you cannot escape it. The most ghastly nightmare!" On the other hand if you read to him certain of the passages in the early Isaiah which describe the beauty of the world . . . then I think you might have given him some sense of what religious believers are talking about. I say *some* idea: I am talking of how you might make a beginning.[75]

To cite one more example of Wittgenstein's influence, Tilghman presents a philosophy of religion that completely shuns the pursuit of evidence. He puts his philosophy in succinct terms: "The concept of God and the concept of evidence don't go together."[76] Tilghman construes his philosophy in terms of restoring an earlier understanding of God and the world.

On the Verge of a Renaissance of Philosophy of Religion

Wittgensteinian, feminist, and continental philosophy of religion are all part of the extraordinarily diverse and vibrant field of philosophy of religion today. Additional movements need to be brought into focus

Language Game," in *The Autonomy of Religious Belief*, ed. F. J. Crosson (Notre Dame: University of Notre Dame Press, 1981), and Roger Trigg, *Reason and Commitment* (Cambridge: Cambridge University Press, 1973). There is a helpful overview of the issues in W. D. Hudson, *Wittgenstein and Religious Belief* (New York: St. Martin's, 1975).

[75] Rush Rhees, "Natural Theology," in *On Religion and Philosophy*, ed. D. Z. Phillips (Cambridge: Cambridge University Press, 1997), 36.

[76] Tilghman, *An Introduction to Philosophy of Religion* (Oxford: Blackwell, 1993), 225.

in our current postpositivist era. This chapter goes on to look at the renewed appreciation for religious tradition and at religious pluralism. To help foster a sense of how the new work constituted a dramatic shift in the world of philosophy, I offer this brief account of a philosophical meeting in England.

In 1957 there was an exchange between Gilbert Ryle, Mary Warnock, and Anthony Quinton on the prospects of metaphysics. The setting is an English-speaking philosophical world where the primary goal is linguistic and conceptual analysis. (One observer characterized this period as worse than in Marx's day. Karl Marx complained that philosophers do not try to change the world; they only talk about the world. Some Anglophone philosophers worry that philosophers not only do not try to change the world, but now do not even talk about the world; instead, they talk about talking about the world.) In this scene, Ryle considered how the traditional philosophers of the past would view the state of philosophy in the 1950s. Ryle imagined a chorus of complaints: "There is Plato, with many supporting voices, asking why we have so little to say about the immortality of the soul.... Herbert Spencer misses discussions of the bearing of evolutionary theory on the nature of man and human society, while Hobbes thinks that it is the bearing of atomic theory that is being unwarrantably neglected."[77]

Ryle summarized two complaints that traditional philosophers would have about philosophers of the 1950s: "They scold us, first of all, for our sedulous refusal to talk about the cosmos.... A second unanimous grumble is that, even inside our constricted horizon, we are diligent about trivialities and neglectful of things that matter.[78] Among the things that at least used to matter, and which fueled heated philosophical debate in the past, Ryle mentions theology. I detect something wistful in Ryle's language:

> In our half-century philosophy and theology have hardly been on speaking terms.... We have forcibly to remind ourselves that there had been an enormously long period during which most of the major theoretical issues had arisen out of disputes between one theology and another, or between theology and science.... When theological coals were hot, the kettle of theological philosophy boiled briskly. If the kettle of theological

[77] "Final Discussion," in *The Nature of Metaphysics*, ed. D. F. Pears (New York: Macmillan, 1957), 156.
[78] Ibid., 155–156.

philosophy is now not even steaming, it is because that fire has died down. Kettles cannot keep themselves on the boil. A philosopher cannot invent conceptual stresses and strains. He has to feel them if he is to be irked into dealing with them. I do not want to exaggerate. The theological fire has died down, but it has not quite gone out and the kettle of theological philosophy, though far from even simmering, is not quite stone cold.[79]

Within several years of this exchange, the *Journal of Religious Studies* was founded by H. D. Lewis, and in 1970 the *International Journal of Philosophy of Religion* was launched. Matters have snowballed since with the emergence nontheistic and theistic philosophies, as well as the development of many philosophical projects on a host of religious concerns from the nature of religious ritual to the religious dimension of environmental ethics. The rest of this chapter covers part of the terrain, while the final, ninth chapter makes an attempt to survey other key components of the field.

Cognition and Tradition

With the retreat of positivism, there has been more sympathy for philosophical projects that commend or constructively explore religious traditions. This change in the intellectual climate has allowed for the revival of arguments for and against the existence of God, and for debate over religious experience, the afterlife, and so on. Chapter 9 addresses some of those themes. In this section I note the appeal of cumulative arguments and then spotlight two key contributions to philosophy of religion, the first of which centers on "reformed epistemology."

The era of positivism, documented earlier, included a take-no-prisoners policy toward religious belief. This hostility was especially apparent in the resistance to a cumulative case for religious belief. Antony Flew, for example, seemed to assume that either an argument for theism was a successful "proof" or it was worthless.

> It is occasionally suggested that some candidate proof, although admittedly failing as a proof, may nevertheless do useful service as a pointer. This is a false exercise of the generosity so characteristic of examiners. A failed proof cannot serve as a pointer to anything, save perhaps to the weakness of those who have accepted it. Nor, for the same reason, can it

[79] Ibid., 159–160.

be put to work along with other throwouts as part of an accumulation of evidence. If one leaky bucket will not hold water that is not reason to think that ten can.[80]

Those defending religious beliefs did not, of course, think that ten bad arguments make a good one, but they did hold that a given philosophy or religion may be supported by a variety of reasons and arguments that, taken together, make a philosophy or religion possible. The word "evidence" comes from the word "to see." With the failure (or presumed failure) of positivism to win consensus, it then seemed fair (in the minds of *some* philosophers) to ask why a secular way of seeing the world should dominate or displace a religious one. Some Christian philosophers have promoted Reformed epistemology according to which certain basic religious beliefs may be taken to be legitimate without having to be vindicated by an impartial, secular review. A leading figure in this movement is Alvin Plantinga, who developed a nuanced understanding of cognition, according to which our warrant for believing something is best seen in terms of what he calls "proper functioning." Proper functioning is then analyzed in a theistic framework where warrant is achieved when cognition functions as it was designed by God. On this view, the Christian community or tradition may be the result or locus of God's actively bringing about religious beliefs.

Plantinga's work is too sophisticated for an easy summary, let alone a comprehensive review of its arguments and the objections it has faced. The three most important texts in which he develops his position are *Warrant and Proper Function; Warrant: the Current Debate;* and *Warranted Christian Belief.* Here is his view on warrant. A person has a warranted belief only if three conditions are met:

(1) It has been produced in me by cognitive faculties that are working properly (functioning as they ought to, subject to no cognitive dysfunction) in a cognitive environment that is appropriate for my kinds of cognitive faculties, (2) the segment of the design plan governing the production

---

[80] *God and Philosophy*, 62–63. Prior to his constructive view of religious tradition (to be reviewed in this section) Alasdair MacIntyre adopted a similar stance: "One occasionally hears teachers of theology aver that although the proofs do not provide conclusive grounds for belief in God, they are at least pointers, indicators. But a fallacious argument points nowhere (except to the lack of logical acumen on the part of those who accept it). And three fallacious arguments are no better than one" (*Difficulties in Christian Belief* [London: SCM, 1959], 63).

of that belief is aimed at the production of true beliefs, and (3) there is a high statistical probability that a belief produced under those conditions will be true under those conditions, furthermore, the degree of warrant is an increasing function of degree of belief.[81]

Plantinga goes on to locate the work of the Holy Spirit in cognitive functioning.

> By virtue of the work of the Holy Spirit in the hearts of those to whom faith is given, the ravages of sin (including cognitive damage) are repaired, gradually or suddenly, to a greater extent or a lesser extent. Furthermore, by virtue of the activity of the Holy Spirit Christians come to grasp, believe, accept, endorse, and rejoice in the truth of the great things of the Gospel.... The principal work of the Holy Spirit is the production (in the hearts of Christian believers) of ... *faith*. ... According to John Calvin, faith is "the firm and certain knowledge of God's benevolence towards us, founded upon the truth of the freely given promise in Christ, both revealed to our minds and sealed upon our hearts through the Holy Spirit."[82]

While Plantinga looks chiefly to Calvin and thus calls his project "Reformed epistemology," his views are not out of step with the Cambridge Platonists discussed in Chapter 1. Nicholas Wolterstorff has shared in this project of Reformed epistemology and critiqued what he sees as the legacy of "evidentialism" in the Enlightenment.[83]

Wolterstorff and Plantinga contend that justification or warrant for belief depends on the persons involved and their circumstances.

> It must be clearly noted that rationality ... is in good measure person specific and situation specific. When I was young, there were things which it was rational for me to believe.... rationality of belief can only be determined in context.... the proper question is always and only whether it is rational for this or that particular person in this or that situation, or for

---

[81] *Warrant and Proper Function* (Oxford: Oxford University Press, 1993), 46–47.

[82] *Warranted Christian Belief* (Oxford: Oxford University Press, 2000), 243–244.

[83] See Wolterstorff's contribution to the collection he edited with Plantinga, *Faith and Rationality* (Notre Dame: University of Notre Dame Press, 1983). See also Wolterstorff's book on Reid, *Thomas Reid and the Story of Epistemology* (Cambridge: Cambridge University Press, 2001). Two other philosophers of religion who offer a high view of the contribution of tradition to our religious beliefs and experiences are William Alston and Basil Mitchell.

a person of this or that particular type in this or that type of situation, to believe so-and-so. Rationality is always *situated* rationality.[84]

Reformed epistemologists thereby insist on the historical condition for forming beliefs:

> A person is rationally justified in all his beliefs until such time as he has acquired certain conceptual equipment and the ability to make use of that equipment. Before that time his system of beliefs may lack a variety of merits, but until, for example, he has grasped (or ought to have grasped) the concept of a reason, he is doing as well in governing his believings as can rightly be demanded of him. According, there is probably a time in the life of each child when he is rationally justified in all his beliefs.[85]

Wolterstorff and Plantinga adopt the view that our beliefs may be justified or considered innocent epistemically in the absence of known reasons or evidence against these beliefs: "A person is rationally justified in believing a certain proposition which he does believe unless he has adequate reason to cease from believing it. Our beliefs are rational unless we have reason for refraining; they are not nonrational unless we have some reason *for* believing."[86] Their stance is explicitly nondogmatic insofar as they commend an openness to reasons against basic religious beliefs as well as a receptivity to positive evidential support. The opposition to evidentialism resonated with a range of philosophers. Norman Malcolm expressed his own opposition to evidentialism as follows: "The obsessive concern [in philosophy of religion] with the proofs [of the existence of God] reveals the assumption that in order for religious belief to be intellectually respectable it ought to have a rational justification. That is the misunderstanding. It is like the idea that we are not justified in relying on memory until memory has been proved reliable."[87]

Consider four aspects of Reformed epistemology. First, Reformed epistemologists seem open to a wide array of ways in which religious belief gets forged. Presumably one way would simply be by being born

---

[84] Wolterstorff, "Can Belief in God Be Rational?" in Plantinga and Wolterstorff, *Faith and Rationality*, 155.

[85] Ibid., 171.

[86] Wolterstoff, "Can Belief in God Be Rational If It Has No Foundations?" in Plantinga and Wolterstorff, *Faith and Rationality*, 163.

[87] N. Malcolm, "The Groundlessness of Belief," in *Reason and Religion*, ed. S. C. Brown (London: Routledge, 1997), 154–155.

into a religious community.[88] But in my view the most plausible cases of (ostensibly) proper-functioning-belief-formation involve religious experience of some sort. Consider Plantinga's description:

> There is in us a disposition to believe propositions of the sort *this flower was created by God* or *this vast and intricate universe was created by God* when we contemplate the flower or behold the starry heavens or think about the vast reaches of the universe.... Upon reading the Bible, one may be impressed with a deep sense that God is speaking to him. Upon having done what I know is cheap, or wrong, or wicked, I may feel guilty in God's sight and form the belief *God disapproves of what I have done.* Upon confession and repentance I may feel forgiven forming the belief *God forgives me for what I have done.*[89]

Plantinga invokes "a deep sense" of God and feelings that seem part of an awareness of God's activity. Insofar as Reformed epistemology draws on a person's experience of God, it will require the vindication of some of the new work on religious experience.[90]

Second, Reformed epistemology seems wedded to a philosophy of human nature. Plantinga writes:

> Belief in the existence of God is in the same boat as belief in other minds, the past, and perceptual objects; in each case God has so constructed us that in the right circumstances we form the belief in question. But then the belief that there is such a person as God is as much among the deliverances of reason as those other beliefs.... belief in God, like other properly basic beliefs, is not groundless or arbitrary: it is grounded in justification-conferring conditions.[91]

As with Cambridge Platonism, which located its view of reason in the context of a philosophy of human nature and the cosmos, a developed Reformed epistemology should include an overall metaphysics showing that such a God-given disposition is possible. I introduce the qualified term "developed" because if Reformed epistemology is right, then someone can know something X (e.g., God exists) without knowing how she

---

[88] But "proper functioning" would presumably have to include no unjust or wicked indoctrination or "brainwashing." Given God's essential goodness, some means for attaining religious belief would be improper.

[89] "Reason and Belief in God," Plantinga and Wolterstorff, *Faith and Rationality*, 80.

[90] See note 44.

[91] Ibid., 90.

knows it and possibly without knowing that she knows it. But I suggest that it is at least philosophically desirable to show the plausibility (or at least possibility) of God's endowing human nature with such a disposition.[92]

Third, Reformed epistemology is built, in part, on skepticism over foundationalism à la Descartes and evidentialism à la Locke, Hume, and so on. It has been important for Reformed epistemology to limit its skepticism to a philosophy of evidence and not to a philosophy of truth.

> It is not the case that one is warranted in accepting some theory if and only if one is warranted in believing that it is justified by propositions knowable non-inferentially and with certitude. From this it does not follow that there is no structured reality independent of our conceivings and believing – though the difficulties of foundationalism have led many to this position. Nor does it follow that we must give up truth as the goal of theoretical enquiry – though the difficulties of foundationalism have led to a wave of agnosticism. Nor does it follow that one belief is as warranted for me as another. All that follows is that theorizing is without a foundation of indubitables.[93]

Plantinga, Wolterstorff, and others have guarded against a broader skepticism through their defense of a realist view of truth and a defense of the overall coherence and plausibility of theism vis-à-vis what they see as the most challenging alternative, naturalism.

Fourth, one of the major challenges to Reformed epistemology involves pluralism (the topic of the next section in this chapter). The problem arises as follows. In Plantinga's case for recognizing religious belief as properly basic, he suggests that the criterion for such beliefs has to be by example. (Recall the discussion of the problem of the criterion in Chapter 2; Plantinga is essentially a particularist.)

> The fact is, I think, that...[no] necessary and sufficient condition for proper basicality follows from clearly self-evident premises by clearly acceptable arguments. And hence the proper way to arrive at such a criterion is, broadly speaking, inductive. We must assemble examples of beliefs and conditions such that the former is obviously properly basic in the latter,

---

[92] Plantinga and Wolterstorff have both defended the coherence and plausibility of a philosophy of humanity and the cosmos that is either theistic or not anti-theistic.

[93] Wolterstoff, *Reason within the Bounds of Reason Alone* (Grand Rapids: Eerdmans, 1976), 52–53.

and examples of beliefs and conditions such that the former are obviously not properly basic in the latter. We must then frame hypotheses as to the necessary and sufficient conditions of proper basicality and test these hypotheses by reference to those examples.[94]

What if the examples Plantinga identifies are different from others?

But there is no reason to assume, in advance, that everyone will agree on the examples. The Christian will of course suppose that belief in God is entirely proper and rational; if he does not accept this belief on the basis of other propositions, he will conclude that it is basic for him and quite properly so. Followers of Bertrand Russell and Madelyn Murray O'Hare may disagree; but how is that relevant? Must my criteria, or those of the Christian community, conform to their examples? Surely not. The Christian community is responsible to *its* set of examples, not to theirs.[95]

But then it appears as though the Reformed epistemologist has laid the groundwork for the warrant or justification of all sorts of competing religious communities. William Wainwright develops this objection:

As a Christian or Jewish theist who reads the Bible, it may seem immediately obvious that God is addressing him or her through the words of scripture. An Advaitins may find it immediately obvious that the Isa Upainishad is a revelation of the eternal truth. Both think that their beliefs are not only basic but also *properly* basic. Why, then, should theists trust their own "intuitions," rather than those of Advaitins? If both are equally intelligent, informed, and religiously sensitive, it seems arbitrary to privilege one set of intuitions rather than the other.[96]

There are several replies. Reformed epistemology is not dogmatically opposed to natural theology. Maybe there are additional reasons making one religion more plausible than the other. A second option would be to accept the conclusion that, from the standpoint of each believer, each commits no "sin" by trusting their intuition. Plantinga's view of warrant allows that persons may be equally justified (from their point of view) in accepting incompatible beliefs, but one person's belief is warranted as a result of the divinely endowed proper functioning while the other is not. Another option would be to look for common ground for these

---

[94] "Reason and Belief in God," 71.
[95] Ibid., 77.
[96] Wainwright, *Philosophy of Religion* (Belmont, Calif.: Wadsworth, 1988), 156–158.

two parties. Could the eternal truth from the Upanishad be reconciled with the relevant truths in Judaism and Christianity?[97]

The new assessment of religious tradition has taken shape through movements other than Reformed epistemology. Alasdair McIntyre has built a case for the role of tradition as a valuable (and virtually indispensable) philosophical resource and tool. A good way to appreciate McIntyre is to read him in relation to the (presumed) failure of the scientifically oriented philosophy of the Enlightenment, the positivists and the like. Bertrand Russell began his famous *A History of Western Philosophy* with this portrait of theology, tradition, and philosophy:

> Philosophy, as I shall understand the word, is something intermediate between theology and science. Like theology, it consists of speculations on matters as to which definite knowledge has, so far, been unascertainable; but like science, it appeals to human reason rather than to authority, whether that of tradition or that of revelation. All *definite* knowledge – so I should contend – belongs to science; all *dogma* as to what surpasses definite knowledge belongs to theology. But between theology and science there is No Man's Land, exposed to attack from both sides; this No Man's Land is philosophy. Almost all the questions of most interest to speculative minds are such as science cannot answer, and the confident answers of theologians no longer seem so convincing as they did in former centuries.[98]

By the time MacIntyre began to write a defense of religious tradition, Russell's "No Man's Land" appeared barren. MacIntyre's main focus in much of his work from the early 1980s onward has been the failure of the Enlightenment (from Descartes and Locke through Kant and Mill) to find a stable framework for morality and reason. Here is his assessment of the difficulty facing the Enlightenment,

---

[97] For additional reading, see H. Hart et al., eds., *Rationality in the Calvinist Tradition* (Lanham, Md.: University Press of America, 1983); J. E. Tomberlin and P. van Inwagen, eds., *Alvin Plantinga* (Dordrecht: D. Reidel, 1985); R. Audi and W. Wainwright, eds., *Rationality, Religious Belief and Moral Commitment* (Ithaca: Cornell University Press, 1986); Linda Zagzebski, ed., *Rational Faith* (Notre Dame: University of Notre Dame Press, 1993); C. S. Evans and M. Westphal, eds., *Christian Perspectives on Religious Knowledge* (Grand Rapids: Eerdmans, 1993); S. Goetz, "Belief in God Is Not Properly Basic," *Religious Studies* 19 (1983); Paul Helm, *Belief Policies* (Cambridge: Cambridge University Press, 1940); J. L. Kvanvig, "The Evidentialist Objection," *American Philosophical Quarterly* 20 (1983); P. L. Quinn, "In Search of the Foundations of Theism," *Faith and Philosophy* 2 (1985).

[98] *A History of Western Philosophy*, xiii.

once it has relinquished the teleology of the ancients (Aristotle) and medievals (Aquinas). (There are striking parallels between MacIntyre and Gadamer, discussed in Chapter 7.)

> The problems of modern moral theory emerge clearly as the product of the failure of the Enlightenment project. On the one hand the individual moral agent, freed from hierarchy and teleology, conceives himself and is conceived of by moral philosophers as sovereign in his moral authority. On the other hand the inherited, if partially transformed rules of morality have to be found some new status, deprived as they have been of their older teleological character and their even more ancient categorical character as expressions of an ultimately divine law. If such rules cannot be found a new status which will make appeal to them rational, appeal to them will indeed appear as a mere instrument of individual desire and will. Hence there is a pressure to vindicate them either by devising some new teleology or by finding some new categorical status for them. The first project is what lends its importance to utilitarianism; the second to all those attempts to follow Kant in presenting the authority of the appeal to moral rules as grounded in the nature of practical reason. Both attempts, so I shall argue, failed.[99]

MacIntyre's more recent work has been refined to promoting the virtues in light of a teleology anchored biologically, much like Aristotle.[100] His defense of Christian belief and virtue is very much a part of his philosophical study of history and the ways in which traditions can develop critically.[101]

MacIntyre argued that what is needed for moral coherence and an intelligible understanding of goods is a stable (but not static) tradition. His immediate interest was his own tradition, Christianity, and the ways in which it evolved in the rational deliberation on goods, practices, and the nature of God and the world.

> What the Enlightenment made us for the most part blind to and what we now need to recover is, so I shall argue, a conception of rational enquiry as embodied in a tradition, a conception according to which the standards of rational justification themselves emerge from and are part of a history in which they are vindicated by the way in which they transcend the

---

[99] *After Virtue* (Notre Dame: University of Notre Dame Press, 1984), 62.

[100] See Alasdair MacIntyre, *Dependent Rational Animals: Why Human Beings Need the Virtues* (Chicago: Open Court Press, 2001).

[101] For related work, see Basil Mitchell, *Faith and Criticism* (Oxford: Oxford University Press, 1994).

limitations of and provide remedies for the defects of their predecessors within the history of that same tradition.[102]

One of the outcomes of MacIntyre's work was an appreciation of practicing philosophy from within and through religious tradition.

> Every tradition is embodied in some particular set of utterances and actions and thereby in all the particularities of some specific language and culture. The invention, elaboration, and modification of the concepts through which both those who found and those who inherit a tradition understand it are inescapably concepts which have been framed in one language rather than another.... The conception of language presupposed in saying this is that of a language as it is used in and by a particular community living at a particular time and place with particular shared beliefs, institutions and practices.[103]

But just how far does MacIntyre go in his emphasis on tradition and language? Has MacIntyre subverted not only evidence and justification to historical contexts but also truth? On this point, MacIntyre insists on truth as something that transcends tradition; traditions may aim at truth.

> Implicit in the rationality of such enquiry there is indeed a conception of a final truth, that is to say, a relationship of the mind to its objects which would be wholly adequate in respect of the capacities of that mind. But any conception of that state as one in which the mind could by its own powers know itself as thus adequately informed is ruled out; the Absolute Knowledge of the Hegelian system is from this tradition-constituted standpoint a chimaera.[104]

What MacIntyre has pressed for is a more historically sensitive appreciation of philosophical arguments for truth about God, the world, and so on. So the rational appeal of a relation may be manifested in how, over time, it solves philosophical problems that arise (e.g., how did Christianity fare in the transition from Aristotelian to modern science?). "The rationality of a tradition-constituted and tradition-constitutive enquiry is in the key and essential part a matter of the kind of progress which it makes through a number of well-defined types of stage. Every such form of enquiry begins in and from some condition of pure historical

---

[102] *Whose Justice? Which Rationality?* (Notre Dame: University of Notre Dame Press, 1988), 7.

[103] Ibid., 371.

[104] Ibid., 360–361.

contingency, from the beliefs, institutions and practices of some particular community which constitute a given."[105] As noted earlier, MacIntyre now welcomes the recovery of a defensible (nonmechanistic) teleology that will bolster and refine traditional virtues.

One other aspect of MacIntyre's work deserves noting. Part and parcel of his positive view of traditions is his view of the indispensability of narratives.

> [M]an is in his actions and practice, as well as in his fictions, essentially a story-telling animal. He is not essentially, but becomes through his history, a teller of stories that aspire to truth. But the key question for men is not about their own authorship; I can only answer the question "What am I to do?" if I can answer the prior question, "Of what story or stories do I find myself a part?" We enter human society, that is, with one or more imputed characters – roles into which we have been drafted – and we have to learn what they are in order to be able to understand how others respond to us and how our responses to them are apt to be construed.... Deprive children of stories and you leave them unscripted, anxious stutterers in their actions as in their words. Hence there is no way to give us an understanding of any society, including our own, except through the stock of stories which constitute its initial dramatic resources. Mythology, in its original sense, is at the heart of things. Vico was right and so was Joyce. And so too of course is that moral tradition from heroic society to its medieval heirs according to which the telling of stories has a key part in educating us into the virtues.[106]

This emphasis on narrative has fueled a major movement in ethics. In narrative ethics, moral reasoning is not like Mill's utilitarianism or Kant's categorical imperative. Rather, one assesses moral life in specific historical contexts and with respect to lives rather than abstract principles.[107]

> The virtues find their point and purpose not only in sustaining those relationships necessary if the variety of goods internal to practices are to be achieved and not only in sustaining the form of an individual life in which that individual may seek out his or her good as the good of his or her whole life, but also in sustaining those traditions which provide both

---

[105] Ibid., 354.

[106] *After Virtue*, 201.

[107] See Robert Robert's "Narrative Ethics," in *A Companion to Philosophy of Religion*, ed. P. Quinn and C. Taliaferro (Oxford: Blackwell, 1997).

practices and individual lives with their necessary historical context. The subject matters of moral philosophy at least – the evaluative and normative concepts, maxims, arguments and judgments about which the moral philosophy enquires – *are nowhere to be found except as embodied in the historical lives of particular social groups and so possessing the distinctive characteristics of historical existence:* both identity and change through time, expression in institutionalized practice as well as in discourse, interaction and interrelationship with a variety of forms of activity. Morality which is no particular society's morality is to be found nowhere.[108]

MacIntyre's view of tradition is complemented in some respects by work by Charles Taylor.[109] Let us now turn to the plurality of themes and religions that are taken up in recent philosophy of religion.

Pluralistic Philosophy of Religion

In the midst of the new work on religious traditions, there has been a steady, growing representation of nonmonotheistic traditions. An early proponent of this expanded format was Ninian Smart, who, through many publications, scholarly as well as popular, secured philosophies of Hinduism and Buddhism as components in the standard cannon of English-speaking philosophy of religion.[110] Smart highlighted three reasons for expanding the cannon to Asian religions.

First, it would free the student from the European cultural tribalism which so bedevils thought about religion (and much else). Second, it would correspond to the real growth of interest in the great Eastern faiths as a possible alternative, and certainly a challenge, to Christianity. Third, out of this subject there arise in a very natural and incisive way most of the philosophical and apologetic issues which the Christian has to face. For example, the Western concept of the importance of the historical process is largely foreign to these faiths, and the notion of a personal God is altogether less prominent. This raises questions about the basis of

---

[108] *After Virtue,* 207.

[109] Charles Taylor's work has played an important role in rekindling philosophical interest in religious tradition. See his *Sources of the Self* (Cambridge, Mass.: Harvard University Press, 1989), especially in his final reflection on community and theism.

[110] See Smart, *Reasons and Faiths: An Investigation of Religious Discourse, Christian and Non-Christian* (London: Routledge, 1958); *A Dialogue of Religions* (London: SCM Press, 1960); *Worldviews: Cross-Cultural Explorations of Human Beliefs* (New York: Scribners, 1983).

theologies in religious experience; and so we are able to gain an insight into the sources of religion from the phenomenological point of view.[111]

Smart championed the thesis that there are genuine differences between religious traditions. He therefore resisted seeing some core experience as capturing the essential identity of being religious. Under Smart's tutelage, there has been considerable growth in cross-cultural philosophy of religion. Wilfred Cantwell Smith also did a great deal to improve the representation of non-Western religions and reflection.[112]

The expansion of philosophy of religion has involved fresh translations of philosophical and religious texts from India, China, Southeast Asia, and Africa.[113] Exceptional figures from non-Western traditions have an increased role in cross-cultural philosophy of religion and religious dialogue. The late Bimal Krishna Matilal made salient contributions to enrich Western exposure to Indian philosophy of religion.[114] Among the mid-twentieth-century Asian philosophers, two who stand out for special notice are T. R. V. Murty (see his *Central Philosophy of Buddhism*) and S. N. Das Gupta (see his magnificent five-volume *History of Indian Philosophy*). Both brought high philosophical standards along with the essential philology to educate Western thinkers. As evidence of non-Western productivity in the Anglophone world, see Arvind Sharma's *A Hindu Perspective on the Philosophy of Religion* and *The Philosophy of Religion and Advaita Vedanta*. There are now extensive treatments of pantheism and student-friendly philosophical guides to diverse religious conceptions of the cosmos.[115]

---

[111] Ninian Smart, "Religion as a Discipline?" in *Concept and Empathy*, ed. D. Wiebe (New York: New York University Press, 1986), 161.

[112] See Smith, *The Meaning and End of Religion* (London: SPCK, 1978). Mircea Eliade (1906–1986) also had an enormous impact in expanding the parameters of religious scholarship, indirectly helping to forge a greater domain for philosophy of religion. See, for example, Douglas Allen, *Myth and Religion in Mircea Eliade* (London: Routledge, 2002).

[113] In Quinn and Taliaferro, *A Companion to Philosophy of Religion*, see the entries "Hinduism," "Chinese Confucianism and Daoism," and "African Religions from a Philosophical Point of View."

[114] See *The Logical Illumination of Indian Mysticism* (Oxford: Clarendon, 1977) and *Logical and Ethical Issues of Religious Belief* (Calcutta: University of Calcutta Press, 1982).

[115] See M. P. Levine, *Pantheism: A Non-Theistic Concept of Deity* (London: Routledge, 1994), and Linda Tessier, ed., *Concepts of the Ultimate* (New York: St. Martin's, 1989).

Along with the proliferation of diverse religious literature and more cross-cultural encounters between religions, questions were raised about the very definition of religion. It was clear that "religion" could not be defined in exclusively theistic terms.[116] But because a positive definition of religion has seemed quite elusive, practitioners of philosophy of religion have often simply presumed that mainstream forms of Judaism, Christianity, Islam, Daoism, Hinduism, and Buddhism are religious and treated other traditions as religious insofar as they resemble these other traditions.[117] There are political repercussions for whether institutions and practices are recognized as religious. For example, identifying Confucianism as a religion in China, rather than as a philosophy, has repercussions for its role in a state-sponsored secular culture. In the United States, religious identity can bring about some protection (in the form of tax exemption) as well as some restrictions (as noted in the next chapter, pluralistic, modern democracies have been reluctant to permit religiously motivated laws). For better or worse, the contemporary philosophical study of religion has not been waylaid by lengthy debates over whether, say, Marxism or secular humanism or environmentalism are religious.

The new appreciation for religious diversity has also fed an appreciation for different views of faith. In this book we have seen religious belief in terms of convictions about the nature of reality and in terms of ways of living; some of the philosophy of religion described is taken up by arguments for the truth or falsity of these convictions, whereas some has focused on making the case for moral faith in the Kantian tradition. Now, "faith" itself is a topic being explored across cultures. Lad Sessions has advance six models of faith. These include what Sessions calls the personal relationship model, the belief model, the attitude model, the confidence model, the devotion model, and the hope model.[118] Each of these models is articulated in different terms depending on the evidence involved and especially the concepts of the one who has faith and the object of faith. Is the one with faith believing propositions? Trusting

---

[116] This is why I believe definitions like W. D. Hudson's are too limited. See Hudson, "What Makes Religious Beliefs Religious?" *Religious Studies* 13 (1977).

[117] I believe it is still notoriously difficult to define "religion." See my *Contemporary Philosophy of Religion* (Oxford: Blackwell, 1998) for an overview of some of the possibilities. Phillip Divine has a rich discussion of the issues in "On the Definition of 'Religion,'" *Faith and Philosophy* 3:3 (1986).

[118] See Sessions, *The Concept of Faith* (Ithaca: Cornell University Press, 1994).

a person? Is the faith all-embracing and defining a person's identity or is it less central? How does faith in God differ from faith in "a non-relational conscious state that realizes [a person's] deeper self, that is characterized by a profound feeling of (self-)confidence (serenity, tranquility, calm, peace)"?[119] The result is a richer vocabulary for seeing similarities and differences across cultures.[120]

From the standpoint of this book, which begins with Cambridge Platonism, it is fascinating to note some parallels in Hindu tradition to some of the themes of the first chapter. Reason is not called "the candle of the Lord," but it is identified as divine in the Bhagavad Gita. Krishna reveals himself as reason and intelligence beckoning his followers to see the divine character of intelligence. "And I am from the everlasting the seed of eternal life. I am the intelligence of the intelligent. I am the beauty of the beautiful."[121] Moreover, while Hinduism does not have the "virtues of embodiment" as the Cambridge Platonists articulated them, there is a widespread affirmation of the good of embodiment as a rare gift and privilege for good.[122] Of course, very different philosophical systems are at work here – that is precisely my point. With the expansion of the field there is a great opportunity to explore the similarities and the differences at work in these distinct religious traditions.

Other themes from Chapter 1 that are fruitful to compare in expanded, religious contexts include the role of virtues in the practice of Hindu and Buddhist philosophy, and the tension between reason and revelation in Islamic philosophy. So, it has been pointed out that Indian philosophy promotes a meditative detachment that is religiously important.

> Against all forms of theorizing and calculating attachment to the world, and regardless of all assurances that knowledge has to have a goal and purpose, and be a means to an end, the Indian tradition has developed conceptions of knowledge and ideals of contemplation which radically eliminate and transcend all goal-oriented interests, and the means-ends-relationship itself. This is not knowledge as "soteriological technique," but knowledge which tries to supersede all technique and instrumentality. Liberation cannot be attained through causal techniques, or the mastery of

---

[119] Ibid., 89.

[120] See Sessions on Hindu and Buddhist faiths in *The Concept of Faith*, chap. 4.

[121] *The Bhagavad Gita*, trans. J. Mascaro (Baltimore: Penguin Books, 1966), 7:10.

[122] See, for example, Shankara, *Crest-Jewel of Discrimination*, different translations.

means-ends-relationships; but it means freedom from such relationships themselves, and from a world which functions and exists through them. It means pure, free, disinterested contemplation in which all causal and instrumental relations, and with them the world itself, become transparent and irrelevant. Knowledge is not something to be done or performed; it is openness for absolute reality (Brahman), i.e. a reality which is not a function and projection of "works" and desires.[123]

In this light, the practice of philosophy has been seen as running parallel with the practice of religion. As for the debate over faith and reason, the recent reexamination of the great Islamic philosophers Al-Kindi (ninth century), Al-Farabi (tenth century), Al-Ghazzali (1058–1111), Averroës (1126–1198), and others sets new historical referents for thinking about the religious significance of evidence and justification.[124]

The new philosophical work coming out of Africa and about Africa has been especially interesting, as one is forced to come to terms with separating colonial and aboriginal thought and to avoid unjustly applying external, inappropriate categories. This has called for a self-critical philosophical investigation that demands a thorough knowledge and acquaintance with the languages, cultures, and histories.[125]

Taking note of parallels between religions, and coming to terms with radically different religions, have been vastly assisted by the journal *Philosophy East and West*, founded by Charles Moore in 1951. While some topics are purely secular, there is an enormous amount of work in the journal over the years by philosophers on Hinduism, Buddhism, Confucianism, and other non-Western religions.

To illustrate further the crossover of diverse material in the philosophy of religion and, thus, the opportunity for fruitful philosophical dialogue between religions, I briefly highlight four areas treated in this book so far that bear on nontheistic traditions. (1) Humean doubts about the substantiality of the self and the composition of the

---

[123] Wilhelm Halbfass, "Darsana, Anviksiki, Philosophy," in *Philosophy of Religion*, ed. C. Taliaferro and P. Griffiths (Oxford: Blackwell, 2003), 304.

[124] As a result of cross-fertilization between European and Islamic philosophy, William Craig has articulated and defended a Muslim version of the cosmological argument in *The Kalam Cosmological Argument* (London: Macmillan, 1979). See also H. A. Davidson, *Proofs for Eternity: Creation and the Existence of God in Medieval Islamic and Jewish Philosophy* (New York: Oxford University Press, 1987).

[125] See the entry "African Religions from a Philosophical Point of View," in Quinn and Taliaferro, *A Companion to Philosophy of Religion*.

world were anticipated in Buddhist philosophy.[126] (2) Buddhist thinkers anticipated what Kant would later formulate as the antinomies.[127] (3) Buddhism can make an important contribution to feminism.[128] (4) Indian philosophers have wrestled with the virtues of working from within and between religious traditions (Hindu-Buddhist dialogue). Consider, for example, Jitendra Nath Mohanty's distinction between tradition and orthodoxy.

> Orthodoxy consists in fossilizing tradition into a lifeless, unchanging structure. Tradition, as distinguished from orthodoxy, is a living process of creation and preservation of significations. When a tradition is alive, it continues to grow, to create, and to respond to new situations and challenges. When it is no longer alive, it requires an orthodoxy to preserve its purity against possible distortions and desanctifications. A living tradition is ambiguous in the sense that it allows for growth and development in many different ways. It is false to oppose tradition to freedom of rational criticism, for rational criticism takes place, not within a vacuum but from within a tradition.[129]

I am not suggesting that in any one of these four areas we have philosophers working on identical problems – as though the eighteenth-century Scottish David Hume was on the same page with Gautama Siddhartha Buddha, or that ancient and contemporary Indian philosophers are wrestling with the same issue as MacIntyre. But I am suggesting enough overlap and a challenging alternative way of conceiving of tradition, reason, and so on to make for excellent cross-cultural philosophy.[130]

Today, most of the philosophy of religion texts used in university and college courses pay some attention to the plurality of religion. The publication in 1987 of the magisterial *Encyclopedia of Religion* was a landmark in reference works for religious pluralism. As one reviewer put it, "The great positive value of the *Encyclopedia* is that it places the

---

[126] See, for example, B. J. Dreyfus, *Recognizing Reality: Dharmakirti's Philosophy and Its Tiketan Interpretations* (Albany: SUNY Press, 1996).

[127] See T. R. V. Murti, *The Central Philosophy of Buddhism* (London: George Allen and Unwin, 1955), part 1.

[128] See Anne Carolyn Klein, "Finding a Self: Buddhist and Feminist Perspectives," in Taliaferro and Griffiths, *Philosophy of Religion*.

[129] J. N. Mohanty, *Reason and Tradition in Indian Thought* (Oxford: Clarendon, 1992), 11.

[130] For what I think is an ideal case of cross-cultural philosophy of religion, see Paul Griffiths, *Religious Reading* (Oxford: Oxford University Press, 1999). Griffiths offers a probing account of religious reading in Buddhist and Christian contexts.

philosophy of religion firmly within the context of a very rich array of diverse faiths and practices."[131] The *Routledge Encyclopedia of Philosophy* similarly includes non-Western traditions. A live, current concern in philosophy of religion today is over how to understand the nature and significance of competing religious conceptions of the divine. A key player in the debate is the British philosopher John Hick.

Hick is the preeminent synthesizer of religious traditions. In an important book, *Death and Eternal Life* (1974), Hick advanced a complex picture of the afterlife involving components from diverse traditions.[132] Over many publications and many years, Hick has moved from a broadly based theistic view of God to what Hick calls "the Real," a noumenal sacred reality. Hick claims that different religions provide us with a glimpse or partial access to the Real. In an influential article, "The New Map of the Universe of Faiths," Hick raised the possibility that many of the great world religions are revelatory of the Real.

> Seen in [a] historical context these movements of faith – the Judaic-Christian, the Buddhist, the Hindu, the Muslim – are not essentially rivals. They began at different times and in different places, and each expanded outwards into the surrounding world of primitive natural religion until most of the world was drawn up into one or other of the great revealed faiths. And once this global pattern had become established it has ever since remained fairly stable. It is true that the process of establishment involved claiming their obedience and demanding a new level of righteousness and justice in the life of Israel. Then in Persia the great prophet Zoroaster appeared; China produced Lao-tzu and then the Buddha lived, and Mahavira, the founder of the Jain religion and, probably about the end of this period, the writing of the Bhagavad Gita; and Greece produced Pythagoras and then, ending this golden age, Socrates and Plato. Then after the gap of some three hundred years came Jesus of Nazareth and the emergence of Christianity; and after another gap the prophet Mohammed and the rise of Islam. The suggestion that we must consider is that these were all moments of divine revelation.[133]

---

[131] Keith Ward, "Philosophy and the Philosophy of Religion," in *Encyclopedia of Religion, Religious Studies* (1988), 24:46. See the other reviews of the *Encyclopedia*, same volume.

[132] This was revised in 1987. See also his contributions to Davis, *Death and the Afterlife* and to H. Hewitt, ed., *Problems in the Philosophy of Religion: Critical Studies of the Work of John Hick* (New York: St. Martin's, 1995).

[133] *An Interpretation of Religion: Human Responses to the Transcendent* (New Haven: Yale University Press, 1989), 136.

Hick sees these traditions, and others as well, as different meeting points in which a person might be in relation to the same sacred reality or the Real. "The great world faiths embody different perceptions and conceptions of, and correspondingly different responses to, the Real from within the major variant ways of being human; and that within each of them the transformation of human existence from self-centeredness to Reality-centeredness is taking place."[134] Hick uses Kant to develop his central thesis.

> Kant distinguished between noumenon and phenomenon, or between a *Ding an sich* [the thing in itself] and that thing as it appears to human consciousness. . . . In this strand of Kant's thought – not the only strand, but the one which I am seeking to press into service in the epistemology of religion – the noumenal world exists independently of our perception of it and the phenomenal world is that same world as it appears to our human consciousness. . . . I want to say that the noumenal Real is experienced and thought by different human mentalities, forming and formed by different religious traditions, as the range of gods and absolutes which the phenomenology of religion reports.[135]

One advantage of Hick's position is that it undermines a rationale for religious conflict. If successful, this approach would offer a way to accommodate diverse communities and undermine what has been a source of grave conflict in the past.

Hick's work since the early 1980s provided an impetus for not taking what appears to be religious conflict as outright contradictions. He advanced a philosophy of religion that paid careful attention to the historical and social context. By doing so, Hick thought the apparent conflict between seeing the Real as a personal or impersonal reality could be reconciled.

> In the mode of I-Thou encounter they experience [divine reality as] personal. Indeed in the context of that relationship it *is* personal, not It but He or She. When human beings relate themselves to the Real in the mode of non-personal awareness they experience it as non-personal, and in the context of this relationship it *is* non-personal. Each of these two basic categories, God and the Absolute, is schematized or made concrete within actual religious experience as a range of gods or absolutes. There are,

---

[134] Ibid., 240.
[135] Ibid., 241–242.

respectively, the *personae* and *impersonae* in terms of which the Real is humanly known.[136]

The response to Hick's proposal has been mixed. Some contend that the very concept of "the Real" is incoherent (Plantinga) or not religiously adequate (O'Hear).[137] Indeed, articulating the nature of the Real is no easy task. Hick writes that the Real "cannot be said to be one or many, person or thing, substance or process, good or bad, purposive or non-purposive. None of the concrete descriptions that apply within the realm of human experience can apply literally to the unexperienceable ground of that realm. . . . We cannot even speak of this as a thing or an entity."[138] It has been argued that Hick has secured not the equal acceptability of diverse religions but rather their unacceptability. In their classical forms, Judaism, Islam, and Christianity diverge. If, say, the incarnation of God in Christ did not occur, isn't Christianity false? In reply, Hick has sought to interpret specific claims about the Incarnation in ways that do not commit Christians to the "literal truth" of God becoming enfleshed. The "truth" of the Incarnation has been interpreted in such terms as these: in Jesus Christ (or in the narratives about Christ) God is disclosed. Or: Jesus Christ was so united with God's will that his actions were and are the functional display of God's character. Perhaps as a result of Hick's challenge, philosophical work on the Incarnation and other beliefs and practices specific to religious traditions have received renewed attention.[139] Hick has been a leading, widely appreciated force in the expansion of philosophy of religion in the late twentieth century.

Diverse pictures of the divine or sacred do not always emerge from non-European sources, as we have seen with Conway, Spinoza, Hegel,

---

[136] Ibid., 245.

[137] See Plantinga, *Warranted Christian Belief*, chap. 2, and Anthony O'Hear, "The Real of the Real," in Taliaferro and Griffiths, *Philosophy of Religion*.

[138] *An Interpretation of Religion*, 246.

[139] Among recent work on religious pluralism, the following are highly recommended: Robert McKim, *Religious Ambiguity and Religious Diversity* (New York: Oxford University Press, 2001); Paul Griffiths, *Problems of Religious Diversity* (Oxford: Blackwell, 2001); Peter Bryne, *Prolegomena to Religious Pluralism* (London: Macmillan, 1995); T. D. Senor, ed., *The Rationality and the Plurality of Faith* (Ithaca: Cornell University Press, 1995); and P. Quinn and K. Meeker, eds., *The Philosophical Challenge to Religious Diversity* (Oxford: Oxford University Press, 1999). For philosophical work on the incarnation, see work by J. Hick, T. V. Morris, P. Forrest, R. Feenstra, R. Swinburne, M. Martin, and S. T. Davis, among others.

and others. Alfred North Whitehead (1861–1947) advanced a comprehensive metaphysic that understands God to be coextensive with the
world, bound up with its process and providing the grounds for its
unity.[140] Whitehead's systematic philosophy is too complex to summarize it here. Whitehead initiated a project of rethinking the concept of
God that understood God to be in much closer unity with the cosmos
than in classical monotheism. Whitehead conceived of God and the cosmos as interdependent; the one transcends but is also immanent in the
other. Whitehead articulates the relation between God and the cosmos
in light of a metaphysics of process and events rather than, say, discrete
atomic objects.[141] Charles Hartshorne furthered Whitehead's work, as
did D. R. Griffin, J. Cobb, and S. M. Ogden. Hartshorne developed an
extensive attack on classical theism, recommending in its stead a neo-
classical concept of God, in *The Divine Relativity: A Social Conception
of God*.[142] Process thinkers tend to emphasize God's *affective* bond to
the cosmos and to deny individual life after death. They also do not
conceive of God as transcendent and omnipotent, but as a reality that
seeks to draw (or call) persons to the good. Griffin is especially clear
on the repudiation of any supernatural causation. "The reason for this
absence of divine interruptions . . . is metaphysical, not merely moral,
being based on the fact that the fundamental God-World relation is
fully natural, grounded in the very nature of things, not in a contingent divine decision."[143] Since the mid-1970s, the British philosopher
Stephen R. L. Clark has contributed a range of works defending a theistic understanding of God with some elements that resemble a process
philosophy.[144]

---

[140] See Whitehead, *Process and Reality: An Essay in Cosmology* (New York: Free Press,
1978), and his *Religion in the Making* (New York: Macmillan, 1926). See also
D. R. Griffin's *God and Religion in the Postmodern World* (Albany: SUNY Press,
1989).

[141] Whitehead addressed several distinctively religious concerns – including his view
that God should be seen as a companion – in *Religion in the Making* (New York:
Macmillan, 1926).

[142] This book was based on his Terry Lectures at Yale University, published by Yale
University Press, 1948.

[143] Griffin, *Reenchantment without Supernaturalism* (Ithaca: Cornell University Press,
2001), 6.

[144] For a helpful introduction to Clark's work and an overview of his books, see D.
Dombrowski, *Not Even a Sparrow Falls: The Philosophy of Stephen R. L. Clark* (East
Lansing: Michigan State University Press, 2000). See also Philip Clayton's work. Of
special interest is Clayton's articulation of his philosophy of religion in his treatment

Of course, process philosophers of religion typically part company with the more traditionalist Christian Platonists discussed in Chapter 1, and yet they (like Cudworth and More) understand God in light of contemporary science. For process philosophers this has involved a more naturalistic theology, one that renounces the appeal to God as a supernatural agent breaking into human history. While process thinkers certainly do not advance a bold hypothesis of "Plastick Nature," their understanding of God's relation to the universe is akin to the Cambridge Platonists in their resisting what they see as the fractured Cartesian model.[145] Process thinkers in fact vigorously oppose the mechanistic account of the cosmos along with Cartesianism. They instead adopt a view of the cosmos that bears a resemblance to Conway's and Leibniz's metaphysic. Griffin calls it "pan-experientialism." He holds that "all true individuals – as distinct from aggregational societies – have at least some iota of experience and spontaneity (self-determination)."[146] A mere aggregate would be a loosely associated group of individuals, like a city, for example. By seeing some mental, experiential character throughout the world, process philosophers do not face the problem of accounting for how experiential, mental reality emerged from purely nonmental, nonconscious forces.

In the next and final chapter, I seek to fill out further a portrait of contemporary philosophy of religion.

of modern philosophy. See *The Problem of God in Modern Thought* (Grand Rapids: Eerdmans, 2000).

[145] For a good overview of the prospects of process philosophy as well as an important contribution, see Griffin, *Reenchantment without Supernaturalism.*

[146] Ibid., 6.

NINE

Religions, Evidence, and Legitimacy

A genuine mysteriousness attaches to the idea of goodness and the Good.

Iris Murdoch[1]

Whose Encyclopedia?

The late twentieth century saw an abundance of encyclopedic, philosophical reference works, published by the leading Anglophone presses: Cambridge, Oxford, Blackwell, Routledge, Macmillan, and others. But for many years, since its publication in 1967, the standard reference work was the eight-volume Macmillan work, *The Encyclopedia of Philosophy*, edited by Paul Edwards. As I write, this work is still widely represented as a substantial reference work in philosophy in North American libraries. With more than 900 articles and an editorial board that reads like an honor role of the most prominent philosophers of the day, this reference work had an easy time commanding and representing the field for almost thirty years. Its editor, Paul Edwards (professor of Philosophy at New York University and then at City University of New York), explicitly identified his bias. "It would . . . be idle to pretend that this *Encyclopedia* is free from bias and that my own ideological commitments have not significantly influenced its content."[2] Edwards identified his slant as analytical philosophy in the Anglo-Saxon world. More precisely, it was an approach to philosophy that was not (in general) appreciative of the positive case that may be made for religious belief.[3] Edwards's own entries are highly critical of religion. "My associates and

---

[1] *The Sovereignty of Good* (New York: Schocken Books, 1971), 99.
[2] *Encyclopedia of Philosophy*, ed. P. Edwards (New York: Macmillan, 1967), 1:xi.
[3] There are exceptions, for example, entries by J. Hick.

I edited the *Encyclopedia* in the spirit of Voltaire and Diderot, of Hume and Bertrand Russell."[4]

Edwards's approach to religion bordered on the hostile in subsequent work, such as in *The Encyclopedia of Unbelief*, where he claims "All the metaphysical claims of traditional religions are untenable" and that "the decline of religion will be of incalculable benefit to the human race."[5] "The sooner these sick dreams [of religion] are eliminated from the human race, the better."[6] In keeping with that spirit, witness these comments from John Searle in a work covering metaphysics and philosophy of language:

> In earlier generations, books like this one would have had to contain either an atheistic attack on or a theistic defense of traditional religion. Or at the very least, the author would have had to declare a judicious agnosticism. Two authors who wrote in a spirit in some ways similar to mine, John Stuart Mill and Bertrand Russell, mounted polemical and eloquent attacks on traditional religion. Nowadays nobody bothers, and it is considered in slightly bad taste to even raise the question of God's existence. Matters of religion are like matters of sexual preference: they are not to be discussed in public, and even the abstract questions are discussed only by bores.[7]

For better or worse, the current status of philosophy of religion is quite different than Searle describes.

The Macmillan philosophy encyclopedia has been superseded by a range of works that display the vibrancy of philosophy of religion. The Cambridge *Dictionary of Philosophy* under the editorship of Robert Audi puts on exhibit some of the best philosophy of religion, as does the magnificent *Routledge Encyclopedia of Philosophy* in which much of the philosophy of religion was edited by Eleonore Stump. Even Macmillan published a supplement to Edwards's work that, much to his dismay, threw off the primacy of his Angle-Saxon analytic orientation.[8] Edwards laments: "The late Jeremiah Kaplan, who was president of Macmillan from 1961 until 1985, and I frequently expressed our

---

[4] "Statement by Paul Edwards...," *Inquiry* 41 (1998):123.

[5] *Encyclopedia of Unbelief*, ed. Gorden Stein, vol. 1 (Buffalo, N.Y.: Prometheus Books, 1985), xiii.

[6] Ibid., xiii.

[7] *Mind, Language and Society* (New York: Basic Books, 1998), 34.

[8] Macmillan also currently plans a second edition of the multiple-volume encyclopedia, with Philip Quinn editing the philosophy of religion entries.

fear that after our deaths my successors would remove all controversial articles from the *Encyclopedia*. What has happened is a little different," namely nonhostile treatments of religion, the inclusion of entries on Simone de Beauvoir, Hannah Arnedt and others, "but no less objectionable. Mr. Kaplan is gone but I am still here to speak out against what has been done."[9]

As for Searle's claim, I suggest he is at least as wrong about religion as he is about sex.[10] At the outset, I note that a new journal, *Philo* was launched in the 1990s with Searle on the editorial board (along with W. V. Quine, D. Dennett, K. Baier, and others) dedicated to debate on theism. One of its editors, Quentin Smith (*not* a theist) writes: "God is not 'dead' in academia; he returned to life in the late 1960s and is now alive and well in... philosophy departments. A hand waving dismissal of theism... has been like trying to halt a tidal wave with a hand-held sieve."[11] More on this shortly.

The Academy

This book began with a political, religious address to the House of Commons by the philosopher of religion Ralph Cudworth. Cudworth's format for philosophy of religion then is different from the institutional settings we find today, with the field supported by established journals like the *International Journal of Philosophy of Religion*, societies like the British Society for Philosophy of Religion, conferences, and departments at colleges and universities.[12] Many scholars readily recognize philosophy of religion outside the academy, whether this is to be found in the life and writing of Simone Weil or in the novels of Dostoevsky – all this despite the fact that academies can be deeply hostile in response to philosophical reflection on religion, as scholars in the former Soviet Union, in Eastern Europe before the collapse of the Berlin Wall, and elsewhere know.[13] Still, philosophy of religion as a field has institutional

---

[9] "Statement by Paul Edwards...," 124.

[10] Actually the topic of sex and religion is quite fascinating and *not* limited to the ethics of censorship or sexual ethics. See work by Margaret Miles, for example, or the magnificent work on Christ's sexuality by Leo Steinberg.

[11] "Editorial Comments," *Philo* 4:2, 197–198.

[12] On one point, Cudworth is actually closer to today's institutionally installed "philosophers of religion," as he was a professional philosopher, whereas many of the philosophers who address religion in early modern philosophy did not hold academic posts.

[13] And the hostility is not limited to the former Soviet Union! Pamela Sue Anderson dedicates *A Feminist Philosophy of Religion: The Rationality and Myths of Religious*

and academic standing, is regularly featured at the World Congress of Philosophy, and is represented in one of the largest formal organization of philosophers in the world, the American Philosophical Association. Philosophy of religion is also well represented in the American Academy of Religion.[14]

This chapter looks at recent philosophical work on the relation between science and religion and at the philosophical debate on the issues that began this book. One way to measure the evolution of the field is to compare present debate with some of the controversies in the seventeenth century. I then offer "a case study" of philosophy of religion today. Examining the problem of evil can bring to light the current breadth of the field of philosophy of religion. After a brief interlude with personal comments on friendship and the field of philosophy of religion, the chapter explores the role of philosophy of religion in political reflection, whether inside or outside the academy. This chapter therefore concludes by taking up some of the same concerns that motivated Cutworth in the 1640s.

Science and Religion

As described in Chapters 1 and 6, the relationship between science and religion has been mixed. The familiar story that pits religion and science against one another has various authors. In the modern era, probably John William Draper (1811–1882) and Andrew Dickson White (1832–1918) were the first to secure a narrative of intrinsic conflict, replacing the more congenial portrait of William Whewell (1794–1866). But while contemporaries like Richard Dawkins would probably side with Draper and White, the Whewell view of science and religion in collaboration has gained ground. Influential work in the twentieth century has suggested that modern science stemmed from theological roots.[15] Highly sympathetic work has been done by Ernan McMullin, Ian Barbour,

Belief (Oxford: Blackwell, 1998) to "the solitary woman who has been forced to struggle with pure thinking, at the expense of her own full embodiment as a female philosopher, in order to succeed in an academic discipline which insists upon the denial of desire, love, and any inordinate passion for true justice" (xiii).

[14] At any given conference of the APA and AAR there are sessions on philosophy of religion. A significant number of past APA presidents have been philosophers of religion (Philip Quinn, Robert Audi, Alvin Plantinga, and so on).

[15] See E. A. Burtt, *Metaphysical Foundations of Modern Physical Science* (London: Routledge, 1932), and A. N. Whitehead, *Science and the Modern World* (New York: Macmillan, 1925).

Philip Clayton, Nancy Murphy, John Polkinghorne, A. R. Peacocke, Bas Van Frassen, Gary Ferngren, Alister McGrath, Wentzel van Huyssteen, Frederick Suppe, and others. This is not a literature focused on Genesis versus evolution but on the ways in which religions (theistic and non-theistic) are compatible with contemporary science. So, for example, Ian Barbour has shown how scientific models of the cosmos resemble religious models. Maurice Mandelbaum is probably representative of many (but by no means all) philosophers of science who reject "the conventional view of the place of religion in the thought of the nineteenth century," which "holds that science and religion were ranged in open hostility, and unremitting warfare was conducted between them."[16]

Although most defenders of the compatibility of science and religion cited here are realists – that is, they believe both science and religion offer accounts of reality that are true or fake – some defenders of religion take umbrage at the way contemporary philosophy of science has questioned the hegemony and impersonal objectivity of science.

In 1962 Thomas Kuhn published *The Structure of Scientific Revolutions* in which he contested the idea that science is a purely disinterested activity operating on the basis of objectively administered principles. "As in political revolutions, so in paradigm choice – there is no standard higher than the assent of the relevant community. To discover how scientific revolutions are effected, we shall therefore have to examine not only the impact of nature and logic, but also the techniques of persuasive argumentation effective within the quite special groups that constitute the community of scientists."[17] Kuhn challenged the idea that scientific change occurred out of an impersonal adherence to rules of evidence. "Chemists could not, therefore, simply accept Dalton's theory on evidence for so much of that was still negative. Instead, even after accepting the theory, they still had to beat nature into line, a process which, in the event, took almost another generation."[18] Kuhn has been read as celebrating a virtually anarchistic theory of reason. I do not think this is quite right. Kuhn saw science as evolving and accountable to the practice and ideals of the scientific community. He did not

---

[16] Mandelbaum, *History, Man and Reason: A Study in Nineteenth-Century Thought* (Baltimore: John Hopkins University Press, 1971), 28.

[17] *The Structure of Scientific Revolutions*, 2nd ed. (Chicago: University of Chicago Press, 1970), 93.

[18] Ibid., 135.

maintain, for example, that Dalton manipulated the data. Still, Kuhn made some philosophers question the notion that scientific reasoning is a straightforward matching of evidence and theory. In Paul Feyerabend's work, we find a radical questioning of strict methods that moves beyond Kuhn.

> The idea of a method that contains firm, unchanging, and absolutely binding principles for conducting the business of science meets considerable difficulty when confronted with the results of historical research. We find then, that there is not a single rule, however plausible, and however firmly grounded in epistemology, that is not violated at some time or other. It becomes evident that such violations are not accidental events, they are not results of insufficient knowledge or of inattention which might have been avoided. On the contrary, we see that they are necessary for progress.[19]

There are abundant defenders of science as an objective normative enterprise. I simply note that some of the confidence in science as an impersonal, objective ideal slipped from, say, early Vienna Circle standards.[20]

Ecology has been an important meeting place for science and religion. There has been enormous debate over the roots of the contemporary ecological crisis.[21] But there has also been a great deal of work on how world religions may generate and bolster ecological responsibility.[22]

---

[19] *Against Method* (London: Verso, 1988), 21.

[20] My own view is that Feyerabend goes too far in his denouncement of objectivity in science. Roger Trigg has done important work on a realist treatment of science and philosophy in general. See his *Reason and Commitment* (Cambridge: Cambridge University Press, 1973); *Reality at Risk* (London: Harvester Wheatsheaf, 1989); *Rationality and Science* (Oxford: Blackwell, 1993). While I believe Trigg's case for realism is successful, I think that much "postmodern" philosophy of science work has also succeeded in raising healthy, skeptical questions as to when science has been a vehicle for specific ideologies. See, for example, Evelyn Fox Keller, *Reflections on Gender and Science* (New Haven: Yale University Press, 1985), and Sandra Harding, *The Science Question in Feminism* (Ithaca: Cornell University Press, 1986). For a balanced overview of the relation of science and religion, see Ian Barbour, *Religion in an Age of Science* (San Francisco: Harper and Row, 1990).

[21] Lynn White published "The Historical Roots of Our Ecological Crisis," *Science* 155 (1967): 37, laying the blame on Christianity. There have been many rejoinders. See the entry on Christianity by Robin Attfield in Dale Jamieson, ed., *A Companion to Environmental Philosophy* (Oxford: Blackwell, 2001).

[22] In *A Companion to Environmental Philosophy*, see the entries of classical India, classical China, Janism and Buddhism, Judaism, and Islam. See also Eugene Hargrove, ed., *Religion and Environmental Crisis* (Athens: University of Georgia Press, 1986); D. L. Barnhill and R. S. Gottlieb, eds., *Deep Ecology and World Religions* (Albany:

As ecology has matured as an enterprise that combines (almost) all the sciences, there has been a revival of philosophies of nature that see the natural world as interwoven with values. This amounts to reawakening the issues of Chapters 1 through 3 over the mechanical view of nature. In *The Death of Nature*, Carolyn Merchant writes:

> The rise of mechanism laid the foundation for a new synthesis of the cosmos, society and the human being, construed as ordered systems of mechanical parts subject to governance by law and to predictability through deductive reasoning. A new concept of the self as a rational master of the passions housed in a machinelike body began to replace the concept of the self as an integral part of a close-knit harmony of organic parts related to the cosmos and society. Mechanism rendered nature effectively dead, inert and manipulable from without. As a system of thought, it rapidly gained in plausibility during the second half of the seventeenth century.[23]

Merchant and others question both the scientific and philosophical foundations of mechanism. Recognizing the good of natural ecosystems and questioning a reductive view of science (in which only physics is really science) has paved the way for reviving scientifically informed religious views of nature.[24]

The dialogue between science and religion is not limited to theism. There has been speculative work on the compatibility of Hindu cosmology and contemporary physics.[25] Some Buddhist philosophers have seen current science vindicating their view of the impermanence and causal interdependence of objects in the world (Pratītyasamutpāda).[26] Confucianism and Daoism – along with Hinduism and Buddhism – have been especially interested in the ethics and values of the applied sciences such as medicine and agriculture. Contemporary environmental ethics texts in English often contain non-Western philosophy of religion.

Back to the Beginning

In this section I survey some of the work that stands in closest relation to the themes of Chapter 1: the articulation, defense, and critique of

SUNY Press, 2001); and M. E. Tucker and J. A. Grim, eds., *Worldviews and Ecology* (Lewisburg: Bucknell University Press, 1993).

[23] *The Death of Nature* (San Fransisco: Harper and Row, 1980), 214.

[24] See, for example, Mark Wynn, *God and Goodness* (London: Routledge, 1999).

[25] See David Gosling, *Science and Religion in India* (Madras: CSL, 1976).

[26] See Martin Verhoeven, "Buddhism and Science," *Religion East and West* 1 (2001).

theism. It needs to be stressed that the philosophical work on religion today includes a great deal of analytic, careful objections to theism. In an appendix to this book I cite some of the leading philosophers working toward positive accounts of divine attributes and theistic arguments. Some critics of philosophical theism may be motivated (as Paul Edwards was) by the view that theistic religion is harmful and void of merit, but others profess a fascination for the theistic concept of God. Anthony Kenny, a nontheistic philosopher and one of the most preeminent living historians of philosophy, offers this assessment of theism.

> If there is no God, then God is incalculably the greatest single creation of the human imagination. No other creation of the imagination has been so fertile of ideas, so great an inspiration to philosophy, to literature, to painting, sculpture, architecture, and drama. Set beside the idea of God, the most original inventions of mathematicians and the most unforgettable characters in drama are minor products of imagination: Hamlet and the square root of minus one pale into insignificance by comparison.[27]

Consider also Roger Scruton who thinks that even if a theistic concept of God were to disappear culturally, philosophical investigation into the idea of God would remain vital.

> Our most pressing philosophical need, it seems to me, is to understand the nature and significance of the force which once held our world together, and which is now losing its grip – the force of religion. It could be that religious belief will soon be a thing of the past; it is more likely, however, that beliefs with the function, structure and animus of religion will flow into the vacuum left by God. In either case, we need to understand the why and wherefore of religion. It is from religious ideas that the human world, and the subject who inhabits it, were made.[28]

The philosophers to be noted in this section are largely in the analytic tradition; they also tend to be realists and adopt a form of fallibilism.

Analytic philosophy of religion – both theistic and nontheistic – has tended to be realist. That is, there is a general conviction that metaphysics is a live option. As Nicholas Wolterstorff puts it, "The situation is not that we [analytical philosophers of religion] have failed to consider the Kantian alternative, and are consequently still wandering about in unenlightened naiveté: the situation is rather that we have considered

---

[27] *Faith and Philosophy* (New York: Columbia University Press, 1983), 59.
[28] *An Intelligent Person's Guide to Philosophy* (New York: Penguin Books, 1996), 85–86.

the Kantian arguments and found them wanting. Kant is not some fact of nature with whom one has no choice but to cope."[29] Substantial work has been done by analytic philosophers of religion to bolster this realist framework.[30]

While it has been realist, analytic philosophy of religion has, in general, been conducted without employing Cartesian standards for absolute certainty. That is, few practitioners claim indisputable, unassailable certainty in their theistic and nontheistic convictions. Wolterstorff offers this view of the field.

> I think it safe to say that almost no one who is today engaged in analytic philosophy of religion accepts the Lockean evidentialist challenge. Some would accept one or another severely qualified version of it; but almost no one would accept it in the unqualified form in which Locke issued it. Almost no one would hold that it is the obligation of everybody, if they are religious at all, to see to it that their religion is rational by virtue of being based on evidence consisting of certainties.[31]

The same is true for nontheists. Various nontheists, including James Harris and William Rowe, do not claim to know with indisputable certainty that theism is false.

In this section let us consider three areas in which theism has (and is) receiving renewed attention in philosophy of religion: divine attributes, theistic arguments, and themes that are specific to theistic religions.

Divine Attributes

There is now a sophisticated body of literature on the coherence and value of such divine attributes as omnipotence, omniscience, goodness, omnipresence, eternity, necessity, aseity, incorporeality, simplicity, freedom, impassability, and passability. Attention has sometimes focused on the analysis of a single attribute. I outline briefly two lively debates and then seek to bring to light what may be called the flexibility of theism. The tools of debate include thought experiments (imagined states of affairs), independent philosophical convictions (so an account

---

[29] "Analytical Philosophy of Religion: Retrospect and Prospect," in *Perspectives in Contemporary Philosophy of Religion*, ed. T. Lehtonan and T. Koistiren (Helsinki: Luther-Agricolo Society, 2000).

[30] See work by William Alston, Roger Triss, Michael Loux, and James Harris.

[31] "Analytical Philosophy of Religion," 163–164.

of divine knowledge will draw on epistemology), and the scripture and practice of theistic tradition.

Let us look briefly to the current literature on omnipotence, as that was the attribute Cudworth highlighted in his House of Commons address that began this book. Much attention has been given historically and since the 1970s to the scope of omnipotence. There is *the paradox of the stone*: If God is omnipotent, God can do any act whatever. If God can do any act whatever, God can make a stone so heavy that no one can lift it. But if there was a stone so heavy that no one can lift it, God could not lift it. Hence God is not omnipotent for either God cannot make a stone so heavy that no one can lift it or God could make such a stone and then there would be an act that God cannot do. There is almost a consensus, I believe, that such a puzzle can be solved by making clear that omnipotence does not involve the power to bring about logically and metaphysically impossible states of affairs. Presumably the following states of affairs involve a logical contradiction: there being a stone so heavy that a being who can lift any stone cannot lift it. The state of affairs is akin to *there being a square circle in two-dimensional* space, an evident impossibility.[32] In setting aside the paradox of the stone, one avoids indefinitely similar paradoxes – for example, can God make porridge so vast that even God cannot eat it?

Matters become more pressing, however, when the paradox is leveled against the compatibility of omnipotence and freedom. It has been argued that omnipotence is incompatible with there being free creatures. J. L. Mackie proposed that an omnipotent being cannot create beings that it cannot control. If God were to create such free, self-controlled beings, then God would cease being omnipotent.[33] There were at least three rejoinders. First, it was pointed out that the state of affairs, *God directly controlling a creature who cannot be directly controlled by God*, is metaphysically impossible and thus not something within the scope of omnipotence (like the proverbial challenge to create a square circle). Second, it was proposed that the creation of free beings would involve

---

[32] See, for example, George Mavrodes, "Some Puzzles Concerning Omnipotence," *Philosophical Review* 72 (1963); Hary Frankfurt, "The Logic of Omnipotence," *Philosophical Review* 73 (1964); and Wade Savage "The Paradox of the Stone," *Philosophical Review* 76 (1967).

[33] J. L. Mackie, "Evil and Omnipotence," *Mind* 64 (1955). See also his "Omnipotence," *Sophia* 1 (1962). For replies to Mackie, see Alvin Plantinga, *God and Other Minds* (Ithaca: Cornell University Press, 1967), chap. 7, and Axel Stever, "Once More on the Free Will Defense," *Religious Studies* 10 (1974).

not the loss of omnipotence but the exercise of omnipotence. A third option is to understand omnipotence as a nonessential or contingent property of God. If God is omnipotent, God would have the power to give up or suspend the attribute. The very existence of free creatures would rest, in part, on God's creating and conserving them in existence with their power of self-determination. Far from diminishing God's power, such self-limitation would be the exercise of an important power.

More pressing than the preceding exchange is one that involves the relation of power and goodness. If God is omnipotent, can God do evil for its own sake? It was argued that if God is freely and truly able to act in good ways, God must be able to act badly.[34] Moreover, if God cannot do evil, wouldn't it be possible for there to be a more powerful being, namely one that does good but can do evil? For Christians who believe Jesus is God and man, there was a reason to believe God can do evil for, according to the tradition, Jesus was tempted to do evil. A real temptation seems to require that the person can follow through with the temptation.

I believe the more plausible replies, among those who assert God's essential goodness, were those that challenged whether the capacity to do wicked acts involves genuine, divine powers. Our ability to do good *or evil* may be a feature of *human* freedom, but in God there may be the higher value of essential goodness. There is some support from Anselm, Aquinas, and others for seeing evil action as an imperfect or impaired power – it is the failure of being perfect or divine. Some philosophers argued that at the root of the religious devotion to God's greatness is a worship of God as an essentially good being and not bare power. "Omnipotence" should, by their lights, be seen as the maximal power of a perfect or essentially good being, a being with the other divine attributes of omniscience and so on.[35] This move to *divine* or *essentially good* power resonates with some feminists (as pointed out in Chapter 7) who lament the philosophy of a God of pure power.

By way of reply to the earlier rationale for acknowledging God's ability to do evil, it has been argued that God's praiseworthiness can

---

[34] See, for example, Benjamin Gibbs, "Can God Do Evil?" *Philosophy* 50 (1975).

[35] See T. V. Morris, *Anselmian Explanations* (Notre Dame: University of Notre Dame Press, 1987); George Schlesinger, "On the Compatibility of the Divine Attributes," *Religious Studies* 23 (1987); Jerome Gellman, "Omnipotence and Impeccability," *New Scholasticism* 51 (1977); Nelson Pike, "Omnipotence and God's Ability to Sin," *American Philosophical Quarterly* 6 (1969); and Peter Geach, "Can God Fail to Keep a Promise?" *Philosophy* 52 (1977).

be delight and awe in God's good nature, and not just relief that God does not exercise a capacity to do evil for its own sake. As for Christ's temptation, perhaps one *can* be tempted to do something if you think you can do it, even if (as it happens) you cannot.[36]

Belief in God's essential goodness has played a part in the philosophical interpretation of God's agency and character as displayed in the Bible.[37] The Bible portrays God as jealous, licensing the decimation of the Canaanites, prohibiting homosexuality, and so on, which some (but by no means all) contemporary Christians find problematic. Those who have a religious allegiance to the Bible as inerrant and infallible either seek to reinterpret this portrait (e.g., the prohibition against homosexuality was against the practice of temple prostitution, not against a loving, faithful, single-sex union) or subordinate their moral judgments to biblical authority, concluding (for example) that the divine command to abolish the Canaanites was compatible with God's goodness. Those who believe the Bible to be inspired and revelatory, but not inerrant and infallible, have greater room to see "the problematic teachings" as more the outcome of human interpretation than bona fide, divinely revealed precepts.[38] Some of the more apparently anthropomorphic biblical language – in which God is said to be jealous or angry – may be aided by belief in divine essential goodness.[39]

In this literature on omnipotence, one can see a variety of positions to contest and develop, rather than a single analysis that must be accepted or rejected. The breadth or flexibility of theism is even more apparent in the literature on omniscience.

---

[36] For a fuller treatment of Christ and temptation, see R. Swinburne, *The Christian God* (Oxford: Oxford University Press, 1994). For a critical evaluation, see Michael Martin, *The Case against Christianity* (Philadelphia: Temple University Press, 1991).

[37] For a good example of the intersection of biblical sources and a philosophy of God's essential goodness, see Morris, *Anselmian Explorations*, especially the chapters "The God of Abraham, Isaac and Anselm" and "Rationality and Christian Revelation." See also T. P. Flint and E. Stump, eds., *Hermes and Athena: Biblical Exegesis and Philosophical Theology* (Notre Dame: University of Notre Dame Press, 1993).

[38] For interesting work on the philosophy of religious scriptures in theistic tradition, see William Abraham, *The Divine Inspiration of Holy Scripture* (Oxford: Oxford University Press, 1981), and his *Divine Revelation and the Limits of Historical Criticism* (Oxford: Oxford University Press, 1982); Nicholas Wolterstorff, *Divine Discourse* (Cambridge: Cambridge University Press, 1995); Richard Swinburne, *Revelation* (Oxford: Clarendon, 1989); Flint and Stump, *Hermes and Athena*.

[39] See the discussion of Demea's anthropomorphic objection in Chapter 4.

At first, omniscience may not seem like the Pandora's box of divine attributes. An analysis such as the following seems straightforward: a being is omniscient if it knows all true propositions. One can tidy this up for comprehensiveness by adding that an omniscient being would know of all true propositions that they are true and of all false propositions that they are false. Troubles that resemble the paradox of the stone emerge when it comes to a finer analysis of propositions. When I am in pain, I know that the proposition "I am in pain" is true, but God does not know that *that* proposition is true in this case but that "Taliaferro is in pain." Presumably this puzzle may be swept aside on the gounds that God and I know the state of affairs *Taliaferro is in pain* obtains; different propositions can be used to refer to the same state of affairs. Omniscience could then be cast in terms of God knowing all states of affairs that obtain – or, for the sake of completeness, an omniscient being knows all states of affairs that have obtained, obtain now, and will obtain.[40] More serious challenges open up, however, as omniscience is thought about in relation to the past and future.

Can God, as an omniscient being, know what is (at least for us) the future?[41]

If God knows now what you will do tomorrow (e.g., you will freely get out of bed), can you do otherwise? God's omniscience is traditionally believed to be unsurpassable in certainty – God does not have to guess at the future or deal with mere probable outcomes. As such, foreknowledge of the future seems to entail or involve the future being fixed or (somehow) already determinate. Linda Zagzebski formalized the puzzle of foreknowledge and freedom as follows:

1. Yesterday God infallibly believed B. (Supposition of infallible foreknowledge)
2. It is now necessary that yesterday God believed B. (Principle of Necessity of the Past)

[40] For discussion of some of the formal paradoxes of omniscience, see Jonathan Kvanvig, *The Possibility of an All-Knowing God* (New York: St. Martin's, 1986).

[41] For an important statement of the problem, see Nelson Pike, "Divine Omniscience and Voluntary Action," *Philosophical Review* 74 (1965): 27–46. The literature here is highly sophisticated. See J. Kvanvig's entry in *A Companion to Philosophy of Religion*, ed. P. Quinn and C. Taliaferro (Oxford: Blackwell, 1997). The leading philosophers who have contributed to this literature include: Marilyn Adams, R. M. Adams, W. Alston, D. Basinger, W. Craig, J. Fischer, T. Flint, A. J. Freddoso, P. Helm, A. Kenny, N. Kretzmann, M. Linville, J. R. Lucas, G. Mavrodes, N. Pike, A. Plantinga, P. Quinn, B. Reichenbach, W. Rowe, E. Wierenga, L. Zagzebski.

3. Necessarily, if yesterday God believed B, then B. (Definition of infallibility)
4. So it is now necessary that B. (2–3, Transfer of Necessity Principle)
5. If it is now necessary that B, then you cannot do otherwise than get out of bed tomorrow exactly seven minutes after you wake up. (Definiton of *necessary*)
6. Therefore, you cannot do otherwise than get out of bed tomorrow exactly seven minutes after you wake up. (4–5, modus ponens)
7. If you cannot do otherwise when you do an act, you do not do it freely. (Principle of Alternate Possibilities)
8. Therefore, when you get out of bed tomorrow, you will not do it freely. (6–7, modus ponens)[42]

As with the literature on the attribute of omnipotence, there are a number of options available. Here are five possibilities.

One can deny that omniscience involves knowledge of future free action. Arguably, the future does not exist (now) and so *your freely getting out of bed tomorrow seven minutes after you wake up* cannot be the ground or fact that makes the relevant proposition about your getting out of bed either true or false. The denial that the future is determinate (and thus not subject to the same conditions as the past) has a lineage going back to Aristotle. So long as God's omniscience involves knowledge of what it is metaphysically possible to know, then God's omniscience does not extend to the future as it is in principle unknowable.[43] The key to this theistic strategy is to limit omniscience at any time to what it is possible to know at that time, for this Aristotelian argument about the indeterminacy of the future can lead to a significant anti-theistic argument: if omniscience requires knowledge of the future, and knowledge of the future is impossible, then omniscience is impossible.[44]

Second, one may deny that God's "foreknowledge" is temporal. Strictly speaking, God is eternal and lacks temporal location. On this

---

[42] Zagzebski, "Recent Work on Divine Foreknowledge and Free Will," in *The Oxford Handbook of Free Will*, ed. R. Kane (Oxford: Oxford University Press, 2002), 46–47.

[43] See J. R. Lucas, *The Freedom of Will* (Oxford: Oxford University Press, 1970); Richard Purtill, "Fatalism and the Omnitemporality of Truth," *Faith and Philosophy* 5 (1988); Joseph Runzo, "Omniscience and Freedom for Evil," *International Journal for Philosophy of Religion* 12 (1981); A. M. Prior, "The Formalities of Omniscience," *Philosophy* 37 (1962).

[44] For relevant anti-theistic arguments, see M. Martin and R. Monnier, eds., *The Impossibility of God* (Amherst, N.Y.: Prometheus Press, 2003), parts 4 and 5.

view, God's foreknowledge is not on the same footing as foreknowledge in time. God does not foreknow your future free acts; God knows them from eternity or atemporally. This is sometimes called the *Boethian solution* after the Roman philosopher Boethius (480–525). Probably the most articulate defense of God's eternity was developed by Eleonore Stump and Norman Kretzmann.[45]

Third, there is what some call the *Ockhamist solution* after the English scholastic, William of Ockham (1290–1349). On this view, God's belief now that you will freely get out of bed tomorrow depends on your free action. Linda Zagzebski formulates this "backward counterfactual dependency" as: "It was within Jones' power at T2 [a future time, relative to T1] to do something such that if he did it, God would not have held the belief [God] in fact held at T1."[46]

Fourth, the *Molinist solution* charges that God has middle knowledge – knowledge in between knowledge of necessary truths and knowledge of God's own will. God also knows what person will do in any (and thus every) possible circumstance. Puzzles of foreknowledge are thereby dissolved (so it is argued) by appeal to God as the Creator. God knows future free acts by knowing which people are created.[47]

A fifth option is to deny that a person's freely doing an act involves the bona fide possibility of her doing otherwise. This option may either take the form of determinism or a different tack in which philosophers contend that indeterminate freedom is compatible with controlled, predictable outcomes.[48]

---

[45] See the following three articles by Eleonore Stump and Norman Kretzmann: "Eternity," *Journal of Philosophy* 78 (1981); "Prophecy, Past Truth, and Eternity," *Philosophical Perspectives* 5 (1991); and "Eternity, Awareness and Action," *Faith and Philosophy* 9 (1972). For criticism, see Linda Zagzebski, *The Dilemma of Freedom and Foreknowledge* (Oxford: Oxford University Press, 1991), and William Hasker, *God, Time and Knowledge* (Ithaca: Cornell University Press, 1981).

[46] Zagzebski, "Recent Work on Divine Foreknowledge and Free Will," 53–55. For an influential essay that revived Ockham's proposal, see "Is the Existence of God a 'Hard' Fact?" *Philosophical Review* 76 (1967). See also "On Ockham's Way Out," *Faith and Philosophy* 3 (1986).

[47] See Luis de Molina, *On Divine Foreknowledge*, trans. Alfredo Freddoso (Ithaca: Cornell University Press, 1988), and Thomas Flint, *Divine Providence: The Molinist Account* (Ithaca: Cornell University Press, 1998).

[48] The literature on this is vast. A highly influential essay fueling the debate is Harry Frankfurt, "Alternative Possibilities and Moral Responsibility," *Journal of Philosophy* 66 (1969). For a recent discussion, see Linda Zagzebski, "Does Libertarian Freedom Require Alternate Possibilities?" *Philosophical Perspectives* 14 (2000).

There is, then, a range of alternative replies to some of the paradoxes of divine attributes. Because of the interwoven nature of the attributes that make up the theistic understanding of God, many works in late twentieth-century philosophy of religion take up projects that coordinate or seek to expose conflicts in more than one divine attribute.[49] Although I have focused on the alternatives for theism, these projects have also provided ample material for the criticism of theism.[50]

Theistic Arguments

There is a very large literature now on the articulation and critique of arguments for the existence of God.[51] In this section I spotlight one strategy that recalls the reasoning of the Cambridge Platonists. In a nutshell, it is an argument from consciousness and teleology.

According to what may be called an argument from consciousness, naturalism faces a problem and theism has an opportunity in terms of accounting for the emergence of consciousness. A range of materialists today concede that it is very difficult to accommodate conscious, mental states as physical elements or processes. Michael Lockwood offers this picture of contemporary materialism:

> Let me begin by nailing my colours to the mast. I count myself a materialist, in the sense that I take consciousness to be a species of brain activity. Having said that, however, it seems to me evident that no description of brain activity of the relevant kind, couched in the currently available languages of physics, physiology, or functional or computational roles, is remotely capable of capturing what is distinctive about consciousness.

---

[49] See, for example, J. Hoffman and G. Rosenkrantz, *The Divine Attributes* (Oxford: Blackwell, 2002); T. V. Morris, *Our Idea of God* (Oxford: Oxford University Press, 1987); E. Wierenga *The Nature of God: An Inquiry into Divine Attributes* (Ithaca: Cornell University, 1989); Swinburne, *The Coherence of Theism*; Richard Gale, *On the Nature and Existence of God* (Cambridge: Cambridge University Press, 1991); Gerald Hugh, *The Nature of God* (London: Routledge, 1995).

[50] Among the many superb philosophers who critique the various theistic projects, see M. Bagger, D. Blumenthal, R. Dawkins, P. Draper, A. Flew, R. Gale, J. Gaskin, P. Grim, J. Harris, T. Kapitan, A. Kenny, R. La Croix, R. Le Poidevin, M. Levine, J. L. Mackie, C. B. Martin, M. Martin, W. Matson, J. J. McCloskey, K. Nielsen, J. Rachels, P. Nowell-Smith, D. O'Connor, A. O'Hear, G. Oppy, D. Parfit, T. Penelhum, W. Proudfood, W. Rowe, J. L. Schellenberg, among others. These philosophers display what may be called the flexibility and versatility of nontheistic projects. For an excellent anthology of some of the best work, see Martin and Monnier, *The Impossibility of God*.

[51] For a novel argument as representative, see R. Gale and Alexander Pruss, "A New Cosmological Argument," *Religious Studies* 35 (1999): 461–476, and their "A Response to Oppy, and to Davey and Clifton," *Religious Studies* 38 (2002): 89–99.

So glaring, indeed, are the shortcomings of all the reductive programmes currently on offer, that I cannot believe that anyone with a philosophical training, looking dispassionately at these programmes, would take any of them seriously for a moment, were it not for a deep-seated conviction that current physical science has essentially got reality taped, and accordingly, *something* along the lines of what the reductionists are offering *must* be correct. To that extent, the very existence of consciousness seems to me to be a standing demonstration of the explanatory limitations of contemporary physical science.[52]

This lament is not isolated among contemporary philosophers of mind.[53] Given a background assumption that the cosmos is thoroughly physical and nonconscious, the emergence of consciousness seems a mystery. As Colin McGinn puts it: "We have a good idea how the Big Bang led to the creation of stars and galaxies, principally by the force of gravity. But we know of no comparable force that might explain how ever-expanding lumps of matter might have developed an inner conscious life."[54] As I noted in Chapter 6, it is largely because of the difficulty of accounting for the emergence of consciousness that some philosophers seek to deny that conscious, subjective states actually exist. Because of the difficulty of identifying subjective experience with "exquisite . . . basic properties of matter and energy," Churchland's elimination of experience is deemed desirable by many materialists though it has also seemed unacceptable due to the evident reality of consciousness.

In this context, a renewed, twenty-first-century theistic argument has taken the following shape in work by Richard Swinburne, R. M. Adams, and others.[55] Given theism, there is a reason for the emergence of consciousness in an ordered cosmos. The existence of consciousness in (what is presumed to be) a good world is a fitting object of a good, intentional reality (God). Given nontheistic naturalism, there is no reason to believe that consciousness and a good world would come to be or would exist at all.[56] If the two most plausible candidates for one's

---

[52] Lockwood, *Consciousness and the Quantum World: Putting Qualia on the Map*, ed. Q. Smith and A. Jokic (Oxford: Clarendon, 2003), 447.

[53] See work by Thomas Nagel, Colin McGinn, Frank Jackson, Ned Blok, and Galen Strawson.

[54] Colin McGinn, *Mysterious Flames: Conscious Minds in a Material World* (New York: Basic Books, 1999), 15.

[55] See, for example, Swinburne, *The Existence of God* (Oxford: Clarendon, 1979).

[56] See Mark Wynn, *God and Goodness: A Natural Theological Perspective* (London: Routledge, 1999).

account of the cosmos are naturalism and theism, there is some reason for favoring theism.

Of course there are many innumerable objections, replies, and revisions to consider: why limit the choice of explanation to theism and naturalism? Current materialists often admit there is a problem about explaining the emergence of consciousness from nonconsciousness forces, but can we adequately conceive of a conscious reality bringing about a natural, physical cosmos such as ours? In other words, can (the materialist) D. M. Armstrong's worry about the physical producing the mental be reversed to create a problem for conceiving of how the mental would produce the physical? Armstrong writes:

> It is not a particularly difficult notion that, when the nervous system reaches a certain level of complexity, it should develop new properties. Nor would there be anything particularly difficult in the notion that when the nervous system reaches a certain level of complexity it should affect something that was already in existence in a new way. But it is a quite different matter to hold that the nervous system should have the power to create something else [mental entities], of a quite different nature from itself, and create it out of not materials.[57]

Taking on board and sorting out objections and replies goes beyond this book. I simply signal here an intersection between philosophy of mind and the revival of theistic arguments.

Theistic Themes

Philosophers of religion now seem more at home with investigating specific teachings and practices within religious tradition than in the positivist era. There are now philosophical treatments of prayer, miracles, religious ritual, the sacraments, the Incarnation, and the Trinity. One popular topic of late has been the development of different accounts of the Incarnation. In one philosophy of the Incarnation, the God-man Jesus Christ is understood as part of the more general, overriding mind of God. In this view, the Incarnation involves a full embodiment by which the mind of God functions physically (in terms of agency, sensation, constitution of Christ's human life) as a human being through a self-limitation of the divine mind.[58] Debate over the Incarnation has also

---

[57] D. M. Armstrong, *A Materialist Theory of Mind* (London: Routledge, 1968), 30.

[58] See, for example, Swinburne, *The Christian God*, and T. V. Morris, *The Logic of God Incarnate* (Ithaca: Cornell University Press, 1986).

provided a fruitful context to compare Christian and Hindu concepts of avatāra in which a divine being is manifest as a human.[59]

At the close of this section on how the current scene in philosophy of religion includes many of the same themes we saw in the seventeenth century, I also highlight the fact that much of the even earlier medieval philosophy of religion has been rearticulated and is receiving great attention. This was spearheaded by Jacques Maritain (1882–1973) and Etienne Gilson (1884–1978), two prominent Thomistic writers.[60] F. R. Copleston was especially distinguished as a historian of philosophy, but he also proved to be an agile contributer to contemporary philosophy of religion. (I think it is safe to say that many secular philosophers were shocked that Copleston, a Jesuit priest, wrote one of the best, least-slanted histories of Western philosophy in the second half of the twentieth century.) For those interested in engaging, historically or philosophically, with the great themes and debates of the medieval era, a range of fine texts and interpretive critical works is available.[61]

To sketch further how philosophy of religion has functioned over the past thirty years let us look briefly at the ways in which the problem of evil is addressed today.

Evil and Philosophy of Religion: A Case Study

Philosophical work today on the religious implications of evil begins from a broader context than Christianity and Abrahamic faith. The opening statement of the problem of evil may, for example, be from the Buddha's challenge from the sixth century B.C.E. "If Brahma is lord of the whole world and creator of the multitude of beings, then why (i) has he ordained misfortune in the world without making the whole world happy, or (ii) for what purpose has he made the world full of injustice, deceit, falsehood and conceit, or (iii) the lord of beings is evil in that

---

[59] See, for example, Noel Sheth, "Hindu Avatāra and Christian Incarnation: A Comparison," *Philosophy East and West* 52:1 (2002).

[60] The relevant literature here is too vast to cite. For a useful overview, see Brian J. Shanley, *The Thomist Tradition* (Dordrecht: Kluwer Academic Publishers, 2002).

[61] An incomplete list of scholars who have done important work to enhance the study of medieval philosophy of religion in recent years includes M. Adams, B. Davies, T. Flint, F. Fredosso, J. J. E. Gracia, A. Kenny, N. Kretzmann, M. Jordan, S. MacDonald, R. McInerny, R. Sorabji, and E. Stump. See J. J. E. Gracia and T. B. Noone, eds., *A Companion to Philosophy in the Middle Ages* (Oxford: Blackwell, 2003).

he ordained injustice when there could have been justice."[62] And the options weighed involve Hindu and other non-Hindu elements, such as an appeal to karmic justice. Radhakrishana, for example, employs karma as well as a strong view of the responsibility for evil that resides in different souls.

> There are inequalities among the souls; some are happy and others un-happy. Does it mean that the Divine has also the qualities of passion and malice? As there is so much pain in the world, are we to treat him as cruel also? For these reasons *Brahman* cannot be the cause of the world. The objections are not valid. The inequalities of creation are due to the merit and demerit of the creatures. They are not a fault for which the Lord is to blame. An analogy is given. As Parjanya, the giver of rain, is the common cause of the production of rice, barley and other plants, and the differences are due to the potentialities of the seeds themselves, even so God is the common cause of the creation while the differences are due to the merit and demerit of the individual souls.[63]

Today there are useful cross-cultural studies on suffering as seen from different religions and cultural perspectives.[64] This has enabled scholars to draw on different views of God's power or the sacred as well as different portraits of the afterlife in addressing evil. For example, it has been argued that Christianity can be enhanced rather than compromised by belief in reincarnation.[65] Reincarnation, of sorts, not in this world but in a succession of other worlds, has also been articulated philosophically.[66]

Although evil is now considered from the standpoint of religious pluralism, much of the debate in the English-speaking world continues

---

[62] Cited in Avrind Sharma, *A Hindu Perspective on the Philosophy of Religion* (New York: St. Martin's, 1991), 46.

[63] Radhakrishnan, cited in ibid., 54.

[64] See, for example, John Bowker, *Problems of Suffering in the Religions of the World* (Cambridge: Cambridge University Press, 1970).

[65] See John King-Farrow, "Evil and Other Worlds," *Sophia* 6 (1967), and his "Evil: On Multiple Placings in Time and Space," *Sophia* 25 (1986). Hick posits a series of reembodiments after death that culminate in a final, ultimate state of unity with the real or the divine. "The individual's series of lives culminates eventually in a last life beyond which there is no further embodiment but instead entry into the common Vision of God, or nirvana, or the eternal consciousness of the atman in its relation to Ultimate Reality" (*Death and Eternal Life* [New York: Harper and Row, 1976], 464).

[66] John Hick, *Death and Eternal Life*, rev. ed. (New York: Harper and Row, 1987).

to weigh in on theism, atheism, and agnosticism. In what follows, I consider six general themes that mark the current literature.

Sensitivity to the Scope and Force of Evidence. At one time it was popular to debate whether any evil whatsoever is incompatible with a good God of omnipotent power and omniscience.[67] Now, it is customarily conceded that some evil is permissible by God if eliminating the evil would cause a greater evil, or if (under certain constraints) the evil was a necessary condition for there being certain worthy goods, or if the evil was somehow an unavoidable aftereffect of a great good. In a highly influential essay, William Rowe writes:

> Intense human or animal suffering is in itself bad and evil, even though it may sometimes be justified by virtue of being a part of, or leading to, some good which is unobtainable without it. What is evil in itself may sometimes be good as a means because it leads to something that is good in itself. In such a case, while remaining an evil in itself, the intense human or animal suffering is, nevertheless, an evil which someone might be morally justified in permitting.[68]

This concession over the permissibility (in principle) of some evil was largely established by arguments from Alvin Plantinga and others that there are some goods such as free will, the exercise of which would warrant permitting evil.[69] This work (if successful) establishes that it is at least logically possible that evil may be compatible with a good God. This strategy has been called a *defense* rather than a *theodicy* as it does not show that the evil that exists actually is permissible. Much of the debate now, however, turns on whether it is reasonable to believe there is warrant for evil. Is it sufficient simply to defend theism? Or does theism require a theodicy?

Rowe develops one of the clearest cases for what he calls "friendly atheism." He is friendly in that while he is an atheist, he believes one

---

[67] See, for example, H. J. McClosky, "God and Evil," *Philosophical Quarterly* 10 (1960).

[68] "The Problem of Evil and Some Varieties of Atheism," *American Philosophical Quarterly*, reprinted in *Philosophy of Religion: An Anthology*, ed. C. Taliaferro and P. Griffiths (Oxford: Blackwell, 2003), 369.

[69] See Plantinga, *God and Other Minds, God, Freedom and Evil* (New York: Harper and Row, 1974), and *The Nature of Necessity* (Oxford: Oxford University Press, 1974).

can be a rational theist notwithstanding evil. Consider, first, his case for atheism in three steps:

1. There exist instances of intense suffering which an omnipotent, omniscient being could have prevented without thereby losing some greater good or permitting some evil equally bad or worse.
2. An omniscient, wholly good being would prevent the occurrence of any intense suffering it could, unless it could not do so without thereby losing some greater good or permitting some evil equally bad or worse.
3. There does not exist an omnipotent, omniscient, wholly good being.[70]

Rowe then presents what is now a famous description of suffering.

> Suppose in some distant forest lightning strikes a dead tree, resulting in a forest fire. In the fire a fawn is trapped, horribly burned, and lies in terrible agony for several days before death relieves its suffering. *So far as we can see, the fawn's intense suffering is pointless.* For there does not appear to be any greater good such that the prevention of the fawn's suffering would require either the loss of that good or the occurrence of an evil equally bad or worse. Nor does there seem to be any equally bad or worse evil so connected to the fawn's suffering that it would have had to occur had the fawn's suffering been prevented. Could an omnipotent, omniscient being have prevented the fawn's apparently pointless suffering?[71]

Rowe's analysis is clear and worth citing, for he does not think the instance of suffering establishes atheism in absolute terms:

> It must be acknowledged that the case of the fawn's apparently pointless suffering does not *prove* that (1) is true. For even though we cannot see how the fawn's suffering is required to obtain some greater good (or to prevent some equally bad or worse evil), it hardly follows that it is not so required. After all, we are often surprised by how things we thought to be unconnected turn out to be intimately connected. Perhaps, for all we know, there is some familiar good outweighing the fawn's suffering to which that suffering is connected in a way we do not see. Furthermore, there may well be unfamiliar goods, goods we haven't dreamed of, to which the fawn's suffering is inextricably connected. Indeed, it would seem to require something like omniscience on our part before we could lay claim to *knowing* that there is no greater good connected to the fawn's suffering in such a manner that an omnipotent, omniscient being could not have achieved that good without permitting that suffering of some

---

[70] "The Problem of Evil," 369.
[71] Ibid., 370 (emphasis added).

evil equally bad or worse. So the case of the fawn's suffering surely does not enable us to *establish* the truth of (1).[72]

In fact, Rowe concedes that, if one had independent reasons for belief in an all-good God, one would be well placed to reply to his argument as follows:

> (not-3) There exists an omnipotent, omniscient, wholly good being.
>
> (2) An omniscient, wholly good being would prevent the occurrence of any intense suffering it could, unless it could not do so without thereby losing some greater good or permitting some evil equally bad or worse.

Therefore:

> (not-1) It is not the case that there exist instances of intense suffering that an omnipotent, omniscient being could have prevented without thereby losing some greater good or permitting some evil equally bad or worse.

But, so Rowe argues, lacking evidence for "not-3" and having the evidence of the degrees and magnitude of the evil we observe, it is not reasonable to believe there are greater goods that require the evil at hand.[73]

Probably the most direct theistic reply has been to contend that there are sufficient goods in the cosmos whereby we may see that (or reasonably believe that) it is good that the cosmos exists not withstanding evil. This is the project of developing a theodicy.[74]

Richard Swinburne has been the most bold in identifying goods in the world that permit evils.[75] John Hick has also developed a positive account of the good of creation and offered an overriding account of how God may bring good out of evil. Hick describes the cosmos in terms of the emergence of moral agents who are perfected through failure, suffering, and renewal. As Hick insists that evil truly is evil (something that ought not to be), he readily sees horrendous evil as something not willed by God.

---

[72] Ibid.

[73] Ibid., 372. Rowe's argument is strengthened by J. L. Schellenberg, who argues that an all-good God would want His creatures to understand the great good that makes the allowance of evil permissible.

[74] Jerry Walls, "Why Plantinga Must Move from Defense to Theodicy," *Philosophy and Phenomenological Research* 51 (1991).

[75] See especially Swinburne, *Providence and the Problem of Evil* (Oxford: Clarendon, 1998).

What does that ultimate context of divine purpose and activity mean of Auschwitz and Belsen and the other camps in which, between 1942 and 1945, between four and six million Jewish men, women, and children were deliberately and scientifically murdered? Was this in any sense willed by God? The answer is obviously no. These events were utterly evil, wicked, devilish and, so far as the human mind can reach, unforgivable; they are wrongs that can never be righted, *horrors which will disfigure the universe to the end of time*, and in relation to which no condemnation can be strong enough, no revulsion adequate. It would have been better – much much better – if they had never happened. Most certainly God did not want those who committed these fearful crimes against humanity to act as they did. His purpose for the world was retarded by them and the power of evil within it increased. Undoubtedly He saw with anger and grief the sufferings so willfully inflicted upon the people of His ancient choice, through whom His Messiah had come into the world.[76]

Notwithstanding such nightmares, Hick defends the reasonability of a hope and faith that an all-good God will defeat evil and bring all people (in the end) to a good life in communion with Him (the Real or an Ultimate, good reality). For Hick, this must involve an afterlife. On this front, Hick is with Demea, not Cleanthes, in Hume's famous *Dialogues*. Hick writes:

If this life, so creative for some but so destructive for many others, is all, then despair at the human situation as a whole is appropriate. Indeed if an all-powerful God has deliberately created a situation in which this present life, with all its horrors, is the totality of human existence, we should hate and revile that God's callous disregard for his/her helpless creatures. If we dismiss the eschatological dimension of the world's religions, Roth's protest against God, instead of being a bold defiance, would be a feebly inadequate response. He goes either too far or not far enough.[77]

I return to the topic of an afterlife later.

Hick, Swinburne, and others argue that God could not have created beings that are free moral agents, interdependent on one another, and guaranteed that all free acts would be good or at least not harmful.[78]

---

[76] *Evil and the God of Love* (Thetford: Collins, 1974), 397 (emphasis added).

[77] "Critique by John Hick," in *Encountering Evil*, ed. S. T. Davis (London: Leiden, 2001), 29.

[78] For other arguments in support of this, see Douglas Geivett, *Evil and the Evidence for God* (Philadelphia: Temple University Press, 1993); Bruce Reichenbach, *Evil and a*

Peter van Inwagen contends that the creation of free beings as well as other goods (nonhuman animal life) inevitably involves suffering.

> Only in a universe very much like ours could intelligent life, or even sentient life, develop by the nonmiraculous operation of the laws of nature. And the natural evolution of higher sentient life in a universe like ours essentially involves suffering, or there is every reason to believe it does. The mechanisms underlying biological evolution may be just what most biologists seem to suppose – the production of new genes by random mutation and the culling of gene pools by environmental selection pressure – or they may be more subtle. But no one, I believe, would take seriously the idea that conscious animals, animals conscious as a dog is conscious, could evolve naturally without hundreds of millions of years of ancestral suffering. Pain is an indispensable component of the evolutionary process after organisms have reached a certain stage of complexity. And, for all we know, the amount of pain that organisms have experienced in the actual world, or some amount morally equivalent to that amount, is necessary for the natural evolution of conscious animals.[79]

The alternative would be a world of constant supernatural interference. Van Inwagen offers this description:

> God, by means of a continuous series of ubiquitous miracles, causes a planet inhabited by the same animal life as the actual earth to be a hedonic utopia. On this planet, fawns are (like Shadrach, Meshach, and Abednego) saved by angels when they are in danger of being burnt alive. Harmful parasites and microorganisms suffer immediate supernatural dissolution if they enter a higher animal's body. Lambs are miraculously hidden from lions, and the lions are compensated for the resulting restriction on their diets by physically impossible falls of high-protein manna. On this planet, either God created every species by a separate miracle, or else, although all living things evolved from a common ancestor, a hedonic utopia has existed at every stage of the evolutionary process. (The latter alternative implies that God has, by means of a vast and intricately coordinated sequence of supernatural adjustments to the machinery of nature, guided

Good God (New York: Fordham University Press, 1982); and Michael Peterson, ed., *The Problem of Evil* (Notre Dame: University of Notre Dame Press, 1992).

[79] "The Problem of Evil, of Air, and of Silence," reprinted in Taliaferro and Griffiths, *Philosophy of Religion: An Anthology*, 396. Arguments to the effect that any evil whatsoever falsifies theism are sometimes called a priori, logical, or deductive arguments. Arguments over whether the amount of evil that seems to exist renders theism unreasonable are sometimes called probabilistic a posteriori, or evidential arguments.

the evolutionary process in such a way as to compensate for the fact that a hedonic utopia exerts no selection pressure.)[80]

Something like this perpetual divine engineering might be called for to secure the kind of universe that Mill maintained that God should have created (as described in Chapter 6). Because it is good that there be a world of interdependent, free beings evolving in a cosmos with laws of nature (and thus not afflicted with massive irregularity), some ills will be inevitable.[81]

An important component in this defense of theism has been the thesis that it is good that God's existence is not overwhelming or obvious. Hick maintains that creation of free beings must have some "epistemic distance" from God; otherwise the belief in God would be coercive and lose some of its virtue.[82]

There are at least two other elements in the arguments over evidence. The first concerns the limits of our cognition. Some theists hold the skeptical position that they do not know the point or purpose of some (most or all) evil. But this is not evidence that there is no point or purpose of evil. Not seeing the point would only count as evidence that evil is pointless if you can rightly expect that you would see the point if it were there. The reason why my not seeing an elephant in my office is good evidence that there is no such elephant is because I would see it if it were here. William Alston, among others, summarizes the many limitations that do not permit us to conclude that evil is impermissible for God to allow (or to conclude that God, if there is a God, should not create and sustain this cosmos).

1. *Lack of data.* This includes, inter alia, the secrets of the human heart, the detailed constitution and structure of the universe, and the remote past and future, including the afterlife if any.
2. *Complexity greater than we can handle.* Most notably there is the difficulty of holding enormous complexes of fact – different possible worlds

---

[80] Ibid., 395. Consider, too, F. R. Tennant, *Philosophical Theology* (Cambridge: Cambridge University Press, 1956), 2:180–208.

[81] For two arguments that link our identity to past harms, see William Hasker, "On Regretting the Evils of This World," in Peterson, *The Problem of Evil*, and R. M. Adams, "Existence, Self-Interest and the Problem of Evil," *Nous* 13 (1979).

[82] See Hick, "Good, Evil and Mystery," *Religious Studies* 3 (1968). See also William Hasker, "Suffering, Soul-Making and Salvation," *International Philosophical Quarterly* 28 (1988), and "The Necessity of Gratuitous Evil," *Faith and Philosophy* 9 (1992), as well as J. L. Schellenberg's *Divine Hiddenness and Human Reason* (Ithaca: Cornell University Press, 1993).

or different systems of natural law – together in the mind sufficiently for comparative evaluation.

3. *Difficulty of determining what is metaphysically possible or necessary.* Once we move beyond conceptual or semantic modalities (and even that is no piece of cake) it is notoriously difficult to find any sufficient basis for claims as to what is metaphysically possible, given the essential natures of things, the exact character of which is often obscure to us and virtually always controversial. This difficulty is many times multiplied when we are dealing with total possible worlds or total systems of natural order.

4. *Ignorance of the full range of possibilities.* This is always crippling when we are trying to establish negative conclusions. If we don't know whether or not there are possibilities beyond the ones we have thought of, we are in a very bad position to show that there can be no divine reasons for permitting evil.

5. *Ignorance of the full range of values.* When it's a question of whether some good is related to E [where E stands for a certain case of suffering] in such a way as to justify God in permitting E, we are, for the reason mentioned in 4., in a very poor position to answer the question if we don't know the extent to which there are modes of value beyond those of which we are aware. For in that case, so far as we can know, E may be justified by virtue of its relation to one of those unknown goods.

6. *Limits to our capacity to make well considered value judgments.* The chief example of this we have noted is the difficulty in making comparative evaluations of large complex wholes.[83]

This emphasis on the limits of our cognition is especially at home in a theistic defense rather than a theodicy.[84]

A related factor that has come into play in such defenses is debate over whether God is obliged to create a best-possible world or God is

[83] "The Inductive Argument from Evil and the Human Cognitive Condition," reprinted in *Philosophy and Faith*, ed. D. Shatz (Boston: McGraw Hill, 2002), 290–291.

[84] See S. J. Wykstra, "The Humean Obstacle to Evidential Arguments from Suffering: On Avoiding the Evils of 'Appearance,'" in *The Problem of Evil*, ed. by M. M. Adams and R. M. Adams (Oxford: Oxford University Press, 1990), and his "Rowe's Noseeum Arguments from Evil," in *The Evidential Argument from Evil*, ed. by D. Howard-Snyder (Bloomington: Indiana University Press, 1996); Alvin Plantinga, "On Being Evidentially Challenged," also in *The Evidential Argument from Evil*; Keith Yandell, "The Problem of Evil," *Philosophical Topics* 12:1 (1981); Clement Dore, "Do Theists Need to Solve the Problem of Evil?" *Religious Studies* 12 (1976).

not obliged to create such a world; the fact that there can be a better world than this is not a decisive objection to theism.[85]

I consider more briefly five other features in this "case study" of philosophy of religion today.

Individuals and Holism. The problem of evil has sometimes been advanced with the insistence that an all-good, omnipotent Creator would insure that each creature has a good life or with the acknowledgment that it suffices that the whole of creation is overall good, even if some creatures suffer unjustly. Back to Rowe's fawn: must an all-good Creator secure that the specific fawn's life is good or is it only essential that there is a deer population, notwithstanding individual suffering? There is an interesting intersection between philosophy of religion and environmental ethics here. Environmentalists can be divided between individualists, whose focus is on specific individuals, and ecologists (sometimes called holists or ecoholists), who stress the good of ecosystems.[86]

Specific Cases. Some of the literature on evil is very abstract with thought experiments and sometimes very concrete with detailed cases described. So, in Rowe's debate with Hick, he has brought into focus not just a case of a fawn but a case of a five-year-old girl being raped and murdered.[87] Perhaps the most common specific case in the literature is the Holocaust. The problem of evil has been articulated by Jewish philosophers of religion in this format:

1. God, as he is conceived of in the Jewish tradition, could not have allowed the Holocaust to happen.

---

[85] See, for example, George Schlesinger, *New Perspectives on Old-Time Religion* (Oxford: Oxford University Press, 1988).

[86] Tom Regan is a good representative of individualism and J. B. Callicott of holism in environmental ethics. Mark Wynn makes good use of the environmental literature in *God and Goodness* (London: Routledge, 1999). It is precisely at this intersection of philosophy of religion and environmental ethics that cases like Rowe's description of nonhuman animal suffering need to be addressed. For a general plea to take animal suffering seriously in philosophy of religion, see Frederick Ferré, "Theodicy and the Status of Animals," *American Philosophical Quarterly* 23 (1986). See also the following three publications by Jay McDaniel: "Physical Nature as Creative and Sentient," *Environmental Ethics* 5 (1983); "A Feeling for the Organism," *Environmental Ethics* 8 (1986); and *Of God and Pelicans: A Theology of Reverence for Life* (Louisville: Westminster, 1989).

[87] See Rowe, "Evil and Theodicy," *Philosophical Topics* 16 (1988).

2. The Holocaust did happen. Therefore,
3. God, as he is conceived of in the Jewish tradition, does not exist.[88]

Responses to the Holocaust have ranged from radically rethinking Judaism in light of "The death of God" to an affirmation of life after death as an indispensable part of a philosophy of providence.[89] There is an interesting matrix in some of this literature that both takes specific cases seriously and speculates about possible ways in which good might defeat or overcome evil. In an important essay, "Jewish Faith and the Holocaust," Dan Cohn-Sherbok writes:

> Yet without this belief [in an afterlife], it is simply impossible to make sense of the world as the creation of an all-good and all-powerful God. Without the eventual vindication of the righteous in Paradise, there is no way to sustain the belief in a providential God who watches over His chosen people. The essence of the Jewish understanding of God is that He loves His chosen people. If death means extinction, there is no way to make sense of the claim that He loves and cherishes all those who died in the concentration camps – suffering and death would ultimately triumph over each of those who perished. But if there is eternal life in a World to Come, then there is hope that the righteous will share in a divine life. Moreover, the divine attribute of justice demands that the righteous of Israel who met their death as innocent victims of the Nazis will reap an everlasting reward. Here then is an answer to the religious perplexities of the Holocaust. The promise of immortality offers a way of reconciling the belief in a loving and just God with the nightmare of the death camps. As we have seen, this hope sustained the Jewish people through centuries of suffering and martyrdom. Now that Jewry stands on the threshold of the twenty-first century, it must again serve as the fulcrum of religious beliefs.[90]

Religious Values. Another feature of the current literature is the debate over the kinds of values that can come into play in terms of understanding good and evil. It has been argued by Marilyn Adams that if only secular values are allowed in our reflection, then the scales tip against

---

[88] See Steven Katz, "The Shoah," in *History of Jewish Philosophy*, ed. D. H. Frank and O. Leaman (London: Routledge, 1997), 856.

[89] See A. Rosenberg and G. E. Meyers, eds., *Echoes from the Holocaust: Philosophical Reflections on a Dark Time* (Philadelphia: Temple University Press, 1988), and M. Berenbaum, ed., *After Tragedy and Triumph* (Cambridge: Cambridge University Press, 1990).

[90] "Jewish Faith and the Holocaust," *Religious Studies* 26 (1990): 292–293.

theism. But why can't the theist look to her own tradition and the values displayed there in addressing evil? Adams proposes that there can be a great good realized through a communion with God in which evils are defeated.

> The worst evils demand to be defeated by the best goods. Horrendous evils can be overcome only by the goodness of God. Relative to human nature, participation in horrendous evils and loving intimacy with God are alike disproportionate: for the former threatens to engulf the good in an individual human life with evil, while the latter guarantees the reverse engulfment of evil by good. Relative to one another, there is also disproportion, because the good that God *is*, and intimate relationship with Him, is incommensurate with created goods and evils alike. Because intimacy with God so outscales relations (good or bad) with any creatures, integration into the human person's relationship with God confers significant meaning and positive value even on horrendous suffering. This result coheres with basic Christian intuition: that the powers of darkness are stronger than humans, but they are no match for God.[91]

Adams's approach to the problem of evil invokes religious experience and unique values such as an inner mystical vision of God.[92] In different respects, Adams and those adopting related accounts, insist that God sorrows over, or suffers in, the ills of creation.[93]

Redemption. Marilyn Adams's approach to evil signals a tendency to emphasize not the justification of evil, but the redemption of evil persons and those harmed. Several philosophers of religion have warned against the way in which a theodicy or theistic defense can lead to ratifying or accommodating evil as actually good.[94] One response has been to insist that evil is not justified and, indeed, there is a sense in which God ought

---

[91] M. Adams, "Horrendous Evils and the Goodness of God," in Adams and Adams, *The Problem of Evil*, 220.

[92] See also Michael Stoeber, *Evil and the Mystics' God* (Toronto: University of Toronto Press, 1972).

[93] Compare N. Wolterstorff, "Suffering Love," in *Philosophy and the Christian Faith*, ed. by T. V. Morris (Notre Dame: University of Notre Dame Press, 1988), and R. Creel, *Divine Impassibility* (Cambridge: Cambridge University Press, 1986).

[94] See, for example, Nel Noddings, "Evil and Ethical Terror," in *Women and Evil* (Berkeley: University of California Press, 1989). On the dangers of theoretical theodicy, see Kenneth Surin, *Theology and the Problem of Evil* (Oxford: Blackwell, 1986).

to destroy all evil, but that it is compatible with God's goodness for God to defeat evil through redemption.[95]

Afterlife. Still other features could be cited as distinguishing marks of the literature today, but I will end with noting how speculation on a next life has an important role. Some philosophers of religion dismiss the possibility of an afterlife as either impossible or undesirable.[96] But others (such as Hick and Cohn-Sherbok cited earlier) see an afterlife as indispensable. The most significant issue in debate is very much at home with the issues that exercised the Cambridge Platonists: what are the implications of materialism for the belief in life after death? A range of materialists have argued that there are ways in which a person may survive death: a person may be re-created by God even after the person has perished; there may be a resurrection of the person's body; God may recompose a person at death, replacing her material body with an immaterial one, and so on.[97]

With the afterlife put on the table for discussion, it should not be surprising to realize that debate over heaven, hell, and purgatory have returned. An important focus has been on whether theism requires a universalism in which all are saved or a more limited view in which some never achieve union with God.[98]

Stepping back from this survey of different aspects of the problem of evil literature, it becomes apparent that there is more at stake than assessing the credibility of agnosticism, atheism, and theism. I already noted how evil is being assessed by different world religions. But these are also approaches to evil that in different ways challenge the kind of theism at stake. Thus, process philosophers (introduced in the preceding chapter) do not view God as omnipotent.[99] For a start, this holds in check the atheist polemic that God, being omnipotent, can freely elect to

---

[95] For the concept of defeating evil, see R. M. Chisholm, "The Defeat of Good and Evil," in Adams and Adams, *The Problem of Evil*. Defeating evil does not make the evil less evil.

[96] See D. Z. Phillips in conversation with John Hick, in Davis, *Encountering Evil*, 71–72.

[97] For two materialist accounts of an afterlife, see Peter van Inwagen, "The Possibility of Resurrection," *International Journal for Philosophy of Religion* 9 (1978), and Bruce Reichenbach, *Is Man the Phoenix?* (Grand Rapids: Christian University Press, 1978).

[98] For an interesting study of two contributors to this debate, see Lindsey Hall, *Swinburne's Hell and Hick's Universalism* (Aldershot: Ashgate, 2003).

[99] See Charles Hartshorne, *Omnipotence and Other Theological Mistakes* (Albany: SUNY Press, 1984).

eliminate all evil at will. Process thinkers also tend to shun any appeal to the individual survival of death.[100] There is also the proposal that while God is the Creator of the cosmos, God is not a moral agent with duties and obligations. God's perfection is not to be assessed in terms of the virtues of human beings. God's perfection lies outside of the domain of moral praise and blame. Brian Davies has advanced this proposal along with historical arguments that this philosophy of God is to be found in Thomas Aquinas and other classical Christian sources.[101]

Philosophy of Religion and Friendship

Before turning to a final section on philosophy of religion outside the academy, I touch on a topic that is more elusive. In several places in this narrative I have referred to friendships – between Henry More and Anne Conway, Lady Masham and John Locke, Kant and Mendelssohn. It is futile to wonder whether the unfolding of philosophy of religion would have been better or worse if there had been more friendships (imagine Descartes and Hobbes going out for drinks), but there are signs that collaborative (and, in some sense, friendly) projects have been quite fruitful.

In an important, recent book, *Can a Darwinian Be a Christian?* Michael Ruse writes in the acknowledgments of his debt to many people – all named – and adds that all of whom "I criticize strongly have been unfailingly courteous and friendly, showing that one can have major differences which need not (and should not) translate into personal attitudes and behavior."[102] My hunch is that there is more openness and collegiality because there is a more widespread realization today that *the one correct view* of an issue in philosophy and religion (the relation between science and religion, in Ruse's case) is not overwhelmingly obvious. Reasonable, intellectually fair-minded, even brilliant philosophers can disagree.[103] Of course, one can still find in the literature some

---

[100] There is at least one exception, however. The process thinker John Cobb allows for some hope of an individual afterlife in *God and the World* (Philadelphia: Westminster, 1969). For a significant process work on the problem of evil, see D. R. Griffen, *God, Power and Evil: A Process Theodicy* (Philadelphia: Westminster, 1976).

[101] See "The Problem of Evil," in *Philosophy of Religon: A Guide to the Subject*, ed. B. Davies (London: Cassell, 1998).

[102] *Can a Darwinian Be a Christian?* (Cambridge: Cambridge University Press, 2001), x.

[103] See the preface to Graham Oppy, *Ontological Arguments and Belief in God* (Cambridge: Cambridge University Press, 1995).

enthusiastic condemnations of opposing views. Here are two: "The God of the philosophers is dead. This God is dead because he is a creature of metaphysics... and metaphysics is dead"[104] And: "The God of traditional philosophy of religion... is a creature of scholastic, modernist, and enlightenment modes of thinking that deserves nothing so much as a decent burial."[105] But in general I believe the tendency to call the views of colleagues dead or liken their work to something like performing autopsies seems to be waning.

In medieval times, the fifth proposition in Euclid's *Elements* was called the asses' bridge, *pons asinorum*, because it was believed to separate the intelligent from the stupid: if you could not follow the proposition, you were deemed stupid. I believe philosophy of religion today has rigorous standards of conceptual clarity, comprehensiveness, command of the history of ideas, scientific literacy, and so on, but there is no *pons asinorum* when it comes to accepting or rejecting the core positions of, say, Hume, Kant, Hegel, Kierkegaard, Wittgenstein, Jantzen, Anderson, et al. Reasonable people can disagree with intellectual integrity and even in friendship.

Let us consider two final examples of cordiality where the opposition is treated with respect. The first is from an atheist J. J. C. Smart commenting on Peter Forrest's book *God without the Supernatural*:

> I believe it is an important work in philosophy, and philosophy of religion in particular. Forrest's study is immensely dense in argument, in new concepts, and in speculation. Even those atheists who are not in the end convinced about it will end up with great admiration for it and wiser by exposure to a plentiful supply of new concepts and arguments.... He is not proposing apodictic arguments. He is certainly not making the silly fallacy that many fallacious deductions can add up to a valid argument. Forrest is putting up many speculations, sometimes choices of alternative ones, all consistent with the modern scientific world view, and his arguments are proposed as plausible, cumulative and mutually supporting one another.... He is a beautifully undogmatic and unfanatical theist.[106]

Alas, some philosophical exchanges at meetings such as the American Philosophical Association are a far cry from this tribute. (Regrettably, some APA meetings can degenerate into cut-and-thrust adversarial

---

[104] Bas Van Fraassen, *The Empirical Stance* (New Haven: Yale University Press; 2002), 1.

[105] John Caputo, *The Religious* (Oxford: Blackwell, 2002), 3.

[106] J. J. C. Smart, "Forrest on God without the Supernatural," *Sophia* 36:1 (1997): 24, 36.

intellectual combat.)[107] But I take heart in Smith's generosity and note as well Michael Rea's conclusion in a book that challenges the adequacy of naturalism. "Naturalism deserved center stage because, though ultimately I reject it, I think that in fact naturalism is the most viable research program apart from a brand of supernaturalism that warrants belief in a suitably developed version of traditional theism."[108] Such respectful appreciation of the merits of the "other side" strikes me as refreshing and creating a context in which philosophical ideas may be developed with dignity, fairness, and enthusiasm.[109]

Philosophy of Religion at Large

The fact (if it is one) that philosophically respectable persons can have serious disagreements over religion plays an important role in a matter of general, public life in the United States. Religious reasons have been given to support legal institutions and practices, and to oppose others, covering almost every area of life. Today the more publicized areas for religious-political exchange involve abortion (or "reproductive rights"), euthanasia and suicide, capital punishment, marriage, sexual ethics, genetic engineering, education (secular vs. religious education; also, specifically instruction in the sciences and history where this involves religious or secular indoctrination), the tax status of religious institutions, and the use of religious practices and symbols in government. In the past, religious reasons have been offered on slavery (both pro and con), the role of women in society, polygamy, alcohol consumption, work on Sunday, the treatment of Native Americans, and dueling.[110] Some of the major modern critics of religion covered in this book (e.g., Marx and Weber) predicted the erosion of religion and thus the decline of instances where religious-political conflict would be vital

---

[107] I should add that one reader of an earlier version of this chapter offered this comment: "Intellectual combat isn't always a bad thing, when important values are at stake. For one thing, it can help avert physical combat."

[108] M. Rea, *World without Design: The Ontological Consequences of Naturalism* (Oxford: Oxford University Press, 2002), 226.

[109] Two different but relevant works on friendship: David Burrell, *Friendship and Ways to Truth* (Notre Dame: University of Notre Dame Press, 2000), and J. Bobik, "Aquinas on Friendship with God," *New Scholasticism* 60:3 (1986).

[110] See John West, *The Politics of Revelation and Reason* (Lawrence: University Press of Kansas, 1996).

to address.[111] Of course, there would be residual issues where a secular state might make allowances for religious convictions (e.g., not compelling military duty for religious pacifists – Quakers and Mennonites – or medical treatments for adult Christian Scientists), but Weber and some contemporary sociologists foresee the privatization of religion.[112] And yet this prediction, at least in the United States and many regions outside of Europe, has failed to materialize. There is, instead, impressive sociological data to support the hypothesis of growth and vibrancy of religion (or religions). Moreover, this is not due to poor or inadequate education measured by non-question-begging standards.[113] The secularization prediction has lost at least one of its major twentieth-century proponents (Peter Berger), and the encounter between "the West" and Islam has given us reason enough to take seriously the relation between religion and politics.[114]

In the English-speaking world there is currently a widespread version of what is often called liberalism (alternatively: *political liberalism* or *procedural liberalism*) according to which citizens should not justify political or legal policies on exclusively religious grounds. In "The Politics of Justification," Stephen Macedo writes: "The only way that we can achieve a public moral framework while accepting the deep and permanent fact of diversity is by putting aside not only the personal interests and religious beliefs, but also the many philosophical and moral convictions with which reasonable citizens will disagree."[115] For Macedo, "public justification" must be based on appeal to a reasonable public. "The application of power should be accompanied with reasons that

---

[111] See, for example, Max Weber, "Science as a Vocation," in *From Max Weber*, ed. H. H. Gerth and C. W. Mills (Oxford: Oxford University Press, 1946).

[112] See R. Wallis and S. Bruce, "Religion: The British Contribution," *British Journal of Sociology* 40 (1989): 493.

[113] See R. Stark and R. Finke, *Acts of Faith: Explaining the Human Side of Religion* (Berkeley: University of California Press, 2000). Thomas Nagel, a political liberal and atheist, offers this backhanded complement to the intellectual prospect of theism: "I want atheism to be true and am made uneasy by the fact that some of the most intelligent and well-informed people I know are religious. It isn't that I don't believe in God and, naturally, hope that I'm right in my belief. It's that I hope there is no God! I don't want there to be a God; I don't want the universe to be like that" (*The Last Word* [Oxford: Oxford University Press, 1997], 130). As Paul Copan has observed, if you hope a view is false you imply that you are not sure that it is false.

[114] See Paul Johnson, "The Study of an Encounter," in *Unsecular America* (Grand Rapids: Eerdmans, 1986), 84–85.

[115] "The Politics of Justification," *Political Theory* 18 (1990): 295.

all reasonable people should be able to accept."[116] John Rawls has a similar view: "The idea of public reason is not a view about specific political institutions and policies. Rather, it is a view about the kinds of reasons on which citizens are to rest their political cases in making their political justifications to one another when they support laws and policies that involve the coercive powers of government."[117] This outlook is, in general, shared by Robert Audi, Charles Larmore, Thomas Nagel, Amy Gutmann, and Dennis Thompson. This political philosophy takes as basic a principle of respect for persons. Robert Audi writes:

> I think that sound ethics itself dictates that, out of respect for others as free and dignified individuals, we should always have and be sufficiently motivated by adequate secular reasons for our positions on those matters of law or public policy in which our decisions might significantly restrict human freedom. If you are fully rational and I cannot convince you of my view by arguments framed in the concepts we share as rational beings, then even if mine is the majority view I should not coerce you.[118]

This secularization of political exchange has much to commend it, and it is not my task at the end of this book to argue for its inadequacy. I advance instead five observations as to why the secular thesis and those who oppose it need to take philosophy of religion seriously.

First, political liberalism does involve a philosophy of religion, an assessment of its universal appeal or reasonable accessibility. In a sense, albeit limited, Rawls et al. have a philosophy of religion. This may seem trivial as it is obvious (to some) that religious reasons are not universally accessible under conditions of reasonable pluralism. But one's philosophy of reasons, evidence, and warrant, and one's concept of "religion" (the necessary and sufficient conditions for being a religion) do come under the domain of philosophy of religion.

Second, the secular hypothesis is not at complete odds with religious conceptions of ethics. As I suggested in Chapter 4 when discussing a Humean philosophy of religion as developed by Smith, much moral reasoning may be read in terms of trying to achieve an ideal-observer point of view, and this view in turn is not dissimilar to seeking what may be called "a God's-eye point of view." In this respect, religious ethics and secular ethics will converge.

---

[116] Stephen Macedo, *Liberal Virtues* (Oxford: Oxford University Press, 1990), 41.

[117] "The Idea of Public Reason Revisited," in *The Law of the Peoples* (Cambridge, Mass.: Harvard University Press, 2001), 795.

[118] "The Place of Religious Argument in a Free and Democratic Society," *San Diego Law Review* 30:4 (1993): 701.

Third, it is not clear that justification for action based on a belief must be based on grounds which *all* reasonable persons accept. Imagine that you believe, reasonably, that famine relief is a grave responsibility of those who are, by contrast, advantaged. Imagine further that this is secured by your first hand experience of poverty. Imagine further that you are in the minority in your society where well-off, reasonable persons with backgrounds and experiences similar to yours disagree with your conviction. I suggest you would not thereby loose your justification and, arguably, you may have an obligation (based on your convictions) to vote for laws which would compel fellow citizens to engage in famine relief. Respect for other persons may require your trying to convince others by, say, testimony, but if you fail to convince, it may still be within your rights to pursue what you see to be obligatory.[119]

Fourth, it has been argued that the ideal of acting only on secular grounds – on grounds shorn of religious identity – is virtually impossible for religious persons. In *Sources of the Self*, Charles Taylor defends this concept:

> The claim is that living within ... strongly qualified horizons is constitutive of human agency, that stepping outside these limits would be tantamount to stepping outside what we would regard as integral, that is, undamaged, human personality. Perhaps the best way of seeing this is to focus on the issue that we usually describe today as the question of identity. We speak of it in these terms because the question is often spontaneously phrased by people in the form: Who am I? But this can't necessarily be answered by giving name and genealogy. What does answer this question for us is an understanding of what is of crucial importance to us. To know who I am is a species of knowing where I stand. My identity is defined by the commitments and identifications which provide the frame or horizon within which I can try to determine from case to case what is good, or valuable, or what ought to be done, or what I endorse or oppose. In other words, it is the horizon within which I am capable of taking a stand.[120]

---

[119] A fuller development of the analogy for philosophy of religion would rest on bolstering a constructive picture of religious experience. Imagine that otherwise reasonable people see some modest but not compelling reason to relieve poverty. Imagine a person who shares this view until she becomes convinced (through argument or religious experience) that God calls everyone to a higher standard of responsibility. Would she be unreasonable to vote for greater famine relief?

[120] *Sources of the Self: The Making of the Modern Identity* (Cambridge, Mass.: Harvard University Press, 1989), 27. For a systematic challenge to liberalism, see C. J. Eberle, *Religious Conviction in Liberal Politics* (Cambridge: Cambridge University Press, 2002).

On this view, our lives may be shaped and embedded by a secular or religious horizon from which we cannot somehow remove ourselves without the loss of our very identity. Given a powerful religious identity, liberal detachment may be virtually unattainable.

Fifth, religion and philosophy of religion may involve goods that are themselves important to protect or encourage even in a secular state. Even if no policy making should be conducted on the basis of exclusive, distinctive religious grounds, it may be good for citizens to have access to religious values and practices as well as to philosophical inquiry into the traditions that make up so much of human history and also define the lives of so many today. Presumably, religious literacy is an indispensable instrument in the encounter with religious, political cultures. Alternatively, if you believe religious traditions involve great ills (sexism, racism, classism, gullibility), you may argue that a society should discourage or at least do no more than tolerate religions. In any case, developing your position will involve your articulation and defense of a philosophy of religion.

I do not want to end this book with the impression that, at the end of the day, I see the prospects of philosophy of religion exclusively in terms of its relevance to contemporary political philosophy! On the basis of the *many* reasons discussed from the introduction of the book onward, I believe that, whether for good or ill, the significance of religion and philosophy of religion extends far beyond our choice of government. And I commend this field to you as a place for constructive and critical, engaging philosophical work.

APPENDIX A

✦

A Guide to Further Study

Philosophy of religion is practiced in a range of centers, societies, conferences, and journals. I list here societies that are also focused on specific philosophers who are featured in this book. Addresses for these may be found through the Philosophy Documentation Center (Bowling Green State University, Indiana) or, in many cases, through a web search. For a good overview of web sites including e-journals, virtual libraries, and the like, see M. Sarot, M. Scott, and M. Wise, "Philosophy of Religion: A Critical Survey of Internet Resources," *Religious Studies* 36 (2000): 355–366.

Centers and Societies

Organizations that promote philosophy of religion include American Academy of Religion; American Philosophical Association; American Philosophical Society; Australasian Association of Philosophy; Boston University Institute for Philosophy and Religion; Society of Christian Philosophers; Buddhist Society; Center for Philosophy of Religion, Notre Dame; Center for Thomistic Studies; Conference of Philosophical Societies; Hume Society; International Association for Asian Philosophy and Religion; International Society for Neoplatonic Studies; International Society for the I Ching; Jesuit Philosophical Association; Leibniz Society of North America; The Nietzsche Society; North American Kant Society; North American Nietzsche Society; North American Spinoza Society; Northwest Society for Phenomenology, Existentialism, and Hermeneutics; Philosophers' Information Center; Philosophical Research Society; Sartre Circle; Society for Buddhist-Christian Studies; Society for Contemporary Assessment of Platonism; Society for Phenomenology and

Existential Philosophy; Society for Philosophy and Theology; Society for Philosophy of Religion; Society for the Scientific Study of Religion; Søren Kierkegaard Society. (If you would like more information concerning Kierkegaard's philosophy in particular, the Kierkegaard Library located at St. Olaf College in Minnesota currently holds about 10,000 volumes including a replication of Kierkegaard's own personal library.)

Journals

Journals devoted to philosophy of religion include *The International Journal for Philosophy of Religion; Religious Studies; Faith and Philosophy; Philo; Ars Disputanti; Philosophia Christi; Philosophy and Theology; Sophia; American Catholic Philosophic Quarterly* (formerly *New Scholasticism); American Journal of Theology and Philosophy; The Thomist; The Journal of the American Academy of Religion; The Journal of Religion; Theological Studies; The Journal of Theology Today; New Blackfriars; Modern Theology; Harvard Theological Review; The Scottish Journal of Religious Studies; The Scottish Journal of Theology, Law and Religion; The Journal of Law and Religion; Literature and Theology; The Journal of Humanism and Ethical Religions;* and *Christian Scholar's Review.*

Books

In terms of series, Cambridge publishes *Cambridge Studies in Religion and Critical Thought*, Blackwell publishes *Exploring The Philosophy of Religion*, Cornell University Press publishes *Cornell Studies in the Philosophy of Religion*; Indiana University Press publishes *The Indiana Series in the Philosophy of Religion*; Kluwer Academic Publishers publishes *Studies in Philosophy and Religion*; Rutgers University Press publishes *Philosophy and Religion*; and the State University of New York Press publishes *Toward a Comparative Philosophy of Religions.*

As for guides to the field, there is *A Companion to Philosophy of Religion*, edited by P. Quinn and C. Taliaferro; *Philosophy of Religion: A Reader and Guide*, edited by W. L. Craig; *Philosophy: A Guide to the Subject of Religion*, edited by Brian Davies; and *The Blackwell Guide to Philosophy of Religion*, edited by William Mann. William Wainwright is editing a *Companion to Philosophy of Religion* for Oxford University Press. Wainwright has assembled a wonderful collection, *Philosophy of Religion; An Annotated Bibliography of Twentieth Century Writings in English* (New York: Garland, 1978). For a more recent bibliography, see Robert Wolf's *Analytic Philosophy of Religion: A Bibliography, 1940–1996* (Bowling Green: Philosophy Documentation Center, 1998). Philosophy of Religion is featured in all of the standard philosophical dictionaries and companions and is a special concern in *The History of Science and Religion in the Western Tradition: An Encyclopedia* (New York: Garland, 2000), as well as Macmillan's forthcoming *Encyclopedia of Science and Religion*. Most of the Cambridge University Press companions to different philosophers have entries in philosophy of religion.

✦

Select Contemporary Philosophers

The following lists of philosophers are not complete; they are offerred as simply a starting point for exploring current work in the field.

Table B1. *Philosophy of Religion*

Buddhism	Hinduism and Sikhism	Confucianism/ Tao	Cross-Cultural/ Comparative	Feminist
J. Cabezona	K. C. Bhattacharyya	R. Ames	E. Deutsch	P. S. Anderson
J. L. Garfield	P. Bilimoria	W. Chan	P. Griffiths	E. Armour
P. Griffiths	S. N. Dasgupta	J. Ching	W. Halbass	B. Clack
J. Gyatso	E. Deutsch	A. Cua	C. Hallisey	S. Coakley
C. Hallisey	M. Hiriyanna	D. Hall	J. Hick	M. Daly
R. Hayes	A. L. Herman	B. Mou	T. Kasulis	H. A. Harris
M. Kapstein	R. King	H. Rosemont Jr.	R. Panikkar	A. Hollywood
T. Kasulis	D. Krishnan	J. Stambaugh	S. H. Phillips	G. M. Jantzen
D. Keown	A. Mandair (Sikh)		J. Runzo	K. O'Grady
S. King	B. Matilal		J. J. C. Smart	J. M. Soskice
D. S. Lopez	H. McLeod (Sikh)		N. Smart	
D. Swearer	J. L. Mehta		H. Smith	
R. Thurman	J. N. Mohanty		D. Swearer	
P. Williams	R. Panikkar		D. Tracy	
D. Wright	L. Patton		S. Twiss	
	S. Radhakrishnan		M. Westphal	
	C. Ram-Prasad		L. Yearley	
	R. D. Ranade			
	A. Sharma			

Table B2. *Divine Attributes*

Omniscience	Omnipotence	Goodness	Divine Simplicity	Necessity	Eternity	Impassibility/ Passibility	Divine Action	God's Moral Authority	Reason and Belief in God	Problem of Evil
M. Adams	H. Frankfurt	R. M. Adams	B. Davies	R. M. Adams	W. Craig	V. Brummer	W. Alston	R. M. Adams	W. Alston	M. Adams
W. Alston	J. Hoffman	C. S. Evans	C. Hughes	B. Leftow	W. Hasker	K. Clark	B. Hebblethwaite	B. Brody	K. J. Clark	R. M. Adams
T. Flint	G. Mavrodes	L. Garcia	G. Hughes	A. Plantinga	P. Helm	R. Creel	K. Tanner	J. Idziak	G. Gutting	D. Howard-Saylor
J. Fisher	N. Pike	N. Kretzmann	N. Kretzmann	J. Ross	N. Kretzmann	W. Ward	T. Tracy	J. Murphy	P. Helm	Saylor
A. Freddoso	G. Rosenkrantz	S. MacDonald	B. Leftow	R. Swinburne	B. Leftow	N. Wolterstorff		P. Quinn	J. C. Mackie	A. Plantinga
J. Kranris	G. Schlesinger	T. V. Morris	W. Mann		J. R. Lucas			L. Zagzebski	G. Mavrodes	W. Rowe
N. Pike	E. Wierenga	P. Quinn	A. Plantinga		A. Padgett				A. Plantinga	S. Wykstra
A. N. Prior		G. N. Schlesinger	R. Swinburne		N. Pike				R. Swinburne	
E. Wierenga		M. Stewart			E. Stump				N. Wolterstorff	
L. Zagzebski		E. Stump			N. Wolterstorff					
		R. Swinburne								
		L. Zagzebski								

Table B3. *Theistic Arguments*

Ontological	Cosmological	Design	Miracles	Values/Moral Experience	From Consciousness	Religious Experience	Cognition
S. T. Davis	D. Braine	D. Basinger	D. Basinger	P. Copan	R. M. Adams	W. Alston	R. Creel
C. Dore	W. Craig	R. Basinger	R. Basinger	C. S. Evans	J. P. Moreland	C. Frank	A. Plantinga
N. Malcolm	S. T. Davis	W. Craig	S. T. Davis	A. C. Ewing	M. Rea	J. Gellman	R. Taylor
C. Hartshorne	G. Grisez	S. T. Davis	P. Dietl	G. Mavrodes	R. Swinburne	G. Gutting	
A. Plantinga	J. J. Haldane	P. Forrest	J. Earman	H. P. Owen		R. Swinburne	
J. Ross	R. C. Koons	R. Hambourger	R. D. Geivell	M. Wynn		W. Wainwright	
W. Rowe	H. Meynell	R. A. Larmer	D. Geivett			K. Yandell	
R. Swinburne	B. Miller	J. Leslie	R. Larmer				
R. Taylor	R. Purtill	R. Swinburne	R. Swinburne				
	B. Reichenbach	M. Wynn	K. Yandell				
	W. Rowe						
	R. Taylor						

Table B4. *Problem of Evil*

Favorable to Theism	Nontheistic/Critical of Theism
M. Adams	P. Bilimoria
R. M. Adams	D. Conway
D. Allen	P. Draper
D. Basinger	A. Flew
K. Clark	R. Gale
S. T. Davis	P. Hare
P. Forrest	R. LaCroix
B. Hasker	J. L. Mackie
J. Hick	E. H. Madden
D. Howard-Snyder	M. Martin
H. Meynell	H. J. McClosky
J. O'Leary-Hawthorne	G. Oppy
M. L. Peterson	D. Parfit
A. Plantinga	W. Rowe
B. Reichenbach	B. Russell
G. Schlesinger	J. L. Schellenberg
M. Stewart	Q. Smith
E. Stump	K. Surin
R. Swinburne	M. Tooley
P. van Inwagen	A. Weisberger
N. Wolterstorff	
S. Wystra	

Select Bibliography

Adams, R. M. *The Virtue of Faith*. Oxford: Oxford University Press, 1987.

Alexander, H. G., ed. *The Leibniz-Clarke Correspondence Together with Extracts from Newton's Principia and Opticks*. New York: Philosophy Library, 1956.

Alston, W. *Perceiving God*. Ithaca: Cornell University Press, 1991.

Anderson, P. S. *A Feminist Philosophy of Religion: The Rationality and Myths of Religious Belief*. Oxford: Blackwell, 1998.

Berkeley, G. *Berkeley's Complete Works*. Ed. A. C. Fraser. Oxford: Clarendon, 1901.

Buber, M. *I and Thou*. Trans. R. G. Smith. New York: Charles Scribner's Sons, 1958.

Butler, J. *The Analogy of Religion*. Oxford: Clarendon Press, 1896.

Caputo, J., and M. Scanlon, eds. *God, the Gift and Postmodernism*. Bloomington: Indiana University Press, 1999.

Clifford, W. K. "The Ethics of Belief." In *Lectures and Essays*. London: Macmillan, 1879.

Conway, Ann. *Principles of the Most Ancient and Modern Philosophy*. Trans. A. Coudert and T. Corse. Cambridge: Cambridge University Press, 1996.

Craig, W. *The Kalam Cosmological Argument*. London: Macmillan, 1979.

Cudworth, R. *A Treatise Concerning Eternal and Immutable Morality*. Ed. S. Hutton. Cambridge: Cambridge University Press, 1996.

Descartes, R. *The Philosophical Writing of Descartes*. Trans. J. Cottingham, R. Stoothoff, and D. Murdoch. Vols. 1–3. Cambridge: Cambridge University Press, 1984.

Edwards, J. *Scientific and Philosophical Writings*. Ed. W. E. Anderson. New Haven: Yale University Press, 1980.

Feuerbach, L. A. *Thoughts on Death and Immortality*. Trans. J. A. Massey. Berkeley: University of California Press, 1980.

Gadamer, H.-G. *Truth and Method*. Trans. J. Weinsheimer and D. C. Marshall. New York: Crossroad, 1991.

Griffin, D. R. *Reenchantment without Supernaturalism: A Process Philosophy of Religion*. Ithaca: Cornell University Press, 2001.

Griffiths, P. *Religious Reading*. Oxford: Oxford University Press, 1999.

Hasker, W. *God, Time, and Knowledge*. Ithaca: Cornell University Press, 1989.

Hedley, D. *Coleridge, Philosophy and Religion*. Cambridge: Cambridge University Press, 2000.

Hegel, G. W. F. *Hegel's Logic*. Trans. W. Wallace. Oxford: Clarendon, 1975.

Phenomenology of Spirit. Trans. A. V. Miller. Oxford: Oxford University Press, 1977.

Helm, P. *Eternal God*. Oxford: Oxford University Press, 1988.

Hick, J. *Evil and the God of Love*. New York: Harper and Row, 1977.

An Interpretation of Religion: Human Responses to the Transcendent. New Haven: Yale University Press, 1989.

Hobbes, T. *Leviathan*. In *English Works*, ed. J. Green. New York: Harper and Brothers, 1929.

Hoffman, J., and G. Rosendkrantz. *The Divine Attributes*. Oxford: Blackwell, 2002.

Hume, D. *David Hume Writings on Religion*. Ed. A. Flew. La Salle: Open Court, 2000.

Enquiries Concerning the Human Understanding and Concerning the Principles of Morals. Ed. L. A. Selby-Bigge. Oxford: Clarendon Press, 1966.

God and Philosophy. Trans. A. Flew. New York: Delta, 1966.

A Treatise of Human Nature. Ed. L. A. Selby-Bigge. Oxford: Clarendon Press, 1948.

James, W. *The Varieties of Religious Experience: A Study in Human Nature*. New York: Modern Library, 1936.

The Will to Believe: Human Immortality and Other Essays on Popular Philosophy. New York: Longmans Green, 1897.

Jantzen, G. *Becoming Divine: Towards a Feminist Philosophy of Religion*. Bloomington: Indiana University Press, 1999.

Kant, I. *Critique of Judgement*. Trans. J. C. Meredith. Oxford: Oxford University Press, 1921.

Critique of Practical Reason. Trans. L. W. Beck. Indianapolis: Bobbs-Merrill, 1956.

Metaphysics of Morals. Ed. M. Gregor. Cambridge: Cambridge University Press, 1991.

Perpetual Peace and Other Essays. Trans. T. Humphrey. Indianapolis: Hackett, 1983.

Kierkegaard, S. *Concluding Unscientific Postscript*. Trans. D. F. Swenson and W. Lowie. Princeton: Princeton University Press, 1941.

The Journals of Søren Kierkegaard. Trans. A. Dru. New York: Oxford University Press, 1938.

Philosophical Fragments. Trans. D. F. Swenson. Princeton: Princeton University Press, 1967.

Leftow, B. *Time and Eternity*. Ithaca: Cornell University Press, 1991.

Leibniz, G. W. *Leibniz: Discourse on Metaphysics; Correspondence with Arnauld and Monadology*. Trans. G. R. Montgomery. La Salle: Open Court, 1945.

New Essays on Human Understanding. Ed. P. Remnant and J. Bennett. Cambridge: Cambridge University Press, 1981.

Theodicy. Ed. D. Allen. Indianapolis: Bobb-Merrill, 1966.

Levinas, E. *Totality and Infinity*. Trans. A. Lingis. Pittsburgh: Duquesne University Press, 1961.

Levine, M. P. *Pantheism: A Non-Theistic Concept of Deity.* London: Routledge, 1994.

Lewis, H. D. *Our Experience of God.* London: George Allen and Unwin, 1962.

Locke, J. *An Essay Concerning Human Understanding.* New York: Dover, 1959.
A Letter Concerning Toleration. Ed. S. H. Tully. Bloomington: Hackett, 1983.
The Reasonableness of Christianity. Ed. I. T. Ramsey. Stanford: Stanford University Press, 1958.
Writings of Religion. Ed. V. Nuovo. Oxford: Clarendon, 2002.

Mackie, J. L. *The Miracle of Theism.* Oxford: Clarendon Press, 1982.

Malebranche, N. *Dialogues on Metaphysics.* Trans. W. Doney. New York: Abaris Books, 1980.

Marion, J.-L. *God without Being.* Trans. T. A. Carlson. Chicago: University of Chicago Press, 1991.

Martin, M. *Atheism.* Philadelphia: Temple University Press, 1990.

Mill, J. S. *Three Essays on Religion.* New York: H. Holt, 1874.

Mitchell, B. *The Justification of Religious Belief.* London: Macmillan, 1973.

Mohanty, J. N. *Reason and Tradition in Indian Thought.* Oxford: Clarendon, 1992.

More, H. *A Collection of Several Philosophical Writings.* Ed. Rene Wellek. New York: Garland, 1978.

Morris, T. V. *Anselmian Explorations.* Notre Dame: University of Notre Dame Press, 1987.

Nielsen, K. *Contemporary Critiques of Religion.* New York: Herder and Herder, 1971.

Nietzsche, F. *Beyond Good and Evil.* Trans. R. J. Hollingdale. Middlesex: Penguin, 1973.
Human, All Too Human. Trans. R. J. Hollingdale. Cambridge: Cambridge University Press, 1986.
On the Genealogy of Morals. Trans. W. Kaufman and R. J. Hollingdale. New York: Vintage Books, 1967.

Oppy, G. *Ontological Arguments and Belief in God.* Cambridge: Cambridge University Press, 1995.

Otto, R. *The Idea of the Holy: An Inquiry into the Non-Rational Factor in the Idea of the Divine and Its Relation to the Rational.* Trans. J. W. Harvey. London: Oxford University Press, 1936.

Paley, W. *Evidences of Christianity.* New York: R. Carter, 1854.
Natural Theology. London: C. Knight, 1836.

Pascal, B. *Pascal's Pensées.* Trans. H. F. Stewart. London: Routledge, 1950.

Patrides, C. A., ed. *The Cambridge Platonists.* Cambridge: Cambridge University Press, 1970.

Perrett, R. W., ed. *Indian Philosophy of Religion.* Dordrecht: Kluwer, 1989.

Phillips, D. Z. *The Concept of Prayer.* Oxford: Blackwell, 1981.

Plantinga, A. *God and Other Minds.* Ithaca: Cornell University Press, 1967.
The Nature of Necessity. Oxford: Clarendon, 1974.

Quinn, P. *Divine Commands and Moral Requirements.* Oxford: Clarendon Press, 1978.

Radhakrishnan, S. *An Idealist View of Life.* London: Allen and Unwin, 1957.

Ricoeur, P. *Figuring the Sacred: Religion, Narrative, and Imagination*. Trans. D. Peellauer. Ed. M. I. Wallace. Minneapolis: Fortress Press, 1995.

Sartre, J. P. *Being and Nothingness: An Essay on Phenomenological Ontology*. Trans. H. E. Barnes. New York: Philosophical Library, 1956.

Schlesinger, G. *New Perspectives on Old-Time Religion*. Oxford: Oxford University Press, 1988.

Sessions, W. L. *The Concept of Faith*. Ithaca: Cornell University Press, 1994.
   Reading Hume's Dialogues: A Veneration for True Religion. Bloomington: Indiana University Press, 2002.

Smart, N. *Reasons and Faiths: An Investigation of Religious Discourse, Christian and Non-Christian*. London: Routledge and Paul, 1958.

Smith, Q., and W. Craig. *Theism, Atheism and Big Bang Cosmology*. Oxford: Clarendon Press, 1993.

Spinoza, B. de. *Ethics*. Trans. G. H. R. Parkinson. Oxford: Oxford University Press, 2000.
   Theological-Political Treatise. Trans. S. Shirley. Indianapolis: Hackett, 1998.

Strump, E., and N. Kretzmann. "Eternity." *Journal of Philosophy* 78 (1981): 429–458.

Swinburne, R. *The Christian God*. Oxford: Oxford University Press, 1994.
   The Existence of God. Oxford: Clarendon Press, 1979.
   Faith and Reason. Oxford: Clarendon Press, 1981.

Taylor, C. *Sources of the Self: The Making of the Modern Identity*. Cambridge, Mass.: Harvard University Press, 1989.

Trigg, R. *Reason and Commitment*. Cambridge: Cambridge University Press, 1973.

Wainwright, W. *Mysticism: A Study of Its Nature, Cognitive Value, and Moral Implications*. Madison: University of Wisconsin Press, 1981.

Weil, S. *Gravity and Grave*. Trans. A. Wills. New York: Octagon Books, 1979.

Wolterstorff, N. *Divine Discourse*. Cambridge: Cambridge University Press, 1995.

Wood, A., and G. D. Giovanni, eds. *Religion and Rational Theology: A Collection of Kant's Texts*. Cambridge: Cambridge University Press, 2001.

Wynn, M. *God and Goodness*. London: Routledge, 1999.

Index

Abraham, William, 122
the absolute, Hegel, 272
Academic skepticism, 66–67
Adams, Marilyn, 13, 410, 421, 438
Adams, R. M., 147, 179, 408
aesthetics
    Cambridge Platonists and, 25
    Dewey and, 288–289
African philosophy, 385
afterlife
    Butler on, 155–157
    Cambridge Platonists on, 48, 422
    conceptual confusion on, 91
    Descartes on, 84, 91
    Hick on, 354, 387, 415, 422
    Holocaust and evil, 420
    Hume on, 161–162, 194, 200–204
    James on, 287
    Kant on, 236
    Locke on, 122, 126
    Mill on, 253, 254, 255
    Pascal on, 105
    Priestly on, 137
    Spinoza on, 151
agnostics and agnosticism
    Cavendish on, 53
    Darwin, 259
    Darwinian evolution and, 258, 259
    Hobbes and, 53
    Pascal on, 104
Al-Farabi, 385
Al-Ghazzali, 385
Al-Kindi, 385
Alston, William, 417
American Philosophical Association,
    424
American religions, indigenous, 135–136
analytic philosophy of religion
    Anglo-Saxon, 392
    Continental philosophy vs., 292

    traditional, 399
    Wolterstorff on, 399, 400
Anderson, Pamela Sue, 330–331, 394
Anscombe, Elizabeth, 363
Anselm, 178
anthropomorphism
    Clark, 144
    Hume, 173–174, 192–193, 210
antinomies, of Kant, 231–234
    and Buddhist philosophy, 386
Aquinas, Thomas, 147
    on Being, 305
    and Hume comparison, 178
    on reality of God, 79
Arcesilaus, 66
Aristotle, 63, 73, 378, 380
Armstrong, D. M., 88, 409
Arnauld, Antoine, 84, 87
Asian religions. *See also* Buddhism and
    Buddhist philosophy; pluralism
atheism
    Bacon on, 55
    Cambridge Platonists on, 53
    Cudworth on, 53
    Darwinian evolution and, 259
    Derrida and, 324
    Hegel and, 269
    Kant and, 234
    Locke, and public office, 125–126
    McTaggart, atheistic idealism, 276–277
    Mill on, 254
    More on, 36, 46, 53
    Pascal on, 104
    secular, 309
    Spinoza, 152
    vs. theism, 278
Audi, Robert, 427
Augustine, 195
Averroës, 385
Ayer, A. J., 337–343, 351–356, 391

443